The
L/L Research
Channeling Archives

Transcripts of the Meditation Sessions

Volume 16
June 14, 2002 to September 19, 2004

Don
Elkins

Jim
McCarty

Carla L.
Rueckert

Copyright © 2009 L/L Research

All rights reserved. No part of this book may be reproduced or used in any form or by any means—graphic, electronic or mechanical, including photocopying or information storage and retrieval systems—without written permission from the copyright holder.

ISBN: 978-0-945007-90-6

Published by L/L Research
Box 5195
Louisville, Kentucky 40255-0195

E-mail: contact@llresearch.org
www.llresearch.org

About the cover photo: *This photograph of Jim McCarty and Carla L. Rueckert was taken during an L/L Research channeling session on August 4, 2009, in the living room of their Louisville, Kentucky home. Jim always holds hands with Carla when she channels, following the Ra group's advice on how she can avoid any possibility of astral travel.*

Dedication

These archive volumes are dedicated to Hal and Jo Price, who faithfully and lovingly hosted this group's weekly meditation meetings from 1962 to 1975,

to Walt Rogers, whose work with the research group Man, Consciousness and Understanding of Detroit offered the information needed to begin this ongoing channeling experiment,

and to the Confederation of Angels and Planets in the Service of the Infinite Creator, for sharing their love and wisdom with us so generously through the years.

Table of Contents

Introduction 6
Year 2002 8
    June 14, 2002 9
    June 21, 2002 16
    June 28, 2002 22
    July 4, 2002 28
    August 9, 2002 31
    September 1, 2002 37
    September 29, 2002 42
    October 6, 2002 50
    October 20, 2002 55
    November 3, 2002 62
    November 8, 2002 68
    November 24, 2002 74
    November 27, 2002 79
    December 8, 2002 86
    December 16, 2002 90
    December 19, 2002 96
    December 19, 2002 100
    December 22, 2002 103
    December 26, 2002 109
Year 2003 114
    January 5, 2003 115
    January 26, 2003 120
    February 2, 2003 125
    February 6, 2003 133
    February 9, 2003 140
    February 19, 2003 151
    March 2, 2003 155
    March 16, 2003 163
    March 21, 2003 168
    April 6, 2003 173
    May 3, 2003 179
    May 4, 2003 184
    May 11, 2003 191
    May 18, 2003 199
    May 25, 2003 205
    July 17, 2003 212
    August 24, 2003 219

September 7, 2003 223
September 17, 2003 231
September 21, 2003 238
October 5, 2003 244
October 19, 2003 250
November 2, 2003 256
November 13, 2003 262
November 16, 2003 269
December 6, 2003 276
December 21, 2003 283

Year 2004 287

January 4, 2004 288
January 12, 2004 295
February 15, 2004 302
March 7, 2004 310
March 11, 2004 317
March 21, 2004 322
April 4, 2004 328
April 18, 2004 333
May 2, 2004 340
May 16, 2004 347
May 17, 2004 353
August 4, 2004 357
August 18, 2004 365
August 22, 2004 372
August 30, 2004 376
September 5, 2004 382
September 19, 2004 390

Introduction

Welcome to this volume of the *L/L Research Channeling Archives*. This series of publications represents the collection of channeling sessions recorded by L/L Research during the period from the early seventies to the present day. The sessions are also available on the L/L Research website, www.llresearch.org.

Starting in the mid-1950s, Don Elkins, a professor of physics and engineering at Speed Scientific School, had begun researching the paranormal in general and UFOs in particular. Elkins was a pilot as well as a professor and he flew his small plane to meet with many of the UFO contactees of the period.

Hal Price had been a part of a UFO-contactee channeling circle in Detroit called "The Detroit Group." When Price was transferred from Detroit's Ford plant to its Louisville truck plant, mutual friends discovered that Price also was a UFO researcher and put the two men together. Hal introduced Elkins to material called *The Brown Notebook* which contained instructions on how to create a group and receive UFO contactee information. In January of 1962 they decided to put the instructions to use and began holding silent meditation meetings on Sunday nights just across the Ohio River in the southern Indiana home of Hal and his wife, Jo. This was the beginning of what was called the "Louisville Group."

I was an original member of that group, along with a dozen of Elkins' physics students. However, I did not learn to channel until 1974. Before that date, almost none of our weekly channeling sessions were recorded or transcribed. After I began improving as a channel, Elkins decided for the first time to record all the sessions and transcribe them.

During the first eighteen months or so of my studying channeling and producing material, we tended to reuse the tapes as soon as the transcriptions were finished. Since those were typewriter days, we had no record of the work that could be reopened and used again, as we do now with computers. And I used up the original and the carbon copy of my transcriptions putting together a manuscript, *Voices of the Gods*, which has not yet been published. It remains as almost the only record of Don Elkins' and my channeling of that period.

We learned from this experience to retain the original tapes of all of our sessions, and during the remainder of the seventies and through the eighties, our "Louisville Group" was prolific. The "Louisville Group" became "L/L Research" after Elkins and I published a book in 1976, *Secrets of the UFO*, using that publishing name. At first we met almost every night. In later years, we met gradually less often, and the number of sessions recorded by our group in a year accordingly went down. Eventually, the group began taking three months off from channeling during the summer. And after 2000, we began having channeling meditations only twice a month. The volume of sessions dropped to its present output of eighteen or so each year.

These sessions feature channeling from sources which call themselves members of the Confederation of Planets in the Service of the Infinite Creator. At first we enjoyed hearing from many different voices: Hatonn, Laitos, Oxal, L/Leema and Yadda being just a few of them. As I improved my tuning techniques, and became the sole senior channel in L/L Research, the number of contacts dwindled. When I began asking for "the highest and best contact which I can receive of Jesus the Christ's vibration of unconditional love in a conscious and stable manner," the entity offering its thoughts through our group was almost always Q'uo. This remains true as our group continues to channel on an ongoing basis.

The channelings are always about love and unity, enunciating "The Law of One" in one aspect or another. Seekers who are working with spiritual principles often find the material a good resource. We hope that you will as well. As time has gone on the questions have shifted somewhat, but in general the content of the channeling is metaphysical and focused on helping seekers find the love in the moment and the Creator in the love.

At first, I transcribed our channeling sessions. I got busier, as our little group became more widely known, and got hopelessly behind on transcribing. Two early transcribers who took that job off my hands were Kim

Howard and Judy Dunn, both of whom masterfully transcribed literally hundreds of sessions through the eighties and early nineties.

Then Ian Jaffray volunteered to create a web site for these transcriptions, and single-handedly unified the many different formats that the transcripts were in at that time and made them available online. This additional exposure prompted more volunteers to join the ranks of our transcribers, and now there are a dozen or so who help with this. Our thanks go out to all of these kind volunteers, early and late, who have made it possible for our webguy to make these archives available.

Around the turn of the millennium, I decided to commit to editing each session after it had been transcribed. So the later transcripts have fewer errata than the earlier ones, which are quite imperfect in places. One day, perhaps, those earlier sessions will be revisited and corrections will be made to the transcripts. It would be a large task, since there are well over 1500 channeling sessions as of this date, and counting. We apologize for the imperfections in those transcripts, and trust that you can ascertain the sense of them regardless of a mistake here and there.

Blessings, dear reader! Enjoy these "humble thoughts" from the Confederation of Planets. May they prove good companions to your spiritual seeking. ♣

For all of us at L/L Research,

Carla L. Rueckert

Louisville, Kentucky

July 16, 2009

Year 2002

June 14, 2002 to December 26, 2002

L/L Research is a subsidiary of Rock Creek Research & Development Laboratories, Inc.

P.O. Box 5195
Louisville, KY 40255-0195

L/L Research

www.llresearch.org

Rock Creek is a non-profit corporation dedicated to discovering and sharing information which may aid in the spiritual evolution of humankind.

ABOUT THE CONTENTS OF THIS TRANSCRIPT: This telepathic channeling has been taken from transcriptions of the weekly study and meditation meetings of the Rock Creek Research & Development Laboratories and L/L Research. It is offered in the hope that it may be useful to you. As the Confederation entities always make a point of saying, please use your discrimination and judgment in assessing this material. If something rings true to you, fine. If something does not resonate, please leave it behind, for neither we nor those of the Confederation would wish to be a stumbling block for any.

CAVEAT: This transcript is being published by L/L Research in a not yet final form. It has, however, been edited and any obvious errors have been corrected. When it is in a final form, this caveat will be removed.

© 2009 L/L Research

Special Meditation
June 14, 2002

Questioner: I feel difficulty in just plain loving so much of the time. What blocks have I created to the love within me? Where or how am I preventing that infinite energy from reaching my heart? What can I do to love and accept my family more? Is there anything I can do to bring healing where it is needed in this family, my father especially? I seem to be very stuck in orange-ray concerns which keep my focus on myself. What can I do to finish my own processes enough that I might place that focus outwards and work to actually serving another?

(Carla channeling)

We are those known to you as the principle of Q'uo, and we greet you in the love and in the light of the one infinite Creator, in whose service we come to you. We thank you for creating this opportunity for us to communicate with you through this instrument. It is indeed a great blessing to join your meditation and we thank each who has laid aside the concerns of the day in order to form a circle of seeking. It is a great blessing to us to share the beauty of each of your vibrations and to be able to serve as we hoped to serve when we joined the inner planes of your planetary sphere. For being called upon to speak upon such subjects as love and its increase is that service which is that which we hoped to offer and so we offer a thankful expression of gratitude for this opportunity and are happy to share our humble thoughts with you, asking, as always, that each choose the thoughts from those that we offer that seem to have virtue and leave the rest behind without a second thought.

When we come to the subject of love we find that there are as many ways to approach the subject as there are stars in your night sky and yet, the energy of each star has its center in the one great original Thought that created all that there is. The expression of discomfort and distress shared by the one known as G is an expression that is very common to those who dwell upon your planetary sphere at this time. It is an ironic truth that before awakening from the planetary dream the mind of an entity is effectively asleep in a metaphysical sense so that the discomforts of being conscious and fully aware of the situation around one are muted by the dream of consensus reality. Whereas upon awakening it becomes obvious that the consensus reality is, in fact, an illusion with a gaudy surface but very little actual content, and that which was before a comfortable sleep becomes an all too sensitized awareness of the seeming gap between that which truly is, in a metaphysical sense, and that which can be expressed by the life of the everyday chores, and duties, and honors of being in the human condition, shall we say, whereas once one was able not to question but simply to abide by those suggestions of that which is worthwhile and that which is not; that which is good and that which is bad. Upon awakening, there becomes the awareness of the state of pain, and difficulty in identifying one's nature, one's goals, one's service and one's path ahead. The life stretches out before the gaze, full of days that are empty of true meaning and vital energy. Within this condition there is one hope, one call, and that hope and call is the call of love. For love calls not only within the being but surrounding and emanating from the being. There is the hope of multiplying, by the actions of the self, the love that is available to the world without one, and the soul begins to wonder if it will ever find that seemingly secret path through all of the twists and changes of the winding road that seemed so straight, when one was asleep, but now opens out into an increasingly mazed and seemingly confused pattern of turns and twists and dead ends.

Many are the souls that sit upon a rock by the edge of this winding road alone, feeling dry as the desert, aching for company and yearning for true purpose. And this is the feeling of the desert within this dry time of awakening and getting one's bearings. It often seems as though the road truly does go on forever with no relief from the smallness of detail in the daily landscape or the yearning of the heart for greater and more abundant surroundings. We come to this group this evening with a very simple message, and that message is that this experience of dryness, and aridity, and difficulty, and discomfort is as the shell or the husk of the self and the worlds that are full of vitality, crammed and stuffed with essence, with meaning, and bursting at the seams with opportunities to be of service to the self, to the Creator, and to the world about the self. Yet, how could eyes that are so open and so aware be missing that oasis of plenty and comfort in the midst of this vast desert of experience?

We would move back with each of you, backwards in time and in mind, to a point before birth, before the approach into this illusion that you call third density. Each of you had undergone a process of planning and prayerfully, thoughtfully choosing the relationships that would serve to bring forth the patterns of catalysts that were those patterns that would engage the self in very precise and intended ways, with certain key lessons that had to do with love, with learning how to love, with learning how to accept the love of others, and learning how to be of true service and how to accept the service of others towards you. Resting in that very supported environment of guidance and planning, gazing at the incarnation ahead, may we say that each of you felt fairly confident that you would not forget your purpose, your dreams, your goals, your hopes, and your desires for learning and for service within the incarnation to come. From that viewpoint beyond the veil of forgetting it truly looked as though it were going to be enjoyable and all too brief an experience. As this instrument has expressed it, each thought this is going to be fun. And then that point of view was lost in the rush of coming into third density fully, of beginning to breathe in and breathe out, of experiencing the limitations of the physical vehicle that must be fed, and clothed, and comforted with sleep and rest in order that it may survive, let alone be of service.

The one known as G wonders why the bulk of its thoughts and concerns at this time revolve about the self and about personal relationships. And yet, we would say that in each entity's life experience there is a constant and never-ending need for the processes of investigation into the nature of the self, and those relationships about one that have been so carefully chosen before times. In each life experience, no matter what the expectation has been beforehand of how enjoyable this experience would be, the illusion itself creates a most efficient feeling of being completely overwhelmed by the ocean of experience. The waves mount upon one another, seemingly often without rhyme or reason, and when one is washed up upon a shore in this archipelago, that shore may well be created from confusion and unanswered questions. We can only suggest to each of you that this is precisely the position in which you desired to be before incarnation. Carefully, studiously and with great love and compassion for the self, each of you planned this descent into seeming madness and chaos. Not to punish yourself, but to give yourself the opportunity to be lost within the body, the mind, and the experience of being fully vulnerable, fully blinded, fully submerged in this puzzle which is never fully worked but which cycles around so that once the puzzle is worked one way, the pieces are tossed into the air and come down to form a new pattern, a new maze, a new puzzle, in order that the incarnational lesson may be viewed once again, and then once again, and then yet again. Again, not to punish but to provide a continuing classroom in which the self begins to know the self, begins to know the mind and the heart of the self, begins at last to refine the self in the sense of coming to a new balance in that winding road of love and light. For balance there needs to be, and it has been your judgment before incarnation that just these lessons and just these relationships would give a rich and varied diet to the soul of choices to make, of puzzles to solve, of keys that unlock chosen doors within.

There is concern within the one known as G that there is a selfishness within that is causing too much the concern of the mind and the heart to rest within those knotty problems of self, and yet we would say that this is precisely that concern which needs to be upon the mind of the individual who is young in years, and, indeed, in a cyclical manner, this process of discovering the heart of self recurs regularly throughout the incarnation. There is no sense ever of being finished. That is a vain and shallow hope, that has nothing to do with the soul within. There is not a curriculum which one may learn and then be finished. Rather, there is an opportunity, for as long as the incarnation lasts, to place oneself in what this instrument would call the refining fire, to allow the soul to be distilled again and again in the distillery of incarnation so that each time the cycle moves a round of catalyst, experience and learning, the soul is more known to itself, more available to the conscious mind, more open and unafraid, more vulnerable to joy and sorrow, and more comfortable in the midst of suffering as well as in the midst of happy times.

Within this cycle of experience at the very center of self lies that same original Thought of love which shines out of the night sky from each star. Each soul within incarnation is also a star. Each drowning in the sea of confusion is also a master. And yet the goal is not to remember the masterhood as much as [to] begin to sense the lack of necessity for understanding. The goal of this sea of confusion is to drive the attention at last from trust in the logic, and the sense of the mind and the intellect, into the heart, to release at last the demand that the life experience make any certain kind of sense, and the creation of that energy of fearlessness that is able at last to say that, "I know that I do not understand and yet, I know that I live in a world that makes complete sense. I know that I do not understand the plan and yet I know beyond a shadow of a doubt that there is a plan. I know that I shall never understand what I am doing but I have come to know that I cannot make a mistake." Then, at last, the soul within is free to take that which this instrument calls the leap of faith, where the meaning and the sense of life, in the metaphysical way of looking at it, begins only when that leap into midair is taken. The demands of sense and logical neatness are abandoned in favor of the full confidence in the support that comes in midair.

Perhaps each of you has seen the cartoons where the coyote dashes off into midair, chasing the roadrunner. Finally, the coyote looks down and realizes that he has run out of cliff, and once he realizes that he is running only on air he sinks like a stone and plows into the ground below. This is the human condition, yet when it becomes possible for the spirit within to cease looking down, each will find that midair is a very firm support. It is written in your holy works that the one known as Jesus was walking upon the water, in the darkness of night in the Sea of Galilee, and when those who were within a boat saw this entity walking upon the water, one of those within the boat started out to join his beloved teacher, and he, too, was walking upon the water until he realized what it was he was doing, and when the conscious mind took over the faith was lost, and the one known as Jesus had to reach out his hand, and when those hands met, the one known as Peter was once again able to navigate the water, and was able to get back safely into his boat.

The daily life is much like this small fishing boat. It is apparent to the conscious mind what is needed. A support is needed so that one does not drown, and, yet, to the soul within, it is perfectly possible to walk upon the water, or, indeed, to move into the water and breathe the water as if it were air. For the soul within is a citizen of eternity and is not limited by those things which seem to limit that human body, which each of you now experiences life from within. To the outer mind, all is this detail and that; to the spirit within, it is a unified experience. Water flowing into air, flowing into stone, flowing into fire. All things transmuting and changing, yet remaining harmonious and connected in a way that is rhythmic and musical. There is a harmony and a dance that is hidden within the folds of the everyday.

The one known as Jim presumes that he is taking large machinery to the cutting of grass and yet, in the metaphysical sense, this entity is merging his energetic being with those spirits of grass, and bush, and tree, and breeze, and dancing with them in such a way that the environment is redolent with the odor of his energy, and the energy of the grass, and the energy of the air, all combining to create a pattern of love and joy. The one known as G has experienced the large machinery of forklift and the bulky boxes and loads which are moved back and forth endlessly in that which is called the warehouse and yet, in reality this entity too dances, in a dance with wood, and dust, and air, and light, in such a way that the atmosphere is forever changed in a harmonious and loving and joyful fashion. For there are no boundaries within the metaphysical world, and that which seems most humble and most usual from the outside in is in fact simply one more way to love, one more way to share the self. So that there is no work that is better than other work, there is no service that is more appropriate than another service, but, rather, there is only that moment in which all that is needed is there, and all that needs you is available for you to touch and bless by your being.

How does one find this being within? Certainly, there are periods of time in which it is appropriate for the entity to be almost consumed with concerns about the self. This entity was speaking earlier of the concept of critical mass, and it is as though within the awakening being, there comes a time of critical mass when that which has been must be laid aside, and that which is to come must be taken up, and it is just such a season that this entity, the one known as G, is experiencing at this time, and, indeed, each of those present happens also to be experiencing a point within the cycle of the experience of learning, where there is the letting go of the old and the embracing, reluctantly or enthusiastically, of that which seems very new. Such times are times when one must move within, more than seems perhaps appropriate to one who wishes to serve others and yet, perhaps we can give you the model of the light bulb in which that light gives light to others only because it is appropriately connected to the source of power, and develops that power in such a way that the filament of that lighting mechanism is activated. An entity is not designed simply to serve others. There is an inner loop of service which is entirely appropriate, which needs to be not only created but maintained so that the filament of self within is whole, and perfect, and free of blockage that it may glow with the love and the light of the infinite Creator. No matter how much energy is developed and given out from such a light, the light itself needs to retain enough power that it may continue to serve as a light. This loop, shall we say, of power within, is fed by a self that sees the value and acknowledges the worthwhileness of that self within. Can each see that it is perfectly appropriate to retain some energy for the self? This instrument has often spoken of being transparent to the energy …

(Tape change.)

… and yet until that instrument is properly empowered it cannot be a lighthouse, it cannot fulfill those services it has intended and for which it took breath.

The love that lies within is waiting at all times and in all places and conditions. There is never a time when this love is not resting quietly, glowing incandescently within the heart of self. The love of the Creator dwells within the heart, and it is the self in its concerns that often lead one away from connecting with the self in the search outward for sources of light and guidance elsewhere, and so we would complete the beginning part of this message by suggesting that for each entity there is a most congenial way to enter into the self through the use of silence and the resting in trust. It is as simple as releasing the breath and the energy of striving so that there is deep breathing in and out, that is not stressful but rather greedy for that life-giving fuel of air that fuels body and spirit. It is possible to breathe in peace and to breathe out stress, to breathe in light and to breathe out weariness. The key always for this kind of inner work is silence. We would encourage the one known as G to take deep breaths of that infinite love and light which are always flowing from the source of all things in infinite supply. There is the desire to love, and yet love is already present. There is the desire to serve, and yet by the beauty of being, each already serves.

We would at this time transfer this contact to the one know as Jim in order that the one known as G may ask any further questions that it wishes to ask at this time. We thank this instrument for its service and would leave this instrument in love and in light and transfer this contact at this time. We are those known to you as Q'uo.

(Jim channeling)

I am Q'uo, and greet each again in love and in light through this instrument. At this time it is our privilege to offer ourselves. We attempt to speak to any further shorter queries which the one known as G may have for us. Is there another query at this time?

G: Yes, there is. For several years now I have been unbearable fatigued. Some days I can literally feel my vitality being sucked from me, I can't find that life force and I've recently begun to suspect an infection called candidiasis. Can you tell me the cause of this fatigue or a measure that I can take to alleviate myself of this condition and ways that I can find that vital energy within?

I am Q'uo, and am aware of your query, my brother. We find that there is some information which we may share without infringement upon free will, however, there is the boundary of infringement which we must serve, for there is catalyst here that is of use in the spiritual growth of your being at this time.

The viewpoint of the self standing upon a prominent precipice and making the self ready to take a leap of faith into that which is your destiny is the basic situation with which you deal. There is the eagerness and the anticipation of the adventure that awaits, for it is that soul's destiny which you have created before this incarnation as the pattern for the incarnation which you feel is now ready to unfurl before you, as the marker, the guide post, the beginning of the great work. The dual feeling of anticipation and weariness is not so surprising when one considers the nature of spiritual paradox. Knowing beforehand that there is a great work to accomplish and yet seeing this work within the eyes of the work-a-day world, the illusion of this density, and translating the amount of work that lies ahead into the ordinary terms, causes one to feel a great burden, a great weight upon the soul, and this expresses itself in various ways in the physical vehicle, in the emotional vehicle, in the mental vehicle, and to a lesser extent within the spiritual vehicle as well.

If you choose to see this configuration of energy within your being at this time as this or that disease, and determine that you shall treat the disease, even in a superficial sense, as well as other levels of interpretation and application of remedy, then it is well to do so and to use the various healing modalities available to you as means by which you shall clear a path for full energy flow through your vehicle.

Thus, this particular catalyst can be used at any or all of the levels previously mentioned to enhance the personal understanding of your need to make a choice, to take a leap, to begin a journey, and to be of service in every manner possible for you, and to learn that which is yours to learn, to give and to receive the love that you feel is within your being awaiting release. It is a choice which you may make upon various levels and it is the key to beginning a great work for you.

Is there a further query, my brother?

G: Yes, I have had many recurring dreams of being in school, of missing homework, not showing up to class, missing deadlines … also dreams of playing in the school band that I was in and having difficulty playing basic songs. Can you give me any insight into what these dreams are tying to tell me? What am I missing?

I am Q'uo, and am aware of your query, my brother. We would again refer you to the beginning of our previous response in which we suggest that it was a matter of a point of view. This point of view in this instance being that opinion of yourself and how you feel that you have responded in your past to various opportunities and challenges that have been significant for you in your own growth in this illusion and within your own spiritual journey as well. It is a point of view which may be enhanced by seeing the self as the Creator, as a co-Creator of all that you experience in your incarnation.

Is there a further query, my brother?

G: Yes, by definition of being a spiritual outsider I am a wanderer. I was wondering if you can answer me whether my spirit is native to this planet or not?

I am Q'uo, and am aware of your query, my brother, and can respond in this case with the suggestion that you are of another planetary origin, of another density of origin, indeed, that which has been called a wanderer by those in this group, who has a mission to accomplish upon this planetary sphere, and who now seeks the nature and the heart of that mission.

Is there a further query, my brother?

G: Yes, I haven't experienced a loving relationship with a female in quite some time now and was wondering if I am, I don't know, meant to have one and where … is…she out there, is that person, if there is such a thing, out there for me? Will I experience something like that?

I am Q'uo, and am aware of your query, my brother. Ahh, this one wants dessert before the main course. There is a great deal of work, my brother, that lies before you before, indeed, you find this friend upon your journey, for those of the nature of the wanderer are quite often solitary for a certain period of time, during which they find the heart of the journey, the road upon which they wish to travel. When the feet are firmly set upon this road then perhaps one day you shall notice another set walking closely beside you.

Is there another query, my brother?

G: Yes, if you need a description I will give you description but I'm sure you can read my mind in a sense. What did I experience the night of June 11th at two a.m. in the morning?

I am Q'uo, and am aware of your query, my brother. We are not usually of the disposition to speak to that which has not been spoken, yet, clearly in this instance we can suggest that this was an indicator, an initiatory experience that will find further repetition and permutation within the life pattern in the days to come.

Is there another query, my brother?

G: Thank you for offering me all these chances to ask my questions. When I am able to meditate, when I'm not very tired, I feel as if I am on one side of my head or my energies somehow are distorted; I'm angled, I'm twisted. Can you offer me some sort of explanation as to what is happening? What this is?

I am Q'uo, and am aware of your query, my brother. As your inner sensitivities become more sensitized to the experience of a metaphysical nature which is being born within you, these sensory perceptions of an inner nature will begin to be aware of the flow, or the blockage of the finer energies as they move through your chakra system. Indeed, as you feel that you feel you are distorted in one direction or another, this is a fairly accurate perception of how energies currently are configured within your metaphysical or time/space being. These energies are those with which you begin to work now as you seek the heart of your journey. The opportunity to balance them shall come to you in each daily round of activities as you are given the opportunity to express various levels of response to the catalyst that awakens these configurations. Thus, we recommend patience and persistence in working with that which is given to you each day.

Is there final query, my brother?

G: In my mother's—if this isn't too long to answer—on my mother's side of my family there's been a big family blow-out, and my mother doesn't speak to her six brothers or sisters, and I've tried to find ways to mend fences and have not accomplished that. I know, I guess anything can be healed and the possibilities are infinite, but do you see it being probable that healing can take place within that family, within that situation, and, if so, can I do anything?

I am Q'uo, and am aware of your query, my brother. Indeed, there is always the possibility of healing, yet the desire to do so being absent in this case from many of those who are involved in the loss and seeking for love, there may yet need to be a time for the inner reflection, even upon the subconscious level, of some of these with whom you are closely aligned, and your part in this process may simply be to offer yourself as you are, to be spontaneous within the moment, guided by love and offering that which you feel, without dedication to any particular outcome. In other words, shining the light of your love as best you can and letting what comes of it be as it is. Perfect in it's own balance, though mysterious in it's manifestation.

At this time we would thank each present for making those sacrifices necessary to join this circle of seeking and for inviting our presence within your seeking this day. We are always most grateful to join you here, upon that dusty path which each pilgrim seeker of truth travels within the great density of choice that is yours at this time. We would remind each that we are but your brothers and sisters, who seek perhaps a bit further upon this same path, and who offer our opinions to you as those who have experienced what you now experience and who wish to be of service to you. Take those words and thoughts of ours which ring of truth and leave all else behind which does not ring of that truth for you, for we would not be stumbling blocks upon your path. Realize that each step you take is perfectly planned, if not upon this level of experience then upon that pre-incarnational level which anticipated the great range of experience that would be yours within this illusion, that you have within you each capability of meeting each catalyst with a successful processing and ability to blend those lessons to the great tapestry of your life experience. Know that others of an unseen nature walk with you to help, to guide, to teach. And finally, we would recommend that each give praise and thanksgiving to the one Creator each day for all experience, whether understood, confused or distraught. For all is a great opportunity to learn the heart of love.

We are known to you as those of Q'uo. At this time we shall take our leave of this instrument and this group. We leave you each in the love and in the light of the one infinite Creator. Adonai, my friends. Adonai.

L/L Research

L/L Research is a subsidiary of Rock Creek Research & Development Laboratories, Inc.

P.O. Box 5195
Louisville, KY 40255-0195

www.llresearch.org

Rock Creek is a non-profit corporation dedicated to discovering and sharing information which may aid in the spiritual evolution of humankind.

ABOUT THE CONTENTS OF THIS TRANSCRIPT: This telepathic channeling has been taken from transcriptions of the weekly study and meditation meetings of the Rock Creek Research & Development Laboratories and L/L Research. It is offered in the hope that it may be useful to you. As the Confederation entities always make a point of saying, please use your discrimination and judgment in assessing this material. If something rings true to you, fine. If something does not resonate, please leave it behind, for neither we nor those of the Confederation would wish to be a stumbling block for any.

CAVEAT: This transcript is being published by L/L Research in a not yet final form. It has, however, been edited and any obvious errors have been corrected. When it is in a final form, this caveat will be removed.

© 2009 L/L Research

Special Meditation
June 21, 2002

Question: This question is from T1, and his first question is concerning the possibility that Earth might be about to experience some major catastrophes in the next eight to ten months. He's seen a number of prophesies that suggest that this could be so, and he feels that, well, if that is so, then he should be spending his time helping people to discover this and take part in the evolutionary process, and get out and be diligent and serious about his service, but, if it's not true, if Earth is not in great danger, then he wonders should he continue to do what he likes in this life: playing games, seeing movies, going dancing in the pub. The second question is, he would like Q'uo's comment on his current progress in soul development, and perhaps some general advice as to how to be more in harmony with the Law of One.

(Carla channeling)

We are those of the principle known to you as Q'uo. We greet you in the love and in the light of the one infinite Creator. His service we are proud to call our own. We thank you so much for forming a circle of seeking at this time and welcoming our thoughts. We are most appreciative of this opportunity to share our thoughts with you and would ask only that, in listening to these thoughts, each be perfectly aware that we are your brothers and sisters, not authority figures whose opinion necessarily needs to be weighted with more importance than your own opinion, your own feeling of resonance with the material. Take what you will, and leave the rest behind. In this way, we are able to share our thoughts with you without being concerned that we will infringe upon your free will.

The questions that you ask this day concern the drama of the end of the age and the beginning of the new age, and the gentle, almost afterthought of a question concerning the general spiritual state of the one known as T1. And yet, in a way, these are one and the same question, for the spiritual state of the whole world and the spiritual state of each entity within the world are very, very closely linked. And the story that this planetary sphere shall tell to the archeologists of the distant future is a story that depends vitally and centrally on the true spiritual situation of each entity upon the planetary sphere that is interested in making a difference in the core vibration of the energy grid and the planetary population of third-density entities upon the planet Earth. It is overly dramatic to say that the fate of the world is in your hands, and yet, in a very real sense, this is so, in the same sense that it has always been so, in that the thoughts and perceptions of humankind have shaped the experience of humankind, and the thoughts of the fathers have often planted seeds that have been reaped by the sons and the grandsons and the generations to follow. So there is a very, very real connection between the spiritual situation of each entity and the way the story plays out upon what this instrument has called the game board of free choice within third density, [the land of Earth's] reign upon your spirit.

Let us for a few minutes focus upon the concerns of the one known as T1: that many sources have expressed in recent months the concern that there is a pivotal period in the beginning of 2003 beyond which humankind shall not be able to pass without a planetary catastrophe occurring. To address this concern head-on, we sort through this instrument's recollections of a period of some decades of experience with such predictions. This instrument has long noticed that the predictions of urgent and critical time periods have never manifested at the predicted time period with the predicted effect upon planet Earth in the physical realm. We have said through this instrument before that it is not that these critical times do not occur but that they are a part of a metaphysical process having to do with the entities upon planet Earth. This metaphysical process has its shadows within the physical consensus reality of your shared outer world, but the depth and profundity of danger of a physical nature is in every case—as it turns out—greatly overestimated and inaccurate.

Continuing to gaze at this question, we would also note that there have been time periods in your recent past, that is in the '70s and in the '80s and in the '90s, when there was a concerted effort on the part of many groups to raise the consciousness of planet Earth. In all cases, what has occurred is that, as more and more entities awaken and join the ranks of those who do consciously work in spirit, in prayer, in meditation, even in worry for the well-being of the planetary entities and the well-being of the planet at this time, the tendency of the Earth itself to express in a manifested and physical [manner] these metaphysical processes has been alleviated and ameliorated so that, while there have been a continuing stream of smaller and non-global difficulties upon your Earth, with tornados and fires, with floods, hurricanes and tsunamis, with earthquakes and terrible fire, none of these occurrences has triggered the predicted worldwide catastrophes. The one known as A has pointed out to this instrument that the one known as Edgar Cayce predicted in 1998 that there would be a global shift, and we may say, since this period has come and gone, that it was entirely due to the awakening and the linking up of positive consciousness upon this planet that this prediction did not, in fact, manifest at that time. What the positive energy upon your planet, as it grows, has done is progressively put off that time period in which third density's shadows shall cease to be present upon your Earth world. In other words, as entities have awakened and begun to offer their hearts, their minds, and their strengths in the service of the planet Earth and its peoples, this mass of positive consciousness has bought time: time to increase the harvest, time to make the most of these latter days of third density upon your planet. Indeed, we may say that at this point you are dwelling within fourth density. That which separates each of you within your third-density bodies from fourth density is nothing more than a state of mind, and this state of mind is far more vulnerable to or transparent to the biddings and the whisperings of fourth-density positive consciousness than ever before because of the fact that your Earth mother is in the process of birthing this fourth density now. And, as we have said before through this instrument, within the next ten of your years, this process shall be complete. We are not suggesting that at that time, either, there will be global catastrophe. Indeed, this future is completely fluid; we would say more fluid than it was ten years ago, and more fluid by far than it was twenty years ago. Your people are awakening one by one, not from a level of authority down, as in the old days of your, shall we say, state religions but in a far more modern and democratic manner, shall we say, in that it is a grassroots movement of soul to soul, of memory to memory, of the open heart being so attractive and calling so strongly to entities that are hungering for that energy that they are pulled into and called into an awakening.

It has become more and more attractive once again within your Earth world simply to come down on the side of love, faith and peace. The humble and the meek are beginning to gain the confidence of their experience with positivity and with negativity. The entities are so close now to that graduation time that the great struggle of choice of polarity is not as pernicious and as painful as it used to be for entities, because there is the underlying strength of many, many entities who are also attempting to open their hearts and to express the love and the light of the one infinite Creator in their everyday lives.

As we said, this is completely a humble and individual movement where entities are being called by themselves into service as harvesters, and, as entities are awakened, then they become as those who awaken others; not because they have gone out and brow-beaten or convinced anyone by fact or data but because it is simply so attractive to awakening entities to experience unconditional love that such entities, once switched on like the lights that they are, call entities to them and help entities to remember why they took incarnation upon planet Earth at this time. For each has that hidden memory of a very good plan; a very good reason to come to planet Earth at this time, just precisely at this time. There is nothing sloppy about the inborn and flowing system of motivations and catalysts that has brought each of you to this present moment. As the one known as T2 has observed earlier this evening, there are many, many ways, but they all lead to the top, and this is precisely true.

The one known as T1 has a particular path that this entity will do well to cooperate with, to explore, to investigate with the kind of curiosity most often found in children and lost when entities become older. It is very well to encourage within the self this infinite curiosity as to why and where and how. This open attitude, this questioning mind, yields great benefit for those who persist in seeking. However, that which is within the mind can only serve an entity to a certain extent. It is the tendency of many who are awakening to their spiritual selves and feeling the distance between themselves and what one might call the world of normalcy and conventional belief and behavior to feel the safety of the philosophical stance wherein one has a very good, distant point of view and is basically an observer that is attempting to figure out the way that things work. This is opposed in our description to the entity who simply opens the heart and embraces the day and attacks whatever comes to him with great love and enjoyment. May we say that, for all of the benefits that wisdom does bring, it is the open heart itself and the passion with which the entity allows that heart to flow that bring the best results in terms of spiritual learning, because, you see, in preparing the self for graduation into the density of love and understanding, that which is most efficacious is the vividness of the entity's experience within third density.

This entity was speaking earlier of its tendency towards being critical of the self when it discovers that it is, yet again, caught in the snares of its bookkeeping software which it seems to have difficulty in learning. The entity spoke of how it had distracted itself with various amusements so that it would not begin one of the many tapes within its head that would bring it from a point of joy to a point of self-critical aggravation and even despair. Such is the nature of the human realm of perceptions that a choice of whether or not to be triggered by the seemingly negative events of the day could be more powerful in creating a positive atmosphere around this instrument than the very serious question of whether or not this instrument was able to perform its duties in an accurate and professional manner. This entity chose to walk away from the problem and to celebrate those things which it enjoyed, knowing that it would eventually move back into that atmosphere of correcting errors and creating the necessary bookkeeping tidiness that a business demands. In a sense of "this world," it is the books that are important; in the sense of fourth density, it is the heart remaining open, undefended, loved, forgiven and accepted that is important. It is very deceptive to attempt to work in both worlds, and, as spiritual beings, we encourage each to consider what is important in this world and what is important in fourth density.

The one known as T1 was thinking concerning what it should do if there were, indeed, a very real possibility of planetary catastrophe. We have never denied the possibility of planetary catastrophe, we have simply been unable to determine whether the probability of a planetary catastrophe is high enough to speak about. We have not been able to determine this because each of you is powerful and has already made changes in the energy level of the fourth-density grid of planetary energies that is attempting to establish itself as the basis for fourth-density positive on this planet. As a race, the human race is more than adequate to maintain this delicate balance between harvest and a comfortable landing into the next density. Yes, there is great potential for difficulty. Look about the Earth at this time, and one sees many difficulties. Yet, is it not something to be encouraged by, that all of these difficulties have been cunningly placed in time and space so that there is not a cumulative effect but rather the ability after each catastrophe for the human populations concerned to help each other to come together and to survive for the most part?

One of the reasons that we encourage entities not to focus upon the negative possibilities involved in global times of shift into the next age is because that which one focuses upon becomes far more potentially possible. If entities all focus upon fear-based information, that will actually greatly help bring about the feared conditions. There is a very careful difference to be made within the mind concerning thinking about information sources such as those quoted to this instrument in preparing for this channeling session. Each of these sessions was couched in spiritual language by those channels of very good intention and positive hope of service who nevertheless were receiving questions of a fear-based nature and responding with the attempt to satisfy the request for specific information as to the schedule of these negative events. And may we say that we in no wise wish to address any specific questions concerning global catastrophe. We simply ask each to choose which thread of meaning and energy to follow: that thread and energy of fear which would guard and protect and make safe and deal with third-density concerns or that energy of unconditional love, faith hope and the desire to serve which translates into a prayerful and confident feeling that all is well and that all will be well. Which energy feels like the one that each of you wishes to choose?

And this is not simply true, as we said, on the global level. For you as a people are saving the Earth, but you as a mind, body and spirit working as one unit to gather experience and enrich the quality of your soul have the self-same choice to make, because each of you faces an individual global catastrophe that is absolutely certain. Each of you faces the death of the physical body; perhaps not today, hopefully not tomorrow or next week or next year, but soon, and inevitably. Each mote of dust that has had life breathed into it by the infinite Creator shall cease breathing and shall once again become dust so that the qualities that bring forth from the subconscious mind to the conscious mind the concerns concerning global catastrophe are those same qualities of personality that bring forth those concerns about the health of the body, the safety of the body, the protection of the body, and the defense against that great enemy which is seen to be death. One can move without a quiver from the microcosm to the macrocosm here and see the same energies at work: fear and love, protection and growth. Do you wish to protect yourself, maintain what you have, guard what is yours and so forth, or do you wish to release all fear, embrace all things in love and trust and believe in all things hoped for but yet unseen? It may help, when there are concerns within the mind about the world, to bring that concern back to the kingdom of the body, the mind, and the spirit of one entity, because each of you is in the microcosm the authentic Creator, the creation, the universe; Creator and created in an infinite Celtic knot that is different for each entity and yet in each entity retains the elegance of utter unity within the complexity of pattern.

The ones known as Jim and T2 were joking earlier concerning part of the query of the one know as T1 concerning dancing and making merry if all things were, indeed, all right and there was not the need to concern himself with warning the world about the catastrophe that is at hand. They were saying, "No matter what happens, we should definitely be dancing," and we would agree with this assessment. For is not the life itself the dance, and is not the secret to enjoying that life to remember that one is dancing; that there is music that is unheard, perhaps, by most? But that music is always playing; it is being played by the petunias and the impatiens; it is being played by the roses and the geraniums; it is being played by the songbirds in the trees and the sky and fire and water; it is being played by every mote that lives and breathes within the creation of the infinite One. This music is forever, it is infinite, and it is closer than the breath that you take. Each of you is living in a wonderful ocean of music and rhythm and dance, and everything in creation is moving in rhythm at a level beyond the capacity of the human mind to comprehend. Even your own bodies are a part of this wonderful rhythm unless the power of negative thought within the mind clamps down so much upon the body that it can no longer express that harmony that it truly does feel with every other living thing that shares its biological space.

Techniques for moving more and more into the Law of One in the way one lives are as simple as the techniques of learning to appreciate anything. It is a matter of becoming sensitized to that which one is attempting to appreciate. When one studies art, for instance, within your schools, one is taught to have taste and to appreciate the beauty of this or that style of expressing images. Each subject that one begins to look into has its standards of good taste in it. As one becomes more and more familiar with that particular part of the universe of learning, one develops taste and knows what is beautiful in that which is said or written or performed or imaged, and just so it is in living the life of the open heart. It is a matter of beginning to see that there is an art and a science to living what this instrument would call a mixed life; a life that is made up not only of third-density or fourth-density concerns but a grand and confused mixture of third and fourth-density concerns so that there is the skipping between the densities in everyday life, seeing the profundity of the tiniest chore; seeing the sacredness of the hardest and most humble work while at the same time seeing the vanity and the uselessness of all efforts whatsoever, because all of these efforts are within an illusion that is brief as a candle and will gutter out for lack of fuel at a certain time not too far in the future. There is a delight in the juxtaposition of beauty and meaninglessness that this instrument has often noted and [it] is very helpful, perhaps, at this point to consider that all things may be turned and looked at upon the other side. And, indeed, what is needed at some points is the ability to see both sides and to come to balance between them.

The one known as T1 has, as this instrument is well aware, devoted a tremendous amount of effort to translating other material that we of the Confederation have produced in the past into its native language so that more entities may grasp this material, and we thank this entity for its great service. It is tremendously helpful, we feel, that this kind of spiritually-based information be available to those who would seek it. It is why we are here. We have remained with this group and with this instrument for many years, because we truly feel that there is efficacy in this ministry that we offer and that instruments such as this also offer. There is a very real purpose to sharing our opinion, and there is a very real purpose for the one known as T1, the one known as Jim, the one known as T2, and this instrument to express those things that each feels are appropriate to the situations that arise day-to-day. We would not discourage the one known as T1 from sharing information that it finds helpful. We would simply suggest to each that there are ways to share information in a positive sense, and there are ways to share information in a negative sense. If one approaches things from a positive sense, this will tend to build up the structure of fourth density; if things are approached in such a way that there is gloom and doom and the raising of fear in those who are being warned, this will not encourage fourth density.

The one known as Jesus said it very simply: when it was asked if the coin of the realm of its time which had the face of Caesar upon it truly belonged to Caesar, the one known as Jesus replied, "Render unto Caesar those things that are Caesar's; render unto the Creator those things that are the Creator's." You may see Caesar strut upon a stage at this time expressing, no matter what nation from which they come, that sting of the dragon's tail; that fear-based concern for protection and safety and the accumulation of resources. The life can be subsumed into the concern for the suffering of the planet Earth, and yet this will not help bring about an increase in the harvest or a softer landing into fourth density.

Consequently, we encourage the one known as T1 to dance, to play the games, and to realize that there are no mistakes. It is perfectly well to work to share the information that it finds important, but it is just as important to share it in a way that expresses the quality of the open and flowing heart that is grounded in trust and shaped to express that love which flows through the instrument of the human body, mind and spirit in an infinite supply at all times. This is the heart of the mission shared by all those who are awakening upon planet Earth at this time. Each of you came here determined to make a difference. Each of you has those tools and resources that are needed. It is a matter of stepping forth in peace, in confidence, and in the sense that each is not alone.

And here we would encourage each more and more consciously to realize the strength of linking up with one's spiritual family. It is as the anchor that truly does help those who were not particularly used to the exigencies of third density to feel more and more comfortable within the realms of your planetary sphere and the incarnation you are experiencing at this time. We are aware that each within this circle has serious difficulties in enjoying all aspects of planet Earth. There are memories, shall we say, of better times, of happier vibrations to rest in, and yet, once one begins to link in a comfortable and subconscious way with one's spiritual family, one is able to recover a good bit of this sense of comfort, knowing that one truly is not alone on the level of intention and desire and group service. For this is a mission that can be done not by one but by a group. The one known as Jesus pointed out that, if an entity has perfect faith, it can move mountains, and that entity known to this group as Ra pointed out that, while it takes a pure entity to move a mountain, if a group attempts to move a mountain, each within the group may have an acceptable amount of distortion, and the mountain will still move. That is the power of the very deeply felt linking into one's spiritual family. We leave this phrase very loose, because you have a very large family. And it is not simply one group that has come into this Earth to serve but, rather, you are experiencing a very complicated, interrelated bunch of groups from fourth density, from fifth density and from sixth density, from the inner planes and from other planets that all have been attracted to the Earth sphere at this time because of the stunning clarity of its passage at this time from one heaven and Earth to the next.

As to what specifically may be done in the life of each present to come more and more into a way of living that reflects the Law of One, we would echo the words of the one known as T2 in the discussion that preceded this circle of seeking: to begin the day with that movement of the mind towards the silence that beckons is to enhance the energy with which one has—we correct this instrument—with which one is able to meet those catalysts of the day. It is as though the day were on wheels, and each day there was the beginning of the movement and, then, as the day moves downhill, it gathers speed. Once the day has gathered speed, it is very difficult to rein that mind's attitude back in and to move on the track of love and light throughout the day. And there is no one upon planet Earth who does this perfectly in any one day, yet that commitment day after day and week after week to spending time with the Creator before the day gets away is extremely helpful. Not everyone is able to do this, and, as we have always said, at any point during the day it is very helpful to tune, to meditate, to walk in nature, but in some way to invite the silence. We are full of words, we can only do so much, but, ah, the eloquence of that still, small voice that speaks in silence.

We commend that wonderful resource to each, and we commend the effort to bring oneself into a heart relationship with all that occurs so that you are aware of the aliveness, the vitality, the infinite worth of all with which you deal. All entities, all qualities, all ideas, all beings whatsoever, all creatures of rock and sky, anything that can be pointed at or thought of, has its own sacredness, honor and worth, and you are among those things which have those qualities. This is the kingdom which does not have Caesar's face. "My kingdom is not of this world." That is what the one known as Jesus stated firmly. And we would say to each, as a metaphysical being, your kingdom is not of this world. You are in the world, you are a blessing to the world, but you are not of it. You dance with your frail bodies, and you dance beautifully.

We thank the one known as T1 for this interesting question and would at this time leave this instrument in the love and in the light of the one infinite Creator. It has been a great blessing and a joy to speak with you at this time. We thank the one known as Carla and would leave this group rejoicing in the love and in the light of the one infinite Creator. We are those known to you as Q'uo. Adonai. Adonai vasu borragus.

L/L Research

L/L Research is a subsidiary of Rock Creek Research & Development Laboratories, Inc.

P.O. Box 5195
Louisville, KY 40255-0195

www.llresearch.org

Rock Creek is a non-profit corporation dedicated to discovering and sharing information which may aid in the spiritual evolution of humankind.

ABOUT THE CONTENTS OF THIS TRANSCRIPT: This telepathic channeling has been taken from transcriptions of the weekly study and meditation meetings of the Rock Creek Research & Development Laboratories and L/L Research. It is offered in the hope that it may be useful to you. As the Confederation entities always make a point of saying, please use your discrimination and judgment in assessing this material. If something rings true to you, fine. If something does not resonate, please leave it behind, for neither we nor those of the Confederation would wish to be a stumbling block for any.

CAVEAT: This transcript is being published by L/L Research in a not yet final form. It has, however, been edited and any obvious errors have been corrected. When it is in a final form, this caveat will be removed.

© 2009 L/L Research

Special Meditation
June 28, 2002

Question from T1: "I have noticed that my human eyes are drawn by beautiful women, while I do not notice less attractive women in the same way. And I know that some beautiful women are cruel, while many unattractive women are beautiful in spirit. I feel that there is nothing wrong with appreciating physical beauty, but I cannot appreciate all women's beauty, and furthermore I find myself fantasizing about beautiful women, even if they are spiritually mean. I find that I am failing to see all equally as the Creator. I'm quite concerned about this. Is this just me or an issue for men in general? I also wish to know about the karmic link between beauty and previous lives, as Edgar Cayce has mentioned in his trance sessions. What role or catalyst does beauty play in our soul evolution?"

(Carla channeling)

We are those known to you as Q'uo. Greetings, dear ones, in the love and in the light of the one infinite Creator. It is a great privilege and pleasure to join your meditation this evening and to be able to share our thoughts with you on the subject of beauty. We find it such a blessing to be able to do this, for this is the service that we have chosen to offer at this time, and you greatly aid us in allowing us to do what we came to your beautiful planetary sphere to share. We ask that, as always, you listen to that which we have to say with an open heart but reject without a second thought any concept or opinion that does not resonate within your heart and your mind and your emotions. For there is a very keen keel and rudder within each entity's spirit that will express itself in sound opinion as to discriminating between that which is for you and that which is not. With this caveat in mind, we are then able to offer our opinions without being concerned that we are infringing upon your free will. And so we thank you for your indulgence in this wise.

This instrument's day has been filled with beauty, and so we find it a happy coincidence to start a conversation about beauty with the emotions and feelings of this instrument towards the beauty that she has been experiencing all about her. The beauty of the lilies, the mimosa, the wildflowers and all of the blooms of this entity's garden have enriched and enlivened this instrument's emotions this day. The way the light glances off this instrument's mate, his face and shoulders, the planes of his jaw and throat, have pleased this instrument as it looks upon its mate. The beauty of kindness and service to others has very nearly swamped this instrument's emotions; the beautiful gifts that it has received this day from those about her; the kind volunteering of the one known as T2, and the gift of just the right stone from the one known as C, and the gift of this instrument's husband: hour upon hour of work, that it may pay the bills and keep this instrument safe, and warm, and comfortable. These things are almost too much for this instrument to express. There is a wonderful feeling of being so richly endowed with beauty that there is not enough expression in this instrument's personality or character to do justice to the richness of the experience of the passing moments of this exquisite summer day.

It has well been said by philosophers that beauty is in the eye of the beholder. What is beauty, indeed? And this is not an idle question. For there is a great deal of similarity between such questions or issues as beauty and the construction of the onion. If you will think about an onion that is cut in half, you will see that there is layer, upon layer, upon layer. All of those layers are onion, but each one is slightly different, and, used as an analogy to the human spirit, mind and body, each layer is of a different constitution entirely. There are different geometries and different constructions of thought and logic upon each layer of the human energy system, and, indeed, one may move through each of the chakras or energy centers of this energy body system and gaze at this onion-like, layered effect. The definition of beauty and the issue of beauty, then, is not the shallow and simple thing that it might seem upon the surface, for each entity is working primarily with one or more of the energy centers, but usually with one primarily. And this colors the way that the layers of self appear to the self, and an entity working primarily through red ray will be seeing different things than an entity working primarily through orange ray or through yellow ray and so forth.

So the question of what triggers the appreciation of beauty is a question that cannot be answered in a simple way. The one known as T1 asked the question from the standpoint of observing physical beauty, and so we shall first address the question from red ray, which is the root chakra and the seat of sexual desire and the desire to survive. Within this energy center, the definition of beauty is colored heavily by the reptilian and mammalian brains, which are instinctual and concerned with nurture and groups, respectively. Instinctually, the great ape is geared to reproduce as thickly as possible. This is a survival mechanism and is a very deep and dependably substantial part of both the constitution of men and of women within your species. The energies of the sexual triggers to beauty are different between men and women because the biological roles of men and women are different. The male of the species is geared towards procreating with as many women as possible who have the markers for fertility and ability to reproduce. This, as the one known as T1 surmised, is not simply the experience of this one entity but is an experience common to the male gender. Within the female, there is also a heavy coloration of biological bias when gazing at beauty through the filter or prism of red ray. The energy in this case has to do with the instinct of the woman to find attractive those qualities within the male of the species that would suggest that this entity would be a good provider, a virile person, and one who would remain faithful to and loyal to the family group over a long period of time. This biases the female of the species towards finding attractive even those males who may not be so physically attractive but yet have attractive personalities or qualities that would appeal to the instinct within the female that suggests to this entity that this particular male would be a good mate. Consequently, those who are male within the human species will predictably and steadily throughout the mature life of the individual revolve around the noticing and the appreciation of those females which seem to be of child-bearing age and of a healthy and attractive physical appearance. It is neither a positive nor a negative quality in terms of service to others and service to self. It is that which is in terms of the experience of the energy body of this particular physical vehicle and the way that it is set up to interact with the many other aspects of the energy system of the soul.

When gazed at through the energies of orange ray, beauty begins to take on more of a depth, both from males and from females. At this point, the energies of communication, personality characteristics, and like interests begin to add to or subtract from the beauty that is perceived by the physical eye. This energy of personal relationships and relationship with the self creates within the eye an esthetic that is primarily focused upon enjoying the self and feeling safe within the self and within the relationship with the other self. It becomes more and more subjective within the choice of any individual as to what the elements of beauty are. Within the red-ray approach to beauty, the culturally-determined points of attractiveness will more or less evenly spread throughout the population so that many, many entities can agree that such and such an entity is beautiful and such and such another entity is not. However, within the dynamics of a personal relationship, the coloration of orange ray begins to spread out the choices that entities make so that there begins to be more of an appreciation for emotional beauty, spiritual beauty, mental beauty and other types of beauty that are not easily seen within the physical skin.

And this is a point worth gazing at for a moment, for there is almost a feeling of being locked in a small room in terms of feeling nearly forced to notice physical beauty from the red-ray level. This is the quality of instinct that is so powerful within the human animal and so important to the survival of the physical mechanism in general. Were such instincts not native to the very bone and blood of the human species, the heart would forget to pound, the lungs would forget to breathe and the body would forget to breed children. This would not be appropriate for the survival of the species. Consequently, there is almost an element of being hounded by one's body, especially for those within the male gender. And we would suggest, for those who feel limited by this compulsion to notice physical beauty, that it is without polarity and without fault to experience momentary attraction and the tendency to fantasize concerning beautiful women. Indeed, this is to a certain extent true for those of the female gender as well. There is, shall we say, a very active sex life for almost everyone upon your planet whether or not the entities involved are having sexual intercourse or even relationships at the physical level. For, metaphysically speaking, that which one fantasizes, one is accomplishing; that which is thought becomes that which is true. This is part of what this instrument would call the background clutter of an incarnation. It is an aspect of having a physical body that is nearly inescapable and, as we said, is a benign and perfectly acceptable function of the soul within incarnation.

Beauty from the yellow-ray energy becomes a far more subtle and rich-textured thing, for within the yellow-ray energy lie family and the mated relationship, and it is within the safety and intimacy of such continuing and prolonged relationships that those who become spiritually mature are able greatly to broaden and enhance their concept of beauty. The qualities of a mate, a mother, a father, a child, or a sibling can be imperfect in the extreme, and yet, over a period of time and the blessing of shared history—we correct this instrument—with the blessing of ever-lengthening shared history, the entities within the family group or within the mated relationship become so over-drawn with the patina of loving and being loved, that even the homeliest entity becomes perfectly itself and therefore beautiful because it is that person. And finally the leaden and heavy weight of physical opinion of beauty becomes that which can take off like the kite in the wind, soaring with the energy of the wind of love.

When the heart is opened and beauty begins to be examined from the green-ray level, then it is that the entire question of beauty is transformed. For, at the heart level, the eyes of the soul are open, and all entities begin to be seen not as bodies but as beings. Within the heart, then, beauty is a function of one's own heart. The tyranny of the outward eye is lifted at last, and the only limitation is with those who have not yet come into an awareness of their own beauty. If an entity cannot conceive of itself as worthwhile or good enough or beautiful in the sense of being a good person, then that poor opinion of the self will cast ugly shadows upon all of the outer world, and entity after entity will come up short within that poor heart that does not see its own sun, that does not see its shining glory. To us, gazing at each of you from the whole system of our bodies, minds and spirits, we see your beauty as an ever-shifting kaleidoscope. Each of you has a beauty that is endlessly describable, and yet it is the harmony and the combination of energies involved in the spectrograph of self that are so fascinating about each entity. Each of you is a vibration that is actually a complex of vibration, upon vibration, upon vibration, endlessly colored by the subtleties of an incarnation full of choices and biases and flowing from moment to moment in a thousand different ways that each of you is most likely not aware of for the most part, yet, within the flowing and subtle regions of the energy body, the changes are constant, and there are no two moments within the life of an entity when that entity is vibrating precisely the same. And yet, as a whole, the energy signature of an entity remains fairly clear and unified throughout an incarnational experience, for each of you comes into incarnation with a tremendous amount of already prepared bias which has been chosen to bring in as a part of the, shall we say, structure of "givens" that form up the structure of an incarnational experience. There is not a person, no matter what his station, his state, or expression of morality, that is not beautiful. Each entity at the soul level is tremendously beautiful. Indeed, each entity—being the Creator—has a beauty beyond all imagining, for each is all that there is; each contains the universe. And would not each, then, have all aspects of beauty and ugliness, the entire range of esthetics within the self, locked in many, many treasure troves within the personality, waiting to be opened by the right combination of circumstance and motivation?

This entity, throughout its life, has had a love affair with beauty in the sense that, as a metaphysically functioning entity, it has long preferred to look at life from the standpoint of beauty rather than from the standpoint of some outwardly determined truth or learned intellectual set of properties or ways of fulfilling the need to be attractive. This entity has long been attracted to the concept of creating a beautiful life. It is not particularly concerned with the beauty of its physical body, although it greatly delights in decorating itself and creating itself as being beautiful, but oftentimes we would say that this instrument judges itself for being too concerned with the esthetics of its actions. What this comes down to, in terms of action and function, is that this entity oftentimes will choose a very impractical and difficult ethical decision, because it is to this instrument a thing of beauty to choose in such and such a way. This has created in this entity's life no end of interesting forks in the road, the path taken being the one that was less traveled. Is this entity correct or incorrect? This entity is itself. The question of beauty is truly a subjective one. However, we would say, as your poet, Keats, has said, that truth is beauty, and beauty is truth. That is all you know and all you need to know.

When it comes to evaluating beauty from the standpoint of the indigo ray, then it is that choices such as this instrument makes become the focus of what beauty is and how entities are seen. Indeed, looking at another being in the physical from the standpoint of indigo-ray beauty, it can easily be seen that the lines of the face, the attractiveness of the body as judged by cultural standards, the gracefulness of expression of communication and personality, begin to pale beside the sheer force of an entity's soul character. For within the eyes of one who is seeing from the standpoint of doing work in consciousness, beauty lies almost entirely in the power and peace of an entity, in its ability to show you joy and bliss and true wisdom, according to the place in the process of spiritual evolution that your particular indigo-ray energy center has found itself enjoying the dance of working within.

Indeed, it is so that such a bias as this entity has towards beauty has, through many incarnations, somewhat biased its soul evolution. Woe betide the entity whose soul evolution is stuck at the red-ray level, for it is as though one were never able to peel the onion, never able to get to the inner surfaces. However, we would say to the one known as T1 that it is extremely doubtful that this entity is much troubled by being stuck within red ray, but, rather, this entity is mistaking a certain type of experience with beauty for the whole gamut of the question of esthetics.

Which energy appeals most to each of those within this circle? That is an ever-shifting question, is it not? Certainly, if an entity finds itself obsessed with physical beauty, there is some balancing work to be done, for it is not acceptable in the sense of metaphysical work overly to be preferring any one situation over another. It is a toxic environment for spiritual growth to be obsessing concerning almost anything, for the great key to spiritual advancement is balance. Rather, we would suggest that the way to work with such a concept or issue as beauty is to move the self through the various experiences of beauty, observing and appreciating the qualities at each level or depth of the energy at each layer of the onion realizing that, as the consideration of beauty rises through the energy centers, the quality of the considerations and the thoughts of such an entity are improving all the while. The experience of beauty is pleasant from any of the layers for depth of truth within the experience[1]. But, certainly, the more profoundly rewarding of the esthetics begin to come in with the richness of the higher energy centers. Yet, we would not for an instant remove that wonderful, primal gusto and brio involved in the physical appreciation and delight in beauty. Should a male not delight in the beauty of the female? Should the female not delight in the handsomeness of the male? Should one not appreciate the delicious taste of good food and good drink? Should one not rejoice in the beauty of song and dance and movement and the physical world and the feast that the eyes and the ears have? Should one not enjoy the touch of soft and firm and rough and smooth? Should one not, indeed, delight as much as an otter

---

[1] Carla: For instance, an experience of exhilaration after a close call may be completely red-ray instinctual responses, yet the feeling is deep and pure. Any feeling, thusly, is beautiful as a *ding an sicht*.

in the play of life? We see no harm or error in such delight in beauty and would only encourage each to open the eyes more and clear the senses more deeply to appreciate every passing beauty of the day. The one known as Jim was saying earlier that it wished to keep a positive attitude, because it so much changed the perception of the life by the self. The one known as T2 mentioned also that the most constant prayer was keeping a positive thought at all times. These, too, are ways of increasing the beauty in the life, of opening the windows of the soul to let the sunshine of love and light in.

We would not have any worship beauty. We would not have any worship at anything that has a name or form or shape. We would suggest to each that, in order to remain balanced, it is well to examine strong feelings about beauty just as one would examine emotional feelings of any other kind. The assumption of preferences and biases is part of that which you came to this incarnation to refine. In order to refine one's concept of beauty, one must first become able to be completely honest with the self concerning opinions of self and opinions of other self. This is not particularly easy to accomplish. The self must be more and more known to the self, more and more accepted and, finally, more and more loved. What is beauty? Gaze within your childhood with the eyes of a small child. Were you not gloriously beautiful? You were innocent of anything except wishing to exult in every experience of life and it is very telling that much of the experience of the young soul of an incarnation tends to be experienced as difficult so that, little by little, that beauty of innocence begins to be warped away and scratched away, and finally knocked into flinders by the seemingly poor opinion of one's parents and authority figures; by the cruel taunts of other children; by the disappointment of the self by the self. All of these things begin to rob the growing soul of its ability impartially and lovingly to feel beautiful and to judge things as beautiful. Indeed, we would say that, for most entities coming into an awakening process, the ability to appreciate beauty has been stunted and warped. And so, there is much work to do within an incarnation to recover that innocence of eye and ear, that allows an entity to sense the beauty of the nature of each thing as it is, or what this instrument would call the *ding an sicht*. Appreciating the real heart and essence of each thing is the key to a balanced esthetic. And when the esthetic is balanced, and balanced for that incarnation, there is no adhering karma stemming from the decisions made within the incarnation.

We encourage, in this regard, the daily balancing of emotions. We have spoken of this often before and in this wise, we would find it particularly useful. Meditation in general is tremendously useful and inviting the silence is a way of saying inviting balance, inviting reality, inviting essence, inviting wisdom. But in a specialized meditation at the end of the day, it is very helpful to pull out all of the experiences of the day from the mental pockets in which you have quickly put them during the day and gaze at each of these emotional moments with a far more thoughtful and judicious eye. Not to judge the self, but to judge the color, the quality, the particular layer of the energy body that was seen through and, basically, to come into more and more of a familiarity with one's own patterns and one's own preferences.

As each preference is identified, then, the technique of balancing meditation is to allow that first feeling, that first bias to flood the emotional self, saturating the self with that precise feeling that was felt earlier in the day. Then, when that has been emphasized and over-emphasized to the satisfaction of the self, the technique involves lifting up from that extreme and allowing the other extreme, the diametrical opposite, to fall gently into and gradually replace the original emotion. And then one encourages that distortion until it, too, is extreme, so that one would see the beauty of a particular thing and one's rush towards it and at the same time one would be able to see the diametrically opposed lack of beauty of a particular perception or opinion or impulse, so that one may see the self as a 360 degree sphere of being that includes all biases. Once one has begun to get the hang of such a technique, one becomes gradually more comfortable with one's biases, whether or not they seem to be fair or just within themselves.

This instrument is informing us that we begin to speak too long and so we would close this very interesting question and our response to it by encouraging each to enter into the essence of the self in silence. Allow the silence to speak, for it, more than words, more than ideas, more than thoughts, have the pith and the heart of the truth. What is beauty, what is truth? Enter the silence, turn the key and enter your own heart and enter a universe of infinite discovery.

We thank the one known as T1 for this question and we leave it and this group in the love and the light of the one infinite Creator. We rejoice and we leave you in love and light. We are those known to you as the principle of Q'uo. Adonai.

Special Meditation
July 4, 2002

Question from V: The question today has two parts.

Part 1: Given the tumultuous history between K and myself I've come to the belief that ours is a karmic relationship. Can you speak to the origin of this karma and if the karma will be satisfied during this incarnation?

Part 2: Several years ago I met with a spiritual entity who identified himself as Kega. Can you tell me if Kega is currently in a physical incarnate form and if there is a possibility of a relationship between Kega and me?

(Carla channeling)

We are those of the principle known to you as Q'uo. Greetings in the love and in the light of the one infinite Creator in Whose service we are. We thank you for the great privilege of being asked to join your meditation and would be glad to speak with you concerning this question concerning a relationship and the one known as Kega, with the understanding that each present take those thoughts of ours which are resonant and meaningful and leave the rest behind. This allows us to share our opinions without being concerned that we will infringe upon the free will of those present. We are extremely appreciative of this opportunity to share our thoughts. For this is the service that we have chosen at this time and it is greatly a blessing to us to be able to do the work which we came to do.

We gaze at the relationship between the one known as V and the one known as K and can indeed confirm that the relationship has what could be called a karmic burden. However, it is our opinion that this is not the kind of karmic relationship which the one known as V suspects, but rather has a metaphysical, that is to say, a non-earth oriented origin and is not indeed a matter of previous incarnations upon this planet, having sown the seeds of imbalance that would produce adhering karma in that sense of the word "karma," but rather is a relationship between, shall we say, one of the children of the light and one of the children of the darkness. This instrument has had a relationship of that same nature with the one known as D and this instrument also was unable to, shall we say, master the dynamics of the relationship from a human level and was able simply by sheer reason and intensity of focus to withdraw itself from energetic bonding with this entity after four years of marriage.

How to understand a relationship in which one mirrors to the other light, the other mirrors darkness? It cannot be taken literally or in a linear manner because the energies involved are more subtle and more profound than those energies produced by an imbalance in a previous incarnation of an earthly nature. Rather, it is as though one of angelic energy were being pursued through various dimensions that only peripherally extend into the physical dimension by that which could be reasonably described as a negative entity of that which this instrument would call fifth-density origin. It is unlikely that such a thing would occur for it is dangerous to those of the origin of fifth density to incarnate into the physical and especially dangerous to the entity who incarnates into the physical and then does not manage to contain or control that energy of light that lives with angelic wings in bone and blood and body.

We can say that [in terms of] such karma as previous experiences between these two entities [is] concerned, there is now a balance and an end of adhering karma of the metaphysical nature. The one known as K is as the entity who is at some level aware that it has failed and yet at other levels much more concerned with the physical body, is unable to realize or process the information or the finality of this failure. Thusly, it is as the maddened bull or the unreasoning anger that possesses entities so that, as the entity known as K lives through its days it is as though the entity were in a dream where the actual personality remains asleep and the metaphysical portion of this entity acts out in a cycling and continuous loop of energy that it is at this time unaware of how to release. This is why the one known as V has not found forgiveness and compassion to be useful tools or resources to use in this relationship. For this entity is as the unreasoning and maddened beast which knows no human behavior but only its instinct and since these instincts are baffling from a linear standpoint and only understandable from, shall we say, a more historical standpoint, it is a situation which this entity has the possibility of resolving within itself but not the likelihood.

Typical of negatively-oriented entities, the one known as K thrives upon fear and pain. This instrument and the one known as V and the one known as Jim saw a movie entitled, "A Beautiful Mind" recently and it is a useful example of how the mind can be cast loose of its moorings to the point that private and metaphysical portions of the personality become segregated from and antithetical to the waking personality and indeed the one known as K is as one who sleeps while, shall we say, a walk-in type of energy lives its life. This entity which overlays the human personality has never been a physical entity and its energies are quite intransigent in their inability to harmonize with the experience of inhabiting a physical body. Consequently, this entity is not vulnerable to the healing techniques that would normally be used to correct such a disintegration of personality. Nor would we be of the opinion that it would be helpful to address the situation within the one known as K in any way. For this is this entity's walk, this is this entity's choice.

Perhaps there is a tiny portion of this entity that hopes for rescue. But it is not situated in such a way as to be accessible to any but the one known as K's own will. It is a situation not penetrable by any other self including the one known as V.

Let us step back and gaze at the underlying energies involved in this interesting relationship. This instrument and the one known as V alike shy away from thinking as the self as angelic or pure or positive beyond anyone else and we are perfectly in agreement that both of these entities are distinctly human, quirky and imperfect in the way that those among third density must be imperfect in order to have a very fruitful and helpful incarnation. However, each of these beings knows too that it carries that which is angelic, pure and positive. It carries it not as a burden but as the breath, as the life, as the [odor], and as the incense. It carries what this instrument would call the goddess, that female energy that makes safe places and whose hearts are full of compassion. This is not an aspect of femininity that is carried except by choice and most usually it is brought into the incarnation with love not for the purpose of helping the self, but for the purpose of being an instrument of the love and the light of the one infinite Creator in the sense of essential beingness so that whether that energy is expressed in changing diapers or in washing the dishes or in teaching or channeling or singing or other activities that would seem far more service-to-others oriented, the incarnational purpose of carrying this energy is satisfied.

There is now activity that an entity cannot accomplish as a vehicle for expressing this angelic, pure love. It is not affected by the cycles or apparent mood swings of the personality but is rather a gift that is firmly and safely hidden in the folds and recesses of the feminine heart. It is part of the very hopeful and energetically radiant attempt by an entire spiritual family of large numbers to balance an Earth that has great need of the fullness of love that is wrapped up in the archetype of the feminine. This energy is using each of these as instruments and we may say that each of these entities, the instrument and the one known as V, have conducted their incarnations with awareness of the gift they carry, respect and honor for that gift, and close attention to preserving the integrity of their positivity as instruments.

On the other hand, the one known as K has moved into the earth planes as a hunter. It has identified a source of light and it wishes to control and take on itself the power of that light, and further it wishes this in a way that is also, in its way, a gift brought into incarnation but as a walk-in in nature, rather than as a part of the personality. In other words, in order for this energy to move into physical form it must be out of balance and wedged into and overcoming the personality of the carrying entity.

It may be helpful to the one known as V and indeed to this instrument, who was earlier expressing its distress at the one known as K's behavior, to realize that this entity is not in the usual sense even aware of its behavior, but rather is as the instrument that is sadly out of tune. It is interesting that the one known as V mentioned that it was surprised that the one known as K still remained in this density. Indeed, we may say that this entity hangs by a thread, both to its sanity and to its physical incarnation. Yet we would not wish to express a complete lack of hope in that there is always the possibility of one shining moment of clarity in which the personality that lies within the one known as K, that is currently suppressed, is able to see that it carries a dark rider and chooses then to shake it off. Were this entity to perceive its true situation, that personality which is the one known as K would indeed ask for help and be the first to remove itself from its dark and overpowering angel.

Thusly the one known as V may pray that the one known as K have a moment of clarity at some point before the incarnation ends, thus becoming able to be vulnerable to healing, health and life in the sense of the greater life within the physical. The one known as V is very much helped by the energies of beauty and harmony and we agree with that which it was saying earlier concerning the need in the life for the providing to the self by self of the magical circumstance. The singing of the sacred songs has been for this entity a very helpful thing in the past and would indeed be that place wherein this entity could derive great refreshment on a daily basis. This instrument, for instance, always includes a hymn along with its meditation in the morning and we might suggest to the one known as V that the discipline of including the sacred breath is a good one that has good results for this entity as well. The silence itself is a very powerful experience for this entity and there is perhaps the opportunity to arrange for the self the opportunity to experience that silence, either within the dwelling or in walking in nature in solitude, to enter into the silence and thus into the tabernacle of the heart. There the Creator waits and there the weary soul may truly rest and find healing. This experience of the beauty of the creation of the Father is most helpful and we would recommend the time in silence and the time spent in praise of the Creator by sacred songs on a daily basis.

In this instrument's mind we find the concept is very helpful. It does not understand this concept completely but we will attempt to use it. It has read a work called *The Flower of Life* by Drunvalo Melchizadek and this entity expresses a way of moving energy through the energy body. This involves moving the energy up into the yellow ray and as it moves into the heart there is a 90 degree phase shift that needs to be taken in this entity known as Drunvalo's system of understanding in order for the energy to move up through the heart and on out into the creation of the Father. Interpenetrated with this concept and helpful to understanding its essence is the advice of the entity this instrument calls Papa concerning retaining energy for the self before allowing the energy to move through the self and out into the world. In this entity's zeal for blessing and sending forth the energy of its love it was reserving, according to the one known as Papa, nothing for itself and acting the role of martyr. Consequently, the image that begins to emerge here is that of the light flowing through the entity into the heart and then back in a loop through the body making sure all parts of the body, mind and spirit are washed completely in the infinite love and light of …

(Tape ends.) ♣

L/L Research

L/L Research is a subsidiary of Rock Creek Research & Development Laboratories, Inc.

P.O. Box 5195
Louisville, KY 40255-0195

www.llresearch.org

Rock Creek is a non-profit corporation dedicated to discovering and sharing information which may aid in the spiritual evolution of humankind.

ABOUT THE CONTENTS OF THIS TRANSCRIPT: This telepathic channeling has been taken from transcriptions of the weekly study and meditation meetings of the Rock Creek Research & Development Laboratories and L/L Research. It is offered in the hope that it may be useful to you. As the Confederation entities always make a point of saying, please use your discrimination and judgment in assessing this material. If something rings true to you, fine. If something does not resonate, please leave it behind, for neither we nor those of the Confederation would wish to be a stumbling block for any.

© 2009 L/L Research

Special Meditation
August 9, 2002

Question from T1: The question today is about pain and suffering, as I am experiencing pain in my nerves around the right side of my waist that leaves me sleepless and concerned about my future virility and health. Why do traumas such as pain and disease occur so often in the lives of spiritually sincere and seeking people? I know I'm a kind soul, so why would I or my higher self include pain in life? His Holiness the Dali Lama said the purpose of life is to be in happiness. I deeply agree with that. Some philosophy books taught us that pains would help us grow. I just don't feel comfortable with such thinking. Should I just communicate with my higher self and say, "Just tell me what to do to make you and us happy? Spare me from such a thing."

(Carla channeling)

We are those known to you as the principle of Q'uo. We greet you in the love and in the light of the one infinite Creator in whose name we serve with joy. We are most happy and grateful that we have been called to your circle of seeking this day. We thank you for allowing us to share our thoughts with you and to be of service in the one way in which we intended when we came to this sphere. We would ask that our words be heard with an open and listening mind and heart but that all of those ideas which do not resonate with the hearer or the reader be left behind. For we would not be a stumbling block before any but only those which are able to add to the resources which each seeker has in the awakening process.

This day you ask about the reason for, the value of, pain and suffering. Certainly, it goes against the values that are dear to the body and to the culture in which each lives to embrace suffering. The instinct of the third-density physical vehicle and the training and enculturation of childhood learning alike suggest the value of comfort, safety and the unimpaired maintenance of the self and those whom the self feels are dependents of that self and worthy of being taken care of. It would in no way be a plan of the conscious mind to invite suffering of any kind, whether physical, mental, emotional or spiritual.

Consequently, the question is most understandable, and indeed the conscious mind of the one known as T1 has not even once requested the painful difficulty that the one known as T1 is now experiencing within the physical body.

To begin to grasp why suffering exists, it is necessary to take a few steps back from the physicality and the immediacy of the experience of pain. So let us draw each with us as we retrain our focus upon, not pain itself, but the mechanism by which physical pain arises.

The goal of third density is the awakening of the self to the true and ever-deeper identity of that self. This involves several key concepts concerning the self.

One concept that is involved is the concept of change. The intent of the soul entering incarnation within the physical plane of your planet is to alter the condition of the vibratory rate and the vibratory strength of the self. That is, the self desires both to change in the way the self perceives the illusion and the power which the self can bring to bear upon that which is focused upon, in the processes of recognizing and dealing with catalyst. The natural tendency of the third-density entity, whether awakened or asleep, is to resist change, and yet the purpose of the incarnation is never achieved without embracing the process of change.

Another concept that is involved in effecting the purpose of third density is an increased accuracy in the perception of that dynamic known to your people as polarity. What is positive; what is negative? What is service to others; what is service to self? How does this creature that you experience as your self respond to perceived light and perceived darkness; to perceived positivity and perceived negativity? Very often, those entities which wandered to this planetary sphere from elsewhere are those who are working very hard in sixth density upon the precise balance between love and wisdom. This means that chances to experience polarity and respond to it are precious, because only by gathering the harvest of catalyst and allowing the winnowing of that catalyst by the processes of conscious and unconscious portions of the self can one begin to redefine and more accurately balance the forces of love and wisdom within the self.

These two concepts work together to create a situation in which each entity receives a series of catalytic happenings, from self, from other selves, and from the creation about one. Each then is responsible for processing this catalyst, using the processed catalyst to incorporate and integrate new learning, so that catalyst is ripened into experience. Thusly, the self comes to know more about the self and about the dynamics of polarity within the self.

Because the self has begun to observe the self making decisions, making choices, especially with regard to polarity, this shows up most often in those choices which this instrument would call ethical. Within the boundaries of the third-density human experience, the illusion is thick enough that the entire experience of incarnation has some of the attributes of a stage play, where the characters are sometimes roughly drawn, the staging sometimes shabby and the lines sometimes poorly written. Every so often, it becomes quite obvious to the self that that which seems to many to be a smooth and glossy-surfaced reality is actually a profoundly skewed illusion in which it is very difficult to see accurately, yet in which one is moved to respond, skillfully or unskillfully.

This being said, we may look at that which the one known as T2 spoke of, in the conversation preceding this meditation, which was that the one known as the Dalai Lama Spoke of being in joy, being in happiness, not necessarily the cause of any perceived catalyst but because the being itself was in that state. This is a challenging concept to one who assumes that, in order to be happy, one must be safe, comfortable and secure. The one known as Elkins frequently said to this instrument, when it was alive in incarnation in this density, "Happiness is not an objective." By this, that entity meant that the state of being happy had little to do with the state of one's spiritual awakening. However, as the Dalai Lama is perceived by us to have used the word, happiness, there is more of the expression of an abiding and universal state of mind which is bliss or joy; not happiness that is the result of a comfortable life but happiness, joy or bliss that is the result of having found the center of the self, found the point of balance within the self and thusly found the peace of a certain degree of self-understanding so that the self is at peace with the self and is able to release all fear.

The one known as T1, in wondering why there must be pain and suffering, is absolutely accurate in feeling that it is not necessary to suffer and have pain. However, it is almost inevitable, for the simple reason that change is inevitable, and the process of change is uncomfortable to almost all entities.

Now, as the one known as Ra has said, the energy of the self is first that of the mind. Catalyst comes first to the mind. The body is the secondary receiver of catalyst, and it receives that catalyst which the mind does not balance. Those who do achieve a state of bliss, joy, peace, realization or happiness in the sense the Dalai Lama used, achieve this state because they have been able to use the catalyst in such a way that the value of the catalyst is honored, the response of the self is known and honored, and those areas within which the self feels it needs more discipline are addressed.

The first receptor, then, is the mind, and when there is catalyst that moves into the mind and is not used by the mind, that catalyst moves into the physical vehicle and resides there as points of distortion, sometimes causing the symptoms which could be considered suffering or pain and sometimes hiding from the detection of the observer because of an efficiency of repression that buries the unused catalyst like a treasure beneath the earth of the body. Indeed, many are the entities who have mental difficulties because of an inability to recognize the truth of catalyst or inability to respond fully to the catalyst.

However, this question has to do with physical pain, so we focus upon those catalytic experiences that are not used by the mind and are instead repressed and unexamined. These move into the portions of the body that represent some aspect of the particular catalyst that has been received.

For instance, within this instrument, the present catalyst has to do with an overload of items that must be handled: chores and duties that must be attended to, physical things that need to be done. Consequently, as this entity began to settle down and prepare for this meditation, it discovered that there was pain within the wrists and that it was substantial enough to require the work braces that this entity often wears. Why would this entity experience pain within the hands and arms at this particular time? Because there is too much to handle. It is not precisely on this instrument's shoulders; it is moving through her hands, and her hands are carrying too many items.

It may be productive for the one known as T1 to examine the area of the body in which this distortion that is causing pain is taking place. The solar plexus energy center is the characteristic energy center that expresses this planet; it is the yellow-ray energy, and included in the yellow-ray energy are issues of society: the relationships with the birth family, with the marriage and children, with the work, with the various groups, such as nations and sports teams and companies, with which the incarnated entity has to do. This is a way of beginning to enter into the process of unraveling the tangles of emotion and fear that have distorted the normal, open flow of energy through the energy bodies.

There is tremendous subtlety to this subject, and we do not wish to suggest that there is a simplistic solution that would render one free from pain and suffering. Rather, we would suggest that there is great strength and power in realizing that the self is not bound by any detail of incarnation but rather is one who is here within incarnation to learn, to experience, to change.

Now, large changes within the physical incarnation do not show up as large changes within the context of the entire soul stream of an entity, that is, that entity which includes all incarnations, past and future, as well as the present incarnation in one great circle of soul being. The changes one is attempting to make are not that which they seem on the surface but rather it is through a filtering system of experience that, very gradually, realization itself begins to alter the perceptions of the entity within incarnation so that catalyst may be more skillfully used, and thusly the perception of pain and suffering will respond to that skill and art of beholding that which seems to be and seeing within it that which is. It is an eternal winnowing of truth from fiction.

And this is not easy when all of the details are steeped in illusion and human opinion. How many are the distortions which are fed to the entity with his mother's milk? How many are those that are added through the processes of schooling, relating with others and, more and more, beginning to tell the self stories about the self that make us seem like this or that character upon that stage of incarnation that you were speaking of earlier?

Sometimes it is possible to have a sudden realization that cuts through all the layers of illusion and distortion, especially within the lives of those who experience an intensity of seeking, whether it be for a short time or for a long time, as any process of dedicating the life to self study. The realization can come quickly, however this is not usual. Usually, there is a step forward, a step back, two steps forward, one step back, and so forth, so that the net result is a very slow garnering of a wonderful harvest which is self-knowledge. As the self-knowledge increases in quantity and in quality, the self begins to discern patterns of distortion that do not serve to increase understanding within the entity. Once these types of unskillful reactions to catalyst are identified, it becomes possible to intervene in the process of distortion in order either to remove or at least to lessen the distortion that is being processed from catalyst into experience.

Many times, the reason for distortion is some opinion concerning the self that is negative.

Sometimes the self interprets catalyst to mean that it has been abandoned; sometimes an entity may interpret catalyst in such a way that he feels that he is not good enough. Whatever the negative perception concerning the self, such perception robs the self of its own peace, talent and magic. If an entity is not pleased with itself, if an entity does not feel that it is doing well, it is simply, by this attitude, hampered in the accurate determination of the nature of catalyst, because all negative perception tightens a net of fear about the soul, and within that net the soul within cannot breathe and cannot express itself with freedom and accuracy. It is only within an atmosphere of love that the self begins to be able to see the self clearly.

This does not mean that it is possible for the self to be, specifically and generally, completely pleased with the behavior and the functioning of the self. The removal of fear from the self simply means that, when the self perceives the self to have failed, that failure is loved, honored, accepted and forgiven with the same facility and gladness with which the self is able to pat the self on the back for perceived excellences and virtues.

Moving back into the thought of polarity, it is important to love the negative portions of self, the shadow portions of self, as much as the sunny, daylight portions of consciousness that one is most desirous of sharing with the world. Blessed is the entity who is not only able to share positivity with the world but is also able to share the perceptions of his own negative nature with a calm and peaceful heart, with a forgiving and accepting heart.

This does not mean that an entity embraces the darkness of self and becomes the murder, the rapist, the thief, the sloth, the prideful one, and the one who disrespects or covets or lives in envy and hate. It means that, when those emotions are encountered within the self as response to catalyst, that the self is able to gaze upon itself with an unblinking eye, not troubled by judgment but remaining within a peaceful and unconcerned heart. To be afraid of the shadow side of self is to invite the entrance into the life of increasing numbers of what this entity would call vampires or those who attack or greet psychically.

For there is the polarity of the light and the dark that is willing and ready to amplify the basic truth of that person as perceived by itself. Thusly, if that person is able to embrace its perceived failures, its perceived suffering, its perceived disharmony, there is no bias incurred towards punishing the self through the contractions of fear that one is not behaving well or not doing enough or not being supportive enough. It is very easy for an entity experiencing negative emotions to begin a spiral that moves ever downward, where there is self-judgment and self-despising and then the outside consensus reality gradually offers an increasing number of mirrors that project the self to the self, showing images of fear-producing feelings. Thusly, the entity considers itself more and more of a failure; it becomes more and more willing to live in fear, and therefore it shuts itself off from those feelings of harmony, unity and the open flow of catalyst and experience. And thusly suffering occurs.

However, there is just as much efficacy in the smallest improvement in releasing fear. As the entity perceives fear where before it did not, thusly it begins to perceive those key elements which provide the catalyst that increases fear. Once these imbedded points of entry for negative catalyst are located, it may be seen that these are like triggers towards contraction, self-protection and fear. Thusly, the process becomes more and more transparent to the seeking self, and the self begins to be able to disconnect the seemingly fear-producing catalyst from the actual process of turning catalyst into experience. It is a matter of identifying that point when an entity is entering into fear, and, as we said, this is a subtle and usually long-term process. It is an awakening that is most salubrious and certainly, usually, most dearly bought.

There are those things which enrich and deepen an entity's ability to work with catalyst, and predictably we feel that this bliss begins with the silence. Entering into silence is an unnatural decision to the earth-bound entity. There is a tremendous amount of letting go implicit in the training of the self to enter into the silence and to release the contents of the intellectual mind. We heartily recommend this entering into the silence upon a daily basis, because it is a kind of training that is like the exercise of the body that strengthens the muscles.

There are improper exercises that are too strenuous for the body, in that instead of building up the body, they break the body down. It is entirely possible to break the self down through an unwise and excessive use of silence. There are few entities who can work with silence all day, every day, for the change rate is dependent upon the amount of time spent in silence. Thusly, we suggest a moderate amount of meditation, producing a moderate rate of change in which the self is not drowned in mind, body and spirit-altering catalyst but rather is able to keep the nose above the water of chaos that describes the nature of change in process.

A further refinement of the entering of the silence which is quite appropriate for the process of getting to know the self well is that which this entity calls the balancing meditation[2], which is recommended to be done at the end of the day, perhaps as one is seeking one's rest, whereby the self moves through the day in imagination, remembering those feelings that were either negative or positive in any degree of intensity and substance. These are the points of catalyst; these are the points of entry into the self of those gifts of destiny and synchronicity which produce for the entity that unceasing flow of incoming catalyst that is designed by the self as it expresses its biases within the incarnative days and weeks and months of its living.

It is an ongoing process, and it does not stop. There is not a point at which one may say, "Now I understand; now I am through with my seeking process; now I am a realized and blissful human being who has entirely awakened and who now is a creature of fourth density, not third density." This is in fact never so. The learning within third density does not stop until the breath is removed from the body, and the consciousness moves on from the physical body to that which this instrument would call Etheria through the processes of the death of the body.

---

[2] From *The Law of One, Book II*:

QUESTIONER: I am going to make a statement and ask you to comment on its degree of accuracy. I am assuming that the balanced entity would not be swayed either towards positive or negative emotions by any situation which he might confront. By remaining unemotional in any situation, the balanced entity may clearly discern the appropriate and necessary responses in harmony with the Law of One for each situation. Is this correct?

RA: I am Ra. This is an incorrect application of the balancing which we have discussed. The exercise of first experiencing feelings and then consciously discovering their antitheses within the being has as its objective not the smooth flow of feelings both positive and negative while remaining unswayed but rather the objective of becoming unswayed. This is a simpler result and takes much practice, shall we say.

It is as though there were a certain amount of food that is on the table, and the food will continue to be brought to the table until the meal is over. When the meal of life is over, the Creator calls the soul out of incarnation and into the beginning of its next experience. Once this incarnative process has been accomplished, once the plan has been completed, the spirit moves on, freely, easily, indeed effortlessly.

So the issue becomes how one wishes to sculpt and self-create the story that is playing out on the stage of incarnation. The one known as T1 at this point is experiencing catalyst that creates fear. How shall the one known as T1 respond? The answer to this lies within the learning processes of the spiritually-awakening and very sincere seeker. We would not solve this puzzle for the one known as T1, but we hope that the thoughts we have shared offer many points that will aid thinking about this situation.

Remember that each is in truth love itself. Love does not contract; love does not fear; love drives out fear. If the entity is at heart a being of love, and if an entity is able to experience the self as a being of love, this is a tremendously important step towards becoming more skillful in the process of experiencing the self as a person of power, peace, bliss and magical effectiveness. That which is perceived as the truth will become the truth. Thusly, be extremely choosy about that which is accepted as the truth.

One can either protect itself, or one can move into a lack of fear, release protection and embrace learning, with all that that suggests. This would seem to increase pain and yet in effect it works effectively to reduce the pain of living.

None within incarnation is ever alone in this *jihad* or spiritual struggle of self with self. It is tempting to sacrifice the self in various ways in order to reduce suffering. However, it is not skillful. Rather, seek to embrace that which is not understood, asking for understanding but not demanding it; not waiting for it in order to forgive and accept the self and to move on without fear into the daylight of each new morning.

We are always glad to enter into the meditation of one who requests our presence in order that we may help to deepen the state of meditation, and there are many, many others within the inner planes that are glad to be of help if help is requested. Within this instrument's spiritual belief system there are angels and archangels and saints, a savior and names of the Creator that color this instrument's ways of addressing the issues which it perceives. Within the mind and the heart of the one known as T1, there are also aspects and names of the Creator as perceived by the self, ways of thinking that have been developed by the self. And these are very personal and intimate and individualistic. Consequently, each entity's path is different.

Each entity's pain is unique to it. Not all entities suffer physical pain, but we assure the one known as T1 that all of those within incarnation are no strangers to negative catalyst or to the suffering that is the inevitable concomitant of life within third density.

We ask you to look at this not as a punishment but as a fertilizer that enriches the soil of self and enables it to grow a better harvest of blossoms and fruit. We wish to each the utter beauty of the blossoming spirit that is increasingly aware of its creator-self and is increasingly willing to lay aside the fears and perceived limitations of the self in order to embrace the one original Thought that is the Creator and that is that Logos which is creative love.

We feel that this is sufficient for this question at this time and welcome further questions if more is desired upon this very interesting subject. For the present, we thank this instrument and those who are members of this sitting group, as well as the one known as T1, and we would leave this group embracing each and enveloping each in the love and in the light of the one infinite Creator. We are known to you as those of Q'uo.

L/L Research

L/L Research is a subsidiary of Rock Creek Research & Development Laboratories, Inc.

P.O. Box 5195
Louisville, KY 40255-0195

www.llresearch.org

Rock Creek is a non-profit corporation dedicated to discovering and sharing information which may aid in the spiritual evolution of humankind.

ABOUT THE CONTENTS OF THIS TRANSCRIPT: This telepathic channeling has been taken from transcriptions of the weekly study and meditation meetings of the Rock Creek Research & Development Laboratories and L/L Research. It is offered in the hope that it may be useful to you. As the Confederation entities always make a point of saying, please use your discrimination and judgment in assessing this material. If something rings true to you, fine. If something does not resonate, please leave it behind, for neither we nor those of the Confederation would wish to be a stumbling block for any.

CAVEAT: This transcript is being published by L/L Research in a not yet final form. It has, however, been edited and any obvious errors have been corrected. When it is in a final form, this caveat will be removed.

© 2009 L/L Research

Sunday Meditation
September 1, 2002

Group question: The question today has to do with the concept of gratitude. We are told by various sources that we should give praise and thanksgiving in all things whether they be what we think are good or we think are bad, and we would like Q'uo to give us some information today about why this is so effective; why giving praise and thanksgiving in all things seems to produce so much of what we call good or the feeling of being in the right place at the right time, of being in the flow. We appreciate anything Q'uo's got to say about giving praise and thanksgiving.

(Carla channeling)

We are those known to you as the principle of Q'uo, and we greet you in the love and in the infinite light of the one infinite Creator. It is in the Creator's service that we find our joy and our employment, and we are extremely grateful to be called to your group by your desire for seeking. We thank each of you so much for the many things that had to be laid aside in order that you could join this circle at this time. It is a great blessing to us to be able to share our opinions with you on this subject of gratitude and thanksgiving. We ask only one thing of you and that is that you carefully employ your own sense of judgment and discrimination as to those things that we may offer, for they are our opinion. We are not an authority of any kind but rather your brothers and sisters. If you will allow us your ability to discriminate, then we feel that we will not infringe upon your free will by those things which we share. We would greatly appreciate that kindness. And we thank each of you for the beauty that you bring to us as we meditate with you and see the wonderful rainbows that each of you carry. It is a great blessing to us to share in these vibrations; to see that each of you, as the one known as H has said, is the master and at the same time joyfully encased in a shell of flesh and playing the part of the clown and the fool.

What is it to be thankful? What is it to give praise? To seek this, we must go a little deeper than zeroing in on that word of praise or thanksgiving or thanks, because the word, "gratitude" or the word, "thanks" does not in and of itself explain the power of the word or the concept that is behind that word. Indeed, in all spiritual realization, the awareness is bounding beyond the ability of words to describe the textures and the depth of the concepts that are moving through the seeking entity.

Let us pull back enough to gaze at each of you as stars or cosmic entities. Each of you, like a star, has an energy. Each of you is capable of radiation. Each of you is capable of being greatly affected by the radiation of other energy fields. It seems within the veil of flesh that each of you is some little pinpoint of consciousness gazing out at a common world; that is, a world held in common by yourself and all those who agree on consensus reality. Whereas in fact each of you is the Creator of your universe, and, as the one known as J has said, sometimes it becomes very clear that the universe lies within, that the reality lies within, that all that seems to be "out here"—as this instrument is pushing at the air in front of her body—that "out there" is that space that is around those fragile, delicate, human bodies that you experience at this time. In actuality, this awareness is but a tiny portal upon the awareness which you carry deep within yourself. You carry it as a precious gem. You carry it in rich and fertile soil. You can, through meditation, find those gems of self and ask them to shine for you so that you may see their beauty. For you truly have not simply one but many of these gems within you, crystallized essences of beingness of various hues and energies that you have, through countless lifetimes, developed and in this particular lifetime have come into a specific and a beneficial balance or shall we say dynamic imbalance seeking towards balance asymptotically. This is your character: you are the crystal, the light, the energy that is the deeper aspect of life rather than being a specific shell, a specific weight, a specific appearance, and all these details that appear to be the most important part of consensus reality.

These beings that you are vibrate to the highest truth of which the crystal of your being is allowed to become aware. If the highest truth which you allow yourself is the truth, for instance, of what this instrument would call right and wrong, then you are established to the extent of the truth of that concept in a vibratory nexus, and your spirit will rest within a comfort zone within those thoughts which identify and specify that which is wrong, that which is right, that which is good, and that which is bad. However, neither that which is right nor that which is wrong tends to create, within the energy of an entity, that emotion which partakes of what you have called thanksgiving, praise and gratitude. Rather, it holds one within the spell of this particular density, which is the spell of polarity. It is quite necessary for your environment while you are learning, that polarity be displayed in a marvelous amount of detail; that the details of the physical universe be actually infinite, so that one can lose oneself endlessly in the examination of the illusion. However, in truth, the energy which created all things, which binds all things together, which unifies, is an energy that is so far beyond words that it is ineffable, and yet perhaps one of the closest locutions to that emotion is gratitude.

We normally greet you in the love and in the light of the one infinite Creator. We do this in a fairly formalized way, because we are indicating to ourselves and to each of you what our vibratory energies are. The Logos which is the one infinite Creator's original Thought is that which we call love, and all that is manifested by the energy of this Thought, acted upon by free will, we call light. Part of that light is the energy of your body and the organs within your body and the molecules within those organs and the atoms within those molecules. Then, upon a completely other level, in the finer bodies, in the energy bodies, that energy is pure and more refined, and what each of you has come here to do is to refine that energy further. Whatever love that you came into this incarnation carrying is a part of the gifts of your previous incarnations which you harvested for this particular illusion. You hoped to add to that store and to further refine and purify your idea of what, who, whose, you are. For investigating essence takes one almost instantly beyond the words, and yet this word, gratitude, is so powerful, because it carries the vibrations of the Creator.

Gratitude is not what it seems; gratitude is not a thanksgiving for blessings received. At its best, it is a way of being so that one breathes in thanks and breathes out praise; breathes in that which is and breathes out, "Thank you," not because of any outer detail but because it is the nature of consciousness to find an overwhelming, ever-overflowing cup of beauty and peace. And as one comes into even the shadow of this energy that lies within your hearts, there is an upliftment, and all of the energies that had seemed chaotic within the being begin to find a rhythm and pulse in harmony with the environment about you and the thoughts within you so that all of the finer bodies and the earthly body that is yours and the bodies that are wind and rain and planets all begin to harmonize and to vibrate and to speak to you. And when the universe is speaking to you, then there is always bliss and joy and peace and praise and infinite thanksgiving. The trick of the illusion is to coax one into the seduction of believing that the dynamic dance between the dark and the light can be solved by choosing the light, or the dark, and turning the back upon the other choice. Certainly, a great deal of third-density existence, especially in the beginning of that process of learning that we call third density, has to do almost completely with sorting out that which you as a soul feel is positive and that which you as a soul feel is negative; that which is desirable; that which is not preferable. Sorting these dynamics out within the personality doesn't take a great deal of experience for many people, for there are many things that seem fair until they have been utilized and experience has been gained that indicate the failure of that beauty over time and experience.

These are the last days of this particular cycle, and each entity that dwells upon this planet at this time has basically chosen its polarity. Perhaps not in a way that activates the spiritual progress that can indeed be accelerated, but the experience of each has been rich and decisions have been made concerning the choice of the light or the dark. What we ask you to think about, in the context of gratitude, is that land which lies beyond polarity, that unification that is very much of higher densities and very much of the fourth density which is at this time coming so close now to that vibration which is your so-called consensus reality that, more and more, there is a transparency that comes and goes for entities, so that suddenly those truths of fourth density and unconditional love are indeed opened to that entity, and that entity feels, understands and sees, as if "real," the perfection of all things and the beauty of the play of light and dark as the soul spins, evolves, balances and regularizes in that spiral towards oneness with the one infinite Creator.

What is gratitude? Gratitude is breathing in and breathing out with the awareness that this act is a gift. Each of you is like a cut flower. You have sprung from the soil of physicality, you have the life of a blossom, and your only responsibility is to blossom, to be, to share that which you are and take in that which all else is exchanging with each other's energy fields, those dynamics which lie between the two of you. It is easy to give thanks when there are good times, but that is not the heart of thanksgiving. The heart of thanksgiving is to see in all things the gift of manifested experience. Oh how precious that is! Oh, how dear! We cannot convey to you our appreciation of the challenges that you face by being in a physical body and in third density, and yet we say to you that such an adventure calls to us simply because each of you is experiencing, within the illusion, the ten thousand colors and shapes and forms[3] that are what the Creator knows about itself so far. As each of you takes in the air and gives it back out to the universe, you are singing a song that no one else has ever sung, lifting to the heavens a beauty that has never before been seen. And the Creator knows more now than before, because you have been open and vulnerable to experience, and the world and all its experience has been opened and made vulnerable to you. This is the heart of thanksgiving—the knowing that every breath you take is significant, meaningful and helpful to the Creator, truly a gift given and a gift received.

We sense that there are other questions, and the one known as J has specifically said that she would like to question upon a different subject. Consequently, we would like to thank this instrument for its offering, and we would wish to transfer the contact at this time to the one known as Jim. We leave this instrument in love and in light. We are those of Q'uo.

(Jim channeling)

I am Q'uo, and greet each again in love and in light through this instrument. At this time it is our privilege to offer ourselves in the attempt to speak to any further queries which those present may have for us. Is there another query at this time?

J: Yes, there is. Hello, Q'uo. I am the one known as J, and I just wanted to tell you that we have golden spiral Milky Way needles, and they're made of gold, iridium, palladium, ruthium and rhodium, and, as we understand it, all those metals work on different parts of the body. We use them as healing instruments, pulling out energy that isn't necessary and bringing in light. We're very excited, and we wanted to share that with you, and to get your opinion about our golden spiral needles. Thank you.

I am Q'uo, and we are aware of your query, my sister. We greet you and we are most happy to attempt to speak to this query. If you will remember that which those of Ra spoke concerning the upward spiraling line of light that is the path all creation takes, then these Milky Way needles may be seen to reflect in a small way this upward spiraling line of light in the healing modality, as you attempt to relieve various distortions and imbalances that the

---

[3] Carla: This expression is a reuse of the Buddhist term of the world of Maya, translated as the world of "the ten thousand things."

human body, mind and emotions are wont to accumulate from time to time due to the participation in your daily round of activities. If you will also remember that there is a phase shift, shall we say, a change of energy that is possible when entities move in a certain direction. When placing energy into that direction which moves at 90° to that direction, traveling at speeds that are in your measurement great, in what are frequently called craft of the UFO nature, then it is possible to change dimensions or densities of light with this phase shift. If you combine this information with the upward spiraling line of light, you may see this spiraling line of light as being a continuous phase shift, so that there is available to each entity that is seeking the healing from these devices a kind of amplified energy that is able to, shall we say, untangle the knots that are within the mind-body-spirit complex of the entities within this illusion. Another way of looking at these Milky Way needles is to see them as one would see the pyramid energies. The pyramid takes the ever-present energy of prana, the love of the Logos, the intelligent energy which creates all things and focuses it in such-and-such a fashion, much as the drain in your bathtub focuses the water as it leaves through the drain. Thus the pyramid and these Milky Way needles tend to focus this upward-spiraling line of light energy so that it is available in the healing modality.

Is there another query, my sister?

J: Not at this time. Thank you so much for sharing that with me.

I am Q'uo, and we thank you, my sister. Is there another query at this time?

Carla: I've got one. I've noticed that two very bright lights have moved to town recently, my friend, V, and the one known as H, and, previous to that, I have very recently met others within this circle that seem to me to be very, very resonant with my own personality. I wondered if there was more than synchronicity involved? Are we of the same soul family? I just feel so much resonance with these people, and the energy change is so sudden. It's just noticeable, and I wondered if you could comment on that.

I am Q'uo, and am aware of your query, my sister. Without infringing upon the free will of any present, we may suggest that those present within this circle of seeking and many others as well have, before incarnational life began, made certain arrangements, promises, shall we say, that there would be the effort made at a certain time within the experience of the harvest to give the life's energy and direction to aiding in this harvest. There is always the ability to share the load, shall we say, that those who are of service wish to partake in, for the joy of seeking and seeing and serving the Creator is multiplied manyfold when there are many harvesters, shall we say, working in the same fields. Thus, one may see those entities who have recently joined this circle of seeking and have relocated themselves to this particular geographical area as hearing the sound of the music, shall we say, the music that is the promise made before the incarnation now come to fruition.

Is there a further query, my sister?

Carla: That's beautiful! Do you have a thought about how we can work together, because I know H and I both, as group leaders, have real hopes of somehow acting to unite the planet in love and world friendship. Do you have any suggestions for how we might collaborate better together or what we may support and encourage in each other?

I am Q'uo, and am aware of your query, my sister. Again, we wish not to infringe upon free will by suggesting that which has not been chosen already in your free will. However, we may suggest that each entity within this incarnation is able to be of most service by being most authentically who each entity is. Each has brought certain skills, desires and talents to this incarnation, and each encourages the other most effectively by encouraging each to be, first of all, to be firmly rooted within the harmony, the love and the light of the one infinite Creator, to be who each has determined before the incarnation each can most effectively be. For each of you is unique, though each of you is the one Creator, each of you has yet another way of shining forth that love and light as a faceted jewel. Thus, encourage each other in whatever direction feels most appropriate. Your hearts can tell you the direction, your meditations can show you your heart. Seek them together however you can, and light and love shall come from this joined seeking, light and love which can heal a wounded planet. We then would suggest that you do as you do seek, share and love together.

Is there another query, my sister?

Carla: No, thank you, Q'uo.

I am Q'uo, and again we thank you, my sister. Is there another query at this time?

R: Yes, I have one. My name is R. With all the earth changes that are happening, the dynamics that are happening with the people that are on this planet at this time, the rage that they're feeling, what is your suggestion to help balance that out towards a smoother experience?

I am Q'uo, and am aware of your query, my sister. We are aware that there are those within this group and within many other groups as well who take time each day to meditate and to pray and to send love and healing energy to all who are in pain; to open their own hearts to the healing love and light of the one Creator; to send that energy to Mother Earth, herself, for her healing as she brings forth a new Earth into fourth density; to send that love and light to each entity upon the planet which feels pain, which feels weariness, which feels the sickness and hate and disappointment and disease and all those other various ailments which can take the attention and turn the mind to darker thoughts and ways of sharing that do not open the heart but close it. We would suggest that, whenever it is possible, upon a regular basis that you take time to pray, to meditate and to send love and light to all who need it.

Is there another query, my sister?

R: I don't know that I have the words for it, it's the astrological things that are going on … how amplified energies are. I'm having a time putting it into words.

Carla: How about "spiritual momentum"?

R: Yeah. There's a lot going on in the positive, but the rage among the people is really amplified. Where's that amplification coming from? Is it just for clarification? It seems like it's more than that.

I am Q'uo, and am aware of your query, my sister. As we mentioned previously, this is the time of harvest, the time of the change of cycles for not only each entity upon this planet but for the planet itself. For all move in the upward spiraling line of light as if in accordance with the hands of a clock striking the hour of change. The time grows short. There is much work yet to do. This planet has for many of your millennia suffered the difficulties of factions warring one against the other. This anger of war and bellicose action has seeped as heat into the crust of the planet, heat which must be released. Each entity, as well as the planet itself, is therefore asked in the spiritual sense to take a larger share of the ability to transmute this heat and anger. Those who have no firm foundation of spiritual seeking or outlet of sharing in a metaphysical manner take this extra share of energy and transfer it as anger. Thus, those who are aware of the change occurring upon the planetary and the cosmic level which reaches into each individual heart, do well to see in their meditations and their prayers hearts that begin to open, minds that begin to open, arms that begin to open, so that there is acceptance and love, compassion and forgiveness, in place of competition and anger, confusion and ignorance. Therefore, we recommend most heartily that the prayers and visualizations be added to you meditations in order to aid other entities in their attempt to open their hearts, which is the purpose for each entity here on the planet at this time. Some are more, shall we say, effective, more able to do this than others. Those who are able to open their hearts first then teach others by example and in their meditations.

Is there a further query, my sister?

R: No. Thank you.

I am Q'uo, and we thank you, my sister, for your query. Is there another query at this time?

(No more queries.)

I am Q'uo. As the queries appear to have been satisfied for the nonce, we would take this opportunity to once again thank each for joining this circle of seeking this day. We are aware that each sacrifices much in order to make the time and space in the daily round of activities available for such a gathering. It is always a great joy to be asked to join you here, and we would remind each that in your own, private meditations, we would be happy to join you there as a conditioning vibration to help deepen your state of meditation. A simple request is all that is necessary, and we shall join you there.

At this time then we shall take our leave of this instrument and this group. We leave each in the love and in the ineffable light of the one infinite Creator. We are known to you as those of Q'uo. Adonai, my friends. Adonai.

L/L Research

Sunday Meditation
September 29, 2002

Group question: Our question today has to do with the concept of balancing. We hear a great deal, from many different sources, that balance is important; that we should be looking for ways to balance our lives, and, since each person lives a unique existence, we're wondering if Q'uo could give some information on how we as individuals could determine what we need to do—each of us—to balance our lives. Is there a good general technique of meditation, of contemplation, or study that you would recommend for us to balance our lives so that the responses we make to people and to new situations are our highest and our best?

(Carla channeling)

We are those known to you as the principle of Q'uo, and we greet you in the love and in the light of the one infinite Creator in whose service we come to you this afternoon. We feel so privileged and so blessed to experience each of your beauties. Truly, each of you is a blessing to us; as a gemstone, as a pearl, as that which is beautiful and unique and utterly essential to the wholeness of the universe. We honor you and we thank you for the desires of your heart that have pulled you towards a seeking circle such as this one. We thank you, for our hope has been to share information of a metaphysical nature with those to whom it would be helpful.

As always, our story is fairly simple, but there are an infinite number of ways to discuss unity. We find that to be somewhat ironic but only due to the nature of language. We ask only one thing, as we share our opinions with you: we ask that you understand that we are seekers such as you, those who walk with you upon a path. We perhaps have had more experience, however, we have not had more experience in third density. In fact, we have not had as much, for our third-density experience was brief.

We consider each of you masters. We know that each of you has the capability of moving from this experience into the next classroom of experience at the cessation of this physical incarnation, and we hope by those things that we offer to provide resources for those of you who seek, as this instrument said earlier, to forge a path that allows light from higher densities into the Earth plane where it is desperately needed at this time.

Each of you is already doing this work by breathing in and breathing out. Whether you feel you are in balance or whether you feel that you are riding the crest of chaos! In fact, the very breath that you share, when shared with an open heart, is of fundamental assistance to the planetary sphere upon which you dwell at this time and to the population of that planet, which is one body, of which each of you is an essential part. Therefore, truly it is said that there are no mistakes, and we simply ask you to realize that, in that context, what we have to say is subjective truth. That concept of truth is a dangerous one for your peoples, and we encourage you to think of our ideas only insofar as they attract you, as they resonate to you, and as they help you to focus with those things with which you are working at this time. We ask you not to see us as authorities or to retain any thoughts of ours which do not seem resonant. With this freedom of will preserved on the part of each of you, then we can feel free to share our opinions with you for what they're worth. And each of you will find different things about that which we say to keep and different things to allow to remain behind. We would encourage this, for, truly, your sense of personal discrimination is a tremendous, powerful and valid resource for each of you. You will know that which is resonant to you. It will come to you as if you were remembering it after a long time of forgetting. It will not feel as new as it will feel familiar and positive. If you do not have this kind of chemical reaction, shall we say, to these thoughts, then leave them behind without a second thought, for the universe, the creation on all levels is full of messages. It does not matter if you miss a message, for another one will be there to take its place. The creation is incredibly, infinitely full of opportunity, and, the more it is realized that the creation is a plastic and even a fluid thing, the more possible it will be for each of you to mine the rich field of experience for the gems that it does contain.

You ask this day concerning balance. This is another concept which is relatively simple to comprehend but infinitely difficult either to delineate or to achieve. We may say a few things concerning balance this day, but by no means could we hope to exhaust the subject. Therefore, if there are remaining questions at the end of this session, we encourage each of you to remember and to bring up those questions that still remain. There will be time at the end of this meeting for questions, and as well it is quite possible to initiate a further question at another channeling if the topic is sufficiently interesting to the group.

Perhaps the first thing that we would discuss concerning the concept of balancing is the model upon which this in built. This instrument tunes according to a certain prayer which is the prayer of St. Francis. In its entirety, it is vibrated thusly:

Lord, make me an instrument of thy peace. Where there is hatred, let me sow love; where there is injury, pardon; where there is discord, union; where there is doubt, faith; where there is despair, hope; where there is sadness, joy. Oh divine master, teach us to seek not so much to be loved as to love; to be understood as to understand; to be consoled as to console. For it is in pardoning that we are pardoned; it is in giving that we receive; and it is in dying that we rise to eternal life.

This is an excellent tuning prayer for this particular instrument. However, we use it [here] to point out the [model's] dialectical limitations. Balance is not precisely a balance between one side of self and the other side of self. There is not a line dividing half of your body into the positive aspect and [the other] half into the negative aspect. While tuning towards the light is a skillful resource with which to address a momentary calmness and stability of point of view, nevertheless, it is not that which constitutes a true model of what it is to become balanced. There is a flatness to the model that could be described by the X axis and the Y axis; those things to the right of the X axis are positive, those things to the left of the X axis negative, and so forth.

Take this model of the circle that this instrument has described and allow it to become a sphere, an energy field around things. This model would indicate that one were in balance—when? When is a circle in balance? To us, a circle is in balance at all times. The spherical aspect of it creates a situation in which there is no possibility of losing one's balance, there is no possibility of falling. There is only the rolling, the being kicked by deity into different circumstances, and the ability to bounce.

So let us look at this model a little more closely. The thing that entities tend to do when they perceive that they are out of balance is to attempt to correct. This is true when an entity is within an automobile and the car goes into a skid. The less trained an entity is in moving out of a skid, the less likely an entity is to affect positively the direction of the car by those actions which are taken after the self-perceived slip is noticed. The more skillful the person in driving, the more experience that person has had, the quicker that entity will correct [the path of the vehicle]. The secret, of course, is refraining from attempting to steer the car while it is out of control.

This relates strongly to that saying from what this instrument calls the "AA Prayer," which is:

> Grant me the courage to change what I can, the peace to leave alone what I cannot change and the wisdom to know the difference.

When applied to bringing the physical vehicle, the emotional vehicle, the energy vehicle, the energy field [as a whole], through a skid within the life experience, the first thing that needs to be addressed is the fear of being out of control. The actual situation within the physical experience is that, there is no difference between the skid and the correction except the feeling that it gives to the entity internally. The situation in truth is that, at all times, metaphysically speaking, there is an element of being completely out of control. This is because the entire atmosphere and environment of your planetary sphere and [its] many supporting sub-densities or inner-densities, as this instrument calls them, are completely focused on creating an out-of-control experience that will be cyclically more and then cyclically less in control, allowing each entity who seeks that proper and timely cycle wherein lessons are addressed, are processed, [and] are either learned or not. The cycle moves around, and either the same situation occurs again for that particular entity on that particular theme, or the cycle spirals, because there is now another level that has opened because of prior learning. Consequently, metaphysically speaking, each of you is in the process of infinite change.

Change is uncomfortable by its very nature. It is confusing, and new patterns that are tossed into the life experience by a most humorous deity have a tremendous ability to appear to the untutored eye like pure and complete confusion and chaos. It is only after processing a good deal of new catalyst that a pattern may perhaps become clear, and it is by hindsight, then, that most of us see the true value and benefit of most of the lessons that we have been offered by our higher selves, chosen before this incarnation with great care and great love. The only difference between before incarnation and during incarnation is that, before incarnation, the reasons for these choices were perfectly clear. Within incarnation, all of the sense of the pattern as an integrated whole has to remain beneath a veil of confusion and illusion so that the fundamental nature of the lesson of this density may become slowly and subjectively clear to each in its own way.

This lesson, as we have said many times, revolves around concepts which have to do with a principle that is of the nature of a Thought or a Logos, and that principle cannot be described better within your language than by the word, love. The Logos or love is an energy that has created each of you, that has created each of us, that has created all planetary and stellar bodies, that has created a house for Itself. The Creator of this house is listening, is fascinated, and is hoping that each of you will attack the school year that is known as planet Earth with great appetite and enjoyment. It is seen before incarnation as a place where it would be impossible not to be merry. As the one known as F has said, "How can one not be in a good mood in a beautiful place like this?" And indeed your mimosa bean pods hang down with a beautiful flair in the autumn sunlight and that particular quality of color within the light of autumn is most beautiful not only on your plane but also in the inner planes where we are at this time resting.

It is indescribably beautiful, and there is only one thing that mars the carnival atmosphere, and that is change: the reason that you came! For only in illusion is the perception of real change possible. It is not that there is not a different thought every moment for infinity, it is not that things do not change, for truly no two entities can breathe the same breath twice; no single entity can breathe the same breath more than once. The philosophical river that has for so long been talked about as not being able to be stepped in twice still runs, still changes, and still brings a fresh harvest every day of things that will place the entity in the position of feeling out of balance. Where lies the love in this structure? Love within the structure lies in that which is not seen. It lies beyond the confusion, it lies beyond the circumstances, and it lies in becoming aware of the self as a unit that contains all that there is, in balance or out of balance. All the ingredients lie within, not neatly separated into those that are identifiable as positive and those identifiable as negative but thoroughly and completely mixed, and mixed yet again with the infinite layers of acculturation that each of you has experienced because of how each has heard what each has heard throughout the incarnation. There are many of those within this group whose early experiences within this sphere have been difficult to bear; whose growth as spirits has been distorted in various ways because of assumptions accepted as true, such as, "I am not worthy," "I am not happy," "I am not blessed," "I am not lucky," "I am not good enough." We could go on, but basically it is that feeling of being not good enough, of being abandoned, of being stranded in an unsafe place, which charges one with the need to put up defenses.

This brings us back to the idea of the circular, ball-shaped nature of self. Does a ball, does a sphere need defense? Indeed not. In fact, within the civil engineering trade, the building of bridges is only possible in some cases because of ball bearings that are placed at points of balance within the structure, because the circle can hold much, much more pressure and weight and more of a changing load than any other structure, anything with corners. This means that people can use the circular form to stabilize large structures, and, if the nature of the energy field is seen to be round and spherical, then it may perhaps more easily be seen that the way to become a balanced entity is not the dialectic of, "Oh, I see the dark; I must replace it with the light." But as the one known as J said, "Oh, I see the dark; let me love it with my light. Let it all become one thing within the heart." The heart that is within each of you is a haven that is already in balance. There is a pre-incarnational setting that you may be able to change somewhat through the course of an entire lifetime. You are hoping that you will be able to adjust the way you perceive information so that the information that you receive is less and less distorted. One of the goals of balancing is to decrease distortion, and, as this instrument has said earlier in this conversation, to become integrated, to become not only that entity who loves but that entity who is loved, so that one begins to feel the fullness of self and the rightness of having all that there is within one entity. This part of balancing simply clears the field by removing as much distortion from the perceptions that are incoming as possible.

So let us move from the concept of sphericalness or not cringing from difficult experiences, to another facet of the balancing experience. That is the great importance of not only allowing oneself to fall, [but] allowing oneself in those moments of self-perceived chaos to move with the chaos. Indeed, to feel as if one is falling down and not coping but also to begin to allow the self to laugh about it, to take it lightly. We have said through this instrument many times that we encourage you to love that which is beyond yourself and take it very seriously but we encourage you also to take yourself lightly. For those things which are the highest and the best within you are those things which simply need to be found within the self and allowed to express. They are already there; they are hiding behind things like defensiveness, fear, all of those reactions that are, as Buddhists would say, not particularly skillful. There is a great deal to be said for this point of view of skillfulness. However, it does not come into congruency with the thought that is behind the skill, which is that of love. There is nothing restrained about the love of the infinite Creator, nor is there anything restrained about the power of those energies that move through each of you at all times. There is distortion in the incoming data that you receive with ear, with eye, from reading, from opinion and so forth. It comes in roughly and raw, and some of it is true and some of it is not; some of it is of good report, and some of it is simply gossip; some is true, some is false. How shall you judge yourself? How shall you look at the momentary experiences of the day and say, "This was a good thought; this was a non-skillful thought"?

There are many ways to address the subject. The best way that we know to tell you is that the key is emotion. You are of the concept, because you have a biological computer called a brain, that you are here to think better, and indeed in many ways as a side-effect of spiritual improvement in the constitution, there is also an improvement in the thinking. However, the harvest of planet Earth is not a thought, not on the level of ideas. Rather, it is a pure emotion. It is a thought that is creative, that has to itself the nature of a principle that engenders more of itself or children of itself, so that each of your thoughts, each of these moments during any day when something crystallizes for you emotionally and you have a specific reaction, whether it is a positive emotion seemingly or seemingly a negative one, offers …

(Pause)

We must indeed state that we cannot describe that which it offers except to tell a story. This instrument was communicating [earlier, by letter,] with an entity who talked to her about "Lunchables," if you are familiar with this product which contains cheese, meat and crackers. She [the writer] was thinking about the difference between perceiving something in one structure and perceiving it in a different structure, and she was eating these little crackers and cheese. She discovered that if she put the crackers, then the turkey, then the cheese upon each other in that order, they tasted one way; if she changed the order, she had a different experience, and yet they were the same ingredients. This entity said to this instrument, "How can it be that Lunchables would teach me a spiritual lesson?" And we say to you that this is the nature of balance. Everything has a message to those whose energies crystallize at the moment that the message is coming through. There will be a continuation of messages for each seeking spirit. There is no concern about whether or not you get them all; there will be another one in five minutes or half an hour. There is no waiting in terms of spiritual learning.

Indeed, all you must decide is how fast you can change; how much you can transform while still remaining stable, productive and all of those other attributes that are valued by yourself and the culture in which you live. It is only that limitation that keeps each entity from progressing very, very quickly. And indeed we would advise against very quick advances and very quick changes. We would suggest to each of you that each find the way to remove toxic intensity from any day in which it occurs. In other words, quite often the reaction of one who has learned something and is excited about learning more is to do more and more meditation, more and more balancing exercises, more and more visualizations, and so forth, which simply creates a faster rate of change until the stable, everyday self is offered a crisis that expresses to that entity the nature of that entity's limitations as far as being able to change beyond a certain rate of acceleration. The thing to be aware of within the self is what this instrument would call burn-out, where there has been a massive application of principle, truth and the various resources of the "spiritual supermarket," as the one known as T has called it, and circuits are blown, and consequently there is that time where distance must be set between the self and the spiritual seeking. Those entities who are not capable of toning down their efforts with the ability to laugh at the self are those who are most vulnerable to spiritual exhaustion. For those who wish over a long period of time to make sustained and serious efforts in opening up the self to the realization of self, we encourage laughter, we encourage good friends supporting each other, we encourage each finding the ways that relaxation truly comes, that lightening-up really happens.

It is not the same for all entities. One entity can relax perfectly well doing stitchery, another entity reading, another entity walking in the woods. Another entity may have the need to remain active at all times. Whatever the pattern, that pattern itself and the emotions that it calls up are those items of real interest. How am I perceiving this structure, this that presents itself to me, this gestalt? How can I juggle and play and dance with this and change the structure of the way I am thinking of the contents of this constructed situation that will improve my capacity to be comfortable while I am not in balance? These are excellent questions to ask of the self, because truly reality is a plastic, illusion that is very penetrable by belief and perception. That which you perceive is that which is subjectively true. If the perception or the belief changes, the body itself will believe the perception rather than the actual circumstance. Therefore, if each of you happened to be hypnotized and then placed in a situation where there was physical discomfort and yet one was told that it was not occurring, the entity's body would not feel pain. Conversely, if an entity is told that he is being touched by fire, in the absence of any fire on the physical, that entity's body may well blister and burn. Belief becomes the reaction to the body.

This means that the belief that you have about what you are experiencing can create a wide range of actual occurrences, for the belief system triggers the response to the situation. The way that the so-called human experience works is not particularly objective. Indeed, it is extremely subjective. It is extremely permeable, and you have much more power over your universe than you know. So another level in working with the balancing is to see that you have the creative power to reconstruct not the situation itself but how it is looked at, what point of view is used. What difference, may we ask, would there be between a drama or even a soap opera and a sitcom? What difference is there between melodrama and drawing room farce except the way that the entities respond to the undoubtedly somewhat mired situation that is required in order for a play of any kind to occur, whether it be a comedy, a drama or a tragedy? How can you create a sitcom, so that there are laughs and saving graces to the life experience that inevitably includes all of the crazy things that occur upon planet Earth; all the things that seem unfair, all the things that pull at one, all the things that create emotion?

For you see, each of you, balanced or unbalanced, is constantly sending a signal. Each receives the same signal; each receives the infinite love and light in infinite supply at all times moving from the roots of being, from the roots of the body, spiraling upwards through the self and out into the universe again. The magic here is involved in your nature and how you refract that upward-spiraling light in such a way as to create your own color, your own luminosity, your own way of offering light back to the infinite Creator. So what you are really responsible for here is simply becoming more who you are, for who you are is a spiritual, energetic being, and it is something that is encased and often buried in that illusion which is flesh and those persuasive seductions that the physical world offers; seductions such as the need to feed the self, the need to create warmth for the self with inclement weather, the need to appear to be this or that way in regard to other people. All of the needs are for a seduction of the senses and a seduction of the emotion. It is as if each were at a magic carnival and one could either spend time upon the rides going around and around, or one could bring one's bounty to the carnival and have it judged to be "best chocolate cake" or "best tomato." It is a choice of where to put the mind, where to put the energy, where to put the love. If you are loving, you are in balance. You can be upside down or sideways or flat on your back in the illusion, but, if your heart is open, we ask you to be utterly pleased and satisfied and to move on into the moment to mind some of the wonderful, spontaneously available breath and spirit and *je ne sais quoi* of that particular moment; that intersection of space/time and time/space in which this perfect moment became possible.

Each breath in and each breath out is so precious. We dwell in our present density in a much more expanded time frame relative to your own, and we see the preciousness of breathing in and breathing out for only seventy-five thousand years, and we see especially at this time the preciousness of breathing in and breathing out for perhaps the last of the series of incarnations within third density. It is truly a transformational and magical time. The subjective feeling of being out of balance is inevitable. The truth always lies in the knowledge that all is well, and all will be well. Where you put your energy is precisely where you should be putting your energy even if, in subjective terms, analytical terms or in the opinion of others, it is incorrect. Know that you will always come about to a new tack when you feel it from within. Know that, until you feel it from within, it is better to continue to collect data, to absorb and to feel, and then to observe the feelings, to learn from those out-of-control, seemingly unbalanced emotions where the mind is, where the heart is, where the catalyst is, what the lessons are.

The lessons usually have to do with the giving and the receiving of love. As the one known as V has said, it is much easier to give than to receive. Many within this group are working with the ability to receive love, so there is never an assumption that this or that situation is helpful and this other situation is not helpful. Know that many times this situation is the reverse of that which it seems to be.

This instrument is informing us that we have been far too wordy, and we shall need to move on. We thank you so much for asking such an interesting question, and we would like to transfer this contact to the one known as Jim so that his energy may be used in answering further questions. We thank this instrument for its service, and we leave it in love and in light. We are those known to you as the principle of Q'uo.

(Jim channeling)

I am Q'uo, and greet each again in love and in light through this instrument. At this time it is our privilege to offer ourselves in the attempt to speak to any further queries of a shorter nature that may remain upon the minds of any of those present. May we ask at this time, then, if there is a query to which we may speak?

J: Yes, hello, Q'uo. This is J, and I was wondering if you could just speak to me briefly about any suggestions you might have about how I can use these healing instruments, the phi-ratio spirals, with my clients to be in service to others, and if you could just briefly speak to me about the clockwise and the counter-clockwise motion of them and how they might send out of the body or into the body. Thank you very much.

I am Q'uo, and I am aware of your query, my sister. As you are working with those who present themselves to you for your healing energies and efforts, it may be helpful to spend a few moments at the beginning of each session in meditation together in order that those energies which are in the subconscious mind and which are attempting to make an impression upon the conscious mind might do so, for it is truly said that all healing will come from within the entity to be healed and simply needs an avenue over which it might travel, shall we say. This avenue can be provided by each of you seeking the resources of the subconscious mind.

As to the clockwise and counter-clockwise spiraling effect of these tools for healing, we would recommend that the attempt to send energy into a body or portion of the body may best be accomplished by using those energies which move in a clockwise fashion. Thus, the prana or infinite love and light of the one Creator may be sent more speedily and precisely to a certain location by using the clockwise spiral and by visualizing this energy moving into the spiral and into the body as this tool is used, so the counter-clockwise spiral then is most helpful in the removing the energy from the physical body or a portion thereof, again, seeking the counsel of the subconscious, moving in the intuitive response from the subconscious in a fashion which allows a visualization to assist the use of the counter-clockwise spiral.

Is there a further query, my sister?

J: No, thank you very much.

I am Q'uo. We thank you, my sister. Is there another query at this time?

Carla: Let me follow up to J's question and just ask if the image that you're offering is that of its coming from the needle into the energy field of the body and then also moving up the spiral so it's not just a one-way energy flow, it's a connection between the infinite and that infinite within self through the needle, but it's also being pulled by the desire from above as it is being sent from above. Is that right? Is the dynamic there one of a partnership between the body that's receiving and the energy that's moving through?

I am Q'uo. This is correct, my sister.

Carla: Thanks.

Again, we thank you, my sister, for your efforts. Is there another query at this time?

S: I have one or two. It's kind of interesting, I've been reading on the spiritual value of mazes and things like that, and there's a crop circle I have here that would be—I guess—a perfect candidate for a spiral maze, and I was wondering if you could tell me what this particular crop circle represented and your ideas on such a maze?

I am Q'uo, and am aware of your query, my brother. The spiral maze which you refer to is a pattern of energy progression which may be projected in a specified fashion according to the intention of the entity utilizing it. This is to say, it is a tool which may function according to your use of it. It may be that which enhances the environment in which it is constructed if that is your desire. It may be that which enhances the health and well-being of those who enter into it if that is your desire; it may be that which enhances the well-being of the planetary sphere upon which you dwell, if that be your desire. Thus, you may see, it is the intention of the magician, shall we say, the entity which utilizes the tool for healing and transfer of energy that determines the effect, the outcome or the results.

Is there a further query, my brother?

Steve: Can it be all of those? Does it have to be a single one, or can it be all three?

I am Q'uo, and am aware of your query, my brother, and this too is possible. It is the desire, the intention, the direction that is important in determining how any such tool is used.

Is there another query, my brother?

S: The last one I have was …There is a lady we work with; she just recently has gotten married, and her husband has some very severe back issues, apparently all his life, and I'm wondering if you had any words of wit or wisdom that we may offer to help her be of assistance to him?

I am Q'uo, and am aware of your query, my brother. In looking at the physical vehicle and the various distortions of such that may occur during an incarnation, the back region is that area which signifies support for the entity. When there is a feeling within the entity's being that it is unable to support someone around it or itself or is unable to be supported by such entities, oftentimes, there will be a difficulty in this physical region. It is therefore necessary for the determination of the specific cause that the entity experiencing the distortion have the desire first of all to untangle the riddle; that some means of untangling be utilized. Whether this be contemplation, meditation, prayer, the intellectual analysis of the experience, or whatever means is useful to such an entity, there needs be some method chosen to seek the untangling of the riddle.

Is there a further query, my brother?

S: Not from me, thanks.

I am Q'uo, and we thank you, my brother. Is there another query at this time?

Carla: I have a question about the music at the beginning. It's in two parts. Number one, was that intended by, shall we say, unseen forces and, if so, was the point simply to make us aware by using a song with no key that changes chords and keys constantly?

I am Q'uo, and am aware of your query, my sister. In this instance for you, this is the correct interpretation. For each other entity present, there may be a different interpretation. For the one known as Jim, attempting to arrange the music, this was a practice in accepting that which was.

Is there another query, my sister?

Carla: No, thank you, Q'uo.

I am Q'uo, and again we thank you. Is there another query at this time?

D: I'm D. I have the observation that came to me as we were discussing the counter-clockwise and clockwise spirals, and that was this: that, if you think of love as one spiral, one direction, hitting somebody else, it's reflected just as in a mirror; reflected in a counter-clockwise direction which again, in hitting another person, another mirror, reversed in a clockwise direction, on and on, clockwise, counter-clockwise, love reflected as it is applied. It's just an observation that came through as I was listening to the discussion.

I am Q'uo, and we appreciate your observation and would note that it is indeed one very valid interpretation of the spiral effect. Is there another query at this time?

D: I'm D again, and thinking about the harvesting process and putting in terms of the time frame that we understand, could you express to us what kind of time would be involved in the harvesting process that we are entering into now?

I am Q'uo, and am aware of your query, my brother. The time of harvest is now. There are many souls who move through the doors of what you call death which move them into the light and [they] remain in that light for as long as it is possible to enjoy the light before it becomes too glaring, too strong and too intense. Then the step from the light is made, and for many at this time the step is into the fourth density of compassion and understanding. The length in your measurement in terms of months or years is not that which any can accurately assess, for it is indeed a fluid process responsive to the group mind/body/spirit complexes that populate your planet at this time and the choices that are made by individuals and groups seeking to share the light, seeking to become the light. Thus, it is possible for a great amount of work to be done in a short period of your time due to the traumatic nature of many experiences and events taking place upon your Earth world at this time. Thus, we cannot with any certainty give you even a general idea beyond a decade or two, which we realize is not terribly specific according to your measurements of time and experience.

Is there a further query?

Don: No, thank you, Q'uo.

I am Q'uo, and again we thank you, my brother. Is there another query at this time?

(No further queries.)

I am Q'uo, and we would take this opportunity to thank each once again for joining us and inviting us to this circle of seeking. We realize that we have spoken overly long, and we apologize for our wordiness, but it is such joy to join you in your circle of seeking, and we rejoice at each opportunity and invitation. We would remind each that we are available at any time that you would wish us to join you in your meditation to help deepen the meditation. A simple request mentally is all that is necessary for us to join you there.

At this time, we shall take our leave of this instrument and this group. We leave each in the love and in the light of the one infinite Creator. We are known to you as those of Q'uo. Adonai, my friends. Adonai. ❧

L/L Research

Sunday Meditation
October 6, 2002

Group question: The question today concerns the power of thought and the power of belief of the words that we speak to ourselves and the images that we create from these words and these beliefs and how this image can be changed according to how beliefs change. We would like for Q'uo to give us some information on how we can create our own images; how we can change the way we talk to ourselves, the words we speak in our minds, and the images that we see. This is, I guess, a personal mythology—the way we look at ourselves and the way we look at the world through the creation of ourselves, so anything Q'uo would have to add to this thought, we would appreciate very much.

(Carla channeling)

We are those known to you as the principle of Q'uo, and we greet you in the love and in the light of the one infinite Creator in Whose service we are. We thank you each for arranging the details of your life so that you are able to join this circle of seeking. We thank you for the opportunity to share our thoughts. We are most happy to do so with the request, as always, that each of you takes what you feel is good from those opinions which we share and by all means leave all of those things which do not seem to be as fair to you behind without a second thought. This will enable us to feel that freedom which comes from being a neighbor and a friend whose opinion is worth sharing, without feeling that we have represented ourselves to you as authorities or teachers, for truly we are as you: those who walk upon a path and those who reach out in service to others. We have a tremendous sea of things in common: the creation that we share is one.

You ask this day about the power one's self-image has to affect one's life. Indeed, this is an endlessly interesting question, because it revolves without end in terms of the effect of feedback and how the echo of feedback never actually ends, so that, not only is there a feeling of progression to the energy of one's being as one experiences the illusion of time, there is also that sense of each moment being its own perfected entity which is established as the truth of that moment and which moves out endlessly into the creation of the Father as a perfect offering of that moment, that time, that space and that truth, so that the truth is always coming from you in its perfect form at the same time that it is forever in development in the process of birth to the ever-new moment.

The one known as J has suggested that it is quite possible that the experience or the illusion that each of you shares at this time is one which has been assisted or enhanced, shall we say, by those beings of higher densities who have compassion upon those who have gone through a tremendous amount of change. In this supposition, the one known as J was indicating that, indeed, perhaps the much talked about latter days, rather than being imminent, have actually already occurred, and, were this to be so, this suggestion is that all of those who indeed did graduate at that time still might have experienced so much trauma at the changes made at the shift between the old world and the new that the souls of those within this room and perhaps within this planet were placed, as it were, upon a stage that was created specifically as a hologram substituting for the world which was the old world. This new world then would be a world which was constructed to be a safe haven for those positive entities whose work was done within third density but who were not quite ready yet to spread their wings and accept the full light of fourth density without their physical vehicles. We do not state that this is true, but we do state that this is a wonderful way to envision the consensus reality which you face at this time, because it is efficacious in allowing you to see that you have an enormous amount of power over your consciousness and the experiences of that stream of consciousness.

Certainly we can say that, regardless of the model used to discuss the transition times into fourth density, the membrane between densities is semi-permeable and increasingly so as the time moves from moon to moon and year to year. Already you have experienced a great deal of shifting and opening up of energies, of patterns changing, and these things have been experienced, not because necessarily they were chosen but perhaps inadvertently, so that change has multiplied upon change, and it is easy to feel that one is completely unable to control one's life. However, we would suggest to you that the issue of control is a kind of seduction designed to limit the ability to envision and to dream when one is allowed to be cast loose from one's circumstances so that one exists in that space between all things: between densities, between energies, in the water, shall we say, that the creation swims within. It can be seen that this "between place" is actually the womb within which the self is birthed from moment to moment, and, as the self is birthed, so is the creation. It is difficult to grasp that one does create the stars, the bodies within the heavens, all of the amazing and cosmic structures of energy and balance that no one's mind in any density could actually grip, wield and change, yet each of you, by the way he thinks of himself and the way he tells his story to himself, creates the stars of a certain color and in a certain order, creates a universe that wraps around him like a cloak and prepares him for that journey which, in his own mind, is the business of his life.

Each of you has this kind of creatorship, and each is feeling this ability to change the feelings with which life is replete. Each has talked before this meditation began of ways in which the thoughts have been used to create a better environment for the self. The one known as Jim was speaking of how he had begun to realize that that which he had told himself made a difference in how he felt. From the tiniest thing that you say to yourself to the largest, each word and each thought is an energy that has the power to create change in your consciousness and in the world around you. The more you are able to focus upon this power to speak truth, the more transparent the environment is to the echoes of new thoughts. The one known as R was creating lists of words that took power away and words that gave power, and they were words like "follow" or "choose," "I can't do it" or "miracle." The possibilities within the mind that are allowed to the self become the possibilities that are possible within your world. If you can allow yourself the time and space to move within that closet of self and simply listen to the self as it is, the information that comes to you is that sense of self that has drifted beyond the campfire of everyday talk and moved into the cry of the wolf, the beaming of the stars, the energy of the Great Mother and the light of eternity. What do you dream? What do you hope? We say to you, as you dream, take that time in which you color your dreams with care and love and the self-respect that all dreams deserve. The ideals that seemed fair at earlier points in the life may indeed have become tarnished. They may even seem to have failed and to have become vitiated and destroyed by experiences which you have undergone.

How much of disappointment within yourself is true, and how much of it is the tail end of other peoples' stories which they have told to you? The one known as T suggested earlier that there was tremendous power in releasing all thoughts of forgiveness in a certain stubborn situation and moving instead to thoughts of forgetting completely the past. To this entity we say, these thoughts have the power to change the life. It is a sweet mystery, the sugar-bear[4] of truth hiding in the forest of

---

[4] Carla: This odd phrase comes from an early poem of mine, written in 1975:

Sugar Bear

I hear crickets outside the car window,
Run my fingers through the damp
Softness of the summer night.

opinion with the undergrowth of words, words and more words. Each word has its roots and its blossoms, and the words that you plant in the flowerbeds of your sentences, your thoughts, the things that you share with others, have their own beauty, aroma and color. We are not suggesting that your life should be a coloring book to dabble at on a day when there is nothing better to do, for we realize that each of you is moving very quickly through days that seem all too short, and we grasp the fact that it does not seem that there is a great deal of time to spend upon the details of each thought, each word used, and so forth. And yet we would suggest to you that any care that you can take with the things that you think to yourself about yourself will be rewarded, and this reward will echo and re-echo and spiral if you are able to continue to monitor your own inner conversations.

In this instrument, for instance, there is a longstanding distortion towards self-criticism, and this is basically an internalizing of childhood voices that this instrument has heard in the past. In no case does this instrument have to continue hearing this particular voice, it being the voice of her parents, both parents having passed from your illusion. However, as is the case with most children, no matter how old the child gets, there lives within that mature person a tremendously powerful memory of every hurtful word that has ever been spoken [to the child]. Unfortunately for the playful aspect of self, the serious aspect of living a life within the physical illusion sounds its steady toll of time and space and calls all to experience responsibility and accountability for the thoughts and desires of one's own heart. When the moment comes that you can see into this conversation that may have ancient and irrelevant voices within it, you will be more able not simply to silence those voices but to lay them into an appropriate and loving place in deep memory with blessing and with love, so that you may indeed forget, not simply forgive the voices that would bring you down and make you feel small, but,

[rather,] forget them. This forgetting and forgiving of the old voices can release a tremendous power of change within the life pattern.

If you do not choose then to say to the self when a mistake is made, "Oh, you stupid person, you have made a mistake," then what would you choose to say instead? Is there indeed any dishonor in making an error? Is there a necessity to judge beyond the need to correct the error? For most entities, there is. There is always the need to make a judgment. The reasons for this, indeed, would be the subject of another discussion, but, for the entity within third density, the tendency is to make a judgment every single time an event occurs. Knowing this about yourself, then perhaps you can think upon what kind of judgments you would like for yourself to make. It may seem pretty obvious that it is not a good idea to tell the self that the self is stupid or getting old or losing memory, and yet each in this room has said these things to the self at various times. What would be your substitute for this self-comment? Perhaps the embracing of compassion for the self and a willingness to move on has more energy for the positive than any words that you might find to soften the blow of judgment.

It is a difficult thing to grasp in the world of the mind where things seem so clear-cut, but in actuality your illusion is set up with some precision to prevent any entity from being correct for very long at a time. The need of this illusion is fundamentally the need for confusion. Too much clarity within third density creates a pleasant and long third density. Each of you is experiencing the culmination of far more powerful ways of experiencing third density. These ways have been rough, and each trail has been mazed, and yet the progress that each of you has made is outstanding. In all of this confusion, each has found the end of a rainbow and is following that vision.

We encourage more than anything else this basic faith in self that sees beyond the mistakes of the moment and trusts in the excellence of that self that lies within like an undiscovered country. Were this instrument never again to say to itself, "You're just not good enough." would she be good enough? Were the one known as Jim never to say again, "I just can't remember like I used to," would he remember as he used to? Perhaps, but the words that truly hurt the self are the words of judgment that create a contraction and a sorrow within the heart,

> The future is laid out before me like roads,
> One turn leading to the next,
> Finally, the driveway and home.
> Except for the crickets, there are no distractions,
> Right and left marked only in a dark tattoo
> Across satin, ebony skin.
> Benevolent creature, Night,
> Furry, honeyed one, sweet, let me see,
> Sugar bear, what is my destiny?

and so we encourage you to cease bringing sorrow to your own heart, for it is in no way necessary. Each lesson that comes before you has its learning curve. Each learning curve has many moments of seeming failure. Indeed, the only way to learn is to fail repeatedly in such a way that learning occurs. The mechanisms of learning are assisted not by resisting the pain of learning but by speaking it, chanting it, expressing it, having a dance with it, so that there is a movement of energy and a lifting of the spirit that deals with whatever is being dealt with at the time. The one known as R said earlier life is not about working, it is about playing, and this is a good sentence to use as an example for how you can speak to yourself in certain ways. All things take effort. Shall you call that effort work, or shall you call it play? Shall you call it walking, or shall you call it dancing? Shall you call it speaking, or shall you call it singing? Shall you define yourself as prose, or shall you allow yourself to be poetry?

There is a way to play with the textures, qualities and tonalities of life. In this playing, all of the forces of nature wait to play with you, and, when the mind is released into this playing mode, there is a tremendous outburst of energy from angelic and from inner-planes nature sources who are just waiting to play with anyone else who is also playing. For the dance is ongoing, and that which you are is that which moves into this dance, becomes part of this dance, and becomes the dance.

What is your self-image? We ask each of you to define this for yourself at a time when you are simply contemplating what your myth of self is. As this instrument has said, she is a legend in her own mind, and each of you is that. Each of you is a story you've told yourself. It is not simply a birth, a childhood, an education, and a series of experiences as an adult; it is a story with shape and moods and energy and fire, that is, if you wish to tell yourself a story that has energy and fire. The one known as Jim can tell himself that he is cutting grass, or he can tell himself he is dancing with the devas. This instrument can tell herself that she is a bookkeeper, or she can tell herself that she touches people's lives with love. Each of you can look at the simple facts of the life and weave many different stories depending upon those things which are chosen to emphasize and those things which are forgotten and left behind. It is your world, and the possibilities of a world that is created just as you wish it are endless.

Imagine the effect if more and more entities within your Earth world truly, deeply and honestly found that energy within which is the energy of peace, that peace which passes all understanding! Have you considered why there is not peace within the world at this time? When there is not peace within the human heart, what story can the human race tell itself? Is there even a belief in the ideal of peace? Is there a willingness to know that peace is the truth and that strife is the illusion? This instrument and the one known as R earlier were working upon the words of a song. It seemed to this instrument at the time that the words were growing like grass; sprouting up and opening to the sunshine. What artful dodgers words are, slippery, forever changing, always shifting in their nuances and their tones. Words are difficult to use with absolute justice, and yet the power of each word is the power of the [spirit of the concept]. The power of concept is infinite; the power of belief is infinite. The beliefs that you have create themselves as true within your body, within your mind and within your life. May you believe well; may you seek truly and deeply your own story.

We would at this time transfer from this instrument to the one known as Jim to complete this communication, and we thank this instrument and would leave her in love and in light. We are those of Q'uo. We would transfer at this time.

(Jim channeling)

I am Q'uo, and we greet each again in love and in light through this instrument. It is our privilege once again to ask if there may be any further queries to which we may speak at this time. Is there another query at this time?

T: I have a question. You said that forgetting was a good idea as a helpful aid in the act of forgiveness. I assume though that there are times when you can't forget, and I don't mean that you're not able to forget but that maybe you shouldn't for other reasons, physical reasons, I don't know, you just come in on times when maybe you should not completely forget. There's a mixture of forgetting and forgiving at that point … or is all the forgiving in the forgetting?

I am Q'uo, and am aware of your query, my brother. The forgetting to its completion is the definition of forgiveness. Most, however, find that there is work to do in forgiving another before one may forget that which brought up the catalyst and placed a barrier between the two. It is not always easy to forget. For as long as one has an emotional investment in the catalyst which has arisen, then there is work to do in communication, in analysis, in meditation and finally in forgiveness as one is able to see another as the self and is able to accept those as the Creator. This usually takes a significant portion of your time.

(Pause)

I am Q'uo, and am again with this instrument. We appreciate your patience. Is there another query at this time?

T: Not from me, thank you.

I am Q'uo. We thank you, my brother. May we speak to any other point at this time?

J: Hi, Q'uo, this is J, and I have a question. I'm not sure, respecting my free will, if you'll be able to answer or not, but I was wondering if you could tell me if my soul has been higher than third density previously to where it is now.

I am Q'uo, and am aware of your query, my sister. To this query we may answer, yes indeed, for this is true for all entities. For all have been complete in their unity with the one Creator. In the sense in which you speak, we can confirm that you are indeed that which may be called a wanderer who has previous experience in densities beyond the third and who has come to this third-density planet for the opportunity to be of service as it is birthed into a new level of evolution.

Is there another query, my sister?

J: No, thank you very much for that answer.

I am Q'uo, and we thank you, my sister. Is there another query at this time?

S: I have one. You mentioned earlier that, say we're [doing] so well. How can we know when we're doing well; how do we see the unseen?

I am Q'uo, and am aware of your query, my brother, and to this query we must say regretfully, for third-density entities, you cannot know. Understanding is not of this density; this density, my friend, requires that one operate with faith, with will and move forward in that strength, for that which can be known subjectively in this illusion is but a poor print. For there is much beneath [and] beyond that which is seen, that which is sensed, that which can be known in any particular way in your illusion. For all is a symbol here; all stands for something else, and it is a great riddle, a great knot, shall we say, that each has the task of untying and untangling, and many lifetimes are spent in attempting to do just this thing; to reduce the great complexity of this illusion to the simplicity of an individual incarnation, and each effort to accomplish this great goal is rewarded by a small amount of a sense of possibility, shall we say, of a direction, of a homing where one feels, where one hopes, where one wishes, and where one places one's faith as surely as one aims the bow and the arrow at a target and strikes that target surely as one has the faith that the arrow flies truly.

Is there another query, my brother?

S: Not right now, thanks.

I am Q'uo, and we thank you, my brother. Is there another query at this time?

(No further queries.)

I am Q'uo. As it appears that we have exhausted the queries for this session of speaking, we would once again pause briefly to thank each for inviting our presence this day in your circle of seeking. It is always our great privilege and pleasure to join you here. At this time, we shall take our leave of this instrument and this group. We leave each in the love and in the ineffable light of the one infinite Creator. Adonai, my friends. Adonai. ☥

L/L Research

L/L Research is a subsidiary of Rock Creek Research & Development Laboratories, Inc.

P.O. Box 5195
Louisville, KY 40255-0195

www.llresearch.org

Rock Creek is a non-profit corporation dedicated to discovering and sharing information which may aid in the spiritual evolution of humankind.

ABOUT THE CONTENTS OF THIS TRANSCRIPT: This telepathic channeling has been taken from transcriptions of the weekly study and meditation meetings of the Rock Creek Research & Development Laboratories and L/L Research. It is offered in the hope that it may be useful to you. As the Confederation entities always make a point of saying, please use your discrimination and judgment in assessing this material. If something rings true to you, fine. If something does not resonate, please leave it behind, for neither we nor those of the Confederation would wish to be a stumbling block for any.

© 2009 L/L RESEARCH

SUNDAY MEDITATION
OCTOBER 20, 2002

Group question: The question today, Q'uo, has to do with what is happening for the individual seeker; [what is] the metaphysical reality of what's going on in our world today as each of us struggles to understand inner spiritual truths [while] we are caught in the swirl of economic, political, social and other activities that are just increasing at exponential rates. We're wondering what is really going on, when you consider that the various religions of the world have all been affected in one way or another by negatively-oriented entities trying to sway our ability to believe and where we put our faith. [They] have had some success, in causing us to have thousands of years of war as the concept of the holy war is born and carried out in each of the religions. In the Old Testament, for the Christians, there was a New Testament; there was a new covenant. Jesus brought the way of loving one's neighbor. There seems to have been for the last couple of thousand years a smaller and smaller group of people who really feel committed to the way of Christ. Could you give us an idea of just what's happening in the way of metaphysical and spiritual evolution planet-wide and individual-wide and how our various religions and their current difficulties are being affected?

(Carla channeling)

We are those of the principle known to you as Q'uo. Greetings in the love and in the light of the one infinite Creator in Whose service we are privileged to be. We thank you for the opportunity to share our thoughts with you on this interesting subject and would ask only that each of you uses your discrimination to winnow out those thoughts that are useful to you from those that are as the chaff that may blow by, [letting them] be released from the need to have meaning. We ask that you not treat us as authorities but as those who have opinions, and subject everything that all authorities or so-called authorities offer to you to the searching gaze of your own powers of discrimination, which we assure you are excellent. Trust and believe in those feelings of resonance and those feelings of flatness that separate out for you those truths that are yours this day and those that are irrelevant to your situation. This will give us the elbow-room, shall we say, that we need to be able to feel that we are not infringing upon your free will but are only sharing the opinion of friends.

You ask this day, what is occurring with the individual who is moving through this particular phase of evolution upon your planet at this time; what is occurring individually, what is occurring in terms of the religions of the world, and what is occurring in that ever-changing intersection between the metaphysical that is unspoken and the metaphysical that has been delineated by those of a certain set of dogmatic beliefs. This intersection changes constantly, and yet it does have fairly consistent, shall we say, structures that are typical, and so we may in some degree generalize about this. But [we] would always point out that there is no generality that is true in all cases. Your world religions indeed have had a long-term habit of turning from the original impetus of a certain way of religious believing to the machinations of what this instrument would call the priestly class, and here is a generality that we share with you that applies to this priestly class: the causes of spirituality are without politics and have to do with an instinct that is bred into the bone of your species. However, the religions of the human animal are those structures that are taken from a spiritual system and recreated in such a way as to benefit or be seen to benefit this particular class of ruling church leaders. The energy of religion, therefore, as opposed to that energy which is purely spiritual, tends towards moving into those areas of dogmatic and rigid belief systems that vitiate the pure strain of compassion and devotion that the religious system, as it is begun, offers; taking away little by little those freedoms to doubt, to disbelieve, and to explore that create the opportunity for the individual entity within human incarnation to seek and know the truth for the self.

The impulse or instinct to spirituality is that which bites at man's heels and calls his thirsting faculty of hope forward at all times, thereby increasing continually the energy towards individual knowing or knowledge. The energy of religion is that which, more and more as the years go by, has a tendency towards removing bits and pieces of the believer's free range of will so that, more and more, that entity which wishes to be part of a religious system must then yield up the right to judge for the self in an increasingly large number of areas of dogmatic belief. Each time that spirituality is hardened into a dogmatic belief and faith is exchanged for the tenets of a creed, the personal power and the personal responsibility for the self, the thoughts of the self and the progression of the evolution of the self is released in order to choose a structure in which there is no further responsibility for knowledge but only the responsibility of repeating those pieces of perceived knowledge that have been handed down from authorities. In this effort to organize and then maintain a religion, the emphasis almost inevitably turns from the excitement, fervor and joy of religious seeking to the maintenance, increase in productivity of, and enlargement of the existing corporate system.

The benefits of spirituality, then, are those which accrue to that careful and thoughtful entity who does not resonate to the defined belief systems that are available and instead chooses to create, day by day and perception by perception, an independent path of seeking. That system of knowledge can never be more than subjective. There is a desire within the third-density entity for this knowledge, and from this striving, on an individual level, has come the term, "gnostic." This term simply indicates someone who is involved in [creating] a personal path of seeking the truth. Those who find resonance within religions are, and, in this way we generalize overly much also, basically of two types. The first type is, as this instrument is, one who has found its niche within an established belief system, has chosen the path of mysticism which simply steps aside from all dogmatic questions and focuses upon devotion and service. [The second] type of entity [is one] which desires to fit into a group, to belong to that group and have choices taken away from it rather than left to it, so that there is not the need to judge that which is truth, that which is gnosis but, rather, only the need to learn the individual points of belief of the system to which they wish to belong, at which point they then feel that they are safe.

The one known as T was asking earlier about why such deeply religious people as some of his friends and relations would be so governed by fear, and perhaps it can be seen in this light that the entity who chooses the established and carefully delineated way of belief that focuses on a specific set of beliefs that make a system are choosing this structure because it feels safe. Thusly, one may see in general that the entity who has chosen to seek a personal path is less a creature of fear than the entity who feels that it is necessary to hew to a dogmatic set of beliefs and to define spirituality in terms of a laundry list of those things that are believed and those things that are felt to be not worthy of attention or even harmful to the developing spiritual entity. Along one path lies an enhanced feeling of chaos, for with free will does come more confusion or, shall we say, apparent confusion. There is less company for the one who decides to make choices for himself, and it is a rockier and more difficult path at the outset. It is our observation, on the other hand, of those who follow the path of religion that there is indeed a tremendous amount of solace in being part of a group. We find that there is a large degree of complete sincerity in the belief system of many entities within religion and those that have the capacity to be of service to others and to think along terms of offering their love in all situations, yet who do not have a grasp of their own spiritual nature, but instead have been content to rest in the structures built by others. For that is what your temples are, those outward structures that have been created as sacred spaces and that do indeed create an atmosphere, through a long number of years and a long number of generations of workers, that is palpable and that can be felt.

We are not attempting by this description to condemn all religions, for all religions began with the yeasty, powerful, muscular energy of new vision, new realization, and new inspiration. Indeed, it is possible for those within church structures, whether they be Christian, Jewish, Muslim, Shinto or other structures of religion, to remain Gnostic; to remain those upon a personal path; to be those who do not compromise that which they feel within their hearts to be true simply because an authority figure suggests that it must be true. However, there is a substantial portion of the population of your planet that has indeed been affected by religion in the way that those detractors of religion have suggested through history, that being that religion is a drug, a kind of addiction which keeps the "little people" contented with their difficult lives as those who have their primary use in making money for other entities. This strays far afield from the simple, single, elementary truth that connects all entities, whether truth is that which is perceived within a pilgrim heart that is moving out into that personal path of seeking, or whether that same loving heart is content with the patterns that it has been given. The vibrations in which the heart is moving, that tune that the heart is singing, has the capacity to be perfectly one with all that there is. And, indeed, at the heart of all vibrations, of all energy fields that denote an entity, there is that perfectly balanced, totally creative, original Thought that is purely true, so that at the heart of the chaos that is each entity's unknown self lies the Creator in all of Its creative genius, in all of Its lack of limits, in all of Its power to create and to destroy.

This is the truth that underlies vast differences in opinion. It is the truth from which stems the completely unpredictable potential of all third-density entities to achieve realization in an instant; to find the epiphany in the turning of a leaf or the turning of a page. It may seem at one moment that two entities are so far apart that they could never agree, yet such is the capacity of the human heart to embrace truth when it is perceived that any two entities may in one, strong, fine moment find that rainbow bridge that unites them and release the bonds of fear which girdle so many entities to the load-bearing help of organized religion.

We are aware of your discussion before this meditation and are very sympathetic with those feelings of disappointment and even betrayal that so many among your peoples feel at the news programs which discuss the failings of those priests within organized religions whose behavior towards children has been undesirable in the extreme. The patterns of service to self and service to others have their cleanest and most healthy expression outside the biasing and distorting energies of organized religion. In particular, we would point out the lack of validity within that church which you call the Roman Catholic Church of certain practices, the specific one which we have in mind being celibacy, which indeed was not part of the original spiritual roots of this fairly mystical and person-driven, gnosis-driven system of spirituality discussed by those of the Essene sect of mysticism within Aramea [such as] the one known as Jesus and the one known as John the Baptist. This generative spark which the one known as Jim has called the New Testament, the new promise, the new plan, was offered as a very simple and unitary way of being.

The requirements of this particular covenant or testament were that each entity would love the Creator and love the neighbor as the self. All of the law and the prophets, then, depended upon this basic truth, and, when there were discrepancies, the simple requirements preceded and updated the requirements of the Old Testament. We do not need to point out to any of you that the origins of this that is called Christianity among your people were not hewn to with much faith for very long, for there soon came to be an increasing effort to regularize, preserve and establish the church of Jesus the Christ as a Church rather than as a community of teachers and students. When this grew to a certain degree, for political reasons and reasons of social and economic power, it was decided that the discipline of celibacy would be placed as a requirement for being a priest in this particular church. When some entities are born, one of their choices for their incarnation may be celibacy. For many others throughout the centuries since this decision was made, not by those seeking truth but by those seeking power, many have been in a position of desiring to be a priest and needing to accept the strictures of that position including celibacy. We would suggest in this instance as in many others in the history of your religions that the requirement in and of itself is an unbalanced one, and it is not surprising that there have been unhealthful and insalubrious distortions that have come about in the personalities and actions of those who truly desired to be of service to others but who, along the way in attempting to deal with an outer, physical organization called the Church, have found themselves in difficult and unbalanced situations which they were not able to control. Please note that there is no political, religious, economic or social system that does not have its imbalances, inadequacies and potentials for abuse.

It is to be noted that the vast, vast majority of those in positions of this kind have pure souls, clean hearts, and no actions of which they must be ashamed. Further, we would suggest that the pattern of distortion remains the same throughout the institutions of the world. We would suggest that there is no more difficulty in one religious structure than in another once the structure has been penetrated and enough has been learned about the abuses of that particular system to be able to speak clearly and without injustice of that particular system. It is, shall we say, the predilection of third-density entities to find ever-new ways to create a sense of comfort, a sense of power, a sense of confidence; to aggrandize the self and to protect the self in some way. These are all ways in which it is the illusion that is seen; it is the illusion that is manipulated, and yet it is the spirit within that loses the opportunities to seek in a clearer, more lucid way because of being caught up in the various distortions of a particular system.

But each of you swims in an archipelago of distortion. There is the distortion from each of the helpers that touch the life of the young and the innocent child: the teacher, the sales clerk, the babysitter, the children of friends, the mothers of friends. All of these comprise part of the world in which the child lives. All of these teachers and friends and parents and those who truly do care for the child have their own biases and distortions, their own fears, and their own projections of their hopes and dreams for that child which they are offering to the child. Is it any wonder, then, that, as the child grows, it becomes more and more steeped in the acculturative forces around it so that, more and more, the child begins to give away its ability to seek, its clarity of mind, its sharpness of questioning? Think of the very young child, and you think of a child who is asking questions. Think of the older child who is at the start of the teenage years, as this instrument would call it, and see how that entity's basis of self has been eroded in terms of that which is that entity's alone, in order to be replaced, by choice, with the look that is appropriate, with the sayings that are those of the group to which this child belongs. In one way and then another and then another, the child's mind has been taught that in this and this and this area, this is the perceived truth, and there is no need or hunger for more. When this has been truly successful, it is that which keeps an entity asleep, which keeps that yearning for true inner vision at a minimum, and I think these are the concerns that justifiably can fill the hearts of those who feel that there is the possibility of subjective, personal knowledge and who mourn those energies within a culture which are attempting to stop that energy from moving forward by, shall we say, the empty calories of dogma rather than faith.

Now let us switch gears and gaze a bit towards the end-times scenario which your conversation previous to this meditation dealt with to some extent. Several of you were wondering what the negatively-oriented entity wants, how the negative entity perceives this time of graduation, and how it wishes to see things go. This is a complex question, for this [group of] negative polarity upon your planet has been to some extent distorted by a group of higher-density negative entities, primarily those of the fifth density, who have found that if entities can be kept from choosing either the positive or the negative path, and if they can be taught a maximum degree of fear, so that their minds are worried and their hearts are troubled at all times, this creates a kind of food which is used by these higher-density entities for the equivalent of an excellent diet.

The political and social history of your peoples—as you were speaking earlier of Atlantis and ancient cultures and then those that are more modern—have been these generations of those whose fear, terror, anger, hostility and pain have been offered up as food to the forces that enjoy that world of dark shadows and negative emotions. Consequently, there is almost no true negative polarity in the sense of an organized group of people that work together for the graduation into fourth-density negative of the planet or even of a group of its people. Those who have truly found the possibility of graduation in the negative sense within this particular harvest have been those whose focus has been extremely self-absorbed and unassociated with the energies that look, from the outside in, like negative polarity. The creators of your present global situation, then, are not entities of tremendous negative polarity but rather are those entities who have been most effective in shaping the society towards maximum degrees of control over others through the uses of what this instrument would call the media, so that these are not terrifying dragons but rather dupes for fifth-density entities who are using them as well as all others within the planetary system insofar as they can be taught to hate, to covet, to control. These are the energies that are encouraged along with the fear that lies beneath such policies.

All of this dwells in the illusion, is washed by the waters of consciousness that stream endlessly through the illusion, carrying the waters of truth and beauty and life. It does not matter how intense the outer forces of fear and negativity are when the heart of an entity rests in faith, in hope and in love: faith that all is well, hope in every hopeless situation, and love of all things, of all biases, of all entities. Rest and perfect peace, how beautiful those words are, and yet this instrument has asked over and over again since 9/11/2001, "What is perfect peace? What is the peace that passes understanding? In what does that consist, is there in my heart already?" This instrument has asked over and over again, "That peace, do I know it already? Am I squashing it; am I pressing it down out of my reach by my choices?"

We suggest to you that this peace is a state of mind, a state of consciousness, a way of vibrating. When fear runs through the system, this state of mind is unavailable. When the fear is dropped from the illusion by the choice of the entity, this state of consciousness becomes available. Many are those among your peoples who have attempted through drugs to find this state of perfect peace, but we suggest that this peace lies within your heart, it is your native and natural environment; it is real, it is not the illusion. It is one tiny, thin veil from you at this time, for fourth density truly is coming upon you. Thusly, your faculties of faith, hope and love have an increasing amount of potential to take hold within your life. We encourage all forms of positivity within your minds, within the way you talk to yourselves within your hearts, for that state of consciousness which you create day by day and hour by hour within yourself is as the training wheels for that spontaneous and unrehearsed state of consciousness that comes to you as you awaken to the new day.

We would at this time apologize for the length of our discussion and transfer this contact to the one known as Jim. We thank this instrument and leave it in love and light. We are those of Q'uo.

(Jim channeling)

I am Q'uo, and we greet each again in love and in light through this instrument. At this time, we would ask if there may be any shorter queries to which we may speak briefly, as we realize that we have spoken overly long to begin this week. Is there a shorter query at this time?

T: Yes, I have a question. I alluded to this earlier. It involves when you see something that may go the way you would like it to go at the expense of another, and you catch yourself having to actively resist hoping that this event will happen which basically will help you but doesn't help the other person and actually could be at the expense of this other person. How does one go about not doing that? It sounds simplistic, but any comments you may have would be greatly appreciated.

I am Q'uo, and aware of your query, my brother. We are also aware that we speak, as the one known as Abigail would say, in an overly-long fashion, and she complains[5].

We shall be brief. As you look at your daily round of activities, you will see various instances in which there is the opportunity to practice that which you know, shall we say, that which is of one piece with the one Creator, the unity of all creation. There are many catalysts that present themselves to you during your daily round of activities that will test resolve, that you may be able to express that which you know in a spontaneous fashion or [that you] will be unable to do so and will mentally take note of this which you may call a challenge, a test, a catalyst, perhaps even a failure.

---

[5] Abigail, a 16-year-old Siamese cat, had begun a serenade of some force. She was calmed.

However, we suggest to you that, as you look at these various opportunities to practice your knowledge and to live your love, it is only natural that you shall come up short in some instances, for you are not perfect beings. There are few within the creation of the one Creator that do not notice the deviation of the consciousness from that which is straight and true, the love and the light of the one Creator. When you feel yourself moving away from that which is part of your being, take note, perhaps pause for a moment in your own contemplation or meditation, seek to heal that which is in need of healing, to make whole that which is broken, to make straight that which is curved, to become that which is your highest ideal. Do not chastise yourself because you have fallen short. Rather, use this opportunity to increase the resolve, to follow the path of the seeker of truth and the one who would serve the Creator in all he or she would meet during the daily round of activities.

Is there another query, my brother?

T: No, not from me, thank you.

I am Q'uo, and we thank you, my brother. Is there another query at this time?

S: I have one. My wife and I have been talking of late and contemplating. We've noticed in our round of activities, I guess, signs or appearances of, I guess to best describe it, it seems like somebody is—how should I put it—messing with her, something or someone or some entity, whether work activities, home activities, other activities, and we just seem to feel there's a strong coincidence and presence of somebody or something messing with her life, as you will. Could you offer any help or assistance or ideas on this situation?

I am Q'uo, and we are aware of your query, my brother. Many entities upon this planetary surface are so full of light and so full of the ability to direct the energy of their own existence that they are attractive, shall we say, to those of the lower astral realms who lack this ability to focus their own energies and accomplish what you might call metaphysical work. Oftentimes an entity in the third density, such as the one known as C, who has these great abilities to accomplish various kinds of work, be it the physical work of this illusion or the metaphysical work of realizing spiritual principles, and who have, for one reason or another, blocked their own energies, create a, shall we say, gap in the faith, an insertion of doubt in one area or another [which] then provides an opportunity for those of the lower astral to attach themselves to this entity at this point of blockage and to begin to utilize that doubt, that portion of fear, that deviation from what is possible within, to energize their own undirected existence. This is more common than one would first imagine, for there are always, within the natural environment, those entities that are seen as the parasite, that which feeds upon the energy system of another rather than propelling itself by its own motivational ability to accomplish that which it wishes to accomplish.

Thus, there is the need from time to time for entities to cleanse themselves—more specifically their auric fields—of such entities, for all who seek sincerely upon the positive path of service to others radiate a kind of light that is seen as a power, a beacon, a resource, that which can be plundered, shall we say, if there are certain circumstances within the third-density entity's auric field. We have mentioned those qualities of doubt, of fear, of lack of assurance that there is a path to follow and a way in which to do this. Thus, we suggest that each finds a means which is effective for the individual to accomplish this cleansing. Whether [you use] what you would call the smudging, as we have heard it called, the use of various elements of water, of salt, of garlic and so forth, to rid the self and the environment of one's own dwelling place of such entities is unimportant. What is important is that you find that technique which has meaning to you and utilize it upon a periodic basis, much as one would cleanse the teeth, wash the body, and so forth.

Is there a further query, my brother?

S: Hmm … any specific recommendations that you might elaborate on in this type of case?

I am Q'uo, and am aware of your query, my brother, and, as we spoke previously, it is necessary that the entity accomplishing this cleansing choose the possibility that is most, shall we say, in harmony or resonance with that that entity's own sensibilities. If the entity is steeped in one of your religious traditions, each has a cleansing method that is utilized. If it is, shall we say, more the case that the entity is a seeker in what you would call the metaphysical or pilgrim's path of the spiritual journey, then there are far more avenues available. We mentioned the smudging, the salt, the garlic.

There are ritual words of cleansing available in the texts known as *The Law of One*; there are other texts such as the one by Dion Fortune available for the choosing of the ritual of the most effectiveness. We cannot be more specific, for to do so would be to choose for an entity that which is most efficaciously [chosen] for the self. Thus, we only can point general directions.

Is there another query, my brother?

S: Not from me right now. Thank you very much.

I am Q'uo, and we thank you, my brother. Is there another query at this time?

J: Yeah … Hi, Q'uo, this is J, and I just have one quick question. I was wondering if you have a color or a certain note or vibration that we can understand?

I am Q'uo, and am aware of your query, my sister. As we are composed of a variety of entities forming this principle which you call Q'uo, there is also a variety of colors and notes that would denote our qualities or purpose. However, we are unable either to voice the note through this instrument or clearly transmit the color which is toward the violet portion of your spectrum but is of another quality. The answer is yes, but we cannot speak or give them through this instrument. We apologize.

Is there another query, my sister?

J: No, thank you. Thanks.

I am Q'uo, and we thank you, my sister. Is there another query at this time?

S: I had a discussion earlier talking about the idea of second and/or third-density humans, *per se*. Could you tell me what you see in, from your perspective, that idea?

I am Q'uo, and am aware of your query, my brother. To the best of our knowledge, the time of harvest upon your planet which is now is that time during which the seniority by vibration of incarnation is used exclusively for the determination of who shall have the opportunity to partake in the third-density illusion at this time. Thus, those who are most able to benefit from the short time remaining are those who are offered this opportunity at this time.

Is there a further query, my brother?

S: Not from me right now. Thank you very much.

I am Q'uo, and again we thank you, my brother, for your query. Is there a final query at this time?

(No further queries.)

Carla: Thanks for all the good energy, Q'uo.

J: Happy full moon!

I am Q'uo, and we will take this opportunity once again to thank each present for joining in this circle of seeking and for inviting us to do the same. It is our great privilege to do so. We again apologize for speaking overly long. We so enjoy these gatherings that we do not keep track of your time, as you may perhaps wish we would.

We are known to you as those of Q'uo, and we would take our leave of this instrument at this time, leaving each, as always, in the love and in the light of the one infinite Creator. Adonai, my friends. Adonai.

L/L Research

L/L Research is a subsidiary of Rock Creek Research & Development Laboratories, Inc.

P.O. Box 5195
Louisville, KY 40255-0195

www.llresearch.org

Rock Creek is a non-profit corporation dedicated to discovering and sharing information which may aid in the spiritual evolution of humankind.

ABOUT THE CONTENTS OF THIS TRANSCRIPT: This telepathic channeling has been taken from transcriptions of the weekly study and meditation meetings of the Rock Creek Research & Development Laboratories and L/L Research. It is offered in the hope that it may be useful to you. As the Confederation entities always make a point of saying, please use your discrimination and judgment in assessing this material. If something rings true to you, fine. If something does not resonate, please leave it behind, for neither we nor those of the Confederation would wish to be a stumbling block for any.

© 2009 L/L Research

Sunday Meditation
November 3, 2002

Group question: The question today, Q'uo, has to do with the intensity of catalyst that we feel. We've heard it said that most learning that is efficient takes place with some sort of trauma. We're wondering why that is. Is it due to the intensity of the lesson we wish to learn? And is the lesson we wish to learn discernible from the catalyst that we experience, or do we need to look deeper than the catalyst we experience? We would like for you to give us some information concerning how we experience our catalyst; how we can be more efficient in using our catalyst? Is it in dealing with the catalyst itself that we see what we're trying to learn, or do we need to meditate more to discover the lesson? Do we need to work with our dreams? Do we need to do essays? Do we need to be doing something besides just looking at the catalyst that is available in our daily lives?

(Carla channeling)

We are those known to you as the principle of Q'uo, and we greet you in the love and the light of the one infinite Creator. It is a true blessing for us to be able to serve your group at this time, and we thank you for the privilege of being called by your request for information. We are most happy to share our humble thoughts with you with the request that you listen with a careful ear to those things that we would say, rejecting all those things that do not resonate to you personally. This will enable us to feel that we have the opportunity to speak without being perceived as authorities or in any way limiting your free will or your ability to choose for yourself those thoughts that you would value and use as resources.

The [answer to the question] which you ask this day resides within the nuances of your everyday experience. You ask concerning the nature of perceived experience, for each has experienced those situations which seem to constitute a challenge of one kind or another, and these challenges are not perceived as being comfortable or convenient. Questions arise when such catalyst is encountered, such as the one known as V asked, "What is the universe attempting to say to me? What am I attempting to say to myself?" And, as the one known as T has pointed out, at the end of all questions of this kind, the one question that is sure to remain is that question that children ask with such stunning simplicity, why does it have to happen at all?

Rather than deal with this question at this level, we find that it would be useful to remove our point of view to a place which is less local than global, is less personal than planetary, and is less a part of culture and more a part of the archetype. The one known as Jim is quite accurate in supposing that there are more levels to catalyst than either literally or figuratively meet the eye. There are, shall we say, three basic levels of catalyst and certainly many sublevels of catalyst. The first level is the level of the surface reality, what this instrument would call consensus reality. On this level, situations have ripened into manifestation, and often there are choices to make concerning physical details such as the setting of limits, the choosing of resources, selection of options.

Upon the second level of catalyst lie the underlying qualities which, in combination, ripening through natural processes of the spiritual evolution as well as physical and emotional cycles, create the shape of the story that appears within the personal movie of the life, shall we say. For each has a long-running, full-color movie which is being made up of the multilayered and many-leveled story of the life of the one known to each of you as "I." At this second level of catalyst, there is a tremendous amount of power within the simple knowing that you are not alone, neither in your suffering nor in your confusion, but rather each of you is the center of concern, care, love and protection of several of those beings who dwell within your inner planes. Each entity who moves through the gates of incarnation into third-density existence has three of these presences. They may be characterized in different ways. This instrument was trained to characterize them as male, female and unified or androgynous. However, in addition to these entities which this instrument has a tendency to call "angelic," there may be added to your panel of support any number of those who are attracted by your energy, your hopes, your ideals and faith or the lovely light and color of your appreciation of beauty or your devotion to service. These entities cannot help directly with the choosing of the first level of catalyst. These entities cannot make decisions for you concerning the setting of limits, the choosing of options, the selection of the various details of surface catalyst. However, if remembered and included, these presences are able to energize the forces around you to vibrate with information that will aid you as you seek to make the choices that the catalyst has brought out. These underlying shapes are shapes made by those who move in the ways of learning to love and to be loved.

When you are asking for the help of angels and guides, it is well to begin with thanksgiving, with praise and with confidence in yourself, in those who are helping you, and in the perfection of that which is quite apparently imperfect.

The third level of catalyst is the archetypical. Within this level of catalyst lie your most powerful tools for transforming the very nature of your state of consciousness in such a way that it remains within a state of bliss even as it is moving through perceived imperfections. Within this level of catalyst, however, the energies are deep, dark and slow to respond to the conscious mind. Working at this level of catalyst, the greatest resource is silence. It is at the foundation or archetypical level that one practices the presence of the infinite Creator. It is at this level that one becomes a creature of one's own heart, accepting the interiority of the self and opening to that unknown room within, which one of this instrument's favorite poets called "the rag and bone shop of the heart.[6]" Yes, each of you does have indeed the rags and the bones, the teeth and the hair, and the memories of how you gained and lost all of those things, and those things lie within the pack-rat heart until the energies are appropriate for cleaning house, for dusting and tidying and gathering up the garbage into a bin for removal from the life, from the memory, from the need to feel responsible.

The one known as T asked a poignant question in the conversation preceding this meditation, describing a halcyon, golden day within his life in which he basically felt that there was some progress made and some realization gained. This entity awoke to a new day and found that with this new day came challenges of such a nature as to remove those feelings of comfort, serenity and joy and replace them, seemingly of necessity, with feelings of limitation, aggravation and separation. "How can we learn to retain that feeling of realization when the next catalyst occurs?" asked this entity, and we feel that this is the question upon which we would focus for the remainder of this instrument's portion of this communication.

That which you experience as a life seems to have a very steady roll and rhythm to it, as if it were anchored with the birth and the death, and the unrolling ribbon between is just long enough to fit. Yet we find that the experiences of a lifetime are only in part that which is trapped within time and space upon the, shall we say, surface of the time/space continuum which you at [this] time travel within incarnation. Fully half or more of that which you experience as part of a seemingly continuous and unremarkable presence that unrolls steadily before

---

[6] William B. Yeats, *The Circus Animals' Desertion* (l. 35–40):

> A mound of refuse or the sweepings of a street,
> Old kettles, old bottles, and a broken can,
> Old iron, old bones, old rags, that raving slut
> Who keeps the till. Now that my ladder's gone,
> I must lie down where all the ladders start,
> In the foul rag-and-bone shop of the heart.

you is actually called to the present from the future or the past by those patterns of thought which circle around the questions of loving and being loved. One of the questions that was asked was, "Can we work with these challenges by identifying the chakra of the energy body which is bearing the brunt of this challenge?" and the answer is in part, "Yes, these considerations are always helpful." However, we would suggest that there is also skill and art in throwing open the windows of the self to the light within, to the hope within, to the faith within, so that there is a growing awareness in yourself, as you work with catalyst, that you are only partially a creature of time and space. In another portion of yourself, you are a universal and infinite being, a dweller in eternity and one who has given gifts to the self from the future and from the past that feed into the present moment, because there is a need for the nuances, for the lessons of loving and being loved. No matter where the energy centers are that are being stressed by the challenges experienced, the lessons will continue to be about love.

As wisdom feeds into the daily life, that wisdom expresses itself as different realizations of what love is, new and invigorating awarenesses of what it is to share unconditional love, and, for those who are in advanced lessons within incarnation, the challenges are nuanced by the shadings of the energies of accepting the love offerings of others. Many are the times that a negatively presenting set of circumstances has as its formative cause the need to learn the lesson of accepting the love that is given to one. It is in almost every case among those who are positively oriented far easier to learn the lessons of loving than those of being truly, unconditionally, utterly and completely loved. The resistance to the truth of that creates a good deal of murkiness within the patterns that are created through the archetypical and secondary systems of catalyst.

Consequently, we would suggest the value of dwelling not so much upon the first level of catalyst in thinking about what to do concerning the challenges of the catalyst [as upon] thinking more or allowing more time to process the secondary level of catalyst and the archetypical level of catalyst. This would translate into actions such as pondering, as the one known as Jim has said, those items which lie before the mind during moments of work where the attention is not taken by detail, musing along one's way as one drives in the car or walks within nature, and always, in order to call in those archetypical sources of information, it is helpful to spend time in the meditative state invoking the silence of self that allows that still, small voice of guidance within to have its time to shine like a daystar in the heart. Angels surround you beating with silent wings, their trumpets raised. They play that hosanna of praise and thanksgiving that fills the universe with song.

The magic of this vision lies all about you. Every corner of your consensus reality is crowded with magic. All of the creation of the infinite One is as responsive to you as the entity sitting next to you and is perhaps more aware of you and who you truly are than any entity whom you may meet within the physical illusion. These entities—these plants, these animals, these elements—have found simpler ways to love and to be loved than are available within third density, and that direct, intuitive and unhesitating way of loving and accepting love is a great lesson that you may pick up at any time from the wind, the rain, the fire on your grate, and the earth of your own body. The more that you are able to rest within this unity with all things at this very simple level, the sturdier your spirit will be at retaining that vibration of praise, thanksgiving and joy which is the steady state of awareness shared by those who dwell completely within the creation of the one infinite Logos.

What is your identity? Whenever you can, keep a part of your identity quite clearly within your mind as being one with all, one with all you seek, one with all that you do not seek, one with all you understand and one with all you do not understand, one with all of whom you approve and one with all of whom you do not approve. It is not that we ask you to ignore the catalyst of daily life. We hope that you will participate to the extent that you feel that you make many, many foolish errors. Why would we hope that you make errors? Precisely as each of you has supposed in the conversation preceding this discussion that we have with you now, there are many times where, according to the plan for learning that constitutes your particular incarnation, you have chosen to [take up] a nexus of decision. On the surface, it is a decision concerning details; at the secondary level, it is a decision concerning love; at the archetypical level, it is always a decision concerning the nature and the mission of the self. Let yourself slide up and down, in and out of these levels, not disrespecting one level or valuing one level more than another but seeing both, that all things are what they seem and that nothing is as it seems, and that both of these realizations may lead you to skillful acts.

As we leave this instrument, we would simply say that, as always, we remain ready to move into meditation with you as you request our presence. There are, as we just said, many entities just waiting for the invitation to be part of your magical world, your blueprint for transformation. It is a good plan. You have all chosen well. You have chosen, indeed, for an intensity or density of catalyst, hoping both to learn and to serve, and each of you is doing well. Naturally, because of the nature of the physical illusion, there is seldom a finished or symmetrical feel to everyday existence, and yet, as this instrument has often said, once one has found that place for the first time, there is a wonderful and ever-present space wherein one is in tabernacle with the infinite One resting in love and in light, and infinitely full of the one Creator.

We would at this time transfer this contact to the one known as Jim, that we may answer any questions that remain within the minds of those within this group. We greatly thank this group for asking this question and would at this time leave this instrument in love and in light. We are those known to you as Q'uo.

(Jim channeling)

I am Q'uo, and greet each of you in love and in light through this instrument. May we speak to any further queries at this time?

V: Q'uo, I was thinking about my pets this week, and just the nature of the pets as they relate to third-density humans. My recollection is that some pets are second density and some pets are even beginning or early levels of third density. As third density is moving into fourth density, will our pets follow into fourth density? I guess it's a multilevel question in that I'm not sure how fourth density works with us moving into fourth density, if we will remain in fourth density on this planet or if we will go to other planets in fourth that will accommodate or support fourth-density entities. At what level are pets capable of remaining with us? Is there any such thing as a pet, *per se*, in the higher densities beyond third or fourth?

I am Q'uo, and am aware of your query, my sister. This is not a simple query, as one might imagine, for the experience of all consciousness is movement toward the Creator. There are for each entity companions, energy fields of intelligence that move in rhythm and harmony with you, at various portions of your evolution. Whether one calls an energy field a "pet" or a "person" is dependent, of course, upon the individuality of that source of energy. When the spirit complex has been awakened within any energy field, then there is that which we have called a mind/body/spirit complex. In your illusion, the third density in which you now inhabit, you have the companionship of those you have called the pet. In many instances, these entities, through long experience with many of those whom you would call masters—some of which have been totally experienced with one such master, others with more—have the ability to give and receive that which we call love. That is the determining factor as to the density level of the entity called a pet.

As these entities are more and more able to appreciate that quality of love, support and nurturing that is given to them by those that are their masters, so then these entities learn to give that known as love as well, so that there is a giving and a receiving that appreciates the balancing nature of fully-developed love. That these entities may approach their own graduation is also certain; that they shall continue as a pet is unlikely, for these entities, then, are able to exercise their own free will in a way which is not as likely for a second-density entity that willingly gives over its care and decision-making to another. That these entities shall continue as companions is likely, for there is always an appreciation that it is possible that there will be a maturation of the relationship which is most likely to occur, for the appreciation for the relationship is that which is based upon love and which is the, shall we say, thread that binds the two. Many times, there is a student-teacher relationship which develops from that which was formerly the master and the pet. There are throughout all of creation relationships which partake of greater knowledge, a sharing with that which calls for the knowledge, the love, the light, and the desire to serve that are the motivating factors for all intelligence within the creation of the one Creator. Thus, you may rest assured that, when love has been given and received, there is a bond that continues.

May we speak further, my sister?

V: No, thank you. I appreciate that.

I am Q'uo, and we thank you, my sister. Is there another query at this time?

Carla: I have a question: The last time that we had a channeling meditation, I got an energy in the channel that was a little different than anything that I'd experienced before in that there was a tremendous amount of energy and pressure behind the source of information, and, even though I talked as fast as I could, I was probably only expressing about 10-15% of what I could have if I'd somehow been able to speak sufficiently quickly to get everything from the stream as it was coming past. I wonder if you could say anything to me about the experience of that. I haven't been able to figure out what made it unique in terms of anybody special visiting the group or any particular great energy that happened to be behind the question. Any comments would be helpful.

I am Q'uo, and am aware of your query, my sister. The cycle which is most in sway for this particular type of service that is the vocal channel is the cycle of the adept, as we have heard this group call it. The eighteen-day cycle moves in the form of the sine wave with certain days being more propitious, shall we say, for such undertakings. The experience of the pressure is the experience of the availability of information to one such as yourself which serves as instrument. When one is able to open one's own instrument in a clear fashion, putting aside the personal drama and coloration of the day, and is able to find the favor of the particular day within this adept's cycle that is at the peak of the ability to receive information, then the information seems to come much more easily and clearly, without the struggle to define the concept, to pick a certain word or feel capable of describing that which is seen before the inner eye. The experience is one which leaves the trace of vividness which you have experienced and which may, with some profit to future experiences, be plotted upon a graph in order to know when this cycle is available.

Is there a further query, my sister?

Carla: Well, further comment, and I would be glad to have you comment on my comment. I discovered in talking to the people that experience that with me, from the standpoint of listening to it rather than producing it, that there was an overall experience of too many words to be able to grasp any of them, so that it seems to me it would be to my benefit to learn how not to do that, how to retain the clarity but remove the prolixity. Any comments you can give on that would be helpful, I'm sure.

I am Q'uo, and am aware of your query, my sister. It is much as the downhill skier, whose image we place in this instrument's mind, taking the corners more swiftly than usual, feeling uncomfortable as the skill is mastered. Though you have practiced for many of your years to serve as a vocal instrument, for all instruments there is a great deal of work that can be done to refine the art. Learning to experience the prolixity of words and to find the heart of the concept and the perfect word to describe it is as the fast turns for the skier and will become more comfortable for you to experience in future sessions.

Is there a further query, my sister?

Carla: No, thank you. I look forward to not … what shall I say … banging on the ears of our meditation group so much in the future. Thank you very much.

I am Q'uo, and again we thank you, my sister. Is there another query at this time?

S: Yeah, Q'uo, could you tell us who of your group are with us tonight? Can you tell us about yourselves and just a general idea of what energies are with us tonight?

I am Q'uo, and am aware of your query, my brother. When we of Q'uo speak with you, there is a joining of a number of social memory complexes which have had previous experience in communication with this group and which have lent their energies in order that this contact might be made possible. Those of Latwii were the first to be in long-term contact with this group, though those of Hatonn, who have later joined as a more active portion of the principle known as Q'uo, were first to initiate contact with this group in its early days. Those of Ra have been a, shall we say, a guiding principle, or over-arching energy, which has made this formation of our group possible by blending their portion of love and light to form Q'uo with Hatonn and Latwii. This is the core, or Q'uo. There are also others from the Confederation of Planets in the Service of the One Infinite Creator that have joined this circle of seeking from time to time as its composition has required or requested certain elements that are accentuated in these other entities, some of which have names and some of which do not.

Is there a further query, my brother?

S: Not from me, thank you, Q'uo.

I am Q'uo. We thank you, my brother. Is there a final query at this time?

V: I have one that's relative to what S was asking. When the principle was formulated, how did you come up with and what is the energy related to the vibratory complex, "Q'uo"?

I am Q'uo, and am aware of your query, my sister. We make this instrument smile. It has been a long time since he saw his 10th grade Latin teacher. In this study of the language known as Latin, there is the word, "quo," which asks who, what, where, when. We were attempting to give this group a clue as to who we were. More specifically, we were attempting to inspire this group to ask who we were. Our efforts were minimal, for it took this group nearly two years of your time to ask.

V: That's 'cause I wasn't here before. I've been wanting to know this for a long time.

[I am Q'uo.] Our choice perhaps could have been more, shall we say, piquing to the interest. We chose as we did hoping that one of the two instruments would remember high school Latin. We appreciate the time factor, for not all learn as quickly as do others. We shall learn to choose perhaps more interesting names in your future. For now, we remain those of Q'uo, and at this time we shall thank each once again for inviting our presence in your circle of seeking this day.

We are known to you as those of Q'uo. We take our leave of this instrument and this group. We leave each, as always, in the love and in the light of the one infinite Creator. Adonai, my friends. Adonai. ❧

L/L Research

L/L Research is a subsidiary of Rock Creek Research & Development Laboratories, Inc.

P.O. Box 5195
Louisville, KY 40255-0195

www.llresearch.org

Rock Creek is a non-profit corporation dedicated to discovering and sharing information which may aid in the spiritual evolution of humankind.

ABOUT THE CONTENTS OF THIS TRANSCRIPT: This telepathic channeling has been taken from transcriptions of the weekly study and meditation meetings of the Rock Creek Research & Development Laboratories and L/L Research. It is offered in the hope that it may be useful to you. As the Confederation entities always make a point of saying, please use your discrimination and judgment in assessing this material. If something rings true to you, fine. If something does not resonate, please leave it behind, for neither we nor those of the Confederation would wish to be a stumbling block for any.

CAVEAT: This transcript is being published by L/L Research in a not yet final form. It has, however, been edited and any obvious errors have been corrected. When it is in a final form, this caveat will be removed.

© 2009 L/L Research

Special Meditation
November 8, 2002

(Carla channeling)

We are those known to you as the principle of Q'uo. We greet you in this novel way of meeting as a circle of seeking, and we thank you for the great privilege of being called to this circle to join your meditation, to plumb those questions which you would ask with those responses which we may feel free to offer, knowing that each will listen with the greatest discrimination to those humble thoughts that we may share. For we are not those who constitute an authority, but rather we are those who are pilgrims upon the path which is the path which you also walk. And in the way of things, like calls to like, light calls to light, and the forces of life call to those who love life those aspects of the self that move from positions within the future of the self which offer guidance, what this instrument would call wisdom.

We greatly appreciate the energy exchange and the commonality of tuning that creates this particular group. We only ask that our thoughts be considered with a jaundiced eye, removing and rejecting those things that do not ring absolutely true, walking ahead without looking back, knowing that the precious burden is that which resonates, that which is helpful, not in the future and not in the past with respect to authority but rather in the very infinity [of] the present moment.

We would at this time, with this assurance that we will not abridge free will by those things that we share as opinions, request the central query of this particular working.

Carla: *(Carla repeats the question from B, who is calling on the telephone.)* "From my exposure to the situation here, I'm thinking that the harvest may be small, and I'm wondering if a motion picture that talks about the harvest might actually be helpful in increasing, at least potentially, the harvest size. If that is so, would it be more helpful to have a screenplay which dealt directly with the harvest, or would it be more helpful to deal with it indirectly through the growth and the learning of the characters, the story that they tell? That is the initial query."

We are those known to you as Q'uo, and we are again with this instrument. We thank this instrument for retuning and refining the calibration of the tuning to recreate the original Vibration, for that is indeed the comfortable vibration for this particular group of three. We would like to parenthetically note that it is very helpful to have arranged so carefully for this meeting in that the tuning of this group is excellent, and we appreciate the effort that each has put into removing this time from the experience within consensus reality so that that which lies within the inner realms may be shared not only within the subconscious area of awareness but, to some extent, in the language of words.

Firstly, we would state with simple clarity that in all cases it is completely up to the creator of the service as to the nature of that service, and the choosing of each aspect moves not within the values of the world but in the metaphysical value of the feel or the integrity of the artistic work which is the sincere and openhearted attempt to create that art form which remains within that ambience which is as the interdisciplinary tour de force or exercise in that mixture of wit and inspiration that creates that which is more than it seems.

The choices are yours, this instrument's, and that of the scribe's. This is the nature of creative service in that a co-creator has that within itself which is the shape of that which is, as this instrument would say, resonant or simply right. Seek that resonance. This is our most general suggestion, for there is within this particular group a harvest, shall we say, of experience, perspective, honesty of intention and stability. There is also a common thread in that there is a strong tendency within each within this particular group to take the self lightly and that which is greater than the self seriously. This trait common to a group shall indeed improve the point of view which may be comfortably shared by the group and by ourselves as we discuss that which you ask. We are glad to discuss each of the approaches which were mentioned.

The first portion of the question has to do with the possibility that the very public repetition of this body of basic information concerning that time of harvest which is occurring as we discuss it would be an efficacious service, and we can say that it is almost completely a matter of the point of view of the responder. It is our bias to say that it will make a difference, because we find ourselves most sympathetic to the agony of your peoples. We would greatly love to enjoy the experience of the peoples of your planet catching fire for love and becoming empowered once again to be warriors for the light rather than against the darkness. It is very tempting and perhaps indeed efficacious to use the blunt instrument. The question then becomes creating the gem that has so many facets within that context.

Similarly, the, what this instrument would call, snob appeal, indeed the aesthetic high road, of writing is to stay within the infinite art of story and, by developing utterly spontaneous and gripping versions of those soul streams with which you are familiar and placing them into the environment which is enchanted with the soul of the story, [embody] forth the information in a way that is as the rapier rather than the mace but perhaps, in pinking the truth, moves to the heart of that truth and of those watching the story unfold, thereby creating an even more persuasive body of work which basically, within this question, is being considered as a kind of propaganda or persuasive information.

May we say that it is very easy to become cynical when one is aware of the cheap tricks of any trade. This instrument, for instance, became extremely depressed and disappointed when she first sang the *Missa Solemnissai* by the one known as Ludwig. The material was ungrateful to the voice, hastily done, and full of the panoply of the tricks of the trade for playing upon the emotions of the audience. It was, as this instrument perceived it, disgustingly effective. It took this instrument much time to forgive the one known as Ludwig for creating as this entity was wont to create. It took even more time before this instrument was able to appreciate the one known as Ludwig's music once again, as listening to the impression of the music rather than the skeleton of it.

Realize, as the artist who deals with a certain genre, that there are limitations to the genre and that these in a metaphysical sense have no emotional charge but simply become that which describes the body of consideration which feeds into the conscious part of a subconscious process of creation in which that which is dark of the self and that which is light of the self combine in a desire to create and to express the self in such a way that the whole self is used. We do not see within our own system of judgment any reason to indicate any bias towards either the blunt instrument or the rapier. We feel simply a complete faith that those involved in such a labor of love shall find a way with that moment-by-moment guidance which never fails. There are times when that guidance does not move quickly, yet always it moves surely and in its proper time.

We believe at this time that we would pause to refocus the questioning. We are those of Q'uo.

(Another question is posed by B over the telephone.)

We are those of Q'uo, and are aware of your query, my brother. We do find that this is a ticklish question from the standpoint of infringement upon free will. You are precisely correct in assuming that this is a vital point. Shall you move into the belief system that chooses quantity and therefore move along the assumption that the entire population of the movie-going world needs to see the information, or shall the effort be made in a modest way to those independent and other film makers who have a love of the smaller film, thus creating an atmosphere for a potentially greater artistic freedom, sensitivity or control? We leave this within your choice-making with the wry acknowledgement that this is, as this instrument would say, a sticky wicket.

May we ask is there is a further query?

(Another question is posed by B over the telephone.)

We are those of Q'uo, and are aware of your query, my brother. The described characters are perhaps drawn with that description which has not the appropriate or, shall we say, truthful allowance for the human within the characters, more so for the heroine than the brother. The character who has no pain has less of a grateful or sympathetic aspect of companionship with the perceiver of this character's flavor.

May we answer further, my brother?

(Another question is posed by B over the telephone.)

We are those of Q'uo, and are aware of your query, my brother. The basic structure of this suggestion is good in our opinion in that it engages the feeling of sympathy and commonality or, shall we say, identity with those within the experiencers of this story. The handling, shall we say, of the difficult aspects of this story is a relatively easily defined issue in that the choice revolves about the creation of what this instrument would call a threat or counterpoint created early within the story, so that first the sympathies of the audience are piqued, and then the concern or spontaneous depth of involvement in the story due to the perceived threat to the character is made evident within the story.

Certainly, it could be seen as a threat that the life is shaken by running into new experiences, new entities, and so forth. We can see the intellectually attractive aspect of this particular scenario. What we basically see here is the choice between creating a mythic character of the, shall we say, genre which is in common with this instrument's area of interest and the choice of choosing a mythic system which is more respectable, such as that of Christianity, Judaism or even that known as Islam. The myth is infinitely various in detail from myth to myth, from culture to culture and from system to system, yet the issues involved, and indeed many of the predictions concerning harvest, remain constant. Consequently, there is a wide palette for the entity who chooses to create a fiction. There is less of a wide palette for the entity who chooses to hew somewhat more to the story of that entity known as L and L Research.

May we answer further, my brother?

(Another question is posed by B over the telephone.)

We are those of Q'uo, and, my brother, the answer is no. Do you wish to question further?

(Another question is posed by B over the telephone.)

We are those of Q'uo, and are aware of your query. Our response was to the question, "Was there a way to tell the story without offering fear-based information?" and the answer is no. The fear-base then is that which is certainly not desired, and any dwelling upon this base of fear shall detune the story itself. Nevertheless, the entire desire of this particular group is to create a body of information which acts as what this instrument would call a snooze alarm in that it rings a tocsin or tolls a bell that says, "No man is an island, and no nation is insular." Certainly, this information cannot be stated without expressing truths that inspire fear.

However, the story can be balanced in that not only is there the story that creates fear because it describes a cycle of slavery that has been pressed upon entities upon your sphere since that which was the time of Atlantis at the time of the last pole shift. The balance to this information concerning the enslavement of humankind is the equally compelling truth that there is a way to create a balance to this situation; there is a way from this enslavement to freedom of mind, heart, soul and strength. There is an empowerment of humankind which moves from belief systems and perceptions into the very DNA, for creative units within the self of the bodies of those upon your sphere. The need to change the, shall we say, mind-set of your peoples is great in that many entities have moved very close to the area of resistance or, shall we say, meniscus between third density and fourth density, and a very little attempt is likely to be sufficient to create a great potential for moving across that area of resistance into a fourth-density point of view which would indeed greatly aid the planet itself at this time of the birth of the planet as well as its peoples.

We believe that we need to refocus the query at this point. Is there a further question?

(Another question is posed by B over the telephone.)

We would ask that the question be restated.

(B restates the query over the telephone.)

We are those of Q'uo, and grasp your query, my brother. Certainly we would agree that the need is to focus within the aspects of love in its unconditional aspect. This unconditional love, or, as this instrument is fond of saying, the open heart, predisposes an entity to dwell within a state of consciousness which is in itself the fourth-density vibration, and the goal of this particular work of art would indeed be firstly, primarily and centrally directly to engage the heart of the viewer in such a way that it would open and create for the viewer within the movie the direct experience of unconditional love.

The most direct way to share unconditional love is to project unconditional love to the viewer. We cannot choose whether it is more effective to engage the viewer in a vision of unconditional love and of seeing unconditional love through the eyes of the splash of the backdrop of history, or whether it is more effective through the smaller canvas of the story of small-life characters. We would encourage this instrument to share her memory of a recent art exhibition to which this instrument went and spent some time viewing various canvases of those painters of the late nineteenth and the early twentieth centuries in France. This instrument relates the painting known as "Landscape with Cottages" to the question of the splash of history, whereas the charm of the smaller canvas called "Pink Tablecloth" or the charm of the relationships and obvious emotions of the figures within the painting called "The Reapers" engage this instrument's sensibilities on a completely different level. Of the two, this particular instrument as an aesthete preferred the painting "Landscape with Cottages" by an artist known as Paul Michel. To the more chatty or cozy frame of the very human, very small-life details of the latter two paintings, it is very much a matter of sensibility, and we would use the term comfort.

We would hope that our version of a wakeup or snooze alarm would be that which was gentle and clear and full of love rather than harsh, hard-hitting and alarming. The challenge then is to create a true story that tells the harvest saga in a way that both engages the realization that there is a threat and opens up the possibility of a solution which is achievable by the entities as they are within the world that they experience at this time. This is another way of saying that the faculty of hope is extremely powerful, and the empowerment of these individuals that dwell within your density at this time is our hope. The underlying question is, "Do numbers count?" and again this is a ticklish ethical question. From a sixth, a fifth, or to some extent a fourth-density perspective, numbers do not count. From a third and to some extent a fourth-density perspective, numbers count. Which truth makes your passions burn, or is there a bridge between those two truths? We do not know, but we recommend some playing with that dynamic.

Is there a further question, my brother?

(Another question is posed by B over the telephone.)

We are those of Q'uo. May we say that the timing has been premature upon the part of the ones known as Don and Carla. The energy between these two entities was of such a nature that there was an opening into what this instrument and this group in general would call the future, so then the gist of a whole cruise became obvious in the sense that the sea lanes which it would travel were lit briefly, and much was seen, although not perfectly, moving far into the future. The power of love has, in this instance as in all, the power that creates miracles. However, the appropriate timing has always been upon the track, and at no time has there been a difficulty in the sense that, may we say, many seen and unseen entities have combined as co-creators in this and related projects which have to do with standing for that which this instrument calls the Godhead principle. Each has that which is the energy of the Christ, just as the one known as Jesus was the Christ and became the Christed one by embracing that which was greater than himself. Each has the capacity to embrace and move into that role in which the self becomes the co-creator in such a way that love is opened from the creative principle through the vulnerability and the imperfection of the human experience and the human choice, and love is made visible by imperfect hands and weak and uncertain wills. They somehow have launched themselves into the midair of faith and inspiration.

May we answer further, my brother?

(Another question is posed by B over the telephone.)

We are those of Q'uo, and grasp your query, my brother. We are not certain as to the most efficacious threat. It is equally threatening, we feel, to look at the simple task of returning to a 75,000-year cycle of incarnation and reincarnation learning the lessons of love as it is to threaten the enslavement of humankind for eons and eons of time. In the long-run, the latter supposition is more frightening, but, in the context of the next 10,000 years, it makes little difference, and it is unlikely that any entities alive within this particular moment in space/time shall see their ten-thousandth birthday. Consequently, each threat is equally binding. One threat moves more into great matters and the other into smaller, and again and again as we speak concerning your queries, we see the seeking within your mind as to the scale of this particular creation, and we admire the courage which we see within the one known as B, in considering a wide range of avenues, for do not all roads lead to Rome?

Is there a further question, my brother?

(Another question is posed by B over the telephone.)

We are those of Q'uo, and no, my brother, the situation has not changed. Those who would appear within your skies are for the most part those with the service-to-self agenda or those who simply move through the windows of opportunity in a random fashion with little polarity but simply are those who move through as tourists or spectators. Our position remains that of being in thought-form within your inner planes, and, although those of fifth density within certain soul-stream families have more ability to create phenomena, we would suggest that it is not a well-polarized concept in terms of the quality or integrity of the positivity of such a project as that which this group is hopeful of envisioning well.

May we answer further, my brother?

(Another question is posed by B over the telephone.)

We are those of Q'uo, and are able to confirm that there are indeed many who have achieved graduation at this time. It is our humble pleasure to state that the great majority of these entities have chosen, once through the healing process, to remain within the inner planes of this planet in order to aid those who become aware of their presence and are able to ask them for their support and help. For these entities, any inner-planes entity or angel or deva or inner-planes teacher is able to lend its love and its passion to the energies of those incarnate beings with which it is in sympathy. For instance, this entity, as a part of tuning before beginning this conversation with the one known as B, spent approximately ten minutes contacting those within the inner planes and asking for their help, because this entity realizes the power of opinion and the lack of pertinence as to whether this opinion is incarnate or discarnate.

May we ask if there is a further query?

(Another question is posed by B over the telephone.)

We are those of Q'uo, and we find that this particular question is one that moves beyond the boundaries of the Law of Confusion. We feel that it is an infringement to state that there are those within fourth density in any way which would suggest groups or individuals which may represent this configuration. We would, however, state that many there are at this time being born into the Earth's sphere who are activated within fourth density as well as third in what this instrument would call an unusual hookup. These entities are as those explorers who blaze the trail and whose work creates training wheels for those to come.

May we answer further, my brother?

(Another question is posed by B over the telephone.)

We are those of Q'uo and, my brother, it has been exponential beginning, as you said, thirty to forty of your years ago in terms of double-activated entities and certainly progressing in the basic phi ratio of increasing numbers as time moves on.

(Another question is posed by B over the telephone.)

We are those of Q'uo, and, my brother, they would not appear different except in the sense that many wanderers appear different in that they perhaps appear more intelligent or simply different. However, this is not to say that there is an alien quality but only to say that many of those who incarnate among your peoples who are not native to the second density of this planet have a tendency to express in different archetypal modes which, though extremely subtle, sound those nuances which alert entities to a difference.

May we speak further, my brother?

(Another question is posed by B over the telephone.)

We are those of Q'uo, and this is correct, my brother. The so-called double-activated child in its young years may well remember far more of the truth than the same entity which moves into the increasing complexities of the illusion. The fourth density itself is one in which there is a glamour or illusion within that which within third density would be considered the emotional or mental self. Consequently, there is the capacity for a certain type of shadow even in fourth-density thought. The forces of emotion through that which is called puberty among your peoples takes a great toll upon the fourth-density as well as the third-density-activated entity, and the entity of either density's activation which survives third-density adulthood issues is a remarkable and unusual citizen of the planet you known of as Earth.

May we answer you further, my brother?

(B makes a statement over the telephone.)

We are those of Q'uo, and we would agree, my brother.

(B concludes his queries over the telephone.)

We are those of Q'uo, and we leave this instrument and this group in the love and in the light of the one infinite Creator. We thank you for the beauty of this session and the energy of this joining and we leave this instrument and this group thanking each. Adonai. We are those known to you as Q'uo. ✺

L/L Research

L/L Research is a subsidiary of Rock Creek Research & Development Laboratories, Inc.

P.O. Box 5195
Louisville, KY 40255-0195

www.llresearch.org

Rock Creek is a non-profit corporation dedicated to discovering and sharing information which may aid in the spiritual evolution of humankind.

ABOUT THE CONTENTS OF THIS TRANSCRIPT: This telepathic channeling has been taken from transcriptions of the weekly study and meditation meetings of the Rock Creek Research & Development Laboratories and L/L Research. It is offered in the hope that it may be useful to you. As the Confederation entities always make a point of saying, please use your discrimination and judgment in assessing this material. If something rings true to you, fine. If something does not resonate, please leave it behind, for neither we nor those of the Confederation would wish to be a stumbling block for any.

CAVEAT: This transcript is being published by L/L Research in a not yet final form. It has, however, been edited and any obvious errors have been corrected. When it is in a final form, this caveat will be removed.

© 2009 L/L Research

Sunday Meditation
November 24, 2002

Group question: Our question today, Q'uo, has to do with the devas in the, shall we say, astral world, the devachanic realms. We would like for you to give us some information about the inhabitants there. We are aware somewhat that there are angels of a very high order, there are regular spirits that are associated with the natural world, the spirits of fire, of water, of earth, of air, and we are certain that there are others as well. We would like for you to give us an idea of the kinds of entities that inhabit the devachanic realms.

(Carla channeling)

We are those of the principle known to you as Q'uo, and we greet you in the love and in the light of the one infinite Creator in whose name we serve. We thank you each for creating this space in this day of rest to have this session of working and especially so since we realize the many demands upon the time of each of you. We thank you for your dedication to seeking and your generosity of spirit. And we thank you for sharing your meditation with us; it is a great privilege to be with you. As always, we ask that you use your discrimination in listening to what we have to say, recognizing and resonating to those thoughts that appeal to you and leaving the rest behind.

This day, your question was somewhat mixed in that we are aware of various names for various of the creatures about which you have asked, and we are also aware that, in terms of the terminology of this area of discussion, the naming of some beings is not consonant with the naming of other beings in terms of the astral and devachanic planes, which are only a small part of the inner planes. However, we assume that the question was intended to be general and to speak of the inner planes *in toto* as opposed to two of the seven. Indeed, our discussion would be very much the same. However, we would not be talking about the wide range of non-human entities that inhabit the great range of inner planes that is local to this particular sphere of your Earth.

Our answer depends upon an initial awareness concerning the nature of the Creator and the creation. This nature is such that, as this instrument was told by the one known as David, the matter which has been considered by those among your people called scientists for some years as a vacuum has been proven now by your scientists to contain more energy by far than the energy which is released both from within [what] you call matter, such as your bodies, or any atom that can be split. The unpotentiated, resting energy of the creation is so powerful that the power released in your hydrogen bombs is very small in comparison to the power that could be released from undistorted, unpotentiated time/space. When there is the creation within third density of life forms such as yourselves, there is an entry into a world of limitation and polarity.

Within the inner planes of third density, however, this limitation is not there, for the inner planes resonate within the energy of the planet itself which creates, at the moment of its beginning, all of the planes in completion as [a] pattern which, through the illusion of space/time, seems then to begin to appear and to develop and so forth. This again, in the visual world, is one of the limitations of your space/time. The conditions in time/space are quite different, and consequently there is not the bar against remembering and being completely aware of the metaphysical nature of what this instrument would call a deeper reality and the passing nature of all things which participate within this world of life and death. The energy of, say, the tree or a person may be seen in the context of this deeper reality as a minor distortion in the flow of unpotentiated time/space. The illusion that is so pointed and so emphatic to the physical eyes which you enjoy is in fact very little different from, but quite pointedly different from, unpotentiated time/space.

This means that each being of third density has, barely leashed within her energy system, the ability literally to move mountains or to make any physical changes by consciousness alone that her imagination and will can focus upon to a great enough extent, with great enough purity of desire and with a great enough sense of purpose. The limited intake of information within third density is that limitation which affects the conscious mind. It does not affect the subconscious mind except in the higher levels of the subconscious mind. Therefore, it is seldom that entities do see those beings of the inner planes with their physical eyes. Indeed, most of those who do see the inner planes entities while conscious are those who this instrument would call children, those who have not been trained that such things are impossible to see.

Further, there is the necessity for retaining an unprovability about all such beings that would increase a third-density entity's faith. In matters of faith, and in spiritual matters in general, there is a great desire not to infringe upon the free will of any entity who is within third density specifically to make choices. Now, with this view of the third-density situation and the situation of third-density biological units such as yourselves, it is perhaps easier to see that the vast array of very real and very substantive intelligence and spirit that the energy of the one infinite Creator possesses almost bursts out of each tiny nook and cranny of each distortion.

Life calls to life, and life within third-density space/time calls to life within the inner planes; the inner-planes life calls to and seeks to serve third-density space/time beings. The nature of angels is not qualitatively different from the essence of beings such as faeries, pixies, Puck, Robin Greenfellow and all such kindly and jovial spirits, and then moving to the devas within all living things of second density and all of those elemental energies of earth, air, wind and fire from first density. All of these energies may be seen either as focused energy that is attracted, as if by a magnet, by certain states of mind in space/time, or they may be seen as intelligences which are drawn by likeness of interest or likeness of vibration into a harmony and an association. Each of you being a significant though small distortion within the time/space and space/time continua, [you] naturally, by your very existence, draw energy and intelligence from the inner planes.

Because of the limitations of the space/time mind or intelligence of third-density entities, there is always the tendency to set the same conditions upon other life as are experienced by the life of the self. This has created through many centuries the naming of vast panoplies of beings of a certain order. For instance, as the one known as V has pointed out, there is a very careful and very large order of various types of angelic beings. There are in other systems of myth and magic many names for inner-planes guides, many names for nature spirits, many names for elemental spirits. They are essences which are beyond the naming much as you yourselves are essences beyond the naming, because they have not any relationship whatsoever with space/time, being completely creatures of thought. They are moved by thoughts. Being creatures of energy, they are moved by energy. The details of desire within third-density beings do not concern those beings of the inner planes that wish to interact with humankind. As much as the energy behind the desire for a particular thing, it is the intent, the purpose, the aim that attracts like energy for inner planes work.

When you wish help, the only bar to that help is the lack of solid knowing that help is available. It is much more difficult for inner planes entities [to aid] humankind if the human is not aware of or calling upon that help. Consequently, we encourage each never to spend the time wondering if such help is available. In our opinion, the universe is literally bursting at the seams with energy and information, and all of it desires to be known; all of it desires to be used. It is at the point of reception by the third-density biological entities that the problems occur. A large amount of help goes unused because it is unasked for and unregarded. Much help from the higher angelic realms is only available to those who ask, for as the energies become more refined and the intelligences more full of the infinite Creator, there is an increasing responsibility for preserving the free will of the fragile, third-density human entities who are moving through this choice-making density.

How greatly each entity's guidance system wishes to help! We give this instrument the image of a dozen angels sitting all about the living room on curtain rods and window sills and the tops of book cases just hoping and waiting to be asked.

The nature spirits and elementals are not concerned with the infringement upon free will, because they are called only by those who know that they are possible: either those whose faith has not been tested at all, such as the smaller children, or those whose faith has been tested and has been tempered in the fire so that there is a knowing that this aspect of intelligence and energy within things exists.

We would at this time transfer this contact from the one known as Carla to the one known as Jim, for we feel that this question has perhaps been discussed as much as we can discuss it before there are further queries to focus or refocus our discussion. Consequently, we leave this instrument in love and in light. We are known to you as Q'uo.

(Jim channeling)

I am Q'uo, and we greet each again in love and in light through this instrument. May we ask at this time if there be any further queries to which we may speak?

T: If one wanted to ask for help from a particular angel or from the elementals, how would one go about protecting oneself and trying to be sure that you are getting positive, Creator-oriented help?

I am Q'uo, and am aware of your query, my brother. We would recommend that the petition for assistance be made while in the meditative state. In this state, you may communicate that which is your heart's desire most clearly to those whose ears and hearts are inclined to a call for service. As you issue the call, having centered yourself and having made known that which is your desire in asking for assistance, then we would suggest [the] engaging of a period of silent meditation wherein you would wait for a contact and assistance, shall we say, that is communicated to you through your feelings, through images, or through intuition. That, when this contact is perceived, you ask kindly but firmly if it comes in the name of … and then you would supply that quality, entity or concept which is sacred to you, be it Jesus, the Christ, the Christ Consciousness, the positive polarity, any of the various saints who have made themselves known as intermediaries in these kinds of situations, and so forth. When you have received an affirmative reply, then you may know that you have made contact with an entity which is both willing and able to assist you in the manner that you desire.

Is there a further query, my brother?

T: No, not from me, thank you.

I am Q'uo, and we thank you, my brother. Is there another query at this time?

Carla: I'd like to follow up. When I was channeling before, I was getting this image of the energies that are a part of everything that you can imagine. I was thinking that we'd get some kind of way to tell what was from first density, what was from second and third and so forth in terms of the inner planes, and I was getting the impression that all of these carefully written down things that various monks and various people have seen through the centuries and written exhaustively about are actually very biased material in terms of culture and so forth, and that was why they wanted to stay completely away from the forms, because these energies, although they would take any form that was comfortable to you, it wouldn't be their real selves. Is that an accurate perception. Is that why you didn't want to be more specific?

I am Q'uo, and am aware of your query, my sister, and you are quite correct, for each culture [contains biases] and indeed within many cultures, there are various teachers, gurus, masters, etc. who have had experience with these types of energy essences and beings of light and who have given them names that are either culturally biased or personally significant and which do not translate well into another culture or experience. Thus, we thought to remain in a general fashion of description so that there could be a transmission of information that was hopefully free of unnecessary distortion that would be confusing.

Carla: Yes, thank you.

Is there another query, my sister?

Carla: No, thank you.

I am Q'uo, and we thank you once again, my sister. Is there another query at this time?

V: I'm not exactly sure how to phrase it, but the source of the question came from my meandering thoughts regarding that particular kingdom or realm, and I would like to know, Q'uo, if you could speak on the origin of those they call the archangels. I know that in general you did give a very good description of the entities themselves. I'm trying to get more specific with those entities that have been labeled archangels and even individually named with, you know, particular names such as Michael, Gabriel, etc.. I guess what I'm trying to establish or figure out is, how does one maintain or even initiate a relationship or even a conversation with such beings?

I am Q'uo, and am aware of your query, my sister. One begins to speak to such a being from the center of the heart. It is well to enter into the meditative state or that which is centered in contemplation and prayer and to offer that which is the heart of one's concern in an open and, shall we say, somewhat dedicated fashion. The dedication of which we speak is that kind of dedication that does not seek a certain outcome but seeks to be of service in a pure and helpful manner.

Thus, as you would begin to open yourself to such communication, it is well to prepare oneself by personal efforts in the way of prayer, analysis of one's own needs and abilities and a beginning realm, shall we say, of consideration of the desired outcome so that there is both a focus for the petition and room within it for the appropriate response. Those whom you have called archangels are those whose desire to serve is not only deep and firm but is practiced and experienced. These are entities who have taken responsibility for a greater portion of your creation than most and who have for many of your millennia been able to offer themselves in a manner which has realized that which you would call success in that they have taken—and this instrument laughs—under their wings a great deal of responsibility and who have done so with a great deal of compassion.

Over seventy-five thousand of your years ago, this particular planetary sphere was placed in what you would call a quarantine, for there have been many entities needing to be moved to this sphere from other third-density spheres that were completing their third density and who had populations of mind/body/spirit complexes that were unable to proceed into the fourth density and who needed to repeat the lessons of third density. They were transferred to this particular sphere by a variety of techniques, some of which were seen at a later time period to have been infringements on free will. Thus, it was necessary to guard this free will as the various populations of recycled third-density planets were added unto this particular third-density sphere. Thus, there was the need for a great deal of care in the overseeing of this process of the beginning of the third density of this planetary sphere, for there were many souls of various origins who would need to be protected, shall we say, [to] be placed in a certain situation that was designed to allow a balancing of distortions.

Thus, there were many hands and hearts engaged in this effort, and there were those who were willing to take the responsibility for a large part of this process, and they were given not only this responsibility but were given the positions that you would see as the angelic realm and the—we correct this instrument—and those who would guide this process in a kind of continuous consensus in the direction of energy expenditure.

Is there a further query, my sister?

V: Yes, and I apologize for lengthening this contact. I have one last question and that is if you would speak to the understanding or belief that, at one time or another, humans have actually joined with angels, I guess, in a mating fashion, if you will; that there have been instances where there were offspring as a result of humans and angels coming together, and there have been statements made at one time or another, "Oh, this person or that person came from the angelic kingdom," and, "That person or this person has that particular energy within them." Can you speak to that?

I am Q'uo, and am aware of your query, my sister. Many of those of the Confederation of Planets in the Service of the One Infinite Creator have been in various forms throughout their history of contact with the population of this planetary sphere. Many have been taken or perceived as being angelic, for indeed their vibrations are similar, and there has been, as we alluded to in the previous query, the transition to this planetary sphere of various other third-density populations seeking to repeat third density in a manner which you would see as the sexual reproductive engaging of energies. This in particular was one of the primary reasons that the quarantine of this sphere was put in place, for there was the changing of genetic codes in order to assist the learning of spiritual lessons that was seen at a later date to be an infringement upon the free will of those with whom the mating occurred.

Is there another query, my sister?

V: No, thank you. That really clears up a lot. Thank you.

I am Q'uo, and we thank you once again, my sister. Is there a final query at this time?

(Tape ends.)

Special Meditation
November 27, 2002

Group question: The topic is: What will be happening physically and metaphysically in 2003 and what spiritually oriented people should be doing and thinking about in order to cope with these things?

Questioner: The first question is, who exactly is Q'uo that we are speaking to, and how does the communication process through Carla work?

(Carla channeling)

We are those known to you as the principle of Q'uo. Greetings in the love and in the light of the one infinite Creator in whose service we are.

We are those of Q'uo and are aware of your question. We communicate with this instrument by means of this instrument's pathways which she has opened within her energy body in order that it may receive messages in a more direct link from those universes which exist beyond the subconscious, of the inner or metaphysical world that dwells within your human brain. We and many other voices reside within that universe and are drawn to help those upon your sphere who are seeking for truth in the way that we might be able to be a resource, for like draws to like, and many are the channels among your peoples who receive various of these voices, depending upon the tuning, shall we say, or the resting balance of energies of that particular instrument.

We were called to this group this evening by this instrument, who asked for the highest and best contact that she may receive in a stable and conscious manner in the name of Jesus, the Christ. Then the instrument called mentally for a contact of this nature, challenging us when we responded in the name of that which she holds dearest and highest and that is, for this instrument, Jesus, the Christ.

We are those who are able to say that Jesus is Lord, for this entity, yourselves, and we all retain from the beginning of that which is infinite the holographic spark of the one great infinite Creator. We have, in the processes of evolution, eventually experienced that which is the consciousness known as Jesus, the Christ or the Christed One. We have found that epitome of fourth-density unconditional love to be the redeeming quality that will create within entities the vibration which focuses the seeking soul towards a graduation from third density into fourth density.

It is, at this time, the graduation day, shall we say, for approximately the next decade of your years. Therefore, this instrument is very open to working with us, for this instrument feels also that the voices of universal guidance, shall we say, are helpful to any who wish to experience them and certainly for the next decade. It is well to attempt to aid those who are working spiritually in this way towards a graduation in terms of service to others and unconditional love.

This quality of Christed consciousness is that which the one known as Jesus, the human, wore and became in his selflessness and in his offering all for the sake of others. And this Christed consciousness awaits those who would seek further in the ways of spiritual solutions. Therefore, this instrument was able to make contact successfully and to assure herself that the contact was that which it stated that it was.

May we answer you further, my brother?

Questioner: What has Q'uo's experience been in the evolution through the cosmos? Was there a third-density experience that was experienced?

We are those known to you as Q'uo and are aware of your query, my brother. The Q'uo principle is made up of three entities: one of fourth density, the identity being that known to this instrument and this group as Hatonn; one from fifth density, that entity being the one known as Latwii; and one from sixth density, that entity being known as Ra. These three social memory complexes comprise this voice. The entities are of this galactic system. One of the entities is of the energy known as Venus, the other two experienced third density within other star systems. All experienced third density in a unique way, each in their own refinement of that experience. Each has had a markedly easier third-density experience than those of your particular planet. This is because the planet of which you are a part has been peopled with those who have been repeating this grade; some of them since before the last seventy-five thousand-year cycle. This is a particularly confused group of entities whose great length of experience has not yet brought them to a clear choice amongst all the variations from service to others to service to self and [so they go] swinging back [and forth] in a random and unfocused fashion. The lack of will amongst those of your peoples can be traced to this history of many, many incarnations which, in some, have not added either to graduation in the positive sense or graduation in the negative sense.

We hope to increase the harvest by sharing such information as we can to those who would wish to hear it. In giving you this information, we would ask that it be stated clearly within your article that we are not those of authority but rather those who come in the name of the one infinite Creator. We can offer our opinion as those who walk upon the same road, that path which is the way, the Tao. And we can share our opinions as we go, but we ask that each who considers these thoughts choose only those amongst these ideas which resonate deeply within, so that it feels as though each is remembering rather than learning. Those things which do not resonate we would ask that you lay aside and forget, for information is everywhere and in every moment, and if that which we offer is not timed right for you for now, then we ask you to let it go, for we would not be a stumbling block before any.

May we answer you further, my brother?

Questioner: Could you explain what you mean by graduation and harvest?

We are those of Q'uo and are aware of your question. All are familiar with the concept of the harvest, and, in this instrument's long experience in her fifty-nine years upon your planet, she has focused attention upon the teachings that are contained within that which is called your Bible. Within this particular book, the image of the harvest has an especial meaning, for the one known as Jesus in his teachings is said to have offered a story concerning the harvest. Indeed, this entity offered many teachings concerning the harvest. In the case of these teachings, all was offered in story and in image, for this messenger of the harvest came two thousand or so years before the actual shift of the planet itself into another density of experience, another area within space/time in the great spiral of the galaxies about the central sun.

The central thrust of the metaphor of harvest for the one known as Jesus was that the fields were white with the crops, and all was ripe and ready to be harvested but that there were not enough workers for the harvest, and there was a call for those who followed this teacher to take up the honor and duty of attempting, each in her own way, to add to the possibility of awakening those blooming and ripened souls that are the pride and the product of 75,000 years of learning, so that they might make that last step over the line, from a faint-hearted will to serve the cause of love, to a passion and a fire to serve in a very focused and loving way for the good of the self those about the self and the planet itself.

Indeed, in one of the other stories about the harvest, this entity suggested that laborers went into a vineyard to harvest grapes and worked most of the day, and there were those who came very late in the day to working upon the grapes, yet, at the end of the working day, all were given the same coin. This is true of the harvest as well. It does not matter when in the 75,000 years of learning the awakening and realization of the true nature of the self occurs, it matters only that it occur. The one known as Jesus the Christ was the first of the messengers of that which is to come and that which is already here in part: that being the age of unconditional love that is fourth density, that is the very nature of the lesson of third density. Graduation occurs when the heart is able to remain open, in more than half of the circumstances of life, to the welfare, happiness, comfort, safety and service of others. The heart needs to be awakened and inflamed with the desire to know the truth that lies within the open heart. By keeping the heart open, the learning process is greatly enabled for the seeker, and, by attempting to serve others, the eyes of love begin to be given reason to open.

May we answer you further, my brother?

Questioner: If you need to exemplify unconditional love in order to make the harvest or to graduate, how do you overcome the negative patterns in oneself that keep you from doing that?

We are those of Q'uo, and are aware of your question. We would first suggest that the process not be thought of as overcoming but rather balancing and moving deeper into the nature of the true self. The self may be seen by the self, and the self may find itself helpful if it is able to retain an objectivity concerning the incoming data which it is receiving.

The very heart of third-density existence is the experience of utter confusion. It is the goal of this density to create an atmosphere in which only by faith can one see the health and rightness of the present moment. The purpose of this confusion is to wean the infant spirit from its biological choice-making brain and into the fourth-density gateway, shall we say, which is the fourth chakra of the energy system of the human vehicle, the green-ray energy center or heart chakra. Once the seeker is able to grasp the value of this opened heart and the limitations of both intellect and personality, the seeker is far more able to retain a certain sector of consciousness which is devoted to refining the accuracy and lack of emotional bias with which it receives the incoming information.

We would suggest that the biological mind has as its purpose the protection and the survival of the organism, and in order to adapt to its circumstances, from its very beginnings in the second-density kingdom of the great apes, it has prospered because of its adaptive nature. Once this occurs—this opening of the heart—once this inner ear is able to begin suggesting to the consciousness as a whole when it is biasing its incoming information, then it becomes far more possible to detect within oneself the triggers that create confusion beyond the necessity of the incoming information.

Even before the birth of an entity, it begins to be acculturated, and very rapidly the process of acculturation, even in childhood, creates a pattern of misperceptions based upon this information passed on by parents, friends, teachers and others about the young soul entering this illusion through the door of birth. Therefore, it is virtually impossible to undo in a literal sense the learning experience that helps create distortion. We would not suggest that entities attempt to eliminate distortion, for distortion is not a pejorative term but rather a descriptive one. The first distortion of the infinite Creator is the free will, the second is love, and the third is light, these being the first three and primal values of this particular system of discussion of the mystery of the one infinite Creator.

Does this answer your query, my brother?

Questioner: It looks like our planet is moving into a very difficult time of negative experience. How can one who wishes to graduate into the fourth density cope with what's occurring now and what will occur in 2003?

We are those of Q'uo, and are aware of your query, my brother. Firstly, we would say that the physical manifestations of political intrigue, unrest, terrorism and war are as they are and are the natural outworking of the processes of graduation in which entities who have chosen [the path of] service to self are attempting to graduate with the same devotion and focus as those attempting to graduate in the path of service to others. The situations, we would suggest, are in the hands of all of those who understand and realize that they are citizens of eternity who came here to learn and to serve and who wish to go on to learn and to serve, for that is the desire of the upward-spiraling cells of each entity and each atom that exists within the physical and metaphysical universes.

We would suggest that the self be attentive. The responsibility of the open heart is to love unconditionally that which it sees and to see each and every thing and person as the self or a part of the self. In times of disquiet and conflict, entities are offered a sharpened opportunity to behold the shadow portion of the self, the wolf that bites at the heart within. This forthcoming year may contain disquiet. We can only encourage each to open the arsenal of inner and outer gifts towards the third-density situation, finding ways to respond appropriately in service to others as inspired and as able.

With this concern reduced to that which is its actual nature, that is, that which can only be affected positively by knowing all is well or negatively by worry, the concern can then be turned to that which is the true business of this hour, this year, and indeed the decade to come. That is aiding the planet itself and aiding the self and each other self to achieve the ability to enjoy an increased density of [the] light that lights your physical sphere. The nature of that light is changing, and it will become less and less possible for third-density physical vehicles to dwell in that light, not because it is damaging to the physical body but because the energy is hardened in a way into a state of mind that is characteristic of third density and is connected with the concept of self-protection and survival.

The enjoyment of [the] light of fourth density is dependent upon being able to move into a state of consciousness in which all other selves are seen as the self and all crimes and achievements are seen as a portion of the universal self and to move that 180 degrees [until] the self is seen as all things and as the Creator. That unification of consciousness opens the self to loving and being loved in a way that the body loves itself rather than the way entities who are separate units love each other.

Each is unique. We do not presume a high mentality, but rather we suggest that, at the subconscious level, all entities within creation are already one, and therefore the process of moving from third to fourth density in part consists of accepting the oneness at a level which has moved into the belief and perception system of the entity. This biases the conscious entity towards retaining the attitude of unconditional love and outgoing radiance of being at times when there is a perceived threat. The one known as St. Francis of Assisi is said to have called the fire, Sister Fire and the pain, Brother Pain, seeing that all things and qualities are a portion of one infinite creation. In each culture, there …

(Side one of tape ends.)

(Carla channeling)

We are those of Q'uo and are again with this instrument. We were speaking to the concerns in a metaphysical sense of the upcoming year, and we were pointing out the enhanced ability of those who remember the mechanism of confusion which is covering the deeper essences of that which is occurring in the infinite play of consciousness.

We would suggest that the coming year is one in which there is an occurrence that is ongoing, and cyclical within that ongoing unity, which is as if there were a ratcheting up of the density actually experienced by those among your peoples at this time. These movements began long ago and are increasing in their frequency as the clocklike motions of planetary movements spiral this planetary sphere into the vibrations of fourth-density time/space and space/time. The mismatch in vibration between [fourth-density space/time and] those who live and dwell within the third-density, choice-making brain is increasing, and it is becoming more difficult to feel comfortable. This experience of discomfort is markedly increased by the toys and gadgets of those among your peoples who are indeed of service to self. These toys include your popular media and the various products of your peoples' service-to-self intrigues. These two factors combine to offer to the third-density entity a remarkably increased experience of rush, stress, uneasiness or even depression.

For those who are awake, the mismatch has a different effect. The attempts to keep the third-density heart open within incarnation are reliably imperfect. However, the sheer desire to keep that infinite love flowing through the energy body has a tremendous impact upon the time/space, rather than the space/time, universe. Within that universe, intentions and ideals are things. Consequently, even though the entity has been thoroughly imperfect in keeping the heart open, the intent, repeated and repeated without tiring, to return to a state of openheartedness allows the entity to respond to the fourth-density portion of the vibrations by seeking [them], and, in so doing, the entity moves into its needed next healing crisis. Many times, these crises are emotional and expressed through emotional, what this instrument would call, conditions. Many other times, there is the actual difficulty with the physical vehicle or other effects which vary with the reactions of the individual to the increased density of light and the imbalances within that entity's energy system.

The goal, then, is not perfection but rather that sturdy returning and remembrance of unconditional love. That is the nature of the one infinite Creator, and that nature permeates and fills the universe that you are aware of and all that you are not yet able to measure. Indeed, the very space that has so long been considered a vacuum is far more intensely packed with the love and light of the one infinite Creator than the atoms of what you perceive as matter.

Does this answer your query, my brother?

Questioner: Can Q'uo give any prophecies as to what actually might occur, so people could prepare themselves mentally and spiritually to handle it?

[I am Q'uo.] We would suggest that the prophetic information is that which would detune this contact to the extent that we would not be able to speak through this instrument. The response must begin, therefore, with our note that we do not feel it to be possible to speak [specifically] upon such subjects without infringing upon free will. We again request simply that each be aware that there may be opportunities to serve in ways which are not presently obvious. The situation as it develops will far better be served by the focusing upon the steadfastness of faith that all is well and that all will be well.

We ask each, brothers and sisters: is it well to dwell on anything in fear when the matter with which each concerns itself helps to shape the future? Is it well, then, to dwell on danger even by way of preparing for it, or is it better to dwell in a universe in which there is no danger and thus affirm that which you wish and desire? The way that entities speak to themselves creates an amalgamated future in what you term consensus reality. Therefore, any attention paid to survival beyond the usual preparation for your power outages and so forth is a way of expressing fear.

There is no portion of the creation which can be labeled safe nor is there any which can be labeled unsafe in terms of the continuation and the thriving and the progression of consciousness. There is no danger; the physical illusion is an illusion. The harvest is only physical in the sense that it is creating effects upon the surface of your planet because of the decidedly lagging vibrations of the third-density population which is creating a kind of resistance of the incoming density. The Earth is, as a planet, as Gaia, far into its labor, and it needs the pouring of light into that which this entity calls the Christ grid and which others have called the fourth-density grid or the ascension grid.

This is the true emergency. In a planetary situation such as this, our focus and perhaps any of those thinking metaphysically is upon the softening of the labor of planet Earth in her harvest and the increasing of the harvest of souls from this many-times repeated cycle of greed, rapacity and war. May we say that the sum total of this tack of defense and aggrandizement is the production of fear and pain. These emotions are as food to negative entities which from the fifth-density level are inspiring and activating the tendencies towards extremist belief systems and the "eye for an eye" point of view of justice. Those who would serve at this time may well attempt to ameliorate the third-density consensus reality, and we encourage those who would attempt to help. The attempt to save the self is one which moves from fear, and we would suggest that this is not a position from which to achieve a truth. Following truth leads to the heart of self, and, in the heart of self, the identity is [as] one with that which animates all things rather than being overly concerned for the physical vehicle. We do not suggest that entities be careless but rather that they respond appropriately as occurrences develop, meanwhile refusing to burden the pathways of the mind with fear-based concerns.

Information will come by many messengers: that which is seen, that which is read, that which is heard, that which moves before the vision of bird and beast, wind and rain. The process of true knowing come to one through one's own systems of guidance from within that universe that dwells in that shadowy ocean of your brain cells which opens a gateway to an infinite universe that is the true place where each lives.

Consider, if you will, that the entity which is watching that which is upon your television is observing a virtual reality. In just such a way, distortions in the infinite love and light of the Creator are, when picked up on third-density's physical channel, translated into this particular channel of existence. At the same time, each entity dwells within the corresponding metaphysical universe. The physical death is the movement from a heavy, chemical illusion to a less distorted and non-physical universe. There is no discontinuation of being. However, each did move into incarnation at this time not to save the self but to reach out a hand to others so that, as each hand reaches out, hands begin to connect, and entities begin to hope in a focused and harmonized manner, becoming part of the rhythm and flow of the very appropriate and necessary changes that are occurring within your planet at this time.

The harvest can truly be greatly increased at this time, because so many entities here are just a tiny step from awakening so that we feel that there is a real possibility that, working increasingly in harmony, light centers such as this one and all positively-oriented groups upon your sphere may begin to look less like solitary lighthouses and more like big cities. The grid of fourth density may be seen as formed by the joined hands of all positive people and all joined hearts as well. In terms of aiding your planet, the seeking entity may look at the globe, and behold many places where the life forces are weak, places that are barren and unfruitful. These are places where there needs to be a strengthening or a tweaking, as this instrument would say, of the grid.

Entities may at any time choose to become radiators of unconditional love to the grid simply by intending to do so and moving into a state of meditation. The process of sending this light forth is one of intending to. There are visualizations which aid in this sending of light for some, such as the visualization of violet light being sent or the visualization of the planet with light streaming into the grid and the grid lighting up. We would note that your scientists have discovered this grid, among others, and therefore there is a panoply of sources which entities may find which offer information of a linear kind concerning specific portals and grid points which this entity has no language for discussing. However, it is not necessary to know the grid's makeup in order to aid by the very being of the self within the open heart.

May we answer you further, my brother?

Questioner: What's the best way to align one's own energy centers to the Christ grid? How do we visualize it in order to send energy to it?

We find that this instrument grows weary. We are those of Q'uo, and we will make this the last full query of this session.

This instrument is familiar with the writings of the one known Drunvalo Melchizedek, and we would say that the attempt to follow the exercises within that particular book having to do with the activation of the Merkabah make up a system whereby an entity may harness and discipline the wandering mind within ritualistic mental activity which tends to open the energy body. There are as many ways to open the energy body as there are inspirational experiences. The mechanical ways of opening the heart such as that of the one known as Drunvalo have as their burden the form and outerness of step one, step two, and seriatim, the list beginning and ending.

There are many suggestions of such rituals of opening the heart, and we would encourage entities who seek such to search the information available for such suggestions. For ourselves, our suggestions are more along the lines of that ineffable and spontaneous expression of joy and thanksgiving which each has experienced in ecstatic moments. We bring to this instrument's mind the experiences of the bonding of a man and woman in love, the bonding of friendships, the discovery that one loves one's work. Such feelings open the heart by their very nature. Beauty, when perceived purely, opens the heart totally.

Therefore, what will open the heart for each seeker is unique. For this entity, it is the returning again and again to the table of Jesus the Christ to take into herself that very being which this entity views as unconditional love. This entity is in ecstasy as she hears the central words, "Do this in remembrance of me," and to that, this instrument replies mentally, "I will remember, Lord." For another, the opening of the heart may involve the beauty of a song, the flight of a bird, the odor of a rose or the abstract dwelling upon an idea. Each entity's place of balance is different.

However, all have in common the need to open the heart, but not from a careless or unprepared position. When the heart is asked to open, first we ask each to ask their energy body to come into balance, to open, and to be unclogged. The simple asking of the mind to the self to take care of this aids in the ability to move into that state of consciousness which is the inspiration of love, the passion of right livelihood or the firm settling upon that which is highest and best for one. These feelings of realization of the nature of the self and the nature about the self greatly aid in the opening of the heart. Certainly, anything which seems inspiring and resonant may be trusted by the discrimination of the entity.

The suggestion with which we would close is that we would ask each to remember that spiritual evolution is a process of change. Change is, by its nature, a condition which biases the consciousness towards discomfort. The more work one does in consciousness in a day, the faster the metabolism of the consciousness rises. It is as though an entity were exercising muscles. It is well to seek using measured times of meditation especially if such practice is being done is solitude. In groups, it is much more safe to meditate for longer periods, and we would certainly suggest that entities in groups are more powerful magnetically than by themselves.

We suggest a gentleness with the self, for the first self which must be loved in order to love others as the self is the self, and it is the hardest of selves to love, for the secret thoughts of the self are known. We would ask that each attempt to keep the light touch, being passionate and fiery as a lover in pursuit of the truth of the one infinite Creator and of the nature of the deeper self while being able to keep the light touch with the surface of the illusion, not disrespecting or dishonoring its importance but recognizing that illusion is involved in the information that is being offered.

We thank the one known as W and the other members of this group for calling for our presence at this somewhat unusual session. We have enjoyed meditating and sharing our vibrations with your own, and we thank each for the sacrifices of time and energy which each has made in order to carve out this time of contemplation and questioning. We leave each of you in the love and in the light of the one infinite Creator. We are those known to you as the principle of Q'uo. Adonai. Adonai vasu. ☥

L/L Research is a subsidiary of Rock Creek Research & Development Laboratories, Inc.

P.O. Box 5195
Louisville, KY 40255-0195

www.llresearch.org

Rock Creek is a non-profit corporation dedicated to discovering and sharing information which may aid in the spiritual evolution of humankind.

ABOUT THE CONTENTS OF THIS TRANSCRIPT: This telepathic channeling has been taken from transcriptions of the weekly study and meditation meetings of the Rock Creek Research & Development Laboratories and L/L Research. It is offered in the hope that it may be useful to you. As the Confederation entities always make a point of saying, please use your discrimination and judgment in assessing this material. If something rings true to you, fine. If something does not resonate, please leave it behind, for neither we nor those of the Confederation would wish to be a stumbling block for any.

© 2009 L/L Research

Sunday Meditation
December 8, 2002

Group question: Q'uo, today we are just going to take pot luck and see what you would like to share with us that might have some use in our spiritual journey and our opening of our hearts to love.

(Carla channeling)

We are those of the principle known to you as Q'uo, and we greet you in the love and in the light of the one infinite Creator, in whose service we are. We thank each of you for laying aside the cares of the world in order to create this time of meditating together and seeking the truth. We thank you for calling for information that calls to us so that we may have the pleasure of sharing our thoughts and feelings with this circle of seeking. We ask, as always, that each takes what she finds to be a resonant and helpful personal thought or concept and leave any thought or concept that does not seem personally resonant and helpful behind without a second thought. We appreciate this discrimination on the part of all listeners, for this care upon the part of the hearer creates a freedom for us to share our opinion without being concerned that we might place a stumbling block in front of any. The nature of spiritual truth is such that it is not necessary to create stumbling blocks of dogma. It is our opinion that the truth, as it relates to an individual and to an individual process, is unique to that entity and to that entity at each point in time. Even for the same entity therefore at a different time, two seemingly disparate truths may appear equally helpful.

You have given us leave to speak concerning our choice of topics that might be helpful to your seeking and your opening your hearts to love, and we thank you for that marvelous freedom to paint whatever canvas that we can of the love and the light of the one infinite Creator.

What shall we draw with this day, my friends? Shall we choose the paint brush of the astilbe, and shall we remember with you all of the colors of the summer as we move the feathery flowers through the canvas of thought? In what colors shall we choose to dress truth and grace and beauty so that each may find a brother and a sister in those ideals, friends among the values of the seeking soul?

There is always a kind of feeling of hallowedness about the search for truth. It is as though there is a spiritual search that is created of the mettle and courage of the pilgrim upon the road, and the many different challenges and obstacles of that road are as the dragons of the time of mythology. One sets out upon a journey to seek truth, and it is a knightly and a noble pursuit.

Very often we find that entities among your peoples do not see this same *beau geste* when they gaze at such concepts as beauty and grace, and yet how simply do concepts of beauty and grace fill the mind which is asked to open to those images that have been held close to the heart in memory, from those times of being vividly, deeply impressed by beauty in a moment, in a pose, in an attitude, in a scene that is perceived just once! How very often has each of you been stunned by the beauty of that which lies beyond the eyes of everyday in the moments of the daily life that are so small and so unremarkable, yet [which] hold such a burden of beauty? And is there not truth in that beauty? As the poet known to this instrument as John said, "Is not beauty a kind of truth?[7]", and is it perhaps not easier to apprehend directly?

These are the gifts of truth to fill out that range of options for those who seek truth. For within the seeking of truth in words there is many a harvest, yet always will those words create their own structures and delimit many aspects of the whole nature of truth from the ability of the mind to express.

We would suggest to this instrument that she gaze inwardly at a tree that she was remarking at upon a recent walk. This particular tree, with its precise angles of branch and its precise knottiness of twig, where leaves had been dropped and where leaves would again bud out in the spring. Each tree has its unique pattern, its unique expression of prayer, praise and thanks. Each tree reaches to the infinite Creator in precisely such and such a way, and the shadows of light, as they strike and play with that particular form, create a system of truth, proportion and elegance that has never been seen before and shall never again be expressed. Such is the dearness of beauty to the eye that is open.

There are many times when we see among your peoples a great feeling of unanswerable depth of confusion. There are many among your peoples whose experiences are at present somewhat overwhelming, and we would suggest that, in these times of increasing transparency to change, it is a very stabilizing and grounding thing, when such restlessness is perceived, to ask the self to look at the objects that lie about one in the natural arrangements of the everyday life: the shape of a tree, the lift of a bird's wing, the direction of flight and the posture of its body; the images that meet the eye. All of them contain information. All elements of your illusion work together to form an infinitely responsive and self-correcting system of information that is helpful to the spiritual, mental, emotional and physical processes of all those within any given environment. It is quite possible, given that an entity is alone within its own space, within its own yard or ground, that each portion of the creation of the one infinite Father is more aware of that which is needed by the self than the self is, for each element of the creation of the Father dwells within an awareness that all energy is one and feeds within the same system. Each plant that shares space with you knows you, cares about your wellbeing and is aware even of the thoughts which you think. The only element within that natural environment of the third-density human self and its second-density surroundings that is kept from the awareness that all is truly one by the so-called "veil of forgetting", as this instrument would call it, is that third-density element that creates an inability within the third-density entity to remember any environment except that local environment in which all entities seem to be separate.

The search for truth, like the search for self, is difficult to pin down, and we are aware of the previous question of the one known as C, "How do I know when I am being most deeply my self? What direction do I go to find a deeper and truer expression of self?" In a world in which entities are simply told how to behave, we believe that this is a most reasonable query, for it is a hallmark of the attempt to create comfort by third-density entities that they would seek, when creating for themselves standards of morality and ethical behavior, a list of desirable elements rather than an open-ended attitude of discovery. The explanation for this way of proceeding to find the self by consulting an outward list of attributes is indeed perhaps the more valued of your so-called parental ways of teaching virtue to the young and growing soul of the child. The virtues are taught as a list: be patient, be open, be loving, share everything, and so forth, the common suggestions for good behavior as each child grows.

The search for self is far more like the search for beauty in that there is no search precisely but rather the opening of the awareness and the realization of the nature of that which one has already been looking at without much comprehension. May we say that it is our opinion that the self that is most deeply true is a variable value depending upon the precise placement of the seeker's mind and will and

---

[7] John Keats, "Ode on a Grecian Urn":
    … When old age shall this generation waste,
    Thou shalt remain, in midst of other woe
    Than ours, a friend to man, to whom thou say'st,
    "Beauty is truth, truth beauty—that is all
    Ye know on earth, and all ye need to know."

desire at the moment of awareness. Perhaps at one point that awareness might be very close to the gateway to intelligent infinity as that person drifts in meditation on a sea of peace and silent fullness. At another point, an entity may be totally focused upon some difficult task, and every nerve may be strained simply to do that one task well, and, in expressing the excellence of that effort, the resonances of beauty explode out of each atom of that moment of intense effort. When the self can feel self being, it is an event that is real beyond the ability of any, the self or an observer, to describe or to identify that which has been realized. When an entity feels beauty, it is simply there. It does not have to be explained. Indeed, it cannot be explained.

How to see what each entity sees is a very difficult subject to examine. The techniques vary considerably from sensibility to sensibility. This does not keep one's perceptions from being very important nor does it keep them from being, no matter how confusing, vulnerable to the essences available through direct apprehension of beauty. So perhaps we would suggest, in seeking truth, in seeking the self, to lift from the literal seeking of that which can be said about the self, that which can be said about truth, and rather find the light and satisfaction in those moments of self-awareness when the heart can feel itself beating, loving, caring, hating, despising, being attracted to, when the self can feel its movements with clarity. In those moments, step back an instant and behold the beauty, the colorfulness, the articulation and the nuances of the one infinite Creator expressing just now, just so, and only because you are where you are, as confused as you happen to be and with all things precisely as they must be for this moment of beauty to burst into the awareness with its present, its gift, of gem-like truth wrapped up in the colors and textures of a whole and undivided moment.

We would at this time transfer this contact to the one known at Jim, that we may respond to any remaining queries in the minds of this particular group. We thank this instrument for its service and leave it in love and in light. We are those of Q'uo.

(Jim channeling)

I am Q'uo, and we greet each again in love and in light through this instrument. At this time, it is our privilege to ask if there may be any further queries that we may attend to at this session of working.

Carla: I have one from B, Q'uo. He says that he's very interested in knowing if the great horned owl that has been living in his family's backyard for quite a long time now, has a relationship with him and his mom or might be helping him and his mom in their spiritual seeking.

I am Q'uo, and am aware of your query, my sister. In this case we would suggest that the entities involved, the one known as B, his mother, and the creature known as the great horned owl have all found the area in which they live to be helpful in the nurturing of the life experience. The owl feeds upon the small creatures which inhabit this wooded area, and the one known as B and his mother are also most appreciative of the beauty of this place and the enhancement that the spirit feels in such beauty. As each spends time with each, there is a shared relationship that is developed. However, the conscious intent is that of the one known as B and the one known as his mother, leaving the choice of the area to these two entities. The great horned owl has found this area to its liking and is willing to accept the human intruders, shall we say.

Is there another query to which we may speak?

Carla: Well, just to follow up on that, then, if they asked mentally, if they projected a request to this owl for a relationship of that inner type, would that second-density creature respond? Is it just waiting to be asked, or is it simply an owl that's hunting food?

I am Q'uo, and am aware of your query, my sister. Your latter query is more to the point. Is there another query?

Carla: Yes, I'd also like to ask a question from C, and she would like to know anything that you could tell her about the members of the Confederation and where they might come from.

I am Q'uo, and am aware of your query, my sister. We of the Confederation of Planets in the Service of the One Infinite Creator are from this one creation that each experiences. However, we are aware that a more specific location has been requested, and we would suggest that we have come from many points within your, what you call, galaxy. Most are beyond your current technology's ability to perceive. We are joined in the desire to be of service to those who call for our aid so that it is the call that is important, not the placement in time or space nor the distance, for in seeking we are sharing steps on a journey with you. There are vast numbers of inhabited planets within your galactic system. The number is large enough to be meaningless; thus, it is well to see the entire creation as alive and intelligent and able to respond to those life forms which move through it.

Is there another query, my sister?

Carla: No. I thank you on behalf of C and also on behalf of B.

I am Q'uo, and we are most grateful to you and to these entities as well, my sister. Is there another query at this time?

(No further queries.)

I am Q'uo, and, as it appears that we have exhausted the queries for this session of working, we would take this opportunity to thank each present once again for inviting our presence in your circle of seeking this day. We are always most happy to join you there. At this time, we shall take our leave of this instrument and this group. We leave each in the love and in the ineffable light of the one infinite Creator. We are known to you as those of Q'uo. Adonai, my friends. Adonai.

L/L Research

L/L Research is a subsidiary of Rock Creek Research & Development Laboratories, Inc.

P.O. Box 5195
Louisville, KY 40255-0195

www.llresearch.org

Rock Creek is a non-profit corporation dedicated to discovering and sharing information which may aid in the spiritual evolution of humankind.

ABOUT THE CONTENTS OF THIS TRANSCRIPT: This telepathic channeling has been taken from transcriptions of the weekly study and meditation meetings of the Rock Creek Research & Development Laboratories and L/L Research. It is offered in the hope that it may be useful to you. As the Confederation entities always make a point of saying, please use your discrimination and judgment in assessing this material. If something rings true to you, fine. If something does not resonate, please leave it behind, for neither we nor those of the Confederation would wish to be a stumbling block for any.

© 2009 L/L Research

Special Meditation
December 16, 2002

Group question: What can I do to be more of an integrated whole and healed being, vital, expansive and radiant, filled with more of the Creator's joyful and creative light, making me a more transparent and humble servant of the light?

(Carla channeling)

We are those known to you as the principle of Q'uo, and we greet you in the love and in the light of the one infinite Creator in whose service we come to your people and to your circle of seeking this day. We thank each for the setting aside of the time and the energy and the care to seek the truth, and we are glad to share our opinions concerning the question of the one known as B concerning how to live a more radiant and service-oriented life, with the simple request that each of our thoughts be taken as an opinion rather than a fact and be subjected to the indifferent scrutiny of that part of the self which is the discriminator. Allow that energy within that knows what is and what is not helpful to make its feelings known, and, when there is resonance, then we are pleased to have been a resource. If there is not resonance, we are simply pleased to have you forget that which was said. For there is always truth in the surroundings of every moment for those who have the eyes to see, the ears to hear, and the hearts to understand. With this caveat, we are able to be comfortably on the proper side of the distortion towards preserving free will amongst all; of being a stumbling block for none.

The one known as B, as well as the one known as Carla and the one known as Jim and in general those entities on your planet which are enjoying third density at this time, indeed do have a tendency to get in their own way, as if there were part of the self that enjoyed blocking the natural light that streams into the body complex, most visibly from sunlight, but, in an energetic sense, moves into the body at all time. Both the physical and non-physical vehicles flow light through in infinitely great amounts, potentially. The energy body is as the electricity, having the capacity for both a large amount of energy carried and a large intensity or resistance of energy carried. Thus, the crystal within you can both be strengthened in terms of more power and can amplify its power by focusing, crystallizing and mythologizing the energy that moves through it and the crystal that bears it and shares it. The higher the desire, the more opportunity or capacity for bringing more light through; the more focused the will upon the dance of creative living, the more intense and penetrating shall be the nature of that widened channel for light. The ability of one entity to be a channel for light is infinite. An unflawed crystal could heal a planet. The secret to doing work in the sense of magnetizing the fourth-density grid or, in a more mythological sense, helping to birth Gaia's fourth-density self, is a helpful way to encourage and align the self with the emotional point of view which will help create a broader and a more intense and pure flow of the Creator's infinite love and light into the planetary grid. We may say in another way, into the hearts of all those that lie within the tidal waves that emanate from your being.

It is said in the holy work known as the New Testament of the Bible that it is not good to hide one's light under a covering, but rather it is good to stand it upon a hill where it can be seen, letting it bear witness to the light. The tendency of this instrument, of the one known as B, of the one known as Jim, and of most of the entities upon the earth is to stand in one's own light. The truth is that each entity is precisely that which the one known as B asked how to become. Each is as the master, the knight in shining armor, the hero or the heroine. Each faces the ordeal of life, the ordeal of personal relationships, the ordeal of creating a living, the ordeal of true communication, and the ordeal of facing the self, in the sense of doing work in the disciplining of the personality. The answer to the question which you asked lives within you already: purpose, already perfect, worthy co-creator, part of what this instrument's teacher calls the Godhead principle.

You are part of the Principle of planet Earth. For the most part, this social memory complex has not been activated, because the fourth-density mass mind has only taken its first tentative steps. Each who is master during this hour plants the seeds of a harvest that will feed those who are able to build upon the work done by this special group of those who come to aid in the harvest. Certainly, as the one known as Brother Philip has said, "… the crown (of co-creatorship) weighs heavy upon the head, and yet you shall wear it, and you shall serve under it."

If each is a master, what is keeping each from the self-realization of mastership? This instrument has been used to calling it "world opinion." All that is within the consensus reality is world opinion. In no case does it reflect reality. That which reflects beyond the illusion is the consciousness within and it is, as all potential things, caged until the reaping hand unlocks the door. In this instrument's hymnal, there is a poem which she is used to singing, which [has] the image of the entity known as Jesus the Christ standing outside the door of one's heart, knocking ever so gently and asking to come in. Doubt, fear and that kind of contracting emotion deafen the ear of faith and blind the eye of knowing. They stop the mouth of hope, and make one's armor permeable.

It is acceptable in the extreme to be doubtful; to, as this instrument would say, "err and stray from the ways[8]" of the infinite Creator, yet the attempt to move gently back into the balanced and centered state of mind which is the open heart ever and always creates a new experience or the potential for the brand new moment. This entity is aware enough of the psychological benefit [of] starting again that it will, tomorrow afternoon, confess its sins, slight though they may be, to that priest which is assigned to her parish. This entity does not believe in sin, only in making mistakes, yet still this entity feels lighter when it is completely empty of un-confessed shadows and forgiven for each and every error. Then there is a new heaven and a new earth, infinity of new possibilities and new beginnings. This is true at the moment, and it does not take a priest unless an entity is fond of rituals and finds it helpful to seek such a practice as this instrument has. The roles of this confession and forgiveness can both be taken by the self. One stands in one's own light, because one is under the impression that it is the proper thing to do.

Many times, it does not even feel incorrect or wrong to express fear in some way, because it seems practical and thoughtful and responsible to be concerned. However, it is well, when the possibility of doing so arises, to take the opportunity to recount one's errors to one's priest or itself and to be shriven with a truly compassionate heart. The addition of the outer priest creates the illusion that there is a Creator moving through the intermediary of priesthood and touching the lowly penitent. The truth is that the instrument creates or projects the priest from the self by fear, contracting against the idea of meeting the Creator directly. This is that which the instrument is aware of and accepts as a part of her earthly personality shell until such time as this practice no longer offers her comfort or a resource in pursuing her desires.

However, for those who are of a more solitary nature, it is well to invoke the priest within yourself, and we would suggest that you create this portion of the self as feminine, nurturing and loving; a part of the self that truly loves with the full and flowing heart, that sees the soul amidst the grime of an entity's inevitable errors. As this instrument pointed out in the conversation before this meditation, errors

---

[8] A phrase from the *Episcopalian Book of Common Prayer*.

are not only necessary but adventurous. They are necessary, because the nature of learning is trial and error, trial and error. Each time, the information of that attempt creates new knowledge. Eventually, an entity increases its knowledge enough to reach its goal, by which time it is involved in a further quest.

So the cycle is a spiral which will predictably address the life's issues of an incarnational level on a cyclical basis. Each time that the theme recurs, the motif is offered in a new instrumentalization, and there are nuances to be learned each time. There is no reason to be discouraged because the entity sees itself slipping into numbness or over-activity. This is another way of making an error and represents that which offers the possibility of learning. Thusly, if it can be seen as "adventures in failure," and if it can be seen that each failure inevitably leads to the attainment of goals that are deep within the desires of the soul stream of the entity, then it becomes easier to have compassion upon the self within its dream of personality and preference.

Carla: *(Sings)*

> Oh, Jesus, thou art standing outside the fast-closed doors,
> In lowly patience waiting to cross the threshold o'er.
> Then come, oh Christian brother, His name and sign who bear,
> And shame, thrice shame, upon us who leave him standing there![9]

The heart is the seat [of] and the portal to the truth of the self. The emotions are the fruit of great refinement through the turmoil and difficulties of turning catalyst into experience and the potential into the actual. It is a short lifetime in which to do such a thing. It is an adventure too great for skin and bones to hold it. The imagination of the entity within the human breast is stellar, star-like, infinite, eternal and several magnitudes larger than life. Yet it glows within as if in a cave until the door is unlocked into the heart, and the self enters fully into the tabernacle of the one infinite Creator. Moving into the silence is like unlocking that door. Even stopping thinking is like picking the lock.

The return to center is a journey from fear to love. When the sun is shining and the pocket is plump with money and the heart and the arm are full of love for a pretty girl or a handsome gentleman, when the breeze is fresh with the smell of spring flowers, such a state of mind as this instrument would describe as centered and joyful is easy to achieve. Yet it is as though the entity played upon the surface of the waves, enjoying the sunlight and basking in the graceful, ceaseless swells of the softly lapping waves. When the storms and extreme tides and waves of inclement weather stir the sea's surface into spume and spray and destruction, the self must needs remove its body from the deeps and become a land creature again, seeking shelter from that which is too turbulent to enjoy. Blessed is that swimmer with the equipment to dive deep, deep under the storm, to the still, crystalline water that is under great pressure and moves only languidly even with the wildest storm upon the surface.

This circle was speaking of points of view. And the feeling and emotion and point of view of resting in the deep of the ocean and the stillness of the ever-moving sea is a helpful way to create a kind of icon on the desktop of being centered so that you may click on that image, and other images that you find instinctually, to create a sense of expansion, stillness and peace. The every effort which is produced with the intention of opening the self to the one infinite Creator, of radiating more of the Creator's light and serving more and more as an agent of light, is in itself the heart of the process of achieving the desired goal. Shall you achieve it perfectly within this lifetime? We would not wish to deny the possibility; though we may that it is a possibility/probability vortex rather than a truth.

The energy to walk a path and to live a sacred life is as the energy of the deep [ocean water,] with little movement but great force. The peaceful soul is a soul resting in love. It has no waves to buffet it, because it is protected by its position, just as the heart is protected within a heavy and very strong cage of rib and spine. The precious interior of the body is well protected, and the precious heart of the energy body is similarly loved. To allow oneself to feel the joy and the passion and the *brio* of one's being is to dare great things. To do so with gentility and honor, with grace and with style is to shine up the armor of life. Rather than shrinking from pain of any kind, we do not say to dwell upon it, but rather to see it as a helpful friend, a sister or brother. You do not know why this friend is helpful; it may seem to be very, very unhelpful. However, the blasting of

---

[9] From an 1867 song by J. H. Knecht and W. W. Howe.

sand against rock creates the removal of grime and grit and the reappearance of the stone in all of its crystalline beauty, and so is the soul blasted to remove the grime of living and learning and failing. The storms come, and to all eyes which look upon the surface, the boat is crashed upon the rocks, the body is thrown into the turbulent and boiling waters, the life is extinguished. Those who are in the open heart simply dive with remembrance, with faith, and with joy, deep, deep into the waters that separate the mind from the heart, the storm from the stillness, the illusion from the truth.

We would at this time transfer the contact to the one known as Jim. We thank this instrument for its service. We leave this instrument in the love and the light and transfer to the one known as Jim. We are those of Q'uo.

(Jim channeling)

I am Q'uo, and we greet each again in love and in light through this instrument. At this time, we would inquire of the one known as B if there may be any further shorter queries to which we may speak.

B: Is S what's known as my twin soul? Are we twin souls, her and I? How may I serve her highest good? Is it likely that love will bring us together in this present world?

I am Q'uo, and am aware of your query, my brother. There are some aspects of this query to which we may say very little, for we do not wish to infringe upon free will. Concerning the concept of love bringing together two souls to sing a song of service together, [this] is to suggest that that which has begun shall continue, and indeed this shall, in some sense. However, the exact configuration of this relationship is even now being turned, and we would not wish to interfere with that which is of perfection.

Concerning the previous portion of the query, we must pause that this instrument be allowed to go deep.

(Brief pause for tuning.)

I am Q'uo, and we appreciate the aid from the one known as B. Will the one known as B re-vibrate the query?

B: Is S what's known as a twin soul, and are we twin souls, her and I?

I am Q'uo, and we appreciate your restating of the query, for the portion which we had responded to was the portion dealing with this illusion in particular. The query referring to the concept of the twin souls is one which goes beyond this illusion and reaches into those timeless states where being is all and service is easy. We would suggest that these two souls indeed have found themselves within each other's hearts and in this respect are twin flames of the heart energy, each expressing in a unique fashion that which is one and which has, through their mutual expression, become two.

Is there any further query, my brother?

(Side one of tape ends.)

B: There are moments of higher consciousness where I think I am piercing the veil, and I would like to know, are these moments more gifts or are they states of consciousness that are attainable? How may I best use these moments, and is there any kind of outer gift of service that I can bring out of them?

I am Q'uo, and we are aware of your query, my brother. We would suggest that these experiences of unity with the one Creator, the experience during which one feels great inspiration and such, may be likened to the stages of a journey, where there is a marker left on the trail by the self for the self, at certain times during which there is an opportunity for an increased level of service. Some may call this initiation; some may call this a reaffirmation or dedication. Indeed, there is a quality of a connection with unity which of itself will be made apparent through the life pattern and the energy exchanges that follow such experiences. For it is not possible to feel so inspired and aware and not be changed to a degree which will be noticed and be a means of service in itself, in that the light from within the soul shines forth in a nurturing fashion.

To most effectively utilize such experiences, it is necessary simply to open the heart and the mind as a natural portion of the daily round of activities in a fashion which says, "Here am I; what would Thou hav'st me do?" When one is willing to serve in whatever fashion it is asked, then one has provided the channel through which any such energies as these of the enlightened quality may flow. Thus, to desire, to intend to be of service is all that is necessary, for the way shall be made clear how one is to serve when one clears the way to the heart and mind.

Is there a further query, my brother?

B: Thanks, Q'uo, for this channeling You know I pore over your words almost daily. To realize my highest known desires, is it necessary that I change or purify my diet, and, if so, to what degree?

I am Q'uo, and am aware of your query, my brother. The degree of purification of one's diet, of one's thoughts, or of one's actions is completely a function of one's free will. As one wishes to increase the level of being with the knowledge that this quality informs all service, then it is well to take an action such as [the one] you have suggested, the improving of one's diet, to serve as a training aid, shall we say, a function or an action in the physical world, which grounds the desires that are spiritual in nature so that the daily round of activities is informed by such inspiration, such desire, and such perseverance. Thus, it is completely a function of your free will as to how your personality sees such physical expressions of metaphysical principles. Trust your own heart, your own knowing of that which is appropriate. "Seek and you shall find," it is truly written.

Is there a further query, my brother?

B: Is it probable, after my work is accomplished in Ohio, that I might move or stay for a time in Louisville and/or Virginia, to help in whatever manner I can?

I am Q'uo, and am aware of your query, my brother. Again, we reach that point across which we do not wish to step, for there is infringement possible when speaking of this kind of future activity. May we simply say that all things are possible for one who desires to serve.

Is there a further query, my brother?

B: Can you tell me what happens to me when I smoke marijuana? In December of 1998, the year I graduated high school, after much time spent smoking the substance, I found my body and mind reacting severely to marijuana. I became paranoid and self-doubting. My thoughts became jagged and conflicting. I couldn't make sense of what was real and what wasn't. My body reacted violently, shuddering sometimes, breathing with difficulty, heart palpitating, unable to interact with anything external, unable to think, unable to function. And every time I have tried to smoke it since, it has been the same experience, sometimes almost fighting for my sanity/survival.

I am Q'uo, and am aware of your query, my brother. We are aware that there are certain, shall we say, parameters which have been drawn by your higher self in your preincarnative choices for this incarnation which were necessary in order to focus the considerable amount of spiritual energy that is available for your service and your learning. The desire was that there would be a near-complete reliance upon your natural ability to access this information without the use of any aid or crutch such as that which you have mentioned, the marijuana. Thus, we find there is a preincarnative choice that has expressed its qualities in your conscious and subconscious response to the experience you have described.

Is there a further query, my brother?

B: I feel very scattered within my mind/body energy. I am either on one side of my head or the other, or in different focal points and twistings and turnings, and I wonder, does the imbalance lie in my brain, in my body, in the chakra system? And how can I bring greater balance?

I am Q'uo, and am aware of your query, my brother. To achieve the balance of which you speak it is well to engage in the meditative state once a diurnal period so that these various thoughts and directions of energies may find their true home. That is to say, as the energy of a spiritual nature, of which we were speaking in the previous query, begins to move through your physical vehicle, there are various, shall we say, distortions which may have an influence upon this energy, so that there is the shattering or the splintering of the integrity of the energy and the information which is available to you. If one is able to calm the conscious mind and present a cry, or plea for coherence, or centering, for the return to the foundation of one's spiritual self, then these various thought patterns may, as the mud within a murky water, begin to settle, [so] that the water be cleared, that the sight be restored, and the vision made whole.

Is there a further query, my brother?

B: You're making a lot of sense to me, Q'uo. I was recently told by a healer that I had done physical and spiritual damage to my red ray and was wondering what steps I can take to heal and open that chakra again?

I am Q'uo, and am aware of your query, my brother. The practice of meditation, of which we just spoke, is again that which is working upon this same, shall we say, distortion, that has its effect in the randomization of the thought process. When you are able to feel at home in your body and in this illusion to a degree where you are ready to express the energy available to you, then you will find both the thoughts and the red-ray energy center will be easily discernable to you. And it will be far more easy to express any energy from any energy center. Thus, the practice of the meditation is that which, when done with the appropriate dedication of purpose, may become a healing for you that is reflected throughout your mind/body/spirit complex. The meditative state is much like the recharging of a battery and a reorganizing of its energy potential, so that as your desire taps this potential, there is useful work in the metaphysical sense.

Is there a further query my brother?

B: You know I'm kind of out. Would you have anything to offer, to say, advice on my work to come, my healing to take place up in Ohio, my interaction with my family?

I am Q'uo, and am aware of your query, my brother. We would advise the worthy seeker to go forth in faith. All is truly well and the Creator awaits the interaction of your love, as you express it, within your family structure. It is much like building a firm foundation for that which is to come. There is much potential. There is the positive direction. There is the realization of a few remaining stones necessary to place within that foundation and this work has begun apace. We say be of good cheer, go forth in love and rest in faith. All will be well. Your feet are firmly planted upon the path of seeking. Continue walking this journey with a happy heart, and with a willingness to accept all that awaits you.

Is there a final query at this time?

B: Surround Jim and Carla with a lot of love and light, and that's my last request.

I am Q'uo, and we assure each present that as each seeks light, the light finds the seeker and there is an imbuing of the seeker with this light, that it may be shared with others. So that each as a candle may alight the earth with the light of love and service to the one Creator, and each face that comes before the pilgrim on its dusty journey.

At this time we would again thank each present for inviting us to join your circle of seeking this evening. It is always a joyful invitation that we gladly accept. We remind each that we are available to help deepen your personal meditations when requested to do so. It is our honor and pleasure to join each in meditation to lend our conditioning vibration so that the meditation might be more stable.

At this time we shall take our leave of this instrument and this group. We are those of Q'uo. We leave each in the love and in the ineffable light of the one infinite Creator. Adonai, my friends. Adonai. ✣

L/L Research

L/L Research is a subsidiary of Rock Creek Research & Development Laboratories, Inc.

P.O. Box 5195
Louisville, KY 40255-0195

www.llresearch.org

Rock Creek is a non-profit corporation dedicated to discovering and sharing information which may aid in the spiritual evolution of humankind.

ABOUT THE CONTENTS OF THIS TRANSCRIPT: This telepathic channeling has been taken from transcriptions of the weekly study and meditation meetings of the Rock Creek Research & Development Laboratories and L/L Research. It is offered in the hope that it may be useful to you. As the Confederation entities always make a point of saying, please use your discrimination and judgment in assessing this material. If something rings true to you, fine. If something does not resonate, please leave it behind, for neither we nor those of the Confederation would wish to be a stumbling block for any.

© 2009 L/L RESEARCH

SPECIAL MEDITATION
DECEMBER 19, 2002

Morning

(Carla channeling)

We are those known to you as the principle of Q'uo. We greet you in the love and in the light of the one infinite Creator in whose service we come today. We thank you so much for calling us to your circle of seeking and for taking the time and the concentration and focus from your very hectic and busy lives for creating a place and a time to seek the truth.

We grasp that this is to be a question and answer session, and so we would ask only that, in our answering these questions, each keep in mind that we, like you, are travelers upon a road, knowing little, experiencing mystery and wishing to share our thoughts and opinions but not wishing [to assume] the vesture of authority. Therefore, we ask each to pick up and enjoy those thoughts that appeal to each. Those thoughts that do not appeal, we ask each to leave behind. With this discrimination on the part of each, we are free to speak without infringement upon free will. May we ask for the first query?

J: Yeah, hi, Q'uo. This is J and glad that you're here with us today, and I'm the one that called you to the channel, and I'm here with my best friend, R, who is leaving soon to move to the beautiful island of Hawaii, and so I wanted her to be with me here today to ask some questions. One of the most nagging questions that I have is I really like what I do; I like being a body worker; I love doing massage with people, and I feel like that's one of the ways that I can be in service of others. However, sometimes I feel like that there's more that I should be doing, and I don't know if I should worry about it. I would like if you could speak about being in service to others and maybe doing body work and if this is really where I'm supposed to be at this time.

We are those of Q'uo, and we grasp your query, my sister. The desire to be of service to others is the arrow that flies without error. It is difficult from within the illusion of third density to have a clear, lucid point of view concerning one's own outer gifts and inner gifts, and one's use of them. [It] is often skewed, because perhaps one misperceives a portion of one's gifts or denigrates it as being not as useful as other inner or outer gifts. We are aware that, in the case of the one known as J, the desire is true, and, although we cannot ask any to be content with our knowledge, we would offer the point of view that the system of incarnational lessons and service works with a great deal of redundancy so that if an incarnational lesson or an incarnational lesson has been planned, it will occur as an opportunity, not once, not twice, but as long as the entity who has set this pattern up is alive and needs the experience of working with that particular pattern or structure of catalyst.

Therefore, it is not that any entity is going to be the perfect understander and scholar of one's own fate or destiny but rather that the redundancy feature ensures that, if one opportunity for a certain type of service or a certain type of learning is missed or unseen at one juncture, it will surely come around again offering another opportunity, and another and another. Nor is there any judgment from self to self, in terms of the self between incarnations that set this plan up, concerning whether or not the entity in incarnation decides to take advantage of a particular pattern for learning. Indeed, it may be noted that many wanderers create for themselves a superfluity of incarnational lessons and service in the same way that a child will fill his plate overfull because it all looks so good.

Not all things in life are requirements as far as the school of living is concerned. As a classroom, the curriculum of Earth is simple: it is love. There are lessons in how to love, in how to accept love from others. These lessons may have to do with loving without expectation of return or, in many cases, learning to accept love without expectation of debt or guilt. As the one known as J has pointed out, it is often far easier to serve and to love without expectation of return than to accept the love offerings of others as a worthy and honorable person. The lesson of acceptance of love is keyed, therefore, to those who are dealing with exceptional clarity in seeing the landscape of their own imperfection. Consequently, that entity which is working upon opening the heart to being worthy of love is also working upon lessons that are linked to the distortion of feeling unworthy. The service of the inner type, as each in this group is aware, is the more central service, since it works upon the soul of the planet, the soul of the entity, and the soul of the group entity that is the self and those other selves that are even now becoming more and more able to form the basic structure of trust and sharing that is the foundation for fourth-density shared memory.

Although the inner service is the central service, it is often the least easy to accomplish because of its very simplicity and its nature of being essence rather than form. Consequently, it is often the more efficient route to rest within one's outer gifts while one is becoming more aware of the beauty of the inner self. There is, as this instrument has often said, a process which this instrument calls falling in love with the self. Until this moment occurs, the self will be seen as imperfect and error-prone. Within the illusion which you enjoy at this time, this is inevitable. However, there is a process of moving beneath the personality shell's turbulence that we encourage each to invite, through silence and listening and the immersion of self in the creation of second density and first density, where the vibrations are without the veil, and there is much grounding and reaffirmation coming from the energetic beings that dwell within air, fire, earth, water and within each plant that blossoms and each animal that shares breath with those upon this planet. This first and second-density entity is extremely helpful to those who are attempting to get a sense of themselves as beautiful and worthy, for each animal, no matter how humble, each plant, no matter if it be called a weed or a flower, has its youth and its blooming and its happy old age and its natural sinking again into the earth. Does the leaf grow concerned because its structure has been somewhat eaten by insects? Does the doe in the forest lose faith in the rightness of things because there is not enough to eat? Indeed, each plant and each animal spends its time in surety, confidence and peace, for it is not troubled by attempting to justify its existence. It is not troubled by its perceived imperfections. Rather, [such entities are] just as the very aged kitty on the instrument's lap. As it struggles with difficult and stertorous breathing it has absolutely no feelings of inadequacy, guilt, anger or fear, but rather takes each breath as it comes while enjoying the most positive and safe and comfortable situation that it can find which, in this cat's case, is to be within the aura of its favorite human.

May we say in this regard that service is often greatly helped by association with those who are able to support, encourage and offer honest criticism of that path which in general is shared by both. The value of spiritually-oriented companions in this wise of seeing oneself, seeing one's service, cannot be overemphasized. All is within the self, and that which is intended to be placed before the view is indeed being placed before the view. The essence of service is that there is not a specific right service, but rather there is an opportunity that will revolve and come about again and again, and each instance of this sort of opportunity to pursue an outer gift will, if pursued, blossom into a viable path. Consequently, you cannot make a mistake; you cannot choose an incorrect road. You can choose only between a more direct one and a more roundabout one.

May we answer further, my sister?

J: No, that was good on that question. Back to the second-density beings. I was wondering if you could speak to me about my dog, Gypsy, who is also getting on in years. She is so loving and so faithful. Is she third-density harvestable at this point in time when the cycle of her life ends?

We are those of Q'uo, and we find that we can confirm this as the one known as J is already aware of this entity's harvestability.

J: Okay, one more question, and then I'd like for R to ask a question if she'd like to. I've been wondering lately if earth changes, things could really occur this year. I see Carla as an advisor, because she really helps me to stay grounded and not have a lot of fear. I'm thinking that possibly I should change residence. Is that something that you can speak to? I do like this place that I live in, but I'm wondering if I move in this coming year of 2003.

We are those of Q'uo, and are aware of your query, my sister. The energy that moves through your peoples at this time is an extremely vigorous one. It is the product of the increasing transparency between third density and fourth density. As this process of transparency continues to intensify, more and more entities will be sensitive along the lines of their distortions, sensitive in all ways. In those who are awake, it may seem to be a vigorous, cleansing wind; in others, it may seem to be the wind of change; in those who are fast asleep, it may seem simply to be a wind of confusion, chaos and disaster. As this instrument would say, it is all in the point of view.

In such an atmosphere of increasing sensitivity of the self to thoughts and subtle energies, it is not surprising that entities whose distortions lie along the lines of quiet and an untouched aura would begin to feel that perhaps dwelling in such a densely populated area might not be as desirable for the peace of the inner self as moving to a less crowded area where there is more space for the aura to flower on its own. We see neither harm nor [true help] in such a move in terms of any deep spiritual motivations but would note that often, when there is within the self the desire for transformation, the movements of the self in the outer sense of literally moving from place to place may well help to create the atmosphere of transformation, in that the process of moving is in itself traumatic and carries an energy which can be added unto by the cleansing and regenerative energies that are felt within the being. Therefore, the move is not just a physical move but a symbol of the felt or perceived movement or transformation of the self. Therefore, it may be that such a trigger, that acts as a suggestion resource for the inner entity, may be helpful to the outer entity.

Is there a further question on that, my sister?

J: No, no, that's good. That explains everything great. I personally want to thank you very much, and, as always, it's good to be around you and your energy. I would like to ask R if she would like to ask a question.

R: Yes, J, thank you, and thank you for honoring me by bringing me here to this channeling.

Thank you, Q'uo. I feel like a lot of what you've spoken already has been spoken to me and my inner self and questions.

I am moving to Hawaii in less than a month, and I feel one of the big reasons is that I want to create that feeling of space and openness for my inner transformation, and you spoke of the first and second densities, of the plants and the animals, and I have a strong urge to submerge myself in that environment of nature. My questions would be, how can I best serve this world, my girlfriend, M, who I'll be moving with, and myself through this move and this transformation, and are there particular energies, whether it be individuals or groups that might … that I might be able to assist and they may be able to assist me in our transformations to be love?

We are those of Q'uo, and are aware of your query, my sister. We are glad to comment upon this exciting and transformative adventure upon which you set out in so brief a period of days and hours. The best way to serve in the new environment is the best way to serve in all environments, and that is to offer the self without pride but with joy, to the moment, to the lifetime, to eternity in purity of being, in the glisten of armor polished by discipline so that the armor of light may shine.

Already the one known as R sees the self as a light. The question always with the light is, where to put it? Shall it be placed upon the top of a building and become a light in a lighthouse that warns those of dangerous reefs? Shall it be a light of hope that is cast into those lives which have been darkened by pain? Is [it] the particular kind of light that is the flame of passion? This is the question that each may ask the self when hoping to serve one's very best. Where is the passion, where is the desire, and where, when one opens one's eyes, is the opportunity?

It has puzzled, confused and baffled many and discouraged more that when the dreams of the heart are to serve by noble and outwardly respected means, [that] when the eyes open to the situation at hand, it consists instead of cleaning a bathroom, washing the dishes, cooking the meals, "chopping wood, carrying water," as this instrument would say. The one known as R also has placed for itself in the coming situation, as well as in the situation it is leaving, ample opportunity for service and for learning. There are entities and groups with whom, as a soul, your soul stream has made agreements. You may think of these entities as members of a large family that has been apart for some time but that, when it comes together, has a certain resonance that speaks of home, anchoring, safety, intimacy and nurturing. Look for the resonances in those that you meet, not only so that you may be of help to them but so that they, in their need to be of service, may be of help to you.

May we answer you further, my sister?

(Long pause.)

Is there a further query at this time?

J: No, I think this is probably about the length of time for this instrument. We thank her, too, for offering herself as a channel and thank you very much, Q'uo, for being with us today.

We are those of Q'uo, and we thank you, too, my sister and the one known as R as well. It has been our privilege and our pleasure to share energy with you. We thank this instrument as well, and we leave each of you as we found you, in the love and in the light of the one infinite Creator. Adonai. We are those of Q'uo. ✣

Special Meditation
December 19, 2002

Evening

(Carla channeling)

We are those known to you as the principle of Q'uo, and we greet you in the love and in the light of the one infinite Creator in Whose service we are ineffably overjoyed to be. We cannot express our thankfulness for being called to this circle of seeking, and, as we prepare to offer our thoughts, we would request that each scan our thoughts and concepts within your process and pattern at this time, looking for resonance and the feeling of recognition. We request that all opposing or separating ideas, in their seeming to you, be released and forgotten, for they clearly are not those which serve as resources for you. With this caveat, we gain our freedom to share our opinions not as those in authority but as friends and fellow walkers of the way of the one infinite Creator.

We greet the one known as J *in absentia* from the physical circle gathered within the walls of the Magic Kingdom[10] and would welcome this entity's first query at this time.

Questioner: J has experienced cancer and its healing, and he was wondering if, in the book he is writing about cancer, Q'uo was involved in providing any of the inspiration for the book, and, if so, would Q'uo have any insight as to its purpose?

We are those of Q'uo, and we are aware of your query, my brother. It is an interesting one, for the answer is yes and no. We are a part of your guidance in the sense of being used for personal guidance or higher self in direct communication as an entity, with you, as the specific guidance which is a portion of the soul stream, shall we say. In the sense of being an entity who chose to contact you from some vantage point which convinced us that we as a group needed to contact you for a certain project, no, we were not those who created the desire or the material for the written expression of your heart and your pen.

The process of channeling, creatorship, authorship or composer-ship is that of the tempering fire of circumstance, the quality, purity, intensity, crystallization and balance of the desires of the deep heart for the truth of the self and the truth of one's service, and the quality of what this instrument would call alertness or awakeness. These are the tools which open the channels of creativity. There is a balance between intuition and guidance and the more artisan-like craft of learning, discovery analysis and synthesis which must needs find an inner bridge in order that the heart and the mind work together as a portion of an extended spiritual family, shall we say. We are that portion of your guidance that we naturally occupy by virtue of the shared soul stream. However, as we have often mentioned, our guidance comes more in the form of a kind of carrier wave that deepens and intensifies or sharpens in

---

[10] Carla's name for the Rueckert-McCarty and L/L home.

delineation the details of the personality shell's own processes of dreaming, envisioning and seeking.

May we answer you further?

Questioner: "Are there any inaccuracies in the book that I've written or are there any areas that could benefit from further amplification?"

We are those of Q'uo and are aware of your query, my brother. We find that this direction of questioning is one which, if followed, would detune this contact, for these are key queries. We remind this instrument of an experience that it had when the course was being studied and the instrument asked the professor a question concerning the book about which the test would be taken. The response to the query was, "I will not answer that question." Consequently, this instrument chose to spend its study time answering that question, and this instrument was accurate in determining the nature of the final test. It was indeed that question that the teacher could not answer.

Sometimes, there are these decisions made which must be the sole concern of the creator dwelling within flesh and the personality shell. It is the quality of coloration within the third-density work of art that so enlivens and expresses the courage and the irony of being a third-density entity. We would simply say that a creation is a world, and, when the world is expressed in the roundest, most clearly delineated topography and detail of which the imagination of the creator is capable, then the work is whole. This instrument, as a writer, has never had the inner discipline to persist in correcting distortion until it was satisfied with its work. This has not prevented the work from being appreciated, and we would share that musing of this instrument's with you, that perhaps something can always be made better, the possibilities being infinite.

May we ask if there is another query?

Questioner: Are there any suggestions as to how best to disseminate this information, any target groups or timing that you could recommend?

We are those of Q'uo and believe we grasp your query, my brother. The target for the audience is that target which focuses upon the greatest concentration of those to whom the message is written. In your case, this would be those wanderers close to awakening within your peoples. The choice of the writing in English and of using story as a means of delineating metaphysical processes is a valid choice amongst the various approaches that could be taken. The target group cannot be said to be entirely of one type, whether that type be economic, age or job-related, for wanderers exist at this point in your planet's evolution at virtually all ages. The initial waves of entities have come through to take incarnation beginning in the [19]20's and 30's and your [40s,] 50's and '60's. Therefore, though it is always the youth of any people which are the most sensitized to deeper issues, yet still there is no clear demarcation between the young and those who do not share youth with those younger, because of the length of time that the harvest has been quite close, and the extent to which those from elsewhere have felt it well to commit themselves to the taking of third-density incarnation in order to aid the planet and its people at this time. Thusly, we would say that the young ones are a substantial portion of those who would welcome these ideas but such a creation as your volume would be very good material for those of many ages and conditions.

As to the timing of this volume, again we come up against the full stop of free will, for that is a matter of resonance for you and those who encourage and support you. Allow this question to resolve itself as far as the particular month or day. In general, we would say that the addition of all sources of sound metaphysical information are to be encouraged at this time and in the immediate days of what you call your future, for natural cycles connected with this planet's sacred harmonics of position will be in crescendo and in coda for your next decade or so in your years. The timing as a particular date—though not necessarily a significant key—is, however, a puzzle that the one known as J may find pleasure in resolving.

May we ask if there is a further query?

Questioner: The last question is, "Would Q'uo honor the book by providing an endorsement or a message which could be printed on the cover, website and/or promotional material?"

We are those of Q'uo, and are aware of your query, my brother. May we say that we are flattered by your desire for the author of cosmic sermonettes through this instrument to give a recommendation for your worthy volume. May we say that your creation shines with its generosity, purity and wit. We are those who honor the heart and the process of forming the point of view that informs your creation has great elegance. The attempt to move from the appreciation of a way of thinking and being to a position of internalizing that system of perceptions is a long journey most often at least partially stumbled through and suffered through. The fruit of such an intense time of transformation is often black and bitter among your peoples.

The energy that is moving through the earth that you enjoy life upon at this time is a cleansing and a purifying energy. Fourth density and third density become more and more transparent to each other. This precipitates, for those who are awake and for those who are asleep, the experiences of a mind and a body which are no longer tuned to the vibrations present in the current ambient experience. The need then is to release the old experience in order to accept that which comes next, and the one known as J has our thanks for being able to express a story in which this shifting of realities is given so many helpful stories, characters and moments. We recommend the reading of all books which may appeal to an entity. We recommend that entities gaze upon this and all volumes looking for resonance. The pleasure of new ideas is that which often sharpens inspiration and clarifies logical processes. Consequently, this and all books may be viewed as possible resources for spiritual growth.

Would there be any follow-up queries that those present might have in terms of these questions and what the one known as J might pursue?

Questioner: I think that's all the questions at this time. We thank you very much, Q'uo, for all of the information that you gave us.

We are those known to you as Q'uo, and we thank you, my brother, as well as this instrument, the one known as T, the one known as M, the one known as J, and those who are with these in thought for asking us to share our thoughts. It is such a precious thing to touch into your energy and feel the shared vibrations of your beings. We leave each of you resting in the infinite Creator. We leave you in the love and the light of the One. We are those of Q'uo. Adonai. Adonai.

Sunday Meditation
December 22, 2002

Question from J1: Can the source of anger, seeming this is the source of the cancer, be inherited? Can it be from past-life programming, or could it be deliberately implanted or consciously created to create a learning opportunity during the incarnation?

(Carla channeling)

We are those known to you as the principle of Q'uo, and we greet you with great joy in the love and in the light of the one infinite Creator in Whose service we are. It is a great blessing and privilege to be called to your group this day to join in your meditation and to offer our humble opinion on the subject of the causes or the providence of cancer. We are glad to share our opinions with you with the request, as always, that each discriminate carefully as each listens or reads so that no idea is allowed to take lodging within your value system that is not resonant to you personally. With this in place we feel much freer to offer our opinion without being concerned that we might infringe on your free will.

The circle of seeking this day queries concerning cancer and certainly we may speak concerning this particular distortion or disease. However, our remarks may in general be relevant to other conditions and estates of humankind's physical vehicle.

We would begin by acknowledging some of the basic structure from which we speak concerning that which is conceived of among your peoples as disease. Since all that has formed is a distortion of the one original Thought, to say that disease is a distortion is not to insult the breed. For, indeed, that which is known among your peoples as disease has its own beauty and function within the system of dynamics of third density. It is a highly convenient and somewhat sensitive means of ending a life span at the just and appropriate time for that entity and, indeed, in many cases the so-called disease comes into play as a result of the filling up of the capacity of the entity's learning system from the wear and tear of the daily incarnational experience once the vital energies of the entity have expended that amount which they have to offer to the challenges and pleasures of having breath and life within third density [which] may have ended sooner than was intended before incarnation.

This is impossible to predict before incarnation, either how catalyst will strike the entity within incarnation or to what depth the increased load of unprocessed experience may go. When such bank accounts of undigested experience rest within an entity so that the amount of unprocessed catalyst is over the full line for an entity in terms of incarnational energy then it is that the physical vehicle may gladly accept the disease in order to plead a sensible and timely period upon an incarnational pattern.

This is most helpful for the entity so that healing may occur as would be needed to create an atmosphere within which the entity somewhat healed from its travels in its personality shell through the incarnation may recover itself, take thought after its healing, and consult with its higher self and all guides in the construction of a new incarnation which would address those unresolved catalysts.

It is for this reason that many entities [who] find themselves dealing with physical difficulties of one kind or another would then end life experience at a younger age than would be, shall we say, the cultural norm among your peoples. Consequently, whatever the condition or disease that is perceived by those who offer tests with the various measuring devices of your peoples, [they] have only the outer hints and clues as to the true cause of the condition.

The shape of unprocessed emotion within the incarnational energy vehicle most closely associated with the physical vehicle has a much more accurate and clear concept of where the opportunity of an ending to the incarnation is coming from in terms of cause. Only the entity and, perhaps, sometimes not even that entity is fully aware of what sorrows upon the heart, what unbalanced emotion upon the emotional body, have created a situation of imbalance which has reached the point where the mind complex of an entity cannot balance it. When this occurs the natural evolution of the distortion known as disease is to move from those difficulties within the mind to the more obvious hints and clues offered by the analogous condition which has been given to the body, for it to, shall we say, act out its distress, sorrow, anger, grief or whatever the imbalanced emotion or unrefined emotion that has been causing the distortion to be chronic within the energy body of the individual.

The query specifically moves to question the three possible causes of the arising of cancer from anger, that is: the predisposition of the genetic makeup of the vehicle, the carry over from past life distortions, and the placing of the illness or condition within the life experience as a response to those things which occur within incarnation, and we would take these one at a time after simply saying that we would agree with the one known as J1 that relating the emotions of unrefined anger to the condition cancer is quite often correct as a solution to the linkage between mind and body in the arising of that particular disease.

Firstly, there is the possibility of genetic predisposition, and while we completely agree that this predisposition is a portion of many entities within your density who do experience the arising of this disease, it is entirely possible for two entities with the same genetic makeup to respond quite differently to stress when it takes the form of the hot and fiery distortions of anger. One entity may be able to allow the refining of that anger by not resisting it or holding on to it but simply sitting with that anger in utter compassion for the reasons for that anger, the hurt and pain and sorrow behind that anger, the entity feeling threatened, fearful, abandoned or unworthy and thus creating the experience of a confused anger that then can be placed in the tempering fire of patience and waiting so that that anger is given time to be refined by the enduring fire of experience.

When that which is creating distortion is allowed to express itself completely in the inner energetic system of the vehicle then it is that the physical distortions that might arise, the cause of genetic predisposition, will not arise since there is not an imbalance penetrating or chronic enough to trigger the stimulus to which cancer is a response. Consequently, the thinking system and the perception system of each entity has the responsibility for determining what is the truth of any particular occurrence and when an entity's information system is able to deliver, shall we say, a less distorted truth concerning the evolution of the emotion of anger, the skill of this draws the sting out of the otherwise triggering perception that the entity is no longer safe and must become one who is on guard and protecting oneself.

This contracting or defending choice when faced with one's own anger defines the perception that the cells of the body will receive. If anger is perceived and yet it is perceived from a viewpoint of safety, compassion and nurturing it will not constitute a trigger for a physical vehicle to produce that which is cancer.

Thus, it is exquisitely central for entities to be alert to the actual nature of their allowed perceptions for what is perceived is what the physical vehicle reacts to. Each has seen the demonstration of hypnotism where an entity is informed that being stuck with a pin will not hurt and, sure enough, the hypnotist is able to demonstrate the changed perception of the client which has been hypnotized. This is precisely the nature of perception, and we encourage each always to gaze with a clear eye and an unbiased point of view at the nature of one's thoughts. For each thought that is processed by the intelligence has its nature, its strength, and its vector in terms of polarity and purity.

The second suggestion as to causes of the cancer, that is, the cause of how the anger expresses itself in cancer, is that which is carried over into a present incarnation from a past incarnation. Often there is in the experience of older souls upon your planet—that is, those who have been through multiple lifetimes upon your planetary sphere—that there is a carry over especially of those experiences that have been involved in a pervious death: the place of a fatal blow, the chakra involved in a mortal emotional dysfunction, even the primary and secondary energy centers associated with certain relationships distortions and imbalances. When such a relationship is central to the incarnation pattern [it] may well constitute an imbalance that expresses even through an entirely new body and energy system the cause of the strength of the previous distortion. Often in the case of wanderers this does not apply because such entities have balanced karma moving into the earth plane and therefore have only the energies of the present incarnation to balance.

When such a lack and imbalance does persist from one incarnation to another we would say that it most generally does not take a certain form in terms of disease but rather constitutes an area of weakness that may be a target of opportunity for those illnesses that are offered to one that is at as toxic state of imbalance. These would then have to do more with the energy center affected by the imbalance than they would have to do with a particular disease.

That is, where the imbalance [was seen] to be a yellow-ray imbalance, shall we say, the disease might be of the organs, it might be cancerous, it might be a nervous [disease], it might have various descriptions depending upon the target of opportunity, its timing, and those illnesses available in the surrounding of the *(inaudible)*. However, such an illness would involve the same basic area of the physical vehicle.

This, then, would not be so much an emotionally caused disease but rather it would be that almost mechanical outworking of previous patterns with the insulating numbness of forgetfulness to ease the outworking of a complex pattern of imbalance from a previous incarnation. The usual expressions of such carryover illness are those expressions such as the colds, the flu, the problems with weight, the problems with the appearance of the skin, those things which are more generalized or simply visit for a time at a time when an entity does present a target of opportunity.

The third suggestion of the one known as J1 was that such anger may create opportunities for such a disease as cancer from inside the incarnation or from just prior to incarnation during the planning stages. And we would say that often this is the cause which is the, shall we say, the efficient cause of cancer among your peoples. For many are the people who are very eager to cleanse and purify their energy body of all imbalance and the guidance before incarnation encourages the self to put in place a possibility of illness in order that should the incarnation not be going as planned there may be set in place the predetermined tendency to form illnesses which create the opportunity for inner work.

A good example from channeling which we find within this instrument's awareness is that of the one known as Franklin who programmed into its incarnation the possibility of crippling polio. This did not occur in childhood as that particular disease normally does but rather it was set in place as a fallback strategy in case the one known as Franklin became led astray from its desires prior to incarnation to become more positive, more openhearted, and more service-oriented.

The practice of politics is, shall we say, not designed to create such opportunities for positive polarity but rather such practice as those of a politician may well lead to service-to-self energies being fairly freely encouraged under the guise of helping groups of people for their own good. When this particular imbalance became marked enough within this entity's incarnation it then chose subconsciously to create for itself a situation within which it would be more able to do inner work and less able to have a breadth and a fast pace of social activity. This did, indeed, in this particular entity's case work well and created the possibility of much good work and balancing the distortions having to do with the right use of power.

When a severe illness comes to one unexpectedly it certainly is appropriate to question carefully all three of these possibilities and many others not yet thought of. It is well to gaze deeply into the self to see as clearly as possible the distortions and glamours and exaggerations and cruel lacks of self-encouragement and self-validation that may have created such an imbalance that the energies of disease were needed. It is well always to see disease not as an enemy but as that friend which has perhaps come too soon and needs to be asked to move out of the stage of life and back into the wings so that more of this incarnation may be enjoyed.

The solution which the one known as J1 [seeks] to the riddle of disease and illness is that which we commend for truly all is love and as each becomes able to see the self with love and all things outside the self with love one is able to create the atmosphere in which healing occurs. It is like giving oxygen to one who is having trouble breathing to give love to the inner self. It may seem that others should love one and one should love others and that self-love is selfish but there is a level at which it is not only unselfish but necessary for health, to come into a sense of peace within the self that is beyond explanation that is the result of feeling unthreatened, safe and nurtured and there is no one but the self that is able to give that resource to the self on a stable, everyday basis.

Certainly an entity may feel safer with a certain companion or with a certain group. However, in terms of the innermost workings of an energy system within the human third-density being the setting of the stage for a balanced and even functioning experience of living is what this instrument calls falling in love with the self.

The energy of compassion is easy to feel for others. It is easy to open one's heart when one sees another's suffering. It is much more difficult to see the beauty of one's own suffering and to see the heroism of one's own endurance and determination to survive. It is very easy for an entity to be blind to his own beauty. More than that it is very easy for entities, especially within your culture, to fear and shun the shadow self, thus alienating that dark side of self in which lies so much strength and health when appropriately acknowledged, loved and disciplined. The one known as John wrote, "Love is all there is." Others have written similar sentiments such as, "Love is the answer," and these simple phrases hold a powerful and unified truth.

We would ask each at this moment to rest and to invite the self to move beneath the breathing, the heartbeat, and to the essence of self. Beyond form, beyond function, beyond explanation, can you feel the jewel-like crystal of you vibrating, radiating and being? Experience that beautiful energy that is yours alone, feel it flowing from the root chakra upwards and out the top of the head. Sense into the entity upon your left; now turn your attention to the entity upon your right. Feel the energy fields mingle and cuddle together and feel the energy of the group entwining itself from the energies that have flowed out of the heads of each so that they begin to spin and form a spiral, upward spiraling, moving on into the eternal realms from each pilgrim heart. This is your beauty and this is the beauty of the group.

We would at this time transfer this contact to the one known as Jim that we may answer any shorter queries that this group may have at this time. We thank the one known as Carla and leave this instrument in love and light. We are those of Q'uo.

(Jim channeling)

I am Q'uo, and we greet each again in love and in light through this instrument. May we ask if there are any briefer queries at this time?

Carla: I have a question from T. She says, "I am interested in the energy exchanges between individuals. I understand the law of squares and was wondering if the benefit is the same …"

(Side one of tape ends.)

(Jim channeling)

I am Q'uo, and we are again with this instrument and we appreciate the patience of each present, and to continue.

When in the meditative state, then, it is well to focus the attention upon some quality that belongs to the entity with whom you wish to link your energies. Perhaps this quality might be the openhearted sharing of energies that is available through this person. Perhaps it is the kind of question which this entity seeks with you to solve the riddle to. Perhaps it is a desire to share a certain kind of future experience, the sending of love and light to various places upon your planetary surface, for example.

Whatever the focusing mechanism, it is well to utilize this quality, desire or goal in order to blend the energies with the other self within the meditative state. It is well to decide beforehand the appropriate time for such an experiment, and it is well to retire to that place that is yours for the seeking within the meditative state, that place which you have made holy by your previous intentions.

When these simple prerequisites are accomplished then one may enter into the meditative state with a certain degree of confidence that what you are attempting to do is indeed possible and shall bed the result of your efforts.

Is there a further query, my sister?

Carla: I was wondering if you could comment on whether it is equal to have a focus group in a physical location and then have others from remote areas focusing on the focus group or is it equally efficient to have no focus group but simply everyone at a remote location connecting to the place itself at a certain time?

I am Q'uo, and am aware of your query, my sister. In the attempt to provide increased energy resources to various portions of your planetary surface we find that it is well to focus upon these places as precisely as one can within the meditative state, for this is a metaphysical working that is being attempted and is not one in which the physical precision is required, for it would be nearly impossible to find the precise location of any point upon your planetary surface that was described by latitudinal and longitudinal lines. Thus, one must rely upon the intention of the group of meditators that sends its energy offering with the precision that is allowed in the metaphysical realms. Thus, it is well to have an entity or a group which organizes such an effort, yet all who partake may do so from their own personal locations.

Is there a further query, my sister?

Carla: So, just let me clarify. So when somebody like James Twyman goes to whatever place he has gone to most lately and then has everybody pray for peace at that place—I think most recently it went to Iraq—the advantage is psychological within this illusion rather than metaphysical. Is that correct?

I am Q'uo, and are aware of your query, my sister, and, in general, this is correct, though we are aware that the entity of whom you speak is one who also performs his own kind of music and magic within the location that is in need of the energy of healing. This is a somewhat different kind of working, for this entity also operates within the social and to a lesser degree the political realm of the area in which he is involved, this adding different levels of energy to the mix, shall we say.

Is there another query, my sister?

Carla: If you don't mind me being persistent, would it be easier for people to focus and become linked concerning a place if there was a small focus group somewhere in the surrounding area at a specific time, or does that make no difference in terms of the law of squares, in terms of the actual faith of entities who are able to join with each other metaphysically? My basic question is does it actually help people with the process of linking up to have somebody to focus on or is it just as easy to focus on the place as to focus on the person?

I am Q'uo, and am aware of your query, my sister. We appreciate your persistence. The query is best answered, we feel, by suggesting that it does not make a difference to those who are from a distance sending their energy resources to have other entities within the area receiving the energy that will focus it. This is an activity which all may accomplish from a distance, shall we say, for it is a metaphysical working that is attempted.

Is there a further query my sister?

Carla: So the only advantage that a focus group would have would be if they produced their own gift to the place and that would be another kind of energy rather than purely metaphysical, is that correct?

I am Q'uo. This is correct, my sister. Is there another query, my sister?

Carla: No, I am done. Thanks a lot.

I am Q'uo. We thank you once again, my sister. Is there another query at this time?

J2: My question is that I am really interested in learning how to start to remote view. I realize that it takes a lot of energy. Do you have any suggestions that you could give me on maybe how I could create more energy to learn how to remote view?

I am Q'uo, and am aware of your query, my sister. Again, as in all metaphysical undertaking it is well that one cultivate the desire to do that which you describe and to set aside a certain amount of your time upon a daily basis in order to practice that which you wish to accomplish. It might also be helpful if you enlisted the aid of a friend or two and informed this friend that at a certain time you would attempt to visualize this friend within whatever surroundings this friend may be currently placed. Then at a later time to check your experience with that of your friend. This done upon a daily basis or some portion of your time might develop the ability to see with the far-seeing inner eye that which is usually missed.

Is there a further query, my sister?

J2: No, Q'uo. Thank you so much for being with us today.

I am Q'uo, and we thank you, my sister, as well. Is there another query at this time?

Questioner: I have a question. I was re-reading Ra in connection to how they came at this time to help correct distortions that they felt occurred from a long time ago. I was wondering if there is any assistance we can provide in helping Ra correct any distortions that they feel occurred?

I am Q'uo, and am aware of your query, my brother. The attempt to alleviate those powers which were given to the Law of One by the experience of those of law with those of the Egyptian culture many thousands of your years ago, is an experience that is profound enough in its fundamental nature. Its ability to influence many of the population of your planet is also that which is difficult to achieve in any physical sense, for there has been the, shall we say, construction of a certain artifice of an intellectual or mental nature that is the result of the reserving of information meant for all by a few.

That this pattern has been reproduced in an extensive sense in the years that followed this experience, that perhaps the most help that can be offered by individuals at this time is to seek to remove these distortions from one's own pattern of experience and personality structure. Thus, the healing of the self as is the first attempt and work of any who would heal others is that which is most helpful to the entire planetary population and not just to those of the social memory complex known as Ra.

This experience of attempting to balance the internal distortion is that which uses the information concerning the Law of One in its most significant sense, for as one is able to find a balance within the self then one radiates this attitude of unity in a way which is much like the broadcast signal from one of your radio or television stations.

Thus, the principle might be stated that one teaches many, for the beacon that shines from the consciousness that has cleared its own system of energy is radiant, is all-pervasive, and is that which enlightens the darkness.

May we ask if there is a final query at this time?

Questioner: Not from me, thanks.

I am Q'uo, and as we find that we have apparently exhausted the queries for this session of seeking, we would again take this opportunity to share our gratitude with those present for inviting our presence in your circle of seeking this day. We are most filled with joy at each invitation, for to share your experiences for but these brief moments is most enheartening and enlightening to us as well, for we see that with which you struggle in your daily round of activities as you move through this grand illusion attempting whenever possible to pierce the veil of forgetting and remember just one small bit more of information and inspiration with which you have propelled yourself into this dimension and these incarnations with the desire to serve and to seek the one Creator.

We are known to you as those of Q'uo. We would take our leave of this instrument and this group at this time. We leave each in the love and in the ineffable light of the one infinite Creator. Adonai. Adonai. ✣

L/L Research is a subsidiary of Rock Creek Research & Development Laboratories, Inc.

P.O. Box 5195
Louisville, KY 40255-0195

L/L Research

www.llresearch.org

Rock Creek is a non-profit corporation dedicated to discovering and sharing information which may aid in the spiritual evolution of humankind.

ABOUT THE CONTENTS OF THIS TRANSCRIPT: This telepathic channeling has been taken from transcriptions of the weekly study and meditation meetings of the Rock Creek Research & Development Laboratories and L/L Research. It is offered in the hope that it may be useful to you. As the Confederation entities always make a point of saying, please use your discrimination and judgment in assessing this material. If something rings true to you, fine. If something does not resonate, please leave it behind, for neither we nor those of the Confederation would wish to be a stumbling block for any.

© 2009 L/L Research

Special Meditation
December 26, 2002

Question from S: The first question today is, "I feel like I'm living simultaneously in two worlds, both with opportunities to love and serve and both lined with fear and "what if's." I feel right in the middle of both worlds, being pulled more and more, not able to discern. In each world, my indecision and neutrality are seemingly causing others some pain and distress in different ways. I've been thinking of R and how she went with N. "Your people shall be my people and your God, my God,"[11] and the possible benefits [to] my husband and symbolically to the fourth-density Earth coming into being [stemming from] that sort of unconditional decision, even to the point of intense sacrifice and standing firm in the open heart and unconditional acceptance. I've been consciously sending love and light through my hands and heart—not mine but the Creator's—and I don't know if this helps. I'm wondering if there's something more that can be consciously done to help serve.

So my question is: Can you comment as specifically as possible on the dichotomy that I'm experiencing in this situation? By what process can I make two worlds one and honor a now-open heart? Is there any significant distortion of my own that's hindering this decision?

(Carla channeling)

We are those known to you as the principle of Q'uo, and we greet you in the love and in the light of the one infinite Creator, in whose service we joyfully take part. We greet the one known as S and thank this entity for its desire to seek the truth and for its queries. We thank those who have formed this circle of seeking with the one known as S and commend each for that driving desire to seek and know the nature of the self and of the one infinite Creator enough to lay aside this time in service to learning, to truth, and to the benefit of all through the increase of light. We ask only that each listen to our thoughts with a dispassionate and open consciousness, looking for that resonance that speaks of recognition and remembrance and that feels like a personal truth. Leave all other thoughts aside, for they do not hit the mark at this time. Perhaps at another time they may, but for now we ask you to lay aside those things which may constitute a stumbling block.

This query concerns the way to serve to the maximum of the ability of the one known as S. We are aware of the purity of intention of the one known as S. Further, we are aware of the resonances between this situation and situations in the past experiences of two of those within this circle, which create for us the delicacy of movement through highly charged emotional issues concerning fidelity, honor and the concept of rightness.

---

[11] *Holy Bible*, Ruth 1:16.

The skill and art of learning the self has a great deal to do with the patience necessary to untangle the self from the, as the one known as S has called them, fears and "what if's"; from the trammels and snares of relative and acculturated variations of opinion, each of which has a rationale and a beauty of its own but which are mutually exclusive.

The situation of third density is that of the falling through midair. The entity is aware of the danger inherent in falling while at the same time being completely unable to affect the direction of the fall. This is the perceived situation within which the consciousness of an individual is very tempted to feel itself [a part].

In essence, the situation is one of complete freedom of action, given that the entity can free itself of the various acculturated and relativistic opinions which divide the self as it is from the self, as it believes it should be.

We would gaze with the one known as S at the concept of rightness. This instrument is aware of cultures within the limited number of societies that are upon your planet and dwell within the recorded history of this planetary sphere.

There are those cultures which value above all things the fidelity of the mated relationship and the exclusivity and permanence of such a relationship.

There are other cultures in which this is a value which has its relative uses but which is outweighed by ceremonial or personal preferences having to do either with personal growth or cultural movement having to do with position, status and so forth.

The concept of rightness, then, is, as all concepts within your conscious mind: to some degree an illusion, the falsity uncovering the truth, and the truth uncovering the falsity.

These are mysteries rather than puzzles to be solved, these questions of rightness. This does not negate the value of a wholehearted and deeply sacred process of plumbing the actuality of that which is most resonant as a path of learning and service in the particular moment of this crux. How is one to release the self from all past opinions concerning rightness? There is only the option for the faithful of opening the self to a higher concept of that which is right. This instrument, in speaking as a counselor to the one known as S, has several times discussed the concept of resonance and has suggested that, when there is a question before the attention, that the question may be taken into the meditative state with a view to finding that path of maximum resonance, and we would say that, for this instrument, it is somewhat simpler to connect the heart and the mind, thereby offering this instrument a more balanced platform from which to release the strictures of past conventional thinking. It is more difficult for the one known as S to release these strictures.

However, we would say that the observation of the one known as S that the neutrality of the present position is catalyst for others is accurate, and we would agree that the present moment is indeed that time during which it is entirely appropriate to ask of the self that it lend its desire to finding that path of maximum resonance creating the atmosphere in which, prayerfully and thankfully, a choice is made and closure found to that structure which at this time resembles, no matter how inadvertently, the triangular relationship. It is well for the choice to be allowed to blossom, and we would simply encourage the one known as S to focus upon the releasing of judgment and all statements containing the word, "should."

What is the nature of preference? This instrument would say that the key to judging preference is the distinction betwixt preferences and obsessions or addictions. Preferences or distortions of opinion or bias are entirely natural to entities as long as they experience identity. We, ourselves, experience preferences at various levels within our own processes at this time. They are part of a net of information and intuition and, within third density, contain a good bit of grist for the mill of third density. The making of choices as an ethical entity is at the heart of the learning process of third density.

We find ourselves up against the Law of Confusion in becoming much more specific about this particular choice. It is a choice betwixt the past and the future, betwixt the conventional and the conventional in that it is conventional within your society both to remain with the relationship in which trust has been broken and to leave a

relationship in which trust has been broken. Consequently, the desire for purity exceeds the limits of the situation, which is in actuality part of the consensual process for these entities involved.

The one known as S has her heart and soul to listen to. We simply encourage honesty, a full examination of preferences and an honest evaluation of the dynamics of inner truth which operate within the one known as S to maximize her learning and service.

This instrument once asked concerning a sacrificial situation, and, when the source was unable to make any substantive response, it suggested to this instrument that the question may be whether or not it was this instrument's time to go to Jerusalem. Is it a time for unconditional love to one direction? Is it a time for unconditional love in another direction? Where is the love? Where is the opportunity? Where is the deeper beauty and the feeling of resonance?

We would end this particular portion of this session by responding to the question concerning the sending of love with heart and hands. It is well to see the energy system of the self as being a system of energy which is enclosed within a self-protected system of energies, so that the infinite energy which feeds the vital portion of the being is allowed to remain at all times at full strength. The image of the self sending light through the hand is distracting in that it suggests that the entity of itself may have energy of that infinite kind. It therefore is perhaps more skillful for the one known as S to experience the way that the fully-functioning energy system opens the centers to being a channel for the unconditional energies of the infinite Creator, which then can rush through the open channel within that energy vehicle.

Thusly, the self is seen as the beautiful, gem-like being that it is and full energy continues moving through the channel, itself, which needs to be honored as the self which is offered in service to the light.

Often, feelings of lack of worth and excessive "humanity" influence an entity quite subtly into feeling that one is unworthy of being honorable, content, happy and so forth. These prejudices against the self have an insidious effect upon the faculties of judgment and may be examined for qualities of delusion. The essential truth of all beings is infinite worth and an awesome amount of personal power. We urge in all humility that humility and self-worth are not incompatible.

May we ask for the second query at this time?

S: You have previously stated that B and I are twin flames of the heart energy. Is this the same as my understanding of twin souls and could you expand on our two particular souls coming into this incarnation and finding each other? If we are communicating and aiding each other outside of our conscious minds, as it seems we have an almost telepathic [communication], we feel we need to know how to deepen that and strengthen that to help serve each other and others through any meditations or practices.

We are those of Q'uo, and are aware of your query, my sister. The terms "twin souls" and "twin flames," in our limited usage of these terms, are equivalent. There are other systems of philosophy in which there are distinctive differences between these terms. However, in our usage, they may be taken to be general terms indicating that entities are part of the same soul stream, which is to say that they represent those who have worked together a sufficient number of times within the same group of wandering souls that they have become one.

In some lifetimes, this might express as being twins; in some lifetimes, this might express as a purely spiritual attraction having to do with that which is greater than both, such as those involved in a revolution or in the mission of sharing the healing or the comfort of spirituality with those about one.

In other cases, it might take the form of the star-crossed lovers.

And in many cases these relationships mingle and have undertones and overtones connected with the many experiences of learning and serving as companions of the heart and as those who are portions of the same social memory complex or those complexes which are allied. For there is a vast brotherhood of allied, spiritual entities, whether they are planetary entities or individual entities of your inner planes, that have banded together at this time and, in many cases, for several thousands of your years to work upon that which this instrument calls the harvest of your planetary sphere. We do not wish to cross that line from describing the nuances of being twin souls to defining the details of a particular joined relationship but would simply say that potentially all entities are twin souls. It is a matter of the two becoming so intimate that the barriers to shared thought are completely removed, and that which is an experience for one is an experience for the other.

It is seldom that entities within third density have the comfort of such companions, and we would suggest that each comfort is also a responsibility and each responsibility, a comfort.

The deepening of any inner relationship is contingent upon resting in the confident silence of knowing and allowing time within that silence for the communion of souls. This instrument uses a small doll to allow a channel for its spiritual teacher to rest physically close to this instrument and certainly the one known as B and the one known as S, in exchanging the many things which they have created with their hands and hearts, have created such talismans for each other that may serve as channels for such resting energy.

These talismans are able to operate because of confident faith that all things are alive and that there is no space or time within love, and we would encourage the moving into the silence and the resting in trust and faith as the primary methods of deepening this service-oriented oneness.

We would at this time transfer the contact to the one known as Jim, as this instrument tires, and we would wish to address the remaining queries. We leave this instrument with thanks and transfer in love and in light to the one known as Jim. We are those of Q'uo.

(Jim channeling)

I am Q'uo, and greet each again in love and in light through this instrument. As we feel that we have spoken to the third query which asks us to differentiate between the terms "twin souls" and "twin flames," and what makes it a unique relationship, we would ask if we might respond to the fourth query at this time.

S: Can you comment on the stress situation in my body and anything I could do to help relieve and release the situations before they become manifest physically?

I am Q'uo, and am aware of your query, my sister. We find that the stress of which you speak in this query is related to the situation that you described and to which we spoke in the first query. Thus, the alleviation of the stress which you feel within your body complex is contingent upon the ability to relieve the stress that you feel in the relationships that are now pulling your heart and your thinking in various directions. It is a situation in which we are unable to participate fully, for we do not feel it a service to solve the riddle which you now contemplate. However, we can suggest that, as you meditate upon the direction in which you wish to move in your relationships and find a ground upon which you may firmly stand, there then will be the reduction of the stress factor within your entire life pattern that you will find reflected within your physical vehicle as well, for, when the physical vehicle is party to catalyst, it is usually so because the mind complex and the emotional complex have not fully utilized the catalyst which has been given to them. Thus, they pass on, shall we say, a kind of doubling effect …

(Side one of tape ends.)

(Jim channeling)

… I am Q'uo, and we are once again with this instrument. We thank each for the patience that has been granted to us.

We were nearly finished with our response to this query, but wished to be certain that it was clearly understood that the ability of the one known as S to find an harmonious solution to the balancing of emotions and relationships is that crux which will determine the ability of the body to deal with less and less of that which you call stress. Thusly, we recommend significant portions of time spent in the meditative state upon the daily basis, during which the one known as S may ponder that direction which is most in keeping with the heart of her own compassion and desire to serve.

We realize that this is not an easy situation in which to find direction, for there are qualities of character that are involved in each instance respecting the traditions of one's own culture and religious upbringing, in the keeping of vows made in marriage, and the direction of the spiritual seeker whose heart has opened and has found directions that move beyond cultural conditions. This is a matter which must be carefully considered. However, we assure the one known as S that there is within her own heart a direction which seeks to be known. Thus, within the meditative state, this entity may seek to be moved by her own heart.

At this time, we would thank each once again for joining in this circle of seeking and for inviting our presence here as you continue to seek means by which to open your own heart and be of service to those who would cross your path at any time in your daily round of activities, for this is the way that each entity affects not only one's own spiritual growth but the service one would wish to offer others. For it is in the non-dramatic interactions of your everyday round of activities that the power of your own choices of service to others and opening the heart may be found.

We are known to you as those of Q'uo. At this time, we shall take our leave of this instrument and this group. We leave each in the love and in the light of the one infinite Creator. Adonai, my friends. Adonai. ✤

Year 2003

January 5, 2003 to December 21, 2003

Sunday Meditation
January 5, 2003

Group question: The question today has to do with the grid of our planet as we are moving from third into fourth density. We are assuming that there are points on this grid that are in need of some attention, some sort of focusing energy which we would like to be able to do, in our meditative state and maybe even in general, just the way we are able to live our lives to produce compassion or love or mercy or forgiveness in our daily round of activities. We would like Q'uo to give us some sort of an idea about how we might be able to be of service in this respect; in strengthening the grid, the road to fourth density from where we are in our daily round of activities in dealing with the catalyst of the day, with our own distortions, with our desire to serve and our feeling like sometimes it's just too much.

(Carla channeling)

We are those of the principle known to you as Q'uo, and we greet you in the love and in the light of the one infinite Creator. We consider ourselves to be those who are part of what this instrument's teacher calls the godhead principle, and we speak to that part of you which has called us here, that part of you which is also the godhead principle. It is in the sympathetic vibration of that likeness of focus and polarity that we link and find ourselves in this most agreeable and blessed condition of sharing this time of seeking with you. We thank you for the privilege of being called and for the careful way in which our nature was defined by the parameters of the tuning and challenging of this instrument. We greatly appreciate the care being taken with the tuning of the connection to enable us to experience clear communication with this particular, shall we say, biological instrument; one of the more complicated wind instruments, shall we say, being the human bodily instrument. In this case, the instrument is also the composer of the song which creates a fascinating context for us to work within in shaping these awkward bundles which are called words, to attempt to speak of concepts which exceed the limit of any words. We ask only that each take what seems sensible and helpful, from those thoughts we share, and leave the rest behind, for we are not those who are in authority but rather those who share experiences as your neighbors and co-creators.

We are glad this day to speak with you concerning the metaphysical road-building in which this particular instrument and the one known as Jim have been much interested in late months, as the experience of entering fully into the twenty first century and dealing with the weight of previously known information has brought these two entities to a condition of perception at this juncture which seems to indicate work in the direction of this metaphysical roadbuilding.

We would first comment upon the concept of time, for much of what we say has a certain timbre which can create sense only within a limited context, that being the illusory context of space/time. The metaphysical universe is not the space/time universe, and so, consequently, a query concerning the physical aspects of metaphysical work draws a response which must straddle both space/time and time/space considerations. The outer activism which is the interest of this instrument, especially, is dependent upon a network of information and data concerning space/time projections of time/space events. If one focuses upon the space/time continuum and its illusory march of progress, shall we say, the energies of metaphysical structure recede, and the more the effort is made to interact with space/time events and space/time values, the less direct will be the effect of such work upon the time/space or metaphysical continuum, which is a consideration when one is attempting to connect space/time to time/space, insofar as each entity involved is capable of embodying that linkage.

In this regard, we would state our observation that fear and fear-based concern is easily the most challenging foe that stands before the faithful warrior of light at this juncture. We do not criticize or judge entities for their fear-based responses to the space/time events which unfold as part of the consensus reality of your illusion. There certainly would appear to be concerning and substantial issues which indicate almost certain disaster. From our viewpoint as those observing this global culture from the outside in, we would state another observation, that being that, although it may have escaped your notice, there have been few years in recorded history in which there was not disaster, catastrophe and war. There also has not been a time within your recorded history when there has not been a wide range of options for solving all perceived problems. That which appears to be worthy of great fear on another level is precisely that which may be embraced with the most surety, because it is in challenging and novel times that one begins, within incarnation, to learn about the self and to be surprised, encouraged, invigorated and renewed by the experiences one has in learning of the depths of the self, the self's emotions, and the self's hopes and dreams.

Is it hunger that is feared? Then, when that time of hunger comes, take what little that you have and give it away to the common good, and you will find that you can create miracles of loaves and fishes.

Do you fear the cold? Take heart, and when you are cold, move to the company of others who are also cold and embrace them, and together you may live through the night and know the heart of another.

Do you fear having nothing? Take heart, for truly all entities possess nothing, but merely share that which comes their way, that which has been allowed to come their way by circumstance, by pre-incarnational request and by the desire to learn.

Do you fear not having enough? Embrace thankfulness and gratitude and count the blessings of what tiny things you may have in the face of deprivation and you will find yourself endlessly giving thanks.

For once the eyes of gratitude, of thankfulness, have been opened, it may more and more easily be seen that all circumstances are those for which one may give thanks with a true, honest and cheerful heart, for insofar as circumstances seem difficult, just so far shall they later be revealed as the healers of those deeply buried sores that must be lanced.

Each entity has placed in its own path those things which look remarkably like stumbling blocks and sources of great suffering, and they can be seen that way with perfect logic and sanity. We do not suggest that losing fear is a logical process; we suggest rather that the way the process of living has its impact upon a given soul is dependent upon that soul's point of view and attitude. We are suggesting that the point of view or attitude is powerful and central to the goal of becoming a working crystal which is indeed sending blessed and transmuted light received from the infinite Creator by personal intention into the planetary fourth-density/third-density connection, creating the lighting up of the fourth-density grid.

Losing fear is therefore a tremendous and powerful resource to pursue. The ways of losing fear often have to do with more and more becoming aware of how fear has embedded its trigger points within the network of antennae which your personal structure of perceptive priorities presents to you: first, second, third, fourth and so on. A great deal of what is gained from the input of data into the mind and the consciousness has to do with how items are prioritized in the consciousness. The process of perception is far other than the way it seems, entities neither hearing with their ears nor seeing with their eyes, but rather forming a digitized information grid from not only the present moment [grid] but previously organized grids of expectations. Changing the expectation grid of one's prioritizing software, shall we say, changes the information package that one receives from oneself as it inputs the data.

In a way, we are speaking very mechanically and yet the mind works along logical, mechanical and habitual routes, taking shortcuts when it can once it has decided upon the priorities. Moving into the prioritizing mechanisms within the self is deep work and takes a good deal of self-awareness that can usually be achieved only through time. Consequently, this is a long-term goal, for fear is not an absence of love; it is not what is left over when love is ended. Fear is the dark side of love. Fear has its legitimacy and must indeed be embraced within the self and asked to avail its gifts to the use of the light. Fear becomes courage when the fear is faced, and the wolf that has caused the fear, rather than being fled or being slain, is invited into the heart to be loved, understood, accepted and charmed.

We ask you to become storytellers to yourselves, telling yourself the story of the hero or the heroine that you are, the warrior of light who makes so many mistakes and must iron its costume daily, and yet somehow, though the costume is baggy and the efforts are unavailing, this story of the self moves on as one of the fighter that will not quit but never fights against but only for. Gaze upon those fear reactions and ask your most intelligent and clever self what creative things that you can do to target, come to understand, and come to have sympathy for each direction of fear-based thought; not rooting it out, not judging the self for fear, but having compassion upon the entity that is involved in a flesh, blood and bone illusion.

Each entity will perish from the third-density experience. This source of fear is, shall we say, the parent of all other fears, that fear of ceasing to be. We would ask through faith that the entity posit to itself whether it is worthwhile to fear death or whether it might not be more skillful to see the inevitability of that, and, rather than shrinking from that inevitability, to turn that story from that fear of death to the love of each and every day and hour that remains to you. Time, in terms of space/time, is an illusion, yet it is within this illusion that each of you dwells; it is within this incarnation that each of you now acts; and within your continuum and your illusion it is indeed a very intense time of transformation and change for the planet upon which you live. Consequently, there are indeed aspects of the metaphysical transformation of the planet's population and its very global entity that poke up rather abruptly as mountains on the topography of the present time and space. Many catastrophes have already been seen of the natural kind and of the, shall we say, human or political kind, and you may see that these forces and energies become more sharply delineated, more clarified and more obvious.

Embrace this time as a time when those who are steadfast shall be those who are able to function as light transducers, keeping the energy moving into that grid which is made up of love. When an entity's heart has been able to relax and free itself from fear and from the need to protect, it becomes soft and fertile and yeasty with the food needed for the seeds of love to blossom into those beanstalks that truly do constitute a ladder between earth and heaven. Each is aware of the story of Jack and the Beanstalk. This entity gave away its cows in exchange for magical seeds, and the entity came home and planted these seeds and grew itself a beanstalk that reached into another world. It is having the faith, in very non-physical ways, to sell the cows that gives to the light worker the ability to grow beanstalks between third density and fourth. The beanstalk is a seed of faith, and each of you is one who gently and sometimes unknowingly cradles that seed. When you birth it, that is the beginning of the self as an impersonal portion of the godhead principle.

When one can see oneself as, shall we say, a priestly or a magical figure, one then is able to move from a metaphysical position, from a position of embracing time/space and time/space values. This is the other side of releasing fear; that is, the discipline of continuing in remembrance of love, continuing in remembrance of who the self is, continuing in remembrance of why the entity is here.

We would close this discussion or, shall we say, this primary discussion by touching upon those interests that this instrument has in more specific details of ways to have organization come to a physical effort to support the concept of helping the fourth-density or Christ grid become stronger; helping the connection between this world and the next to solidify. You may tell from the balance of our cosmic sermonette that most of the work has to do with state of mind, for love and all of the energetic essences which underlie and create your space/time reality have to do with the energies of love, those energies which created you and which you now can focus as co-creators, allowing your will and your desire to direct those healing and infinitely beneficial energies of unconditional love that flow through each entity ceaselessly from the Creator. This state of mind is always the choice of the entity and indeed constitutes the greatest and most continual choice of the incarnation. Where shall the thoughts settle down? In love or in fear?

When one sees the self in fear, do not abandon the self, do not correct the self, but sit with the self and look at the fear. Let it be. Let it wash over and through one seeing the self as permeable, as healable, as fallible but [also] as a shining hero dealing with the most amazing adversity. This is your story; we ask you to stick to it; we ask you to think well of yourself. The one known as S, in channeling, enjoys creating a common ending for these channelings just as this instrument enjoys closing with those words which mean farewell and peace in the Creator. This entity closes its channelings with the thought, "Play well together." This is a great road-building statement. Those who play well, with themselves and with each other, are honoring the Creator and the forces of unity that will release fear and open the heart.

There is some science which can be applied to a linear calculation of those plans which entities may create for themselves in order to give more shape and focus to what may otherwise seem an amorphous goal; that of lighting the planet and creating that solid connection to the next world which is at this time attempting to be born and certainly having its own difficulties.

We commend all and any efforts to serve. Needless to say, we must leave plans which have to do with physical calculations in the hands of those in whose free will these plans are being tossed about as dreams, hopes and visions. We commend the group effort suggested for exploring such services and would echo the sentiments of this instrument as spoken prior to this channeling having to do with being willing to rest in mystery and resonance to a certain extent in feeling one's way towards the blending of the physical and metaphysical in service.

We thank this instrument for its service at this time and would transfer this contact to the one known as Jim, leaving this instrument in love and in light. We are those of Q'uo.

(Jim channeling)

I am Q'uo, and we greet each of you in love and in light through this instrument. It is our privilege at this time to ask if there may be any other queries to which we may speak at this session of working.

S: [I have] questions with me. In each meditation we have with you, we offer the lives of those friends and family who may be in need[12], but, since we may not always ask specifically to do that for them, would that be considered any violation of free will, per se?

I am Q'uo, and we are aware of your query, my brother. There is the gift of the one Creator which is the prana, the love energy which is available to all entities as a source of the life-giving qualities of the one Creator. It is to these energies that one adds when one prays for the wellbeing of another. Thus, the entity has the free will to work with these energies as they are given in the daily round of activities, perhaps enhanced by those who pray, by those who wish the entity well, but these energies are added to those which are usually utilized without one's being aware of them.

Is there another query, my brother?

S: The last one is, I seem to have a great affinity for quartz crystals and points, and I was wondering if there is any other light that you could shed on why that might be so, whether it's past incarnations or just the energies they allow or anything like that that I could contemplate on?

I am Q'uo, and am aware of your query, my brother. We find that there is some general information of this nature which we may share without infringement. We would suggest that there has been within your pattern of incarnations a great predilection towards these means of communication and healing which you have utilized in various ways in different incarnations. Thus, there is within your being a portion of your learning and service which resonates to these crystalline entities and their abilities to enhance one's wellbeing, one's level of *élan vital*, shall we say, the energy which powers one in the daily round of activities and in the geometric precision with which these crystalline entities may be utilized for healing, for communication and for the far-seeing, shall we say.

---

[12] L/L Research meditation meetings are concluded by a release of stored light from the session, while placing in that light the names of those we wish to offer healing prayers for.

Is there another query, my brother?

S: Not from me, thanks.

I am Q'uo, and we thank you, my brother. Is there another query at this time?

Carla: I'd just like to ask, since it was my question and also my channel about the grid, if there was anything that you could channel through the one known as Jim that you couldn't get through me because of my biases? If so, I'd be glad to hear it.

I am Q'uo and am aware of your query, my sister. No, we do not wish to be overly generous in our compliments to your abilities as an instrument. We would suggest that there is a clear entry into your being which we may utilize in speaking our thoughts through your instrument. We feel no distortion or hesitation or bias that would hinder our ability to communicate that which we wish to communicate.

Is there a further query, my sister?

Carla: No, thank you, thank you very much. Thank you for the indication. I'll look at it very carefully.

I am Q'uo. Again, we thank you, my sister. Is there another query at this time?

(No more queries.)

I am Q'uo. We are most grateful for each entity's participation in this circle of seeking, and we thank you for inviting us once again to join you as you walk this path of meditation, of service, of intensification of desire, and of open-hearted sharing, each with the other.

We are known to you as those of Q'uo. At this time, we shall take our leave of this instrument and this group. We leave each in the love and in the ineffable light of the one infinite Creator. Adonai, my friends. Adonai.

Sunday Meditation
January 26, 2003

Group question: The question this week is from J: "My understanding is that free will is based on the right to shift the point from which one views life and experience, while choice deals with the decisions made once you are there on that point of view."

We would like Q'uo's comment upon J's idea that free will is the point from which one views, while choice deals with the decisions made from that point of view.

(Carla channeling)

We are those of the principle known to you as Q'uo, and we greet you in the love and in the light of the one infinite Creator. It is our great privilege to be called to your group for this session of working, and we thank each of you for the seeking that brought you hither. We ask, as always, that each use discrimination in listening to those concepts which we may offer this day, for we would greatly prefer not to be a stumbling block before any. It is never known what reed may break under a general breeze, and truly we would wish to harm no spirit who is seeking this day. We simply urge each to be aware of the power of thoughts, perceptions and concepts, for their energy for weal or woe is great.

You ask this day concerning the nature of free will and the nature of choice, and, as often is the case in such queries, we find it is well to step back from that question and create some platform from which to observe the context of that question. The structure of the universe that is your house is created hierarchically; that is, from that which is above to that which is below or from that which is inner to that which is outer. In this hierarchy of creation, the unpotentiated Creator is that which rests in infinity and eternity.

The first distortion to this one infinite Creator is that distortion called free will. The distortion called free will creates that distortion which is called the Logos, that principle from which the creation is brought forth, that Thought whose power to create and to destroy is absolute.

From this second distortion of unity in its unpotentiated form develops all of the nested series of illusions which you enjoy within your creation. Such is the structure of the house of the one infinite Creator.

What, then, could be described as the nature of this first distortion of that so-called Law of One or unity of all things? Within this instrument's system of studied and practiced religion, there is a concept which is part of the mythological structure of Christianity, as it is called, that entity being one of a triune set of entities or essences which express the relationship of parent-child and that which is somewhat amorphously called the Holy Spirit. It is this so-called Holy Spirit that holds within this mythological system the equivalent position to this first distortion which is called free will, in that it expresses the feminine aspect of the principle of deity; in that it is the fructifying, fertilizing and potentiating force that makes possible the concept of novelty, creation, separation and all of the concepts that flow therefrom, including the concept of choice.

Consequently, this aspect of free will is as an archetype or an archetypical energy which has aspects of the Creator centrally placed within that structure which make free will, as an entity or essence, that mystery which is infinitely feminine in the archetypical sense. Thusly, it could be observed that the energies of femininity can be seen prejudicially as being negative, in the same way that light can be seen to be a negative influence from the standpoint of those who associate light and knowledge with an awareness of sinfulness or wrongdoing. However, the energy of free will is as the energy of the wind, moving under divine influence.

Light, itself, may be seen to be an aspect of divinity, and that which is subsumed under the concept of the tree of good and evil may, endlessly, be seen in ways both positive and negative. Always, when there is such power as free will expresses, there is within the system of judgment of those attempting to grasp the nature of such energies a slight tendency, perhaps, to be prejudiced against the sheer power of such an impersonal and yet highly individuated essence, to the soul stream which is looking out through the eyes of incarnation. The impact of beginning to grasp the actual nature of the nested illusions of experience is daunting and can constitute a time of adjustment in which the nature of the self is allowed to transform itself according to the ways of this free will that enters into the creation upon each level of development. The free will of yourself can barely be distinguished from the free will of that Logos that is your higher self, that overarching Logos that is the group mind of that soul stream, that overarching Logos that is the planetary mind, and so forth. The connections that each entity has with other aspects of an infinite being that is the self are unending, so that free will is, shall we say, that icon of deity which expresses the feminine, the ever-moving, the fructifying.

As we begin to speak of choice, we move deeply within this nested arrangement of illusions into that one which you now enjoy, for this illusion which you now enjoy, which we have often called third density, is that density within which a very pivotal choice must be made, and indeed for almost all of those upon the surface of your sphere at this time, has been made. Indeed, in these so-called latter days, we have begun to release our concerns about choosing, for we feel more and more that people are awakening to their choice having been made, or are becoming aware very quickly of the choice to be made; that is, the choice of service to others or service to self and the making of that choice.

It is a situation in which people are within a very small distance of awakening in greater numbers, and we can say that this is exciting for us to see. It does indeed seem to be a substantially growing energy within our observed routines in watching the energies of your planetary energy grids that there is more substantial light from all over your globe, that there are those within all precincts of your earthly sphere who are spending time within the tabernacle of their hearts offering their hopes, their dreams and their full intentions towards the increase of light, love, healing and peace within your planetary sphere.

These energies are not lost but rather are gathered together, and, as we have shown this instrument before, you may see these angels of light weaving together the many, many prayers and hopes and dreams and visions that are the vehicles for sending light that is blessed by entities such as yourselves into the inner spheres. We may say that many, many are those who have chosen to begin to do this, as people, whenever they can, thinking of those who are in need and sending them prayers of love, light and support. Indeed, we find more and more that entities have made the choice of how to serve the infinite Creator.

Now, perhaps it is valid to build on the choice that has been made; to rest within its commitment as if it were a cleft in the rock, and, from that point of view, which is the choice to be fearless, to allow all other choices to be those choices that optimize the perceived sense of love. The choice of service to others or service to self that so classically is expressed in the archetypical image of the tarot card of The Lovers seems a simple one. It often seems very clear what is service to self and what is service to others. However, many are those who have found that there are courses in polarity given to them by the school of life which are exceedingly subtle and worthy of study. For those who are attempting not only to choose but to choose with grace and deftness and skill, not the most obvious service to others but the highest, there is a never-ending and very rich palate of choices to be made, options to be considered. And always, ever-new each day; a new and newly mysterious universe to comprehend, behold and give thanks for.

Free will blows as it will; spirit moves where "it listeth."[13] Shall your ears be open; shall your eyes see clearly; shall your hearts understand. We salute that universe our poor words faultily attempt to describe, and we salute the questioner for seeking the truth. We hope that our humble words have provided some thoughts that may be helpful and would at this time transfer this contact to the one known as Jim that any other queries that this group may have may be addressed. We thank this instrument and leave it in love and in light. We are those known to you as Q'uo.

(Jim channeling)

I am Q'uo, and we greet each once again in love and in light through this instrument. At this time, we would ask if there may be any further queries remaining upon the minds of those present. Is there another query at this time?

T: Yes, I have a question. Maybe I'm beating a dead horse, but it's back to my attempts to conquer my negativity, and I guess just any help, I mean, my idea is to try to pick out the person that I least like to give positive thoughts to and attempt to do that. Could you comment on this or have any suggestions?

I am Q'uo and am aware of your query, my brother. We would respond by suggesting that, though it is well to send positive thoughts and thought forms to those whom you feel have an emotional attachment to you or, should we say, you to them, it is also well to be able to accept the self, for having this flow of charged catalyst moving through one is much like the meditation in which you attempt to focus single-pointedly upon a concept, a thought, or a feeling or perhaps upon nothing itself, and while you are doing this, many thoughts of all kinds move through your mind and to address them most efficiently with your goal of single-pointed focus in mind, it is well to observe them and let them go. Thus, in your daily round of activities, as you experience these moments of negativity in which you feel anger or frustration or doubt or fear, any of the emotions which would cause you concern, that you also observe these; that you let them move through your being and let them continue through your being unless you feel there is some quality or concept which a particularly recurring thought may have for you. This you may determine by feeling the emotion within you in its, shall we say, aftereffects or long-run impact upon your mind and your emotions. When you feel there is something of importance within the origination of such a thought or the form in which it takes and expresses itself to you, then this also may be examined. However, if you feel there is no emotion that is connected to the thoughts in a personal sense, it is well to allow the thoughts to pass their way and to continue on your way. Is there a further query, my brother?

T: No, thank you very much.

I am Q'uo, and we thank you, my brother. Is there another query at this time?

V: I have a quickie. As you spoke of the concept of free will earlier, you likened it to a house as a hierarchical structure, and what came very vividly to mind was a brief portion of a dream that I had a number of years ago where I am standing in front of a very large house, or not standing but riding in a car and traveling up to the front of the house, and I say to the person with whom I'm traveling, "This is my father's house. It has thirteen rooms." I've never known what that meant, and I don't even know why it came to mind as you were speaking of the concept of free will, but I'm wondering if indeed that is why it came to mind. Can you speak to that?

I am Q'uo and am aware of your query, my sister, and, to a degree, we feel that we may speak, though there is much in this concept which is best left for your discovery. However, in relating the concept of free will as a house or a hierarchical structure, we may suggest to you that, in the dream house with thirteen rooms, that you have within this structure which you have described in the dream as your father's house a room for yourself that is placed in an hierarchical fashion; that [in] this house which belongs to your father there is a place for you, and that place is the point, is the question.

Is there a further query, my sister?

V: No, thank you.

I am Q'uo, and we thank you, my sister. Is there another query at this time?

---

[13] *Holy Bible*, John 3:8, "The wind bloweth where it listeth, and thou hearest the sound thereof, but canst not tell whence it cometh, and whither it goes: so is everyone that is born of the spirit."

Carla: I'd like to ask about a dream I had also, Q'uo. Just anything that you could tell me about its meaning, because it's haunted me. In the dream, I was trying very hard to save a family of royalty from the disloyalty and perfidy of some people that were around them, and I was having to work with a whole team and do all kinds of derring-do, and it was a big adventure, and, at the end of the dream, when I woke up, I had collected all this evidence against the criminals and had taken it to the authorities and then was told that, because I had done it the wrong way, I had not taken the evidence directly to the judge, that the evidence was no good and that I had failed to do my job. And, since I had that dream, I've had several more dreams in which I'm seemingly back in this same, very large hospital and research center trying hard to save the lives of the royalty that the opposition is attempting to kill. If you could give me some direction to go in looking at that, I'd like anything that you have to say, I'd appreciate it.

I am Q'uo, and am aware of your query, my sister. We face the same situation in regards to providing interpretation of this message from your subconscious as we did in the previous query. However, we may suggest that the family of royalty may be looked at as those qualities or concepts that are held most dear by you and for which you would indeed give all of your effort, your self, and your incarnation for the preserving of which. The paperwork may be seen as related to the mundane world and its valuing of such qualities or principles.

Is there a further query, my sister?

Carla: Not on that point. I would like to ask another question with the full understanding that I'm just asking, and you don't have to answer. I would appreciate it if you could confirm that an energy that I've recognized in the one known as K is belonging to an entity that seems now to be visiting another entity known as C. I wondered if you could comment on this or confirm that there is indeed a congruency of vibration?

I am Q'uo, and am aware of your query, my sister, and may suggest that there is a great degree of truth in this assumption, though there is also more complexity than the simplicity of the statement would suggest.

Is there a further query?

Carla: Yeah, I'd like to follow up on that by asking if, by that, you intend to indicate that there is a fairly comprehensive extended family of entities that are not local earth which cooperate together not just on the positive side but also on the side of service to self in attempting to create the atmosphere that would be most conducive to their goals.

I am Q'uo, and am aware of your query, my sister, and would suggest that this assumption is correct except with the use of the verb, cooperate. Those of negative polarity compete, thus there may be more than one negative source.

Is there a further query, my sister?

Carla: No, not at all. I will have much to think about there. Thank you for that. I just really appreciate being able to talk to you. Thank you for everything.

I am Q'uo, and we thank you once again, my sister. Is there another query at this time?

Carla: I guess, could I ask just one last query? And, it is this. A lot of people have asked me lately, how do I look at this world with all of its difficulties and have a good attitude, and I've basically said to them things along the lines of, well, just look and be as accurate as you can and learn it all and know that this is what it is that you're here to love. Is that a helpful way to focus on the things that are seemingly quite appalling that are occurring, is that it's time for us to be steadfast but it's good for us to know what we're being steadfast in the face of?

I am Q'uo, and am aware of your query, my sister. We would suggest that, as you look at the illusion which is your experience at this time in third density, that you attempt to activate and balance all energy centers and the attributes with which they allow you to deal with the solution; that you see with clear eyes and honest seeking for truth that you give wholeheartedly your unconditional love to the Creator in all beings; that you work tirelessly within your illusion to bring these principles to those you love; that you communicate with each entity that you have a connection with to work together for this goal and that you give praise and thanksgiving for the very life you experience within whatever kind of illusion presents itself to you in your daily round of activities. Taken together, these energy centers and expressions of your abilities and desires can form a kind of magical transformation; first upon a metaphysical level of your own being and of the illusion about you, and then may move in a doubled sense each time you are able to share with another these efforts, concerns, dreams and so forth.

Is there a further query, my sister?

Carla: No, Q'uo, thank you so much.

I am Q'uo, and again we thank you, my sister. Is there another query at this time?

(No further queries.)

I am Q'uo. We would take this opportunity to thank each one again for inviting us to join you in your circle of seeking this day. It is always as great joy for us to do so.

(Tape ends.)

L/L Research

L/L Research is a subsidiary of Rock Creek Research & Development Laboratories, Inc.

P.O. Box 5195
Louisville, KY 40255-0195

www.llresearch.org

Rock Creek is a non-profit corporation dedicated to discovering and sharing information which may aid in the spiritual evolution of humankind.

ABOUT THE CONTENTS OF THIS TRANSCRIPT: This telepathic channeling has been taken from transcriptions of the weekly study and meditation meetings of the Rock Creek Research & Development Laboratories and L/L Research. It is offered in the hope that it may be useful to you. As the Confederation entities always make a point of saying, please use your discrimination and judgment in assessing this material. If something rings true to you, fine. If something does not resonate, please leave it behind, for neither we nor those of the Confederation would wish to be a stumbling block for any.

CAVEAT: This transcript is being published by L/L Research in a not yet final form. It has, however, been edited and any obvious errors have been corrected. When it is in a final form, this caveat will be removed.

© 2009 L/L Research

Sunday Meditation
February 2, 2003

Homecoming

Group question: The question today has to do with the concept of self-acceptance. It seems that every seeker of truth at some point needs to be able to accept the self as completely as possible in order to progress in the seeking. It seems like many of us, in order to increase the compassion in our lives, have programmed a lack of compassion for the self, being service-to-others people, and this gives us constant opportunities to accept the self when we fall short of our goals.

Could Q'uo give us an idea about how we can go about accepting the self, perhaps through opening energy centers, through balancing the distortions that we find? Any other information Q'uo would have concerning self-acceptance would also be very much appreciated. And we would appreciate any additional comments Q'uo would care to make about the process of sharing with each other that we've undergone this weekend[14]; we've had a great weekend of sharing personal experiences and our catalyst and our growth and our dreams, and we would appreciate hearing a little bit about what Q'uo might have to say about that.

(David Wilcock channeling)

[(David's Guidance System) We greet you through] … that entity known in this sojourn as David Wilcock. We greet you in the light and love of the one infinite Creator. It is at this time that we shall commence our communications.

Bear in mind that the relevant statistics of proportion have it in your favor that, within the span of this incarnation, you will have increasing opportunities to allow those aspects of self that have been inimical to the greater process of integration to fall away. This process of falling away is fundamentally that of an allowing; allowing the consciousness of the higher self so to infuse you that your every breath is quickened and enlivened by that living essence of the creation that is all there is.

Recognize, as you gaze across the spectrum of experience that you have amassed within this sojourn on the physical sphere, that there are those experiences that were of an apparent detrimental nature, which seemed to remove a certain degree of opportunity for the self to have happiness in function and an ease in mobility, among others. As you are now becoming increasingly aware, the nature of your experience is chosen, and it is the catalyst of the choice that determines the polarity of the entity.

---

[14] L/L Research's annual Homecoming was held at Louisville, Kentucky, at the Rueckert-McCarty-L/L homestead, The Magic Kingdom, from January 31 to February 2, 2003. The sitting group is the Homecoming group, folks who gathered for this time together to celebrate our shared journey.

The progress towards polarization to the positive is indeed, at times, a dark and bumpy road with many false steps and apparent inconsistencies in the path. Recognize that truly all steps do lead back to the Oneness, and thus [regardless] of the apparent discrepancies in the patterning of life, there is always centralizing focused consistence within the sphere. The fact is that you can walk along any surface of the sphere and you will always be the same distance away from the center as you always have been and, thus, progress is made while also the orientation with regards to center has never been lost.

The idea, then, is to recognize those inconsistencies that have developed in what you would think of as the past, regarding times where experiences caused for there to be a mental partitioning and a sealing away of the pains that have been brought about by said experiences. We have referred to these before as fragments. The fragmentation of the self occurs when there is a denial that certain experiences truly exist; not that they have been completely forgotten but, rather, that they are knowingly held down with a conscious exertion of energy by the mind, so as to eliminate the possibility of further apparent suffering or struggle from occurring by the reflection on the hurt.

What we have spoken to you about during the course of this weekend, through the medium of the checklist questions, is that most centralized way in which we can begin to look at the life pattern as a whole and examine the droplets of issues that have [bedewed the] spectacles [looking on] the entire vista of awareness that is the self. Each droplet is, in and of itself, a precipitation from the ocean of Oneness from whence you sprang, and, thus, the differentiation of yourself as being separate from others is but another aspect of this illusion, as is the illusion that any experience is separate from that of the conscious forces.

Thus, you could think of these fragment cells as being akin to droplets of water that have been arrayed across the tabletop of your own psyche. The process, then, is to enable for there to be that centralizing gravity well at the center of the circle that does then call forth all the droplets together once again to merge into oneness. In this rather simple analogy, you see how it is that, by the formation of a sieve or a funnel, so to speak, that the water droplets, in turn, form rivulets which then grow into larger droplets, and then all again returns back to that point of oneness.

These topic areas that we have mentioned speak particularly to the issues of how one's self has been able to enunciate these differences between "before and after," "here and there," "seen and unseen," "form and formless," within the realm of the conscious self and how that consciousness then precipitates into physicality. And so, much as your mouth is filled with teeth which are used to chew and to process that energy which would sustain the physical body complex, we ask that you also sink your teeth into the issues that have been the central, leading motives of your life; and then to spend some time distilling and chewing upon each [of] those experiences that you have processed in the past; to arrive at greater levels of understanding and coherence within the self, so as to eliminate any distinction that these were events that caused you to be a victim or that were unprovoked but, rather, to recognize that all was occurring in perfect, harmonic, sacred ways

There was a question with regards to the self-acceptance aspect of this understanding and how it is that the falling away of these fragments might very well lead to a greater ability to accept oneself. We would ask that you recognize that the intrinsic lack of self-acceptance is a precipitation of the fundamental characteristics of work within third density; namely, this work does not prescribe a certain degree of easy "half-ways" but, rather, it is a path of suffering, or apparent suffering, as the experience is chosen to be labeled by the conscious self. The nature of catalyst, therefore, is for those experiences to come about which create a motivation which allows[or invites] that muse that helps the self to move forward and to make strides towards higher and higher levels of attainment and understanding, towards a greater and greater degree of personality transparency such that the self becomes as a gleaming mirror that reflects back only that which is the true essence of the one infinite Creator, such that those other selves may then see it.

The balanced, self-aware and self-accepting self is one that has been able to work through these processes, then to analyze, understand and accept the experiences of the past and distill the love and wisdom contained within them and to use that as a propellant for the rocket to take off into the ethers, such that the self is no longer encumbered by the gravity of the physical but can indeed rise higher and higher into the firmament, with the understanding that there is only irreducible simplicity in this essence of creation.

The simplicity is that you are the light. The chair that is holding you up as you hear these words is formed of light, as are you. There is only an apparent sense of there being an atomic or molecular structure by virtue of the distortions of this light through the various spiraling movements that then bring about physicality. But, in essence, all begins and ends as light. Thus, more and more, by defragmenting the self, by working through those aspects of personality that have remained compartmentalized from conscious awareness, there [comes] an ability to supersede those feelings of being frustrated by virtue of the understanding that all of your life's experiences have been created only for your own evolution in understanding.

Therefore, you cannot continue to indulge in victimhood. Once you have seen past the illusion, [you see] that there was [not] any experience foisted upon you other than that which you, by your own discretion, created for your greater evolution and path. We ask on this day that you recognize that the brain is but a bio-computer; that the true center of function that you have exists outside time/space, outside of anything within your body; that, at this time, there is a mind being created as you listen to these words, with all others who would seek to find that Oneness. And, therefore, you can never be alone; you can never be outside of this Oneness; there is no differentiation save for that which is consciously elected to be chosen by the higher self as it then exhibits its tendencies towards producing catalyst that will allow the physical self to rise towards higher and higher levels of manifestation and acts of greatness; not acts of greatness measured in your physical terms but, rather, the greatness that can be found in simply being able to let go of the repetitive behavioral pattern that has not been in the highest and best good of all involved; by being able to focus one's efforts towards the greater good and recognizing how it is that, by clapping the hands together in appreciation for oneself and being able to self-accept, that there is an everlasting wellspring that is created within the self and that the chalice of divine self-preservation and self-transformation can be dipped into this sacred water; that you can, then, imbibe these waters of life for yourself and experience that divine communion with the one infinite Creator.

It does, then, allow you to supersede those distinctions of right and wrong, of good and bad, of positive and negative; to recognize that all experiences that have transpired in your life, whether you felt alienated, isolated, alone, victimized or abused, are all emanating from that essence which does have the destroyer aspect or Shiva as well as that positive, constructive aspect. It does, then, form the framework through which you can arise to higher and higher levels of manifestation.

We now, at this time, cast the wording over to that known as Carla.

(Carla channeling)

We are that principle known to you as Q'uo, and we greet you in the love and in the light of the one infinite Creator in whose service we are. May we thank each in this circle of seeking for calling us to your group to share our humble thoughts with you. It is our privilege and our blessing. We would ask of you that you allow the opinions which we share to drift through your mind without attempting to accept them or reject them but, rather, simply listening to them. Those thoughts which are part of your process of truth will resonate to you as though you were remembering them. Those truths that are not part of your personal truth at this time will simply roll over you, and we ask you to allow that to occur and to leave them behind without a second thought. For, truly, that careful discernment upon the part of each of you allows us to share our opinions and our heart with you without concern that we might infringe upon your free will and your learning.

May we say also that it is a great privilege and a great blessing to meet that entity which suggested that it be known to us as Guidance System. We greet the Guidance System of David; that is the chosen name of this entity for us, at least. We are most privileged to be able to share this conversation with the one known as Guidance System.

We would perhaps pick up upon the powerful image that this entity suggested: a way to look at suffering as being that rain which falls in its bitter drops upon the sensitive sphere of the self and which is, then, allowed by the fearless seeker to enter into the energy system of the vehicle and to come through the natural spiritual gravity that moves the energy within that body to pull those energies down from tributaries into rivers and to the ocean of All That There Is.

Let us look at the suffering as it touches the sphere of self. It flows in a muddy, silt-filled rain, touching the grosser of the antennae of the sphere of self that are put out to catch those energies that threaten survival and comfort. The emotions that are brought from the second-density instinctual entity that is your physical vehicle are often clear, but not often of an energy that is at all open to growth. Rather, such energies are protective, armoring, defensive and survival-oriented, and, in such an atmosphere, these droplets simply must slide off. They have stung the [antennae] of the outside of the sphere of self but have not penetrated and begun the process of working through or being refined by the energy system of the physical and finer vehicles of that soul stream in connection with personality shell in connection with physical vehicle that you call a self.

As the self begins to lose the need to armor, the self becomes semi-permeable, and, for the first time, this vulnerable, undefended self is able to suffer, and this is an achievement, in our humble opinion. The achievement of a self-acknowledged suffering is a great achievement among your peoples. When that crystalline moment comes that the self knows its suffering and sees its sorrow, in that moment is born the opportunity to lift, transform and energize that portion of self which has become deadened, that it may once again become enlivened. The process occurs through this simple process of permeability that allows one tributary, and then another, and then another to spring up in that desert of defense until the self becomes fallow and open to the rain of pain; to that which is causing anger, jealousy, envy, covetousness or any other feeling which causes one to feel an adversity.

Look, now, at the color of this rain, as it begins to be distilled by the processes of the energy vehicle. The process of [self-]acceptance moves the pain through the protective layers and into the personal layers and into the depths of the societal layer, the most difficult of all for catalyst to penetrate and flow through.

Notice that this rain seems to fall upward, but this is because, my friends, you are one of the branches of the tree of life, and that tree has its roots in the heaven worlds and only its branches within your earth world. The rain is moving upwards into the heaven worlds; the energy, as you allow the pain to move through the energy body, is moving upwards from the denser aspects of pain into the heart and into that transformation of the heart which is as the ninety-degree phase shift which moves an ineffable part of the self into a kind of time/space in which that higher energy may far more easily be made permeable and penetrated with great amounts of energy and undifferentiated or unlimited light.

In this part of the process, once that simple allowance of pain has been able to create permeability so that the pain falls into the heart, then the energies of the tabernacle of the one infinite Creator are able to exercise their true-color nature upon this dim, many-colored rain, and each drop of envy becomes true-color envy; each drop of grief becomes a true-color grief, and, instead of the muddy palette that you began with, as you allow the truth of your interior self to work upon this catalyst as it will, in wisdom, in rhythm, and in time, this heart energy begins to place true-color value in those things that you have allowed the freedom to be fully experienced.

Once these colors have been achieved, the experience flows on wings of beauty, transformed by that warrior of light that is yourself; that true channel of light that keeps the armor bright, [moving] into that truth which is the newest portion of the Creator's knowledge of Itself. In this process of acknowledging your own suffering, it is perhaps appropriate to speak through this channel of that which it experienced earlier this day as it experienced the feast of the presentation of the one known as Jesus the Christ. This is the last or final aspect of that mythological system which this entity experiences as its closest road to the Creator[15] in its season of acknowledgement of the birth of the spirit within flesh. It is long been our feeling that each within the circle of seeking represents, as the one known as H has said, the Creator Itself, in the aspect not of the Creator-Father but of the child of the Creator, the daughter of the Creator, the son of the Creator, the Christ of the Creator, that which is in the world, that which has come among us in each of you.

The heart awaits the birth of your own spiritual self, realized for the first time as a being of integrity,

---

[15] Christianity.

eternity and infinity that you cradle within the manger of your heart. This seed, this child must be protected, loved, cared for, nurtured, encouraged and paid attention to. In this Christ child dwells all of those things which the one known as David's Guidance System was describing as that house of cards which is the build-up of accreted crystallization of pain. Once one crystal is dissolved, it is easier to collapse the rest of those crystals, which become as the ice that melts into the water or the cards that collapse the space between them. In this presentation, the one known as Jesus was brought, as an infant forty days old, to the temple to be given to the Creator, as is the custom of this particular entity's culture.

Each of you is an infant; you are at the temple; you have been given to the Creator by that parent which is your physical self, and we say to you,

> Lord, now lettest thou thy servant depart in peace, according to thy word, for mine eyes have seen thy salvation.[16]

Behold the self as it is: an outer defense system of clay, bone, flesh and blood; an inner network of feeling, and, within that feeling, an inner network of truth, and within that truth, an inner network of the one infinite Creator. May you rest in that tabernacle whenever there is suffering within your life, and may you rock the child within. Protect that spiritual self with your love, with your compassion, with your acceptance of the suffering that is going on, placing it all within the loving arms of that Presence that rests within the tabernacle of the heart.

We believe that this is the energy that we wish to share upon this subject. However, we find that there have been two queries asked and that they are connected in a very integrated and energizing way, and, consequently, we would move from speaking through this instrument to passing the sacred feather to the one known as David's Guidance System, for there is much to speak on in terms of that movement of the energy through the system of points of energy or chakras of the finer bodies. The techniques involved in removing blockages move into interesting connections with the nature of suffering. The energy system of the physical vehicle, as we have said, moves from what this instrument would consider the lower to the higher, and, as energy moves into the scoop of the root chakra, it has a full and undifferentiated potential. The colors of the chakras of each individual's energy vehicle are unique to that entity. Each entity is its own blossom; each entity flashes in its own colors, and there is, in the fuller acceptance of the self, an increasing scintillation and strength of energy of the energy that is moving through the body that is a product of that acceptance of self that relaxes the strictures that narrow the path of energy flow.

We believe, however, that we would do well at this time to allow the one known as David to speak upon this subject for a time, as this entity does not have the vocabulary that would be helpful in this discussion. Consequently, we would at this time temporarily pause and turn the feather over to the one known as David's Guidance System. We are those of Q'uo and leave this instrument in love and in light.

(David channeling)

[(David's Guidance System)] Your neurological system is not fundamentally related to the cognitive processes of the brain and how the various nerve system impulses do then holographically imprint their matrices upon the tissues of said organ. The aspirations of the higher self, to strive for a conscious mind that does involve a fuller and more complete rendition of the vibratory centers or nexi of the physical form, [functions] in such a fashion as to have the conscious self using a mental process, using a consciousness template that involves emanations from all of these centers.

The issue to which we are speaking is a representation of the fact, as was stated in the Law of One series, that the contents of an ego is so distorted as to be useless.[17] Rather, we would ask that you reflect upon the energy that forms consciousness, and see that the wheels-within-wheels of the chakra system formulate the true consciousness that you experience at any given moment in your illusion. Therefore, potentially speaking, all chakras do then contribute to that which you know as your conscious

---

[16] The Song of Simeon, from the *Holy Bible*, Luke 2:29-32: "Lord, now lettest thou thy servant depart in peace, according to thy word; For mine eyes have seen thy salvation, which thou hast prepared before the face of all people; To be a light to lighten the Gentiles, and to be the glory of thy people Israel."

[17] "QUESTIONER: Can you tell me how you balance the ego?
"RA: I am Ra. We cannot work with this concept as it is misapplied and understanding cannot come from it." (*Law of One, Book I*, Session 13)

process, the conscious process being that which you oftentimes experience as imagination, intuition, hunches and the like.

We are setting up a necessary framework in order to better differentiate between that distorted concept of consciousness which most of your peoples possess, and the truer and deeper essence of awareness as a harmonious function of all the centers. You have seen many examples in your life of what is known as synchronicity, whereby you experience that time where you look up from a book or have some other moment of symbolic importance which is then immediately followed by an instantaneous feedback mechanism from that which you would think of as the physical. You recognize, of course, that there must be some aspect of yourselves which goes beyond that which is physicality. But this is in effect a thinning of the veil between dimensions, causing you to have a greater ability to focus and differentiate on the essence of true individualized creation as opposed to true unified creation. When this differentiation has been accomplished that which is known as form then dissipates into formlessness. This is known in the shamanic traditions as stopping the world. It is by this process that one who has quickened his process can see those other selves around it to suddenly disappear, and perceive that it is the only being in existence. This is a vibrationally uplifting process. The reverberations that we speak to most specifically this time have to do with the relative degree of cacophony that exists in most of your entities as they go about the hustle and bustle of daily existence without care or consideration for the stillness of mind. This causes there to be an extreme vibrational dyslexia, so to speak, within those lower centers. Then the kundalini spirals, so to speak, can only be awakened by the vertical uplift of the vibratory energy frequencies so that to allow the higher centers to be more fully actualized in the here and now.

What we find is that if you do not have a rooftop over your house, then you will never truly be able to experience the shelter from the raindrops of catalyst. You will never truly be able to home in on that which is known as "home," that which is of the warm hearth, the bear rug, and the delicately arranged objects on the mantelpiece that allow you truly to feel at home in your own physical instrument. Relatively speaking, most of those on your plane exist in a homeless condition. They exist in a condition where they drift and wander to and fro, much as do their thoughts. And this does cause there to be a specific vibrational disharmonious complex in the lower centers.

This disharmonious complex can be analyzed for each individual center as a spiraling line of light, so to speak. And as we have spoken before there are those turns of said spiral whereby certain events have transpired. We seek to collect these spirals, to bring them back to a spherical center of one-pointedness or unity. When this spherical point has been readapted, then all experiences that happen in the present moment can be understood within the greater matrix of the soul and the understanding of how past, present and future merge into a seamless continuum, much as would the Ziploc baggies in which you have stored the food that you have prepared in loving service to others.

So, too, do you have the opportunity to take this manna from heaven, this bread that is the bread of life, and to then package it and conceal it from yourself, without the compartmentalized self recognizing that this manna or higher consciousness that breathes into your physicality does then have the opportunity to be differentiated, not for the purpose of partitioning the ego from those aspects of self that would be deemed as differential but rather storing away various nuggets of awareness within the self. So that, as you continue along the spiral, and various experiences arise into your illusion, you have the prosperity that comes from having a storehouse, so to speak, much as would a squirrel store up acorns in the hole of a tree, knowing that when winter comes there will be those hard months of cold and shivering. Thereby there is a supply that has been instilled.

There is the opportunity for greater abundance in those moments when many others would feel distraught and alone. By storing a larger amount of catalyst than is currently being processed, you can then have that background of experience. When these experiences again arise, they can be compared against that newfound wisdom that has been accumulated by the self. In so doing, [the self may] arrive at a greater degree of functionality so as these blockages are then moved through.

With the appropriate requisite collapsing of fragmentariness within the lower centers of your physiological organism, as it relates to the glandular systems, and that of the energetic body as it relates to the chakra system, we do then see a greater opportunity for there to be a relative clarity in these lower centers and this does then allow for the spiraling line of light, or the kundalini in this case, to progress higher up the chakra system into that known as the seat of love, where the heart is centered, into that known as the seat of will and communication, or the throat center, into that known as the seat of psychic awareness, of the unification of love and compassion, or that of the brow chakra, and on through the crown [chakra][18] into the gateway density, in which spiritual gravity[19] is attained and you again begin collapsing into the oneness.

And thus, fundamentally speaking, the acorns of the self have been holed away in this moment as you listen to these words shared by those known as Guidance System and those known as Q'uo and experience for yourself how it is that, though you may not be able to remember consciously all that has been spoken, that which you think of as the conscious mind is actually a subset of your true awareness. And the deeper awareness that you have is that which is existing in all the chakras. The synchronicities manifest by virtue of the fact that your mind does possess those aspects of the higher centers, if you can but remain still long enough for them to bubble to the surface, much as would the precipitation occur as we have previously spoken.

Therefore, in potential, your conscious mind and day-to-day awareness does have the ability to have full access to intelligent infinity. It is [needed] that the cares and concerns that you have can be cleared off the tabletop, so that you can then make a place setting for the Master, the Christ self to be seated before you. As this Last Supper occurs, you can then accept the death of that distorted ego personality that you have created for yourself and understand that it is through the prayer, "Not my will but Thy will be done,[20]" that you can allow this ego sense to be subjugated and recognize the greater degree of personality transparency such that the higher aspects of being do then become, by virtue of proximity, your vibrations.

As there is no proximity within oneness, we thank you and again turn the microphone back to that known as Q'uo.

(Carla channeling)

We are those known as Q'uo, and again are with this instrument and greet you once again in love and in light.

So it may be seen that the rain of catalyst, the cycle of suffering, is that which may also be seen as the sunshine of life and the cycle of joy. There is a healing in that permeation of self with suffering, in that refining of emotion through the processes of dealing with and experiencing those emotions and experiencing their growing nobility within you, their growing beauty and deepness of tone. It becomes clearer that, once this rain has fallen and been accepted, sunshine moves into the heart. For is there not rain and is there not sun, and shall one be surprised at the rain? But shall one not give thanks when the sunshine abounds and when the day is fair, and opportunity is rife. Those days are also part of the cycle of joy and suffering.

We thank the one known as David and the one known as David's Guidance System for discussing the energy centers as they did, for it is beyond this instrument to explain in that detail how one may move from dealing with specific catalyst, dealing with specific flow of emotive material, to moving into the deeper waters, that ocean of processed catalyst which has become beautiful, blessed, transformed and given back to the one infinite

---

[18] This refers to the chakra system by ascending order from green through violet. Green is the color of heart energy in this system. Blue, the throat chakra color, is associated with clear communication, while indigo is the color of the brow or third eye chakra. Violet is the color of the crown chakra, and in the Law of One material, it is associated with the "gateway to intelligent infinity." About this gateway, the Ra group says, "Know then, first, the mind and the body. Then as the spirit is integrated and synthesized, these are harmonized into a mind/body/spirit complex which can move among the dimensions and can open the gateway to intelligent infinity, thus healing self by light and sharing that light with others." (Law of One, Book I, Session 17)

[19] "QUESTIONER: Then when our planet is fully into fourth density, will there be a greater gravity?

"RA: I am Ra. There will be a greater spiritual gravity thus causing a denser illusion." (*Law of One, Book I*, Session 17)

[20] When Jesus is praying in the garden of Gethsemane, the night he was taken into custody before his trial, he prayed to be spared this, but, he said, "Father, if thou be willing, remove this cup from me; nevertheless, not my will, but Thine, be done." (Luke 22:42)

Creator. That is a crystalline and light-filled ocean of experience …

(Side one of tape ends.)

(Carla channeling)

It is as the overarching system that rules the system most proximate to the human or physically human experience. If one can envision, as the one known as V was discussing, diving down that cliff of ocean from the relative shallows of the conscious experience into the abyss of infinite awareness, that infinite awareness has a coherence that is full of information that, in its very transmission, is as the Balm of Gilead, that healing energy that can move into a situation within as those healing waters, as that medicament without description heals by its energy alone, not needing rhyme and reason, not needing logic and possibility, not needing the human acceptance; needing, rather, the acceptance of a state of mind that is other than that which your culture understands, or accepts.

So let us end by looking at the silence. For this is the most potent weapon that the warrior of light, as this instrument has called the spiritual warrior, possesses. The silence has been described as that [which] unlocks the door to the room in which the one infinite Creator dwells. It has been described as that which unlocks truth. It has been described as that which enables and ennobles the process of catalysis, chemical reaction, and result: catalyst and experience.

Silence is as the open hand. Come to the Deity empty, empty-handed, empty-minded, empty of all but the thirst and the hunger for the presence of the one infinite Creator, the one original Thought that created all that is. Come empty, for you shall overflow. What concerns you? Come to your heart, and come empty. Come into the sea and dive deeply. Dive for that deep, deep water where truth has been crystallized within your own process, where you can enjoy the company of the angels of the deep that are there to comfort you, hold you, love you, strengthen you, and send you back into the fray.

And when you come back, into that archipelago that is conscious living, know that each island of chaos and confusion and each stretch of lonely ocean between are one with that deep water. Each drop that touches each island of confusion comes from the One and goes back to that same One.

We leave you with the greatest of love and thanks for each of your hero's journeys. Why are you together this weekend? What have you come to rejoice in? We leave you to each other and we ask you to love each other. Heal each other. Encourage each other. Bear each other's burdens. And bring each other home.

We are those known to you as Q'uo. We leave you in the love and in the light of the one infinite Creator. Adonai, my friends. Adonai, vasu. ☥

L/L Research

L/L Research is a subsidiary of Rock Creek Research & Development Laboratories, Inc.

P.O. Box 5195
Louisville, KY 40255-0195

www.llresearch.org

Rock Creek is a non-profit corporation dedicated to discovering and sharing information which may aid in the spiritual evolution of humankind.

ABOUT THE CONTENTS OF THIS TRANSCRIPT: This telepathic channeling has been taken from transcriptions of the weekly study and meditation meetings of the Rock Creek Research & Development Laboratories and L/L Research. It is offered in the hope that it may be useful to you. As the Confederation entities always make a point of saying, please use your discrimination and judgment in assessing this material. If something rings true to you, fine. If something does not resonate, please leave it behind, for neither we nor those of the Confederation would wish to be a stumbling block for any.

CAVEAT: This transcript is being published by L/L Research in a not yet final form. It has, however, been edited and any obvious errors have been corrected. When it is in a final form, this caveat will be removed.

© 2009 L/L Research

Special Meditation
February 6, 2003

Question from B: The question today has to deal with the concept of empowerment and enslavement that Q'uo mentioned in the last session. We are aware of how enslavement in various kinds occurs through governments, military and so forth, but what we would like to know *(inaudible)* empowerment might even be found in the very DNA that we contain, that would help us to realize our life's goals of serving and of learning, and we were wondering if Q'uo can give us some information about how a person can achieve this empowerment, and what was Q'uo talking about when empowerment was mentioned in relationship to the enslavement. In addition, we would like to know something about what the empowerment in the DNA might actually look like.

(Carla channeling)

We are those known to you as the principle of Q'uo, and we greet you in the love and in the light of the one infinite Creator, in Whose service we are. We greatly appreciate and thank each present for calling this circle of seeking together and calling us to your group. It is a great privilege to speak and share our opinions and we would simply ask that, as always, each idea be taken as an opinion and not as an authoritarian statement, for we would not wish to be a stumbling block for any. With this caveat in place we feel free to share our opinion with you without infringing upon your free will or your learning process.

As we gaze upon your query we realize that there are opportunities to infringe neatly pocketed along the way that we shall need to observe, so pardon us if our information is uneven. It is to be noted that as we tell you this story we ourselves are the legend in the story and when history is revealed in its truth it is almost inevitably made of stories. There is almost never the possibility of achieving a unified truth concerning the events of your peoples. It is possibly to move closer and closer to the full picture but very difficult to move beyond unseen limitations. Some of these unseen limitations lie within us and some within this instrument. Both systems of limitations, whether that be ethical or informational, these things do limit and possibly skew the story that we tell.

The long history of your peoples is preceded by an even longer, unwritten, unrecorded history of those energies and essences and individuals that made their own history at the time of what this instrument would call the last cycle change, or ice age. These entities were plummeted into service of a high second-density nature by entities who wished to have aid and help with their needs. These entities were not intending to be either evil or good, but rather were those who looked upon the second-density life forms of this planet as fair game for molding into the workers that they needed.

Thusly, a new race was created, not merely by the infinite Creator, but by those co-creators which were attempting to work with these life-forms for their own needs. Further energy and further manipulation was offered to these entities, creating within them that which this entity would call soul-streams. These were the improvements, shall we say, that indeed moved into that which was part of the DNA. However, not the same portion of DNA which had been the focus of change previously.

In this second wave of alterations, improvements were made so that entities were of third density, being ensouled and capable of mental, emotional and spiritual evolution in ways which transcended the second-density model of individuals coming from a gene pool and returning to that common memory pool. These entities, then, having been altered twice, were soon joined by other entities from other spheres within your galaxy whose time had run out for their third-density planets, and whose needs led them to this particular sphere that you call Earth.

These entities through the processes of years, generations and millennia gradually continued to alter and continued to spread and continued to learn. With the steady increase in the sources of population to your planet came an increasingly complex mix of archetypical structures, which were in some ways not so much incompatible as cranky with each other. It was not that the differences between populations was impossible to breach, it was that within the biases of the population groups there survived a good deal of territorial energy from second density, the parent genetic structure being that of the great apes.

Consequently, there was an inborn tendency towards aggression which had only been encouraged by the second wave of genetic manipulation. This set the stage for entities we shall grandly call the space pirates. The space pirates were, in these entities' way of describing them, from the fifth density, and they had many minions from the fourth density, but these densities being in the negative sense a very pure path along the path of service to self.

It was discovered that if these entities used those with a hunger for power to encourage and hone their appetite for power and domination, these entities in turn would do their best, through the processes of aggression and war, to conquer and control that which was seen as desirable, whether it be geography, position, money or power. And these entities found, perhaps due to the limitations of your human imagination, perhaps due to the limitations of imagination of fourth-density minions, that their greatest tool was the very blunt instrument of war and consequently, when the forces that learned their trade within the culture that this instrument calls Atlantis, whenever these entities show up their plan is always to encourage division, strife and, if possible at all, the largest war available.

For this in turn [subverts] the energies of youth and maturity towards the entrainment of conscious thought processes until entities moved into that space within their minds where they believe and accept as true the necessity of war, the rightness of the native land's authority figures, and the real and genuine desire to make the world a better place through rearranging the geography, the people *(inaudible)* power in a way which keeps those in power in even more power and simply enslaves the attitudes of the minds of all of those who follow them into furnishing the physical vehicles that march off to the war, and by their dying, their suffering, and their injustice thereby spread the suffering, the pain, and those other negative emotions ever higher, evermore violently, ever at a greater level.

The goal of these space pirates is simply to achieve a *(inaudible)* so that third-density cycles come and third-density cycles go and there is either a very small harvest or no harvest at all, most of the harvest, therefore, being that which this instrument might call spent energy or entropy, except that it has to do with the burden of sorrow, grief, suffering and pain of those who have not made the harvest.

This began to cycle in Atlantis and has moved through its complete cycle at this time. In all three cycles, then, there has been almost no harvest and as your peoples approach the end of this present cycle of time, which is the final opportunity for harvest within this particular planetary third density, the energies of Atlantis remain. There had been incarnations of groups of entities which first did the bidding of these space pirates in Atlantis. Not yet once, but as the gazing eye looks at history this group can be found again and again. Within those of Babylonia, within those of Rome, within those of

Germany, within those of Germany once again, and now within that which is the United States.

These energies have grouped, gathered and arisen as a natural event, since graduation is at hand and these entities are attempting to graduate in service to self. Consequently, once again millions and millions of earth natives who are otherwise very close to being harvested have been entrained in their minds and in their thinking by the discussion of subjects that lead the mind to war and to the just reasons for it, thereby once again placing these millions of entities in the uncomfortable space of being dimly aware that their true freedom is being taken from them, but truly having no real capacity to figure out what is going on and why there is no rest or peace for them.

The one known as B asks concerning the DNA and the empowerment of this DNA, and, indeed, the DNA was carefully adjusted not to move beyond third density by those entities of the first adjustment of the great ape vehicle which was found upon your planet at the end of second density. This adjustment was in its own way a safety precaution, as in a tamper-proof lighter or a child-proof bottle cap, for it was felt that such entities as these great ape beings had been would not be able to withstand the pressure of ethical decisions or knowledge of right actions.

However, the structure of DNA is not limited by these manipulations which may be done by your men and women of science. These spirals of light that cohere for the formation and continuation of [life] are born from states of consciousness or matrices of perception rather than being limited by the current instructions of the current DNA. The energies of unity and unconditional love once welcomed into the heart and worked with in a persistent and conscientious manner begin to lend to the mind of the meditator and seeker of silence access to a state of consciousness in which there are no limitations. In this state of consciousness infinite energies flowing in infinite supply at all times and there is ample energy to fuel any state of consciousness to which the focus, the desire, the purity and the process of an entity has brought him.

Is it easy to attain a state of consciousness that builds new strands of DNA? For a very few it is relatively easy. However, for most it is a great challenge. The hope of the various populations of your sphere, then, may be based upon that hope that springs forever from the heart. That hope to seek and find, to open up that source of magic that makes the impossible possible.

We of the Confederation of Planets have come to tell a very simple story. It is a story of thought. It is a story of the power of thought. It is a story of the power of a certain Thought that created all that is. It is a story of the power of absolute and unconditional love. It is a story of intelligent infinity and the desire of that infinity to know itself. It knows itself with every thought of its children and each entity of whatever density of whatever planet within the infinite creation is a child of the Father, or as many would say in this time of political correctness: Father/Mother.

This work of connecting DNA strands through alterations in consciousness is work that is as accessible as the next moment, that moment when one ceases speaking and enters the silence with a full heart. This moment is as far away as the nearest star. It is the kind of choice that entities may look at from the worldly point of view and say, what a nice structure, what a pleasant fantasy, that fantasy of creating the self anew and transforming the self into an entirely different kind of person. However, from the standpoint of faith there is available another point of view. That point of view is inscribed within what this instrument would call the magical personality.

For a millennia you upon this planet who look straight at the questions of truth, beauty and life have carefully written down this and that observation and experiment with consciousness and with *(inaudible)* fields. Each attempt at inner knowledge have been somewhat successful and there is available to the seeker a fairly substantial supply of excellent information on what it is to become a magical being, what it is to become a nation of priests, what it is to become a tribe of shaman. It is entirely possible through the discipline of the personality, through the seeking after silence, and through the other giving of oneself to the will of the Creator to move into that space wherein there is a true, real possibility of literally designing and building DNA in many of those who come now to birth upon your planet.

The entities you call your scientists begin to find again and again that there are more strands of DNA found within many of the children being born upon your planet at this time and even those who have been born with usual DNA are found to be creating new strands within their incarnation. This is that which we were speaking of when we were mentioning that empowerment of DNA. Indeed, more and more entities among your people are able to share in a charismatic sense a good deal of that state of consciousness for a limited amount of time, it being a yellow-ray sharing rather than that which comes from the truly unified heart. Within this influence it is entirely possible that many would find it maximally potentially doable to lift themselves into a state of mind which indeed is true freedom, that state of mind which no longer is connected to fear, is no longer connected to the desire to defend, but is free to love, to radiate, to embrace.

We feel that we have come to a natural pause and would ask if there are any follow up queries at this time?

Question: Has there ever been a time in the history of this planet when human beings experienced unconditional love in a group way?

We are those of Q'uo, and are aware of your query, my brother. Indeed, at this very moment there are many groups upon your planet who are experiencing unconditional love. Such entities have largely been hidden, entities such as this group, entities who are not at all well known, entities who are completely out of sight of any publicity, have always in these ceaseless changing patterns of energy of groups upon your planet found ways to come together to express love for each other. Sometimes it is the force of an idea that for a time blends people's energies so beautifully that they are able, simply by the force of an idea, to dedicate their lives to that goal, to that ideal. We would suggest those known as the Quakers and those known as the Transcendentalists.

Other groups have been formed because of the charisma or beauty or purity of the service of one entity, a woman or a man of extraordinary capability. The great monasteries of your so-called dark ages were opportunities for entities who wished nothing for themselves but everything for the truth. To serve without *(inaudible)*, without record and with exquisitely positive results. Groups such as these will exist as long as there are entities within third density, for it is the absolute destiny of that which you call the human spirit to seek and know the truth. When that seeking for the truth becomes so pure that it has a force stronger than the need to respect authority or resist change, then such a group moves forward, finds its own strength and serves quietly, lovingly, faithfully and persistently.

Spiritually speaking, history is story after story of those who, for the love of the Creator, for the love of an ideal, or for the love of a wonderful teacher, gave all that they were and all that they had towards the generation and the propagation of unconditional love.

May we answer you further, my brother?

(Pause)

Question: In the Ra books it was mentioned how much of the information that seemed quite sensational was actually transitory and had little importance. When making films, this type of sensational information is usually quite frequently utilized. How best can we balance the need for sensational attraction and the quality information that may not be quite as sensational?

We are those of Q'uo, and grasp your query, my brother. Perhaps we may simply say that when telling the absolute truth the sense of humor is often helpful. May we ask if this penetrates the outer walls of thought at all, or shall we attempt again?

Question: Could you also speak further?

We are those of the Q'uo, and would be glad to do so. It is indeed truth that transient material fascinates the mind of those within the illusion which supports such antics. It is equally true that the substance of metaphysics is naturally and instinctually fascinating to few. The introduction of characters who are wise is often accompanied, because of these biases, by the addition to that character of quirks which while not destroying the creature's wisdom or veracity, nevertheless give a character quirks that are genuinely humorous to that culture. Consequently, the use of humor softens the blow of the use of truth. The use of the various devices of humor, whether those be of language as in the rhyming or in any other …

(Side one of tape ends.)

Question: In *The Law of One* books it was mentioned that Star Wars was kind of like a children's story compared to what is really occurring. So many times Hollywood uses fantastic stories to give a message. Is there some way that we could be more realistic, shall we say, in presenting this information?

We are those of Q'uo, and are aware of your query, my brother. We believe that there are an infinite number of ways for such information to be shared. The truth of spiritual achievement is that those among your peoples at any particular time who are able to do work in consciousness dwell side by side with those who have no claim to an inner life. They dwell for the most part very quietly.

We would ask you to think of those known to this instrument as Native Americans, whose rituals are based within the general category of the magical personality [and seen] by ordinary people as an everyday part of a naturally lived life. To entities within this particular culture all parts of the illusion are alive, all first density, second density, and third density entities alike share consciousness and are part of one ever moving, ever living story of creation. The earth is seen as the body of the mother and all of those upon the mother are seen as the children of the mother. All natural elements and energies and animals and plants are seen as various very lively, very energy filled creation which is full of information at all times.

It is very instructive to see how simple and direct many of these exercises in enlarging consciousness are. The truth of enslavement to fear and suffering and other people's wars, and the possibility of choosing instead empowerment, freedom and the spiritual path is one which lies directly in the path of every day and of every man. It is not necessary to be extreme or inhuman in order to become an entity that truly has a magical personality. Rather, it is a matter of moving through an awakening process and becoming directly aware of the self. Once this point has been reached—and this point is very realistically expected to be reached by one who attempts it—the universe opens and the impossible becomes possible.

The greatest amount of effort for one who is attempting to make this change is the beginning, where it is in the beginning where one must express the faith of that which has not yet occurred. When there is a very good psychological structure which would give characters a reason to pay attention and to begin to work upon the spiritual personality, the magical personality, then it is possible, perhaps, to move into your structure of *(inaudible)* character the logical and persuasive [proximate] reasons for characters to become part of a group which does attempt to seek the truth.

May I answer you further, my brother?

Question: One particular possibility is to have a dissatisfied business man who has perhaps suffered a loss of a loved one who has the chance to risk his life to save another and this other was not really in danger but was a means by which an ancient brotherhood contacts him and through this interaction between the brotherhood and the man many aspects of love *(inaudible)* are brought out. Could you comment on this particular approach to the project?

We are those of Q'uo, and are aware of your query, my brother. As in many good ideas there are inconsistencies within the idea. However, we would say on the whole it is an excellent idea. The difficulty that we see with it is simply that the positively-oriented entity is unlikely to set up a situation that is false in order to make a test. Rather, such an entity or group of entities would observe such an entity as moving into such a role and would, because of the emotional colors shown by this entity, because of its emotional purity and love, become a candidate for further communication.

May we speak further, my brother?

Question: So the situation would really be an actual situation that would be observed by the brotherhood rather than being staged by the brotherhood?

We are those of Q'uo, and we can affirm your understanding, my brother.

Question: Could you comment on a second approach which would have a scientist, a geneticist perhaps, discovering that within the DNA there had been a certain quality that allowed the experience of unity but it had been switched off so he begins to work with himself and his own DNA to switch it back on, which brings him into contact with various villains and other characters.

We are those of Q'uo, and are aware of your query, my brother. And this concept is also an excellent one and also has drawbacks, in our opinion, and we would share that with you. The DNA angle, shall we say, is a very helpful one to bring up for entities as it is, indeed, the heart of the penetration into the illusion of the structure of the spiritually or energetically formed world. The changes that will allow entities within third density to welcome fourth density life are bound up in the further strands of DNA that are formed with the full consciousness of unconditional love.

However, the concept of moving through scientific testing and in some way measurable by scientific instruments at this time discovering how to place unconditional love into the perceptive matrix of an entity is questionable. There is much to study, shall we say, in this angle of DNA research and we would suggest that which has been useful to this instrument has been a specific work called, *The Biology of Perception*. This instrument, we may say, has had its eyes opened to a great extent, far greater than the eyes were open before on this subject by this very helpful bit of research.

We encourage the one known as B to investigate not only this particular source of information on DNA and perception, but any sources which are suggested in the course of investigation into this particular article or video cassette as this instrument would call it.

May we answer you further, my brother?

Question: So when you said earlier that there were children now being born with additional strands in their DNA, is it true then that this would not be measurable by current scientific technology.

We are those of Q'uo, and would say, my brother, that there is always the possibility of doubt when outrageously different or new information is offered, and this has certainly proven to be the case with many other instances of seeming impossible events, such as, for instance, the possibility of meteors falling from the heavens, which was considered impossible at the time that they were finally, once and for all proven to exist.

We find that we are very limited in our ability to speak concerning this because it is more than most of those things that we have offered that which can be plumbed by the use of your techniques of research.

May we answer you further, my brother?

Question: What was the connection of doubt that was mentioned?

We are those of Q'uo, and, my brother, we do not doubt that we used the word but we doubt that we can remember why.

Question: Writing about unconditional love is hard to do from the theoretical point of view. Is there something that B could do in the way of another session with Carla or with Q'uo that would help him to experience this quality in order to be able to write about it?

We are those of Q'uo, and are aware of your query, my brother. Certainly, we would be glad to speak with you upon the subject at another time. The one known as Carla is also most happy to share upon the subject. We would also point out that there are two other sources of strength for you. One is that invisible but very present group of entities that are devoted to the one known as B and that have spent many, many years caring for and accompanying the one known as B. Those presences of support, sanity and encouragement that have sometimes being felt are most real and most loving and these constitutes an unseen band of advisers and helpers. The key in invoking their help is in the word, invoke. It must be asked for, and it must be appreciated. With the request and the thanksgiving being the foundations of such a silent communication with those that have no words, this very powerful help may be activated, enlivened and energized by the living entity's faith that they are there.

The second group that this entity has available to it is that visible group known as L/L Research which has a physical location and a location in time which meet your requirements for being upon the planet at the same time and being able to connect with a spiritual group, or, shall we say, a spiritual clan or family, which in and of itself has the potential to be a great source of strength for those who wish to spend time becoming, shall we say, enchanted or charmed by the magic of that particular gathering of light and energy. Such places, once established, are as the lighthouse which the longer it burns gathers more fuel to burn even brighter.

We are aware that this has been your last query but if we may clear up anything we would offer you that opportunity at this time.

Question: Thank you for your questions, they were very, very good.

We are those of Q'uo, and we would at this time take this opportunity to bless you, wish you well and leave you in the love and in the light of the one infinite Creator. We are always available to you to deepen and strengthen your meditative states. You have only to ask mentally and we will be there in silence and in great love. We are known to you as the principle of Q'uo. Adonai. Adonai vasu borragus. ♣

Sunday Meditation
February 9, 2003

Question from J1: The question today from J1 has to do with the difference between belief and faith. He considers belief to be a lower channel of data and catalyst processing than faith. We would like Q'uo to give us some information on what they see to be the difference between belief and faith.

(Carla channeling)

We are those known to you as the principle of Q'uo. Greetings in the love and in the light of the one infinite Creator, in whose service we come today. It is a great privilege and a pleasure to greet each of you, and we wish to thank you for arranging time in your lives to come to this circle of seeking, to spend time asking and yearning and opening doors in search of the truth. It is those who persist, and those who do not quail at the thought of further truth being shown to the world, to whom that truth comes so richly and so generously.

And for us, you are our truth; you are our primers of beauty, service and learning. We thank you for sharing those vibrations of your meditation with us. As we share our thoughts on belief and faith, we would ask each of you to do us the favor of listening with great discrimination, and choosing only those thoughts that appear fair to you to keep and to think about, letting all the rest go without a second thought. In this way we may be assured that our opinion remains opinion and not authority, as we would not wish to be a stumbling block for any.

We wish to thank the one known as J1 for such a perceptive and probing question. Indeed, we have a very simple story to tell, and our story is in part the story of the difference between belief and faith. Our story is a story about unconditional, pure and creative love, a love so powerful that it has created all that is, all that has been and all that shall be. It is also creative and powerful to destroy, and all that has arisen likewise moves into transformations which remove it from one form into another.

And this same energy of unconditional love is that energy which creates that benign and most kind gateway to that which is the life to come. Thusly, this Logos, this great original Thought of the Creator, is responsible both for your energies of life and your consciousness and for those limitations upon the form which you now enjoy, which shall put a period to the apparent lifetime of you as an individual. And indeed may we say that it is more than an apparent ending, for each personality shell that you choose with which to come into incarnation does indeed have its appropriate period, when that personality shell has done the job for which you assembled it.

It is difficult to imagine, faced with the riches of one's own complex and subtle gradations of personality and beingness, that that which you experience as yourself is only a tiny portion of your true self. And yet this is indeed true. That which you experience within a single incarnation is as that tributary that is a portion of the stream of soul that is you, but it is as that stream flowing from the beginning at, shall we say, a distance from the center of the circle of life, and flowing towards the center that is your soul stream; that is, rather, a soul ocean. And each individual life experience is at the same time, in metaphysical time, flowing towards that center of the ocean of self. Consequently, it is well that you are not able to remember or to know that which is going on in all the other radials of this circle of self, for the information would be too much to bear.

Nevertheless, it is within this rich milieu of discovered and undiscovered self that the question of faith and belief arises in its best context. For it is questions that move beyond transient material that are generally thought of as the life-and-death questions, and these are the questions that seem to ask for belief or faith as that which is used to address the uncontrollable and implacable forces of this great creative love that births and that puts an end to life, with equal generosity.

What is the entity within third density to do with these inarguable forces of life and death, being born and moving through the gateway of death? There is within the heart of your people an absolute instinct towards what you may call either faith or belief, in the general sense that it calls forth a spiritual response. The catalyst of being faced with one's mortality creates the situation in which the self faces the unknown and asks, and there is a great hunger behind that question: What? Why? Who am I? Why am I here? Why am I poised between my birth and my death? Why did I choose birth? Why did I choose a state of mind, body and spirit that will end inevitably in the dissolution of body? These are fundamental queries about which the spiritual instinct of third-density entities will naturally cycle.

When this entity was a young woman of teenage years, this entity discovered that it could not believe in the dogma of its church, this entity being what she calls Episcopalian or Anglican. The point of dogma upon which this instrument choked was the virgin birth. And so this instrument asked for advice from its spiritual advisor, an entity of great authority in this instrument's church. He suggested to her that the Christian story was a mystery which, in the particular church that is Episcopalian, is not expected to be understood, but rather is held as a point of faith, as a mystery to be understood at a later date, not within this lifetime. This view of the story of the virgin birth, and of all the other points of faith in the Christian creed seemed to this instrument to be far more tolerable, and to this day this instrument retains firm and loving ties with its parish church. Nevertheless, this instrument has never been able to absorb, accept or understand the need for dogmatic and dogmatically held beliefs.

However, we believe that we grasp the nature of the need for articles of faith that are dogmatically believed, perceived and promulgated, and perhaps if each will think within its own mind and heart of those times when structure equaled comfort, it may be more easily understood what the attraction might be for those who desire and crave the black and white world of right and wrong, acceptable and non-acceptable, that is implied and created with the acceptance of a dogmatic structure. Basically, that which is belief always has content of a specific nature. This insistence upon the nailing of spiritual value, truth and beauty to specific words and only those words chosen by a specific dogmatic editing of holy works, each point which is used to describe another limitation of specificity, is as the builder who wishes to build itself a house to keep it safe from the whims of doubt and change. There is the desire to create a structure of belief that will be stout and firm against the storms of those issues that inevitably bring one face to face with what seem to be the gray areas of self.

In such times, as inconvenient and limiting as belief systems may be, the comfort of knowing what one must do often seems fairer and more desirable than existing within the outdoors of an unconstructed spiritual path in which the only features of the landscape which are distinct are those features that come at one at their own time, out of their own fog, bringing their own gifts in hands that are open to give, loving, but above all, unknown and unexpected.

And let us look at the processes of faith, for faith is that which accepts a truth without content. For the structure of faith is such that it is expressed in that leap into midair, where all that is known is that it is the Creator's world, and all is well. Thusly, one launches oneself into the abyss of the present moment and what comes next, because one has lost all fear of the consequences of being out of control.

In the Buddhist story, there is a tiger above and a tiger below, and the seeker clings to the side of a cliff, and the question is, "Shall I let go?" That is the question of faith. The question is, "Shall I let go?" Thusly, perhaps it may be seen that the choice between belief and faith is the choice of arranging a protected structure in which faith may stay the same, and arranging an open structure where the sanctuary that is built exists primarily within the heart.

We would pause for the one known as "GuS" [Guidance System] to speak through the one known as David. And, may we say, the pleasure of sharing this communication with the Guidance System of the one known as David is indeed a privilege that we appreciate to our very toes.

We would at this time pause, awaiting this instrument in love and in light. We are those of Q'uo.

(David channeling)

We speak this day as the Guidance System of that entity known as David Wilcock. We greet you in the love and the light of the one infinite Creator.

When enunciating the peculiarities of semantics in such a question as the differentiation between belief and faith, one must pause for a moment and be somewhat guarded in the dissemination of wisdom in accordance with said words or sound vibration complexes, for it is a fact that those of your peoples are more than capable of using either of these words in a variety of contexts.

We do understand the framework of the question as implying a selective bias preferential to the idea of one concept complex over another, and we would ask that you recognize that there are negligible degrees of semantic overlay between these two concepts, such that you may discover one entity using one concept in a completely different fashion as would another. And so, there is certainly one aspect of personal definition whereby the term known as faith would be seen as a less distorted view of the one infinite Creator in all Its majesty and glory, as opposed to that of belief, which, [as a word,] has more of a "herd" mentality [in which the Creator] is apprehended for a sense of purpose or satisfying curiosity, rather than for enhancing one's love and ability to serve. This is the aspect that we will focus on in the course of this session. But let us begin first of all by describing the characteristics of the words themselves, in terms of how they are most commonly utilized.

It is indeed true that both belief and faith can be seen by your peoples as a positive. Both of these words can be used in contexts wherein the entity has found some aspect of meaning that informs existence, and that gives pause before one would otherwise indulge in repetitive behavioral patterns that have become so ingrained as to wear a circle in the rug of your mind, so to speak.

And let us also say that it is indeed quite a fact that in the name of belief and in the name of faith there have been many great evils committed. And thus both of these words could be used in a decidedly negative context, depending on the will of that person, for the benefit of others or for the benefit of self, and how those terms are then contorted.

It has been said that truth is a moving target, and in one sense this is true, and in another it is not—so thus you see the pun. The essence of truth is indeed an individual process. As was enunciated in the Law of One material, the primary gestalt through which one views the Law of One is that of free will. This gestalt implies, fundamentally speaking, that as long as you understand the importance of each individual's path as being totally unique, and its own Christed self in action, then you shall never fall again into the whims of the ego, or that personality-self that seeks self-annihilation, that seeks separation, that would seek to fragment the creation into a series of disparate parts rather than to allow the melting influence of love to form that energy of allowing, which does then cause all of these various separate aspects to again fuse together.

So let us be clear, therefore, that although truth is a moving target, there are those philosophical principles that act as over-arching beams of support upon which the stage of life is being played. It is important to have a steady diet of spiritual materials that gives you an adequate respect for these principles, as otherwise it is all too easy to use either the principle of belief or the principle of faith as your platform through which to expect that a particular belief construct that you would have or a particular aspect of faith that you would experience is also right for others. We are speaking in broad generalities here, because we are aware of the disparate levels of consciousness from which many of our readers will be coming to this material from. And thus this is not to imply judgment or blame in any way, as we are aware that you understand this.

Given this construct of free will as being the overarching support structure through which your game is being played, it is wise to then understand that you are in a system of causes and effects that has a very discrete motivating purpose, regardless of whether or not you are conscious of it. This system of free will shall be preserved. It has been said in the Law of One material that you are free to have any experience that you desire. It is only when these experiences begin to infringe on the free will of another that you then would experience those balancing acts that would manifest into your physical sphere, so as to offset the energetic disruption in the harmonics of your field and in the fields of others that had been produced.

Therefore, if you can step aside from the drama of self, from the passion plays of whether you will be enlightened or whether you will make the ascension or not, you can have loads and loads more freedom and information coming into your being by simply recognizing that every single path that is being followed is precisely perfect for that entity; that every entity at some point or another becomes aware of this under-arching framework often known as karma. This under-arching framework is not something that can be easily stepped aside [from]; in fact, it is our job as your guardian, as your higher support structure, to insure that, without judgment and without blame, karma is carried forth.

And therefore, there are many of those of you who would experience those elements that would seem to be of a balancing nature, that would seem to produce those experiences that you would tend to label as suffering, and therefore there is a subconscious bias in your mind that we, as your guardian, have in some sense cast a foul judgment upon you, that we have seen you as impure, that we have seen you as disgusting, or that in some fashion you have not lived up to our expectations.

We recognize that this is a belief, that this is an essence of perception that is brought forth in the illusion that is wrapped around you, which you perceive as being the three dimensions of length, width and height in which you experience your lives. Understand that outside these three dimensions, there are those densities of higher energy; higher energy that is not directly visible to you but which nevertheless exists all around you. And thus, one possible way that you could look at this is that the energy is beyond the threshold of the speed of light. And thus, were you capable of raising your vibrations beyond the visible speed of light at 186,000 miles per second, you would then perceive other structures that existed around you, such as those angelic beings who are ministering to your very needs.

We want you to understand, therefore, that the beings who are standing around you in the room in this very moment are those beings that exist outside of the apertures of your perception—outside of the capabilities that you have to understand and to resonate with your experience. There are those upon your plane who have not been given adequate compensation by the mainstream media, who are nevertheless capable of crossing this threshold of light and becoming aware of the energies and emanations that surround them. These entities have their own sets of experiences that have informed their faith, and have informed their belief.

In previous epochs of your history, and in those times which are now known as history, you have had other examples of those souls who have come forth and stepped up to the plate, so to speak, to then raise the vibratory frequencies to such a degree that the threshold point of light is then crossed, that these unseen worlds of emanations are then directly apprehended by the sensory organs, such that it is no longer [behind] a veil shrouded in mystery, but rather that of the completeness.

Even as you do this unto others, so are you doing it to yourself. Thus there is that parable in the Bible:

When the Son of man shall come in His glory, before Him shall be gathered all nations; and he shall separate them … as a shepherd divideth his sheep from the goats. And he shall set the sheep on His right hand, but the goats on His left. Then shall the King say unto them on His right hand, "Come, ye blessed of my Father, inherit the kingdom prepared for you from the foundation of the world. For I was an hungered and ye gave me meat: I was thirsty and ye gave me drink: I was a stranger and ye took me in.[21]

In this melting away of the difference between self and others, there is a unity. There is a unity in understanding that if you could go beyond that threshold point of light, you would see that your body is enmeshed perfectly with the others around you. And thus, as the sixth-density entity, Ra, once said, it is impossible for us to see you as separate beings.[22] Recognize this for yourself, and then begin to understand how it is that this universal law of cause and effect, the preservation of free will, is the primary motivating factor behind those corrective experiences that we would then bring about. They are corrective much in the same sense that a chiropractic adjustment would realign your skeletal system so as to be in greater harmony with the necessary functions of the physical body in its optimal state.

You can understand that we[23] are making adjustments to your energy body by bringing about those experiences that cause you always to return to a state of perfect balance. And thus, if you have just found yourself going through a situation where you feel as though some aspect of what you may term "bad karma" has occurred, recognize that it is simply the precise degree of balance that is required to bring you back to being unified.

In that moment of unification, once again you have the opportunity to rest in faith, to rest in belief, to rest in the understanding that, if you choose to believe, if you choose to have faith, you can see that once again we have taken the necessary precautions and steps to bring you back into that state where your karmic report card is 100 percent straight A's—where you have not failed in any way, as there is no concept of failure, but rather that you can see that you have been returned to a state of balance, the balance that you think is implicit within these moments of readjustment.

The balance comes about by virtue of understanding that, regardless of whether you see this unseen structure of cause and effect that informs your experience, it will nevertheless continue. And thus, what we do find is that in that discernment between belief and faith, whereby one would see faith as being the higher vibratory frequency, there is the understanding that faith comes about when one allows the illusion of belief to fall by the wayside.

The illusion of belief is that which can be ascribed to many things. Many of your peoples still would believe that which is read in your mainstream media, such as the newspaper, the television media. Thankfully, this is changing, as this has been a source of many distortions. However, let us remain on this point for a moment and take one of many examples.

It is widely understood that there have been those sightings of UFOs, that there have been those entities who have directly experienced them, including many of your astronauts and many of your best airline pilots.[24] And yet at the same time there is a very curious silence within your mainstream media structures as to any mention of these events. Also we would encourage you to reflect back on the event known as the Disclosure Project conference on May 9, 2001, whereby 39 top-notch whistle blowing members of the government and of military structures assembled together at the National Press Club in Washington, DC to give a final and definitive statement to the world about the fact that this presence was real, and having the proof that was required to show beyond any shadow of doubt that this phenomenon did indeed exist.[25]

What we find is that this conference was only covered very briefly in your mainstream media, if at all. And thus the perception or the belief that there is no such thing as UFOs has continued, by virtue of the lack of support within these structures. Thus, be aware of the fact that belief is highly subjective. It boggles the imagination of most entities to try to contemplate and to understand how something that appears so ubiquitous and overarching as the

---

[21] *Holy Bible*, Matthew 25: 31-35. The parable as channeled was somewhat garbled from its Biblical lines, and so the original story has been located and inserted as per David Wilcock's suggestion.

[22] "The distinction between yourself and others is not visible to us. We do not consider that a separation exists between the consciousness-raising efforts of the distortion which you project as a personality and the distortion that you project as another personality." *Law of One*, Book I, p. 67.

[23] In the sense of the Guidance Systems of Everyman and Woman.

[24] For personal examination of this issue, a good starting point would be www.dreaman.org/usufoirc.html.

[25] Information may be found at www.disclosureproject.com.

mainstream media that you are infiltrated with every day could be actually not entirely believing itself, and actually not entirely informing your belief in a fashion that is most suitable, that is most capable of giving you a true glance of that which is perceived.

Another example that we would share is that of the ruins that have been discovered under the sea off the western tip of that island known as Cuba. These ruins include structures that look just like your Stonehenge, structures that look like pyramids of those step-pyramid varieties known in Mexico and in the central Yucatan area, and even those known as sphinxes. These structures also have inscriptions on them that are clearly written. The problem, as seen by your geologists, is that these structures are only seen as being capable of being above water as early as 11,000 of your years ago.[26] Now, it is the combined team of Paul Weinzweig and Paulina Zelitsky of Advanced Digital Communications, or ADC, that gained permission from the Cuban government, through Fidel Castro, to take sonar readings of these areas, and thereby make a study, as previously the Communist regime in Cuba did not allow such undersea analyses to be conducted. Recognize as well that it has been publicly announced that these entities did sign a contract with the National Geographic Corporation to then bring forth a documentary to the public. Recognize as well that of course, nothing further has occurred, and that this story has never been covered except on certain internet media, such as MSNBC.[27]

Therefore, what we see is something that potentially is an earth-shaking paradigm shift, something that gives the definitive smoking-gun proof that there is a civilization before the one that you now know, and that it exists right now on your sea bottom—that it has been discovered, that it has been photographed. The evidence already exists and has been seen. And yet, it is by virtue of the pall of consensus reality that is drawn over the eyes of many in their desire to believe in what they are being presented that this information goes unreported, and that it is still possible for those entities around you to make choices which say to themselves that there is nothing mysterious in the universe, that there is nothing beyond that which is in three dimensions and is right in front of one's face, that there is no history beyond that which is taught in your books and your texts.

We would ask that you understand more fully now how it is that belief has been instructed, and not necessarily having the greatest degree of discernment in the instruction. Furthermore, we would ask that you understand that faith is a choice, in the beginning. Faith is a choice of moving outside of that which is necessarily presented for you to be spoon-fed as a belief. Faith, as has been expressed by the entity Q'uo, is that of the ineffable. It is not something that can be easily defined. There is no empirical equation or formula that will give you the necessary ingredients to experience faith; that will give you the necessary discernment to understand if your faith is indeed that which will consist of that which is for your highest and best good, or whether there are those aspects that are in conflict.

We say again, therefore, that these underlying support structures of free will, or that which was termed as the first distortion of the Law of One[28], gives that which does inform faith, and does inform experience. If you can understand how important it is not to infringe on others, you then have the game of karma understood, and never again will you have to experience those balancing acts where you are once again brought back to that undifferentiated state of unity by having those karmic events occur.

We want you also to recognize the flipside of karma, and this is where faith becomes so important. The flipside of karma is equally automatic. So many of your people get tied up in the idea that bad karma is destined to happen, and you, in a sense, fear the Lord your God. Recognize that you are just as amply rewarded for the good things you do as for the negative. It is so easy for many of you, however, to

---

[26] Information may be found in Kevin Sullivan's article, "In Cuban Depths, Atlantis or Anomaly?" Images of Massive Stones 2,000 Feet Below Surface Fuel Scientific Speculation. Washington Post Foreign Service, Thursday, October 10, 2002; Page A25, www.washingtonpost.com/wp-dyn/articles/A3507-2002Oct9.html

[27] More information may be found at www.dwij.org/pathfinders/linda_moulton_howe/linda_mh8.html.

[28] *Law of One*, Session 13. "RA: The intelligent infinity discerned a concept. This concept was discerned to be freedom of will of awareness. This concept was finity. This was the first and primal paradox or distortion of the Law of One. Thus the one intelligent infinity invested itself in an exploration of many-ness. Due to the infinite possibilities of intelligent infinity there is no ending to many-ness. The exploration, thus, is free to continue infinitely in an eternal present."

become aware of karma and to become more aware of the negative transpirations as they appear for balanced proportions rather than those of positive feedback for that which you are doing that spreads light and love to others.

Therefore, when you are serving, it is not in vain. We are not asking that you serve as a system of reward or punishment. We are not asking that you do this as a Pavlovian system where, if you hear a bell, you will receive a food pellet to encourage salivation. Rather, we are asking that you understand how it is that by melting into the joy and the beauty of that world of energy that exists beyond the threshold of light speed, you come into an awareness of the scientific reality of the fact that you are connected with all others. Therefore, anything that you would do to another is that which is done to yourself, and you understand beyond any shadow of doubt that there can be no other act but service. Even if you appear to be doing things that are selfish, this too is a service, for the Creator aspect has both the Shiva qualities of destruction and those qualities that would build up and renew and mend fences and heal. But this healing energy does often come through as a result of the destroyer aspect of Creation. Both yin and yang flow together in divine symmetry and proportion, and your life is a balance of this.

We have said that to be harvestable you must be slightly above fifty percent service-to-others polarity. There is still a great degree of service to self within the self [at this point]. Therefore, it is wise to comprehend the idea that there are those aspects that in your historical traditions would be known as "sins" that can still exist within you, these drives that you may have towards service-to-self behavior. And by simply accepting and healing and renewing the fact that these exist, you are coming into a greater degree of faith.

Faith, therefore, is not simply having the faith that you will promote yourself to a point where these distortions will not exist. Rather, faith is the belief that you can have the distortions, that you can have certain blind spots. You can have certain areas where you may rub against something that is not comfortable as you go through life, and nevertheless that point of discomfort is that which calls your attention to becoming ever more optimal in your energetic functions as a divine being.

The more that you understand these principles, the more that you recognize how it is that you can build up the line-of-light spiraling energy within yourself; the more you can again spiral higher and higher into your own awareness. [It is then] that you can see that belief is a choice, and that faith is more of an understanding. Faith is simply an allowing of yourself to be that which you are. There is a certain genius of motivation that must be present in order for you to make this leap into faith, and hence the term "leap of faith" is often used.

You have plenty of evidence that you could choose to "believe," that would allow you to think that faith could not exist, by virtue of the fact that you exist in a Godless universe, or so it would seem when there are so many injustices or apparent injustices around you. In a grander vision of faith, you understand that you can have faith in the process of karma. You can have faith in the process [so] that when you do something that is of service-to-self nature, it will be balanced.

You can have faith in the fact that there is no judgment when this is done, contrary to what many of your peoples have thought. There is no judgment. All experiences are acceptable, and you can move through these experiences, accept yourself as they are happening, and accept yourself in the realization that will allow you to get down to a deeper layer of the onion, so to speak.

And of course, as you do this there are many tears that will be shed. But as you get deeper and deeper into your core, you come into a grander understanding of the positive aspect, which is that by simply allowing yourself to be present with others, to be present in that moment of opening the heart to the Christ self, of opening the heart to universal freedom, to universal bliss, that you have become undifferentiated. And in that moment, if even for just a slight touch of a thought, you can grandly experience the true ineffable nature of your being, where faith becomes a living process, a living consciousness. [It is] a consciousness that transcends all boundaries, all distinctions, that exists in the ever-present now and that is yours in that moment when you have that breathtaking joy and bliss, the true knowledge that you have never been left behind, that you have never been abandoned.

(Side one of tape ends.)

And thus, even in those moments when you have no faith, when you have no belief, the structure exists. And this is a structure that loves you. It is a structure that has an identity. You can think of that identity as the Christ self. You can think of that identity as your Buddha nature. You can think of that identity as the part of yourself that is the one infinite Creator, such that when you are looking into the mirror, you see the face of the one infinite Creator. You see this face when you look into the faces of others. You see this face in the environment all around you. You see this face, indeed, in everything and everyone.

And as these boundary lines and distinctions melt away, you understand that faith and belief also melt away, in a sense. For you become the living embodiment of belief and the living embodiment of faith. Again, we say that it is not necessarily plausible to fully apprehend this in each and every moment, as this requires a great deal of work on the self. But, rather, we do want you to understand that if your humble efforts are significant enough and sufficient enough, then you can indeed tap into this pure state of consciousness. Even just a few moments of it can fill you with the wellspring of emotion and joy that will [allow you to] shed tears as freely as a flowing river. Once again you know that you have never been left behind, that you have always been protected, always been loved and always been cared for, now and forever. Amen.

At this time we return the microphone to that entity now known as Q'uo, and we thank you for this time that we have shared.

(Carla channeling)

We are those of Q'uo, and we are again with this instrument. Grasping the dominance within third-density of that distortion known as the Law of Confusion or free will, it may become clearer why the third-density illusion is made in such a way that it shall always be impossible completely to satisfy the requirements of proof for spiritual truth. It is necessary within third density that all choices to believe in spiritual matters in a certain way be made completely in freedom, that freedom that only exists when there is no proof and it is a matter of faith.

The instinct shall always be within the human breast to reach out to that energy that it senses as being greater than it is. Many are the stories told about this mystery of the Creator, the Logos, the Grandfather, the Father/Mother God. There are many and many a name, and many a story, and in each name and in each story some may find comfort. And in the words that those entities have said that were written down, or that were written down on behalf of these entities, some may find tremendous and substantial resources. Therefore, the spiritual panoply of riches lies open to the seeker. Yet what shall be that which increases faith? What shall be that for you this day?

The nature of faith is that it is a state of consciousness. It is a state of consciousness that already exists within you, within each spark of the Creator, within each of Its children. Not that this can be proven, but that it is the truth that calls the spiritual seeker to awaken, and, once awakened, that calls that seeker onward and onward to find that for which it thirsts and for which it hungers.

We suggest to you that that which aids in inducing that particular state of mind that opens the heart to the awareness of that consciousness state that is unconditional love is that which is available to each of you each day. It is that time which, like this meditation, must be gouged out of a day that is already so crowded with good things to do. It is that time when you give yourself to silence. It might be only a five minute silence, but if it begins your day, or ends your day, it may completely change the attitude with which you look at that which lies before you when you open your eyes.

So we encourage each of you in your own way to find some silence, either by walking in nature, by silent meditation, by taking an image and moving into contemplation from gazing at the rose, or the sunset, as the one known as T was speaking of, or whatever visualization or image takes the mind beyond itself so that it rests in beauty and in truth.

The essence of faith is a realization that all is well, and that that which is needed is in hand. All that you need is coming to you. All that you do not need is falling away. The processes of a loving and nurturing Creator insure that all is well, and that all will be well. Not as the world in which each of you experiences the illusion of life might define wellness, and yet this core attitude, this point of view that states unequivocally and without proof that all is well, is as that seed that grows every time the sun shines, that sun which is the open heart.

This instrument is fond of saying, "Center. Move back to the Center." What are your thoughts this day? Where is your center? Upon what do you rest?

We would transfer this contact as we make this last point. We would transfer this contact to the one known as Jim, that we may address any shorter queries that remain within the minds of this group. We thank this instrument and we leave it in love and in light.

(Jim channeling)

We are those of Q'uo.

David: Can the entity speak to the opposite side of faith and belief, which is when one is scared, when one exists in fear, so that we may better understand the process of balancing, and that we may experience faith without the weight that this fear imposes upon the self?

I am Q'uo, and am with this instrument, and we greet each again in love and in light through this instrument. We are aware of your query, my brother.

As entities begin the conscious journey of seeking that which you may call the truth, and begin to ask those questions of which we spoke at the beginning of this session, seeking to know who is the self, what is this love, what is it that the seeker believes about this life and the journey through it, the fruits of continued seeking for truth; when the seeker begins to fashion some form of concept or quality that answers for it one query or another in relation to those fundamental queries asked by all seekers, this gathering of beliefs, shall we say, is as the beginning of the journey, during which there may be many difficult moments which challenge the beliefs.

There may be fear, doubt, confusion, anger, grief, jealousy and so forth. Each instance of the challenging of beliefs gives the seeker of truth an opportunity to call upon a more, shall we say, nebulous feeling, that being the quality of faith, that is slowly, quietly and assuredly developing as the seeking continues, as the attempt to answer these queries continues, as the facing of difficult catalyst continues.

Therefore, this quality of faith is powered by what you may call the exercise of will; the continuing to seek, the renewing of the thirst, the asking again of questions, the getting up when catalyst brings one to one's knees. To continue, seek relentlessly, persistently, without fail. Even if there is failure to seek at one time, there is the renewal of the seeking at another. Thus, the exercising of the will is that which builds this quality of faith within each seeker; that which will nourish the seeker when the catalyst is fierce, when the doubts rage, when the anger boils, when harsh words are spoken, when relationships are shattered.

The faith, then, is that which rises from the very soul, being called forth by the continual exercise of will in the face of all catalyst, that which you may call good, that which you may call bad. Therefore, we recommend to each that the will be featured and focused upon as one faces all catalyst, including those of the negative nature.

Is there another query at this time?

V: I have one, and with Q'uo's permission, I would like to direct this one to David's Guidance System. As has been done by those of Q'uo and by those of Ra, I would very much like to hear from David's Guidance System what is their point of origin and their identifying vibration?

(David channeling)

We are the Guidance System of that entity known as David, and we have heard your query and shall respond in due course. Understand that the entity, David, has been working with us for some measure of time in various incarnative states, and that we exist through a triumvirate system, or a tripartite system, if you will, meaning that there are three essential aspects. There is, of course, the sixth-density aspect of that known as the higher self or oversoul of the entity David, and this source is the same source as that which spoke in the Law of One material. However, it is wise to reflect on the fact that to have a pure and undifferentiated sixth-density contact requires a great deal of tuning and the assistance of other selves.

It has been the status of David's work up until this time that there was not the capability to bring forth others to the process of this seeking, and therefore we may reflect on the fifth-density aspect of self which also exists for each entity. These aspects may be many in number, but it is very common, as you would think of it, for there at least to be one aspect which is of the masculine propriety or gender in its overall energetic bias, and one entity which is of the overall feminine bias. This refers back to material that is spoken of in the earliest sessions of David's material, whereby the masculine aspect introduced itself with the archetypal sound vibration complex of

Grandfather, and whereby the feminine aspect introduced itself with the archetypal sound vibration complex of Lucia, or Light. Therefore, we see the interesting paradox of the fact that the feminine principle is named after Light, and the masculine principle is named after Love, as many souls have the opportunity to love their grandfather.[29]

And so, what we would ask for you to visualize is simply that we stand before you as three, that there is a process of dissemination of information that involves the inspiration from the higher self which is then transduced through these fifth-density contacts to then impinge upon the energetic fields of that entity known as David, so that the speaking may then occur. We trust that this is as satisfactory of an answer as we are wont to give at this time, and we thank you for your query.

We ask if there is another query present at this time, that it may be posed to any of the three channels on this day.

J2: I have one query and this is directed towards David's Guidance System. I am a bit confused sometimes about clockwise and counter-clockwise in the use of the spiral needles. I just wanted to ask if the clockwise motion is actually pulling energy out of the body, or is pulling energy and light into the body, if this is correct or if it is in the opposite.

We are those of David's Guidance System, and we thank you for your query. It is wise for others to understand the context in which this question has been asked. Recently there has come to the attention of David the work of those Russian scientists that has brought forth new meaning to the understanding of torsion fields, or the spiraling wave of consciousness. There are waves that are of clockwise movement, and that propagate through the vacuum, or aether, as such, as well as those of counter-clockwise movement.

There is also the entity known as Dr. Alexandr Shpilman, who has designed a device which does then create either a left-handed or a right-handed torsion beam. These beams do then have a very beneficial effect in either capacity, by virtue of the fact that this is the energy that feeds the body. There are those times in which entities wear clothes that are made of the synthetic materials which do then act as a torsion shield, such as those known as polyester, and this does then impinge upon the amount of torsion fields that are brought into the body.[30]

There are those upon your plane known as non-eating saints, who do not have to ingest food and water and such, but rather draw directly off of this spiraling energy for their total sustenance and support. Therefore, what we are dealing with in the question of these needles is a particular design of metallic substance that does then have the archetypal shape of the spiral worked into the end of the needle; that spiral known as the phi ratio, of that of 1 to 1.618 in proportion.[31]

Understand that by creating a needle with this configuration, there is a funnel produced, so to speak, for this energy to be circulated. Therefore, what the question deals with is the difference between the left-handed and the right-handed beam, or that of the counter-clockwise or left as opposed to the clockwise or right-handed beam. It is the left-handed beam which actually brings energy into the body and its aura systems. This beam is that which is more fundamental to the basic energy and structure of consciousness.

However, just like any other process of consciousness in your system, there is that which must be purged and released. Similarly, you can eat but you also must excrete in order to remain healthy. Therefore, you see the right-handed beam or the clockwise beam as representing that which takes energy out of the body. Therefore, the needles can be used in such a fashion. We thank you for your query.

J2: Thank you.

Carla: Is there a final query at this time, for anybody?

(Pause)

(Jim channeling)

I am Q'uo. As it appears that we have exhausted the queries for the moment, we shall once again thank each present for inviting us to join you in your circle

---

[29] In the *Law of One* series, Light/Wisdom is often associated with the masculine archetype and Love with the feminine.

[30] Information may be found at www.rialian.com/rnboyd/spin-torsion.htm.

[31] Information may be found at www.mcs.surrey.ac.uk/Personal/R.Knott/Fibonacci/phi.html#golden.

of seeking this day. It is always a great pleasure and privilege for us to be asked do so. We would also remind each that we are available to aid in the deepening of your meditation. A simple request, mentally sent, is all that is necessary. We shall speak no words but simply blend our vibrations with yours in order that your meditation may be deeper and more centered.

At this time we shall take our leave of this instrument, leaving it and this group in the love and in the light of the one infinite Creator.

We are those known to you as Quo. Adonai, my friends. ✣

L/L Research

L/L Research is a subsidiary of Rock Creek Research & Development Laboratories, Inc.

P.O. Box 5195
Louisville, KY 40255-0195

www.llresearch.org

Rock Creek is a non-profit corporation dedicated to discovering and sharing information which may aid in the spiritual evolution of humankind.

ABOUT THE CONTENTS OF THIS TRANSCRIPT: This telepathic channeling has been taken from transcriptions of the weekly study and meditation meetings of the Rock Creek Research & Development Laboratories and L/L Research. It is offered in the hope that it may be useful to you. As the Confederation entities always make a point of saying, please use your discrimination and judgment in assessing this material. If something rings true to you, fine. If something does not resonate, please leave it behind, for neither we nor those of the Confederation would wish to be a stumbling block for any.

CAVEAT: This transcript is being published by L/L Research in a not yet final form. It has, however, been edited and any obvious errors have been corrected. When it is in a final form, this caveat will be removed.

© 2009 L/L RESEARCH

SPECIAL MEDITATION
FEBRUARY 19, 2003

Question from R: What are the disciplines, prerequisite, attitudes and practices that are helpful to me in order to open my indigo-ray center to intelligent infinity at the present time?

Carla channeling:

We are those of the principle known to you as Q'uo and we greet you in the love and in the light of the one infinite Creator in Whose service we are. It is our privilege to be called to this group and we thank the one known as R for this query and the seeking and hungering for the truth that brought this entity to request information that may aid in the evolution of mind, body and spirit. We thank as well those who sit with this group in service and in an equally pure search for the truth. These energies that move into the sphere of this working create that vibration upon which we are able to stabilize and establish this particular channel through this group and through this instrument. It is our distinct pleasure to offer our humble opinions upon this most interesting question of information concerning the opening of the gateway to intelligent infinity.

We would ask that, in order for free will to be respected, each who receives these thoughts feels completely free to disengage the self from any of them which do not seem correct at this time. Those thoughts which are part of the subjective truth of that particular individual at that particular space and time will be very resonant and will seem as though remembered, rather than learned for the first time. Those thoughts that do not seem resonant are those thoughts that we would ask you to leave behind. We thank each for respecting this request, for it allows us to speak freely without being concerned that we will be taken as authorities rather than as your brothers and sisters in seeking and in service.

The request of the one known as R for information is exquisitely phrased and we would thank the one known as R for the care and love with which he crafted this expression of seeking for the truth of the moment, the space, the time, and the ever-full expression of appreciation and thanksgiving for that process which moves into the present moment as the emerging blossom of transformation, new life and new birth. The request for prerequisites, practices, disciplines and attitude that are helpful is a request made by one who has spent a good deal of time and energy in contemplation of the outer teachings of what this instrument would call unchurched spirituality. The question being couched in the language familiar to those who enjoy the wording of those known as Ra creates an atmosphere in which we may feel free to use the cosmology of this system, which indeed is most concisely described or represented by those known as Ra.

Within this system of cosmology, shall we say, the gateway to intelligent infinity rests above the energy center known as the brow chakra or the indigo-ray chakra and hence the work of indigo ray is that work which has most directly or proximally to do with opening the gateway to intelligent infinity. The discipline of the personality and work in consciousness is the precinct and purpose of this energy center and it is within this center that the practices and disciplines requested dwell, for the most part, in terms of their subject matter.

The attitude is certainly a central key not only to the seeking, pattern and process of the one known as R but also the seeking, pattern and process of each seeker of truth within the creation of the Father. This attitude is such a central key that it becomes as the chief rod and staff that support the seeking of the pilgrim. The preeminent position of attitude is such that, by attitude alone, the entity who dwells in faith and lives fearlessly and in an atmosphere of thanksgiving and gratitude has, by that simple token, entered the gateway of intelligent infinity.

Being fearless is perhaps not as simple as it may seem. And the threads of being that move into the lessons of becoming fearless are those same threads of being that move into the lessons of peace and the discovery of its nature. Indeed, it may be said that the redeemer of the third-density world is that which is known to this instrument as love. For the heart of the attitude which gives thanks for all things is the fearless heart that sees the love in all things, even as it sees the distortions to which love has been bent by those co-creators which are other selves. The process of becoming aware of reasons to be grateful in all things is a long and subtle process and one which ties back into the discipline of the personality.

The part of your query to which we have not yet responded, however, the prerequisites of work at this time for the one known as R in opening the gateway to intelligent infinity, moves back into what we would call the metaphysical past rather than the historical past, within the inner universe of the one known as R, for the prerequisite for doing work in consciousness for any is that progressive and conscientious query of energy centers and the preparation for the promulgation of sacred or priestly work, thus giving respect and honor to that energy of self which is as the entity of sacred or magical energy which functions as the priest or minister of that which is the sacred life, the life that has been consecrated by the ever-opening awareness of previous work in consciousness.

With this entity then, the one known as R, we shall walk through some considerations for the work of preparing for a session of work in consciousness. The basic plan for this work would be to choose a single place and a single time of day within which to do this work. This time would be a time of contemplation and what this instrument would call the balancing meditation. This meditation is one in which recent thoughts and biases of the feelings that have been experienced by the self are examined to determine for the self the possible distortions, both positive and negative, that have resided in these pockets of gathered catalyst and e experience.

The one who reviews the self's thoughts and feelings is as one who goes into the storehouse of its grains to gaze at the harvest and judge its worth. As one winnows through one's thoughts and as one reviews those triggers which have caused responses within the self, one may see those areas of lack and esurience which baffle or otherwise distort the flow of energy through the energy body. It is well, perhaps, to start with that which is the so-called lowest, that first chakra or red-energy center in which reside strong and profoundly meaningful responses to triggers concerned with survival, sexuality and territory. It is very often that issues will become caught in this very basic energy center because of this particular culture within which all of those in this circle enjoy life, and its great dependence upon or emphasis upon sexuality as being central to that root ray or red-ray energy center.

However, within the life experience of all those within this sitting circle, the threat of war has been always imminent and at this time continues so. Consequently, there is an issue common to all of those within your culture at this time which has to do with survival. Further, there are those issues concerned with information of the so-called New Age, as this instrument calls it, information which often suggests the sudden ending of certain processes upon your planetary sphere; thereby, in a lesser but equally disturbing way, suggesting threats to survival. These issues create a background area of interference which may only be addressed when acknowledged, recognized and dealt with as part of that which is the milieu.

Within the next energy center lies that which is most visible among your peoples and yet not that which can be overlooked. The culture which you enjoy and the so-called New Age sub-culture whose opinions often affect the philosophy of, shall we say, the surface culture of your peoples, emphasizes and indeed nearly glorifies personal relationships and consequently it is most likely within your day-to-day discussions and communications and with other selves that the issues which truly are informing and consuming the mind and the emotions are known to the self. It is well, however, to gaze at those patterns which are repetitive which do not seem constructive, for energies within this orange-ray system may well be strengthened and crystallized by such work.

A key indeed is to see each entity within a relationship as a flower of an unique beauty which is better beheld than trimmed or plucked. Again, within that which is called the yellow ray or yellow-ray chakra by this instrument, the culture within which you now dwell is likely to bring to the conscious attention of each the over-stimulations and desires for avoidance which are part of the relations of the self such as the family group of birth, the family group created by the marriage of self and other self, the group created by the working for the living and so forth. Again, these interactions are the stuff of gossip as well as the material for learning within the curricula of the school of Earth in third density. However, within these group systems, may we say that nothing is as it seems, in terms of the value of group structures within the learning processes of the self. We can only say that the value of this system of learning which is bound up in the concept of family, clan and other group concepts cannot be overestimated. It is in this direction that progressive concepts may open new ways of seeing that indeed strengthen and further open the yellow-ray chakra in such a way as to improve the orientation towards the green-ray energy center and that tremendous shift of energy which may come as the heart opens.

The next energy center, moving upwards, to consider in terms of the experiences of the day, is that known as the green-ray energy center and in this wise we may say that this is the beginning of work in consciousness. When one has been able to address the issues and look into the feelings and distortions and energies experienced within that portion of the lower energy body, then the entity is ready to move into the open heart, having secured a good flow of energy, that energy of the one infinite Creator, through the roots of the energy system of the physical vehicle into that energy system which does indeed open to the gateway of intelligent infinity as that infinite energy roars through in its ceaseless dance of upward spiraling light.

The heart chakra is not that which is worked with as much as it is that which is entered, as one with great gratitude enters the holy place in which one is safe, loved, cared for, and appreciated as a child of the one infinite Creator, a child and an heir, a rightful and loving heir, and, indeed, a co-Creator. The space of the heart is that which is filled with the balm of Gilead. It is that which beams and radiates as the sun. It is that in which there is no effort, strife, or worry but only the feeling of loving arms, a strong and loving chest and shoulders to rest [the head] upon when one is weary; a capacious lap to sit in, to nestle in, to curl into and to go to sleep in when one is exhausted within the heart. This is the energy of healing, the energy of unbridled and unstinted compassion. This energy is that energy that is the steady state of the creation of the Father, that vibration which is the essence of the one great original Thought of the infinite Creator.

Resting upon the energy of this center, resting upon the open heart, it is then that the disciplines of the personality begin. That which is the blue-ray center or the throat chakra is the seat of the discipline of creating true communication, true speech, and true statements. It is the seat wherein one discovers the art of listening. And these disciplines feed into those conduits that lead to communication that runs clear, as the stream that does not pick up the mud and the silt of the storm but, rather, lets energies be as they express and as they resound and as they ripple, not so much judging as praising the beauty of the ripples, not so much resisting as dancing with the patterns that emerge.

The one known as R has tremendous amounts of dedication and energy in the area of the indigo-ray work and is well aware of issues which it focuses upon at this time, and we would not infringe upon the free will of the one known as R by commenting more closely. We do not believe that there is any lack in this portion of the creative and intentional work in service of the one known as R but, rather, that this entity focuses with great care and love and persistence at this time. As this entity indicates by the very shape of its query, it is well aware of its need to move always back into the whole self as a prerequisite to doing work in consciousness. It is when the bottom is firmly planted and well placed on the ground of true small things that the spirit may soar. It is when the first story of the house of a life is swept and tidied that one may go to the upper room, there to be lifted up into midair with the angels. Let that first floor first be neat as a pin, with each honor which is also a duty seen to, each promise kept, each relationship honored, each thread of self within found like the lost sheep, brought into the loving heart, kept warm, comforted and fed until the self is as loved as those loved ones that are about one, until the self is also seen as the Creator, as the Christ, as the child of the one infinite Creator, utterly worthy of love.

To become fearless is not the work of a moment or a year, yet it is the work of any within a lifetime. At least there is goodness in the intent to discover the nature of true release from fear. For there are two choices: contraction into fear, or expansion into love. It is the nature of work in consciousness that it does not proceed well unless there is first established full energy into the heart and the resting within the heart in unconditional love. With this energy flowing through the heart, the work that is done in consciousness is well powered, well fueled, well supported.

Above all, we would encourage a releasing of heaviness. It is a time within your peoples' experience when there is every energetic reason to become more and more wound up, distracted by the nature of the illusion. Yet this is precisely the time when it will be most effective to express, in whatever way is felt appropriate, those positive feelings having to do with the certainty that all is well. For as the fourth density becomes closer and closer, it becomes more and more important to remember the increasing transparency of thought to materialization. Thoughts are becoming things. States of mind are becoming DNA. Lean into, then, the advantages of an increasingly metaphysical atmosphere. If there is a fear-based concept which moves into the awareness of the self, encourage the promulgation of a positive gratitude and confidence-based response. For there is love in each situation, and the expression of that love is as the sun that radiates and warms the chilled soul.

Lift up the heart. Lift up the eyes. Lift up the hands. And lift up the voice in singing and praise and thanksgiving and in joy. The opportunity to express and bear witness at a time of such powerful illusion and seemingly unlimited potential is a wonder. We bless the journey and celebrate the process of the one known as R and encourage him always to keep the light touch in the seeking that honors the ideals of the self beyond all words and yet may take the self lightly.

We leave this instrument with blessings upon its sacred and glowing round, and we offer to this entity our presence within the silent communication in order that we may aid in deepening the meditation for this entity whenever this entity might wish to request our presence mentally. We thank this instrument, this group, and the questioner known as R, and we leave this group in the love and in the light of the one infinite Creator.

We are known to you as those of Q'uo. Adonai. Adonai, vasu, borragus.

Sunday Meditation
March 2, 2003

Group question: The question today has to do with, what we, as we talked around the circle perceived, as an increase in the level of energy, the tension, the intensity, the amount of things and difficulty that people are going though. And we had the idea that maybe what's happening for people now is they are reflecting this increased energy by having whatever catalyst [that] is ready to come up in their lives come up—whether it's getting out of one relationship and into another or transitioning from one place to another, one life to another. We'd like to have some information on whether this might be a correct perception. Any type of elaboration on this topic would be appreciated as well.

(David channeling)

We speak as the Guidance System of the entity now known in this sojourn as David Wilcock. We express our heartfelt gratitude for the opportunity to be present this day upon the cusp of the awakening of the human spirit and the treasures that are cherished in those moments of quiet solitude when the distinctions of self and other-self melt away in the blinding light of realization once duly applied to the conditions of personality. We approach you from a perspective of knowing that you are not separate beings, and of seeing you in your totality, as you exist even now.

In this totality your experience is a great chain of being. It is a chain that continues to cycle through the gears of your life and thus it is a chain-driven life, so to speak. As you move through these experiences you have opportunities to choose how you will label them and identify them in your mind. We have frequently spoken in these sessions of the importance of stepping outside of the perspective of right and wrong, good and evil or of joy and suffering and to simply remain steadfast in the understanding that the creation moves in cycles of creation and destruction. There are those times for the building of stones, there are those times for the casting away of stones.[32] The perspective of the present moment is the focus that allows you not to get caught up in the dramas and mundane realities of apparent daily living as expressed through "ordinary" circumstances, as this word is then used to describe the rather immobilized state in which most of your people exist at this time.

The lack of mobility comes from the fact that there are blockages in your energy centers, or chakras, and those blockages only allow for a certain portion of the light/love energy of creation to stream and flow through you properly. The question pertains to the exact nature of how these blockages are being opened up by virtue of the shifting energies that are

---

[32] *Holy Bible*, Ecclesiastes, 3:5.

present in your time/space and space/time nexus. We have spoken of this in the last session and the session before, and thus we do not need to repeat information. Suffice it to say that, as of your date, February 19, 2003, you have crossed the next major hurdle in terms of intergalactic astrology. You are now moving into a higher zone of energy, to put it in the simplest possible terms.

When there is a heightened amount of energy on your plane, there is the opportunity for the cleansing of those aspects of self that have so far remained cloaked in cobwebs and stuffed away in some far corner of the closet of your mind, so that you are not capable of truly bringing them out and looking upon that which you have chosen to hide away. Now is the time to step outside of those boundaries and distinctions that have limited you to the perspective of seeing yourself as an ego, as a personality that is beset with various experiences that are of a less than positive nature, and thereby [as one] experiencing a certain sense of despair and longing for a life that is somehow separate from that which you have previously obtained. If you could but recognize that you are truly divine, that you are truly pure love and pure light in this moment; if you could see things as we do, you would recognize that any distortions that you may have in your personality are just brimming with light and love, waiting to spill over the fences and burst into your awareness, much as would the crashing of the tidal wave sweep away those pockets of civilization that had grown up and allowing for there to be a cleansing and renewal thereafter.

Now, of course many of your people might think of these earth changes as being negative in nature. However, it is more akin to the idea of lancing of boils on the skin that have grown too large. Recognize that these boils are in your mind. These boils are in the patterns in which you have lived your life. It is a pattern that extends itself through every activity and focus of your sphere. These patterns have enabled you to continue enacting the same behaviors without really thinking about what you are doing. You consider that you are apart from your experiences, that your experiences are happening somewhat automatically, and that you do not have the power or the ability to change them. You see these forces as acting around you, swirling and spiraling, seemingly chaotic, out of your control.

It is our perspective, this perspective of boundless light and limitless love from which we look down upon you, [that we] recognize how carefully you have created every single aspect of that which exists in your sphere of influence. And therefore you can never have any sense of guilt or blame towards others for that which you have experienced.

Now is the time, for many of these lily pads will be forming on the surface of your lake. You will have the opportunity to skip from one to the other, skipping away from the shoreline of limited possibility and moving out towards the horizon where the sun is again rising in your life and where you have the opportunity for the dawning of the new phase of your awareness. This time is one of growth, healing and renewal. It is a time where you do not have to be the wizard any more and try to cook up these elaborate and arcane spells and magical tricks that will allow you to function somehow within the distorted circumstances that previously existed. Now is the time for you to step outside of the need to "cook the books" with wizardry and to try arcanely to adjust yourself to that which has already been in place. What has been in place will have these upheavals that you had not planned on and that therefore it will be falling away. Your opportunity now is to bless this process instead of trying to fight against it. The energy will seem to move so fast that you have not the time really to consider your actions but rather simply make these actions. This is the case in the lives of those of the L/L Research Team and that of David Wilcock at this time, since there has been a partnership that has been engendered. This is but a subset of the much larger gestalts of change and consciousness of fluid movement that are occurring within the human energy field, as a totality-consciousness, in its own limited state. This moves towards greater concrescence[33] with each step of consciousness, much as do all the rivers pour into the sea.

So, too, you can allow yourself to refrain from blaming yourself over the past; to refrain from having any sense of shame over those opportunities that you have missed. Now you have the purest of opportunities to start everything afresh, to have a complete tabula rasa, a blank slate, on which you can etch your own engravings. It is the engraving on the tombstone of the life that you have left behind. You can allow this death to occur, you can bless the death

---

[33] concrescence: the act of growing or increasing by spontaneous union.

within yourself and recognize that from death comes life. From this change comes renewal, comes prosperity, and comes the opportunity once again to revivify within the heart the longings of desire that have welled towards seeking to know the face of the one infinite Creator and recognizing that face as your own.

When you have these opportunities present before you, it is akin to stepping in front of the mirror and seeing a new visage, a new conception of your own being. We recognize that there is a great deal of apparent suffering that is involved in these transitions. It may not seem evident or obvious that these transitions are good or beneficial. Instead you may find yourself experiencing more and more a sense of despair over what you have left behind and, in a certain sense, expecting to be paid back by the universe for all the sacrifices that you have been asked to make. We would ask that you simply look beyond the apparent disorder and dysfunction of that which is occurring, and instead recognize the perfection that comes in the joy of sacrifice, in the giving up of those aspects that have not suited you, including the releasing of many physical possessions, as is the case with the L/L Research team and with many others on your plane.[34]

By allowing yourself to step outside of the boundaries that have encircled your consciousness, you allow those previous dispositions that have weighed on your consciousness to fall by the wayside. And you find that it is only by cutting these tethers that your hot air balloon is then allowed to rise so that you can once more alight into the heavens and find a greater sense of peace and stability and renewal from the light that becomes yours, in those moments when you have overturned the false longings of the past by recognizing that those cards were dealt to you by your choice. Since you have chosen every aspect of your reality, you chose the very things that you would put your heart's desire on, the things that you would wish for, the things that you would desire for most deeply in your heart. Some of these desires that you have had may include the desire to prolong a situation that is not in your highest and best good. You may find that you desire for a situation to be better without realizing that there are [other alternatives]; other fish in the ocean, other wildlife outside of your own forest.

In one sense, it could be seen as wild living to step outside of this pattern of predescribed distortion and habitual circlings around the same target of interest. However, you can also step outside of having any blame over yourself for having desired these aspects of stability or apparent stability. Now is the time for the overturning of the patterns that have become well worn, as would ruts grave themselves into the roads where the ancient wagons once traversed. How easy it is to allow these shifts to happen, once you understand that you can let go of your pride, of your ego feeling dissatisfied unless you can make the best out of a situation that has become dysfunctional.

We would ask that you also look upon your political sphere at this time. Many of you are now falling out of love with the idea of a benevolent government that will save you from the fears and the illnesses of the outside world. The terror that can be bestowed upon those who would be jealous of your freedom, so to speak, has been presented by those of your American sphere at this time.

The events that occurred on February 15[35] are recognized very strongly in higher consciousness as an event whereby the collective free will of humanity has voted to have a higher consciousness on the planet. We would ask that you think back to the Law of Squares as it was defined in the Law of One series and recognize that for each entity that marched, of which there were approximately six to ten million, there are an infinitely larger number of requests that are made by virtue of the intent to serve that stand behind these entities, and by virtue of the fact that your Logos is biased in the direction of service-to-others polarity. When you understand this, you step outside of those feelings of despair or doom that hang over your head.

There are many times in your individual life where you will have an experience that appears that something negative is going to happen to you. In the preparation of the self for said negative event, there are those appropriate shifts and realizations that are made in consciousness. You come to understand that, because of the bourgeoning event that is

---

[34] Both David and Vara were moving from independent domiciles into one room. For Jim and Carla, the giving up of two of the rooms of their living space also resulted in a grand paring down of material goods.

[35] On this date, millions of Americans and those all over the world protested for the cause of peace.

transforming you, you can let go of many things that have formed stopping-blocks and holding points in your life in the past. Now you have the opportunity to let them go by the wayside. It is only after you make these shifts that you discover that the negative event itself does not need to transpire, as what was truly required was the change in consciousness and not the essence of actually going through said event.

Similarly, there are many scenarios being bandied about regarding the idea of apocalyptic doom or nuclear conflagration or some other aspect of mass destruction that would take you outside of your zones of comfort and put you into a "Mad Max scenario," as some would call it, some form of complete disruption and chaos. There are adjustments that are being made to planetary consciousness. There are carefully placed strictures involved in what your negative elites are actually capable of performing in terms of physical acts on your plane.

Thusly you see the detention of one known as Jose Padilla, who was accused of having been a terrorist without any supporting information and was apprehended and held in Guantanamo Bay, Cuba, without being able to contact his lawyer or otherwise have access to the normal rights in the Constitution. From this one case, one may project a fear that this will become commonplace; that ordinary anti-war protesters will be denied their citizenship and herded off to detention camps or such things. Since the beginning of our work with David, we have always stated that although these potentialities would appear to be possible, that they will never actually arise into physicality. This is by virtue of the fact that your planet is essentially positive and that there are simply not enough of your peoples who are willing to turn their backs upon others, especially within their own country, and in so doing, create this nightmare scenario that is such a virtual re-depiction of previous negative scenarios on your plane. Therefore, you can choose to have a fear reaction, if you want to, to the events that are transpiring on the Earth at this time. However, we would ask that you make this choice with the understanding that it is only useful to you insofar as it leads you to make realizations about your own life. To put it in a more blunt fashion we can say that as you fall out of love with your negative elite and no longer seek to give them the god-like status that the media would convey, you also take yourself off of the pedestal that you have erected and recognize the ways in which you yourself have allowed negative situations to propagate and to fester. When you become more and more cognizant of the ways in which some of these negative actions in the grand political scheme play themselves out in your own world, you begin to understand how ascension truly occurs.

As we have said, ascension is a process not a conclusion. Ascension is not something that you are simply going to watch happen in newspaper headlines. It is an intimately personal event that transpires within your own life. It is an intimately personal event that transpires within the lives of all as they move in synchrony together, as one, through these energetic changes. And thus we want you to understand that as you will be seeing the dissolution of these strictures on government and on politics in your sphere throughout this year, so too will you have opportunities within your own personal sphere of influence.

Those aspects in which you have had dysfunction with your family members can become renewed into a grander light and a grander love by simply allowing the various distortions of personality to be OK without feeling that you need to identify and classify each little wrong that is done against you and to rage against it, insisting that you will not proceed forward in your life until every item on your laundry list has been duly satisfied and mitigated through intense discussion. Rather it is OK to allow that ego to die, to allow the personality that clings to the idea that all of its needs must be met in that itemized list to fall away.

You are not here to get along with each other and to have everything be perfect. Rather, you are here to agree to disagree, to allow those distinctions that make one different from another simply to stand as they are. If you are in a situation right now, it is best to choose whether or not the situation is acceptable to you as it is right now. Forget about those goals that you have laid upon yourself of how you want things to be, and of what you appear to be working towards with another person in terms of what you would like to have as the eventual outcome for how you will engage in behavioral interactions. Instead, simply accept the situation as it is. Once you do this, then ask yourself if the situation, as it is right now, is indeed suitable for your patterns. What we often find is that when it is not suitable for you, there is a tendency towards the argument and towards the fracturing of your energetic body. This fracturing does cause a wound, and the wound needs to be healed somehow. This often leads to the psychic vampire effect, where you will attack those around you and seek to find those little things that are inconsistent and amplify them to such extremes that there is then this great conflagration that unfolds.

We ask you to see that the negative elites in your sphere of American influence are seeking to find anything they can possibly get their hands on to justify bombing Iraq. Your "global village" as a whole is seeing that these [justifications] are ludicrous and certainly inconsistent with any chain of logical thinking. Therefore, the situation that now occurs, with this country desiring to bomb Iraq so strongly, is very similar in many ways to the situations that occur in your own life when you have found your own Saddam Hussein, your own petty tyrant, someone in your sphere whom you have labeled as being the cause of your ills. And that you seek to find any small inconsistency in their behavior that would allow you to feel that you have now the claim ticket, the right, to lash out, to drop your bombs of fury and anger and hatred, to cause that scalding, with the hope that, after you have duly caused shock and awe to occur and your bombing campaign is complete, that you will then have unconditional surrender, and all the petty things that you have wanted will be given to you without conditions and that the white flag will be duly raised before the scorched battlefield.

We ask that you not think about this in terms of anything that is a metaphor, for we are speaking in very literal terms here. We want you to understand that those events that transpire on the physical plane are entirely mirror images of exactly that which is occurring in your own sphere. Thus we ask for you to draw these analogies between what is happening in your own life and in your own mind, and that which is occurring in the world.

The consciousness of humanity in general is moving towards a greater acceptance of others. This persistent anti-war stance that is coming out more and more contains the realization that there is nothing virtuous in bombing others for the sake of their leader being inadequate. Similarly we would ask that you not bomb the other-selves around you for those small fragments of their consciousness that indulge in negativity. We ask that you also become aware of the inventory of overall treatment that you receive, and as we said, to see if it is indeed suitable for you.

You may find yourself being led to quite unexpected circumstances as they shift [your thinking] outside of the perspectives that have encased you in this apparent amber whereby you become like the frozen mosquito in time for millions of years to be fossilized, unable to move, unable to grow, unable to strive towards the light and love of the one infinite Creator. The amber that has encased you is melting. You will ascend with your wings to the firmament and again find the peace that "passes understanding," the peace that moves outside of logical thought or rational/intuitive thinking, either one, and instead moves directly into the zone of being. If you can allow yourself to be, without attempting to have a goal, without attempting to notch things on your bedpost that can say, "I did this," "I did that," "Look at what I have gained," "Look at what I've attained," you move out of having that awareness of past and of future and become in the ever-present and omnipresent Now. You can have this consciousness in this moment as you contemplate the words that we have spoken.

At this time we shall shift this work over to those known as Q'uo for additional perspective on the matters upon which we have spoken. We thank you this day for having had the opportunity to be present with you in this aura of thanksgiving. This is truly a time for the renewal of the human spirit and we are appreciative of the opportunity to catalyze your growth in this matter. We thank you.

(Carla channeling)

We are those known to you as Q'uo, and we greet you in the love and in the light of the one infinite Creator, in whose service we are. It is a great blessing for us to be called to your meeting and we thank each of you for creating this circle of seeking, this opportunity for us to share our thoughts with you. We would ask only that each of you listen carefully to that which we have to say, with an eye to keeping those thoughts which appeal to you and have a resonance to you, and laying aside all those that do not, for we would not wish to constitute a stumbling block to any. We ask that each of you trust your discrimination for there is that within you which recognizes that truth which is yours.

Each within this circle has a tremendous amount of experience at thinking about spiritual structures and the spiritual life. And each realizes already, as the one known as David has said, that there is something going on and there is change in the wind, shall we say. Now let us pull back a bit and gaze at the sphere of consensus reality that this instrument sometimes calls the world of Maya.[36] It is the nature of illusion to appear quite real. It is the nature of reality to be an illusion. The essence that is not illusion is unfindable, existing in potentiality only. All of which you may become aware with your present—or with our present—organs of sense or instrumentation is illusion. You are not moving from a third-density illusion into a fourth-density position of no illusion. You are moving from an illusion in which there is a relatively small amount of light into an illusion in which there is a fuller or more generous brand of light, a different animal, shall we say, a new kind of light that has different characteristics and that supports different life forms, different planes of existence, different lessons, and so forth.

This is occurring within that which the one known as GuS[37] called the time/space continuum. And may we say that we are most grateful to have the good offices as the one known as GuS and it is a great pleasure to work with this beautiful spirit. The experience of each of you, as you begin to become aware of those things which built your question this day, the increased energy, the increased [rate] of change, the increase of suffering, the increase of stressful things, is receiving experience in ways other than they seem on the surface. The third-density kind of light casts a certain construction upon events which transpire within the day-to-day living. The same events gazed at from the standpoint of the next density are seen in a fuller and more generous light. The key to adapting to this time of increased light, increased transparency between third density and fourth density, and increasing amounts of the light of honesty within the self as it matures and grows, is to offer that which is wrapped up in the fuller and more generous light. The information coming into your very body, into the energy system of the body, at this time is information that is light, that is the limitless light of the one infinite Creator, carrying with it overlays of the increasing fourth-density energy which is, as this instrument said in the discussion prior to this "cosmic sermonette," bringing things to the surface that were hidden and making the rough places plane.

The energies of fourth density are those energies which look at distortion with full awareness of the beauty of each distortion and awareness also of those harmonics and harmonies of undertone and overtone that create avenues of progression in which the biases, which may seem less than harmonized, may blossom and open in the sunlight of compassion until a fuller view is seen, a larger area constituting a point of view in which not only can a distortion be seen but also the surrounding energy that creates the distortion and that place which seems to be blocked.

It is, from the third-density point of view, very tempting to make judgments, especially concerning the self. It is very tempting to make these judgments far below the level of conscious thought. In this atmosphere of judgment, whether it is known by the self that the self is judging the self, or whether it is only known to the self that there is judgment against the self and the entity experiences that judgment as being projected from others, yet still there is that spiky, thorny energy of judgment which can catch an entity up into an endless round of self-examination and attempts at healing. So we would suggest that there are things about the fourth-density point of view which are increasingly available to those who look for them.

The fourth-density energy is not an energy in which it is possible to make a judgment. Rather, it is an energy in which distortions are seen in their colors. Let us say there is a different kind of judgment in assessing the beauty, the truth, the purity of a color. Gazing at a distortion it may be seen, shall we say, as green, but is it a beautiful green? Or is it muddy with the overlays of judgment? It is possible in many cases for an entity to sit with the self and ask, "Is this feeling, this color, this bias, a thing of beauty, a thing of honesty, a thing of truth within my being? Or do I carry that which is not intrinsic to myself? Do I carry armor to defend against an enemy? Does this bias carry the pain of self-judgment, the opposite of armoring in which armor is tossed away and the self is flayed by the judgment of the self?"

---

[36] From the Sanskrit Maya, another name for the Hindu goddess, Devi or Sakti, consort of Siva, meaning in Hindu philosophy "illusion." In magical lore, Maya is the densest of all planes that ascend the tree of life.

[37] GuS: Guidance System.

Come to a feeling concerning that bias, that color. See that as yourself and accept that bias, not as a third-density entity would, judging its worth, but as the fourth-density energy would gaze upon any vibration which crossed its path. This enables each entity as a person, as a seeker, to have a way of assessing inner feelings, inner biases, without calling the self in any way incorrect, wrong or unworthy. We do not mean to suggest by this that there is no structure within which one may judge for the self the ethical rightness or wrongness of action. This is indeed a very helpful and driving part of the spiritual life. Metaphysically speaking, entities move from decision to decision, from choice to choice and those choices build the polarity which is intended by the intensity of the desire to make the most positive choices.

What we are attempting to move into here is the pattern wherein entities set, deep within themselves, as the one GuS noted, the habit of being a certain way, the habit of accepting this and that as true about the self and those other things as untrue. As change inevitably occurs, some of those things which have been true concerning an entity change and this process is cumulative, so that many is the person who gazes at the self one day and realizes that a change has occurred and it has been missed until this instant. It is a wonderful time when that realization occurs.

While [each is] the entity who lives within the flesh and bone of third density, we assure each that these changes and disruptions will continue and increase, for there is a time of transformation for this entire planetary entity. The actual changes that are occurring, while exquisitely articulated, are in fact relatively slight. Consciousness among your peoples upon the metaphysical level is heartwarmingly, shall we say, close to jumping that area of resistance which is as the meniscus upon the surface of water, which is as the ocean which runs betwixt the densities, that area of resistance or quantum boundary to cross. You are much advanced as a people in doing this, to the extent that we can begin to address those of Earth as a social memory complex in the metaphysical sense. Certainly there is a good deal of development that shall take place before this process of birthing …

(Side one of tape ends.)

…that work of being, as the one known as GuS has said. Yet in that being you can become far less troubled by yourself by doing what this instrument has called falling in love with the self. This is the essence of the fourth-density way of dealing with distortion. Each is aware of entities they know which have quirks and habits that are laughable or ridiculous. This entity's love of clothes, for instance, is well known to many within this circle. Yet were those within this circle to speak of this quirk of the one known as Carla, their tones would be fond and their voices would hold nothing of judgment but only affection. For it is seen by all others within this circle that the personality shell of this instrument, while silly, is not criminal. It is simply distortion, and each has its patterns of distortions. Thus, each can see that [it] is possible to love the quirks and distortions of another, finding them loveable and forgivable. Yet as this instrument turns its eyes on the self, this instrument, in the past, has been known to judge itself quite harshly for having this predilection and it has, for various portions of time within its life, simply refused to allow itself to purchase any new garments, feeling that it had quite enough. And yet, within this instrument there was the constant craving for something new to put on the body. Is this a clever, intelligent or sensible way to be? No. And yet it was the work of literally decades for the instrument to come to a day in which she gazed at this distortion within herself and realized that she had fallen in love with herself, that she could forgive herself this: that there were, in her newly expanded way of looking at herself, more important things to focus upon than the details of a personality shell.

Once this lack of judgment began to filter into the roots of personality, relaxing this skein of judgment that had netted and twisted itself about the personality shell, that energy to judge the self faded for this instrument, thus freeing the ability of this instrument to love other flawed personality shells and the souls which they contain. The fourth-density attitude begins with the awareness that each entity is divine, yet a portion of that which we may call the "Godhead principle." The physical being, the personality shell, the thoughts of the surface of the mind itself, are layers of an illusion which is held in place by that system of energies which is at this time beginning to falter and weaken, beginning to give way to a fuller and more generous light. Allow and call for this golden light. Know that you are as capable of receiving it as you are as asking for it. We encourage each to begin to find ways to fall in love with the self. This resource that you have within you of forgiveness is extremely powerful and it connects within the tree of mind with those energies which are far more powerful than those archetypal rulers of third density. This is, may we say, a fascinating subject which we could speak upon for some time yet, but this instrument informs us that we must stop speaking and so we accept that it is time for us to release this instrument from discussing that main query.

We would move to the one known as Jim to pick up any brief queries before we would leave this group. We thank this instrument and this group for bearing with us while we attempt to articulate that which is not particularly easy to say in your words. We thank this instrument and we leave it in love and in light. We are those known to you as Q'uo.

(Jim channeling)

I am Q'uo, and we greet each again in love and in light through this instrument. At this time we would ask if there might be any shorter queries to which we may speak in a brief fashion. Is there another query at this time?

(Long pause.)

Carla: I guess not, Q'uo.

(Jim channeling)

I am Q'uo. We are most grateful to each for inviting our presence this day. We realize that we have spoken over-long and we ask your indulgence and your forgiveness for causing you to have to sit for this period of time. We are most grateful for your patience and for your desire to seek that which is loosely called the truth. We share with you that which is our opinion and we ask that you weigh each word carefully, leaving behind any that do not feel right to you. We do not wish to be a stumbling block in any path of seeking.

At this time we would take our leave of this instrument and this group. We are known to you as those of Q'uo. We leave each in the love and in the light of the one infinite Creator. Adonai, my friends. ✤

Sunday Meditation
March 16, 2003

Group question: The question today has to do with how light seems to respond either to impending catastrophe or out and out catastrophe. So many people are marching for peace, now that it seems war is so likely. The women in Rwanda have had a chance to bring the feminine principle and the nurturing of their being into their country now that the men have been killed, pretty much. It almost echoes the veil between the consciousness of conscious mind, and the possibility for two paths, whereas before there was just positivity.

Would Q'uo talk to us about how the possibility of catastrophe and disaster can help to being the light to being in our world today?

(Carla channeling)

We are those of the principle known to you as Q'uo, and we greet you in the love and in the light of the one infinite Creator, in Whose service we are. As always, we thank this group for creating an opportunity for us to share our thoughts and we are most happy to do so on this occasion, with the request, as always, that each evaluate our thoughts on the basis of those thoughts alone and not on the basis of our authority. The resonances of personal truth have nothing to do with authority. We ask you to use your discrimination carefully, for there is much information and much of it is excellent but there is always that precise choice that is possible of that which is truly your own. The great challenge of the maturing spiritual entity is to move beneath the surface of things and to begin to see things not from an historical or political point of view but rather from a spiritual point of view, a stance or attitude which has its basis in those dynamics which truly are functioning within the heart of that situation which is called "history" in its outer manifestations.

The dynamics of harvest for your particular planet at this particular juncture are not those of what could loosely be described as a normal third-density harvest. This instrument has frequently made jokes concerning the status of Earth or Gaia as a planet for juvenile delinquents who have repeatedly flunked third grade at other schools and are finally sent to Earth when it is felt that they are incorrigible.

The profoundly militaristic energies that your peoples experience at this time are, as has been discussed by the one known as J and the one known as Jim, the fruit of repetition and iteration over many civilizations, many wars, and even many planets. Those upon your sphere have experienced misalignments of energies and misjudgments of polarity in honest but misguided efforts to attempt to serve and to grow. And the nature of the decisions which have capitulated previous societies into catastrophe, catastrophic war, the leveling of that which was wealthy and sophisticated to the so-called dark ages, is a pattern that has been repeated not once or twice but many times. Consequently, your present harvest has overtones and undertones from many previous expressions of the iterating mechanism which turns love into fear and fear into aggression. The energies that are present at this time are iterative energies, energies that have become mindless, that have, in a tremendously profound sense, become obsessed, obsessed to the level of the archetype, so that it is as though your harvest expresses the archetype of the lightning-struck tower with an intensity that could only be achieved by mindless repetition past the point of self-knowledge and into a state of mind of slavery of which at this time we see your peoples attempting with ever fresher energy to snap and break the control, so that the human spirit might once again become liberated from this endless round of fear and hostility.

The reason that the so-called disaster is found to have a silver lining is simply that your peoples, beneath the veneer of those decisions made by few which affect the culture or the experience of all, are as the rind of dead energy that is enclosing a very fresh fruit that has been growing from the inside out and is coming to a state of ripeness. Consequently those who are in power at this time, being more of a service-to-self tribe, shall we say, create the apparent history, the apparent news, the apparent on-going story of your peoples. Whereas the true story of your peoples is that story that moves from the heart, that moves from the seed of the fruit that has ripened within the rind of militarized thinking that infects your planet at this time. The inner fruit is healthy. And in times of disaster the rind of militaristic thinking is chipped away and people suddenly become aware that they are alive and in considerable and substantial opposition in feeling and in mind to those militaristic actions which tend to be the agenda of the day for any group of those who hold power at any time.

We cannot say that it is impossible for entities to hold power without becoming service-to-self oriented. We can only say that it is catalyst for all entities to respect those moments when power is offered. Each of you has a power in this situation, each of you who are part of the healthy fruit of Earth, that fruit which is being harvested at this time has that power, passion and energy of a growing, living, thriving being. That energy is of the One, connected to the root, to the womb, to the Earth, to the Mother. The goodness that springs forth in almost all entities' breasts is that goodness which is the truth of the human race, just as the militaristic shell of humanity's behavior is a truth. It is a part of a truth that attempts to take over the entire consciousness of what the human entity is. In assuming that such separating ideas as aggression have worth, the standpoint of those with power is continually biased more and more towards that attitude which accepts the power to change others for the better. This is the innocent beginning of that which can become a monstrous evil, as this instrument would call it.

What a flower does to praise the Creator is blossom. And what each of you may do to praise the Creator is allow yourself to blossom. Those elements of cultural thinking which have infected each mind to whom we speak will show themselves to you with their thorns, their warts, and their scars. And you will gaze upon them and they will not be fair. There will be thoughts of anger, jealousy, retribution. These will not be true thoughts, yet these are thoughts that are pressed upon you daily, and have been since your youth. There is no judgment in thinking these thoughts, and we would not ask you to judge yourself for finding yourself with the capacity to think them. But indeed, you have the capacity to be conscious of them, to evaluate them and if you find them to be those thoughts which do not allow you to blossom then you may, by choice, pluck that thought from ready memory and replace it with one that is more close to the heart of that which you truly feel to be the spiritual truth of the situation. Each shadow that you remove from your own flowering being is one less barrier betwixt you and the sun that gives you life, the Logos that sends the energy that creates each moment. As the crisis period continues you may find yourself in any number of situations in which there will be the choice of moving from the militaristic rind of thought that infects the planetary thought at this time at the level of those in power or choosing to think from a spiritual point of view in which all entities are seen as souls in the service of the one infinite Creator in various ways.

As the one known as J has said, some entities must draw the short stick, some entities must accept being the bad example. Each entity which is perceived by the seeker to be a service-to-self entity bent on the destruction of the good is also a soul who is serving perfectly, in his own way, attempting to learn the same lessons, those lessons of love and how to love always the choice of how to love. For those who are on the service-to-self path also have passion, but it is the passion for the self, to arrange the world in which the self is satisfied, safe and comfortable. It is easy to see a display of evil and good, dark and light, yet we ask you to move beyond this somewhat limiting image of the present harvest, for it not a battle betwixt good and evil. It is, rather, a battle for thought. It is a battle betwixt those who would wish to enhance and lift and enlighten in a great outpouring of radiated love and those who would control, contract and shepherd the world as they would wish it to be controlled. Expansion or contraction? You are experiencing the contractions of fear of those who are in power and, yes indeed, because of these encroachments of aggression, upon the very citizens in whose name they are promulgated. This pressure has produced a kind of explosion of healthy, blossoming, passionately engaged human beings who have now experienced themselves as souls; who have a deep and passionate feeling about that which is the appropriate action for themselves, their families, and their country.

It is indeed a precious moment and a promising time of rapidly awakening consciousness planet-wide and it has been pressed into being and encouraged by the seemingly disastrous policies of those who wish war among your peoples at this time. And we may say without expressing any unknown information, certainly, it is not one entity or a small group of entities which wishes the engagements of war and the reallocations of territory and power. There is pressure planet-wide, at the level of those who remember whole societal-wide catastrophic scenarios and wish beyond all reason to reinvent them, that presses these entities onward. Much of this harvest, then, expresses enormously deep archetypical energies that have been stuck for an unusually long period of time, repeating seemingly endless cycles of rising towards the light, rising towards union, rising towards an awareness of love in its unconditional and redeeming aspect, only to fall back to the level of the great apes and their tribal loyalties and the protection of the family group. It is a great ascent that the human attempts in third density, to move from beast to angel, from a mute and unspeaking love to a supernal, wordless expression of love. In between those two lies the third density and in that density you have the forgetting that allows your voice to be uncertain; that allows your mind not to know; that allows your heart to make foolish choices and then to experience change because of them.

Each of you is a wonderful flower that blossoms daily, that opens to the light, that has your own unique aroma and habit and form. Each of you is a tremendous blessing to this planet by your being. You are as those who have fought alongside each other for many, many years. This is another time, another opportunity to stand together and to fight for the light, not [to be] against anything, but to do the inner battle that wins through to the armor of light, to face the self in every day, in the morning light that shows all flaws clearly. This is your *geste*[38], to gaze in that mirror and see the flaws and see also the one infinite Creator, to gaze into the world as it is and see past the rind of militaristic thinking, see past this deadening infection that has blotted the surface of your thoughts with a kind of mildew. Remove yourself from the surface, remove yourself from that which is not truly your own thinking. Come back into the heart of your flowering being and feel the strength, the passion, the love that resides and rests there just as it has always rested over the deep before any form was. That is the peace that lies within your heart. It is a sweet peace, it is a true peace, it is the original peace. And it is a piece of you, that which can never be separated from you. Nothing can separate you from the love of the infinite Creator. Nothing can separate you from the truth of your being. Nothing can separate you from yourself.

We wish to express thanks to the outer expressions of this group in the context of your political situation, for those who light a candle for peace express a beautiful thought and it is very appropriate, we feel, that such lighting of candles about the globe may be seen from your satellites, so that all the world has become, in its own way, a rock concert. We enjoy that image of all of those lighting the flame and this time not for the love of a good song and a good time, but for the love of the world.[39]

We would at this time transfer this contact to the one known as Jim, in case there are other queries that may be answered at this time. We thank this instrument and leave it in love and in light. We are those known to you as Q'uo.

---

[38] A romantic story of daring adventure (*beau geste:* beautiful gesture (French)).

[39] L/L Research held a candlelight vigil for peace at 7:00 PM on this day, in conjunction with over three thousand other groups around the world who coordinated this global candlelight peace vigil.

(Jim channeling)

I am Q'uo. We greet each again in love and in light though this instrument. It is our privilege at this time to ask if there may be any further queries which we may attempt to respond to with our opinion.

J: Hi, Q'uo, this is J and I have a question today from R. She's in Hawaii and she complains that recently her dreams seem to be invaded, as Carla would say, from psychic greeting. Several years ago she had experienced a period of time where she was a willing participant in some ritual sex and she feels that those cords are still connected and the thoughts are pervading her dreams. So her question to you is, do you possibly have any suggestions or anything that you could speak to on how she might be able to disengage these connections, these cords that were made at that time? Thank you.

I am Q'uo, and I am aware of your query, my sister. As we observe this entity we see that which she and you have called the cords that connect her to a previous activity of a ritualized nature which had its place in magic, shall we say. That is, in the changing of consciousness by the effort of will and ritual combined. We would recommend that that which was formed may also be removed or cut, shall we say, by once again utilizing the force of the will and a ritual movement that would be accomplished within the meditative state. After the meditative state has been achieved and the entity feels calm and centered within its being, it may visualize these connecting cords with as much detail and clarity as possible, seeing the source, the origin, the connection with the self and the place upon the physical body that the connection is observed. Then this entity may, during the meditation and in a mental sense, take the scissors and cut these cords, bidding farewell to that energy in love and light, in peace and in joy, bidding that energy to go its way, as the one known as R goes her own way, now unencumbered by these cords. When this has been successfully imaged in the mind, then there may be the completing of this ritual of freeing oneself from unwanted energies by the grounding of this ritual either by the words, "So may it be done," or similar words or by the stamping of the foot upon the ground, or the hand upon the surface, with this motion completing the ritual.

Is there a further query, my sister?

J: No, Q'uo, thank you. Thanks for being with us today.

I am Q'uo, and it is our great privilege to be with you this day and to respond to your query. Is there another query at this time?

Carla: A question about direction of thought that I'd been taking with P. He asked me to get you to confirm that a very viable way for us to go at L/L Research to help to promulgate the Law of One is to form an Essene Teaching Circle. It's not a very elaborate plan yet but he asked if I would ask you-all about this concept, if you had any comments or you could confirm that it was a good idea.

I am Q'uo, and am aware of your query my sister. We can confirm that whenever entities who wish to be of service to the light gather together in any ritualized form to pursue an understanding and a service of that light there is an advantage indeed to this blending of energies. For when there is the addition of wills to a central purpose there is far more possibility that the purpose shall be realized. For as those of Ra have well said, "When those of like mind together seek, far more surely is it that they shall find."

Is there another query, my sister?

Carla: Do you have any recommendations for a budding community such as ours?

I am Q'uo, and am aware of your query, my sister. We can recommend that which you know already to be true, that is that it is well to communicate in an open-hearted fashion, in a frequent fashion, for many are the opportunities for misunderstanding when there is more than one entity in a group.

Is there a further query, my sister?

Carla: No. Thank you, Q'uo.

I am Q'uo, and again we thank you, my sister. Is there another query at this time?

Carla: I'm out.

I am Q'uo, and we seem to have exhausted the queries somewhat earlier in this day!

(Laughter)

We are very pleased with our efforts!

Carla: On behalf of S, I would just ask if my Annsy is happy in my lap?

I am Q'uo, and we are happy to confirm the joy of your Annsy.[40]

Carla: I just thought that you might enjoy that.

I am Q'uo. We have the greatest of appreciation for your effort to stand in for the one known as S.

Carla: I love you Q'uo. It is so good to be with you.

I am Q'uo. And we are most overjoyed to feel the love and compassion, the sense of proportion and dedication from this group. We are always pleased to be able to join your group and this day has a special feeling about the open-hearted sharing that has occurred.

We thank each for this offering of love and for the invitation to join your group. As always, we are most privileged to be able to do so. We are known to you as those of Q'uo. At this time we shall take our leave of this instrument and of this group. We leave each, as always, in the love and in the ineffable light of the one infinite Creator. Adonai, my friends. ✤

---

[40] S is a seeker who often asks such stellar questions as, "Who will win the Derby?" and "What are the lottery numbers to pick?" Since our group tries to eschew specific and transient information, these queries by S have become a group joke. Annsy is Carla's doll.

L/L Research

Special Meditation
March 21, 2003

Question from J: "Please describe the contractual design and service to the one Creator, service to others and to mother Earth which my divine essence through love and service has created, agreed to, and desires to fulfill at this current space-time."

(Carla channeling)

We are those known to you as the principle of Q'uo, and we greet you in the love and in the ineffable light of the one infinite Creator, in whose name we come to you this day, [to] this part of that which we may call the "Godhead Principle" for all entities are a portion of this Godhead Principle, each splintering as gems from a mother lode or sparking off [as] sparks from a glorious and sacred place of Creatorship, always and ever retaining, in the microcosm of the macrocosm, a holographic expression of the infinite reaches of the one Creator and Its creative Thought of love. We are most happy to share our thoughts with you upon this subject and ask only that each thought that we offer be appraised and estimated with quite careful discrimination, seeking and searching always for the personal resonance, for that peculiar sensation of remembering that which you have already known and simply had forgotten. This is the mark of personal truth. All other ideas, be they ever so attractive as toys for the mind, need to be left behind as stumbling blocks, if that essence of remembrance and resonance is not there. With this freedom granted us, we may then express ourselves without being concerned that we, as incorrectly perceived authority figures, might cause any to stumble.

The life of any, the incarnation of the flesh, is brief and dense with possibilities. For us to be able to express to you the whole of those things which you planned as possibilities within this incarnation which you now enjoy would be a very long discussion, comprising many avenues which you have not chosen, which you have left behind for the glory, the service, the sacrifice, that love requires of those who choose the path that is, as the poet said, less chosen. And it has made all the difference.[41]

---

[41] "The Road Not Taken," by Robert Frost
  Two roads diverged in a yellow wood,
  And sorry I could not travel both
  And be one traveler, long I stood
  And looked down one as far as I could
  To where it bent in the undergrowth;

  Then took the other, as just as fair,
  And having perhaps the better claim,
  Because it was grassy and wanted wear;
  Though as for that the passing there
  Had worn them really about the same,

  And both that morning equally lay
  In leaves no step had trodden black.
  Oh, I kept the first for another day!
  Yet knowing how way leads on to way,
  I doubted if I should ever come back.

  I shall be telling this with a sigh
  Somewhere ages and ages hence:
  Two roads diverged in a wood, and I—

We can say that there is for you perhaps one leaf to fall from the tree of fruit. Yet it is that which will come naturally to you and it is a roundabout route indeed, were one to gaze at the route from the air of hindsight. But upon the ground of time it is a good way to go, and all things shall transpire in their time. This is the essence of that which we are able to tell you in any specific way.

We would then spend the balance of this reading discussing that which you have asked in the light of a point of view which is perhaps broader and less specific than you would prefer. However, we wish very much for you to work this last puzzle, to experience the faith that springs from the leap into midair; to place the self not only upon the line but happily over the line, because it gives joy and it expresses the deepest passion of the being.

These choices are those which, if relaxed into, seem sometimes to flow with uncanny precision and speed. At other times the lesson includes waiting. And there are both aspects within the present puzzle, those things which need not to be resisted and those times faith alone can express the quality of serenity that does not blink at apparent challenge, difficulty or lack of manifestation.

What is the shape of service to the Creator? We suggest that the contract that you speak of is [a] contract that you have attempted to keep for some time. It is a life-long contract. It is elastic. It is in force as long as you breathe. This contact is common to many who at this time express upon the surface of your planet, both those who are in last incarnations, or hopefully last incarnations, as an earth native and those who have come here from elsewhere from higher densities in order to be of service upon planet Earth at this time. This basic mission which all hold in common is perforce a generalized expression of the essence of the self, for are not all selves part of the infinite Creator? So that there is that spiritual paradox, that is so precious, of the absolute equality of all souls and the absolute uniqueness of each gem of personhood that is the soul stream that is represented so sketchily in the illusion of flesh by the personality shell, which those about you experience as yourself. That which you came prepared to live for and to die for is the cause of love and light. The need at this time upon the planet which you now serve is great. The time is Harvest and those who have awakened have awakened to the memory that they are here to serve in a specific way.

This specific way is so completely other than the culture in which your peoples experience life, see contracts and jobs, that it is very different to wrap the mind around the job at hand. However, this job is to live a life which contains as much consciousness and awareness and accurate observance of all that is seen as possible. It, then, requires the instrument that is your soul to aid as a shuttle in bringing into the physical body and out into the metaphysical inner planes of this planet, by intention, the infinite love and light of the one Creator which at all times is moving through the openhearted entity and being sent by intention either to the Creator, to the fourth-density grid of this planet, which this instrument is so interested in strengthening, and to the people that one comes in contact with on a daily basis, that can be served and can be prayed for by the simple level of consciousness expressed within, that sanctum sanctorum which is the opened heart wherein the entity is in tabernacle with the one infinite Creator. To carry this persona into the world is to carry peace into the world, to carry light into the world. To carry this consciousness means that you begin to see yourself as the Christ. You begin to see others as the Christ. You begin to see the creation as an expression of the Father and you begin to see that in being the most essential self that you can, you are moving closer and closer to the selfhood that is the Christ, that is the "I" of "me."

We do not wish to indicate the literal Christ, that body, that personality shell. But we indicate the consciousness that is the Christ within, that consciousness which the one known as Jehoshuah carried so elegantly and so bravely and with such tenacity. Yet it was a cloak, and that cloak is the cloak of the Godhead Principle, shall we say, or the divine spirit, or as this instrument likes to call it, the Holy Spirit, that which is Christ without the body, that divine fire which flows, that wind of spirit that "bloweth where it listeth."[42] This is the consciousness that is your basic contract. This is what you came to do and this is not easy work. For this is a work that exists throughout the day, throughout the waking time that is left to you upon this sphere and so it is essential, in the practice of those who would

---

I took the one less traveled by,
And that has made all the difference.

[42] *Holy Bible, King James Version*, John 3:8.

maximize their service, that the entity be more and more aware of the thoughts and the feelings that are occurring, of those triggers that pull the self from the self which rests in the great ocean of divine consciousness into the murk of the archipelago of confusion and chaos that is the usually segmented daily experience.

The deep waters that surround each moment are not apparent to one skating upon the surface of life. It is those who are brave enough to dive into the present moment and to gain its fruits by thirst and hunger, seeking like the hart that "pants after the water brook"[43] as this instrument would quote from her Bible, that the self becomes a honed instrument, a crystal radio, that is waiting silently, empty handedly, to receive the information that comes through the shuttle of the gateway to intelligent infinity that is the spiritual body.

The strategy that we would recommend for working upon this primary contractual obligation or what the Ra group called "honor/duty" is that heart-opening discipline, for which the one known as J has so richly prepared himself by many resources and many experiences that hone and refine the strategies and processes that this entity may bring to bear upon that seed that is within that blooms in the spring of awakened consciousness. The seed has fallen in good ground and there is every hope of a good spring and we just encourage the one known as J to bend to the Earth of its planting, to tend the buds that come, with great love, with great awareness of the sacred honor in drawing breath at this time, in this place. We encourage the openhearted attempt in each day to gaze at the household of the self with first interest upon the lowest of the floors, that level of survival and sexuality that perhaps the cave and the more primitive parts of a house would suggest, the first floor, a ground floor of personal relationships and the family and group relationships that are intimate in the personal life. These small concerns, these incidental chores and experiences of day-to-day life contain most of the grist for the mill of the metaphysical learning which you indeed did come to do.

The learning will take place whether or not all relationships are used that have been prepared. And indeed in most incarnations many relationships are allowed to lapse or may not even occur simply because of the road not taken—so that there is no way of exhausting the possibilities of any incarnation.

The gift that you give in this contract is the enormous gift of a life that is lived for the Creator, a life that is lived in remembrance of the Creator, a life that is lived in devotion to the mystery of Deity, a life that is lived in faith that all is well, and that all will be well. These energies are the energies which allow the heart to open when the entity is comfortable in its own skin, when it has a home life in which it is functional and content, when it has obtained some grasp of the good and the seeming challenge inherent in the worldly work of gaining supply, then can the heart begin to open and feel safe in an undefended and relaxed state. And in that state full energy begins coming through the heart and according to the will of the entity which is the crystal being doing the work, that energy then can then move in to work in consciousness, for the self, for the planet, for entities about the self or for, indeed, the Creator Itself. All of these energies are part of a life lived in faith and in gratitude, if it can be remembered to give praise and thanksgiving for all that occurs. The resources which the one known as J has so ably stacked up in the years of experience, of service, and in devotion will be able to come into play as they are needed, not because of the cudgeling of the brain or the intellectual sophistry of thinking, but those things which point and hint and suggest shall be bubbling up from dream, vision, bird, bush, sky and unusual, unexpected synchronicity. We encourage, then, the attention to the information that flows from the devas of second density who are in complete harmony with the needs of your soul stream. We encourage those awarenesses of synchronicities and of good words spoken that are given from the actions of angelic aid in fourth density, of higher teachers in fifth density and sixth density and of the Creator's whimsy, which operates at an even higher level than even these teachers. Indeed, many times the Creator's dry and attic wit[44] has salted the sad and sorry [earthly] tragedy with ironic yet bittersweet humor. This too is a teaching of a very deep kind.

---

[43] "As the hart (deer) panteth after the water brook, so panteth my soul after Thee, O God." (*Holy Bible, King James Version*, Psalms 42:1)

[44] attic wit: a poignant, delicate wit, peculiar to the Athenians.

You are a crystal that has the entire spectrum of energy. You can generate and focus upon any of these colors. And by the responses that you give to catalyst —in the daily life especially, in the small life— you can refine, articulate, purify and crystallize these colors that are your emotions. There is such beauty in the human heart and, as you give yourself to the Creator day by day, you are as the flower in the field that shines with your very own array of colors. These are the palette that you have created to give praise and honestation to the one infinite Creator. What then are your thoughts this day? What then are the feelings that you have produced?

This instrument was saying earlier about itself that in a recent situation it had, on the worldly level, a great success, but on the personal level felt disappointed with herself, for she had not taken the opportunity in every case to see new people, or that is, people new to her, as souls, but rather personalities, becoming involved in the intricacies of very social rituals and aggravation that is inherent in these to this particular entity. Why did this choice get taken? Why was the attention straying from the center of devotion, which this instrument hopes is lit as the lighthouse upon the hill at all times? Nay, this lighthouse sometimes seems to get very faint and seems not to shine very brightly.

These are the times that are precious for learning, these moments of awakening awareness that one has been drifting off of one's focus. Then it is that it is time— not to discipline the self, rebuke the self, or scold the self—but rather to correct the error of thought, speaking out loud perhaps the principle involved in seeing entities as the Creator, seeing the self as the Creator, and seeing the creation as the Creator's world. These are those things which you have contracted to do. It is very easy and completely understandable within the culture that you enjoy that you would equate contractual missions with outer gifts. And yet we may say without any feeling of personal wrongness that were this instrument never to have channeled, to have written, or to have sung in this incarnation, this instrument would still be appropriately and properly pursuing that which she calls the King's Highway.

There is nothing of outer gifts that is contractual but rather the contractual obligation, the honor, and the duty is to the being that you hope to allow to flower within this density and within this lifetime specifically. There was a hope of one who would come to the Harvest, harvestable and shining as brightly as the sun, and thus harvesting those about it as the radiance lights other people and begins other people's journeys toward awakening simply by the radiance of being that they experience. This is a very subtle, a very hidden service. It is one which takes tremendous discipline yet gives great joy and is actually what this instrument would call the fast track to inner learning. For in this particular state of mind you are as the tuned instrument that is able to observe, from a standpoint of compassion and thankfulness, the unfolding plan of the one infinite Creator.

This is the time wherein many are being called to awaken and take up their part in this effort to build a road to fourth density that is a safe one for those who come after this generation upon planet Earth. The work with third density of this group of entities called human beings is largely at an end and the, shall we say, political, global score does not look very good. It looks as though we have as entities not proceeded to a very appropriately harvestable place for those interested in love and in light. Yet these appearances have no substance.

A microscope taken to anything physical may show that there is virtually no substance in matter but, for the most part, space. Energies are what have substance within the metaphysical world. The energy of intention and the absolute fidelity to focusing upon the center of your desire are the basic prerequisites for the work ahead. It will bless many, yet it will often be hidden.

We do bless and encourage you to follow those paths which lead to outer service as well. These are less central to the energy which causes you to ask these questions, yet we feel that you will be feeling delighted as well as in some consternation as things unfold. There is much of interest to come so we simply encourage the feeling that all is well, the feeling that the road is beneath the feet. That which this instrument calls the King's Highway, that Tao, that Way is beneath the feet and you are on the road. This is the bulk of that which we would say to respond to your query with one more thought concerning the work with the environment that you mentioned.

The one known as Gaia or the Earth or Terra groans in a despairing labor at this time. She has become somewhat encouraged as more and more entities send light and begin to grieve for the suffering and feeling of fear that is being cast about the surface of your globe like a pall. This is encouraging to Gaia yet she needs ever more reassurance that her children love her and wish her well and assist her in the travail of the birth of her fourth-density self. Entities such as this instrument and its group and other groups like it have begun to become aware of ways to intensify and strengthen the one known as Gaia and especially that fourth-density labor. The tool, as is so often the case, is the human crystal placed in visualization or meditation at a particular time, thus joining wills into a more and more giant and strong will that may bring many others to it by the sheer energy of its light.

There is, inherent in the attempt of Wanderers to, shall we say, infect the Earth with heightened awareness of love, that dependency upon what this instrument would call the One Hundredth Monkey Effect, the hope being that eventually more and more entities are forming lighthouses, light groups, study groups, meditation groups, groups of all shades of devotion and way of expressing devotion to the infinite Creator, yet groups that harmonize in wishing light and love to planet Earth and its people. These goals are moving along with speed and we see many more places of light coming to be where entities may come into small groups and form spiritually oriented friendships, fellowships and families. These possibilities for increased light at this time are great blessings and we encourage those opportunities that come one's way for these are opportunities to add one's light to the light of many others. And these opportunities are occurring with greater and greater frequency for those of your peoples who have awakened.

Know that the Earth will be fine. It is the sadness and the sorrow that shall occur if the Earth must give up upon humankind that is the tragedy here. Therefore love the Earth, express that love by direct relationship with the Earth, spending the time with the nature and the state of nature and simply sharing love with the Earth, experiencing loving and being loved as you breathe the carbon dioxide for the trees to inhale and as the trees exhale their oxygen so that you may have life, rest in the harmony of the one infinite Creator, and be healed.

We would at this time ask if there are any follow-up queries that we may help you with at this time?

Jim: I would like to know about that tone that he has experienced in his right ear for a number of years, a very light tone, what that tone might be for, what it might be a symbol of or a result of?

We are those of Q'uo, and are aware of your query, my brother. This tone is that confirmation of a positive conclusion that you have set for yourself. The similar tone upon the left side would then be the indication of a negative response to a conclusion that had just been reached. This is not a fast rule, for other causes can produce tones within the ear. However, it is helpful when such a tone is perceived to think back upon that which was the issue upon the mind at the time the tone was heard and see if there might be some information within that sound that is perceived within the inner ear.

Is there another question, my brother?

Jim: When J does breathing exercises he goes into a certain state of suspended animation where he hears another tone. Could you explain what that tone might be?

[We are those of Q'uo.] The one known as J has the separation of a slight nature of the inner bodies from the physical body as the complete cessation of the respiration occurs. The inner bodies are lifting somewhat up into the gateway and moving up, shall we say, the silver cord or the spiritual shuttle resting in the information stream that is down-pouring from the one infinite Creator. This indeed does alter the consciousness, and the noise is as if the car window were cracked a bit allowing the universe of airflow outside to enter the protected shell of the physical vehicle.

May we answer you further, my brother? We are those of Q'uo.

Jim: J feels a connection with those of Ra, with the Great Ones of the Central Sun, and with those of Metatron. How can he make that connection more apparent and how can he use it in his own spiritual journey?

We are those of Q'uo, and are aware of your query, my brother. The precise status of connection to entities with these names is …

(Tape ends.)

L/L Research

L/L Research is a subsidiary of Rock Creek Research & Development Laboratories, Inc.

P.O. Box 5195
Louisville, KY 40255-0195

www.llresearch.org

Rock Creek is a non-profit corporation dedicated to discovering and sharing information which may aid in the spiritual evolution of humankind.

ABOUT THE CONTENTS OF THIS TRANSCRIPT: This telepathic channeling has been taken from transcriptions of the weekly study and meditation meetings of the Rock Creek Research & Development Laboratories and L/L Research. It is offered in the hope that it may be useful to you. As the Confederation entities always make a point of saying, please use your discrimination and judgment in assessing this material. If something rings true to you, fine. If something does not resonate, please leave it behind, for neither we nor those of the Confederation would wish to be a stumbling block for any.

© 2009 L/L RESEARCH

Sunday Meditation
April 6, 2003

Group question: The question today, Q'uo, has to do with what it seems like a lot of people are feeling these days, because the United States is engaged in a very destructive war with Iraq, and times just seem like they're full of stress. There's more to do than there's time to do. A lot of people are feeling sadness, anger, frustration and doubt. These things just seem to come bubbling out. We're wondering if there is a way of maintaining one's harmony in such times; if there is a way of dealing with these difficulties that will bring us back to harmony? We appreciate anything that you might have to say about how we can deal with the difficult times that are within us and about us.

(Carla channeling)

We are those known to you as Q'uo, and we greet you in the love and in the light of the one infinite Creator, in Whose service we come to you this day. We wish to thank you for the great blessing of your company and the beauty of your vibrations as you sit in this sweet circle of seeking. We thank you especially for taking the time out of that life which, by your question, is represented as being most busy and somewhat difficult. Yet you have found the time and the place to come together simply to seek the truth. For this we thank you, for it is a great blessing to us to be able to share our thoughts with you and to be called to your meeting.

We share these thoughts with you with the request that, in listening to them, each be very discriminating as to those thoughts which you accept and use as resources. We would not ask that you look upon us as authorities but rather as those with an opinion which we are glad to share on the basis of our being friends and neighbors with you, not simply in terms of time and space but in terms of the nature of our beings and the journey which we share. If you are able to use your discrimination in listening to our thoughts then that will free us to be able to express them without fear that we would be infringing upon any entity's free will.

You ask us this day concerning the peace and harmony that is so beloved and so dearly sought among your peoples and yet is seemingly quite elusive at times for many of your peoples. The description of the times as being troubled and the self as being troubled seem to be that truth which lies upon the surface of the minds of many of those present and certainly it echoes those thoughts which are upon the minds of your people in general, for upon a global basis the great cry of your planet and its people is for harmony and peace.

This instrument wished to use the term "grass roots," and we stopped this instrument from using that term to describe that energy which is bubbling up. For in "grass roots" we would not make the pun without intending to! And we wish to say that the energy of harmony and peace is indeed bubbling up out of the grass roots *themselves*, out of every seed and every living thing that takes its life from the soil and turns towards the sun in your second density. The energies which turn towards harmony and peace are those energies which you possess in each cell of your vehicle upon the physical level, and in your finer bodies within the inner levels as well.

There is an instinct within each spark of the Creator's light for the balancing of the energy to a default setting of peace and joy. The impulse and energy which nurtures this into manifestation, however, is the impulse—not towards joy or towards peace—but that instinct that lies in the direction of single-mindedness or, as the one known as V has said, the discipline of the personality. So we would take some time to discuss this concept of the default setting of joy and peace.

It is our bias as we look upon this circle of entities, with their beautiful energy vehicles shimmering, that we see that view which lies the deepest most easily and that portion of you which lies upon the surface least easily, whereas within the physical incarnation such as you now enjoy, unless the vehicle in which you enjoy living has been born blind or there are other perceptual difficulties of a substantial nature, that which comes easiest to your senses and to your observational powers is that which is seen, heard, smelled, tasted and felt. The priorities of your earthly experience, then, focus upon those things about you as an entity which are the least authentic or real. And yet, it is at the level of these inauthentic and illusory structures which this instrument calls "consensus reality" in which you spend your days and your working hours. And we do grasp that there is every temptation and every logical reason for each of you to wander far from the concept of the self as one whose mind is on only one thing and that is the love of the one infinite Creator.

We gaze within this instrument's mind to find description of this paradox and find her experience of long and busy and well-crafted days of toil in which many chores of varying kinds are approached, organized and removed from the list of things to do. This, within this instrument, we find to be the source of almost no stress, and this is remarkable, for among your people there is the tendency, not only to have too much to do, but also to find oneself being concerned about the fact that one has to much to do. This kind of energy then snowballs upon itself and creates an ever greater sensitivity to one's lacks and failures to achieve that which has been expected of one either by the self or by others.

Within this instrument's mind we also find constant efforts towards the re-tuning of the mind and it is in this direction that we would like to go in discussing ways to work with the situation which you now enjoy, which is, basically, a very good environment: observe, analyze, and alter the priorities of thinking which cause your particular mind and attention to focus upon one thing rather than another of the details of those things which are occurring at any particular moment.

At any particular moment an entity may be experiencing a multitude of catalysts. There are catalysts that come to the ears, the trains that pass, the telephones that ring. There is catalyst for the eye in the passing view and catalyst for all the senses in that which is occurring. There is catalyst for the mind in those thoughts which are sparked by the sense impressions of the moment. And there are those thoughts involved with the reactions to the original thoughts that have been thought by the self. In all of this arrangement, there has been no thought described which has not been caused by the outer environment impressing itself upon the being. The one known as C was expressing her desire to move beyond the thoughts of that level, to move into those thoughts which are authentic, original and her own thoughts, moving from the inside out and not from the outside in, so that there is a feeling of being, shall we say, as the flower that blooms to meet the wind, rather than as the scrap of tattered rag which the wind blows any way that it wishes to, for there is no root in the tatter but only material that has been beaten and torn.

Each of you feels at times as a tattered rag, as a thing for the wind to make sport of and play with and indeed it often feels as if the wind of spirit has picked you up and put you down someplace where you would rather not have been placed.

To the mind that is focused upon the love of the one infinite Creator, the view of all that comes through the senses, the thoughts concerning those sense impressions, and the thoughts judging those thoughts about sense impressions are all seen as the bits of froth upon the surface of the waters of life that they are. If the single thought that the mind is stayed upon is the love of the infinite One, then the being within has the opportunity to choose to maintain that focus, not only in those moments of silence but also in moments in the noise of culture, of warfare, of crowded conditions, of distressing amounts of inequality in a world which yearns and hungers and demands absolute equality.

In your prophetic literature, in your myths and in your sagas, there is much concern for transformational times. Within ancient Roman literature there is Ovid gazing at the metamorphoses of nature and of humankind. Dry-as-dust historians have gazed at the rise and fall of empires. The energies of spiritual leaders such as Jesus the Christ have focused upon the transformation of that which is material into that which is spiritual. And this instrument has followed a long line of studies of various religions and mythologies and philosophical systems in which this matter of how one helps oneself to transform from the lesser into the more noble aspect of self. The stuff of transformation is the stuff of waking from a sleep.

Fortunately, we have that very humble and accessible example of the kind of change that you all face at this time. It is a time of transformation, perhaps most importantly for your planet. The very Earth which has bred you and nurtured you is itself now being born, and this effort and labor go well. Yet there is difficulty. The difficulty is critical in that if the delivery continues to go poorly there will need to be the equivalent of the Cesarean, the removing of portions of the skin of the Earth that the new configuration of the energy-body of the Earth may have room to be born in its appropriate shape and arrangement of energy nexi. It is more for the planet than for the people that many of you have chosen to be in incarnation upon the planet at this time. It was your hope that you would be able, by awakening within the dream of physical life, to become a magical person, a person able to act as a crystal entity, receiving energy, transmuting energy, and sending energy out into the fourth-density web of planet Earth.

That which distracts is always a detail, that which calls you back to remembrance is always discipline. Very seldom does nature so configure experience that it is impossible to miss the spiritual signals. Most usually the hints and clues of spirituality are so configured as to be completely able to be missed, able to be glanced over, able to be prioritized below the threshold of awareness, [displaced] by the affairs and details and chores of the day. Each is aware of the spiritual figures who have indicated through history that, when they are busy, then is the time to rise earlier so that they may pray longer, for it is in the praying that the work gets done rather then in those long daylight hours of toil. This is a great key for those who have ears to hear. We are not suggesting that entities must get up early and meditate before they begin the day in order to prepare, but we are suggesting that the mind of an entity is that which is in a state of extreme vulnerability to the mental conditioning. The power of suggestion is great. Each entity has seen many examples of such suggestion, the most common perhaps being that when one entity yawns, those about that entity will quite often catch the yawn and find themselves expressing similarly.

So it is too with the mass media, the television and the newspapers, those agents of consciousness of which J was speaking, that tend toward creating cookies of the right shape out of the dough of entities' thoughts so that entities' opinions upon certain subjects bear a remarkable similarity. They have been listening to one source and in that source lies a structure which seems to explain or justify actions. And [yet] in the details of these actions there is no end to the shades of gray, the ethical questions, the causes for sorrow or anger or concern of one kind or another.

The simplicity of the solution is funny. For the solution to the awareness of trouble is in the turning of the consciousness to the love of the infinite Creator. We do not intend this as a greatly abstract concept. We intend this in another way and we would ask you to open yourselves to the concept that you *are* the peace and harmony that you seek, for you are a spark of the one great original Thought of the infinite Creator. Say that the Creator, in its infinity, in its impossibility of being described, is a vibration. You have that original vibration, which is unconditional love, as the basis of every cell of your being. Without that Thought of love has nothing been made that is made. It is not something you possess, it is your very nature, it goes far deeper than the marrow of your bones, it is far closer to you than your breathing. It is far more real then the impressions of sense. For it is that impulse and spark without which you could not take thought, take breath, or enjoy existence or consciousness. This nature of the principle of Deity is the heart of you, is the truth of you. You are as the stone within which the perfect sculpture hides. Each detail, each chore, each duty, each disturbance, each warfare chips away, pounds away, hammers away, rattles away, and aggravates away bits and pieces of detritus, of those things that are not you, gradually beginning to shape that faceted gem that lies within the details of a busy, earthly existence. How blunt are the instruments of catalyst! And yet how effective.

When one begins to become aware of this process of catalyst and experience, learning and transformation, one begins to be able to pick up some tools to use that are not as blunt as the blunt instruments of outer experience, things learned the hard way. And once again, the key to making use of these finer instruments, of removing and distilling from the self those impurities which one targets and wishes to see fall away, is the will. And each time the will is used to lift the self from that archipelago of small confusions to a place of spiritual attitude and consciousness where these details are seen as details like any other, a burden is lifted off of the attention. It is as though blinders are released from the eyes and for the first time, by asking of yourself this discipline of attention, you may begin to experience the unreasoning feelings of joy and peace of which this instrument was speaking earlier. For it is our opinion that it is this instrument's long years of attempting to be disciplined about returning the mind to the silence from the details that has gradually enabled this instrument to find a measure of peace that does indeed pass understanding.

The Creator within you, the Truth of yourself, is happy to live your life. You have sufficient spiritual impulses within you to move through your incarnations in a state of true peace and undiluted joy. Yet it is something for which permission must be given from the self to the self. One must give oneself permission to be content and happy and blessed, for these are not things which are in the training which your culture offers its people. It is not taught among your peoples that happiness is a natural state, but rather that struggling and competition are the natural state. And each is aware of many ways in which the culture itself offers these lessons to those who are growing and in need of instruction. Always it is the spiritual sense alone that is able to release the conflicts, the struggles, those things which are the truth of the illusion, in order to turn once again to the stunning mystery of oneness, to the love that is all that you see, to the light that has created all that is, without blinking at those things which seem good and which seem evil.

The life that is lived is a work of great subtlety. There is an unlimited potential for transformation within the physical illusion and the limits are released one by one by that entity who is willing to ask of the self, "Yes, but who am I beneath that detail; yes, but who am I beneath that action? Who am I, whose am I, why am I here?" When faced with disharmony it may be a resource for you to think to yourself this thought: "Who am I? In terms of that situation that is 'out there,' what's the situation with me? If I am a creature of love, then what am I doing in this situation?" To look at the situation and to react as you see it from the outside in is often less than helpful. To gaze at a situation from the inside out is to find the love within that particular structure and then to be the defender, the protector, and the expresser if need be, of that love. Whatever it is that you gaze upon, whoever is reaching out to you that asks for a reaction from you, attempt if you can to leave that situation, that relationship, that moment in a little better order than you found it, with a little more love, a little more understanding, a little more of the Creator's freedom in the atmosphere.

In almost any situation it is easy to lose the tuning of mind which is that tuning of yourself that holds remembrance that the "I" of you is an "I" that is far more than the personality shell and that self which lives the surface life. Who is truly living your life? Infinite Consciousness would like to live your life. It is a matter of getting out of Its way.

Those who remain silent may be those who have the most wisdom. Those voices that speak the loudest in your society may well be those voices which offer the deepest confusion. Consequently we encourage your appetite for the silence. We encourage plunging into that muscular silence that is the speech of the one infinite Creator and going as deep as you can for as long as you can whenever you can. If you only have thirty seconds or two minutes, or five, you may visit the gateway to intelligent infinity. Take the time, whenever you can, to release your energy body from its very strictures to refresh it, open it up. And when you find yourself in the open heart, we greatly encourage your sitting there for awhile with that one great original Thought that is love itself. Rest in the love that lies within the heart and know that it is the truth of you, it is your deepest self. And then go forward in your armor of light, knowing that those things which are of earthly origin will express as they must and that all things that live shall die and all that passes from illusion shall once again come into being. Rest in those cycles that lie beyond sense. Rest in that mystery that lies beyond mind. Rest in the feeling that you have …

(Side one of tape ends.)

(Carla channeling)

In order for personal learning to occur and in order for you to do your service we are always happy to join you in your meditation in order to deepen that state of meditation that you may enjoy. And there are many entities in the unseen worlds which are alert to those who seek in various directions. Consequently, it is a matter of knowing that which you are and that which you believe and then asking for help from those structures within which you feel comfortable asking. This instrument would call the help angelic. Others would describe various entities of various levels of the inner planes by various technically more accurate names. Our point is simply that there is tremendous energetic help for those who have become clear as to what it is they seek, who it is that they are, and why it is that they have chosen life at this time.

Move into a feeling of as full an awareness of the self as can be had. Ask for the help that is there. And then find that courage which releases the self, in a state of complete vulnerability, to face the next moment without preconception.

We are informed by this instrument that our time with her is up and consequently, and with good grace and humor, we gladly leave this instrument and transfer this contact to the one known as Jim, that any questions remaining upon the minds of those present may be addressed. We leave this instrument in love and in light with thanks. We are those of Q'uo.

(Jim channeling)

I am Q'uo. We greet each again in love and in light through this instrument. It is our privilege at this time to ask if there may be any further queries remaining upon the minds of those present to which we may speak.

T: Yes. I have a question that continues right off of what the entire channel was about. I've never believed too much in entities from outside of myself influencing me, but I'm coming to believe that, in the last year or so, that due to whatever reason, I'm drawing more attention to myself. Could this just be the general upheaval which everyone is experiencing? I don't know how far you can comment without going beyond the Law of Confusion, but please comment as to whether I am being specifically targeted or is this just a general thing that everyone's having to deal with at this time?

I am Q'uo, and am aware of your query, my brother. As we look upon the experience which you describe we see that that experience is one which is common to many people at this time. For there is within many such as yourself the great desire to be of service in a situation which does not allow the service in the manner which you desire to give. Thus, you feel a great deal of powerlessness. This powerlessness is full of desire to serve which has been blunted. This causes there to be a blockage of energy, shall we say, within your system of energy centers. There is a kind of fracture of the crystal that may be observed in such a situation where the energy applied by those of negative polarity to those who wish to aid but are blocked in their aid causes the fracture, a catalyst, to become apparent and to vibrate in an overactive manner and then to express as you have described. There is the need, shall we say, to examine the fracture, the catalyst, that triggers the difficulty within the meditative state. It might be well done to feel these feelings and to examine their origin. When one is more aware of the composition of the self, of the means by which energy moves through the body/mind/spirit complex, then one is less liable to suffer the intensification of difficulties that one has freely chosen. It may be well to find a positively-oriented project where one can construct a symbolic mending of the fracture within one's energy centers. For example, there may be various small projects or items about one's dwelling place that need repair, that need cleansing, that need attention. This can be a symbolic expression of energy that then is felt within and allows healing to occur within, therefore repairing the fracture.

Is there another query, my brother?

T: No, thank you very much.

I am Q'uo. We thank you very much. Is there another query at this time?

S: I have what I wouldn't say is really a question but more of a statement. I notice as I go through life with family and friends around me, that sometimes I take [them] for granted, and don't always show my appreciation and gratitude. I'd like to include you, Q'uo, and, as you say, the heavenly hosts and to express my gratitude and appreciation of [your] being there when I feel like talking to you or just knowing that you're there, and the help and love that you've given. I just want to express my love and gratitude again for all that you've done.

I am Q'uo, and we are most filled with the same love and gratitude, my friend, that you have expressed for us. We feel this for each entity such as yourself and all those who seek to be of service in this illusion that you now inhabit for it is not an easy task to move through the darkness with but a small candle to light the way and there are many missteps in the darkness. We are happy to join any entity who asks our presence for the purpose of, as you say, listening, to blend our vibrations with your own, to perhaps offer a bit of inspiration that may aid in the movement through the daily round of activities and the many experiences of catalyst that are part of the third-density experience that each of you now inhabits.

Is there another query at this time?

S: Not for me, thanks.

J: Yeah, I have a quick question, Q'uo. Do you express yourself in other groups such as this one, in this world?

I am Q'uo, and am aware of your query, my sister. We of Q'uo are privileged to speak to this group using the verbalization technique of channeling, as you have called it, but restrict our contact with other groups or individuals to a more personalized sense of blending our vibrations with theirs. There are, however, portions of our principle, such as those of Hatonn, which do speak to other groups and have for a great many of your years. The mind-to-mind contact that produces the channeling phenomenon is one which is difficult for most to initiate and more difficult yet to maintain. So even though there have been attempts to make this kind of contact with other groups, for the most part they have been short-lived. However, we do not measure our success at service by the channeling type of contact which we now enjoy with this group, for we find it is possible to reach with our hearts in love and light to all the creation and are pleased to feel the loving response of the great majority of the creation with which we are one.

Is there another query, my sister?

J: Well, I, like S, would like to really give a heartfelt thank-you. I do feel your presence. I feel like that when I work with other people and do massage work I feel your presence. I've been feeling it more and more since belonging to this group. You're a big part of love in my life and I really do appreciate that.

I am Q'uo, and we return your loving respect and pleasure of company, my sister, for it is our great joy to be able to be with each in this circle and with any entity who requests our presence, for when we tabernacle with any we tabernacle with the one Creator. Your experiences are unique to yourselves and each time we are able to blend our vibrations with yours we find new ways of expressing and experiencing love and light.

Is there a final query at this time?

(Pause)

I am Q'uo. As it appears that we have exhausted the queries for this circle of seeking, we would once again thank each present for inviting us to join you in your circle of seeking. We are always overjoyed to be able to join this group and we look, as you would say, forward to these gatherings though forward is perhaps a misnomer, for we live as one being at one time at all times. The illusion which you now inhabit is one which plays a trick, shall we say, in order that you may do a certain dance, make a certain choice, give of yourself in love and move one step further in your union with the All.

At this time we shall take our leave of this instrument and this group. We leave each, as always, in the love and in the light of the one infinite Creator. We are known to you as those of Q'uo. Adonai, my friends. ✤

L/L Research

L/L Research is a subsidiary of Rock Creek Research & Development Laboratories, Inc.

P.O. Box 5195
Louisville, KY 40255-0195

www.llresearch.org

Rock Creek is a non-profit corporation dedicated to discovering and sharing information which may aid in the spiritual evolution of humankind.

ABOUT THE CONTENTS OF THIS TRANSCRIPT: This telepathic channeling has been taken from transcriptions of the weekly study and meditation meetings of the Rock Creek Research & Development Laboratories and L/L Research. It is offered in the hope that it may be useful to you. As the Confederation entities always make a point of saying, please use your discrimination and judgment in assessing this material. If something rings true to you, fine. If something does not resonate, please leave it behind, for neither we nor those of the Confederation would wish to be a stumbling block for any.

© 2009 L/L RESEARCH

SPECIAL MEDITATION
MAY 3, 2003

Question from R: This evening R would like to hear whatever words of wisdom or love or enlightenment that you might have to offer him concerning the journey that he has taken and what would be most appropriate for him now.

(Carla channeling)

We are those known to you as Q'uo and we greet you in the love and in the light of the one infinite Creator. We are most blessed to be with you this evening and we thank you for the care for your soul's truth that has led you to set aside this time and this energy for this purpose. This instrument also has set aside this time and this energy which are hers for this purpose, as has the one known as Jim. Consequently we are honored and privileged to be able to share with you these thoughts that form the message which we have for you this day. Please be aware that we would greatly appreciate your utmost discernment in listening to that which we say, keeping only those thoughts which resonate deeply within you as personal truth, having the character of a memory recalled. Leave aside all those things which may trouble you or not fit those parameters of your discrimination which are such faithful sentinels of your own truth, which is unique. This will enable us to speak our thoughts without concern for encroaching upon the freedom of your will and we appreciate it greatly.

We see the landscape which you offer at this time as the man solitary and alone upon the hill, gazing out over a vast and trackless land. We see the attitude with which this figure is viewed as seminal in this circumstance, for the trackless waste may be desert, or it may be the fecund and infinite ocean out of which all life springs. It can be the desperate regions of the Sahara or it can be the gentle shore of the ocean of life. Such is the case of the solitary man upon the hill. Is it a hill of good dreams, or a hill of nightmares? Is it a hill from which one is looking upon the past, or is it a hill from which one is gazing upon the possibilities of the infinite divergencies of the present moment going into the future?

We are gratified, my brother, that you chose to refrain from delimiting the parameters of that which we had to say, for we are therefore much more able to use those images and words that move beyond word into emotion of which this instrument is capable. So are we able to speak in this way, when complete freedom of expression is offered and pot luck is taken, shall we say. For we care deeply to answer that which has been asked, not to answer that which has not been asked, and not to infringe upon the learning that is implicit in the question. Consequently, rather than asking, you knocked, and a door may open and for this we thank you.

This instrument had been discussing the broad range of clients with a fellow counselor. And the other counselor suggested to this instrument that the vast majority of his counselees were experiencing the feelings of guilt and unworthiness that come from not setting down the catalyst and experience of the past, not attending to the releasing of old energy and thus being stuck between the past and the guilt thereof, and the future and the fear thereof. This conversation was not without its rhythm in this own instrument's process, for it deals with continuing triggers which open into unworthiness, which effectively deflate the blooming of this instrument's joy in the present moment. Consequently this comment went deeply into this instrument's heart and we share the gratitude that this instrument has felt for this very common-sense observation.

The deep wanderings of any entity will include many episodes during which the knight in shining armor errs in judgment or in intention and consequently loses the luster of the feeling of honor that goes with the appellation of knight. While in the metaphysical realm, error is not seen in the same light, shall we say, as within your density and within your illusion. Nevertheless, within the metaphysical worlds there may be found in any incarnation those spots which did not come clean, those stains of judgment which became catalyst for growth and cause indeed for those extremely understandable emotions of regret and self-doubt. We would not take from you the sting of this learning. For it has been helpful and will continue to be helpful in the way of the ore that is flung into the machine which whirls rocks at high velocity in order to crack them and to open up the ore within them. This kind of action is the corrosive and concussive kind of catalyst that truly creates the feelings of the darker side of the palate of colors of emotions that tell the truth about the essence of any biological entity which you may call a soul. This catalyst is that which is as the Beatitudes of this instrument's Bible. Those sayings, of the one known as Jesus, describe the poor in heart, and those who mourn, as blessed.[45]

We ask you: why are these things a blessing? And we say unto you: as always in the gaining of truth, there is usually within your third-density illusion the necessity for sufficient discomfort to rock the boat of complacency and pride that are the besetting errors of those who strive with every fiber of their being to be honorable, ethical and spiritually compassionate entities.

All other sins, or errors, as this instrument prefers—and so do we—to say, have this characteristic of disappearing beneath the compassion of the awareness that it is impossible not to err while within the third-density state. The releasing of the catalyst, then, has to do with an increasing ability to recognize the value of that which is known to you within this density of yours as the past. Indeed, it is the past only in the sense that your thoughts are those which are formed from that which is in space/time, that which is within this illusion. Consequently, the thoughts themselves deal completely with illusion unless the choice is made firmly and constantly to move the seat of perception from third density to that which is known as fourth density to this instrument; we believe that you are aware of these terms also.

How is it possible then, to find those moments when the mind and the thoughts become unskillful? For this is the basic nature of the state of mind into which you, as a personality shell, have stumbled, shall we say, in the way of left foot, right foot and perhaps not looking up often enough beyond the next step and the next, to see, shall we say, "the big picture." To see that point of view which does not shift with the passage of 10,000 years and to see one's learning and one's service in that light.

We would wish to say, my brother, that in no way have you been deficient. In no way have you stepped away from every challenge. In all things you have attempted your best. And we share with you the fundamental and absolute perception that this is enough. This is what has been. Were it not enough, yet it would be enough. For it is what has brought you as a blooming, gem-like, crystalline entity to this moment, which is full of infinite possibilities. Had you hoped to be closer to your goal at this point, my brother? How do you know how close you are to a given goal? How do you know what the nature of

---

[45] The Beatitudes:

Blessed are the poor in spirit, for theirs is the kingdom of heaven.

Blessed are the meek, for they shall possess the earth.

Blessed are they who mourn, for they shall be comforted.

Blessed are they who hunger and thirst for justice, for they shall be satisfied.

Blessed are the merciful, for they shall obtain mercy.

Blessed are the clean of heart, for they shall see God.

Blessed are the peacemakers, for they shall be called children of God.

Blessed are they who suffer persecution for justice's sake, for theirs is the kingdom of heaven.

your future may be? Indeed, no one, and we say this absolutely, no one caught within the bounds of space/time can know the future. For although the future has been formed from the standpoint of eternity, it has most decidedly not been formed from the standpoint of third density. Indeed, you at this time, shall we say, are on a time lateral, a sidetrack, not even upon the main track of evolution, as you work to move through this illusion which is so cleverly designed to give you the maximum opportunity to change, to transform, to make new choices and find new balances within the spiral of ongoing learning, evolution and service that is the essence of the love and light of the one infinite Creator.

You stand upon a hill. You gaze. And where shall you gaze? And what shall be your thoughts? Shall they be those thoughts that measure and judge the self as though there were a score beyond which one would succeed; in lack of which one would fail? My brother, this is decidedly not the case. The score of which this entity is aware in a quantitative sense is the score of 51% service to others by intention and we hope that you are aware that you are vibrating as service to others at this time by a comfortable margin. There is great purity and sweetness in your desire to serve purely. We ask you to know, for the first time, your nature. To know and begin to have faith in that essence which you have chosen as your essence.

Have you erred in some way in the past, as this entity has, as the one known as Jim has? Yes, my brother. Blessed are you, for you have erred and now you can begin again as if for the first time except that now you have knowledge. There is a knowing within you that you will remember because it is burned and etched into you by the corrosion of catalyst. But you have sweetened this catalyst, little by little and it is that energy which we would encourage you to shed upon this entire concern at this time. We give this instrument the word, *forgiveness*.

You have harmed no one. We may say that the attempt to take on another entity's difficulties in order to free him of them is, to our way of thinking, somewhat distorted. Might we ask in this case if it would not have been more skillful to take on that entity's perfection and know that it was the truth? By believing that which you saw, and not believing that which you did not see, you were more skillful upon the level of what this instrument would call the akashic plane and less skillful upon the level of what this instrument would call the outer planes. Universally, it is less skillful to choose the near target, of working with the pain, the behavior, and the illusion. Always, knowing the truth of perfection is the more universal and the more truly metaphysical solution to gazing at distress, difficulty, damage and distortion in general. That which seems utterly dark is also the light. It has become distorted. As this instrument often says: it has departed the factory specifications. Yet it is still the light. Like all true vines, it is attached to the one great original Root, the Thought, the Logos that is love.

What can there be besides love in a universe in which all things are one? That which you see in others you may work upon within yourself. By knowing the truth, it is true for you and it is true for that entity. You see that the dark side is an illusion which may be charmed with the art, the pretty stories, the songs, the lilts, the melodies, the gentle motifs, of the storyteller, the poet and the singer.

When that choice is yours again, we suggest simply attempting to see in a more balanced and more universal way that which you actually are seeing. Attempt to see *into* and not *at* the situation, seeing beyond the apparent into the divine that surrounds and penetrates it. This knowing is not an infringement upon anyone. It does not need their approval, their agreement, or their understanding for it is not a thing. Rather, it is an essence. Share your being, share that which is in you, that which is the true self of you, that which is what this instrument would call "the Christ within." That consciousness that is unconditional and that knows that all entities in absolute equality of essence are one with the divine.

We stand with you upon this hill in all times, in all places, in all seasons, those who have heard your call. Nothing can separate us. There are energies, which are yours, which guide and aid and give encouragement and support even to one who is in solitude of being. It is well to lean into this support as you would into an extended family. There are energies of fourth density, fifth density, and sixth density that are connected with you. These extended families are energies and essences of a light that cannot be subverted. They can be activated by the focus and the surety and confidence of your …

(Pause)

We find that this instrument has no word for the feeling of knowing that someone is ineluctably a part of your family. The more that you can rest in total confidence that this feeling, this support, is there and able to help, the more this shall calm the troubled waters of the inner ocean.

Before we leave this instrument, we would wish to be sure to speak concerning the state of mind of the boiling and turbulent anger and so forth which you experience when you wish to meditate deeply.

As you may have inferred from that which we have said previously concerning your previous practice of aiding those about you by taking upon yourself their distortions, by moving into the astral and becoming an uninvited guest within their distorted worldview, shall we say, if we could call this situation an entity called "Weltanschauung." For instance, we could say that you invited Weltanschauung into your aura—to use the term very loosely. Within your energy body there then lurked Weltanschauung, who was not the entity that you attempted to help, but rather a thought form, consisting of your intention and this entity's distortion. Thusly, in affecting what this instrument would call a yellow-ray energy exchange with another entity, there was the shadow that free will had been gently nudged, if not infringed. It is a shadow area, that helping of another by the force of physical will.

Again this is a portion of that which is past and need not concern you at this time, except in that you may forgive yourself unconditionally and release the past, thanking it for the tremendous gifts of instruction which it has given you and turning towards a blessed future with confidence. This attitude will bring about that which it expects. That which an entity thinks and focuses upon is a strong power to alter the course of a very possibility-strewn existence. There are more choices to make than we can express through this instrument. Every instant abounds. Consequently we simply encourage those who seek the truth simply to be alert for there is information thick-strewn about the path.

The situation then is that there is an amalgamation of Weltanschauung energies which has gotten into the section of the aura which this instrument would describe as being mostly in the orange and yellow ray, those energies of resistance and other difficulty that you have picked up being mostly involved with issues of personal relationships and the relationship of self to various groups such as the family, the marriage, and the working colleagues.[46] These are invited guests and consequently have enjoyed a pleasant ride within your nature. It is time to invite them to leave. We would suggest that you create for yourself, in the privacy of your contemplations and reflections, that which this instrument would call an exorcism. You may investigate the [Roman Catholic] rite of exorcism to see the fundamental shape of such an invitation to leave. Within the works that this instrument calls the Law of One there is some discussion of such a cleansing. And certainly within this instrument's mind lie many other avenues which can be fruitfully investigated, such as the American Indian tradition and the Hindu tradition.

One very simple method of releasing these thought forms is to remember the essence of each distorted thought form, whether by the name of the entity which had it or by some description of the shape of that suffering which you invited in. Write each down and then ritually and with solemnity burn each piece of paper upon which these essences are represented. It need not be complex. Yet [if you wish] it certainly may be so, and we suggest that the inner self be invited to create the most acceptable and appropriate words and actions for you; ones that express most purely your acceptance of yourself, your acceptance of these thought forms, your invitation for them to depart and your inviting them to do so in the name of that which you hold the highest and dearest of all things, that for which you would live and that for which you would die. Stand upon that which you are, that which you know, that which you believe and have faith in and say, "Goodbye. I thank you, God bless you, be on your way now. Be gone."

---

[46] Carla: I read this sentence through a lot, as I felt sure the Q'uo group did not intend to suggest that one exorcise the family and friends one loves. I believe they were talking here about the times R had taken on some sorrow or time of suffering for such people and suffered with them to the extent that he was suffering for them. Insofar as he as a person and healer would be distorted about the nature of that suffering and the nature of true healing, to that extent would R's own perception of the energy be skewed, and since what we perceive is truth to our minds, R's memory was keeping "untrue" versions of these relationships, based on past times of sorrow and his joining the suffering one in confusion rather than "knowing" the truth of perfection and rightness. However, I leave it just as transcribed. My interpretation could be all wrong!

We would now at this time ask if there be those follow up queries which you may have upon your mind?

(Long pause. No verbalized question.)

We are those of Q'uo, and we are with you, my brother.

We are most aware of the lack of what you call ego and we find your imaging charming.

A point we would make as we depart is that there is, for each choice to martyr the self, that choice to use slightly more wisdom and to extend the time within incarnation. This is not meant upon the literal level. It is quite subtle but is the level at which you function at this time. It therefore is at a deeper level than words and we cannot express ourselves directly.

We at this time depart this instrument and this contact with feelings of joy and of gratitude so, so full in our hearts. We leave this instrument and this group in the love and in the light of the one infinite Creator. Adonai vasu borragus.

L/L Research

L/L Research is a subsidiary of Rock Creek Research & Development Laboratories, Inc.

P.O. Box 5195
Louisville, KY 40255-0195

www.llresearch.org

Rock Creek is a non-profit corporation dedicated to discovering and sharing information which may aid in the spiritual evolution of humankind.

ABOUT THE CONTENTS OF THIS TRANSCRIPT: This telepathic channeling has been taken from transcriptions of the weekly study and meditation meetings of the Rock Creek Research & Development Laboratories and L/L Research. It is offered in the hope that it may be useful to you. As the Confederation entities always make a point of saying, please use your discrimination and judgment in assessing this material. If something rings true to you, fine. If something does not resonate, please leave it behind, for neither we nor those of the Confederation would wish to be a stumbling block for any.

© 2009 L/L RESEARCH

Sunday Meditation
May 4, 2003

Group question: The question today, Q'uo, is please expand on the difference between serving and pleasing. It is mentioned in the [L/L Research] transcripts many times but it is mentioned as though we should already know what they're talking about. So we appreciate your giving us the difference between serving and pleasing.

(Carla channeling)

We are those known to you as the principle of Q'uo and we greet you in the love and in the light of the one infinite Creator, in whose service we are. We thank each of you so much for the privilege of sharing this meditation with you and for taking the time and the energy from the busy schedules, about which you were speaking earlier, in order to seek truth. We are happy to share with you our thoughts as they come to us on the subject about which you asked, of the difference between pleasing and serving others. We, however, would ask that each of you use your own personal discrimination in listening to that which we have to offer. For we may offer some things that are helpful and other things that simply are not and we would greatly appreciate each of you accepting only those things which seem fair and resonant and right to you, allowing all of the other thoughts that do not ring true to be forgotten. For we would not constitute any sort of a stumbling block in any entity's progress.

As we gaze upon this interesting question, the memory which this instrument has of many attempts within this instrument's earlier life to be of fuller service that were rated by this instrument as unsuccessful, come before us as that about which we would speak as the beginning of this topic. This instrument is, and has been, at a greater extent than is usual upon your planet, one who has been centrally concerned with the question of how to serve for all of its incarnational existence. And in this instrument's early years she lived a childhood that was unusual compared to the cultural norms of your peoples in that this entity was more responsible and had a work and duty-ridden existence such as that of an adult at a very early age because of the circumstances of her family's life, lifestyle and the occupations of the parents of this birth family. Consequently, this instrument was constantly serving others: babysitting, cooking, cleaning and doing those services that are common to all who maintain a home and take care of the creature needs of the family. However, this particular instrument enjoyed the company of two parents who were very intelligent, very naturally critical, and due to lifestyle considerations, often very far from sober, thus creating a situation where the instrument was constantly serving and indeed, serving well for its age and abilities. However it was being told constantly that it was not serving well, and indeed, nothing was ever "good enough."

Consequently, this instrument worked for many years as an adult, consciously moving back into the child years and comforting and loving that child self, which even now sits upon this instrument's lap, a beloved child at last, adored, pampered and given every creature comfort of which this instrument can think.[47] For truly this instrument has discovered that the secret to recapturing its magic of youth and innocence and dream-vision was connected with the lack of forgiveness which this instrument had toward its child-self, having judged, not as a loving entity would judge the self, but as a thoughtless and critical entity would judge the self. This healing has been an ongoing process within this instrument's experience of regathering its child self to its heart and becoming that mother and father that truly adored this very human and error-prone entity known in this incarnation as Carla. This ability to move back in thought and to do work in consciousness, having perceived a lack of love, is very helpful as a resource for an entity who is working upon how to serve others in the highest and best way.

Now let us back up from this storytelling to a far hill where we stand to look over the terrain of this metaphysical land within which we traverse as we discuss the question of how to serve. In terms of the cosmology of which this instrument is so fond, the Earth and its experience is the realm that could be called a school. It is a beautiful, marvelous, magical schoolroom called Earth upon which the entity is born, upon which it receives every catalyst which it needs in order to think new thoughts and transform into a new being, not just once but as a continual spiraling progression. And it gratefully accepts the [return to] dust of the physical body when that soul which has done its work within bone and flesh finds that the Creator has called it onward, the lessons here being finished.

It is a specific kind of classroom. The subject of this particular grade which this instrument calls third density or human existence upon planet Earth is, "How To Love And Be Loved." The paths that each entity enters into in this life are in one way fated and designed ahead of time; in another way, completely and specifically a matter of free choice, so that each turning in the road offers the choice of one or more differences of direction which may seem small at the time. But down the road a few paces one finds the roads diverging rapidly. A few paces more, and the two roads, or three roads, have moved in such different directions that one road no longer gives a view of any other. And then within *that* road that has been chosen, another series of choices opens up that may just as rapidly move one forward into yet another situation. This is a beautifully designed, though paradoxical construction of synchronicity and will, in which the soul coming into incarnation, along with its guidance, decides upon what particular lesson shall be the focus of the incarnation.

All lessons have to do with love. But there are different threads of understanding having to do with loving and accepting the love of others that create many, many, different choices of incarnational lesson, some having heavily to do with the responsibilities of loving and expressing that love in very fundamental and practical ways; other entities having fierce but unseen catalyst having to do with a resistance or inability to accept love and to greet the love offerings of others with trust and faith. In each case the lesson is unique to the entity and the way that it comes into the life is carefully guarded. One way to pinpoint one's own incarnational lesson is to look back over the incarnation and to begin to see where the spirals have returned to the same theme again and again throughout the incarnational experience. In this instrument's life, for instance, the incarnational lesson has, in part, been how to love without expectation of return. This particular lesson, therefore, has come up not simply with the birth parents, but with other relationships that this entity has had that feel resonant and correct and right and yet have posed this same theme, motif and question as catalyst for this instrument's spiritual growth.

[This instrument] also has had to do a great deal of conscious work upon how to accept the love offerings of others. For, damaged and bruised by the catalyst of its early life, it became, unawares to itself, of the opinion that there was an unworthiness to that entity called Carla which must endure, for there was no hope of becoming adequate or worthy. It is ideas such as these that create a situation in which, rather than feeling confident and sure within the self, the self becomes cast adrift from that center of emotional security within the heart that knows itself to be a worthwhile person. And cast adrift thusly, such entities are ever prone to the self-doubt and the feelings of unworthiness and depression that concur

---

[47] Carla: My teacher, Papa, sent me a Raggedy Ann doll a year ago, which I declared to be myself as a child, and have subsequently loved with all the fervor of a new Mom! I ask her to tell me her dreams, and she does!

with, or occur at the same time as, these particular distortions in the life pattern.

Now, in this instrument's case these relationships which occurred were carefully chosen, not for that which would be considered happy reasons, but precisely because they set up the dynamics in which this particular lesson might be best learned. The incarnational plan therefore has functioned beautifully. However, had this instrument not chosen to engage with that birth family in relationship work and therefore had this instrument never grasped what the lesson was or how to work on it consciously in this relationship, there were repeated instances where this instrument had planned carefully to meet other entities which would have been just as helpful in setting up the dynamics of a relationship of this instrument with an entity who was profoundly worthy of love but who was incapable of giving emotionally in return.

Thus, this instrument was teacher to those with whom it came in contact who were incapable of loving, for they received love even though they could not return it. And this instrument in turn gratefully drank in that seeming corrosion of difficulty in the relationship because of needs seemingly unmet which then cause this instrument to place itself within the spiritual regions of seeking, asking and silence: the listening, the waiting for the return of the voice that speaks.

In general, it is easy to identify when an entity wishes to be pleased. It is easy to identify that which an entity who wishes to be pleased wishes. And it is usually fairly easy to obtain that which is desired. Thusly, we do not feel that we need to speak about pleasing people. Indeed, it is endemic to this culture that those who are born with the biological persona of femininity have an enormous amount of cultural and familial training in pleasing entities. It is the way of this culture that the feminine aspect focuses upon pleasing and making comfortable those about it. And certainly the feminine persona is most gifted in this way by nature. Thusly, each may rest in the knowledge that when entities ask for something and entities say that they shall be pleased, there is a fair probability that that entity *can* be pleased, that the need can be met, and that the entity will be "happy."

To serve someone is a far different matter. Serving someone is not necessarily pleasing the entity. Serving someone is not necessarily doing anything to, with or for an entity. Serving someone is fundamentally the awareness that you and the person you are serving are one entity, united, singular and absolutely equal. Rejoicing in the apparent differences, a servant of the light relates to other selves as "themselves," knowing that the self and the other-self are a certain kind of entity, citizens of eternity, dwellers beyond time and space, within a universe that is as wide as infinity and as small as the interior of the human heart. Indeed, may we say that from our perspective, the universe lies within each of your hearts and all the stars and all the galaxies actually reside within. So as you sit upon your blanket and gaze at the outward stars, you are also gazing within at precisely the same view. That which lies within you is infinity, blessing, grace and the infinite Creator Whose consciousness is all that there is.

Service is bound up in the knowing of this relationship and this nature so that when one who is a servant of the light and of the Godhead principle, shall we say, gazes upon an other self, no matter what that self is asking, the basic service is the connection of unity without judgment of any kind but with absolute faith that this entity is a spiritual entity and is to be honored, loved, respected and treated as a spiritual entity.

What is it to serve? Upon the surface it seems a thing of question and answer: "Ask and you shall receive, knock and it shall be opened"; "Can you make me a peanut butter sandwich?" "I certainly can"; "Can I have half of your peanut butter sandwich?" "You may have the larger half." This physical kind of service is easy to see. The problems begin to multiply in wishing to be of service to another when the lines of relationship have become tangled into the energy nexi the body of the relationship, so that blockages have been set up which create the inability to communicate fully. In this atmosphere there are hungers that cannot be fulfilled. There are thirsts that cannot be slaked. There are needs that cannot be met, or so it would seem. And in such a pickle it seems as though the universe has become full of centers of trouble, what this instrument might call "trouble bubbles," which keep coming into what would otherwise be a very simple equation and creating such confusion that no clear path to the most high or the most loving service can be seen.

Certainly the one known as T1, who has asked this question, is aware in many ways that there is no firm ground upon which a conversation concerning things dear to the heart of either self or other-self may be voiced. For the blockages and distortions within the body of that relationship have become by repetition hardened in the way of thought forms into that which is set up as the situation in which the feeling of being of service is impossible to receive because the capability of other-self to express to self and the capabilities of self to express to other-self have been compromised. When service reaches an impasse in a deeply central relationship, such as the one known as T1 experiences at this time, the possibility of being gratified by a sense of having served becomes distant and rare. For that other-self which is being served is unable to become aware of the nature or the purity of the service. May we say that this in no way etiolates or annuls that service of true love freely given which the one known as T1 offers. This is a service. There is no hesitation in our stating that all who love serve.

Let us examine what occurs when one loves. When one loves, one is expressing the self, the nature of the self being love. The one great original Thought is a Thought of love. When this Thought of love decided to know Itself, each of you, as sparks of the divine, was created and then all of the worlds, densities and creations were created in order for the Creator in all of Its parts to have a place to play. The [classroom] level of this school of love which each of you enjoys at this time carefully hides the simple truth of this unified and loving nature. It is not apparent that all entities are one, for each seems to have an end at the skin and the hair and the appearance and all others seem to be separate from the self. It is the work of the student who seeks within to move beneath the veneer, the flesh and appearance, and especially the apparent firmness and stability of all things, for things are much more plastic and pliable than is usually thought within the illusion. For those who are able to move into the heart, and to open up into that self that is love that is the heart of each, the illusion begins to shimmer and waver and finally to drop away from time to time completely, showing the great ocean of unity and love and tremendous emotional support which the Unity of the entire creation offers to the one who is able to move beyond appearances. To the one who has become able to rest in her own skin, in the knowledge that she is a perfect and worthy spark of the infinite Creator, as well as a bozo, and a wretch, and a sinner, and all of the other appellations with which humans are wont to name themselves when they see that they have made what they would consider mistakes. It becomes clear at last, as the mists lift, that all is well, all is One; the being is the service, and the doing, a secondary and distant detail.

Now this translates into rethinking the nature of service from a doing to a being. That which is done unto another is subject to the rules of free will. It is not well to infringe upon the free will of another. It is not well to criticize or judge another. It is not necessary in any case to do these things. Yet, there is the drive to serve that is or becomes a frustration for one who is having difficulty shifting back and forth between the world of appearances and actions, and the world of essences, energies and intentions. We would say then, focusing into service, that the heart of service is the full acceptance, respect and honoring of other-self as the self, and treating other-self as the self is treated. Within each entity's progress in evolution in mind, body and spirit, there needs to be careful and continuing attention given to the working with the self alone. Wherever an entity sees damage elsewhere, no matter how clearly that energy is another entity's, a key to working out this quandary of service and its appropriate nature is to do the work upon the self that the entity would wish to do upon the other-self.

Thusly, if there is great projection from other-self of judgment and control and this kind of careful tension built as a barrier between self and other-self which seems to be projected towards the self from the other self, then it may be skillful for the self to move into that area of self that is being criticized, that judged, controlled, unhappy area, as if self were other-self. As if there were a self that was able to come to the aid of the self that is being criticized, judged and limited. The self then, who is attempting to be of service to other-self works upon the self to affirm the self's value, to honor the self, to ask the self what it needs and in all ways to turn the attempt to serve other[-self] within so that the self seems to be serving the self, yet it is the self who loves, serving that self within, which is studying the incarnational lesson of loving, without expectation of return, loving, independently of the reaction, loving beyond condition.

What does this develop into then, as one shifts from the being of the loving heart to the doing of the outside world and the conversation at breakfast, and the conversation during the night-time news? We do not know, we cannot know. Each entity and each moment are as those stepping-stones which springboard into "we do not know," for each of you has an exquisite amount of free will and each of you has infinite possibilities.

When service is occurring it will become clear to the self only gradually and only by hindsight. And the hallmark of that service will be the awareness that the heart remained open throughout the decision-making processes of everyday life. There shall be many words in working out any tangled relationship; there will be many feelings and many balancings and rebalancings of the energy between the two. Yet when service is being successfully offered, there will be the continuing stubborn, quirky and absolute insistence upon continuing to see self and other-self as both worthy and loving and compassionate entities who are striving to solve that mystery which is implicit in humanhood: how to express the metaphysical nature of the self within the material world. The material world seems often inimical and unfriendly to the spirit. Yet indeed it is not, or need not be. For within that material world lie not just concrete and computer chips and men's dreams of empire but also the call of the birds that the one known as S was mentioning earlier in your conversation as being such a blessing to him within his new abode, the feather of the eagle as the one known as F. was mentioning, and all of the blessings of earth and water and fire and air and the plants and the animals which make up your second density. All of the entities and energies are messengers, easily impressed and magnetized with news that is just for you, just for today, just for right now. We cannot tell you ahead of time what winged or furry beast, what street sign or road sign or chance-read word shall be a signpost for you but we can assure you that, as you look for them, they will crowd around hoping to be noticed. Information lies thick upon the ground, flies in the air about you and comes to you in every ray of light that the infinite Creator sends. The universe is alive, it is intelligent and it is working as one infinite being. You are a part of that. Not a mechanical part, but a living, breathing entity which breathes the air of eternity and whose concerns are beyond the trammels of the apparent passage of time.

When an effort to serve seems amiss, we simply suggest that the self take a very deep breath, in and out, in and out, and begin coming back from the details of the tangle to the truth that lies beneath the tangled surface of the waves of life. Picture the surface of your life as the choppy waves that seem to crash upon the shore, and know that deep within you, the truth of your being is as the liquid core of the Earth itself: calm water, quiet, deep, powerful, infinite and strong. This is your nature. This is your very essence. You are love. As you allow the surety of this one Thought to pervade your being, feel all concerns drop away leaving only the flame of spirit, only that love which created all the worlds that are and all that shall ever be.

We would at this time thank the one known as T1 for the excellent question which we have enjoyed working on with you although we fear our words are very poor. And we would at this time thank this instrument and leave it in the love and the light of the one Creator as we transfer this contact to the one known as Jim. We are those of Q'uo.

(Jim channeling)

I am Q'uo, and we greet each again in love and in light through this instrument. It is our privilege at this time to offer ourselves in the attempt to speak to any further queries of a shorter nature which may remain upon the minds of any of those present. Is there another query at this time?

S: I had one that C requested I ask. In a previous session it was mentioned about psychic greeting[48] and it seems more and more obvious that it is something that she is suffering through and I was wondering if you could elaborate or shine any words of wisdom or light on this situation.

I am Q'uo, and I'm aware of your query, my brother. When one feels that one has become the focus of the attentions of a negatively-oriented entity, and that one's behaviors, thoughts and actions have begun to reflect this interaction in a negative fashion, then it is well to incorporate some means of examining the life pattern and seeking a means whereby the openings that offer access to such entities may be closed by the efforts of the self. Thus, we would recommend that the one known as C begin a daily practice of meditation; whether at the beginning or the end of the day or some time in-between is of her choosing. It is often easier to do a

---

[48] psychic greeting: psychic attack by non-physical service-to-self entities.

meditative practice at the day's end, when one can assess the qualities of one's experience during the preceding day and work upon these perceptions that focus one's attention upon one's behavior, one's thoughts, and one's responses to them.

Thus, during this meditative time it would be well if the one known as C could examine the recent events within its life pattern that have made an impression, whether to the positive or the negative, whether of joy or of sorrow, whether of what you would call good or bad. Then take this inventory of events and examine it with an eye towards choices made which may be less harmonious than are possible for the one known as C … Examine those areas in which she has offered herself in a manner which she would choose to improve, shall we say, if possible. When there is seen a pattern, then it is well to begin a process of balancing this energy. The pattern may be of any nature, may be choices made in certain areas which were seen to be deleterious at a later time and then may be relived in the meditative state so that as the energies are once again felt that were felt in the beginning of the day and these energies can begin to be balanced by the conscious knowledge of the one known as C and of the natural balancing within the human soul that is possible when one has made a discovery that is in such need of such balancing attention.

The effort to make what we would call a cleansing is also helpful. This was our previous suggestion, that the one known as C attempt to find a way to purify her environment.

The environment of the mind, of the attitude, of the being, within oneself is also a good place to begin, but would need to be supplemented by the daily meditation so that there may be a continual effort to examine the part that one plays in the opening of the self to the possibility of psychic greetings. For such greetings do not occur by themselves. There is a choice that each entity makes somewhere within the life pattern that opens the self to the possibility of such greeting, whether negatively-oriented entities find their ability to work in any life-pattern when such openings are made either wittingly or unwittingly by the third-density entity. Thus it is well that any entity who feels that such negative greetings are a portion of its experience begin to examine that experience with care upon a daily basis so that these openings may be reduced and healed.

Is there a further query, my brother?

S: That was interesting, thank you very much. Just one last one on a lighter note. You don't think that Funny Cide is going to win the Triple Crown, do you?

I am Q'uo. We are aware of your query my brother. And we find that we are less talented as racing prognosticators than as those who are able to comment upon the daily round of activities. We are sorry that we are not more helpful in this regard. Is there another query at this time?

S: No, I always ask every year. I just thought it was amusing, thanks.

I am Q'uo. We thank you for your levity and for your concerns. Is there another query at this time?

C: Yes, Q'uo, I have another one from T1. She says, "We are told that love is not an infringement on free will. What actually happens when that love is sent? Does it provide an increased probability or potential for love to be assimilated into that entity's life unconsciously? What happens on a metaphysical level? How is it a service?"

I am Q'uo, and am aware of your query, my sister. When love is sent to any entity, it then is a resource which may or may not be used by that entity. Most often there is little conscious recognition of love which has been sent from, shall we say, what you would call a distance or through time. But there is the unconscious recognition, by the receiver of such love, that one's beingness has been enhanced, that the possibilities are greater, that the resources have increased, shall we say. For at the heart of each seeker, there resides a supply of love that is the daily round of gift, shall we say, from the one Creator, the intelligent energy by which the Logos creates the one creation; by which the Logos provides each entity within the one creation the energy to partake in that which you call life. Thus, when one sends love to another, one amplifies that which is already there and sets up what might be seen as a harmonic wave that moves within the metaphysical realms of one's consciousness there to enhance that ability to perceive and utilize the gifts of the one Creator.

Is there another query, my sister?

C: Just a follow-up from me on T1's behalf. So there isn't any way in which loving someone can be considered an infringement on free will?

I am Q'uo, and am aware of your query, my sister, and this is indeed so. However, we see that many entities have differing definitions of what they would call love. The primary quality that we recognize is that it is unconditional.

Is there a further query, my sister?

C: I do have another question from another person. I would like to ask on T2's behalf: "What is the metaphysical meaning behind SARS? If AIDS reflects the public fear of sex, what does SARS reflect? What can we do to treat SARS positively?"

I am Q'uo, and I am aware of your query, my sister. We find that there is much within this query which would infringe upon the free will of many, so there is but little we may say in this regard. As to the metaphysical implications of this disease, as you would call it, we would suggest that there is much occurring upon your third-density illusion at this time in which there are populations of peoples being experimented with, shall we say, so that there is an added degree of difficulty in the life experience. Beyond this we may respond no further.

Is there another query, my sister?

C: Yes, T2 had a follow-up and I will ask it on his behalf although he did say that he realized that you probably could not answer it: "Is SARS a biological weapon that is being used by people against other people?"

I am Q'uo, and I'm aware of your query, my sister. We may speak in general terms and suggest that the gist of this query is basically correct.

Is there another query, my sister?

C: T2 asked specifically, "Was SARS made by China's government?"

I am Q'uo, and at this juncture we find the full stop of free will must be enforced. We may say no further. Is there another query, my sister?

C: No, and on T2's behalf I thank you so much, Q'uo. And also on T1's.

I am Q'uo, and we thank you and they as well, my sister. Is there another query at this time?

(Pause)

I am Q'uo. We would be happy to respond to a final query at this time if there may be one.

(Pause)

C: There don't seem to be any more questions, Q'uo, but we surely do thank you.

I am Q'uo, we are also most grateful, my sister, and we are grateful to each entity within this circle of seeking as well for inviting our presence this day. It is a great privilege and pleasure to be asked to join your circle of seeking. We ask that each utilize the powers of discrimination so that there is no word or concept which we have spoken that becomes a stumbling block in your area of seeking. If any word or concept does not ring of truth to you, we ask that you leave it behind without a second thought.

We are known to you as those of Q'uo. We shall take our leave of this instrument and this group at this time. We leave each in the love and the ineffable light of the one infinite Creator. Adonai, my friends. Adonai. ☥

Sunday Meditation
May 11, 2003

Group question: We've had a general discussion that has touched on several key topics, the focus of which is that self-acceptance seems to keep coming back to center stage, regardless of what one thinks its importance level is. As one moves further along the spiritual path it continues to be the ultimate focus. Now, we also had a brief discussion about what it truly means to be a mature soul and how that involves loving yourself and thinking for yourself and not going along with mainstream consensus. So, with this as our basic background of discussion, we've decided to leave this session open to the forces to take in whatever direction they see fit for our mutual good.

(David channeling)

I am the Three. We greet you as three in one, the triune aspect of the higher self of entity David Wilcock. We are pleased with the opportunity to share our words of good fortune and commerce of energetic exchange. In our heart of hearts we appreciate greatly the opportunity to share these words with you, and only remind you that you can take as you will these seeds of thought and if there are those complexes of understanding that seem to surpass your own capacities, they may be best dealt with by allowing them to fall away as the rains naturally wash clean the buildings in the aftermath of a hurricane.

As the racetrack commentator would say, "Gentlemen, start your engines." So too is there a time of acceleration happening on your planet. It is this time where the gate bursts forth and the race is then run. The race is a symbol of this capacity for each soul to move beyond cleverness and into compassion. It is the race towards unconditional love for the self and for all others, seeing them as only reflections of the self in the various forms that it exists in oneness. You may smell the enamel coming up from your teeth as we drill through the cavities of your understanding. And the burn of catalyst can seem rather jolting at times, as it certainly can tap into a nerve. Those in this room in which we do these workings are not different from the mass of humanity at this time in that the catalyst of self is accelerating, much as in our racetrack analogy.

It is a dizzying process at first, to experience the releasing of those aspects of living that had seemed to be fixated before. One can be fixated on beliefs or on social structures of various sorts. The prospect of releasing these strictures is one wherein the inanimate difficulties of life's travails are then made animate or, in other words, where those issues of mind spring forth into physical form and become those which by necessity must be confronted directly in one's physical experience. In this sense, one could say that physical experience in the tangible and direct form is the final result of catalyst that has remained unprocessed by other means such as the spirit and the mind complexes.

With this key you can unlock the door to the variegated mystery of self through experiencing quite directly those apparent punishments that life has provided.

We ask only that you recognize that the orchestrating forces of life make it clear that there is to be no larger experience of rather catalytic and suffering nature than is warranted for the evolution of the soul to occur in due course along a pre-described plan of action scripted by the higher self. You may see the octagonal red symbol, known as the stop sign on your racetrack, and feel the need to halt or to put on the brakes on this dizzying spiral of experience. This is akin to those who cling to the riverbanks, seeking the solace of fingers trapped in mud rather than letting go and allowing the eventual reunification into the ocean of oneness to occur.

We have spoken of the variance between a soul that perceives itself as mature and a mature soul. Many of those on your plane seek to embellish their true maturity by pursuing the avenues of distinction typified by that known as the status quo. This ability to refine one's understandings with the monkey-mind mentality, if you will, is indeed a skill, it is a skill of denial and dissociation. The collective understandings would support the war mongers, as some have called these entities, in order that there be a sense of satisfaction in oneself over what is occurring. It is much easier to confront the aggressor with love than with internal condemnation. It is, however, prudent to ensure that love not be confined to one's own social class or grouping but rather to expand to a more universal perspective and thus, though these words must seem very basic to some of you, see those Afghanis or Iraqis who are hurt, maimed and killed by bombings as being equal to yourselves and respect the fact that any support for a governmental figure should not exclude the full ramifications of their actions.

At this time there are those who choose support out of fear. They recognize that these patterns have established [themselves] within their own lives as well. We speak of the relative nature of the pecking order in a family for example, where perhaps the oldest sibling has an unequal amount of control over his or her brothers and sisters. There is a desire to see the object of one's authority in a favorable light, as this allows the conception of the world being a good place to continue. There is a strong desire not to see the negative, not to face that which exists quite plainly for those with eyes to see and ears to hear. Many of you have lost your ability to speak, have lost the energy in the throat chakra, by failing to grasp the information that is present in your mind and taking an easier path of watching television for your news rather than studying those sources that are easily available on the internet and in certain venues of talk radio and satellite-dish television. These issues are only relevant insofar as they are the current catalysts that are the architecture upon which your lives are being led. May we point to the persistent cyclical nature of these events and in so doing explain that what we speak of now is as but the current foundry in which the steel is being hammered into swords rather than plowshares. This foundry exists whenever the populace of third-density [feels that a] vortex of being separate from God exists. Once this connection is again reestablished with oneself inside, there is the extrication of external authority figures from one's immediate influence and this is one aspect of the maturation of the soul.

The soul coming into maturity accepts self in spite of the apparent inconsistencies that are set before the entity. The deeper core of this realization is that the clock is ticking and each one of you is wearing a watch. On some level you all understand that this is the end of a cycle and that the changes that are occurring such as the nearly 300 tornados that occurred in the last week of your time, as we do this reading. [They] are symbolic of a change in consciousness that is happening. This change has been predicted for many thousands of your years of time as you measure it, Christian predictions only being a more recent example, and thus there is a deep knowingness that this is the last chance for third density in this current capacity. There is the often unwavering support for one's leaders despite the nature of nuclear holocaust that could be unleashed if there was not a greater degree of prudence of thought and action.

We feel that the entity known as Q'uo has more to speak on at this time regarding these "space pirates," as they have been called. And thus we transfer this channel. We thank you and we consider you to be our allies and equals in this quest towards infinite knowingness. Peace be with you in the light of everlasting love.

(Carla channeling)

We are known to you as the principle of Q'uo, and we greet you with great joy through this instrument in the love and in the light of the one infinite Creator in whose service we are. We thank the one known as David and the Three and honor them and may we say how much we enjoy working with these energies and how much we feel thankful for the ability to share in the energies of these entities and of each of you. We thank each of you for seeking the Truth, and not by a passing thought, but by setting aside a significant amount of time, energy and love to honor the hunger and the thirst within you for that which is true, beautiful and noble. For indeed, you are experiencing a life in the fire of experience, in the foundry, as the Three have called it so well. And we would use another name as well, the athanor, the oven in which the alchemist places a base metal and ennobles it by knowledge of those higher truths which come from higher to lower, from above to below, faithfully to limn the nature of archetype within the fire of the crucible of living at third-density incarnation upon you present time lateral of third density as you are experiencing it.

This is not what could be called the average or normal way of the ending or the graduation from third grade or third density. In the case of many other sub-logoi, third density's endings have been breached with considerably less difficulty. The so called "space pirates" that you now experience as what this instrument would call "the Bush Boys" have to a fair degree been able to reinvent and recollect many of the tools and many of the subterfuges of past incarnational experiences. And many [of the] fairly small group of influential American statesmen who are following "the Bush Boys," are also remembering and feeling comfortable within the structure of support for such ideas as this instrument would describe as tribal and second density in nature, and falling, then, into a pattern which has indeed placed this particular planet for the last good bit of your experience of time in this density on a local time and space system which is as cut off from the main track as any shunt.

The way back onto the track happens at this time to be the graduation of the entities who are ready for harvest from this planet. The challenge for all of those who feel called into service upon a global level at this time is to identify the purpose of the incarnation, to identify the best way to pursue this purpose and thusly to find the peace that lies within the self which has reckoned with both the situation that it believes that it has come to see before it, and the structure of—this instrument would say virtue—but we would ask her to pause while we find a more neutral emotional word for the way of the highest and best. This instrument has often been able to use the terms of knighthood: honor and chivalry, courtesy and that round table feeling of one for all and all for one. The *beau geste*[49] for many musketeers of Earth at this time is, from the round table of shared experience and concept, to create the fourth density by the way each entity within the round circle lives, moves, thinks and has its being. This is subtle work, yet each of you is, by this work, moving into the place within your nature for which you sought incarnation.

Now, you sought incarnation for several reasons. Many are the tales of suffering that have been spoken within this group this day. And many are those which have not been spoken. We may say that each within this group has, as this instrument has called it, experience in the "school of No."[50] These are all true experiences and excellent in their way. And it is the skillful seeker of spiritual maturity who reckons with these companions of the fire with enough respect and honor to sit with and keep company with these shadows of self, these powerful or troublesome indications that the self indeed has 360 degrees of self to experience.

This instrument has been encouraging each in counsel to investigate and get to know that dark side, for it must be loved also, and more, it needs to be disciplined and to be brought into the circle of self that is working together, for there are many selves within. And there are many voices that come to one who is seeking upon the path. Not [only is there] the voice of guidance that is primary to a certain entity, but also many other voices that, as an

---

[49] *beau geste*: A graceful or magnanimous gesture. [F, *Lit.*, beautiful gesture.]

[50] Carla: When Don Elkins and I first came together, I felt that I had entered into the school of No. May we be married? No. May we have a family? No. May we settle down in a home? It was a challenge for a 25-year-old woman who had intended firmly to have six children! Many preconceptions of what I wanted in my life eventually fell away because of this catalyst.

entity moves through initiations and various levels of realization, will come and be attracted to that seeking self who is blooming in a certain way which calls to the sense of beauty or the sense of spirit, these two things being so close within fourth density we find trouble choosing our metaphors, which, by the Law of Attraction, bring these, as this instrument would call [them], angelic entities, these essences of spirit, these entities that are based upon purified emotion, into the extended family of guidance which increasingly becomes available to the entity that begins to take hold of the process of spiritual evolution and begins to make those difficult choices of what to observe, of what not to observe, what to pick up and what to put down. Indeed, these ways of becoming more aware of the true nature of the self are very important to the eventual success of the mission of each of those within the sphere of the planet Earth at this time and incarnation.

There is the opportunity for that which is already present, but in a very hazy way, to become locally strong. The Earth, with the continual putting of the hostility and bellicosity of many of its entities into the energy of the its mantle, has virtually no choice, as an entity of muscle and blood of its own kind, but to shift the heat that is occurring naturally into a far more balanced way within your planet, into those areas which previously had not experienced so much difficulty with heat below the surface of the mantle of the Earth. When one considers that the heavier materials of the Earth, the oils, the metals, have consistently and for a period of your years been more and more focused within your particular continent of North America, it may be understandable to see the increase in seismic activity for the Earth entity which this instrument calls Gaia is more and more finding it necessary to express some of this heat in ways that it would not have previously, because there was not such a concentration of the heat within your particular continent. The very comfort of your physical vehicles at this time has the potential of becoming greatly disturbed because of the simple lack of awakened and focused compassion that is that which is the prerequisite for bringing in whatever stronger help those vibrations of unconditional love which are as the tie-down points for, shall we say, the airplane or the winged creature of unconditional love. How can you tie down unconditional love, after all? It is infinite; it is mutable in terms of how the energy even expresses within your density.

As the one known as Carla stated, there are partial ways, so far, that your scientists have found to pin down the energy nexi of the incoming grid. There is only that portion of the science of consciousness which has been available to be examined by your scientists. The cosmic sector, as the one known as Larson calls time/space, only shows up as the infinitely changeable, yet always dependable presence of that which cannot be pinned down, cannot be solved, cannot be located and reined in. Rather, it is a harmonic and each of you are as the tuning fork. If you begin to start your own "tuning-forkness," your own emotional essence, vibrating in unconditional love, and allowing that vibration to continue. all of those within your purview have an opportunity, of which they may be unaware, to allow that portion of them which vibrates at that level to join you … And so you have the experience of entities who are able to be seeds of light and love, who seed a group and, by focusing on love alone, are able to begin the process where one heart fires another into spontaneous harmonic vibration as a resonance of that first heart that has found infinity and then another and another and another begin to light up.

This instrument saw a movie, as did the one known as E, in the previous diurnal period. And within that movie there was the vision that this hero within the movie had of all of the entities upon the planet, all of those who were unawakened, and all of those who had begun to change. When this instrument was very, very ill and in the hospital fighting for her life, as she prayed she began to see precisely the same kind of vision but it was the vision of all of those who were praying, not necessarily for this instrument but simply praying for all of those who were suffering. They shone in millions and millions of lights, and there was hope and certainty there that was precious and miraculous in this instrument's process at this time. And indeed, was one of the keys to her rapid rehabilitation from that point.

And this instrument has also seen that there was an entity who was forced to mutilate itself by removing its own arm, for it had been trapped in the mountains by a boulder upon its arm. This entity also, in the powerful and challenging situation of pain and survival that this entity faced, prayed. And when it did so, it also reported the same vision of all of the souls that were like lights, millions and millions of lights, that were lighting the planet keeping watch in the room of prayer that is common to each of you in this circle; common to every entity upon the planet; common to princes and paupers, Afghanis and Iraqis, and wealthy, wealthy Americans, and every other entity: intelligent, barely sentient, and everything in between, that lives and breathes and has taken a body so that the ensouled entity within may gain experience, may go into the furnace and may come out of that furnace with a gift for the infinite Creator of dearly bought and precious experience, and more than that, dearly bought and infinitely precious emotion. Never doubt the importance of those emotions that move beneath the surface of the situation, beneath the anger, beneath the grief, beneath the emotions of any descriptions which are easy and come immediately to mind. And indeed, simply sit with those first shallow reactions watching the self at work, watching the triggers go off, watching all of the playacting that you have learned to do in order to cope with a very difficult environment and a heavy illusion.

If you have the patience to watch *through* the processes that the mind puts you as an entity through, you may come to these peculiar moments of awareness, as this instrument would call it, where you are beyond the details and into that spacious part of the self that moves beneath that dense geometry of the surface experience into the much broader and more mystery filled caverns, mountains and ranges of the archetypical mind. This works, for the most part, on image, on myth and idea, and the connections that create new places within the mind. So each of you is extremely powerful to deal with this somewhat discomforting situation as you gaze upon the Earth plane. Each has the capacity to generate focus, to generate intention, and thusly to open the door to such disciplines as maintaining silence, reaching through that silence to ask, and then finding the discipline to wait in faith for the movement of spirit.

At the same time, may we say what a joyful thing that we see in each of your hearts! There is a joy, a feeling: "*that now I believe I may have the possibility of service,*" true service, beyond the self, beyond time and space. And we say to you this is the time that you have waited for, in many ways, for each of you. This is the time of opening and flowering development. And we find our hearts so full of pleasure and joy in sharing a bit in the experience of your awakening that we cannot express it.

We feel that we have spoken long enough for this group at this time and would ask the one known as J which the one known as Carla set this up with beforetimes to read that query which comes from the one known as B.

(J reads a question from B.)

"It appears that the fourth-density harmonic grid forms the requisite structure for social memory between living organisms. Can you confirm this? And please feel free to make any comment that you feel would be helpful without infringing upon free will."

(Carla channeling)

We are those of Q'uo. And we find that, as this instrument said in her perfectly conscious state, there is some knowledge missing which would helpful for a responding in specifics to the one known as B. However, we will use this instrument for a while before we transfer this contact back to the one known as David and the one known as the Three.

The concept of social memory, while in a linear way perfectly understandable, is less understandable in terms of its venue, its place of occurrence. It occurs within what this instrument would call the cosmic sector. And yet the cosmic sector appears within third density only by anomalous behavior recorded in otherwise traditionally and classically accurate experiments having to do with the Einsteinian view of the universe. Thusly, the concept of social memory has anomalous characteristics. It may be said that such forms training wheels for social memory and creates the necessity for learning. However, we may say that there are other approaches—or another approach—which also yields social memory. Perhaps we could look at the two as inner and outer in their pathways. Or in another way we could say that the local, as opposed to the cosmic, both have their ways of developing fourth-density characteristics.

With that said, we would transfer this query to the one known as David and incidentally, as we will not speak with each again through this instrument, we leave each at this time with many, many thanks in the love and in the light of the one infinite Creator. We are those known to you as Q'uo. Adonai.

(David channeling)

We are those of the Three, and we greet you in the light and love of the one infinite Creator. Bear in mind that the verses that are uttered at this time bespeak of distortions that are unavoidable due to the mismatch between your current physical conceptions and those of the templates of universal consciousness. As the one known as Ra has stated: Understanding is not of your density and there are those elements that remain inscrutable. With this disclaimer in place, we may enunciate further on this query.

The geometric structures so often sought after in your sacred science teachings, whether secret or public, have their importance as the solidified forms of vibration, and this is the ultimate point from which all other queries branch. They, i.e., the geometries, correspond literally to the solidified essence of light or sound, if you will, and the civilian victims of a holocaust may not be likely to understand such pains as can be wrought by the separation from understanding that comes about when this important truth of creation is lost once again. Your crop formations have been given by the Confederation to help enunciate the importance of these structures, for as a mandala of thought, they are unsurpassed in the capacity to align one with the vibrations of the one infinite Creator. It is for this reason that many of the cathedrals in the European continent have been built by those of the Knights Templar to utilize this system of sacred geometry in their construct, as have the temples themselves. The cloak and dagger capers that have occurred within self start to be erased as the geometries are contemplated and the greater capacities for self-acceptance are made clear in that transformation that then occurs.

The geometry itself corresponds to a crystallized consciousness template and therefore is indeed crystallized thought. Thoughts manifest as vibrations of neurons, if you will, in the electrical pathways therein. And, it has been discerned by your scientists that these neural pathways are holographic in nature in that a given sector of the brain is activated contemporaneously with other sectors and thus the information of memory is stored holographically rather then linearly in one area such as the pons or the cerebral cortex or medulla. With respect to the structure of the thought forms it will be eventually discovered that these energetic pathways are geometric in nature and this is the essence for the roughly spherical orientation of the brain itself.

The neural information is a nested structure of geometries with infinitely intricate and ornate patterns that subdivide within the major geometric gestalts much as could be seen in the patterns of a paisley shirt, as this instrument calls it. These fractal patterns are also typical of what is seen on your Earth itself based on the positioning of conscious intelligent entities, whether in the form of your body complexes or in the form of second-density life including that of the vegetative nature. And so in the duplication of the ability to respond to this geometry within each soul comes the strengthening of the particular ornate inlay work on that aspect of the grid allowing there to be reconciliation in that area causing the oppressive heat to be released in such a form.

Much as the grid exists in a bare-bones skeletal fashion it forms the template for the structure of continents on your planet and in turn forms the structural regions known as mountain ranges, based on the energetic upwelling of the core magma that then punctuate the lithospheric area, as this is known, forming these structures of passive energetic generation, causing the energy to be released into the atmosphere much as would a firearm release a projectile if not duly taken care of to avoid such energetic releases. The mountain ranges can also be chaotic in their activity as can be seen in the Flatirons in that region known as Boulder, Colorado whereby there is obvious evidence of a sudden breakage of the crust, causing a rather violent disturbance in the geotectonic outlay of the corresponding structural intricacy of that area. These mountainous formations come about when the energetics of consciousness have not been duly grounded by the aspects of selfhood known as third-density entities and thus the formative structures of fourth density consciousness have a great degree of importance in how they are corresponding to the relative efforts being made by entities in a given area.

May we state that the power of prayer can be utilized much as the shoebox organizes a pair of shoes not yet walked upon, to then box up those loose energetic vibrations in areas where the physical presence of entities is otherwise not possible, such as in the Siberian regions of the Asian sub-continent of Russia. With these abilities for prayer to cause a structuring of chaos in given areas comes also the lessening of disturbances to your planet by virtue of this release that occurs.

It is the release of each soul's condemnation of self that forms the elastic to allow this grid to bend and fluctuate in an appropriate fashion. The movement into fourth density is a swelling of the physical geotectonic size of the Earth, if you will, with the corresponding increase in intricacy of the grid matrix substructure through the ornamentation of the given geometry in its blossoming, flowering formation to a new structure. Thus, the Becker-Hagens unified vector geometry 120 polyhedron, as it is known, is indeed a structure that will continue to provide accurate coordinate information as it then evolves or flowers into the corresponding formation, as can be seen in the evolution of the Earth whereby the original landmass was subdivided along the equidistant points known to you as the tetrahedral formation. And these points continued to be vortices of influx of energy as the cuboctahedral and now icosadodecahedral forms then took its place. Similarly, the essence of social memory is one wherein souls form a collective, as there is a geometric structure to consciousness within the brain and within the greater soul matrix at large, based on the instreaming of different chakral regions.

There is value in seeing the grid as the template of consciousness for the social memory complex, if you will. We do ask that you recognize that there is a disparity between the degree of completion of the grid itself and the degree of completion of those who would exist on said grid even in the formative structure of social memory. And thus one could think of this grid as being a *library of light*, an everlasting template of information which does then lead to the formation of consciousness. But, much akin to your internet, [it] cannot be searched in totality due to the degree of complexity within said structure. And thus the interface between entities on the planetary grid and the grid itself is not one to one, but rather it is akin to the prop or support structure through which consciousness is then informed by experience. This may help to enunciate more completely how these structures of consciousness emanate from the realm of light into the temporal fluid crystal form of geometric template, then into the mind/body/spirit complex of the entity itself as it struggles to form a unity with other entities.

In this capacity, then, the car pulls out from the garage and the free will is utilized in the journey through the awakening of self with the understanding that the car is garaged at the end of such sojourning. The garage for each entity is that area in which it lives upon the global grid and therefore each sojourn out from the house forms another loop or whorl in the structure of energy on the grid itself. Thus you can indeed thread the beads together of different areas on your planetary surface and in so doing form that string of pearls that is of greatest price that can then be worn as the crowning achievement of the overlay of the super-consciousness onto the conscious templates of manifestation.

We appreciate the opportunity to share on these matters of great importance to your planetary evolutional catalyst, as it is a deemed to be essential that such a grid be worked with in the capacity of the healing of the informational structure through the correspondence of the healing of internal landscapes therein. In the ancient lore, various cultures corresponded to certain aspects of the zodiac, if you will, and this has to do with the geo-astrology, as this science is then known. Therefore when certain astrophysical influences flow into the grid there are those given geometric areas that have an activation experience. And thus when this geo-astrology is understood for given areas, it can then be used in concert with the sign in which given planetary conjunctions are occurring at a certain time. Thus we would ask that you watch for these conjunctions of less than spurious nature, with the understanding that those areas will then be energized and the corresponding Earth change events will occur if there is not a fully awakened consciousness therein. In this matter then, a form of spectatoring of possible advance disaster may be undertaken and the prayer power utilized to form the shoeboxes, or the healing balms for those particular areas of the grid. We speak of "b-a-l-m-s," not "b-o-m-b-s" as this instrument has spoken, as the bombing is not a healing by any stretch of the imagination.

We thank you and want to remind you that you are loved more than you could ever possibly imagine, bearing in mind always that it is yourself that seeks this love. What you feel, of God being abandoned from you, is truly the sense of God in the self that wants so dearly for you to reunify. It is that loneliness that you then project onto the others around you and seek their acceptance fittingly. Whereas indeed, if you can find that peace that knows no boundaries within one's self, all others will, by their very nature, be correspondingly resonant with higher aspects of the conscious self and in so doing heal the apparent indiscretions that have persisted in what you would think of as the past. Thus by transforming oneself the holographic reconstruction of one's external environment is made complete. And by extrapolation we are referring to your grid, and [the] Earth at large.

We thank you. Peace be with you in the light of everlasting love. We shall exit this instrument and require a period of approximately one and one half of your minutes of time to reintegrate this consciousness into physicality. We thank you. Adonai and amen. ✤

L/L Research

L/L Research is a subsidiary of Rock Creek Research & Development Laboratories, Inc.

P.O. Box 5195
Louisville, KY 40255-0195

www.llresearch.org

Rock Creek is a non-profit corporation dedicated to discovering and sharing information which may aid in the spiritual evolution of humankind.

ABOUT THE CONTENTS OF THIS TRANSCRIPT: This telepathic channeling has been taken from transcriptions of the weekly study and meditation meetings of the Rock Creek Research & Development Laboratories and L/L Research. It is offered in the hope that it may be useful to you. As the Confederation entities always make a point of saying, please use your discrimination and judgment in assessing this material. If something rings true to you, fine. If something does not resonate, please leave it behind, for neither we nor those of the Confederation would wish to be a stumbling block for any.

© 2009 L/L RESEARCH

SUNDAY MEDITATION
MAY 18, 2003

Group question: Our question this week has to do with how we can maintain our spiritual centers in our desire to seek in a spiritual sense, when there are so many things in the world around us to which it seems to be necessary for us to pay attention in a very focused fashion, whether it is the children that we are raising, the family to which we are relating, the job that we are working, or the friends with whom we wish to interact. We would like any information Q'uo could give us about how to maintain this balance between the worldly things that seem to take so much of our time and attention and the spiritual things that we have to work so hard to make time for.

(Carla channeling)

We are those known to you as the principle of Q'uo, and we greet you in the love and in the light of the one infinite Creator, in whose service we are. May we say what a great privilege and pleasure it is for us to be able to share in your circle of seeking and to be asked to share, as well, our opinions concerning the balancing of the busy life between the two worlds of doing and being. In order for us to speak freely we would ask one thing of you and that is that you exercise the most stringent discrimination in listening to those thoughts that we share. We are not those of authority but rather those who are your neighbors, your friends, your brothers, and your sisters.

We have perhaps walked, in your way of thinking, more miles along the road of spiritual evolution, yet we are not those who have infallible opinions, but rather those who are like you: pilgrims upon the road, those who seek the truth. Therefore, in order for our reassurance that we are not infringing upon the free will of any, we would greatly appreciate your using the utmost discrimination in judging whether or not the thoughts we share may have some use for you. If they do not, please leave them behind.

We gaze within this instrument's mind for the flavor of the experience about which you question in this session and see that this instrument, as all of those within this room and indeed within your culture, has a marked tendency to find herself physically running out of time, not just from time to time but in each and every day, before the list of things that were hoped-for-being-done within that day is finished. And indeed, often in this instrument's mind, we see the rueful assurance that a hard working and productive day can go by completely full of hard work yet without even beginning to cross an item off the list of those things that the instrument thought that she was going to do that day. Indeed, the illusion is quite efficient in creating ever more confusion and ever more catalyst for growth, learning and service. As the one known as V has said, the universe is doing its job.

It is our feeling that each creates, before incarnation, a plan for those themes of choice within the incarnation to come being set as default, repeating markers within the life experience. Whatever the lesson of service is, whatever the lesson of learning is, these things are provided as if they were food. Sometimes the food is black and bitter fruit, or so it would seem within the physical life. And yet this fruit is that which is prized in terms of its effectiveness in placing the essence-within-the-entity in situations in which the themes of the incarnation may be explored, and that which M called the processes of spiritual evolution may take place upon whatever level.

Certainly, most of the solid, serious work of spiritual evolution is done with conscious intention. But for the most part, in terms of the content and the substance of the work done, that work is done below the level of consciousness, fed by the intention as if the root or source of the stream were within the mental/emotional/spiritual worlds, shall we say, but springing forth into the life in terms of experience, intuition, dream content and so forth. Consequently there seem to be fountains of events of a certain type that periodically or perhaps constantly just keep coming, keep springing forth. And together with those sprays of the water of catalyst come sprays of the minerals within that water which are emotions connected with the events that are occurring, so that as you, as a soul, are flowering, these rains of catalyst and emotion come to feed the fertile soil of your learning. You have every opportunity to grow that crop of knowing, that crop of realization, what this instrument would call "grokking," that these themes that spiral again and again into the life experience help one to explore.

Let us take a step back now from this query and look at the entity that each of you is and how that entity experiences, or experiences not, what it sees, and stores in memory. Neither the present nor the past is in the kind of sharp focus that they seem to be within the physical illusion. The one known as D has pointed out that we do not see with our eyes nor do we hear with our ears. Rather, there is a kind of composite that is made up largely of pre-assumed vision, which fills in the background of most entity's organs of awareness[51]. But one is not seeing it clearly, indeed one may not notice a great deal of what one is gazing at because of the way the mind receives data and forms it into a picture.

The structure of memory, similarly, is such that the true memory is being harvested to the soul quality essence or higher self of each entity and only the shadow of the experience, or shall we say a copy of the data, remains within the bio-computer of the mind. Consequently, much that floods the awareness is the result of poor or actually incorrect information. Therefore, the task of untangling one's organs of awareness from pre-assumption is a difficult one, a lifelong one, and one that cannot be done without help.

We encourage each in this wise, then, to pursue those resources that will aid in allowing the mind to reassess each pre-assumption that can be found within the mind, assessing it anew for its accuracy, its place within the value system which you enjoy and so forth, giving the self the chance to look anew at all of those things which you are quite sure you have gazed at already and concerning which, [you have] come to a settled opinion. Always, there is new truth for you in situations which are puzzling you. Always, there is a great deal of fertile growth which may occur rather quickly in understanding a certain structure which is puzzling, such as the challenge of the childrearing about which the one known as M was speaking.

The instinct is to assume, since one is within a physical body and it seems quite obvious that one is a limited entity and must take care for the self as a frail and limited entity, that one must be strong, one must be sturdy, one must be upon one's guard at all times. Upon one level this is completely and absolutely true. Within the illusion, in terms of extra pairs of hands, when there is one parent in a house with children, those hands need physically to be looking out for those children, doing what needs to be done for those children, and so forth.

However, your query concerns the state of mind within which these duties which are so dear to the heart may be done. It is not the chores themselves, as we gaze around this circle, that seem to be troubling the mind of any within this circle. Each entity within this sitting group seems to have a strong

---

[51] This refers to the fact that we "see" through a digital process within our bio-computer minds which assumes, from general details of the sight presented to the eyes, the background to be of a certain place, and places that in our sight only vaguely, zeroing in only on details such as the identity of people in the eyesight range, what they are wearing or holding, and whether there is danger in the scene.

yellow ray, or physical/environmental presence. That energy is flowing well. There is not the begrudging of the working time, or the dislike of that which one is doing, to be stumbling block to enjoying that time of labor to which each has committed the self. Rather, it is the experience of each that the physical doing that consumes the time within the day also seems to consume that space within the mind, the heart, and the being which is spacious and has that feeling of comfort and emotional security which gives one that point of view which is full of joy, cheerful and simply having a good time, having what this instrument would call fun with whatever one is doing. Once an entity has moved through those reexaminations of the default settings of the mind, shall we say, one is then perhaps more in touch with where the self meets the process of spiritual evolution today, at this time, at this instant.

Then the soul may begin to become conscious about its choice of points of view. The choice is not what it seems, for it is not the choice between one mental view and another. It is not a choice that can be pinned down to thinking one way or disciplining oneself to behave in one certain way. Rather, it is a growing awareness that the self is magical and the environment of the self is also magical. In the realization of the profundity and the depth of that magical self there comes a realization that much of the most important part of you, as you view yourself and your gifts, is impersonal, that you are living a personal life with perhaps 20% of your energy and living an imperishable, impersonal life with by far the majority of the life energy that is invested within the personality shell which entities relate to as each of you.

You are so much more than you seem. And so much of what each seems to be is only the shadow of the essence of the gifts that are burgeoning forth from that fountain of catalyst and emotion. Each gives so many gifts that each is unaware of through each day. Within the confusion and the turmoil of the rat-race, the crowded schedule, the endless chores, there is no end to the interaction which each has with all the inner sub-densities of this particular experience which you enjoy at this time. At the level where the resource of intent is most effective, intent may be set in such a way as to call in help which is unseen and which is the other side of the story of that physical persona which is flesh and blood and has only two hands and must be responsible. This help has no hands, has no feet, and for the most part it has no voice. This help is unique in its pattern, its structure, and its way of communicating to you. For each of you is a very special and eccentric kind of "energy ball" that draws to it, because of its beauty, entities from the inner planes which this instrument would call angelic, which wish to help. They wish to help with gifts of spiritual presence, inspiration, laughter, healing, and any number of invisible yet very real sub-rays of that sun of love, that Logos of unconditional and infinite love. They will not aid in doing more chores more quickly, but rather the help, when remembered, is as that blessing which pours like rain upon the thirsty soul, smoothing and washing away the corrosive acid of catalyst and offering the healing balm, the inner touch of that company which touches the heart, enters the heart, and settles there, spreading like the balm of Gilead the feeling that all is well; in the midst of this chaos, all is well.

This instrument at one time had a motto that hung on her wall and it said, "Bless this mess." And we find that the energies involved in this sentiment have a good deal of the energy of which we are speaking: that feeling that it may look as though I am alone, and yet I am not; this may look like a mess and yet it is a blessing; this may look like confusion, yet all is well. The key to this expanded kind of awareness is remembrance. It is very helpful, as the one known as T said, to place within the consciousness little helpers that bring the mind back to the vital questions, "Who am I and what am I doing here?" Quite often, "Who am I?" is a very provocative question and very pointed. "Am I the mother? Am I the seeker? Who am I? What am I doing here?" Usually when that question is asked it is in the context of a relationship. And we may say that a shortcut to the second question's answer is to know that love is always the reason that each entity is in a given situation at a given time. Consequently, the question becomes, "Where is the love in this moment and how may I witness to it?" When that realization comes, the ensuing action carries with it the energy of soul growth. For in dealing with the practicalities of the small significant life, the fundamental bases[52] for that life have been invoked and, consequently, the energy body is balanced within the awareness of identity and purpose.

---

[52] Plural of "basis."

We realize that it is most easy to lose sight of this identity and this purpose as being fundamentally spiritual and, consequently, if there are the heard signals within the day, such as this instrument's memory of noon whistles and bells to mark the beginning and end of classroom periods [or] the tones of the clock as it marks off an hour, this kind of sound is a good trigger to place within oneself, so that when one hears that noon whistle, one has a moment of memory and remembrance of who you are and why you are here. It is tremendously centering to have those moments of recollection and truly they need be no longer than a second or two, for to the soul who is eager the possibility of returning to that place of remembrance brings forth a quick and eager response.

Within each entity there is a link between that which is measurable and that which is not. Within the measurable world, within the daylight world of consciousness, entities have the opportunity to choose what they wish to intend. It is a choice which then may be held in remembrance, in intent. If, for instance, one goes into the sleeping state with intention to remember the dreams and explore them, that intention begins to have strength as the new resource is used. If one goes to bed and places a glass of water by the bed and then, holding that glass, one places the intention within that water that asks what this instrument would call the inner alchemist to supply those things that are needed for the next day, and then one takes the time simply to drink that water in thanksgiving and praise and in gratitude for the gifts that have been given, that intention sets into motion powerful energies which use the crystalline nature of the water to magnetize intention. Any opportunity that you as an entity have to remember such intentions are important to you. [As you] simply think upon them, each thinking drives the intention deeper into the subconscious processes that are powerful to prevail in the ways of developing spiritual clarity within one's life

Remember that the deeper self is seeing a different kind of light. The inner self is already dwelling within that state of knowing which exists within all densities but your own. The plants, the animals, dwell in a state of complete knowing that all is one, that all is in harmony, that all is working out as it should. Those within the angelic realms of your planet are also full of this consciousness. It within the physical illusion, that is made with the light of photons, atoms, molecules and much, much of what you call space creating this vast illusion that you now enjoy, that power is limited within the physical body. Within the mind, it is operating as the second density, as the fourth density, in a state of unity and awareness of infinite consciousness. In that light there is no space. In that light, there is more peace. In that light which is that shown by unconditional love by the open heart, the stresses that wind one up like a spring are released gently and repeatedly as the moments of remembrance circle around and a deep breath may be taken in and out, pulling in the oxygen to the mind, pulling in remembrance to the intention. There is no physical action that is proof against the consciousness that is hungry to remember the vibration of unconditional love. In the seeking for that one great original Thought of love, the seeking itself develops its own answer within you so that as you seek, already the answer lies within the open heart.

We would at this time rest this instrument, for we feel that we have perhaps said enough on this subject to generate other queries and, consequently, we would at this time leave this instrument and transfer the contact to the one known as Jim. We thank this instrument and leave it in love and in light. We are those known to you as Q'uo.

(Jim channeling)

I am Q'uo, and we greet each again in love and in light through this instrument. At this time it is our privilege to offer ourselves in the capacity of speaking to any further queries which may remain upon the minds of those present. Is there a shorter query at this time?

J: May I ask about something that came up in the channeling? It seems you can prepare yourself [for the] next day by thinking about what you're going to do before you go to sleep at night. In other words, let it work out through your dreams. Is there anything else that can be said about that, about the dreaming function and how you can best focus your attention on it to use it to work and serve and grow. If there are no other questions I'd be interested in hearing more about that.

I am Q'uo, and am aware of your query, my sister. It is well, if one wishes to work with the dreams, that one indeed prepare the self to do so. For in working with the dreams, one is working with the deeper portion of one's own conscious and subconscious mind. At this level of awareness there is a perception of experience as a whole. There is the unification of that which seems broken to the conscious mind that resides within the deeper portions of the mind. And as you are able to work with this portion of your own mind, you develop a pattern or relationship which can be built upon, expanded and relied upon in all future endeavors. It is well therefore to, shall we say, convince the subconscious mind that you do indeed wish to seek that treasure which it has to offer. This may be accomplished by simple things that are repeated; that is, [make] the suggestion to the conscious mind, to yourself, as it would seem, that as you retire for the night and enter that state called sleep, you wish to remember those dreams which follow and that you have indeed prepared yourself to work with these dreams by placing, next to your sleeping position, the necessary writing utensil and paper or pad upon which you may record the dream upon waking. Perhaps, as you are more adept at this work, one or two or more times during the night you will be able to write the dream upon the pad, so that when you awaken in the morning, there is a written record that will, shall we say, jog your memory and allow you to access further information as you begin to ponder the dream, to think upon the dream and to record the dream. Record all impressions that come to you at this time and when you have more time later in your daily round of activities, perhaps you will be able to meditate upon the dream, its imagery, its message, [and] its importance. If you are able to make this time in your daily round of activities for this process, then you will find that the subconscious mind gives more and more symbology, more information, that you may use to unlock, shall we say, other doors within your mind which also have information which is pertinent to your query.

Is there a further query, my sister?

M: Is it okay if it's unrelated?

[I am Q'uo.] Mm-hmm.

M: My husband is having health problems and I wanted to try and heal him. But I feel for some reason that I'm not sure that it's okay. I don't want to infringe on his free will even though he says it is okay. For some reason I am holding myself back. I don't want to interfere with his free will. I'm wondering if you can shed some light on that.

I am Q'uo, and am aware of your query, my sister. Indeed there is the concern for free will in this instance, for there is a portion of your own being which is not certain that this is the course of action which you wish to follow. It is first necessary for you to make this decision within yourself and perhaps the working with your subconscious mind though the dream recording is a portion of that process which you may utilize.

(Side one of tape ends.)

(Jim channeling)

I am Q'uo. We are once again with this instrument. Is there another query at this time?

M: Well, I guess I do have another short one. You had said that I have to ask myself if I have any further blockages, and I know I do. For some reason I'm hesitant to try to do healing. I feel like I'm not qualified to do it. I think it's because I don't feel like I know enough to do it. I seem to have a particular blockage about healing. I'm not sure where it's coming from.

I am Q'uo. We will speak a few words further upon this topic but do not wish, ourselves, to infringe upon your own free will, my sister. As you examine your own opinions concerning healing in general and your ability to accomplish it in particular, we would recommend that you employ a process of essaying, so that you might write down the feelings that you have concerning this healing process. Explore upon the paper that which is upon your mind and within your heart. Allow this process to become a portion of the working with your dreams, so that there is a dialog which is set up between your conscious and subconscious mind. In this way perhaps you will be able to reveal to yourself that which is the major blockage that stands between you and your ability to heal, which, we may comment, is substantial.

Is there another query, my sister?

M: No.

I am Q'uo. We thank you for your query. Is there another query from anyone else?

D: I'm being asked to ask a question in the form of a riddle. It's not transient. This riddle relates to all the questions of the entity, M, and the content that we've talked about. It's phrased in symbolic language: "What is the difference between the symbol of a sphere and the symbol of a washing machine as it relates to these questions?"

I am Q'uo. We shall allow the one known as M to "work" the riddle. Is there any other query at this time?

V: On a more humorous note and purely transient … Hiccups seem to be obviously catalyst pointing to some function that's going on in the person's being or mind, but is there a physical reason for them?

I am Q'uo. And though we are aware of your query we are unaware of the ability to express an appropriate response.

(Laughter)

V: Thank you, Q'uo

May we ask for a final query at this time?

Carla: I'll just ask the question that I ask from time to time. And that is, do you have any new thoughts upon the adventures that I'm attempting to embark upon? Especially as concerns the gathering of G and E?

I am Q'uo, and am aware of your query, my sister. We are most pleased that there is an effort underway to add to the ability of this group to be of service to others, for this time upon your planetary sphere is one which will require a great deal of effort for the healing of Mother Earth and the population that inhabits her at this time. For as you are well aware there has been a great deal of adversary relationship that has in many cases caused a movement away from the path many would have wished to travel before the incarnation began. Therefore, when any group joins in service to the one Creator, there is an increase in the possibility for all entities upon the planet and for each entity that seeks in service to others. As you seek together there is far greater chance that, as a group entity, you shall find that which you seek. For there are many entities who have incarnated with latent abilities that come to the fore when there is the opportunity to share in service with others. Each entity will add that which is his or her own ability to the group's energy and will find that there is a multiplication factor that returns the energy in a greater sense so that there is a dynamic ability to grow in ways and degrees that were not previously possible for the individuals within the group, for the group itself, and for the planet as a whole.

We are pleased to be able to work with this group, whatever its number might be, and we remind each in this circle of seeking that we are happy to join you in your private meditations, to help deepen the meditation, if you but ask or request our presence. We will speak no words but will simply offer our conditioning vibration in order that each may feel a deeper sense of the meditative state and a centering of the self therein.

At this time we shall take our leave of this instrument and this group. We are those of Q'uo. We leave each in the love and the ineffable light of the one infinite Creator. Adonai, my friends, Adonai. ☥

L/L Research

L/L Research is a subsidiary of Rock Creek Research & Development Laboratories, Inc.

P.O. Box 5195
Louisville, KY 40255-0195

www.llresearch.org

Rock Creek is a non-profit corporation dedicated to discovering and sharing information which may aid in the spiritual evolution of humankind.

ABOUT THE CONTENTS OF THIS TRANSCRIPT: This telepathic channeling has been taken from transcriptions of the weekly study and meditation meetings of the Rock Creek Research & Development Laboratories and L/L Research. It is offered in the hope that it may be useful to you. As the Confederation entities always make a point of saying, please use your discrimination and judgment in assessing this material. If something rings true to you, fine. If something does not resonate, please leave it behind, for neither we nor those of the Confederation would wish to be a stumbling block for any.

© 2009 L/L Research

Sunday Meditation
May 25, 2003

Group question: The question today has to do with the concept of free will, as regards to how the Confederation of Planets in the Service of the One Creator has related to the population of planet Earth for as long as there has been a relationship. Considering all the dirty water, the dirty air, and the nuclear proliferation, warfare, disease, poverty and so forth that are rampant upon our planet now, especially after the graduation of the Harvest, we are wondering, are there any circumstances under which the Confederation of Planets would consider abridging free will and stepping in and cleaning up the air, cleaning up the water, destroying nuclear weapons, providing food and services for people that need it? Or is there some other consideration that we should think about? We would appreciate anything Q'uo has to say on that topic.

(Carla channeling)

We are those known to you as the principle of Q'uo. Greetings in the love and in the light of the one infinite Creator, in whose service we are. We greatly thank this group of seeking souls for coming together in meditation and for calling us to your circle. It is such a privilege and pleasure to share your meditation and so heartwarming for us to be able to offer our thoughts to you, humble though they may be. As always, when speaking with you we would ask that you use the utmost discrimination in listening to and considering those things which we offer, for truth is a very personal thing and it is not our intention to remove the joy of learning from your path or to infringe upon the free will of that Godhead principle which is as yet under construction.

Your query this day revolves around that very topic of free will and so we are delighted to share some thoughts upon this most interesting and very rich topic of conversation. Firstly, we would look at free will without looking further than the creation itself. See the Creator-Self prior to the creation, which includes that which emanates from the Godhead principle in the many, many sparks of the Creator which you see about you as stars, planets and those entities about you who are yourself and other selves. In this pre-creation Godhead, the Deity's first distortion from absolute and complete unity was free will. It was this principle which allowed the Creator to ask, "Who am I?" and to follow through on that question by the very personal and utterly committed act of entering that question into the vibrations of Self which the Deity experienced upon asking Itself that question. That which It was able to think was the original Thought and that Thought, as we have said many times, was that pallid word, love[53].

---

[53] Carla: For those wondering why we do not capitalize the word, love, when it is used to indicate the Logos or Word which is the Creator, we refrain from focusing on this word, since it is so greatly overused in common, everyday language. The "love" that would be capitalized is a love far beyond the general usage of the word, which tends to be used for romantic, sentimental and casual feelings.

Now the love of a Creator is a love that cannot be said to be pallid for it creates, it destroys, it makes manifest, it hides, it is mystery, it is experience, it is nothing, it is everything. Yet this Thought has a certain vibration. This vibration has the power to create movement. Movement is that distortion that you call light. So Creator, then free will, then the Logos, then light, in the manifest universe. That is the progression we would describe to you as a way of saying that free will is not binding merely upon us. It is the first and primal characteristic of the creation of the Father, or that which this instrument often calls the Logos, or the Godhead principle. It is the nature of the Creator; it is the nature of the Creator's parts.

The question of intervention contains distortions along certain lines which we would like to explore. Your query had to do with what the situation might be within which we would find it possible or desirable to abrogate the free will of those entities upon your sphere which are imposing these difficulties and distortions upon the hapless remainder of the body of population of humanity upon your planet. However, this query is a query which in its very nature asks that which cannot be answered. For it is not possible for each of you to remove from yourselves the privilege, the responsibility, the honor, and the duty of serving as witnesses to the light at this location which you now enjoy at this time, and in this situation which you now enjoy.

Upon the level of the surface life, upon the level of your mass media and the details of politics and policy, it is indeed clear that your sphere is controlled by the few for the sake of the few and to the detriment of many. Gazing at the Earth sphere from the stance of spiritual responsibility or maturity, there is another picture entirely. In this picture, no power is given away to any thought form or actual entity. Rather, each is in relationship with the power, the discipline, and the focus of the self. Insofar as there is no discipline, then there is likely to be very little power. However, your environment is an environment in which the planetary venue was chosen and the ingredients of the life experience of each of you were chosen for an agenda which only peripherally involves the ways of politics, policy and power. In the outer sense, rather, each of you came here to dig a bit deeper within your particular bit of the Godhead principle, that which you have chosen to filter into incarnational existence within the carriage of the personality shell, welling up within the earthly home of your body, that structure that houses and carries you about. Each of you came here hoping to use the illusion's corrosive and harsh ways to thrash and pound and uncover the jewels of creatorship within the ore of self. Within the rubble of bits and pieces of the shale of the details of the day and the gravel of, "what I do for a living," there lie great jewels within each, undiscovered facets of self, undiscovered crystalline formations, nuggets of insight, awareness and realization. Many of these insights are very close to the surface and have been salted within the soil of your most available levels of subconscious mind by the self before incarnation, in order that each of you might have real fruit from the digging, real substance from the probing and the examination of the thoughts of the self.

When this work is done deliberately, consciously, and over a period of what you call time, the energetic body of an instrument of light begins to tune itself as would the piano tuner tune the wire. Tuning, tuning, until the pitch is right for that wire. Each of you has a true pitch and you are tuning that tone of self as you seek the way of the Creator within.

As you dig with a trowel of, "Who am I?" and the weeder of, "What am I doing here?" you are preparing the ground and planting the seeds that blossom into the gifts that you came to share, the essence of self [that blossoms into] the committed and loving compassion of those dwelling within the illusion but knowing that they are not trapped in the illusion. The one known as E reached for his pillows of Faith and Hope, those words written upon those particular pillows[54], and we encourage each to take those pillows, those words, those tools, those resources that hearten and strengthen each of you. For you came here to be strong, you came here to offer the power that is yours in active and personal compassion that reaches out and embraces the planet and its peoples. Not because there is a wish to rescue them or to change them in any way but because entities are there to love, just as the you are the object of the love that is all about you, not simply from those entities within the flesh that may express

---

[54] E had exchanged his throw pillows, which he was using to prop himself up with for meditation, for ones that had the legends, "Faith" and "Hope," saying that he had need of those qualities.

love in their halting words but more, from those entities which are unseen and whose presence uncovers in silence that state of unconditional love in which the self can finally feel safe, secure and able to rest within that holy place that is the heart, the heart of self, the heart of the planet, the entity of self, the entity of [the] planet. Are these not one thing? Need we intervene to rescue your planet when there are millions of sparks of the Creator upon your planet which are capable of tuning themselves until they burst forth into the most beautiful and harmonious song of love that the world has ever felt?

Each of those awakening upon your planet at this time, and there are many, is awakening at a time when the aura of fear, terror and discomfort has never been greater among your peoples. Even under this barrage of fear and negativity, entities are awakening because of the service of those who are already awake, those who find ways to express the thoughts that encourage, and cheer, hearten, and strengthen the light within those with whom they come in contact in one way or another. It is easy to think very quickly of the performers, the singers, the dancers, those who are very visible in public situations as being good examples of those who use their power well. Yet, each time that the one known as G, for instance, offers heart and car ride and help to an entity whose name is not known but whose heart is, the universe has become a sweeter place. Each time that each of you smiles at the stranger who frowns at you, who offers a soft word in response to a harsh one, each gentle or loving act of friend to friend, as in the one known as J, who generously offers her bodywork to this instrument's most accepting vehicle, is making the world a more tuned and peaceful place in which to dwell.

One cannot address your world's situation, may we say, to use a cliché, upon the level of the rescue of third density. Entities shall move into early fourth density no matter what happens to your sphere as the density changes and [they] will repair the planet with the planet's cooperation. Indeed many entities even now are repairing their little bit of the planetary surface by loving and talking to the Earth, by cooperating with what this instrument would call nature deities or divas, by relating to the surroundings of self with the understanding that all things are alive, all things work in rhythm and in harmony, and all things except those sunk in the mire of third-density forgetting not only love each other but know that they are one. In this atmosphere, the possibilities of becoming a powerful, magical person are great and as the time sharpens the focus right unto the moment of birth of fourth density, there is in effect a fourth-density energy that is now as real upon your sphere as the third-density energy. It shows up within the physical world only by creating anomalous effects [in terms of physics' sub-atomic particles] but it shows up within the inner life of that wonderful multilayered being that each of you is in a much more clear and obvious way, as the interpenetration of the two densities becomes such that it is much easier for nature, or for the forces of coincidence, to work in order to bring things to your attention which you have asked to be brought to your attention. That is why, in the midst of such challenging times, such times of transformation and change, yet still each of you has had the feeling of entities helping along the way, unseen hands giving a boost and angelic guidance coming through unexpected and unusual means.

The *beau geste* of each of you at this time is, among other things, to reclaim and recapture your own freedom of will at the level of spiritual endeavor, at the level of will, at the level of choosing to become personally involved in compassion towards entities of flesh and blood and bone. Move into active compassion, focus upon the eyes within the photographs of the media rather than the details of horror and terror. Focus upon the process of souls learning, being transformed and being lifted away into new lessons and new densities. Many are those who have already been cleared, out of third density and into a fourth-density environment. Many are those who are coming back at this time with the altered DNA possible with fourth-density consciousness. The so called indigo children and crystal children are those who have already been harvested and have begun their new life in a new density in which they begin as the equivalent of an indigenous species, within the context of fourth-density life. Each of you has perhaps an overweening opinion of the gadgets and the trickery of the present level of technological expertise of your peoples. Yet, indeed, the next level of expertise flows with cooperation with the light rather than control of the light and this in turn opens those abilities which create the impression that that which you think of [as] advanced technology is, in fact, the knife, the flint pounder, the fish hook.

Much simplicity lies in true love. Living in this simple atmosphere of the open heart, entities are able to do precisely that which they can focus into, love with all their hearts, and release all attachment concerning outcome. This instrument, for instance, has great hopes to serve the planet by the campaign of information and persuasion which would coax all entities into tuning to that harmonic tuning of love and light and personal compassion which is the true tuning for you. Yet she is aware that, of herself, she can do nothing. But what she can do is pray, daily, sincerely, wholeheartedly, "Creator, teach me your ways. Show me the path that you have prepared for me to walk in." This in a sense is the giving over of the power into guidance, yet it is the taking of power to ask for guidance and to use it. This is a different matter than asking to be rescued because each feels powerless before the problems of the world. We assure you, in the ways of spirit, each is profoundly powerful and as each becomes aware of the dynamics and the strength of groups who are together tuning their will to love, this power and this *beau geste* shall come clearer and clearer into the vision, so that it can be seen in ways that are difficult to describe but very real. [The vision is] that the truth can never be hidden, that the light has never been extinguished by darkness, that all is well, and that there is the profound satisfaction and the responsibility of knowing that the combined energy of groups such as yours, in coming together to affirm love, light and unity, have already made a tremendous difference in the progress of this shift into fourth density.

For two decades of your time at least, we have seen what this instrument would call the rubber band effect, as the light generated by those who are awakening affected the planetary shift. So that it was as if the band was being released very slowly, by a tiny increment each time. This is the reason for the many earthquakes and other changes in the planetary experience, none of which is so earth-shattering that it does indeed shatter the earth or remove the general population. Those who have been actively involved in this lightening of [the vibrations of] planet Earth are perhaps five percent of the population and yet much has been accomplished because of a few. And that few has begun to grow exponentially as more and more entities begin to wake up and then, by their influence, begin to lighten the atmosphere around them to enable others the freedom from fear which it takes to begin to wake up.

It is not for you to give up your free will nor for us to intervene. Rather it is for you, each of you, to move internally from the third-density perspective to the fourth-density perspective, gazing at this Earth sphere of yours with a fourth-density perspective. Each has a very sturdy point of land to stand upon to gaze at the chaos of your illusion. That land is the firm *terra firma* of the truth, that which you know. What is it that you know? What is it? When you dig within yourself and come to the center, what is that that you know? It is the Creator. When all is taken aside and the last veil is parted, that which lies within your heart, that which is your very nature, is the infinite Creator, waiting for you. And in that place of the heart, with the Creator, in that tabernacle of the spirit, the difference between your free will and the Creator's free will falls away and there is a love that exists that balances, heals and restores. We encourage each to spend as much time as possible in the precincts of your own heart. For even a moment in that holy of holies that lies within informs and enlivens the day, the experience, the reality, if we may call it that, for an entity.

By free will each of you decided to come to try to make a difference—for yourself by learning, and for the planetary light by serving. These aspects of learning and service intertwine like the ropes of a strong ship's hawser and cannot be taken apart. Living, learning and serving, are all wound in together and there is no telling when one stops and where another begins. We assure you that all is well with your people. The harvest has grown substantially and we are most pleased to see the situation as it is. From our standpoint things look very good. The vibratory energy of your planet begins to lift. Much has been accomplished. Much has been begun of goodness and substance. It remains for those of you awake to be aware of this time and its possibilities, to follow through day upon day, and act upon act, year upon year, and thought upon thought, decade upon decade, and realization upon realization. That is the real heart of the job, the mission. The service is in the being, and in the being lies the tuning that will bring the Earth and its peoples to health within early fourth density. This is early fourth density, you vibrate now in fourth density. Certainly your third-density vehicles are having their challenges in accommodating the new vibrations. And yet the body is the creature of the mind. And as your consciousness begins to feel comfortable swimming in the waters of unconditional love, so the bodies shall find themselves more and more able to enjoy fourth-density vibration.

It is in your hands, each of you. We would not take this learning or this service from you. The energies of your planet at this time are, as this instrument has heard it described by her teacher, off on a side track: a time lateral. The train of yellow-ray third-density Earth has been shunted into a lateral experience by the determined and repeated actions of what this instrument would call the Sons of Light and the Sons of Darkness, or those who promote peace and joy and those who promote war and suffering. In the outer sense, these few entities have again and again, upon other planets and upon this one, in many different societies, chosen the ways of war and chosen them for reasons unknown to themselves; being manipulated by those far cleverer than they, who use the suffering and the pain of third density, in its endless repetition of war, as food. It is time to stop feeding fifth-density entities who feed on fear. The only way to move back onto the normal time track of this planet is to find ways to lose fear and to respond to all situations not with hesitation but with confidence, not with the feeling that something needs to be done but with the knowledge that something is being done. It is being done with the mind and with the heart. The power of each to help each in these realizations is great. We are most pleased to encourage each to listen to and to respond to each as the seeking and the processes of learning go on. Each is teacher to each and there is a circle of learning.

We would at this time leave this instrument and transfer this contact to the one known as Jim, for there are questions within this group and we would like to leave this instrument, as her energy becomes somewhat low, and to use the one known as Jim's rather more capacious physical energies, although we do find that there is a limited amount of energy within the circle of all of those at this time. Consequently, we would thank the one known as Carla and in time transfer this contact to the one known as Jim. We are those of Q'uo, and we leave this instrument in love and in light.

(Jim channeling)

I am Q'uo, and we greet each again in love and in light through this instrument. It is our privilege at this time to offer ourselves to speak to any further queries which may yet remain upon the minds of those present. Is there another query at this time?

G: Q'uo, if it's not too large, I would like to know, metaphysically speaking, from your perspective, from love's perspective, what happened in the middle of the last century when the Hindus and the Muslims set down their weapons, ending a downward spiral of violence, death and bloodshed in order to end Gandhi's fast, in order to save him from the termination of his own life?

I am Q'uo, and am aware of your query my brother. We find that this experience was one in which there was a great deal of the opening of the …

(Side one of tape ends.)

(Jim channeling)

I am Q'uo, and we are again with this instrument. We shall continue.

These two great faiths, the Hindu and the Muslim, had through the actions and the service of the one known as Gandhi been able to appreciate this entity's open heart to the degree that they were willing to set aside age-old differences in order that this entity whom they revered so greatly might stop his fast and continue to live among them. For it is well perceived, when there is an entity such as the one known as Gandhi who has opened his heart to that degree, that there is no boundary beyond which love cannot be given. This entity was successful in opening his own heart so that the will of love moved through him in a way which was easily recognized by those whose lives he touched. Thus, when it became apparent that this entity was willing to give his life and the remainder of it for the cause of peace between the warring religious factions, those religious factions found the way to their own heart in relation to this entity and were willing to cease the hostility in order that this entity might cease his fast and remain among them.

This was a shining moment for these religious factions for there has been little before or since that has galvanized them to lay down the differences, as did the one known as Gandhi's actions.

Is there another query my brother?

G: Not from me. Thank you.

I am Q'uo, and we thank you my brother.

J: Yeah, Q'uo, I have just a quick question. I was hoping that you could give me some clarity on this. Before I came to the Earth is it possible that I came from the Pleiades and the particular star that I am thinking of is Alceon. Can you confirm that for me?

I am Q'uo, and am aware of your query, my sister. We find that there has been some influence in your previous incarnations from this particular star system which you call Alceon. Not necessarily that you have originated there but that you have had experiences there as you have had upon the planet Earth.

Is there another query my sister?

J: No, that's all for now. Thank you for being with us today.

I am Q'uo, and we thank you as well, my sister. Is there another query at this time?

G: I have one, if nobody else does. Q'uo, in seeking love there are different moments in a seeker's life when he is overcome with the emotion and desire to seek and find and feel and know love, and there's dry times in between. And I was wondering what you might have to say on the effect of just putting forth the intent to see love, just that motion, just that request. Whether it's felt in the heart or not, whether it's just empty words, what kind of effect that has?

I am Q'uo, and am aware of your query, my brother. As the seeker of truth moves upon the journey, there is for each seeker those times of increased seeking, increased desire, increased passion for the purpose of the life's path. It is during these times that there is built within the entity a metaphysical foundation, shall we say, that is added to by each additional seeking desire. Each time the seeker renews its quest for the open heart, for sharing with others the love that creates all things, then the seeker has added yet another stone, shall we say, to secure the foundation of its metaphysical journey. As you also mentioned, there are those times when there is less passion, less desire, perhaps less expression of the desire to seek love. These are normal experiences for each seeker. For there are seasons, cycles, periods of increased awareness, increased strength in seeking, increased compassion within the heart. This is as the seed which has been nurtured by attention and has begun to sprout, cracking the hard shell of the exterior, sending forth the first roots, sending forth the first small leaves, beginning to express in the way in which love has been encoded within each entity, each seed, each seeker.

Thus you find periods during which there is a great wave of energy that moves through your being. It is at this time that the desire to know, to seek, to share, and to love is nurtured, is brought forth. As you continue to move upon your journey of seeking, you will begin more and more to create this desire for yourself rather than feeling the normal rhythms that move throughout all creation. This is the conscious portion of the journey of seeking. Each entity has the subconscious or unconscious motivation during which the upward spiraling line of light begins to manifest more through the seeker's journey. When the seeker has become enough aware of this type of energy moving through its being then there is made a room, or a place for it by the seeker, so that there may be a more, shall we say, conscious application of the energies of awareness. Thus there is the completion of one portion of the journey; that is, the subconscious movement in rhythm with all creation, that becomes the conscious creation of the mind of the seeker that seeks to know the source of love within the self, and within all creation, upon a more continual basis.

Is there a final query at this time?

G: Not from me, thank you so much, Q'uo.

Carla: I have a question. This is from K, and she says, "In the story of Job, God seemingly inflicts horrible events onto his faithful believer named Job. With regard to this parable I have two questions. One, why was the Creator portrayed in such a dark manner? Is this story accurate? And two, does the Creator have a dark side and what is its nature?

I am Q'uo, and aware of your query my sister. The story which is spoken of in the book of Job, in your holy work known as the Bible, is an example of the entities that were of what we call the negatively-oriented nature, who were attempting to pose as your Creator in order to control the actions of many of the peoples that you may refer to as the Jewish race of that time, who had long-established relations with many sources of information from elsewhere, shall we say.

The experience of the one known as Job was along the lines of giving and taking in order to control the behavior of these entities. There is, of course, a source of love which is truly of the one Creator which has, as you have mentioned, a complete identity in that it is of all things, both manifest and unmanifest, that which you would call the light and that which you would call the dark. However, there are lesser entities who have traveled from distant star systems to various planetary spheres such as your own Earth and have placed themselves in the position of one which would be the one Creator, in order that they might exercise a kind of control over those entities that they were able to convince to worship them as the one Creator.

We apologize for the somewhat scattered nature of this instrument's work this day, he is somewhat distracted and we have been able to utilize this entity only in some degree of effectiveness. We would ask if there may be a final query, my sister?

Carla: OK, just on my own hook, my question would be: Given that I perceive the pyramids with the knowledge that they would be a complete mystery, and given the knowledge that the time for the pyramids is over, I was thinking that the crop circles are one of the Confederation's ways of actively putting mystery into the fabric of our third-density experience, so that in actuality, in your own way you are continuing to offer mysteries for us to solve or to use. Would you say that that is accurate?

I am Q'uo. I am aware of your query, my sister. Indeed, this is one means by which mystery has been presented to your peoples by some of those in the Confederation of Planets in the Service of the One Infinite Creator. The concept of mystery is the opening into the consciousness which we have found most effective to utilize and it is that which seems to fuel the desire to seek further along the lines of love and light that so many of your peoples now express as a result of coming into contact with various sources of mystery.

At this time we shall take our leave of this instrument and this group. We are known to you as those of Q'uo. We leave each in the love and in the light of the one infinite Creator. Adonai, my friends. Adonai. ✸

L/L Research

L/L Research is a subsidiary of Rock Creek Research & Development Laboratories, Inc.

P.O. Box 5195
Louisville, KY 40255-0195

www.llresearch.org

Rock Creek is a non-profit corporation dedicated to discovering and sharing information which may aid in the spiritual evolution of humankind.

ABOUT THE CONTENTS OF THIS TRANSCRIPT: This telepathic channeling has been taken from transcriptions of the weekly study and meditation meetings of the Rock Creek Research & Development Laboratories and L/L Research. It is offered in the hope that it may be useful to you. As the Confederation entities always make a point of saying, please use your discrimination and judgment in assessing this material. If something rings true to you, fine. If something does not resonate, please leave it behind, for neither we nor those of the Confederation would wish to be a stumbling block for any.

© 2009 L/L Research

Special Meditation
July 17, 2003

Question from G: How may I be free of my own self-created prison walls and free of the resulting pain that keeps my energies internal and my heart, that wants to connect, so distant from others? How may I be free to love, to love at will, and free to channel love as universally and unconditionally as did the one known as Jesus?

(Carla channeling)

We are those of the principle known to you as Q'uo. We greet you in the love and in the light of the one infinite Creator, in whose name we come to you this evening. We thank you for the great privilege of being allowed to share our thoughts with you at this time. To be called to your group is a great privilege, never more so than at this time, as we feel the purity of desire within this group is most gratifying. We are extremely happy to share our thoughts with each of you with the request, as always, that the utmost care be taken to discriminate between those thoughts which may seem fair for a time and yet may not be, and those thoughts with truly do resonate and do seem to be those personal truths that are meant for this time and this circumstance especially.

There is a tremendous skill within each of you, that listening ear and understanding heart that can discern and can know, in that knowing that is beyond proof, that this is for you, that is not for you. That is that judge whom you must trust more so than any other party, for it is a unique thing to be incarnate within this illusion and it is central to the more subtle reaches of understanding, if we may call it that in this density, that the trust be first within the guidance of the self. Only after that primary judge has been accepted as the true arbiter of that which is true for you personally can you rest and enjoy the interesting opinions and concepts of many others who may indeed have part of the truth that is yours, and may not.

We are delighted to share with you upon the subject of true freedom. It is a much overused and misused word. For what is freedom? In the context of third density, it is an illusion to speak of true freedom, in that the circumstance of incarnation, in and of itself, is that which may seem to be as the prison, through the bars of which one may gaze upon eternity without being able to slip the bars of the cage and enter its untrammeled reaches. And yet that too is an illusion. What is true freedom? To examine this, one must examine what is the nature of the self. What is the nature of the self that is free to love?

We ask you to move into a space within your mind in which every stumbling block is removed, all direction is lost, and from which all concept of color or distance or size is missing, so that which you are, that infinite spark of the divine, is able to rest upon the waves of unknowing. These are the underground caves of freedom. These are the dark waters where there is no light, where prayers are true and the delusions and illusions of color and form have no meaning.

What has meaning in these caverns of self that lie beyond limit? Rest and know the strength, the absolute power, the infinity of self. Feel the self that has no need of boundaries, that has no need of bone or flesh or the illusory energy fields of form, texture and color, all of the details so dear to the eye and the ear and the senses. This state is as close as we can come with words at this time to describing the Creator that exists without the need for expression. In this state of absolute freedom from form, there are no boundaries, there are no limits, there is no personality, there is no distraction, there is no imperfection, all is truly one and everything is infinitely possible.

Lift the hand of the mind as if it were reaching for a string of a balloon and tug down to limit, to color, to personality through densities and dimensions, one after the other in a kaleidoscope—down, inward, until you reach the moment before this incarnation, before these details, before these personalities, when you decided, out of all the wisdom you had amassed, out of all the possibilities you could imagine, that this particular planetary sphere, this particular time, these particular relationships and these particular goals of service and learning are the very things out of all of the infinite possibilities available that you would choose at this time for your learning, for your joy, for your evolution. It is this juncture at which you both placed yourself in servitude and opened the doors to a different kind of freedom. For within the trammels of what this instrument would call this Earthly veil, lie the opportunities to love, imperfectly, brokenly, foolishly, again and again feeling the stumbling ways of humanhood, the clumsiness of limitation, the challenges of dwelling in a world where many things seem to be known which do not make sense and few things are known which make any sense.

A boundary is crossed when an entity chooses to enter incarnation. In some ways it is a boundary from great freedom to infinite limitation. Great vistas of awareness are shut down, closed as if they were slats in a Venetian blind which are simply turned and pulled shut to keep out the light of true awareness, of unlimited light, of unlimited knowledge. It is as if the soul coming into incarnation comes in from outdoors and forsakes the illumination of the sun in order to turn on the puny bulbs of 100 watts of artificial light that may or may not be there, depending on whether the power is on, whether the jerry-rigged ways of producing an equivalent light, without the infinite love being the source of that light, have sway.

It is a shock to the system to come into the body and there is, from the moment of entering the physical vehicle, the necessity to breath and to work and to exist through time as a human being. There is a sense of unutterable loss and yet it is that which has been chosen. So, gazed at from that simple perspective of choice, the entrance into the morass of limitations and confusion that is the Earth plane is the entrance into true freedom. The entrance into confusion is that pearl beyond price which has been paid for ahead of time by the soul who risks everything in order to learn and to serve.

There is in any incarnation a sense of sacrifice, a sense of loss, and so the question becomes, for what did I take flesh? For what reason was I called to this path? And this is a key question for each entity. What was the motivation? Was it utterly, purely to serve humankind? Was it to serve humankind in a certain way? Was it to serve humankind in a certain way, with certain people? Precisely how was this arrangement created and blessed? May we suggest that an effort of the intellectual mind to organize detail as in an outline and therefore understand, intellectually, the reasons for incarnation is to allow to slip away the opportunity to move beneath the surface of the intellect and beneath the surface of the acculturated, societally vetted, or accepted version of that which the life is and that which the goals of life are. We do not need to express [more] to you for we are aware that each within this circle is already aware that those things which the mind can come up with are those thing which are not satisfactory as full explanations for the reason for incarnation.

Truly, if you allow the heart to express, the heart itself with every beat, rhythmically, profoundly, simply expresses the truth of incarnation: love, love, love, love, love. The pump that pumps blood through the veins of the physical vehicle moves in waves of love. The second-density body which carries you about has no thought that is not steeped and marinated in love. The second-density vehicle is aware in every cell that it is the Creator and that it has no need of reasons to exist or to learn or to serve or to suffer and die. Is it ignorance or is it freedom that allows every cell of your body to give one hundred percent of itself in every moment for its continued existence and no less for the existence of that whole being of which it senses itself to be an integral part. As an entity, one not yet fully in communion with all other entities within its, shall we say, soul group, you have a great lesson to learn from those simple cells of your body, each of which is instinctual and vital with its identity, its every possibility and its readiness to respond to the stimuli that meet it in any given moment and so does your body, without question, without doubt, respond to that which it perceives. Is it experiencing freedom? Or is it experiencing a mindless, reactionary, slave's existence?

Let us draw back a step further and gaze at this body that is not you, yet which expresses as a great part of you within the solution. Your body perceives not according to the wisdom of the body alone; rather, the body accepts the information which that entity which you are comes to believe is true. If the entity which is you comes to believe that it cannot feel pain, then it can walk across hot coals or accept the needle in the arm, as has been demonstrated time and again by those who do hypnotism. And each cell of the body is free to ignore as completely unimportant and irrelevant those bodily sensations that otherwise would create great agony.

Similarly, that spirit and soul which you are, which is only imperfectly contained within the lantern of the body that holds the candle that is you and the light that is you, is only limited by its perception of its limits. And when that entity that is, at the soul level, the essence of you, is able to rest in peace, in power, within the temple of flesh that has been prepared for it, without strife and without argument, then that which the soul entity perceives is true. And those confusions and difficulties which may seem to be the case upon the outer plane do not have the necessity to impinge upon the inner essence of being that is you.

Naturally we are not suggesting that, as an entity becomes spiritually more mature, it may then stop listening to those voices that are around it. We do not for a moment suggest that ignoring those precious other-selves about one is in any way a useful exercise for one wishes to know how one may serve, how one may be served, how one may love, how one may be loved. One does not come into incarnation to avoid catalyst, yet at the same time one does not come into incarnation to become a slave to catalyst. One is neither greater than catalyst, nor less than catalyst, but rather, one is one with the catalyst.

The skill that feeds into the concept of freedom is that skill which is able to see the energies, the thought clusters, and the directions that those thought clusters take in their inferences and their suggestions of further thought. In other words, it accepts all of those thoughts as interesting, useful, beautiful, intriguing and equal. And all of the thoughts may be enjoyed, appreciated, respected, honored and followed as one would follow the strengths of a beautiful painting, the motifs of a beautiful piece of music, admiring, appreciating, moving into new places within the mind, within the feelings, because of this catalyst, these works of art that the people around you and their situations offer you in terms of the feeling clusters, the emotional and ethical challenges that are unique to each situation. And as a connoisseur, there is great appreciation in your heart for each offering, whether it may seem to be positive or negative, whether it may seem to be helpful or a hindrance. There is the connoisseur's appreciation for all the sweet and bitter tastes that make a full palate of experience and always, whether it is full of light or seemingly full of darkness, there is a feeling of privilege and even thanksgiving that one is able to meet this moment, to have these experiences, to accommodate this utterly unique opportunity, to see the Creator within the endless mystery of appearance.

Why did the Creator choose to make creations? Our comment has often tended to be, "The Creator is attempting to gain in knowledge and appreciation of Itself. The Creator wishes to know Itself. Thusly, it sends forth parts of Itself within illusion to see what will happen and to learn from the colors created in the palate of emotion that you have created through many experiences and incarnations, that contains your beauty and is unique to you, so that you can teach the Creator that which no one else in all of Creation is able to [teach]. For you are the only one of you in all of the infinite universe; thusly, it is your gift to the Creator, that comes from you, that is greatly desired. You cannot please the Creator by being someone else but only by being most truly and deeply yourself."

Is that freedom? If so, within incarnation, you are at your most free. You have the chance to make mistakes, to do things wrongly, to become utterly confused, to bomb out, to make mistake after mistake, according to your best light, and yet you do not have the freedom to make the Creator disappointed in you. You have the freedom only to disappoint yourself. But, to the Creator, all that you explore is new and all that you choose is brand new in that moment of choice.

How may you be free? My brother, your freedom was never in doubt. It is the life itself, the incarnational illusion that is full of doubt. Is it happening? Is it real? Is it a dream? All of these things are true. It is real. It is happening. It is a dream. It is both valid and illusion, real and imagined, full of power and a vain and empty nothingness. And in these paradoxes, in these impossibilities, in these extravagances that we attempt to place in your mind as being irrational and noumenal, lies a resting place for gathering experience. This is what you have chosen.

So perhaps freedom lies in having the most utter faith which is possible for you in the moment. Faith in what? Faith in the self, as limited as that self may seem. Faith in the energies that delivered you to this present moment, as peculiar, odd and unlikely as they must seem. You are indeed, most free to love at will. The life experience may be seen, in one way, to be that environment in which the will itself, that is, that energy of the soul piercing through the illusion of mass and time and space, chooses its light, focuses its love, and opens the door to the great mystery that lies within, that mystery that is love, that is loving, and that is loved.

We thank the one known as G for this query and we transfer this contact to the one known as Jim, realizing full well that we have only begun to utter the first sentence, in the first paragraph, of that which we could say concerning this most deep question. Yet the time wanes, the energy wanes and it is time for us to open the meeting to those questions which the one known as G may continue to have upon his mind. And so we will leave this instrument, thanking it for its service, transferring this contact to the one known as Jim. We leave this instrument in love and in light. We are those known to you as Q'uo.

(Pause)

(Jim channeling)

I am Q'uo, and greet each again in love and in light from this instrument. We would ask the one known as G if he has another query to which we may respond.

G: I certainly do. Thank you Ra, Hatonn and Latwii for being such loving guides to me during my own journey. My first question is: can you tell me what the splintering agent is that you mentioned in my last reading and what I can do to heal myself of its effects. Is there anything I can do to heal myself of its effects besides engaging in daily meditation, so that I may become whole again, restoring the vision and restoring the sight?

I am Q'uo, and am aware of your query, my brother. The splintering effect of which we spoke at our previous meeting is a point of view, shall we say, an attitude, which you have adopted or had adopted for yourself in your past. We find that your current experience is one which has caused you to change much of that point of view. There has been much healing of your fractured viewpoint concerning various aspects of yourself and how you would be able to accept these aspects in your daily round of activities. Thus, our recommendation remains that which it was then: to meditate and to consider carefully your point of view as regards the self and the self's interactions with others.

Is there another query, my brother?

G: Am I by any chance an indigo child or a wanderer of the type with the dual-activated body, or both?

I am Q'uo, and am aware of your query, my brother. We would go to the limits of our ability to respond without infringing upon your free will by suggesting that your nature, at its core, is more attuned with the status of one who seeks to serve as a wanderer to distant areas of consciousness. Thus, you are one who has journeyed to a distant point of your own thinking, which is now symbolized by this planetary sphere.

Is there another query my brother?

G: What is the nature of the deep fatigue that comes and goes and what can I do to increase my energy levels?

I am Q'uo, and am aware of your query my brother. The …

(Side one of tape ends.)

(Jim channeling)

I am Q'uo, and am again with this instrument. We shall continue. The fatigue of which you have spoken is a product of the rapid change that has become a part of your daily round of activities, as you have been much involved in the realigning of the physical attributes of this dwelling place. There is a deeper type of change that is symbolized by the rearranging of the physical objects that also is occurring within you at this time. This is the, shall we say, quality of bearing a burden that you have felt as a result of responsibilities, of familial ties. There is the enculturation process that is natural to all third-density beings upon this planet that has, for you, culminated recently in a choice to follow your own lights, shall we say. This choice to move as an independent creature has brought the feeling of a responsibility for your own movement, so that you place a kind of pressure or burden upon your metaphysical shoulders.

This is a somewhat roundabout way of looking at your opportunities for growth. However, we find that each seeker has its own way of approaching the journey that beckons. It is a matter of what is more efficient for you. As you continue upon this journey you will find an ease to your movement which is not now present in its fullest degree, shall we say. As you move more and more freely upon the journey of the change of self that continues until one sees there is a self that does not change, then you shall feel more of this weight removed from your shoulders and your being. It is again a matter of being able to accept yourself and your opportunities for growth.

Is there a further query my brother?

G: Thank you, Q'uo. I have a cluster here. Are my twin soul and I adhering to the preincarnatively chosen plan that we had set before us, for the course of our earthly relationship? Is there anything more I can do to help her to free herself from her own confusion? And is there a higher road of service that I might walk, higher than the one I currently walk now?

I am Q'uo, and am aware of your queries and the concern which generates these avenues of inquiry. We feel that you are well aware that there are no mistakes in any seeker's journey. There are, however, expectations. Oftentimes, it is more efficient for the seeker to remove expectations and to be able to accept that which occurs as that which is appropriate. However we are aware that catalyst does not usually work as easily as this simplistic description within your illusion. There is oftentimes much angst between the desire to serve and the actual service as perceived by the self.

The path which you and the entity which you call your twin soul have chosen is indeed appropriate for your own movement into service at this time. We are aware that each would, in what each would call an ideal world, wish to serve in another fashion, one which was more proximate, shall we say, each to the other, in more obvious service and types of learning. Again there is the matter of [allowing] catalyst for growth to occur truly. There is, shall we say, a weight or a resistance against which each moves or pushes so that there is an exercising of the spiritual muscles or ability to conceptualize that which is yours to seek and to serve, to give and to receive. There is always a means by which one may serve more efficiently. That is another way of saying there is always growth potential available. It is well to refrain from taking one's spiritual temperature, judging oneself, attempting to evaluate just exactly where and how one moves upon the path of service to others.

Again we return to that lighthearted feeling which the childlike nature of the true self demonstrates without effort. This childlike nature has taken on an earthly form, with various abilities to express, various difficulties in expressing. Thus, though there are goals towards which each moves, there is the movement, the perception of the movement, and so on, which when examined without too much dedication to an outcome, can give one a hint, a direction, a possibility. But when focused upon too intensively shall we say, when obsessed about, [they] may become a stumbling block upon the journey. Thus do strengths become weaknesses and weaknesses strengths.

Is there another query my brother?

G: Marvelous answer, Q'uo. I have seen enough 1:10's, 11:10's, 12:13's to know that a message is being communicated to me. Can you provide me any sort of insight as to what is trying to be conveyed to me with these one-minute-off "synchronicities"?

I am Q'uo, and am aware of your query, my brother. And though this query upon its surface appearance seems to be one steeped in innocence, it is with this query that we must be most careful that we do not infringe upon your free will. Thus, we have only a suggestion that you look at the symbolic nature of the numbers involved and how this symbolism resonates to a certain point of view that you hold towards seeking and serving, of being of service, and of how this is offered.

Is there a further query my brother?

G: Thank you Q'uo. Why do I feel like there are holes, that is, missing pieces of identity and memory, in my soul?

I am Q'uo and am aware of your query, my brother. This sensation which you describe as "holes" within the soul of one's being is a most interesting and perhaps literal way of looking at those portions of the self towards which one moves in the spiritual sense. To regain one's identity is to fit together many pieces of a great puzzle of many dimensions. When one has a lack of understanding of any portion of this puzzle, there is a hole, shall we say, a gap, a place or way of being that is yet to be discovered. This is the nature of the journey for each seeker of truth—to find the trail of pieces to this puzzle and follow till one is whole, till one is unified, till one feels the unity of self with all other beings. This is a grand journey upon which you travel. Follow that feeling of the whole within until you find that which plugs or fills the hole.

Is there another query my brother?

G: Thank you, Q'uo. Another cluster. Somewhere along the way it seems my memory has been impaired somewhat and I was wondering if you could tell me how that happened? Was it injury done to myself by myself? Or the process of ascension? And, how might I be able to regain it enough so that I can again learn and absorb and synthesize new information?

I am Q'uo, and am aware of your query, my brother.

When there has been a forgetting of that which has occurred within the conscious memory, it is either because there was little value to the self in retaining this experience or because there was some difficulty in accepting the experience, so that there was instead of acceptance, rejection. These experiences are critical portions of one's formative years, shall we say. To explore the primary cause of such rejection, it is often necessary to look within the dream state or the deep meditation, which may uncover these types of traumatic learnings. Thus, we suggest that you take what you can of the current memory, the place where the memory stops, and attempt within your dream state or within your meditative state to take the next step in experience, to open the self to receiving that clue or quality of feeling that will begin to reveal to you that which you have hidden from yourself.

Is there a further query, my brother?

G: Q'uo, you rock. Give me one second, Q'uo.

Carla: Could I ask a question while he is gathering his wits, Q'uo?

I am Q'uo. We would welcome your query, my sister.

Carla: On the question about weariness and food intake and so forth, I've been going from the assumption that it might be substances or it might be the quality of love in the food and so I have focused more on putting love into the food than in being really sensitive about certain substances. Could you make any suggestions as to whether this is a basically good way to value and also if there are substances to which this particular soul either has need for or needs not to have? Is there a possibility that you could share those with me?

I am Q'uo, and aware of your query, my sister. We find that the menu is heavily laden toward the quality of love, which is most nutritious to each seeking soul. We are also aware that the one known as G has a quite clear understanding of his own dietary needs. Perhaps there could be the inclusion of more substances which this entity prefers. However, that which has been prepared is prepared with care, concern, love and great affection. Thus, we cavil not at the diet and applaud each in his and her approach to the intake of foodstuffs.

Carla: Thank you.

Is there another query at this time?

G: Thank you, Carla, for the very considerate question. Q'uo, can you tell me how I reacted to this world as a child? I ask you because I don't recall much of my childhood.

I am Q'uo, and aware of your query, my brother. We examine the life pattern of the one known as G, seeing the innocence of the newborn babe carried through into the childhood, so that there was a freshness of learning that was both comforting to the one known as G and somewhat disturbing to those who were the parents, for there was more ability in abstruse areas of comprehension than was expected. Therefore, there has been a loss of innocence and of the ability to grasp new experiences easily and quickly. This is a portion of that filling in of the hole aspect of which we spoke earlier as well as the beginning exploration of the traumatic learning of which we spoke earlier as well. There has continued to be a great thirst for knowledge and for being of service which both were present from the earliest of ages. This is the sum of that which we feel we may offer without infringement.

Is there a final query at this time?

G: That answer is such a gift, thank you, Q'uo. Am I any closer to the course of dessert? Have I moved on, or am I still on my main course? Or am I almost done?

I am Q'uo, and am aware of your query, my brother. We find that you are well along the consuming of the main course, which we suggest will be a somewhat lengthy meal within this illusion! From time to time you may find a taste or two of dessert. However, we suggest that prepare yourself for a great feast.

It has been our great privilege to be able to speak to your concerns this evening for we feel that you have a great desire for seeking and serving which needs but little guidance to find its fullest flower within the present environment.

We are those known to you as those of Q'uo. We would take our leave of this instrument of this group at this time. We thank each for inviting our presence this evening. It is a great honor to join you in this circle of seeking.

Adonai my friends. Adonai.[55]

---

[55] Immediately after the closing prayer, G looked down at his wristwatch and exclaimed, "10:10!"

L/L Research

L/L Research is a subsidiary of Rock Creek Research & Development Laboratories, Inc.

P.O. Box 5195
Louisville, KY 40255-0195

www.llresearch.org

Rock Creek is a non-profit corporation dedicated to discovering and sharing information which may aid in the spiritual evolution of humankind.

ABOUT THE CONTENTS OF THIS TRANSCRIPT: This telepathic channeling has been taken from transcriptions of the weekly study and meditation meetings of the Rock Creek Research & Development Laboratories and L/L Research. It is offered in the hope that it may be useful to you. As the Confederation entities always make a point of saying, please use your discrimination and judgment in assessing this material. If something rings true to you, fine. If something does not resonate, please leave it behind, for neither we nor those of the Confederation would wish to be a stumbling block for any.

© 2009 L/L Research

Special Meditation, Belknap Campus, University of Louisville
August 24, 2003

(Carla channeling)

[I am Q'uo.] … [Everything,] the body, the sound, the music of life, the color of it, all of these things that fill in the colors and the shapes and the form of consciousness; all of these things exist as vibration. You, yourself, exist as energy fields of vibration within which are many other energy fields. The energy field of the body itself, the energy fields of the organs and of each cell of each organ and each portion of the body, the energy cloud, shall we say, that is made up of this circle of seeking, the energy of your planet, the energy of your solar systems and of the creation of the Father as a whole, in its infinite reaches, and the Creator, Itself—all of these things are energy. All these things are vibrations and complexes of vibratory levels working in harmonics and sub-harmonics together to create the shape of the world that you see before you as you open your eyes, and that create the shape of the world that you cannot see whether your eyes are open or shut.

All that is visible, all that is invisible, is vibration. The vibration of the Father, as this instrument is wont to call the godhead principle, is a singular vibration which we are used to calling that term, the Logos, which is a term in this instrument's vocabulary from its Christian heritage—Logos, the Word, the Word which is love, unconditional love. That vibration is the vibration of the Creator. Those vibratory nexi that manifest as each person here, each of you being a sub-logos, in part, of the infinite Creator, have the goal of moving in vibratory level more and more close to the vibration of the Logos, to the energy of unconditional love. Regardless of what outer gifts you have, this gift is at the heart of your experience of yourself as an essence, of your getting to know yourself as a true being. As you are able to come more and more into an awareness of what the energy of unconditional love feels like, you are coming closer and closer to your own heart.

The days begin to grow shorter at this time, and your planet turns on its axis in such a way that the seasons turn with it, the days grow shorter, and the dark grows larger until winter comes to your planet. And in the heart of that winter there is always that moment of what this instrument calls Christmas when attention is paid to a tiny child that is love made visible within this instrument's religion, that time when Jesus, the Christ, comes into the world as a tiny, helpless baby. We ask each of you here to open your heart and to see yourself in a manger, a new being, my friends, a soul, fresh, untouched, inviolate, waiting, hoping to be loved, to be recognized, to be swaddled and nurtured and held and taken care of and protected. This child within you is the spiritual self that you came into this world to find, to embrace, and to nourish and nurture with your outer life and your inner life, always opening to the vibration of unconditional love that floods the heart when there is no resistance, that waits within the heart, that is surrounding the manger of spirit within you. Pay attention to that child that is your spiritual self, for it is tender and young, and while you have become experienced and wise in the ways of the world, perhaps that has caused defenses to rise within each of you so that you are defended and armored against those who would hurt you. Yet, to those who dwell in unconditional love, there is no man, no woman, who is an enemy. There is no entity whatsoever that is not part of those souls which are yours to love, to help, and to wish well on their way if they perhaps do not agree, but never to armor against, to defend against, or to harden the self against. For the gift of the heart, the gift of love, is that it is fearless. It does not need to defend; it does not need to protect, for it rests in the vibration of unconditional love.

We would take a moment to experience the silence with you. We ask you to allow that silence to blossom within you, that you may feel that love of which we speak. We shall pause. We are those of Q'uo.

(Pause)

We are those of Q'uo, and are again with this instrument. Continuing to feel that energy within you, now, we ask that you begin to allow it to rotate about the circle from you to the person to your left and so forth, receiving the energy from the person on your right and moving it on. Feel that energy begin to spiral and grow; feel that sacred space that has been called into being by the one known as M and then fill it with the flame of love unconditional.

We would speak to you, as this energy rotates and builds, about mission. We do not mean to imply that anyone comes into the world with a contract, "I will do this and this and this, and then I shall be ready to abandon life." Rather, we suggest that each of you, before this incarnation, along with your guidance, sat together and planned, oh, what a glorious plan, choosing parents and mates and siblings and friends and that which is called among your people, enemies, all so that certain lessons, which you had decided upon beforehand, would have regular opportunities to be visited and revisited. For there are certain things which each of you hopes to learn, to work on, not simply learning for the first time, but refining and exploring the subtler reaches of these themes of incarnation for which you did take on flesh. There are other gifts which you chose because you felt perhaps they would be helpful at this particular time, at this particular juncture. The learning and the service bring certain people, certain lessons, certain themes into the life again and again, and we ask that you do not be discouraged when you see these lessons seeming to repeat. Rather, think to yourself that you are spiraling, you are visiting these lessons again, not at the same place, for you are not at the same place, nor is the lesson in the same place, but, rather, each time you visit it, if you are working with the lesson, you learn more, you go further, you become wiser, you become more compassionate, or you simply become more balanced between the all-embracing love of compassion and the more intelligently-guided wisdom of compassion touched with that wisdom which suggests limitations, boundaries, precision, where before there may have been a vagueness or an unsureness. These do not add up to a "mission"; these add up to a life experience in which the possibilities are literally infinite but in which there are, as Dr. Thompson said, certain avenues which open up before one as the blooming of a flower, and things begin to fall in place, and there is that feeling that one has caught the rhythm of destiny and one is now cooperating with it.

What we suggest, if you do not sense where destiny is taking you, is simply, each day, to sit in meditation and listen. The silence expresses much, as well as those undertones and overtones that your dreams and your visions and the street signs and the birds and all of the information thickly strewn in life seems to bring to you. The silence organizes and reorganizes and gradually there comes an inner sense almost as if the creature within you that has energy has found a way to take a deep breath, not the physical breath but the metaphysical breath of, "I can expand; it is safe." Move into that space whenever you can. Certainly attempt it daily, for there is information for you in that silence. And that guidance system that loves you, is part of you and is always with you will find it easier and easier to touch the life of you with this and that hint and inkling until you find it easier and easier to cooperate with the forces of what seem to be destiny but indeed are rich in free will.

We ask simply, if you think about mission, that you think first of the mission that is common to all who take breath upon the planet. You came to love and to be loved; you came to learn about unconditional love; you came to choose between love and fear. When you see fear within yourself, your mission is to sit with that fear, not necessarily to kick it out.

You may not be ready. But, strand by strand, you take it away just at the rate of speed which makes you comfortable. That idea that continues, the idea that lifts and helps, is that idea that love is the truth and that fear is independent of that truth. So, where there is fear, all openings to love that can shine light upon that darkness are encouraged.

Before we leave this instrument, we would ask if there would be perhaps three or four questions that we may answer?

M: *(Reads from an audience card.)* Okay, the first question is, "Why must the children suffer so?"

We are with this instrument and are aware of your query. All of those within this particular plane of existence, all those who are in the flesh and experiencing the energies of a physical body, are also prone to experience suffering, and indeed it often seems unfair, for the children experience the suffering without having the choice of creating the situations that produce the suffering. There are those children who are born into times of war who must suffer therefore. There are those children that are born into those structures of family which seem to create abuse of various kinds and consequently create suffering for an innocent. There are as many instances of innocents suffering as there are innocents, for all do suffer.

The question of suffering is indeed a universal question, and the response that we would offer is that each entity deliberately chooses to enter into a physical vehicle and to forget almost everything that the entity is aware of before incarnation. This instrument has called it the veil of forgetting. There are other terms for it, but, as Wordsworth the poet has said, "We've come, each entity, into the third density streaming clouds of glory which rapidly dissipate with the onset of breath into the body."[56] Focus upon your own birth cries and remember the first suffering that you felt, the cold air, the shock of having to take breath within the lungs, the loss of the warm darkness and the rude intrusion of life. Suffering begins early within the third density and continues in some form or another for almost all those who are in incarnation as the personality aligns experience to some degree or another. The why of it is wrapped up in the purpose of losing that memory. It is important to lose the memory, to become stupid, and to be quite confused and dismayed and taken aback, because it is that point of deconstruction of the self which is that which sets the stage for transformation.

Each of you hoped to rebalance that balance between love and wisdom when you came into this incarnation. You hoped to refine yourself. It is as though each of you has within you a wonderful gem, yet, in order to polish that gem, much surface material must be taken away. And so the suffering is that which blasts and chips and picks at the outer shell that is not the gem, knocking away all of those things that are not the real you. The suffering is that sense of pain as the emotions and the mental structures are in the process of changing. It is the change that is the root of most of the suffering of your species. It is the kind of pain that exercise creates. It is flexing the muscles, perhaps beyond the capacity of the muscles before this exercise. Yet, each time that entities undergo this suffering, they learn or have the opportunity to learn more about how to sit with that suffering, how to take it in, to love it, to work with it, and to allow it to seep through the self, doing those things that it came to do, easing the imbalances in the energy body and approving the overall situation which exists in your soul stream, not simply in this time and space. But you are doing work which transmits itself to the infinite and eternal stream of energy that you are.

Is there another question, my sister?

M: *(Reads from an audience card.)* There is. "What would benefit me the most to hear or know at this time?"

We are those of Q'uo, and are aware of your query, and we would say to you: all is one. Hold to that sense of unity within yourself; know that all that is good and positive to you is you and all that is distasteful and hateful to you is you and that all things whatsoever are you. Look at this instrument, see the Creator; look in your mirror, see the Creator; look into the eyes of the person next to you and see

---

[56] The quote, from William Wordsworth's *Ode*: Intimations Of Immortality From Recollections Of Early Childhood:

> Our birth is but a sleep and a forgetting:
> The Soul that rises with us, our life's Star,
> Hath had elsewhere its setting,
> And cometh from afar:
> Not in entire forgetfulness,
> And not in utter nakedness,
> But trailing clouds of glory do we come
> From God, who is our home
> Heaven lies about us in our infancy!

the Creator; look into the eyes of your dearest enemy and see the same Creator; look into the sky, look into the depths of the sea, look into all of the elements and see only and always and ever the Creator. You are all things. We would say that this would be that thought which would be most helpful, and we thank the entity that has asked that query, for it has many good vibrations within, and we appreciate that exchange of energy very much.

May we ask, my sister, if there is one more query?

M: *(Reads from an audience card.)* There is. "Would you speak to the entering of the fifth dimension and the process of our and the Earth's transition?"

We are those known to you as Q'uo, and we are delighted to speak of those shifts which are at present occurring. The terminology varies from instrument to instrument and structure of myth to structure of philosophy, or whatever, and so this instrument would perhaps call the next density the fourth density rather than the fifth. However, this instrument is aware of those who use the system in which the fifth is that which is opening at this time, and this instrument is of the opinion that these are relatively acceptable terms to use interchangeably in this general context.

The next density is the density of love or understanding, to use general terms. This density is that which seeks to learn the lessons of love. Unconditional love is the chief lesson of your density. Once an entity has grasped the beauty of unconditional love, once the entity has placed itself into a practice of self-sacrifice, of loving others to the extent that they would give their lives for the others, if they could, in order to spare them, once this has been taken as the path that is desired, then the earthly journey becomes a life of service, a life of giving and, increasingly, a life of receiving. For, as the one known as Dr. Thompson says, all that is given out comes back again in a way that is irresistible and cannot be stopped, so that you are soon surrounded with the lessons of how to accept love from others. For you have learned how to love others. When you are at this state, then you are ready to live in a more love-filled atmosphere, and that is what the next density is in relation to third density. The fourth density, then, has a different kind of light, a light that is more densely packed with light, so that there is actually more light in an atom, in a particle, of that energy. It is that shift which is now occurring upon your own planet. Your entire planetary system has spiraled into a brand new area of space/time in which the energies are different, the energies are shifting. There is dramatic change, and your entire planet is recreating itself from birthing itself as the fourth-density planet. Consequently, as each entity reaches the point of leaving the earth plane through the normal processes of what you would call death, there is the opportunity at this time to graduate from third density and move into the fourth density and what is often called ascension. In this process of ascension, the soul energy that is you, the essence of you, takes up a fourth-density body for its next incarnation and therefore takes up a whole different environment with a whole new set of lessons. So, in general, moving into the next density is as moving into the next grade in school. It is an exciting thing to move ahead and start the first day of the school year, when all the lessons are brand new and all the lessons seem good. And this is the experience to which you may look forward, as you look into that next life that may come after this one.

We take this time to thank you once again. It is a pleasure to share our thoughts with you. And, once again, we ask you please to take those thoughts of ours which seem fair to you and to leave the rest behind without a second thought, for we would not be a stumbling block before you.

If you wish to deepen your meditative state, you are always welcome to call the Confederation of Brothers and Sisters of Sorrow. We are happy to lend our energies to your meditation that you may feel a deeper sense of stillness inside. We are happy to come to you in dreams and to be part of your guidance. You have only to ask. We, however, do not wish to speak through any but simply to share vibration at this level.

We thank you for this time together. It has been a blessing to us. We leave each of you in the love and in the light of the one infinite Creator. We are known to you as those of Q'uo. Adonai. Adonai. ✣

L/L Research

L/L Research is a subsidiary of Rock Creek Research & Development Laboratories, Inc.

P.O. Box 5195
Louisville, KY 40255-0195

www.llresearch.org

Rock Creek is a non-profit corporation dedicated to discovering and sharing information which may aid in the spiritual evolution of humankind.

ABOUT THE CONTENTS OF THIS TRANSCRIPT: This telepathic channeling has been taken from transcriptions of the weekly study and meditation meetings of the Rock Creek Research & Development Laboratories and L/L Research. It is offered in the hope that it may be useful to you. As the Confederation entities always make a point of saying, please use your discrimination and judgment in assessing this material. If something rings true to you, fine. If something does not resonate, please leave it behind, for neither we nor those of the Confederation would wish to be a stumbling block for any.

© 2009 L/L RESEARCH

Sunday Meditation
September 7, 2003

Group question: The question today has to do with change and how we respond to change. We've talked around the circle today and it's the common theme for everyone that there have been a lot of changes. And as we look at the situation in the world today, we see rapid changes, some of them violent, drastic and catastrophic. We were wondering if there is a particular response to change that could be recommended? We are forming a community. It seems to be a very good thing to do in the way of providing support and inspiration and encouragement and reinforcement to individuals. People seem to have a way, whether they live together or talk together at work, of sharing their energies and lending their support to each other. Could you talk to us about change and community and the best way to respond to change?

(Carla channeling)

We are those known to you as Q'uo, and we greet you, with great delight, in the love and in the light of the one infinite Creator, in whose service we are. It is a great pleasure to be called to your circle as you convene your public meetings and we can not thank you enough. We thank each of you for the beauty of your vibrations, for the pureness of your hearts, for reserving the time for the seeking of truth and for the steadiness of your dedication which has caused you to create this time from your busy life.

It is a great blessing to us to be called to you and to be able to share those thoughts that we would share.

We ask only that each who hears these words realize they are the words of friends rather than those of authorities. Therefore, in order to allow us the freedom to speak our thoughts, we ask that you discriminate carefully with each and every thought that we share, choosing to remember those which seem to be helpful to you and discarding the rest without a second thought. We are most pleased to share on this most timely question of change, how to respond to change well and how to think of change.

The first change that each experiences within incarnation is that change which brings one into incarnation. As this instrument has noted from time to time, the birth is as the dropping from the plane, with or without parachute. There will be a landing! And there will be an ending to the incarnation. That which arises from dust goes again to dust. In truth, the experience of incarnation, in itself, is an experience rooted in, steeped in, and moving towards change. It is not a circumstance but rather a progression, a developmental cycle; if we could use your terminology, a grade of your school, visited for a semester. This is your course, Life 331-B. We joke about the number, but the concept is true as far as we know.

There are certain organized features of the change within an incarnation. There is an organization of lessons, shall we say, a curriculum, that was chosen by you and your higher self prior to incarnation. Those who incarnated at this particular time within your planet's density have incarnated because there was a desire for a more intensive experience of change and transformation and the opportunities for rebalancing the wisdom and the energy within the energy body of the self that was irresistible. Consequently, each of you has chosen certain courses for the particular term that is your incarnation. These courses or lessons or curricula have names such as "Loving Without Condition," "Creating Sacred Space," "Sanctifying the Rays of Living," [including] the ray of survival, the ray of relationship, the ray of working, the ray of communicating, and so forth. Different entities have chosen to take somewhat different courses. Each has a different course load; a slightly different experience.

Yet each is moving through a process that is very regular and guarded and safe from the standpoint of the spirit or the soul stream of the self. However, within incarnation this is not obvious. Consequently, the illusory experience of taking this course of Life 101 is much more chaotic in its feeling, in its perceived nature, than would be the perception of your self outside of incarnation and outside of the veil of illusion that is this particular organization of time and space in such a way that it is, shall we say, space/time rather than time/space.

Thusly, the first thing we would say about the way to deal with the concept or the perception that one is in a process of change is to remember the structure that supports this perception. That structure is your eternal and infinite soul stream, that energy that is you, now and forever. A part of that energy has moved into the habitation of the physical body or vehicle and at this time you are inextricably intertwined, energetically, with this physical vehicle. Yet you are not this physical vehicle. You simply reach into the physical vehicle with the ties and bonds of [your] dedication of self to the incarnation and connections within the energy body that move into the connections in each chakra. As you present yourselves to us at this time, you sit in the jars of clay, shall we say, that are the vehicles of your physical body, which cannot contain the rainbow self that is your energy, or energetic, body. This rainbow self shimmers and glows and exceeds the boundaries of physicality. And in the balance of each of those chakras, we see much that is not apparent within the veil of [third-density] illusion.

One interesting exercise to use, when one wishes to learn more about the self and where the self is blocked, is simply to rest with the self in a meditative state until one is able to begin to see how the energies of the body are balanced. There is perhaps the technique of asking oneself, "Let me see my energy," and then allowing the rainbow (red, orange, yellow …) to come to life [in your inner vision] as you call the colors, so that you are able, in an intuitive way, in a direct way, to gain access to that part of you which is not verbal and which is far more connected to the truth of your energy body. This can be evoked simply by asking, with great faith that you are asking an actual part of the self that can respond. The talent here is not in technique but in the trust and the "allowing-to-be-true" of the technique. It is not a skill of the mind but rather a skill, as the one known as G has said, of the will, or of the heart and the will together.

When one is aware of and centered within the fundamental perception of the structure of incarnation, then one is aware that one is within a process of change; that one has chosen what one wishes to examine during the process of change; and [that] one is then free to trust the lessons that appear before the face, to lean into them in terms of doing the homework, of doing the mental analysis, of going to the library of self and asking those questions which need to be asked, [of] doing the research that needs to be done in order that one feels one is beforehand with one's lessons. That [may] mean, for you in particular, the process of getting meditation more into a daily habit, or the process of journaling one's dreams or journaling one's thoughts, or the use of other techniques with which you wish to examine the life as it is lived and to ask of the self, "Who are you? Why are you here? What is your mission?"

The energies of reaction to change, which may include much panic and feeling of loss and the stumbling effect of not knowing the path ahead, can be mitigated. The simple trust that all is well, and that this that you experience, whatever it may be, is valuable, worthy of attention, and worthy of your best effort, is very helpful in smoothing and regularizing the process of change that is inevitable and desirable.

As we said earlier, there is at this time a particularly intensive process of change moving through the planetary energies as a whole. It is the end of several cycles within your planet, small and large. The planet itself transits at this time. Consequently, many of you came here in incarnation at this time with extra-curricular activities planned having to do with service to others, service to the planet, and/or service to the people of the planet. We put before you these two slightly different vectors of service to others because that is the mix that we are experiencing within this circle. There are those within the circle that feel that they are Earth natives, that that they have a love of Earth, an affinity for the Earth, and a long association with this particular planet that you call Earth, which we call Atlantis, actually, this being the name of your planet among the metaphysical or time/space entities which live within what you would call circular time and have experienced the entire gamut of the various experiences of your planet through what you would call your past and what you would call your future.

The energy of your people is that energy that is called Atlantis. And this at this time becomes more pointedly relevant in that your peoples as a whole are visiting at this time and attempting to rebalance those energies of Atlantis; those energies that fed into the build-up of the civilization of Atlantis and of Egypt; the civilizations that learned technology and skills of the scientific kind and did not learn the disciplines of the personality that would enable them to make use of such technical expertise in a way that was positive and unconditionally loving.

The very stuff of your density is love. The overriding lesson of your density is love. And yet, it is not a romantic love, it is not the love of brothers, it is not any love that you can imagine or speak of or wrap your words around and contain. It is that love which is the infinite Word. It is that love which is the one infinite Creator. It is that love that destroys and creates equally, generously and eternally. The concepts of love and wisdom seem separate, yet they are simply two shadows within illusion. That truth which lies beyond all illusion is the infinite love of the one Creator. Consequently, when you are attempting to learn love without end, sacrificing, giving, crucifying the self for others to the extreme of the myths of humankind for describing unconditional love, this is but one aspect of love. There is the aspect of love also wrapped in fear, in negativity, in contraction, in darkness, in the shadows, in the depths within the self that gives substance and structure to the whole and creates within infinite light and unconditional love a place, a habitation, not for the soul only but for physical vehicles, for physical feelings, experiences and intensities [as well]. In other words, one of the blessed aspects of third-density incarnation is the ability to feel pain, the ability to be confused, the very precious ability to lose the self and to be forced out of the mental constructs of a lifetime of learned untruths and half truths that your outer civilization offers to each of you.

It may seem perverse for the self to cheer for the self when the self realizes it is greatly confused and stumbling and wandering, as the one known as S has said, and yet this too is a blessing. It is the blessing of opportunity. It is the blessing of darkness. For each of you has within you the potential to be a light that enlightens the darkness, that illumines the shadows, not chasing them away but simply exposing them for what they are. Darkness is rounded in light and light rounded in darkness. That is the way of your circadian cycle. Yet we ask you to see beyond the light and the dark, to see into the nature of your lessons, of your service, of love itself. To see that which is "beyond variation[57]," as this instrument read in her church service this morning. The Creator comes from light with no variation due to change. There is no change in the One Who is all things. Change is an illusion, which is very helpful in the process of the Creator knowing Itself, and for this process the Creator has given Itself to you, to this instrument, to all, in discrete, illusory sparks of light that can experience, and register that experience, and feel and create from those feelings a process of refining and deepening and purifying, until those emotions become truth. And that which before was the babbling of children, becomes, in the ordered experience of the true and deep emotion, a giving of the self that is a harvest of a lifetime. For as the truer, deeper emotions begin to be refined from the welter of shallow feeling, those emotions begin to contain information which is as food to the Creator, a delightful and refreshing food that informs the Creator of Itself.

Now each of you, in this rainbow self that you have, is constantly creating and re-creating the truth of yourself. You are in a constant state of flux. The "name" of yourself is this complex of vibrations, this

---

[57] *Holy Bible*, James 16-17: "Every good endowment and every perfect gift is from above, coming down from the Father of lights, with whom there is no variation or shadow due to change."

rainbow self. When your passing moods strike you, they may well change some of the colors of yourself and tell less of the truth about you. So it is well, when you think of how to respond well to change, to look at the self and ask the self, "Of all of these aspects of the present scene are there those that could be harmonized within the self? Could I, speaking as each of you, find a way to add harmony, to rebalance for more truth, to more center a relationship, a conversation, a group situation, in a way that balances the energies of love, wisdom, will and so forth?"

The time is such that until far beyond the end of each of your incarnations, experiences shall be very intense, for the energies of change have begun long ago and are now in full swing and move towards a conclusion that is not a moment in time precisely, and yet there is a point at which your planet shall be fourth-density positive and those who are within third density upon the planet shall only be able to endure and remain within the planetary atmosphere because they have begun living and thinking in a fourth-density-compatible manner. So the third thing that we would say, concerning responding to change, is to ask yourself, "If I were in fourth density, how would I perceive this situation?" As the one known as Ra has said to this group before, "Where is the love in this moment?" This is the thinking of fourth density. It is that thinking that assumes total acceptance of all beings, total equality of all soul streams, total oneness with everyone, and an inability not to harmonize. When one, as a third-density self, feels the disharmony, one may be aware that one is simply living and thinking and reacting according to the illusion of third density. We ask that you consider this as one of two choices. One of indeed infinite choices! But the other choice that we would recommend is that choice of moving into the sacred region of the heart. For the heart has never left the unconditional love of the one infinite Creator that exists within first density, second density, third density, fourth density, fifth density, and so on. Third density is that density wherein the mind portion of the body/mind/spirit complex is veiled. The body is not veiled; the spirit is not veiled: the mind is veiled. This is simply to produce the ability to experience this process of change, this feeling of chaos, this experience of illusion, of disillusion and recombining and creating the self as one goes. We do not have, in higher densities, that privilege. Consequently we can not work vividly, quickly and effectively to retune or to rebalance our energies. Rather, we are refining the choices already made.

There are other entities within this circle that are not Earth natives but rather those that and that have chosen to return for a program having the experience of learning and service. Again, some of you may have come to work with the planet, for it is being birthed into fourth density as we speak. Some of you may have come to work with the planetary ethos at this time. For there is great energy forming at a global level within many, many peoples of many different cultures and ways of thinking. Yet, the unification of this energy is beginning to be marked, and that is simply that all souls count, all beings deserve the same respect and honor, all entities are sacred.

This energy is a simple, almost primitive realization, that realization of the goodness of the self and the goodness of other selves and of the world. And this basic realization is summed up within your Christian Old Testament statements by the very questionable God—as this instrument would call it—Jehovah, who kept observing as He created that "this was good."

So we ask you to move into the realization, more and more, that you are the chooser of your experience, you are the creator of your truths and you can indeed move more and more, as you experience the feelings of the open heart more and more, into that open heart, into the rush of infinite energy that is moving through that heart at all times, into that atmosphere of support that the one known as G spoke of that exists not without the self, but within the self, and that is only projected outside the self in order to be visible, in order to be seen, in order to be understood. For who can understand one's own heart? Yet we ask you to trust that heart and whenever you can, move into that space of remembrance of who you are, of remembrance of yourself as a spark of Creatorship, of "Creator-in-training-ness," as this instrument has said before. That is your true nature. You are very young. Yet you are moving inevitably and inexorably towards your source, your ending, the one infinite Creator. You are gaining spiritual mass and at this particular time, your goal is to be yourself, for within the heart of self lies this truth, that is fourth-density reality.

And may we say that all densities grow in reality, yet all remain illusory. Each illusion, as it moves towards the octave of Creator-ness, becomes more able to contain truth. As the light itself changes, it is able to hold [more] information.

We ask you to imagine your heart opening and yourself allowing the portions of your mind that are not at this time awakened, to be awakened, of resting and asking for more. For truly those who ask shall receive and to those who knock, the door shall be opened. There is this energy of fourth-density that is actually currently at least as strong within your planetary atmosphere as the third-density energies of chaos and revolution.

Your question spoke of the tremendous changes going on within your world at this time. Indeed we do see the energies of your peoples ripening towards the destruction of entities by their brothers and sisters, moving into larger-scale slaughter of innocents. We see this as a possibility. We see the possibility also, of a grassroots movement, as this instrument would call it, that is impossible to stem, that is a true revolution of energies melding and entities coming together in harmony to work together for restoration, for equality, for justice, for truth, and for the cause of being. How we encourage this, how we urge you to lean into this. This is where your sense of the group's being important comes into play. Fourth-density energy, unconditional love energy, is embattled within a third-density atmosphere. In fourth density, entities work together, harmonizing, combining, each giving their own best, with the result being far better than any of the entities within the circle of creation's [individual] skill, because that which joins together is not added but multiplied and multiplied again. The group effect is tremendously supportive. This is part of why your particular group has been together for some time, and why energies are moving into it at this time.

It is time, as the one known as Jim said in the discussion preceding this meditation, and we would agree. It is time for those of like mind and like heart to come together, to serve together, to learn together, and to support each other. This entity has a favorite song:

> Love one another as I love you,
> Care for each other as I care for you.
> Bear each others' burdens,
> Share each others' joys.
> Love one another and bring each other home.

What is "home," my friends? Home is that place where you belong.

Belong to each other and open your arms, that all entities may belong to you. And take care of each other, and care for each other and bring your planet home.

We would at this time transfer this contact to the one known as Jim that more questions may be asked. We thank this instrument and would leave it in love and in light and transfer at this time. We are known to you as Q'uo.

(Pause)

(Jim channeling)

I am Q'uo, and we greet each again, in love and in light, through this instrument. At this time it is our privilege to offer ourselves to attempt to speak to any further shorter queries which may be presented to us. Is there another query at this time?

S: I have one. When, in your spiritual seeking, you hit a brick wall, stumble and fall and you're not sure what to do to get up, where to go, what to do, do you have any suggestions and ideas of how to get back, brush yourself off, and move forward?

I am Q'uo, and am aware of your query my brother. Oftentimes when the seeker of truth finds that there has been the brick wall of which you speak placed within its path there is the possibility of doing nothing until one is moved by an inner desire to continue the journey. There is the possibility of exploring within the self what are the new priorities, what is it that moves one in any direction. What is it that gives the sense of purpose and meaning to the self as it seeks …

(Side one of tape ends.)

(Jim channeling)

I am Q'uo, and am once again with this instrument. Is there another query at this time?

Carla: I have a question from B. It says next time you're online to the Confederation, please ask, "What aspects of consciousness were developed by the use of fourth-density social memory, from a fourth-density perspective?"

I am Q'uo, and am aware of your query my sister. We find this query to be a very interesting one in which we may explore an idea or two. The social memory aspect of consciousness is that which begins to explore the intimate work entities may share, one with the other, by relying upon those resources which each brings to the group consciousness. Thus, it is much more likely that the group consciousness will be informed concerning any particular point of view when there is a great variety of experiences upon which to draw, in confronting or dealing with any particular situation.

We have found in our own experience that there is much of the support that may be shared in the motivation, shall we say, to explore those areas which are new to us by doing so as a group consciousness.

(Pause)

(The instrument excuses himself from channeling anything further.)

(Carla channeling)

We are with this instrument and we are those known to you as Q'uo. We attempted to contact this instrument after the one known as Jim created the changing of the tape and this instrument was puzzled by the surprise of a new routine and did not respond. Consequently, we recontacted the one known as Jim and this entity attempted to continue to speak. However this entity, in its integrity, quite rightly expressed the desire to leave the contact as it did not feel it was performing its function as an instrument with the highest of purity. And may we say that this often occurs and is very seldom owned up to. When entities are moving from the impressions of telepathic perception, indeed, the line between good contact and questionable contact is, for the most part, the hair's difference between alertness and trust in the self and, for whatever reason, the movement from that rest into a state of energy movement or strife. Once energy begins moving in terms of the human personality shell, it is far more difficult to keep a telepathic contact, for the single-mindedness or single-pointedness of thought that enables an entity to lay the self aside and to respond simply to that which is given is sometimes very much lacking. For this instrument, it is more stable as a setting than most and so we pick the contact up at this point as there is energy within the circle that requires, if possible, a slower termination of the contact. And so we would ask again through this instrument if there are any further queries at this time?

G: Q'uo, in the *Law of One* series, Ra says that there is an incompatibility between the third and fourth densities in respect to the electrical body. They say that if a third-density entity had full awareness of the fourth density, that its electrical body would fail. So my question is, how aware in third density can we be of the fourth-density energies?

We are those of Q'uo, and we grasp your query, my brother. Entities within third-density vehicles are protected from full realization of the fourth-density energies of the electrical nature for the reason that they are unable to express or to have the wiring for the running of those energies in their fourth-density form. It is perhaps confusing that we encourage you to live within fourth density in your third-density self. And yet the shadow of fourth density, cast in third density, is sufficient, just as the light under the door that is closed still signifies the awareness of the light in the room and the awareness of the room in which that light resides. What we are suggesting is that you look at the light under the crack of that door and know by faith that that room is lit and that light is true.

May we refine upon this answer my brother?

G: Not at this time, thank you Q'uo.

We thank you, my brother.

G: If no else has one, Q'uo, before, during the beginning of the round-robin discussions, I was becoming very jittery, very nervous, my heart was beating hard, and I was becoming extremely cold and I have a hunch that its beyond standard nervousness. I was wondering if I was the subject of a psychic greeting?

We are those of Q'uo, and are aware of your query, my brother. In the manner of your speaking, this is correct. We are also aware that you are cognizant of the internality of such greeting. That is, that it comes from that portion of the self that is the mirror of those energies, for the self indeed contains all energies that are possible to express. Consequently, there was indeed that which you may call a greeting and it was indeed of the psychic type and at the same time we encourage the awareness that such greetings are not those of enemy energies. Those greetings are of that which feels unloved. So we encourage the response of opening the arms and hugging to the heart that shadow, that coldness, that jitteriness and accepting and loving it as it is. We suggest that this shall tend to balance and integrate these energies that seem to be attacking, so that they may become those energies that support and defend the self.

May we answer further my brother?

G: No, thank you, Q'uo.

My brother, we thank you greatly. Is there another query at this time?

G: If the instrument still has energy, I have another one. Q'uo, in the *Law of One* series Ra says that "… our very being is hopefully a poignant example of both the necessity and the near-hopelessness of attempting to teach." I was wondering if you could expound upon that any further?

We are aware of your query, my brother. As that known to you as Q'uo, we encompass a great deal of teaching. The energies of the ones known as Hatonn have long taught; the energies of the ones known as Latwii and those known as Ra, have long taught. And indeed those of Hatonn and those of Latwii accept as their teacher those of Ra. Consequently, we have bonds of teaching and of learning even within our principle. And our entire *beau geste* as a principle is to teach and yet, if we were to use this instrument's slang, we would say, "LOL." It is to laugh, it is to chuckle, for how can we teach? What do we know? We know only opinion. We can only toss our words into the wind and hope that some helpful aspect transfers from creation to creation, for we speak across worlds.

We gaze at each of you in your creation. You are masters. Few of you know it. We hope to encourage you to be aware of your nature, yet we have only a simple story to tell. We have only one basic thought to share. You are one, we are all one and that one thing is love. We attempt to be creative, we use channels such as this one so that we may flash all of the colors of that channel's personality and weave such tales as that person's energy and personality shell have to give. Yet our story is the same, and it is inadequate to fuel the realization and the transformation of a single entity.

Yet we shine out our light and we ask you to shine your light, to tell your shining truth when you feel it within. And when your shining truth is that you know nothing, let that shine, let that be a good thing to shine. For it is in our way of perceiving, an excellent thing. So we teach those who are already masters and who have forgotten. You who are learning could take our places, were the veil to drop. Yet you have placed yourself in this darkness which you experience, so that you can change.

Consequently to teach is almost hopeless and yet, what else does a human or the spirit have to share? The rest is love and has no words. When there is the attempt to share, it must be that sharing through the structures and the limitations and the exigencies of logic depending from each structure. These limitations are almost hopeless; that is, they create a hopeless situation in which one throws pebbles at the great eternal truth that is too simple to articulate.

May we answer you further, my brother?

G: No, thank you Q'uo.

Is there a final query at this time?

T: If the instrument has energy and the answer does not infringe upon my free will, about a month ago one evening before I went to bed I had a tremendous emotional energy and wonder if that was a kind of initiation? Are you able to comment upon that at all?

We are aware of your query, my brother, and are able to confirm that this was a type of initiation. May we answer you further, my brother?

T: Are you able to explain the basis of that initiation, the effect that it was taking?

We are able, my brother, only to say that there is crystallization of those energy centers that this instrument would call orange and yellow. The vector of this change, then, is towards the opening of the heart. We find that this is the limit of that which we are able to share with you at this time.

As the energy wanes, we thank this circle. Our hearts go out to this circle, for each in your own way has struggled with much in this latest season of transformation, chaos and change. We ask that you take heart and that you rest in knowing that no mistakes have been made and that all is on track in your curriculum. Whatever it feels like, each has done beautifully and has been brave and true. We would simply encourage you to continue with faith in yourself, faith in your catalyst, faith in the rightness of the plan. Rest in that faith, rest in the memory of those times when you were immediately connected with that understanding. And trust, through the dark night, through the difficult time, through the confusion.

The trees bow before the wind, the seasons change. The winter comes and the leaves must fall and all seems to die, only to rise again in the resurrection of shoot coming through dark earth into the light of spring.

All is well. We meet you in meditation, in that house of prayer, as this instrument calls it, where all time is One, and all beings One.

It has been a pleasure to speak with you and again we encourage you to think carefully before accepting anything that we or anyone else has to say, living, dead, terrestrial or extra-terrestrial. Guard your thinking and discriminate, for your truth is a living thing. We are with you in that holy war, that holy seeking that is the struggle that has been called the *jihad*. Move forward, trusting that the darkness and the light are one and the same thing.

We leave this instrument and this group in the love and in the light of the one infinite Creator.

Adonai. We are those of Q'uo.

L/L Research is a subsidiary of
Rock Creek Research &
Development Laboratories, Inc.

P.O. Box 5195
Louisville, KY 40255-0195

L/L Research

www.llresearch.org

Rock Creek is a non-profit
corporation dedicated to
discovering and sharing
information which may aid in
the spiritual evolution of
humankind.

ABOUT THE CONTENTS OF THIS TRANSCRIPT: This telepathic channeling has been taken from transcriptions of the weekly study and meditation meetings of the Rock Creek Research & Development Laboratories and L/L Research. It is offered in the hope that it may be useful to you. As the Confederation entities always make a point of saying, please use your discrimination and judgment in assessing this material. If something rings true to you, fine. If something does not resonate, please leave it behind, for neither we nor those of the Confederation would wish to be a stumbling block for any.

© 2009 L/L RESEARCH

WEDNESDAY MEDITATION
SEPTEMBER 17, 2003

(Carla channeling)

We are those known to you as the principle of Q'uo, and we greet you in the love and in the light of the one infinite Creator in whose service we are, and by whose joy we are enlivened.

We thank the one known as T for requesting this time of asking and we are most happy to share our opinions with the request that, as always, all the things we have to say be carefully reviewed and examined for their helpfulness to you personally. For many things are interesting but there are those few things which are indeed yours by that internal and intuitive process of discrimination that the spirit has for those things which impinge upon its evolution. There is a resonance to those things that fit into that subjective search for the truth that is ever and always the same. If this can be done then we may feel free completely to share our opinions as what they are, mere opinion, those thoughts of a friend rather than those great teachings of some authority.

May we ask for your first query, my brother?

T: Q'uo has often spoken of the validity of both dramatic and non-dramatic forms of service to others. At this stage in my development, I feel that I may possibly be of service in just being and radiating love. Can you comment on this?

We are those of the principle known as Q'uo, and we are able, my brother, to comment on this. We would suggest that your sense of the paramount importance of the faculty of being is indeed the correct impression, not only for yourself but for all souls involved in incarnational experiences upon the Earth plane at this time.

The function of the illusion is, in some part, to distract one from the essence of the self. It is the delight of the machinations of the forces of what this instrument would call "consensus reality" to bring into the awareness a nimiety of detail that so exceeds the ability of the conscious mind to assimilate in a direct or linear fashion, so that the mind shall be put to the task of prioritizing and sorting incoming data and so that the heart may have the opportunity to be sought when the mind has become useless as an instrument of wisdom by virtue of its over-stimulation. The effect of this structure of illusion is that the self tends to be tempted towards a state of permanent distraction, thereby blunting or lessening the impact of the spiritual portion of the mind, the body, and the spirit in its interconnection within the emotional body. In the face of this condition of distractive environment, it becomes the central challenge of all entities seeking to live life well to begin to penetrate the glamour of the constant rain of detail, and to find beneath the details of an everyday existence those markers that only give a hint upon the surface of their depth and their sacredness within the very framework of the destructive elements of life as it is normally lived. It is a matter of a turn of the mind, so that while a portion of the mind continues to deal with those physical priorities that are necessary for the movement of the honors and duties of a life lived in accordance with ethical beliefs …

(Pause, waiting out a disturbance in another part of the house)

We are those of Q'uo, and find that this instrument has been somewhat distracted from her train of thought and so we shall begin again.

These markers are as the iceberg, barely sticking up into the sea of chaotic detail of an everyday life, yet these markers are everywhere, as the whitecaps upon the waves, and yet unlike the whitecaps, they do not go away. They merely are obscured from time to time by the swells and the restlessness of that archipelago of infinite detail that is the ocean of consensus reality. Consequently, the challenge of being within a lifetime of doing becomes the challenge of simple and utter focus and attentiveness to that sea of detail, not being in any way overwhelmed by the flood but rather trusting in the craft of self, that frail barque of body and sensibility and awareness that is you within incarnation. [The challenge is] to have the persistent vision to gaze into and through all detail, seeing and appreciating the momentary interest of each detail, yet always looking for that whitecap of indication that this contains a marker that moves down through the shallow surface of life into the depths of the being of the self, so that one may, many times within an hour, and many, many times within a day, take those arrows that lead downward into the self and ride them as far as you can, opening the intuition, opening the heart, and allowing the self to move as spirit would have you move.

There is a tremendous amount of trust of the self and of guidance involved in this technique, yet it is one which we offer to you because of the way that your particular mental, physical and emotional make up creates for you genuinely advantageous, shall we say, "fast trains" to the depth of being which are marked by these little whitecaps that flash in the sun, that are not after all foam and spume as part of the water, but are instead that which comes [barely] out of the water but extends in much larger bulk beneath the water. Discerning between the evanescent whitecaps of detail that are whipped up from the bergs or avenues that lead down into the essential self is subtle work, yet it is that which, once opened as a technique, becomes ever more pliable and flexible and easy, shall we say, for the use of the person within the rush and the turmoil of a normally lived Earth life, as this instrument would describe it.

Dramatic service, as this instrument has termed it, is no less service than the service of being. It, however, addresses a different level of the tree of life, as this instrument would term it; a level that is closer to the archetypal and therefore more powerful to serve, although within your human consensus reality terms, such work as essential being offers has virtually no recognition or respect. And many will be the time in which you as a soul stream, within incarnation, are quite fully engaged in being of service and are wholly caught up in the honor and duty thereof, yet will find others about the self not able in any way to grasp that which is being done within the mind or to value it were they to be given an explanation of this technique. We suggest that it is well to disregard the opinion of others who do not at this particular point in your space/time dwell with you, for this particular service has both the glory and the great challenge of being utterly unique. No one, in all of the infinite creation, not even your own soul stream in other incarnational experiences, has developed this particular essence, this particular group of colors or collection of scents. There is a tactile, sensual aspect to being for which it is impossible for this instrument to find words; that is, we cannot find words within this instrument's mind to express the particularly personal and deeply intimate nature of the service of being. It is a demanding discipline to seek, to find, to accept, to love, and to give up the self.

There is in this instrument's experience the repeated occasion of what she calls Holy Communion, in which the one known as Jesus the Christ describes itself as the body that is broken for many, which one takes in remembrance of that being. This entity also offers its own blood, which is shed for many so that the being may take on this persona of the Christ, and in the way of "As above, so below," become that which is held in utter ideal. Within each self there is the Christ or the Christed consciousness that is the very essence of self. That self of Christhood is pure and is uncolored by that energy or entity which wears the cape or coat or cloak of Christhood. Each entity, in coming into incarnation, is as that being which is the Christ, yet which may be in any stage of development within the heart of the incarnational being. Consequently, the hope of one who is seeking to serve in the ministry of being is seeking to open the self up from the level of the personality shell, with all of its limitations, its desires, and its needs, so that, more and more, the self may descend from the surface of self, which is those honestly felt things which bear little of truth, to that inner level of self that opens and opens again and opens again, as the self is able to become honest with the self, to gaze within especially those shadow portions of the self, so that, as those shadows are found, they are welcomed, accepted, loved and used to move ever deeper into a state of unconditional love of the self as it is perceived by the self to be imperfect. To have love for the self at this level flies in the face of culture and nature in terms of the human tendency towards thinking less of the self and more of outward authority figures and other perceived judges of the self.

The environment for work upon the self needs to contain safety. To be safe for the self to the self from the level of self is a challenge that will continue until the moment of realization occurs in which you as an entity are able to know beyond question that you truly are part of the godhead principle and that, as you dig in the perceived dirt and earth of your humanity, that which you toss up is not the best you will see, and that which is hidden is worth the digging. So you may think of yourself as digging for buried treasure. Yet always, when the digging is done, and the self is at last satisfied with that work which the mind and the feelings can do, there is the infinitely shorter route to realization of the true nature of the self that is involved in moving into the open heart and sitting within that tabernacle in which the Creator is always waiting, to share silence with that Creator, to share being with that Creator that is the deepest part of you and is therefore never away from you.

Consciousness is that which you partake in, in the semblance and illusion of individuality. As you hook into that consciousness from the eccentric surface of your personality shell, [you] become more and more able to trust that path of light that leads from that crooked and sometimes tormented surface to the still, clear, lovely waters of the deep self. It is not that the one known as T has no capacity or opportunity for dramatic service in the sense of teaching or offering other outer gifts to be shared by those in need upon the Earth plane. Each entity within this circle came into incarnation with some plans in that regard, with some hopes of sharing deeply felt gifts with those who might appreciate them. Yet those dramatic gifts have a way of being offered only when the time has been put in, in clearing the energies, in disciplining the personality, in falling in love with the self, and more than all else, in becoming aware of the way the self is, the way it feels when one is in that holy of holies in which all things are one. Become more and more conversant with moving through the levels of being, knowing that perhaps for many a month after starting to gaze at the various depths of perception, there will be some real question about what level the thought is upon at a particular time, and ah! the mind has many twists and turns to cause the surface mind to misperceive. However, there is always a stream of information coming from the system of guidance that is your own and this stream will for the most part be in synchronicities and coincidences that point up, certain trains of thought that isolate and underline, shall we say, or emphasize certain key concepts. Once the entity begins looking for such, the incidence of them begins to rise until one begins to feel that indeed the universe never stops speaking to the self. And indeed this is so.

May we ask for your next query, my brother?

T: Thank you, Q'uo. I think you answered many of my questions. My next question is, can you comment on ways in which I can best support the development of the community here at L/L Research?

We are those of Q'uo, and are aware of your query, my brother.

As we, shall we say, riffle through the pages of this instrument's mind, it is at the surface of this instrument's mind that the one known as T serves as he speaks, as he sits. He has been a part of this group for the last several of your days. During the weeks of visitation, there have been energies exchanged upon many levels. There has been the obvious exchange that strikes the eye of physical interaction and the sharing of energy moving in a common goal that is greater than the self. There have been those energies exchanged which move far below that surface energy, [which are] far more important in their energies. Those would indeed be in the areas where the one known as T has, in its own process, in its own studies, developed a steadiness and a sturdiness of stability and dedication which enables him to remain in a most equitable and, as this instrument would say, cheerful state whether faced with an enjoyable and easily contained challenge or with a seeming disaster or a situation which seems to have become too complex to handle easily. This ability to enjoy the process of dealing with items large and small, be they physical, emotional, mental or spiritual, is that energy within a mixture of rays, in terms of chakra points, which this particular group does not have in abundance. Consequently, the chemistry, shall we say, or the coloration of energies as they are exchanged around the circle of community are of such a nature as to clarify and strengthen the energies and stability within the energies of those with whom energy is exchanged.

At the same time, there is within the group an abundance of certain energies which the one known as T has in lesser degree than perhaps others within the circle of community and is of service therefore to the community in being able to accept and appreciate those love offerings of energy in which inspiration and to some extent information is exchanged that creates a sense of appreciation and a sense of being at home, which in turn reflects back into the group in a way that increases the energy of all. This particular entity fits into the circle of growing group energy which the entity known as L/L Research has begun to build with this new grouping in a way that is most beneficial.

So, these are obvious ways in which the energy exchange with those of the community is being helpful. There is always the possibility of developing those energy exchanges, of creating more linkage and, by collaboration, more focuses for the shared energy that is being raised into a dome of light by this group.

May we answer you further upon this point, my brother?

T: Yes, thank you, Q'uo. Can you talk a little bit more about how I can collaborate with the group to raise this dome of light?

We are those of Q'uo, and are aware of your query, my brother. While there is what this instrument would call the luxury of presence, it is well to share presence, to share beingness, and to share tasks. When the space/time continuum moves to that point at which the one known as T is upon the other side of your beautiful planet from this particular group, then it will be that this same energy exchange may continue within the heart, for once entities have connected and bonded in the emotional and mental and physical and spiritual bodies, as each within this group has with the one known as T, there is a connection that cannot be broken, neither in life nor in death. Each has become part of the net of being that is the other and indeed each within this particular group has worked together before and so there is that sense of camaraderie and being warriors together, not against any but for the light.

As to the nature of collaboration, as to the nature of shared support, we would suggest that each day and each choice shall be that which blooms and develops and leads to other choices and other decisions which in turn develop that shared energy. The thing to remember always is that there is a general, well-thought-out plan not for one particular project but for one general shared mission of lightening the planet with beingness and with other, more outer, services as well as seems indicated by the highest and best guidance that one is capable of receiving from day to day to day.

Thusly, we could not offer one specific answer but rather the suggestion to look within the self for those things which might forward or further collaborative projects that the group as a whole has begun and to feel free at all times to share impressions, to make suggestions from those feelings that come from being guided that such-and-such resonates and is a good thing to bring up, is a good intuition to share.

May we answer you further, my brother?

T: Thank you, Q'uo. Can you suggest ways in which I might refine my current form of Gaia meditation?

We are the Q'uo, and are aware of your query, my brother. We find that this is too close to your process for us to be able to comment upon it at this time other than by saying that there are materials upon this organization's website and upon other websites which deal with the quest for a planetary visualization of peace and of planetary restoration that can be sought while the self is tuned not just to those suggestions but to that which draws sparks from the inner fire of self. So, our suggestion would be, first, to find that inner fire to refine the focus of desire and, when it is one-pointed and singular, to open the self to some suggestions from others and to find those threads which lead to other threads which lead to a feeling that, yes, this feels very rich for me, this is my method of bonding with the Earth, of loving Gaia, of relating intimately to those energies of restoration, peace and safety that are the hallmarks of fourth density.

May we answer you further, my brother?

T: Thank you, Q'uo. Can you provide any information on the spiritual theology I have been told that I taught in ancient times linked to the obsidian stone?

We are those of Q'uo, and find that to work upon your process does indeed cross the boundaries of infringement on your free will. We would however confirm that this is an interesting avenue to investigate, not just in terms of thought but in terms of feeling.

May we answer you further, my brother?

T: Can you help me to understand in which areas I have yet to forgive myself and how I can best achieve this forgiveness and acceptance?

We are those of Q'uo, and aware of your query, my brother. We make this instrument smile with our smile, for truly this is a most central query and one which cuts to the heart of process, for forgiving oneself is forgiving the world. Working on peace in the world is a matter of seeking that place of peace within the self where the self is forgiven.

Entities within incarnation upon planet Earth tend to build for themselves a defensive shell designed to protect the self against the slings and arrows of outrageous parents, teachers and other critics of the small child. The criticism begins early and stays late and so the self becomes more and more embattled behind the armor of defensiveness. And this is held together with the rivets of fear. There is the fear that one is not good enough. There is the fear that one will never be good enough, but good enough for what? That question is seldom asked because it has no answer. How can one be good enough in a situation in which each and every human, by virtue of its incarnation into the state of humanhood, is imperfect? The human animal, as it were, is designed to be imperfect. It is not intended that any human being learn the ways of love to such an extent that they become flawless. It is not intended, it is not expected by those who appreciate and love each and every soul stream that is taking incarnation at this time upon planet Earth. You are greatly …

(Side one of tape ends)

(Carla channeling)

The challenge of forgiving the self, then, is not an individual challenge based upon those items which remain unforgiven. For there is always that which is unforgiven, since it has not yet been discovered. No matter how many times you as an entity are triggered by fear and the working of, what this instrument would call, old tapes that have to play within the head once they are started, of the old, unforgiving voices of authority within childhood which somehow have become the interior voices of self, there remains something as yet undiscovered that will, one fine day, rear up out of the sunlight and astonish you with the depth of your imperfection. And you will, once again, be offered the choice of judgment or forgiveness of the self. We do not discourage the faculties of review or oversight. It is perfectly acceptable and useful to critique the self and to say, "I would prefer I had not done this," or "I would prefer I had done this and yet I have not." These perceived errors are very helpful because they help the entity you are to behave better.

Yet we attempt in forgiving the self to move beneath the level of behavior so that you as a being are able to link together the good things about yourself with the perceived imperfections of the self, seeing that you cannot have the one without the other. You cannot have the virtues without their shadows, seeing that every virtue, self-perceived as virtue, if stood on its head and placed in a situation which makes it turn backwards or athwartships, will result in the shadow side of that virtue, which will be astoundingly imperfect.

So, we are unable to suggest specific areas for the work of forgiving the self. Rather, we suggest that in every area where you catch yourself in the process of judging the self, it useful, then, to take the time at some point as close as possible to this time of perception, to move back into that situation and that equation of evolving process that is occurring, with an eye to moving beneath both the imperfection and whatever virtue you may identify as the flip-side of that imperfection, to the sacrament of being and essence that lies beneath both the imperfection and the balancing virtue. For each perceived virtue, if balanced within the self, will reveal its shadow, and vice-versa.

We do mean to be necessarily confusing here. We may take a simple example of the feeling of impatience. Where is that coming from? It is well to look at such a perceived imperfection. And yet what is the virtue that makes entities impatient but a well-perceived sense of duty, a well-disciplined sense of planning and scheduling and prioritizing, and many other aspects which are extremely virtuous and full of character? The idea of forgiving the self is not to find a strand here and a strand there and a strand in the third place of perceived unforgiven self and pluck those out. It is to embrace such perceived moments with the hope of opening the self to the unity of that imperfection with the perfection it balances, so that you may see that you are not a "good" being and attempting to destroy the "bad" being that may exist beneath the floor of the "good" being. Rather, you are attempting to become a full, circular and robust self that knows its shadow side, knows its virtues and knows that neither is the true tale of the self but only the process that is occurring to allow the self to move ever deeper into that self, that interior road to the centre of self that lightens as it goes until, in the very center of self, in the heart of self, in the tabernacle of the Creator within the self, there is a stunning, flooding white light that melts every consideration and allows one to rest in adoration and faith.

May we answer you further, my brother?

T: Thank you, Q'uo. Can you offer any advice in relation to the two Vipassana retreats that I plan to complete?

We are with this instrument. We are those of Q'uo, and are aware of your query. We would offer three suggestions. Firstly, we would suggest attention to the details of sleep so that there is the opportunity given to the body to rest completely at times deemed appropriate by you so that you are able to withstand the catalyst of intensive realization.

Secondly, we would suggest in the matter of clothing that care be taken to be comfortable so that the chafing and other disturbing of the skin by the clothing is kept to a minimum, again in order to remove a stumbling block from a one-pointed focus upon the work itself.

Thirdly, we would suggest working with body and structures that support the body in various ways to identify and, as far as possible, improve the sitting posture, for there is within the discipline of Vipassana meditation, or any prolonged sitting meditation, the challenge of the inner body and its previous habit of movement being so firmly overset in such a short amount of time.

These three minor details, when seen to, set the stage for that which is your process during this period. Certainly, we cannot suggest to you those spiritual tools and resources which are part of your learn/teaching process at this time. We simply ask you to have faith in the ability of the self to discern that which it needs to hear amidst possibly a welter of detail it does not need to hear, trusting always that sense of rightness for the self. We wish you the joy of such intensive work, my brother.

May we speak further upon this?

T: Thank you, Q'uo. If the instrument still has sufficient energy, can you give me any information on Earth chakras near Brisbane, Australia and maybe how I might be able to use them to enhance my practice?

We are those of Q'uo, and are aware of your query, my brother. We find that in the particular entity that you are, your most helpful portals will be those involved in the nearness of water and, if at all possible, the nearness of crystals. The caves and grottos which may contain crystals especially are helpful. The coincidence of hollowed spaces and water create portals anywhere so that we feel that these perhaps are your best opportunities in terms of your geographical location and your own system of sensitivities which includes that towards water.

We have energy left within this instrument for one last query at this time and would ask for it.

T: You mentioned crystals. Are there any certain types of crystals which may be beneficial to have near me, perhaps when I practice within my home?

We are aware of your query, my brother. May we say that water itself is the crystal to which you are most strongly attuned. Other crystals may aid from time to time and we would suggest a testing of the self, either with pendulum or simply with presence and familiarity with certain crystals, in choosing those stones which you feel to be most apt for you at a given time. We find that in your energy environment, the environment of your energy body, there is a very stable, cyclical turn of energy that ever spirals and is ever changing, so far from being a settled or fixed being in terms of energy body, you as an entity are always in motion and consequently, the stones that have crystallized down into solid matter are less powerful for you than charged water.

May we answer you further, my brother?

T: Only if the instrument has sufficient energy. I have felt a connection with water and I think you have really answered my question but there were a lot of coincidences with water-based events in my past. Was that a symbol of my connection with water?

We are those of Q'uo, and may confirm this, my brother.

May we say what a pleasure and privilege it is to speak with you and to each within this circle! We thank you with all our hearts for taking the time and the energy and the focus to be with spirit, to be with guidance, to be with those forces of love and wisdom as you know them. We are poor messengers indeed, yet we offer ourselves in the hopes that we may be of some help and we thank you for the tremendous … we cannot find a word within this instrument's mind, but it is a treasure that we hold dear to our hearts to have this time with you. We thank you. We leave each, as always, in the love and the light of the one infinite Creator. We are with you by request whenever you enter the silence of that great tabernacle of the heart.

We leave you in the love and the light of the one infinite Creator. We are those of the Q'uo. Adonai vasu borragus. ✥

Sunday Meditation
September 21, 2003

Group question: Our question today has to do today with mated relationships. We would like Q'uo to give us some information that might give us a better idea as to the potential of a mated relationship. What difficulties might one expect in entering into a mated relationship? What kind of attitude is most helpful in dealing with the difficulties? Please add anything else that might be of use or interest concerning mated relationships.

(Carla channeling)

We are those of the principle known to you as Q'uo, and we greet you in the love and in the light of the one infinite Creator in Whose service we are. We thank you for the great privilege of being called to your circle of seeking this day and we find the beautiful experience of joining your meditation to be a real pleasure. Blessings to each of you and many, many thanks for clearing the time in your schedule to spend time seeking for the truth. Truly those who seek with an open and loving heart shall be answered. Those who knock with empty hands shall find the door opening.

We ask but one thing before we share our opinions with you and that is that you do realize that our thoughts are simply that, opinions. They are fairly settled and we are glad to share them, but we have found that truth is a various thing, a thing that is part of a personal and intimate network of true things for each entity. And we ask each entity to respect their own universe, their own creation, and to be guardians of what goes into that creation and becomes a part of the network and the fabric of living. Examine each thought and, if it pleases you, work with it. This is why we come to you, so that we may share these thoughts. But if they do not please you, we humbly ask you to leave them behind without a second thought, for we would not be a stumbling block to any. With this said, we are most happy to speak upon the most large subject of the mated relationship and its possibilities and challenges.

We found the conversation preceding this time of working most interesting and were pleased to hear the one known as R say that when she was seven years old, she decided that she loved herself and wanted herself and was there for herself and that this was the foundation of her ability to love and to be loved in the rest of her incarnational experience. May we agree with the one known as R that this indeed is the foundation for all relationships. This instrument has often spoke of the first challenge of spiritual seeking [as] being that of falling in love with the self. Not because the self has become perfect. Not because the self has many virtues. Not because of anything except the fact of being. Each entity is a being of a certain kind. That certain kind happens to be a very specialized way of structuring a being. It is multi-leveled. There is a portion of the being that you are that comes from eternity and that dwells in infinity, so that there is no limitation to the circle of self. It is infinite and eternal. Out of that being has come a spark of that soul stream that is you. And you have found a habitation within a temple of flesh and bone. And again, as the one known as R has said, it is as a vehicle that is able to motivate, to move you physically through the many levels of physical, emotional, mental, and spiritual catalyst that you have received and that you will continue to receive during your incarnational experience.

This self is at once the most simple of things and a complicated thing. In its simplicity, the self of all beings is that of a spark of the creative or Godhead principle so that each of you is a perfect, unique expression of the Creator, as if the Creator was colored with your particular way of loving, expressing and being. Each is as this note, or to be more precise, chord. As the vibrations of your being, which have their own element or range, find their ways to harmonize the various energies of the various chakras the infinite love and light of the one Creator moves through those chakras that are colored with your special blockages and over-energizings and other distortions from a totally balanced energy center. There is nothing neutral about each of you. And this is a wonderful thing. The vividness of those chords of being that each of you is, is a beautiful, breathtaking thing. Each of you is that entity that is vibrating as a melody, or as the scent of a flower. This is your gift, this very simple, very momentary expression of the essence of self. This is your gift in each moment and in each moment there is a new self, a new registering of coloration of being. It is not that all of the notes change, for indeed in many ways, that with which you move into incarnation is that which you take from incarnation. The bones, shall we say, are the same, coming in and going out. The changes that have been made, that can only be made in third density, the density of experience you now enjoy, are in the way the energies are balanced within each chakra and from chakra to chakra, so that these bones are fleshed out with different garments every day. Some of the changes are very slight, other changes, that you may feel that are very slight, go deeper, and have a more profound energy to them that makes a bigger change than you are aware on what this instrument would call the soul level.

So this is the simple being that you are. You are a vibration of the Logos. You are a sub-sub-Logos, a part of the creative principle. And each of you is that which includes all other beings, not simply upon your planet but within the entire creation of the infinite One. To narrow the focus a bit is to discover, in great profusion, the complexities of these connections [between] that which lives and dies and that which is just visiting the experience of living and dying while it is picking up the lessons that were prepared for this time of incarnation, and attempting to use this particular vibration that you experience for finding the self, finding ways to love, finding the grace to allow the self to be loved. In the explication and exploration of these large subjects come many, many lessons, one after another after another. In the school of life, as this instrument would call it, there are many tests. Some of these tests are never perceived by the student, other of the tests are perceived all too well and become great causes of concern, thereby snarling and sometimes baffling the energies that otherwise would be free to work. It is, as the one known as V would say, a puzzle to be solved, in many cases. The experience of a tangle or a difficulty, as this instrument was speaking of earlier, is an opportunity to gaze upon the self in the mirror of perceived experience and perceived difficulty, looking at the nature of the experience, the nature of the perceived blockage or over-activation within self or within other self and the finding of the way through the maze that does not partake of judgment, that does not partake of the consciousness of sin or error and yet that stays persistently and accurately upon the focus of self so that the maze is followed not from either emotion or intellect but rather from the heart.

The heart itself has a working knowledge of these complexities that create the mazes of a puzzle to be solved. And there is no maze created that does not have a solution. Within these boundaries of self lie not only complexities but complexities of various levels of profundity within the essential self so that there is much skill, when dealing [with] the self up close, in being able to slip from level to level and being able to work the maze, from level to level, so that there is a feeling of movement through time, movement through the spaces of self, movement not linear in nature but rather that movement which may seem to be very tedious and turning back upon itself and winding tortuously. Yet, in terms of the maze of self, such wanderings within the self are skillful and useful and very productive. Therefore, the first work, when gazing upon the mated relationship, is the work of coming into a fuller and fuller awareness of the self, of falling in love with the self, of becoming able to see the self without pride or humility but rather as that which is, that which has met the day, that which will express in honesty and sincerity for that day. When the self can meet the self and smile and go, within the mind, "Oh good, I get to spend time with me today," then the self is ready to spend time with [an] other self.

The one known as G has not asked about relationship in a vacuum but rather within a situation in which the heart is leaping like a stag, happy and joyful in the rushing energies of honest and deeply felt, unconditional love. Therefore, as we speak we are not dealing with the ins and outs of making the commitment for the mated relationship. We are responding to this query assuming that the relationship is positive, mutually felt to be positive and inclusive of a third entity, that entity being the one infinite Creator.

Mated relationships are a triad. They are not two partners against the world. Rather they are a temple that has been enlarged so that two entities' lives may be dedicated to that which is larger than themselves, larger than their worldly hopes, constituting that ark which contains those things that one couple wishes to save from the flood of the everyday. Into this ark of mating each may pour their ideals, their hopes, their dreams, their desires, their intentions, and every precious truth and spark of beauty that they have found and loved and made their own. Two entities offering these gifts to each other and to the Creator create a temple with a dome of light that, as that mated couple works through time and through circumstances which try every nerve and every part of the self, [becomes] stronger and stronger. Every time there is a situation met together, and energies are allowed to move between the two and the Creator is included in all discussions, no matter what the outcome of such a situation is, no matter how difficult the catalyst or how long the journey towards a solution seems, the dome of light is being strengthened because the journey is being made heart to heart, hand to hand. And always with the realization that the Creator and the Creator's love is a huge part of the relationship. Indeed, this instrument can speak for herself, but we gaze into this instrument's mind to find memories thick as falling leaves in the autumn of precious, well-remembered moments of this entity and the entity known as Jim coming together in tears or in joy or in trouble, offering each other honesty that is painful or wonderful or simply puzzled and again and again, finding in each other the light that had failed for the self, finding, because of the good mirror, information that was needed by the self. This instrument's memory of self becomes that which is the memory of two selves, as one. And this plinth of shared memory is a substantial platform upon which to build the journey of seeking. This instrument has often said, the mated relationship is the fast track to spiritual evolution. And why is that? If you can think back to the last time that you were alone and had to deal with a situation without help, you can remember those feelings of isolation, even though one is never isolated from the Creator of all things. Nor is one isolated from a guidance system that is strong to help[58]. Yet when one is alone there is a sense of the light failing and the atmosphere becomes close and stuffy because there is simply no air, no mirror, no light, there is not that life that another entity brings into the dealings of self with self. In the interior of self without an entity to serve as an accurate mirror, the mirrors within the self may be very distorted and may not show the truth. There may be too much interference from previous assumption that has not been let go when those assumptions were no longer accurate.

Think back to the last time that you dealt with a situation with a friend, with a mate, with a partner, and that partner, that mate became a mirror or a teacher to you and you had the gift of sight, the sight that is not insight, for it comes by projection and reflection. Yet that sight, perhaps called "outsight," is as the insight that has been the gift of that entity in the mated relationship whose catalyst it is not and who simply is able to gaze into your eyes, see you in the situation and reflect back that which she sees. The blessing of this shared vision becomes the greater the less clear one's own vision is. So mated relationships, and indeed close partnerships of all kinds, if based within spiritual parameters, have a wonderful, flexible ability to have two seemingly imperfect and confused people become to each other the knight in shining armor and the lady in shining armor, those who are wiser than they know because

---

[58] Carla: I believe this phrase comes from my Episcopal/Anglican background, where the prayer book language has the holy spirit as "strong to help," "strong to save," etc. It has the same meaning as would the phrase "… that is a strong help."

love has entered into them and that guidance system that is not working for the other self is able to work through the love within the heart of that entity for the other in ways of creating the opportunity to find a novel and creative way to witness to the truth and the love that is seen in the other self.

The makeup of the human heart is such that as the one known as R has said, when there is the ability to share with another self, that which is a burden to one, by that very sharing, by that very hearing, by that exchange of energy, the sharpness of the pain of living is lightened and the suffering that one perceives [one] to be undergoing is cut in half. All things that can be spoken of can be healed. The great gift of a mated relationship is that all things can be spoken of and may be spoken of. There is permission given from one open heart to live fully as one. Were only two to become one, this is indeed a great thing. Yet, the added gift of the mated relationship is that there is normally some sort of ceremony within which the Creator is invited to join the union and to give life to the union that is so dearly wished. It may be seen simply as a blessing by those who attend the religious service and gaze upon such ritual as a social exercise or indeed a business proposition in which a contract is made with no small print and a long term. The value, however, within the spiritual or metaphysical universe, that universe that does partake of infinity and eternity, is that metaphysical values are specifically brought into the relationship to enhance the pairing so that it becomes a much stronger three-legged entity that can stand on its own and be that house in which two entities may live, the walls of which are made of hopes and dreams and love, but the floor of which is made of real effort, substantial work, and deep sacrifices between each to each.

And we would speak of sacrifice, for there is within the human experience that which can be perceived in many cases as sacrifice, which ensues from the commitment to a relationship. The essence of love in the sense of the love of the infinite Creator is open-hearted giving and open-hearted receiving of energy which passes freely between two people. Within this atmosphere then, two people turn and face living a life together. And as the everyday life moves on from the committed relationship's start, those energies that have been working through each to create and direct the path of seeking for each become those energies that intertwine in new and original ways because of the proximity of the two and because of the continuing accretion of shared memory and shared catalyst.

There is that figure in the archetypal mind which has the entities upon the wheel of life and as the wheel of life is turning, the entities are turned upside down and all the money in their pockets is falling out and falling upon the fruitful earth. And indeed in marriage, the wheel turns and sometimes one is receiving the gifts of others and sometimes is losing the coins out of one's pockets, perhaps on purpose, perhaps not. Yet, it may be perceived when one is at the top of the wheel, upside down and serving by giving, that one is being badly used, that one is sacrificing and not simply able, because of that position on the wheel, to offer a certain kind of love and support to the whole. It is well to be able to gaze steadily at the possibility, going into mated relationship, that there will be times of substantial, apparent sacrifice for, as this instrument has said many times, if two people feel that they are sacrificing almost a hundred percent for the relationship, with the other entity doing almost nothing, then it is possible that they are [each] doing their share. It is very difficult from close up to see the self and its efforts in balance with the efforts of the other self. It is sometimes hard to see the efforts of an other self and easy to see the efforts of self, and again there are times when the self is already seen as failing in a certain situation, and therefore the self is seen as not giving enough and the other self is seen as being overbalanced towards the giving.

We do not know and could not say if we did, what the catalysts shall be for any mated pair as they begin to ride this ark of hopes and dreams along that endless ocean of perceived experience within incarnation. It is only possible for those upon the ark that they have made by their mutual love, to shine the wood of it, to polish the brass, to clean the head, to trim the sail, to keep the keel even and steady and to gaze at the stars with sextant in hand, remembering your hopes and dreams and renewing, daily, that pride in being that makes the chores of living as one joyful. We encourage, in the dailiness of a mated relationship, the continual return to the place of marriage where two souls united with the Creator to create the temple of a lifetime of dedicated and committed loving. Move into the silence of that tabernacle which is within the heart. Move into that shared silence in which each may hear the Creator speak. Let love be that which it is but allow a love which you know not to undergird and support that which you know now as love. For love has infinite lessons to offer and the more one is able to open the heart to the infinite consciousness that is love, the more one is able to open even further and even further. So that, as this instrument would say, one comes into one's bliss, and more and more is at rest and at peace within.

We thank the one known as G for this query and at this time we would open the meeting to any other queries that any might have the desire to ask at this time. We are those of Q'uo.

J: Hi Q'uo, this is J and I wanted to say hello. I wanted to ask a question about something I read in an interesting article today that stated that there might be beings that aren't necessarily someone that we know that has a post set up north of Russia and it said these beings protect the Earth from asteroids, maybe from other interferences, and I was just wondering if you could confirm that or speak of it anyway?

We are those of Q'uo, and are aware of your query, my sister. We find that this energy is both true and untrue in terms of that which you have read, and to explicate, we would say that there are many energies within the inner planes which are detailed to work with perceived difficulties that might impinge upon those dwelling within third-density Earth at this time. These energies are not physical and cannot be found in dwelling places and so forth. Yet they are real, they are simply not those within third-density or physical bodies. This entity would call them angelic but this does beg the question of their nature, for we find no real word that lacks emotional energy for beings without bodies, shall we say. These energies, however, are positive, loving and very articulated.

May we answer you further, my sister?

J: No thank you, that's good for now, thank you.

We thank you, my sister. Is there another query at this time?

G: Q'uo, beyond entering or moving through an initiation through the Great Pyramid, is there anything that an entity can do to become an initiated and purified channel of the Law of One that is as substantial and definitive and transformative? Can an intense desire effect the same type of change?

We are those of Q'uo and aware of your query, my brother. We cannot give you a general answer for entities besides yourself. We can say that there is for each self the possibility of creating and sustaining a successful effort towards realization. However, entities are variously blocked with regard to subtler work. There are densities and sub-densities within the inner planes where the structures of realization are promulgated and crafted by guidance systems that wish to aid and serve you in your evolution which must come into play when entities are within a certain frame of mind and when they have experienced a certain preliminary set of necessary …

(Side one of tape ends)

(Carla channeling)

These experiences may not come at the time that they are useful but like treasures, they are stored away against the proper moment and then, in that moment, entirely unpredictably for the most part, the frame of mind and the moment and those things which have needed to be ingested beforehand, in terms of experience, all come together and an epiphany results. We cannot say that there is one ritual which, when done with integrity and impeccability, will yield the result that you wish. We can only say that energies build to a moment and, in that moment, there is a crystallization of previous experience, and realization that occurs. It is a great gift and a great blessing. And in your case we may say that there are no adhering limitations or blockages which would keep the soul stream that lies beneath your personality shell from coming to that moment with those things which are necessary for realization. We simply suggest that the energy of faith be remembered and centered upon when there is doubt that one is able to become a purified instrument. Each is able to purify the self. That indeed is the very nature of the refinery that is the school of Earth.

May we answer you further, my brother?

G: No, thank you Q'uo.

R: May I ask, I seem to be many people in one physical body and there are times that I feel that I am a fraud and I have wondered how this can be because I have thoughts and often desires that seem foreign. I wondered if there is an explanation?

We are those of Q'uo, and are aware of your query, my sister. Indeed, the explanation is fairly simple, my sister. When an entity is honest and has insight and has moved through many experiences, it is natural to feel that one has become wiser and wiser and wiser. However, it is also true that in spite of or around any integrated, conscious, daylight personality there lies that which, culturally speaking, is simply not accepted or admitted among your peoples, and that is the full 360-degree self which contains every shadow, every evil, every darkness that can be imagined by the mind, the heart, or the soul of human beings. All of those things that have ever been imagined, good or bad, according to various people's lives, are part of that which is R and equally that which is Carla, or Jim or J. There is no lack of evil, so-called, within the heart of any, for all were greatly accepting of and wanting this precise 3-D self that has all of the light and all of the dark. As experiences continue to flow in, there are moments when the integration falters and thoughts are separated out into the shadow side and the positive side. Neither side is a fraud. Both sides are real. The action of the self towards other self expresses that which is the perceived truth of the self. Many, many shadow, dark, evil parts of the self, then, stay within the self, are processed only by the self, there being no need to have the outer mirror of other self in order to be able to see one's shadow self. The challenge then becomes internal. When the self is perceived as self-inconsistent, then whatever is perceived as the "bad self" is to be taken into the arms of that self which you experience as yourself so that you can rock that unloved portion of self in the arms of true compassion; so that you can say, "I fell in love with you a long time ago."

Then there is the joy of telling that shadow the story that will charm it and will allow it to find its freedom within the interior portions of self where it can begin to be transformed into that power and grit of self, that, purified of the baser darkness, uses the power of darkness to assist the will of the daylight self.

May we answer you further, my sister?

R: Thank you.

Is there a further query at this time?

T: Q'uo, if it's possible and appropriate, would you be able to touch me with your energies so that I could feel you?

(Pause)

We are those of Q'uo, and we have touched you.

T: Thank you.

Is there a final query at this time?

V: A couple of years ago I asked about the nature of the entity I know as Turquoise and I wonder if Q'uo would speak to whether enough has changed in my perception, in my environment, and my incarnation to be able to answer that query?

We make this entity smile, my sister. We are those of Q'uo, and we may say only that you are quite correct, that this matter is upon the cusp at this time and that you are dealing with it in a brilliant manner. We are sorry that we can not speak further at this time but there is that which shall take place within your process before we are able to speak without infringement. We thank you, my sister.

We are those of Q'uo, and we thank you again for the lovely experience of sharing in your meditation. We pray you may go forth from this meeting in joy and in peace. We are always with you by request as you meditate, to strengthen your meditation and to make the room of silence just a bit more sturdy and safe.

We are those of Q'uo. We leave you in the love and in the light of the one infinite Creator. Adonai, adonai. ☥

L/L Research

L/L Research is a subsidiary of Rock Creek Research & Development Laboratories, Inc.

P.O. Box 5195
Louisville, KY 40255-0195

www.llresearch.org

Rock Creek is a non-profit corporation dedicated to discovering and sharing information which may aid in the spiritual evolution of humankind.

ABOUT THE CONTENTS OF THIS TRANSCRIPT: This telepathic channeling has been taken from transcriptions of the weekly study and meditation meetings of the Rock Creek Research & Development Laboratories and L/L Research. It is offered in the hope that it may be useful to you. As the Confederation entities always make a point of saying, please use your discrimination and judgment in assessing this material. If something rings true to you, fine. If something does not resonate, please leave it behind, for neither we nor those of the Confederation would wish to be a stumbling block for any.

© 2009 L/L Research

Sunday Meditation
October 5, 2003

Group question: We are going to take potluck this evening and hope that Q'uo will speak to the group energy. We've gone around the circle today and we've shared a lot of very intense, interesting, involved and complex information dealing with personal lives, opening the heart, and new directions, and we would like Q'uo to take a look at these energies, look at our hearts and speak to the concerns that are foremost in our own spiritual journeys.

(Carla channeling)

We are those of the principle known to you as Q'uo and we greet you in the love and in the light of the one infinite Creator, in Whose service we are and in Whose service we delight. We thank you with all of our hearts for calling us to your circle of seeking this day and are glad to share our humble thoughts with you as long as each is able to agree to listen carefully for those thoughts that appeal and those that do not, keeping the first and leaving behind the second. We appreciate this, as it gives us the freedom to speak our minds and share our opinions without feeling that we are attempting to infringe upon your free will or to speak as authorities since we honestly feel that we are not authorities but friends. We offer our thoughts with a hope that they may help, that they may be of service, and that they may be useful in your process.

But, my friends, that is that which our thoughts are made of: process—ours, yours and the Creator's. It is unknown to us, just as it is unknown to this instrument, what we shall say at any particular session of working. When we are given the opportunity to speak according to the energy in the circle, it is a marvelously freeing thing in that it enables us to lift from the logical association of subjects into a more feeling and sense-oriented way of attempting to work with those things which lie beneath the words, which can be used to describe situations, reaching down into the feelings and the structures of those feelings that have existed for some time and that have shaped those ears and those eyes that each of you brings to new catalyst, so that the person that experiences the momentary catalyst is experiencing that catalyst through the eyes of a lifetime of coloration. Many times the skill involved in processing experiences involves not accepting the first structures as being the whole truth of the situation, either its surface appearance or its deeper meaning. We thank you for lifting up from the iron grip of logical ratiocination[59] and intellectual processes. For when an entity is dealing with a new and unknown situation, as the one known as S has said, there is the desire to make progress. And in that desire to make progress, the ruthlessly literal third-density bio-computer/mind, as opposed to the consciousness of each entity, wishes to apply logic to those things which defy logic because of their novelty. When one is wishing to begin a new

---

[59] ratiocination: the act or process of reasoning or of deducing consequences from premises.

structure, certainly one may go into the work having some idea as to what that new structure will be. For instance, this channel had spoken earlier concerning the way a new structure of a spiritual circle or a communal spiritual group might be organized, pointed and motivated. Yet, because of the fact that this is a structure that has yet to be built and because of the fact that it can only be built by those involved in the new structure during the catalyst and the process of so building that structure day by day, the grasping mind of the instrument has nothing immediate upon which to take hold.

Similarly with each within this circle who is beginning a new pattern, it is as that entity who is moving into a new abode, a new structure within which to live the entire gamut of third-density incarnative life from the smallest, simplest and most nitty-gritty of chores and activities having to do with the natural functions of the human body and fulfilling the needs of the human body for sustenance and warmth, all the way to the most abstruse imaginings of one who truly desires to make of the life a gift to the Creator in so many ways, small and large. Each within this group gazes now at a life that is completely new. In many ways this is beginning to become the standard situation among your peoples at this time. For, as many in the group have noted in the conversation preceding this meditation, the world is moving ever more swiftly and ever more intensely in its great rush towards the culmination of what this instrument has often called third-density life. We are not saying that there will come a great catastrophe and all will be finished. However, we are saying that the energies that are moving into place in order to birth the fourth density of your planet Earth move in ever-decreasing circles of attraction to that moment when fourth density shall be the officer of the day, shall we say, rather than third density. There shall be a time in your not-too-distant future when those efforts that you have made to become aware of what it is to open the heart will have culminated in that which can be done within incarnation in third density at this time upon your planet as you know it. Beyond that point there well may be years and years of service and learning for those within this circle. However, the nature of that learning and the nature of the service will no longer carry the burden of the attempt to graduate from third to fourth density. For indeed, those who are able to live in an open-hearted way to a sufficient extent during this time of transition will be able to live within the fourth-density atmosphere.

However, those who are not able so to begin to open their hearts will find that the difference between the vibratory level within the consciousness and the vibratory level within the environment shall be great enough that the discomfort of living within the fourth-density Earth energy shall be too much for the physical vehicles to enjoy without significant distortion, which shall in many cases shorten lives that would otherwise have been far longer and more open to many options involved in structures of those with open hearts. In this atmosphere it becomes more and more obvious that, in the face of new structures, there is only one directive that we may offer that you may trust completely. That directive is to open the heart. This instrument said earlier, speaking for herself, that she found it impossible to keep the heart open for a prolonged length of time; that there was the natural cycle of ego and so forth that would call to any seeking soul those temptations that would take love and replace it with fear. And such temptations are many and varied. Some are obvious, some are subtle. The true nature of such temptations becomes clear usually only when one is in the middle of having closed the heart and then having discovered the closing of the heart and beginning to work backwards from that place of being stuck, or being over-stimulated, or being blocked, so that the uses of hindsight may help the seeker discover the genesis of the conflict that has caused the previously open heart to move once again from love to fear.

We give this instrument the picture of a moonlit ocean. The water is black, sparkling with that infinitely subtle pattern of white that comes from starlight and wave motion. The roar of the ocean, being so familiar, becomes silence and the pounding of the deep becomes stillness. And the soul, in its frail barque, is as the Indian braving the ocean in his canoe. How dare such a feeble and easily extinguished light set off into the darkness! There is the guidance of stars and the song that is not heard but felt, of the ocean speaking to itself, of that great power and magic of water hoarding its information, rolling with the movement of the stars, responding to each and every cosmic energy. And these subtle but very real energies strengthen and focus the attention of the Indian in the boat in this tiny bark canoe. Does this entity, this representative of the seeking soul, choose to have fear of the deep? Does this entity choose to share itself with the deep? Where is this entity going?

The stars do not concern themselves with the movement of the canoe. They smile their cheerful smile, coming from out of the past and into the future with their light and their information. The energies of fire gently wrap themselves about this figure as he allows his craft to move with the waves or attempts to direct it with his paddle.

Each spirit moves across a great and infinitely deep ocean of energies and structures and these entities and the structures, in their shadow form, have form. In their less shadowy reality, which is still illusion, they have no form, but only the shapes of the feelings that have been experienced while working with the moment and its structure and its past, its present, and future. We might suggest to each the growing familiarity with each thought, especially those thoughts that repeat and reappear in the mind. It is well known, in many different ways, that what one says to oneself is heard. And we would take this opportunity to say once again that each of you is a powerful and magical person. Each has words of power and each has been speaking these words of power to the self for many years. In many cases those things which have become habitually said to the self have to do with structures that existed far into the incarnational past of the seeking soul and voices that originally were outer voices—the voices of parents, teachers, authority figures and friends—are allowed to become those voices that have been internalized and validated by the self, not to the self's advantage but indeed, to the self's detriment.

Some examples are quite obvious. If this instrument says to itself each time that it forgets something that it is a fool, it will not only be forgetful but it will feel unworthy[60]. Take this example and apply it to those things which each says to herself. They may be true in a literal or surface way and yet, as you note those particular truths, is there a positive advantage to prioritizing this information? What is it? If there is a positive way to absorb this information, has the voice within you found that positive way or has it allowed laziness and carelessness to blunt the great power of choice for you? Choose carefully that which you communicate to yourself about yourself and, if you find yourself moving into patterns that create feelings of unworthiness, stop; not to correct what may be a true set of facts, but rather to gaze at that little node wherein lie the nerve endings from the past, the circumstances of the present, and the ideals and hopes of your future.

What can sitting with this node of activity and process yield for the honest and, in a way, ruthless seeker of inner balance? In each case where there is a perceived node of feelings and process, there is pay dirt. There is treasure to be found. And it is worth the time that it takes to rest within that pattern, in terms of being able to become more and more skillful in knowing the self and in seeing those habits and triggers from yesteryear, shall we say, that have crept into the present mechanism of the way the mind works, hears and sees; all of which are choices very much up for grabs many times. It is not that we wish to cause self-doubt or to invalidate the thoughts that you have and the feelings that you feel. Rather, we ask you to stay with them, to experience through intensity and time, allowing energy to move as it will and as it must, neither hurrying it nor resisting but rather embracing it with as much love as you can and thanking it for the opportunities, be they challenging or pleasant or elating, as they come up and as it is time to deal with them.

Keep in mind that no matter what it feels like you are never running in circles. You are always on a spiral. You cannot stay in the same place. In terms of physical things, certainly, an entity can choose to stay in one place and end up pushing up the daisies not ten feet from where he last went to sleep. These things are possible for the physical body. However, your spirit, that consciousness which is part of the Godhead principle, cannot stay still. It can move forward in a direction that seems fair or it can move forward in a direction that seems de-structurizing and debilitating. The one thing that the spirit can not do is stay in one place. Like the water upon which this barque of being flows within incarnation and out of it, there is no staying still. Even when one is moored, one tends to go to the ends of the mooring rope, as the influences in the water move that spirit evermore, not resting, not stopping but moving with the gentle patience of eternity.

Let the sun be away when it seems to be night and let the moon be that witness that says to you that the sun is a reality that shall cycle into the awareness once again, in its time. Allow the roll of the pain

---

[60] The instrument has a lifelong absentmindedness in her personality makeup.

that you are experiencing to continue so that the night hours are spent in an engaged and embracing way that enables one to be grateful for the sleeplessness of the dark night of the soul. Know, by the moonlight, that there is a sun that is still reflected into your node of catalyst. And let that reflection, dim though it may be, be that witness for the light and love of the infinite Creator and the rightness of the plan of the Creator for you. Then you are able to release the fear of the night and the fear of the water and the fear of being at the mercy of an ocean that seems, at least on the surface, to be a dangerous place to be. This instrument would say, "life is hardball." There are no soft pitches for the school of love on planet Earth.

The tangles will come. This is why you jumped into Earthly incarnation. You were not unaware of the difficulties of living within an illusion and being cut off from that embedded knowledge of rightness and goodness and identity that you have lost in entering the Earth plane. These things are now unprovable, unknowable and only trusted by faith. We speak of a mystery. It is a mystery that necessarily involves both suffering and joy, both the deeps of night and the brightest noonday. The contrasts are amazing and as this instrument said earlier, it is a very bright experience within the Earth plane in these days of great light, both for service to self and for service to others. Entities all about you, and you, yourself, are attempting to deal with a great bounty. That bounty is an opportunity to move profoundly within a short time both in learning and in service, beginning to move from [being] one who does not use the paddle to one who decides upon a course and indeed starts applying the paddle with great diligence and passion.

As each of you becomes more and more familiar with the way the new structures of being and living feel, each will have many opportunities to get to know the self better, to become more self-supporting, to fall in love with the self, as this instrument would say. May you find the self that you are to be half as beautiful as we find you to be. As you begin to see more and more clearly into yourself, you shall indeed see things in yourself of which you shall not be fond. We ask you not be discouraged. Each of you has all things within. To expect never to encounter the shadow part of self is to expect far too much from the very dynamic energies of any human existence within illusion. The creation is designed to bring you out of yourself and into empty rooms where there is as yet no structure. Let those times be your friends, for they are part of a greatly beneficial and satisfying process.

We would at this time open the meeting to further queries if there are any. Is there a question at this time?

G: Q'uo, if it's possible could you describe to me what I faced within myself two nights ago during an hour and half bout of tears and if an experience like that is something that should be sought or should be allowed to happen as it comes on its own?

We are those of Q'uo, and are aware of your query, my brother. We may say about your experience that certainly it includes those things of which you are letting go, those shifts within your own definition of yourself that require the loss of structures that were in place and that are no longer appropriate. We may also say that it is extremely positive to move through such times and we see, in the way that you shepherded yourself through this time, that love of self that opens the heart and teaches it how to love others as well.

The time of such movement cannot be planned. It is only necessary to set the mind towards service and love and the heart towards living, open and vulnerable to the catalyst that arises in a moment. The natural rhythms of experience shall bring to you those moments as they are appropriate.

May we answer you further, my brother?

G: No, that was excellent. Thank you, Q'uo.

We thank you, my brother.

G: I am full of questions! Q'uo, if an entity's power is not "over" another, or even over oneself, then what is truly the power of a positively-polarizing entity?

We are those of Q'uo, and are aware of your query, my brother. The power of a service-to-others entity is that power to love without reservation. The way of love is simple in the extreme in its effect. However, as the one known as S noted, in the energy system of a physically incarnate entity, there are many ways to become hindered or blocked, in which one becomes the one who cuts off the power for oneself. There are many ways to choose to diminish the forces of love within the self. It is a challenge indeed to find those ways in which love has been too tightly held or too dearly given, given as a miser or a pinch-penny, or given without thought when thought might create a better gift.

The province of power is the province of essence. The basic source of power is that knowledge of self that enables one to stand on one firm place and say, "This is who I am." Once that becomes a joyful and amalgamated, integrated sense, there is within the self a metaphysical center to which an entity may return by taking thought. What is the use or the goal of power? For service-to-others entities it is the power to help others. For a service-to-self entity it is the power to manipulate the environment for the benefit of the self. In both cases there is an environment to be manipulated. For the positive entity, that which is to be manipulated is not physical but rather is the stuff of consciousness itself. Therefore, an entity seeking power in the service-to-others polarity shall be seeking to know in order to serve and to create changes in consciousness rather than changes in status or other aspects of a physical environment.

May we answer you further, my brother?

G: Before I ask again, I'd like to open the questions to anybody else that may have one.

(Pause)

G: Okay, Q'uo, assuming that the work of power is the work of higher energy centers, I know that green ray is the great resource of all spiritual work and that the blue and indigo-ray activities await only the will of the seeker once green ray has been activated. My question is, the moment that love is felt, can an entity "move up," so to speak, and immediately do blue and/or indigo-ray work in that moment, if only for what I would call a short period of time? Or does the state of the open heart need to be reliable and consistent for work to proceed into the higher rays?

We are those of Q'uo, and are aware of your query, my brother. The ability to do work in consciousness is momentary and there can be times of brilliance and clarity for any soul who is able even momentarily to enter the heart. It is to be noted, however, that the more work that is done in the first three energy centers, and that on a daily basis, the more opportunity that a soul may have to rest within the open heart.

The stumbling blocks to living open-heartedly are only partially "out there," only partially the effect of catalyst that is incoming to the consciousness of the seeker. Again, the places where energy is held in the energy body often have to do with the past and those things that are, to all intents and purposes, dead. Yet, somehow, the function of memory has enabled them to have a spurious and untrue life within an entity, which has for the most part moved from those stumbling-block areas of misperception concerning the self.

When the evening of the day comes we have recommended before through this instrument that it is well to examine, as one may, the points which hooked one during the previous day's experience, either for happiness or for woe. Gaze into the way the mind works when it is triggered. Find those triggers. Name them. Get to know them. Begin accepting yourself for having them. Begin attempting to create for the self a safe place where these things can be looked at …

(Side one of tape ends.)

(Carla channeling)

… for however long they need to stay. In reality, much of getting to know the self is not pushing the self around as much as it is gently sitting around the campfire with all of these different parts of self and allowing each to tell its story. For there is good in many different points of view within, all of which may come together in ways that are not helpful. Yet each item within the mix is helpful to consider, helpful to gaze at, perhaps over time. It is a subtle thing to become more familiar with the self without judging the self, and this is the goal of one who is attempting to free up those stuck places within. Once one is relatively balanced within the energy body from red, orange and yellow then the heart is able to get full energy and that full blast of unconditional love that the Creator puts out in infinite quantity and quality at all times. Energy is finally able to move through into the heart in a powerful way.

Many who attempt to do work in consciousness are working on that green ray, working to get the heart to open, without taking the tedious and often unrewarding time to enter into the self in an ever deeper way, making the connections that explain patterns that are long-standing and gradually finding ways to remove the triggers that are hidden within everyday experiences and processes.

We find that this instrument's energy begins to wane and so we will leave this group at this time, thanking this instrument for its service and thanking each within the circle for the crystalline beauty of their beings. Your colors and energy are beautiful to us in ways we cannot ever express and our love for you is great. We thank you for your love of seeking the truth. As you seek, every door shall open.

We leave this instrument and this group in the love and in the light of the one infinite Creator. We are known to you as the principle of Q'uo. Adonai, my friends, adonai. ❧

L/L Research

L/L Research is a subsidiary of Rock Creek Research & Development Laboratories, Inc.

P.O. Box 5195
Louisville, KY 40255-0195

www.llresearch.org

Rock Creek is a non-profit corporation dedicated to discovering and sharing information which may aid in the spiritual evolution of humankind.

ABOUT THE CONTENTS OF THIS TRANSCRIPT: This telepathic channeling has been taken from transcriptions of the weekly study and meditation meetings of the Rock Creek Research & Development Laboratories and L/L Research. It is offered in the hope that it may be useful to you. As the Confederation entities always make a point of saying, please use your discrimination and judgment in assessing this material. If something rings true to you, fine. If something does not resonate, please leave it behind, for neither we nor those of the Confederation would wish to be a stumbling block for any.

© 2009 L/L Research

Sunday Meditation
October 19, 2003

Group question: The question today has to do with fear and love. We are assuming that fear and love are on a spectrum of … there's a connection between them and we would like Q'uo to give us some information about how we can deal with fear, any kind of fear. Fear of doing something we haven't done, the fear of doing something that seems difficult. V mentioned that focusing on the love aspect tended to make the fear dissipate. Is that correct? Is there anything else we can do to deal with the fear when we feel that it's taking too much influence in our lives?

(Carla channeling)

We are those known to you as the principle of Q'uo, and we greet you in the love and in the light of the one infinite Creator, in Whose service we come. We wish to thank each of you for creating this time and space to seek the truth. We are humbled before your energy, your beauty, and the focus of your desire. We are most grateful that you have called us to your circle of seeking. Please know we are happy to share our opinion with you, with the request that at all times you listen with great discrimination, accepting those truths that sound good to you for further consideration and banishing all those that do not sound good to you from your mind. This will allow us to speak freely, knowing that you do not see us as authorities, but rather as those having a certain kind of conversation: a conversation about ideas and about those concepts that move too deep to be expressed directly in words, those concepts of which the one known as D was speaking earlier, the various archetypes, whether they be four or twelve or twenty-two, that in some way or another give one another structure or ways to think about the Creator and one's relationship to the Creator.

There are two questions posed within the energy of this instrument's mind, although we have only the one on the tape recording which was done prior to our speaking, and we find it interesting that although these two subjects seem to be so far apart in nature, they benefit from being looked at together. The two subjects, being that of fear versus love and what the nature of various kinds of nature spirits is, would seem on the face of it to have little or nothing in common. And yet, indeed there is a great essence which they share.

The great *jihad*[61] of the struggle of love and fear is that rock upon which many have shipwrecked their lives, their spiritual ambitions, and their hopes of progressing according to some self-made, or authority-driven plan. Energy gets stuck. Energy that has been bruised and stricken defends itself. Everything that can be imagined has an energy, if it is imagined. This is not to say that when we are speaking of nature spirits we are speaking of

---

[61] jihad: "a campaign for or against an idea; a crusade" as well as the more usual meaning of "a Moslem holy war." The Q'uo intend the first of the two meanings, the campaign in question being for love and against fear.

imaginary beings, for we are not. Rather, they are imaginary in the same way that you are imaginary. You are illusory in a certain order, or grade, of illusion. You vibrate in a certain series of energy fields or spheres, which have their own order and their own purpose. And they communicate with each other throughout that grade or gamut of energy vibration. Consequently, all physical bodies are communicating.

The same is true of the first-density entities and the second-density entities among your peoples. These too, birds, animals, trees and plants of each kind, have their own nature, their own essence, their own energy. And insofar as they are given life, there exists within them a corresponding spirit to your spirit. Is the spirit of a flower or a tree or a stone or the wind the same thing as your spirit? Not at all. In the case of the elementals of first-density, there is a tremendous amount of infinite wisdom in such strong and powerful purity that there is an essence that is indescribable to entities as transparent and ephemeral as living flesh. That energy of fire, the energy of wind, the energy of earth, the energy of water, is that of the everlasting element, not simply in its physical characteristics but in the corresponding spirit of those characteristics. You have only to sit at the edge of a great body of water to begin to know or become acquainted with[62] the essence of water. You have only to stand in the high wind or to bow beneath it and, indeed, crawl on hand and knee to shelter against such a wind to understand the kind of energy that the wind offers. And the same can be seen of the energies of fire, and of earth.

This group has spent a couple of days exploring caves recently and has a special reason to become more and more aware of the power of the everlasting rock-ness. Many are the spirits that can be seen from these elements. They are seen by an eye that is not physical because their energy is that of the metaphysical energy that occupies time/space. Consequently, it has no body in space/time but only the impression, or the shadow, of the truth of such an entity. It is as though you were attempting to prove that you had ideas, ideals, hopes and dreams. Can you show them to someone? No. Do you still have them? Oh yes. In just this way, the mountain, the ocean or the wind has the expression, the thoughts, the hopes, the ideals, the process of its nature; and because it has no hampering of self-awareness, it never moves from love. It remains blissful in its ignorance of any other choice and simply expresses its essence in a dynamic combination with those energy fields of time/space and of space/time that it may meet. Consequently, as you walk in nature or down the urban sidewalk, you are coming in contact with the sprites of the air and the undines of water and the salamanders of fire and the gnomes of earth, all unknowing because you cannot see them with the eyes of daylight. There are always special people who can see into inner planes, for weal or for woe.

Now let us say here that in discussing the inner planes, we discuss a universe vaster than the physical universe and greatly populated with a very wide gamut of personalities. The most tremendous wisdom, compassion and mastery lives within the inner planes. We ourselves dwell in, shall we say, a parking garage in fifth density, as it were, as we are involving ourselves with your vibrations at this time. We are part of that network of inner planes that includes all of the spirits that seek to serve. Those within first and second density, those within fourth, fifth and sixth density; all seek to serve by their very nature. It is impossible for them not to be prompted to share energy and therefore to serve.

Those elementals of second density are far more complex and far less solid in their nature, as would be expected from beings which are, like yourselves, those who live and die fairly quickly. However, the subtlety of second density, with its movement to the light and its relationships within the tribe or pack, create a far more exotic and far more whimsical panoply of figures and of stories in which those figures have found each other and have joined worlds. And so creation becomes added to creation becomes added to creation, and, in the inner planes, there are many exotic kingdoms which have been created so that the essences of all of these energies, in the relationships with various humans and their cultures, can play. There is a tremendous joy and a feeling of play about the free essences of plants, animals, wind, storm, ocean and so forth. When an entity becomes self-aware in third density, she becomes cut off from the joy, the play, and the ever-continuing presence of all of the other members of the inner plane.

---

[62] This phrase "to become acquainted with," is a typical way of defining the word "gnosis" in Gnostic literature. It suggests a kind of knowledge beyond words or explanations.

Each of the sub-planes of those inner planes has its own environment. Those who are able to sift through the planes have that experience, that feeling, of almost going through different grades of water as they move through the sub-planes to that precise vibration of energies that is equivalent to their most comfortable place within the inner planes. Entities who are able to do this come into a land of milk and honey to which they may go in their meditations. Each of you has one; and each of you has, in that vibration, helpers, those whose delight it is to find a way to make that experience which you—that individual soul, that very unique soul—will have to be joyful, playful and as the one known as J was saying earlier, a product completely of the spontaneity of the now. The energies that lie all about third-density humans as they earnestly struggle with their catalyst are energies that encourage the deepest response to the feeling which lies in the environment about the self.

Coming to a moment is coming to a banquet. How shall you enjoy the rich array of incoming experience? Shall it be a thing of love and joy and laughter or shall it be a thing of fear and defending? Each of you is painfully aware that you are not a flower, you are not the wind, you have not been a tree for years and years. And as a person you have been cast forth into an illusion which is bound to hurt and disturb and upset any shred of routine and surety that you may have; for all things pass and the experience of the third-density entity within the illusion is that infinitely renewable feeling of being behind the power curve, unaware of those things which it would have been good to know in order to plan for this change that seems somehow to be taking place. The one known as John[63] wrote in a song, "Life is what happens to you while you're making other plans." This is the cartoon-like nature of the catalyst that is available within your third-density world. It is always aimed at moving you from a balanced and comfortable place into a place where there is a risk to take, a challenge to meet, a cliff to walk off of, so that you may have the experience of choice. That is the one thing that is your glory and your challenge. You have the responsibility that is God-like: of choosing how you shall go on, how you shall think, how you shall meet the day, how you shall treat yourself if you're not happy with how you met the day, and how you shall treat those other-selves that are a part of you. Shall you see them as other? Or shall you see them as the self?

There is a great journey to be taken in that regard, for third density begins as the great ape that you are is barely beginning to move into the traditional, cultural societies, forming tribes, forming instinctively those tribes that describe self and other as the tribe and not the tribe. That great sadness that we see within your political and societal planning these days is that seeming return to late second-density where there is tribe versus tribe with no hope of communication and parity becoming possible between them. Consequently, each entity moving through the various sub-levels of third-density is attempting, more and more, to move from the uneducated idea of self, as only self and other-self that looks just like you because it is the same tribe, to self being the same as other-self, because self and other-self are both ensouled parts of the same Creator.

The education between those two points is vast, immense and unimaginable. Each of you has spent lifetime upon lifetime attempting, with a pure heart and a good will, to penetrate the mystery of oneness. In a world where nothing looks like it is one with you, how can you catch on to what is not being seen? How can you hear what is not being said, what can not be said, for there are no words? The secret is energy, that energy about which the one known as J will speak[64], sharing her passion for the beautiful simplicity of the healing touch, and not even the healing touch, but the energy of the healing heart. Indeed, it is that environment that is beyond words that moves into that walk of faith that exists only in midair. For in that particular discipline, as in so many disciplines that go under the modality of the laying on of hands, the true healing is not in a touch, but rather, in the love that that energy of the touch carries, because of the work that that particular instrument has done as a messenger of healing. The energy of other-selves can be a palpable thing and interestingly enough, you can affect the energy of others. How can you do this? You may do it mechanically by thinking to yourself, upon looking

---

[63] John Lennon, from "Beautiful Boy," on the album *Double Fantasy*. The actual quotation is, "Life is what happens to you/While you're busy/Making other plans."

[64] J, a Reiki healer, was speaking to a college class about healing energy in the week ahead.

at someone else, "This too is me. This is my brother and I love him," or alternately, "Thou art God." Or alternately, as this instrument often says, "You are my mirror." You too are a mirror. What you forget, because you are sitting within your own space, is that you are radiating. Each within this circle is very powerful, has done a good deal of work, no matter what the biological age of those in the circle. Each of you has a metaphysical essence that is powerful. As you allow that feeling of your own self to open up, as you simply allow yourself to be yourself, to flower, to look out of yourself at the beauty of all of those around you, as you listen to each energy and "feel into" the energy of those who are speaking in desultory tones about the room, you can begin to make those heart connections with each mirror, with each part of yourself, thanking each part of yourself, knowing that if you were to pursue that particular person, that particular relationship, that would be a very valuable mirror that you could not get from anyone else. Each person then becomes a treasure trove of undiscovered things, [undiscovered] simply because you have not spent the time to open up to that person and to share what the energy has to offer each of you in that dynamic between you.

When you can, for the first time, move from an intellectual appreciation of the oneness in all to a feeling within your own heart that you are looking at the Creator as the Creator, there is a magical occurrence that reduces fear. That magical occurrence is love, a feeling of love that springs forth like a fire. In the glow of that fire there is a communication from essence to essence and the hearts of those that you are speaking to know that you love them. And there is that within their being that again opens and then, they love you back. And the supportive energy of that relationship, once begun by the open heart, is irresistible. Trust the energy that is yourself. We do not say, "Put aside all fear." We would not do that to entities that might feel undefended and naked and vulnerable beyond their ability to enjoy creation and existence. We are aware that for some it is powerful even to take part of the armor away, to lighten it, to shorten it, to leave it off for small periods of time. Have the feeling when working with fear of "a little is a lot," because it is so difficult to judge the self, and it is so seldom accurate when attempted that we would suggest, rather, focusing simply upon the process, upon giving it a good try and upon being extraordinarily good to yourself no matter what the perceived outcome.

What you are attempting to do as you filter the experiences of your life through the processes of the disciplining of the personality is to become easier and easier with yourself, and easier on yourself, while at the same time, remaining honest concerning your process; that is to say, it is well to be ruthlessly honest with yourself and with the Creator, in your continuing conversation with the Creator, but it is not a good idea, no matter what your basic feelings of irritation may be at the self, to berate the self, or to lose respect for the self, or to act in such a way that there is the expression to the self of dissatisfaction, of feeling that the self is unworthy. These things are all too easy to promulgate within the inner life. They are those stumbling blocks that trip up your feet and keep you from moving forward. They have been put there by voices not your own, but in many cases you have accepted them, internalized them, and made them live far past their time of truth, if there ever was a time of truth for some of those deeply painful childhood insults. See the pain and the suffering that has been endured by you, that has caused fear to become a habit returned to again and again. See with eyes of love and compassion. This instrument carries a doll frequently when it is at home. It talks to the doll and it asks the doll to tell her its dreams. It is in this way that this particular entity seeks to undo damage done to her as a child by those who did not make her feel wanted, needed or listened to. There are ways to work on these difficulties that can be perceived as perhaps being the foundation for those fears that now trouble the seemingly grown and adult life. It is most helpful to open heart and mind together to the processes of seeing where these threads of fear take you. They are the breadcrumbs along the trail that will lead you to a deeper appreciation of self and a deeper ability to interpolate and amalgamate the self of all of those perhaps slightly separated parts of self that have moved away from other parts of self because of wounding, because of difficulty in holding the energy of self completely together.

We would at this time ask if there is a continuing query upon this subject or if there are other questions at this time. We are those of Q'uo.

J: Hi, Q'uo, this is J. I really appreciate what you said and I just wanted to ask you a quick question. I was told this weekend that I'm an adult indigo and I was wondering if you could speak to this and if that's why I have been so attracted to doing energy work and vibrational medicine. Does it have to do with the fact that I am an adult indigo?

We are those of Q'uo, and are aware of your query, my sister. That phraseology is acceptable as a way of designating a particularly opened-up and lively, shall we say, energy of the merkabah or the—I give this instrument [an image] of the spirals of the DNA and [that] there is more light there than is normally carried. We are having difficulty because of the phraseology of "indigo child." There are those who are wired strictly for third density, there are those who come into incarnation with some of the wiring for fourth density already in place and simply needing to be, shall we say, hooked up, and that is your designation. There are others who are completely activated and some of those designated as indigo children are of the latter type, others being of the middle type.

May we answer you further, my sister?

J: No, that's all for now, thank you very much.

We thank you, my sister. Is there another query at this time?

T: Yes. I have said several times that the need for polarity in our illusion can be fulfilled by using the memory. In other words, you don't have to have good and bad or good and evil right directly in your experience every day. You can look at the negative aspect and draw from your memory of negative aspects in your life, in the past. Will that suffice for the polarity that is necessary to stay in this illusion? Could you comment please?

We are those of Q'uo, and are aware of your query, my brother. Indeed, there are those whose discipline is such, and whose imagination has focused so, that this is possible. For, shall we say, the majority of entities, a purely inner vision lacks satisfaction, whereas we would say that, as the one known as V had noted in conversation not too long ago, the function of the video game is so to populate an imaginary battlefield with imaginary enemies that one may bash heads in glorious carelessness of the propriety of doing so in the outer culture, for there is only the image that is being bashed. Nevertheless, when it is done as a spiritual practice it is amazingly efficient. The key is the imagination and the discipline to make the connection between those energies which need disciplining and the seeming abandon of the so called video game.

May we answer you further, my brother?

T: No, thank you, that's fine.

We are those of Q'uo, and we thank you, my brother. Is there another query at this time.

G: Q'uo, if it's not too large for this working I was wondering if you can comment on how one can distinguish between one's own feelings and those of another? How can one protect against the negative feelings of others, and how one can transmute those feelings taken on from others within the self?

We are those of Q'uo, and are aware of your query, my brother. You are indeed correct that it is a larger query than some, and perhaps we shall make this the last query of this particular session because of that fact. For most entities brought up within your culture, the difficulties of knowing what feelings are one's own and what feelings are not, is not a problem because there is a characteristic self-involvement that dictates that there will be no confusion between the feelings of self and the feelings that are not of the self. However, when one has begun a process of opening and sensitizing the self to that which is more real, more true, more beautiful, more to be admired, the self does become less aware of the boundary between one's own universe and the universes of others. This is due to the fact that there is no boundary between the universe of the self and the universe of others except those boundaries that are created by the mind of the person. If it is assumed, as this instrument often does without realizing it, that all are one and all are thinking as one, then one sees one universe and one's feelings naturally move in that one big happy universe where all is known, all is good, and all is loved. This instrument has done a great deal of work in the past few years learning how to make boundaries so that it is able, as a person, to take care of itself and also to have the ability to love others as the self; as opposed to thinking that all feelings were her own and all needed to be addressed equally. It is a very confusing universe to one who has become unable to make those boundaries between self and other-self and as you have said, my brother, it is especially difficult when those feelings which are being imported into your system from a system of another are perceived as negative. It becomes a most uncomfortable and pertinent question as to how to make the boundaries that create comfort zones within the situation where there is overlap in aura, as there is in virtually every urban setting, and certainly in a household such as you enjoy at this time, where there is a constant presence within the dwelling of people whose auras do indeed overlap.

This is not, per se, a negative or positive thing. It can be either. What is occurring in a situation where there are overlapping auras is that there is the opportunity to exchange energy. The downside of this exchange of energy is when the exchange …

(Side one of tape ends)

(Carla channeling)

(A portion of the channeling was not recorded.)

The question of how to determine one's own boundaries can become very subtle. It may be as easy as physically removing the self from an environment, repeatedly, to see what changes may occur when one is in the environment and then out of it. It may be that there is talking to do to the self; that there are voices within the self that need to speak and say, "This is not me," and, "This is me," and, "Let me get you to understand this point of view even though it is not me." One can have some interesting conversations around the campfire of self and in some cases talking out loud to the self, about the self, one may begin to hear the true self and hear what one has picked up as a rider, and hear the difference between what really is the self and what has been simply picked up and started to be carried around on the coattails of the self.

There is also the entire arena of physical cleansing that is helpful in creating boundaries, the smudging of the self with the sacred sage; the ritualistic immersion in meditation of the preferred kind in which that question is put to the self, "Show me myself, show me the shape of myself." There are many ways to ask and indeed, for each person this is a very personal and very idiosyncratic work. Be open with the self, feel confident in following the intuitions and the hunches of self. Use journaling, use the dream process of writing the dreams down and thinking about them, use the conversation of others, and use all of those mute signs of the energy of the environment about you, the wind and the birds and so forth, all of those messengers that have spirit and wish to share energy with you. There comes out of all this amalgamation a growing sense of being able to be a discriminator and that is a very important feeling to gain. So we greatly encourage those disciplines that put one in touch with one's own powers of discrimination. It is a beautiful thing to know that all is one, [but also] that each of you is unique, each of you has your own shape, your own bloom, your own pollen, your own scent. Nobody like you ever was, nobody like you ever will be again. Only you have that breath to breathe, those words to say. We bless each of you as you move into your hopes and your dreams. May you walk with faith, may you walk with joy and may you know that you are never alone, and as the one known as D so often says, that you are loved more than you can imagine.

We leave you in the love and in the light of the one infinite Creator. We are known to you as the principle of Q'uo. Adonai. Adonai vasu. ✣

Sunday Meditation
November 2, 2003

Group question: Our question today concerns free will. We would like to know what Q'uo could tell us about maintaining free will and why free will is the first distortion of the Law of One. Why not the second or third distortion? Why did the Creator of all things feel that free will was the most important of the distortions in order to be listed first?

(Carla channeling)

We are those of the principle known to you as Q'uo, and we greet you in the love and in the light of the one infinite Creator, in Whose service we come to you. May we say what a privilege it is to be called to your circle of seeking? As the shadows lengthen upon your world in the environment of this instrument, we rest in the beauty of the combined energy and essence of each of your souls as you blend and meld into a true circle of seeking. It is a great blessing for us to be here and to share our thoughts with you. As always, we ask that you may use your discrimination in listening to those things which we have to say, for those things which we offer are opinions and are not to be confused with some source of final wisdom or absolute knowledge.

You ask this evening concerning free will and why it has been called, in the words of the Ra, "the first distortion." And we are glad to speak upon this topic. It is certainly a challenging and interesting topic, for it is the penetrating simplicity of the Law of One that it does begin with the free will.

Firstly, we shall address the subject from the standpoint of what this instrument would call logic, although it is a specific kind of logic which is perhaps not entirely linear. The creation is, shall we say, a figment of the imagination of the Creator. The Creator exists in a state of absolute rest within which all things occur, a primal paradox to be sure. The first distortion of this perfect balance and peace is choice, or the use of the will. In this case, it was the will of the Creator to know Itself. Consequently, it is that distortion which precedes the great original Thought, for that original Thought is an active thought—a creative and destructive thought, a powerful, active principle. The one known as D was speaking earlier concerning love and light and saying that the fundamental energy was love, that wisdom was important, yet love in the end was more important. In actuality the love that is the one great original Thought, the Logos; is that which is completely beyond that which the word "love" can express and completely beyond that which the word "wisdom" can express. It is as though one were attempting to name that which can not be seen, held, heard or in any way imagined. Consequently, the first distortion, that distortion moving away from utter potentiality and utter peace and rest, is that freedom of will, employed first by the Creator Itself, to know Itself. In making this choice the Creator became, shall we say, the one great original Thought. It is more of a shift between potentiality and actuality or kinetic reality, shall we say.

However, from this Thought, which was love, there came into being that material which the Creator used to build Its universe, and that is light. Consequently, when we greet you in the love and in the light of the one infinite Creator, we are greeting you with the very stuff of the creation itself and placing ourselves, and you and all things, within this framework of all that is, which does indeed exist only in the sense that, as the one known as G was speaking earlier, the word "now" exists.

The creation may be thought of, in a way, as that moment in which all of time and all of space has its heartbeat of a moment. The illusion is that there is a vast march of consecutive moments, consecutive nows, that create years and decades and centuries and millennia and eons. It is just as useful, however, in terms of spiritual growth, to think of the momentariness or the circularity of time. For each of you is far from being a prisoner of space and time. Within your noonday perception it would appear that you have many limits; you are just this tall, just this wide, you have just these experiences, just this knowledge and just these actions to make up the passing of a normal day. Yet in reality, there is communication occurring, even in the daylight consciousness, between conscious and unconscious perceptions; between the limited consensual reality and the surrounding and permeating metaphysical reality that escapes the senses of the physical world but speaks very clearly to those great centers of knowledge and experience that lie deep within what this instrument would call the frontal lobes, that area which has such great strength and power to offer to the consensual reality self. So there is always, in any situation, a part of you that has escaped all of the limits that seem to hem you in. There is no time at which you are truly a prisoner of your body.

Certainly it may seem so. Certainly within each of the memories within this circle there live those times when the self was very limited, unable to move because perhaps a bone was broken and needed mending or there was an illness that laid one low and there was a need to recover quietly. There are many ways that an entity can feel limited and trammeled and yet, always, there exists that continuing communication with all of those forces of the creation which indwell each tiny speck and iota of creation; for all things are alive. That intelligence, which is light, is infinitely full of information and, as the physical vehicle of the self moves through the dance of the daily life, the interaction between that metaphysical side of self and the daylight self is continually going on. The communication can indeed be encouraged by the choices made by each of you. And the first of these choices, as the one known as G said, is simply to ask to be aware of the communication that is going on. Each asking alerts the unconscious and expresses to it a preference. The unconscious portion of self receiving this permission is then given strength. That is how faith builds upon itself, by using it as if it were a muscle. When muscles are not used they become flabby and, sooner or later, an unused muscle will atrophy and become dysfunctional. So it is with the power of faith, which, in a way, may be described as that certainty that there is communication between the seen and the unseen or perhaps more simply, that certainty in the unseen.

It is very possible to catch this as if it were a cold, by contact with other entities who have it. And that is why so often it is helpful for spiritually motivated people to gather in groups such as this one, to share the awareness that moves too deeply for words in the being of each and yet will not be denied. There is strength in a group of entities, all of whom have agreed to posit, as at least a possibility, the reality of there being greater, deeper, higher vistas, views and truths concerning the self than are immediately apparent [within an environment] that seems steeped in trivia, inanity, and folly. We are most pleased to see groups such as this one and may we say how powerful such groups are, not only to help each other within the group, although this is certainly the case, but also the energy created by a group such as this one as it seeks truly is as that light which lightens the darkness, that lighthouse which stands upon the promontory, blessing all with its guidance.

Our first point, then, is that free will is the first distortion because it is the first distortion, that distortion which made all the other distortions possible, which made creation possible, which made each of us and you here present, possible.

There is a second and equally profound thread of thought concerning this first distortion of free will. This entity worships in a Christian manner and within this particular mythological system there is a three-fold designation to Deity—the Father, the Son, and the Holy Spirit. One may gaze at the Father as the one great original Thought. One may gaze at the Son as that Thought made into something, that Thought made into light. One may gaze at the Holy Spirit as the personification of free will. These are not directly logical connections and we would not ask you to attempt, literally, to understand that which we are saying. We are simply attempting to show a kind of connection between the Christian way of thinking about the mystery of Deity and the similar construction within the so-called Law of One concerning that same mystery. When those within the Christian system, writing early in church history, were attempting to describe the Spirit, when the one known as Jesus was talking about the Spirit, there were similes to fire and to the wind, those things which are not controlled, those things which "bloweth as it listeth,"[65] the wind of spirit, the flame or fire of spirit, coming down into the crown chakra and down into the system of those who pray to that spirit. [They] are asking for the wind to blow them, for the fire to burn them; they are asking for transformation, they are asking for change, they are asking to be changed, and they are asking the agent of that change to visit them.

It is difficult to think of free will as that which must be asked for and yet it is important to move into a space within the self where one is able to lay all aside except the desire to know the truth. And in that place of utter humility and unknowing, in that stance of a person with empty hands waiting to receive, the request may be made for that enlivening, empowering Spirit that is free will. It is yours if you claim it. It is yours if you ask. Again, if you do not ask, if you do not claim it, little by little that muscle atrophies and it becomes more and more difficult to move with the winds of Spirit, to move into changes that are truly moving you towards the center of yourself, helping you to know more, and that more deeply, about yourself.

So one may look at this first distortion not simply as an unnamed wind or a random fire but as one's very own wind and fire. For the whole concept of guidance from the inner planes is wrapped up in that asking which is done by free will. One cannot drag oneself, reluctantly, to embrace transformation. It certainly can happen that way, for the energies of transformation are absolutely unstoppable. Evolution will occur automatically. It is just rather slow compared to the rate of change that is possible when an entity has decided to cooperate and to lean into the process of transformation.

Again and again it is necessary to come to the center of self with open hands, empty hands, full of unknowing, full of all of the colors that have painted your world within the last little while, whether those colors be bright and cheerful chintzes or deep purples and browns and blacks coming from difficult experiences. All of these gifts may be taken into that place and laid before the infinite One, so that you have empty hands, you have an open heart, and you are on your knees, in terms of being without pride, without arrogance, without the need to be sure or to be right. In that state you may ask that guidance system which is yours, that personification of free will which is yours, "What is the truth? Who am I? Why am I here? Whom shall I serve?"

And each time of asking is its own experience. Perhaps you shall not hear words. Perhaps you shall not have an experience that you can talk about; perhaps you shall. But those things that you ask, when you ask the Spirit, are far too deep for words. They move far beneath personality and that brittle shell of civilization and culture that are as the clothing that you wear in order to relate within this incarnation to those about you. And finally you stand naked, glorious in the beauty of the self, that self that is a spark of the one infinite Creator. And when you can stand there, or kneel there, content just to be you and to feel that yearning and that asking rise up, then truly have you offered the greatest gift to the Creator that you possibly could. For that Creator truly wishes to know you. And It can only know you as you know yourself. What It knows about you is that which It has already experienced. What It does not know about you is that which you have not experienced, that which you have not run into. It is as though within that so-seductive appearance of personality and face and body there lies an undiscovered country of enormous size, with mountains and plains and rivers and deep underground caverns, all of which are yours to explore. And that which is free will is your guide.

We believe that this is sufficient for this asking and consequently we would open the meeting at this

---

[65] *Holy Bible*, John 3:6-8: "That which is born of the flesh is flesh. And that which is born of the Spirit is spirit. Do not marvel that I said to you, 'You must be born anew.' The wind blows where it wills [in King James version, 'bloweth where it listeth'], and you hear the sound of it, but you do not know whence it comes or whither it goes; so it is with everyone who is born of the Spirit."

time to further questions, if there be any. Is there a query at this time?

J: Yes Q'uo, I have a query. Two weeks ago I asked you a question about DNA set ups and you told me that my designation was third and fourth-density set ups but not quite turned on. So I am asking your opinion about what I can do to turn that fourth-density connection on?

We are those of Q'uo, and we understand your query, my sister. The DNA of which you speak is affected by thought. Consequently, if, by the disciplining of the personality, an entity is able to begin to tune the heart to living in an open, loving, and vulnerable state, such as that state fourth-density entities [experience], the perceptions that come into the mind and that tell the body what is occurring are those perceptions which will automatically hook up that which is not hooked up within the DNA strands. The stimulus for the body is the mind; so in working with the mind to move from what this instrument would call mental thinking into heart oriented thinking, it is the movement from third-density to fourth-density thinking. As the heart is allowed to think and to be strong in moving into a major part of the process of perception, the body will follow, being a creature of the mind.

May we answer you further, my sister?

J: No, that's good.

We thank you, my sister. Is there another query at this time?

T: I have a query, Q'uo. I realize that the channeled meditation is mainly a metaphysical event, [and] my being at a physical distance[66] is probably not too important, but I was wondering whether there are any precautions or special preparations that would be useful for me to undertake so that I would not hinder the contact or cause any other difficulties?

We are those of Q'uo, and we grasp your query, my brother. We do not find that there is any concern necessary upon your part. Indeed, as you surmised, the physical location does not matter. We did find at one point in our discussion, when we were talking about the beauty of the lengthening shadows, that we became confused because we were also seeing the beauty of the morning, and we had to smile at our own version of being out-of-towners and not quite used to the experience of working with entities who are not in the same physical location. However, this was in no way a hindrance but rather for us something to chuckle at and enjoy. We are always learning from those within third density and once again we discover humor within your technology.

However, in terms of doing anything to better prepare for a contact with this group and with us, the process which this group goes through, of speaking around the circle, seems to be a very powerful and simple means of melding or combining the group so that it is indeed beating as with one heart and asking as with one soul. Consequently, we are pleased that you chose to join in the discussion beforehand and we feel that certainly, other than that, you bring to the group a great deal of light and we are most pleased that you are with us.

May we answer you further, my brother?

T: No, thank you Q'uo, that was very helpful, thank you very much.

We thank you, my brother.

G: Q'uo, I've discovered, with the aid of a reading I had through D, a pattern where I am bodily present, but a portion of my consciousness will evacuate in a moment in any conversation and I was wondering if you might have anything to offer me concerning how that pattern developed within me? Are there any techniques or exercises that I can utilize to stay present and to inhabit my body more fully?

We are those of Q'uo, and are aware of your query, my brother. In terms of the genesis of this particular mental distortion, it is, as in many cases, the far reaches of early childhood which must be moved into in order to see where the pattern has begun. It is quite understandable that when there is disharmony that is present at a level which is painful to experience, the choice of a sensitive entity, in order to protect the self, is to remove the self mentally from the circumstances, since it cannot do so physically. Certainly the processes of schooling and religious education create further times when it is desirable to put psychic distance between the self and situations which do not please the self for one reason or another. And this also has had its effect upon your personality shell.

---

[66] T sits as part of the group, which meets in Kentucky, from his home in Australia, by telephone link.

The pain which is being avoided is not a physical pain and yet, because of the sensitivity of the particular physical body that you have and its way of being connected to the mind, there is a habit that has been formed which is as the nervousness or tension that another might feel, say, at attempting to move through a door and being unable to get it open. It is a feeling of being closed in or frustrated and yet physically there is nowhere to go to get away from that feeling. Consequently, the trip must be taken mentally. And this habit has become somewhat regularized within your personality shell.

Now in terms of how to work with it, we would suggest that you be creative and start with the premise that you are operating with faulty software and that you need it re-written to some extent. How can one work with one's mental settings to change the default? That is the question! And we leave it to you, for this is your work to do. You have tools at your disposal. You have the dream work. You have meditation itself. You have prayer. You have many opportunities to connect with guidance, to connect with the guidance that is found in nature and so forth. All of these are at your disposal. We would also suggest the light touch, the gentle nudge, rather than a ruthless or full-scale-house-cleaning-type attempt to change the self. This is not the desirable way of dealing with the self. Rather, see the self as lovingly and as compassionately as a father would see his son or as a mother would see her baby. Ask the self, "What do you need?" And then see what you can do to …

(Side one of tape ends.)

(Carla channeling)

… satisfy those needs. If there is the need for solitude, cooperate with that need and enter into solitude passionately. If there are suggested to you other things that you may do or things that you may cease doing, follow your instincts, follow your heart, follow that guidance which comes to you.

May we answer you further, my brother?

G: No, that was excellent. Thank you for the most thorough answer, Q'uo.

We thank you, my brother. Your kind words make us a blush. Is there a final query at this time?

S: I have a question. I guess you've heard the story I told earlier. I've been looking for other thoughts, other opinions, other ideas about what is going on with me and my life. I would very much like to get your thoughts and ideas, what you see from your perspective.

We are those of Q'uo, and are aware of your query, my brother. From our perspective, my brother, we see beauty. We see strength and courage. We see deep humility. We see gentleness and yet at the same time we see strength. We would ask that you may see these things about yourself as well. See that beauty which is yours. Let that beauty light you and light your way. See the sweetness and the kindness and the gentleness that has been your gift throughout your incarnation. And let yourself feel that kindness, that gentleness, that sweetness. You need that for yourself at this time.

Picture yourself holding yourself as if you were a baby. Rock that baby, and rock that baby, and rock that baby again. And rock that baby all night if that baby is upset, because sometimes only human touch, only the human love of a parent can get a child through a cranky night. Perhaps we could say that we see you cutting new teeth, as children will do. It is a very painful process. One cannot move with one's normal comfort. One does not understand why it must hurt so badly because one is, after all, just a baby. We would say that this is the equivalent of that which has occurred within you. It is a natural process. It is a process that promises good growth and new "teeth." However it is a process that is most difficult to move through.

So we would ask that you nurture yourself. Realize, whenever you can, that there is a tremendous amount of love around you, not simply from friends such as these within this circle or from family but from a very extended family of those who are with you as guidance and simply those who are with you because they have been attracted to your goodness and to your seeking. This support system is strong to save and quick to respond, and we encourage you to use it. We, ourselves, are available at any time to give you a deeper meditation or a stronger feeling of presence. Lean into the help that is there and above all, believe in yourself, believe in this process, and know that each dark night ends with a beautiful sunrise.

May we answer you further, my brother?

S: I appreciate your kind words. I've even got some that you had spoken two years ago that I keep with me and read. I do appreciate the support and the kindness. From my perspective it's so hard to see, but thank you for now.

We thank you, my brother.

It is with profound gratitude that we say our goodbyes to this group. Thank you for the pleasure of your company. Thank you for sharing with us your hopes and your questions and allowing us to share with you as well. We leave each of you in the love and in the light of the one infinite Creator. Adonai. Adonai. ✸

L/L Research

L/L Research is a subsidiary of Rock Creek Research & Development Laboratories, Inc.

P.O. Box 5195
Louisville, KY 40255-0195

www.llresearch.org

Rock Creek is a non-profit corporation dedicated to discovering and sharing information which may aid in the spiritual evolution of humankind.

ABOUT THE CONTENTS OF THIS TRANSCRIPT: This telepathic channeling has been taken from transcriptions of the weekly study and meditation meetings of the Rock Creek Research & Development Laboratories and L/L Research. It is offered in the hope that it may be useful to you. As the Confederation entities always make a point of saying, please use your discrimination and judgment in assessing this material. If something rings true to you, fine. If something does not resonate, please leave it behind, for neither we nor those of the Confederation would wish to be a stumbling block for any.

© 2009 L/L Research

Special Meditation
November 13, 2003

Question from Y: The question today comes from Y, who asks: What do I need to do to have conscious contact, other than in sleep, with my higher self and channel the light beings who are assisting and others in this incarnation?

(Carla channeling)

We are those known to you as the principle of Q'uo, and we greet you in the love and in the light of the one infinite Creator in Whose service we are. It is our great delight to be with this group this afternoon. We thank each of you for setting aside that precious time that you have so little of within your incarnation for the sole purpose of seeking the truth. We are that vibration which has been called to this group by this question and this channel and we express our great gratitude to you for so calling us. It is our pleasure to share our opinion with you and we would ask but one thing, that being that you listen to those things which we have to say with the greatest care and discrimination, rejecting all of those things which do not seem correct to you and only embracing that truth which seems to resonate within your very heart and soul.

You ask this day what you can do to come into conscious awareness of the communication that is going on betwixt you and your guidance system, and all of those who cluster about you wishing to help as you move through your incarnational learning and service at this time. Perhaps, from the way that you have phrased your query, you already know, my brother, that you are in communication with your guidance and that it has already given you many gifts. So we feel that your question perhaps has two parts and we would address the more general part first, and that is that situation which already exists, and which it is possible that you may not have fully appreciated.

Within you there blooms a flower of great beauty, its petals moving towards the sun with great awareness and intelligence, its blossom opening and the work proceeding as your higher self had indeed hoped before your incarnation at this time. The gifts that you brought in with you into incarnation have brought you far, both in terms of the gifts of the personality shell, such as intelligence and sensitivity, and those gifts which are perhaps not so obvious to the outward eye, those gifts of inward intensity, deep searching, and a discontent with that which seems to be, all those things which appear. There is within you a great yearning for purity, that which is not a little of the light and a little of the dark but all together, that which has been lifted above the seeming muck and mire of consensus reality and some of its more shadowy aspects.

And yet we would assure you, my brother, that it is well planned that you observe, and to some degree, participate in that muck and mire, that stress and tension of consensus reality. For there is within you the incarnational lesson which is to be addressed, which has to do with working with that which this instrument calls the "shadow" side of self. In the yearning for purity, ofttimes that shadow side of self has this tendency to be separated in thought from the so-called "light" side of self, shall we say, that side which seeks purity, which loves the light, which is a creature of love, a creature of eternity, and which truly wishes to experience only that which is beautiful, true and honest. So much that you see seems to lack in this quality, so much in which you participate has its disappointments, as far as that judgmental and intellectual side of you goes. And yet, for what reason would a true seeker wish to put himself into close association with the darker side of life? What would encourage such an entity, before taking up an incarnation, to place this in his way? We do not answer this query. Rather, we leave it for you, for this is yours to ponder and yours to learn, little by little, as though you were in a maze or a puzzle and you were attempting to track your way out of the maze or to fulfill the pieces of the puzzle in such a way that the picture becomes whole.

Perhaps we like the latter simile better, for rather than seeming to escape the page of consensus reality, shall we say, by taking oneself out of the maze, rather, it is easier to see in the puzzle simile that you are simply putting the pieces together, not attempting to escape the puzzle but, rather, attempting to see it as a whole, in its entirety. As you work the pieces of the puzzle, in some cases you will be granted great light, in other cases you will be granted none and the puzzle will seem quite murky and difficult. It is then that the incarnational lesson comes directly into play. We may say about that lesson that it does involve the active use of the will, in the absence of proof, when there is a choice between that which is seen and is unacceptable, and that which is unseen and is acceptable. Within any incarnation, there are many times when a choice to believe or have faith in the entirety of self is to shift the way of attending to the self when it is seen as the shadow side of self, when it is seen as that part of self that is less perfect or less than perfect and therefore, less than desirable.

We cannot offer more clues than this. However, the general gist of that which we wish to offer here is that within that which has already occurred, within that which is now your present experience, there lie great gifts which have been given as a puzzle for you to solve, piece by piece, or as the maze for you to solve, one wrong direction after another discovered and turned back from in order to explore another way. May we say to you, especially in this regard, that it is never necessary to be at all discouraged or in any way to lack confidence. It is not the darkness of a night; it is not the depth of a suffering that reflects the degree of one's success at apprehending the catalyst that is offered. Indeed, the darker the night, the more difficult the experience, the more completely the incoming catalyst may have been received. What remains then is that subtle, complex and fascinating work of unlocking the self, opening the self to the self, piece by piece, step by step, within an inner atmosphere which partakes more and more of that trust and faith of which we were speaking earlier. That gift is one which has been offered you as part of your incarnational personality shell. You have within you already a gift for the use of the will, but is it for faith or is it for other sorts of seeking which rely more on the physical world than on the metaphysical? As you move back in mind through your childhood, through your early experiences, we simply ask you to cast your mind into those recurring themes of light and darkness, to begin to see that incarnational pattern that you have given yourself. You have many good clues, as this instrument would call them, many pieces of the puzzle. And we encourage you to move forward with confidence, self-assurance and a quietness of spirit that comes from a lack of striving. For what, my brother, is there against which to strive?

The second part of our response concerning conscious communication with that system of guidance which is yours is more literally connected with your question. We are aware that you would very much like to make some sort of positive, absolutely certain contact in the way that we are speaking to you through this instrument. In terms of that particular way of becoming more in touch with your guidance, we would recommend never attempting [the technique used] to come into conscious communication such as this instrument is now using, without the careful dedication of self for a fairly long period of training and a process of the initiation during which we, as members of Confederation, offer to those who wish to learn the channeling of spirit such as this instrument does, that which they wish to learn. It is impossible to say how long it would take, but we may say certainly that it is never a project which one may safely undertake alone. The strength of a group and the experience of a more seasoned channel are both necessary in order to regularize and protect the energies that are involved in communication such as we offer through this instrument at this time. We do not wish to be those who create fear, we are simply saying that because of the nature of the physical instrument that is your body and those linkages to the finer sensibilities of the energetic bodies, such communication is almost reliably guaranteed to, as this instrument would say, "come a cropper."[67]

The problem is a simple one, my brother. It is the problem of an entity who contains a powerful tool but who does not know how to use it. Attempting to learn to do what this instrument calls channel is like a toddler attempting to pick up a power tool, turn it on, and use it correctly. The chances for accident or disaster are high, and we would not in any way encourage such a rash and thoughtless method of attempting to gain contact. We do not suggest that you avoid it because you have no possibility of success. Quite the opposite. We suggest that you bate this desire in any outward verbal form because you have great possibility of success and yet without training, without a good long time of consideration and dedication of self—the practice, the self, and the life—the experience would be as that entity who wishes to tune to a certain radio station but yet who is incapable of moving the dial, so that the dial moves without your conscious ability to tune it, moving you from one source to another depending upon various situational details about which you cannot know and which cannot be taught but rather, can be learned without the words during the process of such initiation as that of which we speak.

Were you as an entity enough desirous of following this particular way of coming into conscious contact with guidance, there would need to be a geographical relocation, or at least the ability to visit within those areas where this instrument dwells and this group dwells, not once, but numerous times. Therefore, we might suggest that this be considered with great care and over a long period of time. For that which you would be asking of yourself would be that the life experience be dedicated, from beginning to end, from top to bottom, waking and sleeping, until the time that you separated from your physical vehicle. You would need to be able to dedicate yourself, your time, your essence, and your heart to living the life that you are learning from those things which are channeled to you and which you channel. This is the kind of responsibility that this particular outward expression of the gift of channeling requires in order that the self is protected.

There are, however, ways in which guidance may be sought that are far safer and far more able to be done on one's own than the formal gift of channeling. We begin with that which you mentioned first, the dreams. The dreamscape, as you are well aware, has tremendous gifts to offer the conscious self at a level of which very few entities are aware. When awake, that communication is ongoing. It is not stopped because an entity is conscious and working within the world. What has stopped is the awareness of that connection and that communication. However, the spirit portion of your entirety is quite aware of this communication, as is the body itself.

Let us look for a moment at the mind and the confusion that entities upon your planet have about this organ. There is a mind that came with your body. That mind is that which was created to make choices for survival. Call it the choice-maker. It thinks in terms, partially, of physical instinct, survival, the gathering of the things that are needed for survival, and so forth. The choice-making mind shall always look for advantage. It shall always look for that which is useful, functional, able to offer advantage. You are very familiar, all too familiar, with this mind. Few of those who are awake and aware of the nature of the spirit are very fond of the mind that is the choice-maker.

However, there is another kind of mind that exists within the same space, shall we say, within the same "gray matter"[68] as the mind of the body, and that is the mind of your heart. It is that portion of the mind that comes from the metaphysical side of the creation rather than the physical, from the time/space portion rather than the space/time portion of the creation of the Father. The mind of the heart is not bound by the need to survive, for it is eternal. It is not bound by the need for advantage, for it knows all things are one. That mind is, when allowed to be completely uncluttered, as free and full as is the universe itself; as aware, as gentle, as powerful, and as all-knowing. This mind has few or no words. There are many times when its nature suddenly springs forth and you are suddenly aware that your mind indeed has a consciousness that is

---

[67] To fall heavily or headlong; to come to ruin or to fail.

[68] The grayish nerve tissue of the brain and spinal cord.

eternal and that is not bound by those human fleshly desires and needs for advantage. Usually it is because you have come into the radiant aura of someone who is acting from the open heart. And, in one way or another, you see an entity that is loving and you catch it, you pick it up as if it were a communicable disease, which indeed it is. Like any other state of mind, the state of mind that is unconditional love communicates from one entity to another and it is through contact that most entities within incarnation begin to form their ideas about what it would be like to be a creature of soul, a creature of the spirit, an angel that is here on Earth, but is not of the Earth. Perhaps you have someone in mind that has been to you such a loving presence, that has given you that blessed aura in which the consciousness of your heart can come alive and communicate freely. Does not your heart soar within you when this occurs, when the fetters of earthly thinking fall away and the only horizon that is yours is the horizon of the highest and best that can be imagined by you?

In the dream state many things are offered to you. And we feel that you have some capability already in working with those images that are given to you within the dreams. We would encourage you within this work; it is excellent work. We would ask that you bear in mind that such work is not always literal. In fact, rarely is it completely literal. Usually the mind has a great deal of whimsy and humor in the way it puts together messages that it wishes for you to receive. So we would suggest that you not only look at the dreams, look at the images and so forth with an eye to what they say literally, but also we would suggest that you look at them sideways, as this instrument calls it, letting the brain sag in the middle and make connections that are not at all obvious or likely, and playing with those images that have been given you, looking for inner resonance and provocative images that turn you in a different direction in thought. These are part of that work of coming to understand the self that is very precious.

Further, we would discuss a second line of work which is very available to you as a person by yourself. That is the work of the meditation. My brother, when we say meditation, we do not define that word to suggest that there is a best way in which to meditate. When we use that word, we are meaning to indicate simply a turning to the silence within. When you turn within, you may silence the outside world by ignoring it, but the first stumbling block for most entities in meditation is that the inner self is not silent but rather it continues its habitual discussion with itself. We cannot help you through this except by encouraging you to ignore that conversation just as you are ignoring the catalyst coming in through the ears and the other senses from the outside world while you meditate. It is not a matter of turning the back upon oneself. Rather, it is a matter of allowing all thoughts to arise and then allowing them to die away in their own time, not giving them energy, not ignoring them, but sitting with them, observing them as part of what is occurring within the self. Without their being given energy, they will by their very nature die away. It is interesting as you work with the silence within to see those thoughts that arise not once, or twice, but again and again. One may look at these, not within the meditation but at other times. When you are contemplating the thoughts of the day, you may look at those patterns of thought that habitually arise when the mind starts talking. As you begin to see the patterns of your concerns, you begin to see into that nature within you that is emotional, and that has antennae that have been created to stick out into the world, both within and without, to sense when a particular catalyst is coming towards that antennae. When that antenna finds that it is triggered, that antennae begins its work of tracking that thought.

What antennae do you have, my brother? Where are the triggers that move you from your silent, infinite self back into the world in which you must make choices, in which there is fear and in which one must defend and find an advantage? It is those triggers, when identified, that you may then work on in a conscious manner, consciously doing the work of disciplining the personality so that it begins to recognize, to accept, and to smile at those triggers that would plunge the soul within into that dailyness and everyday world, which is the world of fear and desire. In meditation, in the silence, you move beyond fear and beyond any desire except for that utter focus upon the truth. The seeking that is at the heart of you can then be allowed to have its beingness. And as that seeking is allowed, in the place where desire and fear were before, that focused, inner self becomes an asking, a desiring, a yearning, and a question. Yet that question is within eternity and the answers that come in that muscular, strong silence are the answers of eternity and infinity, moving deeply beneath any possibility of words, moving into the heart of self, the essence, the pith of that part which is as the truest part of you.

It is as though you came into incarnation with a treasure trove inside you, within which lies infinite life, eternal life, complete truth and utter oneness with all things. It is not locked against thieves from the outside. Rather, it is locked against casual entry by yourself. Perhaps you have heard the old saying that there are always guardians at the gate of any temple. You have found an excellent guardian at the gates of the temple of your heart that guards against casual intrusion, shallow caring, incomplete dedication; that guards that which is you in a truer and less fettered state but which does not have form, from that within which partakes of form in your thought processes, that is the choice-making mind, being part of that which is attempting to gain entry into the sanctum sanctorum of your own heart, this treasure trove within in which the Creator awaits. Consequently, as you come into the silence, empty the self, open the self, and allow the self to become utterly humble, utterly quiet. Assume that pose of the one who waits. And listen, my brother, to that silence with all your attention. This is easier said than done and certainly this instrument would say that she is still very poor at practicing the gifts of meditation. Yet the attempt to do such in a purer way is that which gains the ground, that which makes the progress, for so much of the metaphysical process is based in intent rather than in any perceived achievement.

Further, when a practice of meditation has been established in a way that is satisfactory to you yourself, it is entirely possible for you to dedicate a time to what this instrument would call conscious journaling. Perhaps you may be familiar with this method of seeking. It is one in which you either write that which comes to you or in which you write down a question and then let your pen begin to write as if you knew the answer. Little by little you may find with this way of conscious journaling that you are beginning to be able to hear those inner voices of guidance within you that would wish to speak.

The only suggestion that we would have in order to safeguard you during these times is that you not use them in working with other entities but use them only for your own growth and your own learning. For as they are part of your inner guidance, they are privileged information for you. It is a very intimate and personal connection that you have with guidance and it is not that which would give guidance to others. Were you to begin giving guidance to others with your own personal guidance, then there would come to be a difficultly with infringing upon the free will of others and offering information that was not, shall we say, tailor-made for them but rather for yourself. Therefore, offering it to others is offering it through distortion which was not intended by the guidance that gave it.

We hope that we have explained the difficulty here, for it is a subtle one. But it does have to do with the free will of all and the very intensely personal nature of truth. Your creation is yours alone. In a way, all is one; but in the way of learning and teaching, each entity has its own creation. Each who sits in this circle has its own creation and the rules, the study, the progress, the evolution of each of you is unique. You cannot transfer truth, wisdom and perfection as perceived by one person, whole and complete, to another entity. One can only move up from one's essence to the level of words, to that level which is so shallow and frustrating and, by open communication, share those gifts which have been yours to receive without any attachment as to whether any other soul appreciates or responds to that same information.

My brother, we believe that this is the extent to which we would wish to speak upon that main question. May we ask at this time if you would like to follow up with another query or if you have another question at this time?

Y: Thank you for your guidance. What advice can you give me about my physical problems—my stomach, my back, and my emotional problems?

We are those of Q'uo, and we are aware of your query, my brother. We make this instrument smile, for she also has her stomach, her back, and her emotions in common with yours. They are not doing her their best, shall we say, either and yet somehow we shall speak to the both of you.

In the matter of physical ailments, the body is always the creature of the mind. Certainly this instrument has done a good deal of work, moving back into the early days of her incarnation and discovering those threads of fear and crassness and roughness that, even before this entity was born, created for her a disgust of the ways of thinking that exist within consensus reality, or the outside world as you know it. Let us say simply that it is well to become aware of the self as an entity which has come into an environment with which it is not particularly familiar and in which it is not comfortable. The choice to come into this arena of catalyst and choice was a heartfelt one and it came from a desire to serve; and so you and this instrument and many others have come through the densities, knocking at the door of third-density incarnation asking to serve, asking to walk among those native to third density on planet Earth at this time in order to do all that you may, in your humble way, to join in the response that you truly felt to the suffering of the planet Earth and of its people. A call had gone out, you see, not simply today, but for millennia. As this seventy-five-thousand year cycle, that has been talked about often in this group, was coming to its end, the cry was going out from those of planet Earth and from the planet itself, a cry of suffering and sorrow, a cry of seeking and hoping; and it is in response to the suffering of Earth that you decided to apply for the privilege of incarnation in what this entity who channels would call the "heart of the beast,"[69] the crowded byways of your globe in which the business of humankind has for so long included trauma, hardship, war, disease and suffering of all kinds.

You yearned to help. You examined what could be done without coming into incarnation and you were not satisfied. You truly wished to make a difference, as did this instrument, as did all those within the circle, and you knew that you could not make that difference unless you had the right to it by birth. And so you took birth. You were born into this situation, this environment, which does not agree with your sensitive nature any more than it agrees with the one known as G, with the one known as Carla, with the one known as V, or with the one known as J. None of those within this circle find it comfortable to experience life as it comes to them from the everyday experience of untuned conversation with others and the everyday, workaday world. It is that mismatch of vibrations that is the root cause of the difficulties that you now feel.

It is well to examine those areas in which you have discussed feeling discomfort. The area of the stomach is that area of orange and yellow chakra energy in which personal relationships and interactions with groups such as family and jobs are experienced. As you sit at the end of the day, it is very helpful to look back upon those things which have moved you one way or the other during that day, which tightened your stomach, which tightened your shoulders and your back, which made your emotions tighten up. In all of these contracting energies lies fear. Where have you picked up that fear? Where are the threads of that fear? That is for you to examine and to probe. And we may say that in some cases, entities have chosen the recurring of physical symptoms to nudge them back on a track towards the inner life during times when they have taken on inappropriate amounts of physical work. In this instrument's case, this instrument often will take on physical work because the instrument, unconsciously or consciously, realizes how much easier it is to do something in the outer world than it is to turn within and seek service in that way. The instrument has been raised in an atmosphere of the work ethic and perhaps you also share in that prejudice towards rejoicing in those things that are done, those items that may be checked off of the list of chores, the list of duties. And yet many chores and duties are those things that lie within, that take time and delicacy of thought to plumb, even to begin to understand. So we would suggest the evening discipline of moving through the thoughts of the day and seeing how the self is reacting, seeing what is causing those contractions. For every contraction is that which we would call fear. It is the opposite of that expansiveness, that radiancy which is light. When there is no fear, and there is only love, then the energy body is flowing completely. When there is a contraction in any of the chakras, then that infinite light of the Creator that always is flowing through one begins to find its way trammeled, blocked or partially blocked. This in turn communicates itself to the body so that, if the emotional self has not been able to open the heart, then the physical body will express the imbalance that the mental bodies were not able to work out. When you see physical illness or conditions that do not seem propitious, think of those as the last stand, the last way that your system has of expressing, "Stop. Look. Listen. Think about this, for there is imbalance here."

May we answer you further, my brother?

(Pause)

---

[69] A vaguely Biblical term implying that the earth is a place seemingly ruled by evil.

We are those of Q'uo, and we do not perceive that there is a further query, my brother. Is there a final query at this time?

Y: Yes, there is a final query. What is, if you can tell me, my connection to the sacred place known as the Dome of the Rock?

We are aware of your query, my brother, and we find that we cannot speak upon this subject, that it would interfere with your learning processes at this time. However, we do feel that you are, shall we say, on to something and would encourage you to move into that perceived feeling of connection to see where it might take you. For this is indeed promising in your process at this time.

My brother, it has been our great pleasure to speak with you and we are just sorry that the energy does wane at this time. We thank you for the privilege of speaking with you and for sharing the energy of this group. We would leave you, with all of our blessing, in the love and in the light of the one infinite Creator.

Y: Thank you.

We are those of Q'uo. Adonai. Adonai.

Sunday Meditation
November 16, 2003

Group question: Q'uo, our question today concerns the eternal present moment. A human author[70] urges us to access the power of now. He states that in the present, suffering cannot exist because suffering depends on time. We are told, time and time again, that time is an illusion. So we would like to know what exactly is the "power of now"? How can we gain access to that power? How can we live more and more in the moment? How can we realize that we are creatures of the moment? What does the present moment look like to one that has discovered it? What results can be expected in a seeker who indeed has discovered the present moment?

(Carla channeling)

We are those of the principle known to you as Q'uo, and we greet you in the love and in the light of the one infinite Creator, in Whose service we are happy to be and in Whose service we come to you today. We thank you so much for calling us to your circle of seeking by your desire to seek the truth. It is a great honor to us to be asked for our opinion and indeed it is our method of service at this time. So it is a great help to us to be able to speak with you since that is our method of service to others. It is a very precious thing to us and we shall do our best to share thoughts with you that will be helpful. However, in order for us to be able to speak freely, we would ask of you, as always, that each of you employ your discrimination very carefully in listening to those things which we have to suggest. For we are in every case not those of authority but those who are as you, students and seekers of the truth, of that great mystery. We do not know the mystery but we seek it as do you and we are glad to offer our notes from the road with the understanding that you will take only those things which are fair to you and leave behind without a second thought anything that does not sound just right. For truly each of you can recognize and resonate with your own personal truth.

You ask this evening concerning the present moment, the now, and how it may be discovered, recognized, entered, enjoyed, appreciated and, above all perhaps, how it may be learned from. In order to speak about this interesting subject we would begin with some thoughts regarding time itself.

The illusion of time is that which allows your experience to occur within your being. Without the illusion of time and space, without the structure that the Creator has built for your particular body, mind and spirit to dwell in, you would not be able to process catalyst into experience. You would indeed not have catalyst, you would simply be. This is in fact your true state. You are, period. It is not that you are a human or that you are a soul or that you are any quality or condition, you are a part of all that is. You are an Is-ness. It is very difficult for us to

---

[70] Eckhart Tolle, in his book, *The Power of Now; A Guide to Spiritual Enlightenment*: Novato, CA, New World Library, [c1999].

express this concept through words. But beneath all movement, you already and eternally are.

Since that sounds like such a delightful state, one wonders perhaps why the Creator would indeed create a house, such as the universe which you enjoy, which is nothing but an illusion, or a system of illusions that are interpenetrating. The reason is that about which we were speaking recently, that first distortion of free will. The Creator chose to know Itself. And in order to know Itself, It created, with love and with light, a creation in which entities could examine whatever of the material of their essence or Is-ness that they wished to examine, against a backdrop that seemed plausible and solid so that there would be a believable, self-correcting, consensus-reality dream in which all of those within a planetary system, such as yours, could take part and help each other to learn more about that entity which all of you are or which each of you is. For, again this is difficult to say. While each of you is utterly unique, at the same time each of you is a part of one energy system which is the Creator. You are in the process of learning from your inner self with the help of your outer or other selves.

The world, then, may be seen as a dream, as a kingdom, or as a prison. But certainly your physical world, though an illusion, is quite solid, quite substantial, and quite believable. Without time, you would not be able to have the experience of consecutivity; you would not be born, live and die, rather you would exist in a being born, dying and everything-in-between-state, all in a big soup. The desire of the Creator was that hope of becoming a fuller, more richly realized beingness. There was a dedication of the principle of Godhead to an examination of self, a celebration of self, and a learning about self.

Each of you, then, is a spark of that Creator Who has chosen at this time to come into this particular environment of what this instrument calls third density, to live in incarnation amongst others of your kind, being mirrors for others, to reflect to them that truth which they offer you, seeing the mirrors of others that reflect the truth of you back to yourself, and, through all of the mazes and mirrors, beginning to come to a competency of understanding regarding the nature of the illusion that allows you, as a spirit who is seeking the truth, to penetrate more and more that which is not of the essence of self; so that more and more, you are able to take life lightly, to remove from the self the feeling of prison and to replace that with the feeling of the dream or of the kingdom.

There are many ways to lose that feeling of being a slave to time or being imprisoned within time and space. We certainly recommend meditation, as always, but there are many ways to shake the trammels of the noon-day thoughts and chores and businesses in order to lift up from that mental narrowness of thought that does not remember who you are or why you are here. It is very easy to be caught up in the never-ending series of lists, as the one known as T1 was seeing; the doing of things on a daily basis, as the one known as Jim was saying to this instrument earlier, the never ending mountain of chores to be done and duties to be fulfilled. How easy it is to become completely convinced that these are the building blocks of a complete existence! Yet, in and of themselves, there is no real substance or meaning in these things. There is simply that structure which allows experience. Without further seeking, then, the world may seem a kind of prison where the sentence is life and the eventual sentence is death. One cannot escape the life except by the door of death and when one escapes by that door, as far as those remaining can see, that entity has become nothing, dust has returned to dust and the cycle of life and death is completed.

And so for the first cycle of seeking, shall we say, there is that tendency for the new seeker to begin to feel that life is a dream. There is that realization that these seemingly solid building blocks of chores and days and seasons are not substantial. And there is a tremendous feeling of relief and freedom of the lifting up from having to take the work time, the chore time, the time of duties, too seriously. Within one of your philosophical distortions there is that phrase, "First there is a mountain, then there is no mountain, then there is." The time of experiencing life as a dream within a dream is that time when there is no mountain. It is a time when sudden realizations and new information may create tremendous excitement within the self and a time when the dark night of the soul can plunge one into the abyss of the deepest sorrow and grief, and yet always with the feeling that one is actually a spirit rather than a body and that one is experiencing a dream and that nothing is terribly important. It is a precious time in many ways and much good comes from the seeking that is done during this time.

Beyond that time, there comes a time of reintegration, the dream and prison coming together to form a new picture, which is that of the kingdom, a realm, a magical place. We find that this is where many of you within this circle are attempting to live at this time and we commend you for having moved along the path of seeking, through so many bends and curves and difficulties in the road, that your spiritual maturity has begun to allow you to see the riches of the illusion, the tremendous richness of the environment that has been provided for this school of life that you experience during incarnation. It is a time when the bitterness begins to dissolve. There is no longer anger at having to work for a living or feed the body or cleanse the body or take of the environment that one has chosen. The prison doors open because there is freedom to see the blessing of everything. There is no need to justify suffering and duty and all of the unpleasantness of life because it is finally seen not as that which limits and narrows the light, not as that which may be attended to but not taken seriously, but that which has been given as a tremendous gift, each gift, each moment coming fresh from the Creator. That is the time of kingdom. That is the time of jubilee. And it is truly the first place, shall we say, within the mind from which a point of view may be taken that has great depth, so that you may survive those realizations which shall come when you have become unafraid of the prison and unafraid of the dream.

Most entities among your peoples live a kind of inner life that we would describe as horizontal. The world of things spreads out like the skyline, full of detail. And it is that within which one lives. One drives the streets, one walks the sidewalks, one moves horizontally along the face of the planet. To all illusory intents and purposes, it is a flat existence. If that horizontal life were called the x-axis, then the world of spirit could be seen as the y-axis, the vertical life. Imagine standing upon the ground, seeing with the physical eyes that it extends flat in each direction, horizontally as far as the eye can see. The feet meet the ground in just so and so a place. There is contact between the soles of the feet and the ground. And that thin meeting place represents the depth of reality. But imagine suddenly realizing that precisely where the sole of the foot meets the ground there is an infinite opening, upwards and downwards; upwards into the world of ideals, guidance, godhead; downward into the ground of being. It is as though chasms open beneath you and above you and suddenly you are not standing upon a thin slab of ground but upon the razor's edge, in intersection with eternity and infinity.

This is in fact, your situation. You are in the position of being able to live both a life in space/time, the horizontal life, and a life in time/space, the vertical life, simultaneously. We might say that the ability to remember this image, the ability to remember that which is unseen, that which opens to the Creator and to the essential self, is a measure of how well you are doing with the simple act of remembrance that is the key in many ways to progressing in spiritual, mental and physical evolution of self. How to remember that what you see is not all that you get? How to remember the intersection with wonder and magic and infinite possibility? This instrument pursues a daily and weekly spiritual or religious program which includes group worship within that distortion of spirituality called Christian. This is one way in which she attempts to be a creature of remembrance. There are many ways to be remembering who you are and why you're here. That is one way, the simple act of setting aside time, such as you have this day, to seek together. No matter how the meditation goes, no matter how you feel that you have been as a part of a seeking circle, the intention, the dedication of time, are the things that create the feeling of remembering and honoring the portion of yourself that is living that vertical life. In moments such as this, as you allow the energy to move around the circle, we feel sure that each of you has that riveted feeling of opening to the infinite possibilities of the moment.

But there are, as the one known as T2 said, so many different ways of coming into a state of remembrance. Each of you has five senses in the physical. The example that the one known T2 gave of washing the hands and becoming aware of each characteristic and nuance of feeling in that experience operates on the principle of using the gifts that are given to you. Each sense is evocative. Each sensibility may be triggered, tuned and even transformed by choosing to be alert, to be watchful, to be attentive, to pay attention to the little things. This instrument is fond of saying, the smaller the thing, the more common and everyday, the more sacred it seems [to her]. And while we find everything equally sacred, we understand what this instrument is attempting to express. Consider that act of washing the hands, of emptying the bowels and rising from that natural function to wash the hands and to go forth to meet the day. It must be done every day, perhaps more than once but certainly in the morning. For each of you this is a life sentence of natural function that must be attended to for the sake of the body. But that is a heavy energy, that is a grudging life when one "has" to perform natural functions. However, if one enters into those natural functions and the natural ways of cleanliness and preparing for the day with every sense awake, each humble, necessary chore can become a symbol, in the physical, of processes which are moving on within the inner being, processes that move from nuance to nuance and half tone to half tint. And the ability to enter into the joy of removing the old from the system and clearing it for the day and then rising and washing the hands and blessing that event, experiencing that magical flow of water as it cleanses, experiencing all the feelings that are attendant upon the cleansing: the pleasant smell, the texture of soap, the texture of the towel; attending to each of these to see the beauty in them, softens and gentles the harsh edges of necessity into things of unutterable beauty. And as each tiny thing begins to become open to that view, the sacrededness of things emerges and lifts one up into the glory of the illusion of incarnation. Each moment is a bounty, a feast, a banquet. It is brimming with information, it is whole and perfect and one. The only way to come into that sense of consciousness is to learn the attentiveness to the sacredness of everyday things.

Within a sacred space, with altars and pews and vaulted ceilings and stained glass windows, it is easy to feel that one is in a sacred place. Yet every child of dust within the illusion of earth stands on holy ground, whether they are starving or fed, whether they are cold or clothed, whether they are sick or healthy. No matter what state or condition they may be in they stand upon holy ground and they themselves are holy. And you, child of dust, also are infinitely, ineffably, holy. You are a sacred essence of the divine.

How may one begin to experience this point of view? In some ways it becomes a matter of sheer discipline. There is a certain amount of what this instrument would call struggle involved in training the mind to come into a state of remembrance. There is much help which is available to those who wish to become present. And it is indeed a noble task to set for the self, to become present. It is not that one wishes to be without a context. We do not call you away from the world, we do not look down upon any part of the life lived by the ordinary human being. We do not suggest the need for retreat and alteration of the outer circumstances. Certainly, times of quiet, such as the one as T1 has described, are extraordinarily helpful. When there is the sabbatical there is the opportunity to take stock, to express the self as a seeking entity rather than as one who must attend to the ordinary challenges of making a living and coping with the financial side of life. And yet life for the most part is lived in the hurly-burly, in the spotlight of the passion play[71], as the scenes upon the stage revolve.

We give this instrument a view of a complete lack of location. Picture, if you would, the sensation of weightlessness, of lack of input into any of the senses. Lifted from the constant contact with the senses, one is left within a kingdom which is within. Within that inner kingdom of self lies the truth and a great deal of distortion. Where did this distortion come from? An entity is born into incarnation with certain preconceived distortions already. Each of you has chosen a personality shell that is rich in gifts and in challenges. Each of you has scripted for yourself incarnational lessons which will occur thematically, repeatedly, during the incarnation, teaching you the lessons that you have chosen and offering you the opportunities of service which you have hoped for. In this inner life no mirrors exist and it is exponentially more difficult to see the self clearly than when one is receiving information from the mirrors around one. So, while we value time spent in a completely inner search, we feel that the more efficient path, in terms of the rapidness with which evolution may occur, is an environment in which the inner life and the outer life marry. Rather than fighting and dividing inner life from outer life and struggling to get more inner life, we would suggest every way which you may think of personally to stamp the outer with the inner and to relate the inner into the outer, making every connection that you can, so that all of experience becomes one and the physical and the metaphysical become a dance

---

[71] The instrument was drawing from an album by Jethro Tull, called *Passion Play*, in which the suggestion was that we are all living our own "passion play." In medieval English literature, a passion play is defined as "a mystery play representing the passion of Jesus."

for two that carries both the male and the female aspect of living within one consciousness.

By male and female aspects of living, we are, in our distortion, suggesting that the outer or horizontal life is masculine, or "yang" as this instrument would say, in its activity, its reaching, its power to do, whereas that inner vertical life is as the potentiator, that which awaits the reaching, that which does not have the form but which is productive of all form, that which may be called guidance or inspiration or infinity or eternity. To allow the infinite and the eternal to become a part of the passing scene and to allow the passing scene to become stamped with infinity and eternity is to make that marriage within the life of those aspects which otherwise might fight for dominance. We assure you it is not at all easy to do this, it is much easier to compartmentalize and to do the spiritual practice and to move into the daily mode and then back into a spiritual practice and back into the daily mode. Yet we may say the fewer transitions that you must choose to make, the more often that you are able to blend the inner and the outer being, the more substantial will be your stance, and your point of view will benefit from this unification of inner and outer living.

What is the essence of you? That is the question, you see, and the answer is so simple. You are. You are not creating yourself, you are simply discovering the self that is there. You do not choose from nothing, you came into this incarnation a very real citizen of eternity. You are simply peeling away layers of distortion to see yourself clearer and clearer, to have a deeper and deeper sense of your own essence. It is a fascinating journey and we are so glad to have you as companions upon it.

This instrument is informing us that we have spoken long enough upon this most fascinating subject and we bow to her wisdom. We confess that in this particular case we could go on talking for quite a while, for this is a beautiful subject and we thank you for asking [about it]. But at this time we do relinquish this subject and ask if there may be other queries that we may respond to at this time?

V: Q'uo, you've spoken before about the use of the imagination to discipline rogue energies in the personality and I wonder if you would expound on that some, and specifically with regard to affirmations and why it would be so necessary to state affirmations aloud or write them down, to externalize them in some form in order to make manifestation possible?

We are those of Q'uo and we grasp your query, my sister. Perhaps you are aware of the kind of personality which thinks repeatedly about doing something but does not do it. All the thinking in the world is not productive, in terms of creating something in the consensus-reality universe, without action. In the case of making affirmations, the disciplined soul may well be able to make affirmations within the mind without writing them down and having them become "real" things; such is the power of the disciplined personality. However, for the soul who is attempting to become more disciplined, it is well to marry, again to use that simile, the inner intention with the outer fact, to make from the inner dream the outer reality. The act of writing on paper or speaking into the ether where sound may be heard is the act of putting inner vibration into the outer vibration and blending, or marrying, the two. You are aware, my sister, of the old adage, "As above, so below." The idea of externalizing these affirmations is the idea of bringing them into reality. It is an interesting thing that it is more easy to believe in the self when one can see the words that one has written and when one can repeat them and hear the sound.

May we answer you further, my sister?

V: Yes. Actually, I would like to ask about the discipline of the personality and a thought that I had the other day regarding what my mother used to say to me which was, "Guard your tongue." It occurred to me that, in fact, what the discipline is about is guarding the thoughts and creating the truth within you that says, "I see the beauty, I see the perfection," rather than looking at it and seeing the cynicism and only expressing the beauty. Could you illuminate that for me?

My sister, we feel that you have illuminated it very well. The only thing that we could add is an encouragement to play with this awareness that you are a creator, a co-creator and that, as you think, as you actually begin to train yourself to think, you do not narrow that which you comprehend. You are as able to see the thoughts of cynicism, sarcasm, anger and so forth as you were before, perhaps more able. What you are doing as you use the discipline is shaping your heart or— we correct this instrument—shaping your mind to be able to contain the thoughts of the heart, rather than simply the thoughts of the mind. It is not incorrect, we feel, to be aware of the ridiculousness, the sorry-ness or the wretchedness of any particular situation. It is not wrong to have sarcastic thoughts or to react naturally, and fervently even, to those things which make one uncomfortable or create catalyst. The heart, however, thinks substantially differently from the mind, the thoughts of the heart coming from that vertical part of living, that time/space or metaphysical portion where the thoughts are the thoughts beyond incarnation, beyond circumstance or estate. Those thoughts are the thoughts of the infinite being that you are. They are the thoughts of the consciousness within and that consciousness is safe within your heart. It is a matter of opening your own doors into that heart, sitting there and gazing from that heart out into the world. One still may have all of the inner opportunities for making the self laugh to the self with cynical thoughts, such as this instrument does as a hobby, we should say! But allowing the shape of the heart's thoughts to be the shape of the thought as it evolves in the awareness of the inner self gives one grace and distance and remembrance of who you are, so that your expression, even to the self, is a kinder and gentler thing. And certainly the expression to the outer world carries with it that maturity of thought that keeps that heart open and does not consider the imperfection of things as a reason to lose faith or to become embittered.

May we answer you further, my sister?

V: If you are so inclined, I would love for you to answer further but I don't have a further query so I'll pass it to T1.

T1: I've been reading a lot of the material channeled by the Seth entity and one of the constructs that is causing some confusion in myself is that of probable realities. The choice. Seth indicates that in each decision in this incarnation there are infinite other versions of the illusion in which other decisions were made. The teachings of the Confederation state that the aim of third density is the choice [of] service-to-others or service-to-self. Which [choice] one has made is due to [one's] polarity. Taking these two together, probable realities and choice, it seems that the choice is made separately and differently by each probable self projected by the soul. Perhaps I'm just wrapping myself up in constructs here and becoming confused but is there a way which Q'uo perhaps could untangle some of my thought processes there?

We are those of Q'uo and aware of your query, my brother. Indeed, we do not know if we are able to untangle your thoughts but we are glad to share ours with you and in their own tangle, my brother, the self is a concept which understandably within humans is limited and defined by the shape of the physical body and the inevitable flowing forward of sequential time. At each decision point, at each fork in the road, the choice of which fork to take obviously creates a different probable reality than the one that would occur if the other fork in the road were taken. However, perhaps it may clear this up for you a bit to contemplate that whichever fork in the road that one takes one is still equipped with the same incarnational lessons, the same things upon the scroll of life, that will come up repeatedly, so that it is impossible to avoid one's plan. Certainly, one may see that there are widely divergent paths and the tuning song that this group enjoyed this day asks that question, "Is there any other way I could have lived but this one? Is there anybody else I could have been?"[72] Certainly there are other choices that could have been made, but would the person that made those choices have turned out differently, or would those same choices have appeared no matter what road was taken?

In the physical life you walk down paths and turn corners and there is a new place. Turn another corner and there is another new place. Living the vertical life of which we have been speaking, the path is a spiral weaving always around and always anew; not the circle that becomes old, for every time that these themes come around again you are approaching them from a new standpoint, from a new place in your process, a new state of realization.

May we answer you further, my brother?

T1: No, thank you Q'uo. I think I need to read through and think about the explanation that you offered, thank you.

---

[72] From the Dave Matthews Band album, *Under the Table and Dreaming*, the song, "Dancing Nancies": "Could I have been/Could I have been/A millionaire in Bel Air/Could I have been/Lost somewhere in Paris/Could I have been/Your little brother/Could I have been/Anyone other than me/Could I have been/Anyone other than me/Could I have been/Anyone other than me/Could I have been /Anyone"

We thank you, my brother. Is there another query at this time?

G: Q'uo, you have often described the process of coming into that relationship with that self, that undiscovered self beyond the personality, of accessing those deep stores of self-knowledge, as a process of "courting" the subconscious mind. My question is: how does one go about, as you say, "wooing" that lover, and courting the subconscious in order to retrieve that needed information and to create that authentic contact with love and with light and with the Creator?

We are those of Q'uo and are aware of your query, my brother. Each lover must woo in its own way. Let us consider the object of love here. That object of seeking is the self within. It awaits the reaching in the archetypical manner of the Matrix and the Potentiator. The self within is as the unread book, the unknown mystery. In the archetypical tarot images, that is pictured as the woman who is veiled. One can barely see the book of wisdom that she holds at her heart. You are attempting to lift the veil from that book of self. How would you court that self within? We have at times suggested to you to think of that not as courting but as parenting, as if the self within were a child that needed comforting so that you take that self within and rock it and ask it what it needs, what its dreams are, what its hopes are, and then spend time listening to that self.

The ways of courtship are slow and sweet, they are full of passion and yet full of restraint, for the object of love is sensitive, young, inexperienced. And certainly as an essence, living within consensus reality, your hearts are indeed innocent babes in a wicked world. So there are the hints that we give you. It is not seeking as a man seeks a woman and yet it is, in that there is passion, there is true love, and there is the hope of serving.

Find the ways that your own inner self wishes to express itself. Is it walking in nature? Is it filling your mind with great music or great words? Is it the act of service? We find within this instrument's mind an example from earlier this day as she was speaking with the one known as Jim and he was expressing to her how he feels grateful for the opportunity to cut and trim the lawn of the client so that he creates a place of beauty and as he leaves, he looks back over his shoulder with great affection and pride because he has loved that place and danced with the love that is in that place. Perhaps that undiscovered country within you is a place that you may love and that you may dance with and in.

May we answer you further, my brother?

G: No, that was beautiful, thank you Q'uo.

We thank you, my brother. Is there a final query at this time?

G: Q'uo, I'll take the opportunity if no one else does. I have an e-mail that has the potential to create great change sitting in the pending file and I know you can't offer me advice on right or wrong, because there is no wrong, no mistakes, but could you help, give me some info, offer me some advice on what I might consider before I send it and what it might do to the energy configurations between me and this distant person?

My brother, we are aware of your query and find ourselves full up against the stop of free will. We can give this instrument the image of one of her favorite sayings from the Psalms concerning the entity whom everyone thought was a fool until he opened his mouth and removed all doubt.[73] Every word spoken changes the shape of your world. Look at each word for its truth, its compassion, and its service.

We are those of Q'uo. It has been enormously pleasureful to us to speak to you. We find the beauty of your seeking most delightful and we thank each of you for that beauty that you share with us so freely. The energy exchange has been most salubrious for us. We leave you in peace. We leave you empowered with hope, with the awareness of your own magical natures. We leave you in the love and in the light of the one infinite Creator and of each other. We are those of Q'uo. Adonai, my friends, Adonai. ☙

---

[73] This quote is actually from the *Holy Bible*, the Book of Proverbs 17:27-28: "He who restrains his words has knowledge, and he who has a cool spirit is a man of understanding. Even a fool who keeps silent is considered wise; when he closes his lips, he is deemed intelligent."

L/L Research

L/L Research is a subsidiary of Rock Creek Research & Development Laboratories, Inc.

P.O. Box 5195
Louisville, KY 40255-0195

www.llresearch.org

Rock Creek is a non-profit corporation dedicated to discovering and sharing information which may aid in the spiritual evolution of humankind.

ABOUT THE CONTENTS OF THIS TRANSCRIPT: This telepathic channeling has been taken from transcriptions of the weekly study and meditation meetings of the Rock Creek Research & Development Laboratories and L/L Research. It is offered in the hope that it may be useful to you. As the Confederation entities always make a point of saying, please use your discrimination and judgment in assessing this material. If something rings true to you, fine. If something does not resonate, please leave it behind, for neither we nor those of the Confederation would wish to be a stumbling block for any.

© 2009 L/L Research

Sunday Meditation
December 6, 2003

Group question: This week, in the spirit of the season that we are entering, we would like some information on the entity that we know of as Jesus the Christ, Jesus of Nazareth. We would appreciate any information about this entity or his incarnation very much.

(Carla channeling)

We are those known to you as the principle of Q'uo, and we greet you in the love and in the light of the one infinite Creator, in Whose service we come to you. We thank you so much for calling us to your group by the intensity and the energy of your seeking. It is a great blessing to us to be so called and to be allowed to offer you the humble service of sharing our thoughts and opinions with you. We are part of that Confederation of entities whose only hope is to offer such thoughts to those who wish to accelerate the pace of their evolution of mind, body and spirit at this time. We come in response to the cries of sorrow of the entities upon your planet and we can only hope that our humble thoughts may open windows and let in some light and some air where perhaps there has been a darkness of thought. May we lighten it! This is our hope, to lighten, to energize, to enable those beautiful spirits to whom we speak today. We thank you for sacrificing the time and the attention, of dedicating such a time to seeking. And we would ask only one thing of you in return and that is that you listen to us with a great deal of discrimination, keeping those thoughts that you like and leaving the rest behind.

You ask this day concerning the one known as Jesus. This entity has been known by several names. The name of his youth was Jehoshua. The name of Jesus is not that which this entity heard, unless it was spoken by those not of his own country, for that particular name is the Greek version of an Aramaic name. However we shall call this entity Jesus, since that is the name under which each of you calls to him when you speak in your conversation with those entities you can not see but whose influence you certainly feel. The request from the one known as G was to speak concerning this entity's life.

The life of the one known as Jesus was indeed somewhat unusual in that the entity was an unusual being, sharing—in company with many of those within this circle and many of those who call themselves wanderers—the facility of mind and the sharpness of intellect that enabled this entity at a very young age to be one who was intellectually able to study and to grasp abstract concepts in such a way that this entity was, by its very nature, prone to thinking upon the mysteries that it could not solve, the greatest mystery of all being that mystery of the lack of limit to the imagination.

This infinity and eternity that the one known as Jesus felt within him pulled him ever forward. And being fortunate enough to dwell in what this instrument would call a small town where his family had a humble but adequate home and a community of those who could teach spiritual or religious subjects, the one known as Jesus was one who hung about such teachers, reading and asking questions and reading again, until at a young age, as a teenager, this entity was considered a kind of rabbi. Along with the scholarly pursuits that this entity pursued as his principle hobby, the entity also spent many hours at the side of his father and his uncle, learning their trades and working with wood and gathering various herbs and those natural substances which were known to have healing benefits.

The one known as Jesus tended to be somewhat of a loner and liked nothing better than to steal away at nightfall. There was, near the village in which his parents lived, a high place in the surrounding terrain. It was nothing more than what this instrument would call a knob or a small rise of rock, yet the climbing of this modest knob to the ridge of it created within him a feeling of peace that he did not find elsewhere. It was his habit to gaze at the stars and imagine the lack of limit. The overriding sense of infinite possibility would rest upon him at those times and much of the actual substance of this entity's spiritual maturity was gained not because of the teaching of his parents or the teaching of those spiritual leaders which the small town offered but rather the silence which he was able to find within himself while gazing into the depths of the night sky.

At the age of approximately fourteen, this entity was offered the opportunity to study with two other entities from the same small town who were also those who had an interest in the spiritual studies that the village rabbis were glad to offer. And so there ensued a period of some years where this entity studied, prayed and meditated with a group of what this instrument would call Essenes. This further enabled the one known as Jesus to discipline his somewhat mischievous and wayward personality and to refine within himself the hunger that he felt for the truth.

Gradually, as he began to mature into an adult person, it came to him that he must travel and so he began to walk upon a path that was as varied as his sense of each day's shape. He set off upon a pilgrimage, although the one known as Jesus certainly did not think in terms of such but rather simply that he was called to the road. And guided by spirit and silence, he walked through parts of Africa and parts of India. (We have difficulty using place names with this instrument as she has no familiarity with those regions.) Braving hunger and extremes of weather, the one known as Jesus walked many a weary mile and visited the campfires and the caves and the holy places of those who thought along the same lines as those he was taught and those who did not, learning always, accumulating wisdom, and sifting it, winnowing it, and gradually coming into a fuller and fuller sense of who he was, not as the one who had learned these things but as the one who the witness of the process of that learning and its tumbling about and settling into those patterns of thought that he found truly helpful.

It was during this phase that the one known as Jesus gradually became more and more aware of the shape of his future ministry. We give this instrument the image of mountains and sweet water and the name Kashmir, as the furthest that this entity walked before he began the journey, not precisely home, but the journey towards what this very dedicated entity felt was his future and his chosen ministry.

While this entity had been traveling, one of this entity's relatives, the one [known] to this instrument as John the Baptist, had begun his own ministry. Feeling under a real compulsion to purify himself and to allow to fall from himself all things that were not holy, the one known as John began to attract followers to himself with a very simple and direct message, the message of prophets from time immemorial: return to the Creator, cease from error, and serve only the highest and best. This entity had begun what he called baptism, the washing of the self in symbolic and ceremonial manner in such a way that the water was seen as that emblem which washes away all sin. The power of this entity's purity and his charisma created an ever larger group of followers wherever this entity chose to appear from those reaches of the desert into which no one went. And it was at the place where the one known as John the Baptist was baptizing that the one known as Jesus found [both] the inspiration to set a beginning and the beginning on his ministry.

It is remarkable, given the fact that the one known as John was a family member, that this entity recognized in his cousin, the one known as Jesus, not a cousin, not a relative, but the Messiah, as he understood that term, the "one who comes in the name of the Lord."[74] A tremendous amount of power was transferred from John to Jesus and from Jesus to John at that time. It truly was a remarkable day and one which may be seen to be the point at which the one known as Jesus moved from witness to actor, from being to doing, from potential to actual, from inner to outer.

If we might, we would pause to note at this time the length of time that the one known as Jesus had walked through wilderness, talked to all those men of wisdom that he could find and went through the purification of the pilgrimage wherein there is no provision made for food or comfort but only two feet upon a dusty road and strangers at the end of the day. Such training is essential if one wishes to create the life which has depth and power. And this was done by the one known as Jesus, not because he felt it was right but because the thirst and hunger for truth drew him ever onward and the beauty of the search was irresistible, so that there was both the stick of his hunger and the carrot of the beauty of those spaces within which he found himself able to occupy because of the long acquaintance with silence, the long discipline of the body, and the long times of listening, both to others and to what they had to say, and to the voice of his own thoughts.

Indeed, it was mentioned by several entities in the conversation preceding this meditation that it is a very interesting thing simply to watch one's thoughts and to be aware of them as they arise, not to judge them but to become aware of the content of the thought, especially those thoughts that repeat themselves. It is a process wherein one is able to go deeper and deeper within the self simply by careful observation.

During this period, the one known as Jesus had for the most part kept himself apart from any personal relationships, either with men or with women. But certainly this entity was not without those men and women that he loved. The life of a wandering preacher is not a life which can easily be accommodating to a mate and a growing family and it was the one known as Jesus' feeling that these were not pleasures of which he might partake. Consequently, for the most part, this entity held himself apart and was content to have unspoken yet very deep relationships with his mother, his brother, his cousin, and those disciples, both men and women, whose hearts he could see to be of that same thirst and hunger for truth that his was.

Almost all of the writings concerning the one known as Jesus have to do with those stories that this teacher told during the three years or so of his active ministry. We do not find it possible with this instrument in a conscious state to move into such details as are perhaps wished for, for there is an intrinsic shallowness to such stories which, since this instrument has asked for a certain kind of contact, do not fall within the parameters of that contact.[75] In terms of the essence or the gist of this entity's life, we might say that this entity was a sweet yet fierce entity by personality, ruthless in seeking, ruthless in self-observation, and gifted with the ability to grasp peoples' nature and, in some cases, even what they were thinking. This did not endear him to most people, for there is something frightening about an entity who can gaze not at you but into you. And so he was often an intimidating presence. Certainly those who were in the structure of authority in the religious life of the surrounding society found the entity more and more disturbing. In part, it is because this entity dwelt in a part of the world in which he was a marginal native, which is to say that he was dwelling close to a large number of those whom one could call Judeans or those of the tribe of Judah. This tribe happened to carry with it a very, shall we say, "right-wing" or conservative point of view in which a great deal of emphasis is placed upon the attitude of the body, the dress of the body, the proper ritual for each day and each hour of the day, and so forth. There was a feeling that these religious observances created a spiritually well-lived life, whereas, to the one known as Jesus' point of view, all of these rules and regulations were, far from being helpful, actually those things which obscured one's view of the Creator.

---

[74] This phrase is traditionally connected with the Messiah. It is first seen in Psalm 118, verses 22-27: "The stone which the builders rejected has become the head of the corner. This is the Lord's doing. It is marvelous in our eyes. This is the day which the Lord has made. Let us rejoice and be glad in it. Save us, we beseech Thee, O Lord. O Lord, we beseech Thee, give us success. Blessed be he who enters in the name of the Lord." This passage is quoted by the gospels of Matthew, Mark and Luke as being the cry with which the one known as Jesus was greeted when he entered the gates of Jerusalem in the last days of his life.

[75] The instrument always asks to be given the highest and best contact within the consciousness of Jesus the Christ which may be carried by her in a conscious and stable manner.

This entity greatly wished for people to do precisely that which his cousin John suggested, to change their life, as this instrument heard in the sermon at her religious observance this morning. That priest who offered these thoughts was saying that the term "repent" literally means "to turn around," to turn the life around. This was the conclusion to which the one known as Jesus had come, that there was more to that metaphysical entity which was called Israel than the tribe of Judah. There was more to being a spiritual seeker than the outer forms. Naturally, since this entity had had years of training in mysticism and those practices of silence that mysticism encourages, he had little patience with those who identified spirituality with religious observance.

Further, this entity, having been on the verge of big towns, not truly urban in nature and not truly those who wander the nomadic portions of his people, became convinced that his basic mission was to wake up all of the scattered tribes of Israel. This instrument has taken time to study, with the one she calls Papa, the make-up of these other tribes of the so-called nation of Israel. In working with this concept, this instrument discovered that the scattering of the tribes of Israel has resulted in not simply a large number of dispersed Jewish people, but rather those that have become the Orthodox Christians and the Protestant Christians; simply because of the pattern of their dispersal and because of the march of time and because of the march of Christian and world history. Therefore, it may be said honestly that the one known as Jesus, to a great extent, over a long period of approximately two thousand years, has indeed had his message shared amongst all of those who were lost.

And the message always remains simple. Even when the one known as Jesus was in the most mortal crisis, what this entity did to position his disciples, those who were going to carry on after him, for their own teaching was to, as the one known as T said, use something very familiar. In this case it was not water, because there was not the water to drink with the meal but rather the wine. But this entity chose to take meat and drink as symbols of his nature and what this entity said was, "When you eat bread, remember me. When you drink wine, remember me." Again, the word "remember," like the word "repent," is key. To remember is to gather the members together. The one known as Jesus wished to gather all of those together who had come to learn and to serve in the grist mill of planet Earth.

The one known as Jesus had an awareness that the time was short, that same awareness that you may see again and again whenever entities of great inspiration and purity have come to grips with the deeper tides of time and space. In the sense of actual time, two thousand years does not seem to be a short time. Gazed at across the expanse of a cycle of time which is perhaps seventy-five thousand years long,[76] the last two thousand years, the cycle of Pisces, indeed would seem a short time, especially because the one known as Jesus had, to some extent, developed the ability to work within what this instrument calls circular time and so was aware both of linear time and that level of consensual reality that all here share, and also of the underlying reality of the inner planes, in which the end times, as this instrument is used to calling them, had already begun. Things occur within the inner planes long before they begin to appear within the physical plane. The roots of physical experience are often figured as a tree which grows in heaven and whose branches only reach the Earth, so that things have already occurred in the root of the tree and in the trunk of the tree of destiny long before they appear as leaf and blossom upon the branches of consensus reality or physical life.

This entity did not precisely see himself as Jesus the Christ, Son of God, that is preached by many, in that he saw himself [as] one who had emptied himself out in order that he might take on a larger persona. He saw it as the taking on of his life mission. He saw it as his acceptance of the return to the Father and his immolation of himself in the Father. He saw himself as that entity whose only desire was to fulfill those plans that he sensed the Father had. And indeed it is notable that at one point he said to his disciples, " I have meat and drink that you know not of,"[77] and his disciples were

---

[76] This Age is much shorter than that in classic astrology, being one twelfth of the approximate 25,800-year precession of the equinox, or 2,150 years. The cycle to which they are referring is the third-density cycle. The major cycle, or the third-density length, is broken into three 25,000 year "harvests" as the Confederation calls them, and in turn those 25,000-year periods are divided into the twelve signs of the zodiac.

[77] *Holy Bible*, John:4-31-36: "Meanwhile, the disciples besought Him, saying, "Rabbi, eat." But He said to them, "I have meat to eat of which you do not know." So the disciples said to one another, "Has anyone brought Him food?" Jesus said to them,

puzzled because they had not given him any food. But he said to them, "My food is to do the Will of the Father who sent me." Again the figures of food and drink are used to indicate that which truly nourished this particular entity.

This entity was not one who castigated himself or tried to beat down his human nature. Rather, he was one whose hunger for purity was such that he very much wanted and leapt towards the ability to lose himself, lose that ego structure which would have its desires and wants apart from the will of the Father. To the one known as Jesus all else was as nothing and simply was allowed to fall away. Not that this entity denied his roots, his past, and so forth, but that the entity had embraced a life which he saw truly as his destiny. And that destiny was only defined day by day. He could not know the will of the Father for any day but today. Thus the prayer which he taught focused upon one day and asked certain simple things. Let Earth be like Heaven. Let us bring Heaven to Earth. Let all people take care of each other. Let people judge each other as they wish to be judged and let all praise, glory and power be given only to the Creator.[78]

These are some highlights, some notable parts of this entity's being, that really stand out to us as we gaze at this entity's incarnation. The cloak of Christhood was not always light. The one known as Jesus suffered and indeed laid his arms out upon that tree of which the one known as Dave Matthews sang,[79] and gave up the life, the cloak, and all. As we gaze at that moment of sacrifice, we offer the words, "Not my will, but Thine," to indicate the strength of this entity's dedication. It was not that he had no ego. It was not that he was not human. He had personality, humor, anger, all of the emotions. He was a normal entity, within the parameters of normalcy, shall we say. He was fortunate in his gifts and pure and thorough in his dedication.

This entity informs us that we must move on and so we do, but not without thanks to the one known as G for asking concerning this entity. Indeed, this entity's life is greatly to be admired and gazed upon through the smoky glass of imperfectly written and poorly remembered stories. Even the imperfections and distortions cannot hide that message of oneness, what this instrument would call the Law of One, that he brought. Much has been said within this group and within your culture concerning that which this instrument calls the second coming. And we say to each of you, the cloak of Christhood is each entity's destiny. The walk from Earth to Heaven, from third density to fourth, is a walk that all shall take. Each has ego, each has personality, yet each has gifts and dedication, two feet and a dusty path. Blessings abound.

We would ask at this time if there are any further queries?

G: Q'uo, was Jesus aware of his status of being a wanderer to planet Earth? And how did the one known as Jesus approach his suffering? What did he tell himself when he felt the emotions of anger, or doubt, or frustration, or pain, and so on?

The one known as Jesus was in no way aware of any cosmic past or indeed the possibility of other worlds or other entities upon other worlds. However, this entity was well trained as a mystic and had the sense of limitless space within.

In terms of how this entity dealt with its own ego when facing suffering, this entity moved almost entirely upon what this instrument would call resonance. When faced with suffering, this entity would step into a place within its consciousness in which he was able to drift in silence and wait for resonance. And when that resonance would come, it almost never would come with words but rather with purified emotions, as this instrument would call them, those feelings that move far beyond the surface feelings of anger or pain, those feelings that are of connection and lightness, so that the one known as Jesus was able simply to disconnect from the suffering that it was going through, not denying it or repressing it but allowing it and even leaning into it and dedicating that very suffering to the

---

"My meat is to do the will of Him who sent me, and to accomplish His work. Do you not say, 'There are yet four months, then comes the harvest?' I tell you, lift up your eyes, and see how the fields are already white for harvest."

[78] And, of course, "Give us this day our daily bread."

[79] From his song, "Bartender," comes the quote: "Bartender please, fill my glass for me with the wine you gave Jesus that set him free after three days in the ground. I'm on bended knee. I pray Bartender please. Oh when I was young I didn't think about it, But now I can't get it out of my mind. I'm on bended knee, please father please. Oh if all this gold, should steal my soul away! Oh dear mother of mine, please redirect me. If this gold … Bartender you see, this wine that's drinking me came from the vine that strung Judas from the devil's tree, roots deep, deep in the ground."

infinite One in total faith that it was the perfect place to be.

The mantra always was, "What will Thou have me do?" There was one blazing concern that overrode every emotion and every pain and that was the absolute determination to penetrate what the godhead wished and to accomplish it. And to this entity, that meant bringing all of the scattered people together and bringing them into an awareness and a remembrance of who they are and why there were here. The genius of this entity was that his goal was high enough to last a thousand years.

May we answer you further, my brother?

G: No, thank you Q'uo.

Is there a further question at this time?

T: Q'uo, I have a question about music and sound. Can you talk a little bit about how music, sound and vibration can be used as a resource in the spiritual seeking?

We are those of Q'uo, and are aware of your query, my brother. The musical tone is literally a vibration and the range of musical tones is directly connected to the range of the chakras, shall we say, or the energy centers of the energy body. Each being upon your planet and certainly each being and iota of the creation itself, each snowflake sings, each stone has its tone, each flower, each bird, each entity of any kind has a song and the spiritual significance of tone is that it helps to move, by sympathetic vibration, the energy body into a more helpful configuration.

May we answer you further, my brother?

T: No, thank you Q'uo, that was very helpful.

We thank you, my brother. Is there a further query from the group at this time?

S: Yes, I have a question. Recently C had what Carla calls a psychic greeting that she seemed to have dealt with effectively but just before that she had the thought of Q'uo. Were you there to offer support, whether just a thought? Perhaps you can tell me a little about the situation?

We are those of Q'uo, and are aware of your query, my brother. We may say only that it is quite true that whenever there is the thought for us, we are there. We do not intrude but we are tuned to those entities who have been tuned to us, if you may follow our thinking. The one known as C is aware of us, is aware that she may call upon us, and we are there instantly when the thought of us is brought up with the hope that there is help in that thought. It is our distinct and great privilege to serve during times when sturdy help is needed and we are most pleased that the one known as Cindy had the feeling that we were of aid at that time.

May we answer you further, my brother?

S: I've had some insights, intuitions, of work that I would be doing and though it may be much the labor of love, there is a certain lump of fear in me. I know I shouldn't have that but it's there and I was wondering if you could give me your insight on a way to get past that?

We are those of Q'uo, and are aware of your query, my brother. The object of fear is to derail progress. The way of fear is to blot out the sun with shadow. We may say simply that there is nothing intrinsically unhealthy or wrong about feeling unsure of the future or [wondering] if one is equipped to serve in the future. However, in terms of dealing with such feeling, we find great virtue in that dealing with [it] one day [at a time] that the one known as Jesus was so good at manifesting in his own experience. The concept is familiar from the many times that Alcoholic's Anonymous has entered the culture with its motto of, "One day at a time," and this instrument knows the song, "One Day at a Time, Sweet Jesus," which is, by the way, a very appropriate prayer.

What we are trying to say, and not very well, is that each day is its own entity and in each day that large knot of fear may show up here or there. When it shows up, it is very local and it is focused and specific and in the context of one day, and the one thought, and the one process. It then becomes possible to take that specific fear and be with it. We would not suggest attempting to solve, repress or overcome any doubts or fears that may occur. Rather, we encourage you to be with them, as a witness to them, to listen to the story they have to tell and to react within as witness to that story. "What do you think? How do you feel?" Always moving deeper, looking for the next layer within, so that fear becomes a springboard to help you remember that you are seeking who you are and why you are here.

The shape of service is wrought in the furnace of roiling, daily purification and attention. The sheer ability to pay attention that you were speaking of earlier, to be aware of the actual nature of motions that are coming from you and are being offered to you, the energy exchanges that occur between you and yourself, between you and others, between you and the forces of nature that so move you and are so important to you—all of these things are elements of a life that is a kind of blossoming of the self that you may encourage, you may water, you may offer fertilizer to by those things to which you pay attention.

May we answer you further, my brother?

S: I think that's one of those things where, like many of your other words, when I read the transcript over and over, think about, and read it again and again, has offered me great comfort in the past. So for now I'll think about what you said and keep in mind my undying gratitude.

We thank you too, my brother. It is our pleasure and privilege. Is there a final query at this time?

V: Q'uo, I have a ritual that I use internally when I go into what I would call a working meditation, and I wonder if you could speak regarding the efficacy of that ritual? How could it be made more so? What is the function of what I would call the points five and six and seven in my compass?

We are those of Q'uo, and are aware of your query, my sister. The best we may do in terms of not interfering with your process is to encourage the awareness of the silence that shapes the form, the essence that shapes the symbol. Place the feet, metaphysically speaking, and allow with lightness of heart each form to have its jewel-like articulation.

May we answer you further, my sister?

V: Well, since I spoke cryptically I deserved a cryptic response. Thank you. I'll work with that for now.

We thank you, my sister. It is a great joy to be with you and we are sorry that it is time for us to leave this instrument and this group. Know that we are always with you, as we said to the one known as S about the one known as C. At any time, if there is a desire for us to be of aid, we will be aware of it in the manner of your inner planes in what this instrument would call circular time, so we are there the instant that you ask. We assure you, however, that we are not there if you do not ask. Consequently, if there is a presence, especially an annoying repetitive presence, that calls itself by our name, we suggest that you challenge it in the name of Jesus the Christ, for that will scatter any forces that do not come in unconditional love and service to others.

We leave you, as always, in the love and in the light of the one infinite Creator. We rejoice with you and we bid you adonai. Adonai. ☥

L/L Research

Sunday Meditation
December 21, 2003

Group question: Today we are taking pot luck, so, Q'uo, we would be glad to hear anything you'd like to share with us.

(Carla channeling)

We are those known to you as the principle of Q'uo, and we greet you in the love and in the light of the one infinite Creator, in Whose service we come to you today. We thank you for the great privilege of calling us to your group by your desire to seek the truth. It is always a pleasure to be called to this group. We would ask only one thing of you and that is, as always, that you listen to those things which we have to say with a jaundiced and careful ear, being quick to discard and toss away any idea or thought that does not suit you and keeping only those things which seem to you to have resonance and a personal meaning that speaks to you specifically. We feel that we are no authority figures but rather those companions who walk with you upon the road of the seeker. If you will guard your own thought processes, we shall feel free to share our thoughts with you without being concerned that we infringe upon your free will.

We find that this group does not have any opening question for us and that gives us the opportunity to move into those energies that are unspoken and that may perhaps be addressed in a less than specific and direct way by those things that we might share. We are aware that the energy of the time you call Christmas is very much within this group and within your culture at this time. And it is interesting to observe the lack of joy with which many entities approach the dark times of winter solstice, for indeed that is the energy of this particular season of the year, that energy of the dark and the sleep of hibernation and winter. It is a time when it is very easy for those entities who are close to passing from the incarnation to have a more than usual opportunity to greet the dark, with its invitation to all to come and be a part of that darkness. It is a seduction that brings many to that passage betwixt incarnation through what is called death to the next stage of consciousness for that entity. The inner planes having received all entities who pass through the gateway of death; it is then the opportunity of each entity, having made that passage, to discover, for himself and herself, what the next step is. Is it a step of healing, a step of review and examination of the life just passed? Or is it, in some cases, that entities who pass through the gates of death are quite conscious of the opportunity being offered to work within the inner planes and so are most eager to move on into new work, new projects, and new service?

For those who are at all drawn to the dark, this is that time during the season of the year when that invitation will seem more seductive than usual. It is, paradoxically, a time when the deepest impulses of entities are to lighten the darkness, to energize that darkness with gaiety and noise and movement, as if such hectic pleasures might distract the souls dwelling within from their preoccupation with the gathering darkness. That invitation, that seduction of the dark, is often [set] very deeply within the gaiety of your celebrations. It is as though the energies of humankind, not knowing how to cooperate with the darkness, find it necessary to throw up defenses against the darkness and deny the reality of the darkness. For darkness is not simply a physical thing. It is not simply the absence of a sun body within your atmosphere. Certainly that physical darkness is a huge part of the way darkness feels, that experience of the lack of light. Yet, the energies of this season are more than, and other than, physical. In part, the darkness that is physical darkness is complemented or paired with the shadow of self, the darkness of self, that entities such as this instrument would always prefer not to deal with, because it is, while undeniably a part of the personality, not considered a desirable part of the personality. We feel that perhaps this might deserve a good look, this attempt to make all things bright, to lift everything up to the light, and to have a merry and a happy season.

Certainly each within the circle has experienced the hectic nature of this particular season in, as the one known as T said, the cycle of Christmas and Christmas doings. The one known as T was saying that it would seem obvious that entities could wish each other good and send thoughts to each other without the necessity for purchasing items, without the necessity for getting certain items and yet, year upon year, and century upon century, entities faced with the shortest of the days and the longest of the nights of the year turn hungrily towards the festivities that make a brave show in the face of all of that darkness and shadow.

Let us look at the story of Christmas, in that it is a story with darkness within it. The biblical story that this instrument knows from its Sunday school has a beauty to it, the beauty of innocent birth and angelic visitors and wise men of the Earth who also come to honor a tiny child. Yet, it is perhaps not emphasized, but certainly part of the story, that the mother of this entity, the one known as Jesus, was brought to childbed without the convenience or the respect of having been married first. Further, this entity was then asked to marry an older gentlemen who was not particularly amused by the pregnancy that presumably happened by spirit's hand alone. And further, in the very last extremities of pregnancy, this odd couple was forced to travel in the middle of winter, in inclement weather, to a place where there was no bed waiting for them at the other end, so that when the one known as Mary gave birth, it was in a stable and the infant Jesus slept in a manger that was full of hay. These details speak of the physical and the metaphysical darkness of the season, the inconvenience of spirit, the demands of the spiritual life, the demand of this infant to be born—not waiting for marriage, not waiting for propriety, but insisting upon being born, in the darkness, in the cold, in the stable—without convenience, or planning, or foresight. Simply, "It is time, and now I shall appear."

Such is the nature of your own spirit. It is nurtured in the darkness of the season and you are brought to childbed with it as the timing of your own process pulls you into new birth; the birth of your own spiritual self, within incarnation. For that is one of the great values of being in incarnation. You are able, when you become conscious of the situation of incarnation and its advantages, to determine within incarnation to awaken that sleeping soul within that has been brought along into incarnation within you but certainly hidden, sometimes fairly deeply, within the stuff of personality, culture and conditioning.

In the darkness within the self lie both the riches of the soul and the less appreciated of the riches of the shadow side of that soul. As you bring this infant that is you as a soul into conscious awareness and begin to nurture that part of yourself as if it were an infant that needed love and tending, you begin to pull that structure within you that is the witness to all that you undergo in incarnation into more clarity. It is that witness that can release thoughts of the darkness and thoughts of the gaiety and simply continue witnessing as that child within begins to express itself, to reach towards the light that it sees, to begin to have the energy and vitality to move upon its own and to begin to grow within incarnation. As you go about nurturing this beautiful portion of the inner self, we would ask you also to look very carefully to find the wolf that bites, to find the murderer, the thief, the adulterer; to find that entity within the self that truly does partake of the darkness of self-good, that part of selfhood that is self-involved, that has the impulse to think first of the self. This is a good time of year to focus into that neglected portion of the self and to invite it into the warm and gently lighted circle of your own heart's hearth.

It is as though there are parts of the self that have been denied because they are too dark, they are too seemingly selfish or evil or harsh or rough. And yet, that whole entity which you are cannot function without all, both the light and the dark, of its nature. Many times entities who polarize towards beauty and truth and purity feel that they must deny and leave behind those shadow portions of self. And yet we would ask you not to leave behind one iota of that 360 degrees of self that you do possess. For all of the voices within you, all of the 180 degrees of "good" and 180 degrees of that which you label "not good," are necessary to integrate into one peaceful kingdom within.

Many are the times that this instrument has asked the question, "What is peace?" For she meditates on behalf of peace each night.[80] And one of the keys to understanding peace, the concept of peace as a living thing and not as a dead idea, is to realize that peace is the complete and harmonious integration of light and dark, so that all is in balance within the whole entity and all of that entity's faculties are brought to bear on a situation; not simply those faculties towards the good but those faculties that might be considered towards the negative. For the thief, the coveter, the lazy one, all of those dark voices within, can be charmed into becoming the bedrock of will that puts grit into the expression of love that the "light" part of self has no trouble expressing. Yet when the going becomes rough, it is that dark side of self that is able to take hold in difficult situations and endure. That same darkness that could be the wolf that bites, then, has become the best support possible for the light. And this is the hoped-for result of an incarnation full of both the light and the dark as the seasons revolve and as the seasons of inner life revolve as well.

So we take this opportunity to praise the dark as well as the light and to ask each of you to work on embracing all parts of the self, loving, honoring and respecting each and finding ways each day to come into more conscious harmony of being. As you are able to find your kingdom within becoming peaceable, just to that extent shall you be able to be a force for peace to those about you. No matter how you strive, if you do not embrace the dark side of self, you shall ever be less of a messenger for peace and more of a voice that has not the force and directness to project into the Earth plane with all of its inner planes of energy.

This instrument's head is full of angels at this time of year, the angels of heaven, praising God and saying, "Glory to God in the highest and peace to men of good will." We wish you those angels, we wish you the truth of this precious dark time. May each of you move into that time with quietness and confidence, allowing the great washes of emotion and memory to move through your thoughts and your feelings, washing you and leaving you golden and rested and truly at peace.

We would ask if there are any queries at this time before we leave this instrument.

J: Yeah, Q'uo, I've got a question. The veil is very thin at this time and I was wondering what your impression is? I know it's always a good time to meditate. Are there any suggestions that you could make? Is there a way to connect with the thinness of the veil, right now, today, tomorrow? Is there anything that we can do to share in that thinness?

We are aware of your query, my sister. Certainly there is truth to your concept. It is indeed a time when the energies of the Earth and its inner planes are very transparent to the outer world. The idea of meditation is certainly a good one. (We have difficulty imagining a situation in which we would say anything else than that about meditation!) However, one item that is possible in order to connect with the energy of this time would be that which this instrument would call a solstice declaration. At the solstice, it is a very efficacious time to express those things which you wish to give to the dark: the greed, the world hunger, the illnesses of the world and so forth, all of those things which you may consider to be less that optimal. These can be named and given to the dark and the health of this action is in releasing those energies from the consciousness within your self. It is as though this is a good time to connect with the energies that this instrument knows of as Shiva the Destroyer,[81] to

---

[80] These meditations are held each night at 9 PM, Eastern time. People from all over the globe join us, and you can, also. For more information about the daily peace/Gaia meditations, please see the Gaia Meditation page on the L/L Research site.

[81] "Shiva is the great Yoga ascetic, the Lord of the Dance. He is the universal teacher, the omnipresent and all-knowing. Shiva assumes all forms. Originally known in the Vedas as Rudra,

hand those things to the Mother, as it were, that you wish to release from your self. "World hunger, I give it to the dark! War and the bestiality of war, I give it to the dark!" It is well to create more of a festive party atmosphere to this energy, so that those who take part in it may feel the joy of the release of these impressions.

May we answer you further, my sister?

J: No thank you, Q'uo, and happy winter solstice to you.

We thank you as well, my sister. Is there another query at this time?

As we seem to have exhausted the queries of this group, we shall take our leave of you, thanking each of you for taking precious time to sit in a circle of seeking and ask. We are with you, whenever you would ask us to be, to help you with your meditation or to be a presence that makes you feel safer. You have only to ask mentally and we shall be with you.

We leave each of you in the love and in the light of the one infinite Creator. We are those known to you as the principle of Q'uo. Adonai my friends. Adonai. ♣

Shiva is also identified with the god of fire, Agni. As the Vedic Rudra, Shiva appears to be a terrible god—the Destroyer—who always needs to be pacified. When worshipped, however, Shiva/Rudra becomes a beneficent deity." (From www.courses.rochester.edu/muller-ortega/rel249/siva/Shivahome.html)

Year 2004

January 4, 2004 to September 19, 2004

L/L RESEARCH

L/L Research is a subsidiary of Rock Creek Research & Development Laboratories, Inc.

P.O. Box 5195
Louisville, KY 40255-0195

www.llresearch.org

Rock Creek is a non-profit corporation dedicated to discovering and sharing information which may aid in the spiritual evolution of humankind.

ABOUT THE CONTENTS OF THIS TRANSCRIPT: This telepathic channeling has been taken from transcriptions of the weekly study and meditation meetings of the Rock Creek Research & Development Laboratories and L/L Research. It is offered in the hope that it may be useful to you. As the Confederation entities always make a point of saying, please use your discrimination and judgment in assessing this material. If something rings true to you, fine. If something does not resonate, please leave it behind, for neither we nor those of the Confederation would wish to be a stumbling block for any.

© 2009 L/L RESEARCH

Sunday Meditation
January 4, 2004

Group question: The question for today, Q'uo, has to do with how a person can really know another self without projecting a portion of one's own self on what you're seeing. When do we start seeing more clearly what's already there?

(Carla channeling)

We are those of the principle known to you as Q'uo, and we greet you in the love and in the light of the one infinite Creator, in Whose service we come to you. It is our great privilege and pleasure to be called to your meeting this day and we thank this circle of seeking for choosing to come together to seek the truth. We are most pleased to share our opinions with you on the interesting question you have asked this day and would ask one thing in return. We would ask that you please engage, respect and use your powers of discrimination, for we are not authorities who wish to impress with our opinion; rather, we are your companions on the road to seeking the infinite One. In order for us to feel free to share our thoughts, we need to know that you will be able to reject those things that we say that do not resonate for you personally. We ask you to keep only those things that do resonate and seem to have a real value to you. With that understood, then, we feel free to share our opinions concerning the question of how one may know another entity without distortion.

The word "distortion" suggests in its derivation that there is a twisting, a pressure of twisting change that is being applied to that which is being distorted and, in that wise, it is perhaps not the clearest possible term. However, we are unable to find one within your language system that is any closer to that which is meant by "distortion."[82] Indeed, nature is as it is; the creative principle is as it is; the one great original Thought, the Logos, or the Creator is precisely what it is. And yet since that beingness or essence comprises all that is, the creative principle is an immense, or perhaps we should say an infinite, term, disclosing a Being of infinite essence. In the heart of your selfhood, as a person within incarnation, this Godhead principle, this one great original Thought, functions as the self. The way this instrument is fond of putting it in her Christian walk is a quotation from the one known as Joel Goldsmith: "Christ is the 'I' of me."[83] Each entity, then, has the same basic essence. However, this essence is carried within the heart of each cell of the body, within the heart of each thought, within the heart of each true emotion.

---

[82] From *Webster's Unabridged Dictionary*: Distortion: from the Latin, *distortio*, which is from old Latin, *distorquere*, to turn or twist. It is defined as "the act of distorting, a twisting out of regular shape, a twisting or writhing motion."

[83] This basic concept is repeated many times in Joel Goldsmith's Infinite Way material. Here is a typical expression, from p. 97 of Goldsmith's *Living The Infinite Way* (London, George Allen and Unwin Ltd., [c1954]): "One of the first things we have learned in the Infinite Way is, in quietness and meditation, to give up the search for God in the realization that I and the Father are already one …"

It is not the whole of that apparent cell in the body or thought or emotion. It is the enlivening principle.

Now, all that is brought into incarnation, in terms of your experiences as a human being in incarnation, is distorted. You and your guidance system, the higher self, have created a kind of clothing for your beingness within incarnation that is what this instrument calls the "personality shell" and what your psychologists have called the ego. Perhaps you have noticed in your own life that when they are born, children do not come into incarnation as a blank slate. Rather, they enter the incarnation with a decided personality, personality shell, or ego structure. Each entity has created a personality shell in order to have the resources necessary for studying and working with some few key incarnation lessons or issues. Each entity within this circle, for instance, has chosen two or three, or in some cases four, incarnational issues. In most cases these were chosen in order to better the point of balance within the energy vehicle that contains many aspects of the overall essence, not only of yourself within incarnation but of yourself outside of incarnation and of the nature of the family relationships that have been your support and your context as a soul through many, many cycles of learning. This is an extended self, and each entity's extended self eventually connects with all other entities in a living and real bond, so that all are quite literally one within the stream of humanity, shall we say, that is in incarnation and is within the planetary influence, outside of incarnation in the physical sense.

It is apparent, on the consensual reality level, that each entity is a mystery to itself and to others. It is never apparent that all entities have a living, solid, connectivity. It is never obvious that the ties that bind, shall we say, in terms of energy fields and the accommodation of other energy fields by one's own energy field, are of a unitary nature. From the conscious mind's standpoint one cannot know the essence of another's thoughts. One cannot know the true motivations for their actions and so forth. Consequently, entities spend incarnational time not being aware of the present moment, as the one known as G would note, but rather working to improve the information base which they have about other selves close to them in order that they may more accurately predict the thought processes that are being hidden from view by other selves. In some cases the exercises of open communication reduce the anxiety and the sense of confusion that come from not knowing what another entity is thinking. But in most cases, there is little opportunity or realistic chance of creating a perfect communication in which all distortions are balanced and all projections balanced in such a way that they are transparent rather than reflective.

From this standpoint, then, it would seem that it is not possible to know another entity without distortion. But as the one known as V suggested, turning the gaze inward, is the situation any different? Are you not a mystery to yourself? Do you not question your own motives endlessly? Are you not honestly puzzled many times by that which is being felt by the self within? Is there any time in which you are able to say of yourself, "I know myself backwards and forwards. I know what I am capable of and what I can do. I know who I am and why I am here. I know all of it, I have no more questions, I am completely aware." We salute those within the circle who may feel that they can say absolutely that they know who they are. We find in this instrument's mind that she is always surprising herself by what her responses are in the moment. Sometimes this entity is happy with those responses and sometimes she judges herself perhaps harshly for those same responses. Whatever her processes of judgment, however, the surprises keep coming because the novelties of new situations, new energies, and new combinations of events create situations which have not been met before. As the response to the novel situation develops, the first person to be surprised by that response is the self before it ever gets out into the world of other selves. The self is learning about the self at all times. Indeed, this process recapitulates the action of the Creator in knowing Itself. If one could see the vast creation of entities who are working their way around this circle of being to the Godhead principle once more, one could see the process of planting the crop of consciousness and reaping the harvest of new experiences, new thoughts, and new learning. This is a process that is attempted by the self within incarnation but always with imperfect results because of the fact that this particular illusion has its finite boundaries and its preset distortions, shall we say, built into the illusion so that were one to become immensely skilled at manipulating the consensus illusion of your reality, one would still be skilled [only] at understanding and using that which is a very tiny part of a larger system, most of which cannot be known within incarnation, but only seen as if by reflection or by the silhouette of light being stopped by an object so that the silhouette of a system may be suggested as on the wall of Plato's cave.[84] Yet one is not actually able to see into the essence, either of self or the other self.

---

[84] This discussion is from the website www.philosophypages.com/hy/2h.htm.

The Allegory of the Cave

Plato recognized that the picture of the Divided Line may be difficult for many of us to understand. Although it accurately represents the different levels of reality and corresponding degrees of knowledge, there is a sense in which one cannot appreciate its full significance without first having achieved the highest level. So, for the benefit of those of us who are still learning but would like to grasp what he is talking about, Plato offered a simpler story in which each of the same structural components appears in a way that we can all comprehend at our own level. This is the Allegory of the Cave.

Suppose that there is a group of human beings who have lived their entire lives trapped in a subterranean chamber lit by a large fire behind them. Chained in place, these cave-dwellers can see nothing but shadows (of their own bodies and of other things) projected on a flat wall in front of them. Some of these people will be content to do no more than notice the play of light and shadow, while the more clever among them will become highly skilled observers of the patterns that most regularly occur. In both cases, however, they cannot truly comprehend what they see, since they are prevented from grasping its true source and nature. *(Republic 514a)*

Now suppose that one of these human beings manages to break the chains, climb through the torturous passage to the surface, and escape the cave. With eyes accustomed only to the dim light of the former habitation, this individual will at first be blinded by the brightness of the surface world, able to look only upon the shadows and reflections of the real world. But after some time and effort, the former cave-dweller will become able to appreciate the full variety of the newly-discovered world, looking at trees, mountains, and (eventually) the sun itself.

Finally, suppose that this escapee returns to the cave, trying to persuade its inhabitants that there is another, better, more real world than the one in which they have so long been content to dwell. They are unlikely to be impressed by the pleas of this extraordinary individual, Plato noted, especially since their former companion, having travelled to the bright surface world, is now inept and clumsy in the dim realm of the cave. Nevertheless, it would have been in the best interest of these residents of the cave to entrust their lives to the one enlightened member of their company, whose acquaintance with other things is a unique qualification for genuine knowledge.

Plato seriously intended this allegory as a representation of the state of ordinary human existence. We, like the people raised in a cave, are trapped in a world of impermanence and partiality, the realm of sensible objects. Entranced by the particular and immediate experiences these things provide, we are unlikely to appreciate the declarations of philosophers, the few among us who, like the escapee, have made the effort to achieve eternal knowledge of the permanent forms. But, like them, it would serve us best if we were to follow this guidance, discipline our own minds, and seek an accurate understanding of the highest objects of human contemplation.

Nevertheless, in unknowingness, in mystery, the work, the joy, the process of discovering the self continues. And in that process there lie sources of information that are wonderfully rich and abundant. These sources of information begin with the self, continue with interactions with other selves, and are rounded by interactions with a vast panoply of energies within your natural world, within the world of ideas, and within discarnate principles and entities with which the essence of the inner self interacts on the unconscious level. All of these sources of information fall like rain and sun[beams] and all manner of life-giving attributes into the field of self, causing those seeds that have been planted in the personality shell to begin their process of seeking the light, expressing their form and their habit, and developing their characteristic blooms and blossoms of being. Each of you is a very organically, muscularly organized entity. The structure of your deeper mind is as well put together as your skeleton and has as many appropriate functions. It is rather difficult to express to you the complexity of your system as a living being but perhaps it is enough to recall the way the energy body is made, within your density of the yellow-ray body. You have the sub-densities of red through violet within third-density. And each of those sub-densities: red, orange, yellow, green, blue, indigo and violet, contains seven sub-sub-densities so that each chakra, shall we say, in the energy body is a fully integrated system within itself. Then as a system it is further fully integrated as one being. This layering of bodies or states of beingness within the system that is you is infinite, potentially. In most entity's cases there are perhaps three or four levels of beingness which are plumbed during incarnation. In a circle such as this, with entities that have been doing inner work and spiritual processes for a considerable time, perhaps you begin to penetrate into more and more layers, or levels, of being. Each one has its characteristic environment, experiences and learnings to offer. All of them are colored by the characteristic nature of their place within the energy vehicle.

In this complexity, it is as if you were a world, a globe, or an orb that rotated around the sun of your origins—the one infinite Creator. Within that orbit, then, each of you is as a star, as a live-giving, radiant being. And so as you in your orbit meet others in their orbits, there is a strength and a power to each entity which comes from its orientation within its own orbit. One may observe that some entities have very even orbits and this is expressed within consensual reality by the impression that such an entity is stable or has a characteristic point of view that can be well known. Other entities have more of an eccentric orbit, as though their roundness as an entity were not yet completed and as though there were irregularities which would cause the eccentricities of an unequal orbit. And in your consensual reality, this would appear as entities who do not seem to have very well-integrated personalities, who perhaps are fooling themselves or unable for some reason to come into a comfortable relationship with the self, in an integrated way. Sometimes these entities will appear to be mentally disturbed, as this instrument would say. In other cases it is almost impossible to detect the eccentricity in the inner orbit that has been carefully compensated for within the entity's outer life. Yet, still, that inner lack of harmony or roundness of the orbit has its fruit in that sense one gets, when attempting to understand the person, that one has not quite "gotten" that person. This is generally due to the fact that such an entity has not been able to "get" her own nature, so that the lack of clarity may well not be that which is a part of the being that you are attempting to understand. In other words, it is often the case when an entity is feeling that there is a lack of clarity in his understanding of another self, that that other self has that precise difficulty with the self and consequently is not capable of offering the self in a non-eccentric way but rather must hold, in somewhat randomized form, the various aspects of the personality shell.

It is a part of the eternal wisdom to assume that what one thinks about another entity speaks more about that person than about the other entity and we feel that this is part of that which the one known as G was attempting to balance when the question was formed. And it is our opinion that this universally accepted bit of wisdom is the truth. The impressions and opinions that each entity forms of another self will always have a significant bending or distortion which is the result of the self picking up those qualities and aspects of another self's personality shell which speak either well or poorly to the self about the self. Many is the time that this instrument has formed a judgmental opinion of another self only to reflect, at a later and less stressful time, that the reaction which she had was an indication of a part of her own self's dark side, at which the self did not wish to look. So the other self that is being perceived judgmentally is simply the bearer of the news, if it could be called news, "That is the shadow side of the self and this is what it looks like. Here is a mirror." This is the other self's gift to you.

You, meanwhile, are, by your honest and unstudied reactions to that which occurs around you and to the other selves around you, performing the vital and valuable service of mirroring to others, so that they may see themselves in you. It is a part of the endless process of getting to know the greater self which is you, all those with whom you come in contact, all those with whom you never come in contact as far as you know, and those beyond the purview of the planet, such as ourselves. It is a dynamic, infinite and ongoing process. And each creation of the Father, with all of its infinite time and space and process, is just a heartbeat of the infinitely extensive experience of the Godhead principle knowing Itself.

Can one find resources for knowing another without distortion? We believe so. But we couch that with all the foregoing limitations to attempt to indicate the difficulties involved in attempting to understand the system from within the system. It is very difficult, if not impossible, to be clear. However, there are resources available for demystifying and simplifying relationships with other selves and for bringing clear sight to the vision. This work is not concerning the other self, as the one known as V intuited. It is work done within the self. If you consider yourself as a crystal, you may see that some crystals are reflective and others are transparent. The reflective personality is that personality that is not known to itself; the transparent personality is one that is known to itself. This instrument has often said that her goal was to become transparent. And her strategy has been to live as open a life as possible so that others may know all about this instrument, whether it considers those facts good or not good, positive or negative. By opening all parts of the known self to being known by others, this instrument's hope has been to become that personality shell which may be seen through, so that the love and the light of the infinite Creator are able to penetrate the personality shell and become that selfhood that is chosen as the truth of the self. We see in this instrument's thoughts that she does not consider that she has done very well with this goal but she continues to work day by day upon being a self better known to herself, a self more freely and unselfconsciously revealed to others. It is as though she were wishing to lose solidity or density of being in order to be clear and transparent and able to be seen through.

This kind of energy, this kind of intention, is very helpful for several reasons. First of all, the energy put into the self is never wasted. It may seem as though it were selfish to take time with the self, to sit with the self, to listen to the self, to go beyond the self and rest in Creator-ness. It is not at all selfish, however, to spend time in these pursuits, for you are improving the characteristics of your energy field in the direction of clarity and balance. Further, work done upon the self is rest taken from work done attempting to control or manipulate other selves. When there is more self-knowledge, there is almost automatically less need to control situations or to manipulate other selves, for the energies of the self are felt to be strong and powerful and there is not a concern that one's strength and power might be taken away or limited by the narrowness of another entity's perceived viewpoints. Further, with self-knowledge comes that which we would call kindness or gentleness or humility. There is a softness that comes with self-knowledge so that an entity that is another self, though she perhaps cannot explain why, feels more comfortable and more herself when with you. In this atmosphere, self is able to reveal self to you, in an unthreatened and secure manner and consequently knowledge of self creates an atmosphere in which open communication may be sharpened, heightened, deepened and enhanced.

We encourage time with the self, whether it be walking in the woods or gazing at a candle in the dawning hours or in the meditations that many within this group observe as a daily ritual. These forms of moving within the self and asking, in the silence, for awareness to come are all very helpful in terms of strengthening the energy field of the self and at the same time creating the atmosphere in which energy fields are able to encompass and embrace other energy fields without any sense of threat or judgment. Because of the eccentric orbits, shall we say, the choppy waters of some personality shells, some entities are much more grateful to be around than others, in terms of what is perceived from the energy emanating from that other self. And this cannot be, shall we say, fixed or balanced by the self. However, within that limitation of seeing accurately that which another self is putting out, the more self-aware an entity is, the less distorted will be that channel between self and other self and the more accurately the information from other self to self and vice versa, may flow.

So, in sum it is our feeling that the intention to know the self or another self without distortion is the intention to seek the truth. When the truth is being sought within the self, that intention will communicate to other selves and, as this energy improves within the self, the information stream coming from other selves shall also necessarily improve. It is not a matter of literally figuring someone out, for a person is not a closed system. A person is an evolving part of an evolving Creator. Rather, it is a matter of dwelling within a mystery, of delighting in that which is seen of the mystery, and in telling stories to oneself about oneself, about the experiences of living, in such a way that the self is opened more and more to the amazing amount of information that is falling from the inner planes and from the world about one and from the self to the self at all times.

The intention to know the truth is key. Keep the intention pure and the heart open so that all has the benefit of that great sun which is unconditional love. That shall ripen the fruit of your acquaintanceships like nothing else can. Resting in love, letting unconditional love flow through the being and out into the world, is the best start one could have at seeking the truth of another self.

At this time we would open the meeting to short queries if there be any. Is there a query at this time?

G: Q'uo, if you could, why is this statement spoken by Ra, true? "There is but one technique for the growing or nurturing of will and faith and that is the focusing of the intention."

My brother, we are aware of your query. We find that as you ask the question, we have no way of answering it. Is there a way in which you could restate your query?

G: I'll give it a shot. If you can't answer, it's acceptable. How does the focusing of the attention, which is a practice taken on in meditation, cause an increase in the faith that an entity has and how does that strengthen the will at the same time?

We are those of Q'uo, and are aware of your query, my brother. If you will think of the process of going under hypnotic control, being hypnotized by a hypnotherapist, perhaps you may see that the hypnotic induction to a trance is basically a means of focusing the attention. The hypnotherapist will say, "Listen to my voice, listen only to my voice." And little by little such a therapist will simply talk an entity down from the scatter-shot conscious awareness of everyday life into a state in which the attention has been focused and concentrated on one point and that point is the interface between the therapist and the self. As the therapist asks questions, in this focused state then the self is able to penetrate the various surface layers of self to move down into that area of self which is less limited by time and space and which therefore has a greater source of knowledge and information than is available in the conscious state.

In just such a way, as a spiritual seeker chooses to focus his attention, the effort put into that focus will create an evolutionary pressure towards the object of that focus. If an entity has chosen well as to the kind of focus on which it chooses to work and its intentions concerning this focus, the work done will necessarily change that entity in ways that automatically will be defining for the self, to the self, that which makes the self tick, that which motivates the self. And that translates into an improvement in the will. As the process itself moves forward and the self is more collected and therefore receiving better information, the nature of that information, which is based on the nature of the intention for that information, creates catalyst in which faith will be tested in a certain way. And with each test, the faith becomes stronger.

So it is not that there is a one-to-one relationship betwixt focusing the attention and increasing the will and faith; rather, the intention to gather one's self, gather one's powers, energies and being into an ever more coherent and expressive, crystalline self, will create pressures that will more and more define for the self, to the self, its nature, its motivations, its goals, and its discipline.

May we answer you further my brother?

G: No, as always, that was excellent, Q'uo. Thank you and thank you, instrument.

We thank you too, my brother. Is there another query at this time?

G: Q'uo, I will take the mike. I would like to know what the nature is of the right and left ear tones that are inaudible but are heard within?

We are those of Q'uo, and are aware of your query, my brother. The concept of using the pendulum is helpful in this wise, the rotation one way indicating a "yes" answer, the rotation in the opposite way indicating a "no," or some dynamic which is chosen. In each being's energy system, there is a natural right/left dynamic. Some entity's energies are such that the right ear tone indicates a positive and the left ear tone a negative; in others it is the opposite. Consequently the nature of one's pendulum must be ascertained by the self. However, it is or can be considered to be a system for checking the validity of one's thoughts. If there is a positive ear tone towards a thought one has thought with some force, then it likely that there is confirmation from what this instrument would call spirit, or what we may call guidance, that such a thought is worthy of thinking about and considering further. If there is a negative tone heard when one is thinking a thought, then there is a suggestion that there may be something distorted about the thought that needs more consideration and musing in order to penetrate that which one is being basically warned about or told to take with a grain of salt, shall we say.

May we answer you further, my brother?

G: No, that was more thorough than I would have imagined. Thank you very much, Q'uo. Q'uo, if you deem that the instrument is okay, can you speak on a time period on this planet in which a great portion of the population of the continent of Europe died because of an epidemic we call the Bubonic Plague?

We are those of Q'uo, and aware of your query, my brother. We may speak generally concerning this period within your history. The query is very general so we shall simply say that the conditions which brought about this correction in the density of population was one which was brought about by the lifestyle, shall we say, of the entities which occupied your planet at that time. As you gaze back into the reaches of history and prehistory, you may see that there was a gradual increase in the density of population. Whereas before there were people scattered in agrarian lifestyles, with few large cities and those cities being centers for trade and for culture, as the "Christian Era," so-called, came into what you call your Medieval times, cities began to be developed that were much larger and that had much greater density of population than had previously been seen. However, conditions, in terms of health and sanitation were not equal to the rapidly increasing density of population. There were no sanitary systems for sewage and sewerage; there was no way to keep food from rotting and there was no technology which would surely and safely limit populations of rodents and insects that prey upon the dirt and the offal that such a society begins to put out in more quantity than it can clean up. It was this situation which deepened into a runaway epidemic. In a less densely populated situation such a plague would not have had the ability to run so rampantly through so many entities. In a more urban situation, this became inevitable.

May we answer you in a further way, my brother?

G: No, thank you, I was trying to grasp the cause for that particular type of horrible suffering, why it needed to be and it seems it was more of a purely physical source rather than a metaphysical basis. So that was very sufficient, Q'uo, thank you.

We thank you, my brother. Is there a final query at this time?

G: Q'uo, one short one. In the Law of One series [Don Elkins] asks about the one known as FDR and asks if his evolution could be traced for that incarnation and I was wondering, if the person is deemed acceptable by you or removed away enough that you could speak on them, if it is possible, in the future, could we give you an example of an entity and you could give us some kind of brief or general chart or tracing of their growth in their lessons, in a similar fashion?

We are those of Q'uo, and are aware of your query, my brother. We are able to do this within limits, those limits being the conscious nature of channeling that this instrument uses. If this instrument is unaware of an entity, it is likely that we shall not be able to offer particularly valid information. So such questions would be of limited accuracy, my brother. Within those limitations we may be able to discuss entities with you.

May we thank all of you for resting so sweetly within this circle and sharing energy with each other in such an unselfish and beautiful way. It is a great inspiration to us to see entities come together on levels that are deeper than words and deeper than the conscious mind. We thank you for helping to support and enrich each other with your thoughts, your experiences, and your sharing. We thank you for your studies and your seeking, and for all that you are. Each of you is most beloved to us and we appreciate the beauty of each. Thank you so much for sharing this time with us. It has been a great pleasure.

We leave you in the love and in the light of the one infinite Creator in the remainder of your day and your evening. May you find reason to rejoice and give thanks. We leave you in the love and in the light of the one infinite Creator. We are known to you as the principle of Q'uo. Adonai my friends. Adonai. ❧

L/L Research

L/L Research is a subsidiary of Rock Creek Research & Development Laboratories, Inc.

P.O. Box 5195
Louisville, KY 40255-0195

www.llresearch.org

Rock Creek is a non-profit corporation dedicated to discovering and sharing information which may aid in the spiritual evolution of humankind.

ABOUT THE CONTENTS OF THIS TRANSCRIPT: This telepathic channeling has been taken from transcriptions of the weekly study and meditation meetings of the Rock Creek Research & Development Laboratories and L/L Research. It is offered in the hope that it may be useful to you. As the Confederation entities always make a point of saying, please use your discrimination and judgment in assessing this material. If something rings true to you, fine. If something does not resonate, please leave it behind, for neither we nor those of the Confederation would wish to be a stumbling block for any.

© 2009 L/L RESEARCH

SPECIAL MEDITATION
JANUARY 12, 2004

Question from G: Q'uo, I would like to request that this be a potluck reading, but before you begin, I would like to share some of myself and my seeking.

I begin with a few intellectual understandings. I have heard you speak of the process of spiritual evolution as a long and endlessly subtle one. I have read Ra's words in which they say that catalyst must be appreciated over a long period of time. I know, on some level, that I have everything I need and I know, on every level, that I have what I consider to be the greatest outside source of advice available contained within the treasure trove of the L/L transcripts.

Still, I can be a very confused personality. I have reached into those places which I have so eloquently heard described in your words shared with this group and I have just barely touched what I feel to be Christ consciousness and have had brief moments of feeling what freedom might feel like in an awareness that has penetrated the veil to some extent. I see these places and burn to live an identity from those spiritual altitudes; I yearn to be a representative of what true life is to the people of this planet who only know of it in myth, religion, story and dreams; and desire with all my heart, in moments when I actually feel "all my heart," to serve as a channel for a higher will, a higher love, a higher light and a higher way to a world that chose to forget their rightful and divine place in the kingdom of the Creator.

There are so many invisible walls of fear and unknown self, however, that, if not prevent, than surely offer me great challenges in merging my identity with those barely brushed-upon places of truth. What I have felt deep down in those depths of self are only momentary gifts that don't stay, but visit a me that is dry, serious, hurting, confused and off-center more days than not. Much of my time is spent either in places of nothingness, or places without the softness of compassion, and even places that are pure and raw pain which are grueling in their intensity and constancy and impossible to escape no matter my approach.

This is all my catalyst and all my creation, this I know. I feel that I am "on the path" and heading for those realities in which I have seen the truest picture of myself, but have not been strong, integrated or disciplined in personality enough to actually live there. I know, or at least I like to tell myself I know, that I will be on the "other side" of this. What I ask here, from entities I hold most dear, is for guidance, advice, and the compassionate wisdom to help guide me to that other side. I understand that I am so much more than these limitations which I experience and [which] cause me much distress, as you assure us we all are.

What I seek is to transform it all and become empowered because of it. Sometimes that desire burns so strongly that I would like to, probably with great naiveté, put myself through a pyramidal initiation in which I can, once and for all, squarely face the self, drop my illusions, and be who I am and always have been; i.e., the Creator.

So I humbly ask that you guide me please. Give me the great Q'uo perspective which I so cherish and point me towards that light which I seek. Let the potluck begin!

(Carla channeling)

We are those known to you as the principle of Q'uo. We greet you with great joy in the love and in the light of the one infinite Creator, in Whose service we come to you. We are part of the Godhead principle, as this instrument has grown used to saying, as are you, and as are all those who sit in this circle of seeking this day. We thank each of you for taking the time, the energy, the attention, and the care from those many other concerns of your daily lives, in order to seek the truth. That simple laying aside of time is that step so often not taken, for it is difficult to lay aside that precious commodity of time in a thoroughgoing chemical illusion built upon time itself. It is a magical thing you do to open the self to those springs of truth that come from depths below the surface of ordinary subconsciousness.

We pray that that which we offer to this instrument for your consideration may have meaning for you and be helpful but, more than this, we pray that the one known as G and all of those who are in the circle may be very responsible and careful in discriminating between those ideas which may sound good but have no real substance for you personally and those ideas that seem to come from your own memory, as though you had known but had simply forgotten that which we say. In the latter case those thoughts are useful for you and are worthy of consideration. In all other cases, those thoughts are better left behind, for they are not alive for you and truth is a living and changing thing. With this discrimination in place we feel far more free to share our thoughts without concern that we may infringe upon your free will or hamper your own learning process.

This instrument was much moved by the reading of that more elaborate letter that follows the basic structure of the opening statement but in far more detail.[85] We find that the instrument's heart was touched and confused, for in her own personality the instrument has no awareness of the neighborhood and precincts of despair which have been some of the places into which your mind and spirit has wandered. This instrument's incarnational gifts have been far more of, shall we say, a match with the one known as G than this instrument's particular lessons. Consequently, the flavor of deep suffering which came through to this instrument's senses in that letter, have no answering echo within this instrument's experience. And as is natural with those whose hearts are full of love, there is a sadness and sorrow for a fellow being in pain. Yet from our standpoint, the raw and harsh feelings described within the letter are a cause for rejoicing. It may perhaps not have been fully seen by the one known as G that the greatest breakthrough in dealing with a strain or thread of deep fear is to become aware of it fully, to face it, to rest with it. As this instrument is fond of saying, sitting with the pain is the beginning of transformation.

Now, what is the peculiar nature of this pain? For pain it is and we do not quibble with the words used by the one known as G in describing the depth and the jagged and toothed nature of this particular inner torment. Certainly, that nature is hidden in the folds of personality in its endeavors to protect and defend those gifts with which the entity known as G came into incarnation. It is as though having come into a place that was alien and strange, there was, in the entrance into incarnation and in those early and powerfully shaping experiences, a desire to remove the self from a perceived pain that was sufficiently powerful to create, for the self, as it were, a mental, emotional and spiritual closet—a safe place which could only be protected and defended by unknowing. It is as though there is within the mind a door behind which there is safety; there is also a loss of those accoutrements to everyday thinking and living which might open the door of the closet before that sensitive entity, the one known as G, feels able to rejoin what can be only be described as a subjective madness. That is the orientation of the entity as it came into incarnation. It was unexpected by the soul that is your deeper self. It was not expected that there would be this instinctual reaction of revulsion and distaste. However, it is not a

---
[85] Carla had been given a long essay by G and had read it in the days before this session was held.

reaction that is inaccurate or in any way wrong and needing to be removed. Rather, it is a fundamental attitude of the self in conflict that is within red ray, connected to the survival of the being.

Therefore, the blockages or, shall we say, the limiting of the possibilities for expansion of the infinite instreaming energy of the one infinite Creator, are in place not only for the red ray but for the energy body as a whole, for the life force, as it were, is that which is narrowed in order to move through the unbalanced energy body in a safe and optimal pattern. This blockage or inhibition that locks down some expansion possibilities in the energy body, again, cannot be said to be an incorrect action or a negative result. Rather, it can be said to be a very sensible and useful way to create a place for the self within a very alien illusion from which that entity can fulfill as much as possible those intents and driving desires for learning and for service with which this entity came into incarnation.

This entity has spoken of the feelings of numbness and sleep, the feelings of life as a place where drowning is always possible, a place where there is the desire for the light and the life-giving air and yet tremendous instinctual warnings that surface regularly and repeatedly in a cycle that has been life-long, that say to the conscious mind of the entity, "Shut down and escape; close and retreat." To some extent, all entities need and provide for themselves some retreated place within the mind and the heart. When such a safe place has outworn its welcome, it takes on the semblance of a prison and that which previously was the inner closet of safety becomes the cave of fear.

The one known as G is very aware of the strides that he has made in study, in learning, and in clarifying some of these deeper places of mystery within the self. We would suggest that it is not well to break out of prison. The self has placed self in safekeeping and that place of safekeeping has served its purpose. Yet when a larger and more currently adequate safe place is desired, there is the instinctual reaction of fear in leaving the only safe place that has been known. And we speak not literally in terms of the safe place being a physical place, such as the room, the car, the solitude, but a safe place as being within the heart. It is that closet within, that sanctum, that holy place within of safety and succor, that has grown too cramped for the being which has begun to manifest out of the potential of the incarnate self that has been brought into the personality shell for this incarnation.

Perhaps one thing that may help as you work to enlarge the tents of your safe place, is the memory of the fact that you are not the personality shell, you are not the fear, you are not any of those quirky and unmanageable emotions that create your feeling of being knotted and tangled and in need of escape. None of these is you. These are experiences which you are witnessing. But they do not define or limit the being and the essence that is the one known as G. It is as if light were coming through a window that has been covered with paper, that is for the most part opaque in order to block out what is perceived as harmful rays of the sun or of the source of light. The techniques of working with this situation can make use of this trope,[86] of this image of the window which cannot possibly bring through accurate images, for the windows themselves need to be reworked in order to remove the wax, the coating, that prevents clear illumination.

Fear is a word that entities use upon your planet as though it were fear of something, as though fears had a reality only in contact with a certain vector, and this is not accurate. It is helpful in working with one's deeper fears to realize that fear is a state of contraction away from love. It is not, in its essence, connected with a source or a cause; it is the instinctual contraction around information that concerns one. When the feelings of contraction occur, the emotional body is moving away from love and towards fear. Fear does not always look like fear. More often than not among your peoples, fear is experienced as anger. Whatever the muddied emotional set which is the product of this feeling of fear, its message is always unitary. It acts as a siren that says, "Look out, there is an emergency"; it acts as the watchman ringing a tocsin that says, "There's someone breaking into the storehouse."

There is within that emotion a great instinctual urge towards some movement that will counter this cautionary situation that has brought up the emotion of fear. And to some extent these feelings of the need for movement are wise, in that oftentimes there are situations within the illusion which need to be addressed. And when one feels that one does not have the luxury of taking time at a particular

---

[86] A trope is "A figure of speech using words in nonliteral ways, such as a metaphor."

moment to deal with emotion, it is not only acceptable but appropriate to move away from both the fear and the situation in the condign[87] service of becoming able to deal with the human situation that is in the present moment, in the illusion. Yet, at a deeper level, the presence of fear may be seen as a clarion call to that portion of self that is able to rest on the hard and often uneven ground of discomfort and limitation. For the first job of a contracted entity is to rest in that contraction, to look around, to see it not with the feeling of, "Here we go again," but with the feeling of, "Let me look, as if it were the first time—to see, to feel, to sense into this fear. Let me sit with it."

In a way, that safe place of numbness can be seen as a cave with many strands of fear that have formed a curtain that sways with the wind, that is thick enough because of having so many threads to act as a door that keeps one from feeling more afraid. Even that cave has enough fear in it that there is the human desire to escape from that cave that, as the one known as G has said, if there is already a place of numbness and unthinking, where then is any escape? Where is the divine loophole that allows one to escape from this seemingly airtight cave? Yet in the compassion that you feel for yourself, it is well to take the practice of awareness of this fear to the level that, as a soul resting in silence, you are able to visualize taking down just one thread, and then just one more, and then just one more. As the mind gazes upon that fear, as it begins to sense into some of the emotions that have become trapped in that safe place that has become that prison, it is possible, only through the mercy of one's own heart, to become able to look at the fear not with judgment but with understanding and compassion. And with the willingness to exist in that fear as long as is necessary, that the being not be forced into a feeling of more risk, less safety.

In truth, transformation involves the movement created by the pressures of seeking that lift one from a current perception and place the self within a position or point from which stance the entity may look with new eyes, not because the situation has changed, but because the point of view, the place from which the view is presented, has changed. Transformation is not the result of hard work.

Rather, transformation is the result of having done the work and becoming able to release the process. The harder one works at a spiritual process the more likely it is that there will be contamination of spiritual processes by the machinations of the mind. We have often spoken of the mind as a great choice-maker but a poor spiritual support. The mind knows how to do one thing well and that is to position information in order to make patterns that produce choices that seem to aid in improving the likelihood of survival and comfort to the entity. This does not speak well for the mind as a spiritual resource. The best that can be said of the mind for one who is working in those deep areas of spiritual discipline to which the one known as G has great hopes of penetrating, is that it is a very poor choice-maker. Rather, the choice needs to be that which allows movement upon waters which one does not know, which are directed by energies and essences which you do not understand in any conscious way.

It is as if you were attempting to unravel a mystery, a "whodunit," as this instrument would call it. There has been a murder and that has been the murder of the peace of mind and the ability to rest within incarnation for the one known as G. Whodunit? It wasn't the butler, but who was it? What was it? What's going on? What is going on is the deepening of the life from the everyday to the magical and as the desire for that magical life grows, the friction of that old and limiting fear becomes more and more obvious.

We do not in any way suggest that the experiences in escape-ivity and the desire for removal of the self from all things are experiences that are trivial or that can be removed in any easy way. However, we do suggest that in persisting while in a state of unknowing, energies deeper than you can know at a conscious level shall be moving in a most helpful and appropriate manner that will, in a spiral fashion, bring the connections between mind, body and spirit in the one known as G into a progressively more and more balanced and useful state for enlarging the tents for that spiritual place of safety within.

We would at this time ask if there is a further query that may more carefully shape our comments? We are those known to you as Q'uo.

G: Thanks so very much, Q'uo. You've given me a lot to chew on. This is a specific and important

---

[87] Condign is defined as "Deserved; adequate: 'On sober reflection, such worries over a man's condign punishment seemed senseless' (Henry Louis Gates, Jr.)."

question. It is something that I have so wanted to ask since our very first meeting and that is, for better or worse, can you describe to me as thoroughly as is allowable, what effect the multiple ingestions of LSD have had on my mind, body and spirit?

We are the Q'uo, and are aware of your query, my brother. We may speak to some extent and will attempt to shape our answer in ways that will guard your free will. The crucial injury to the mind/body/spirit of the one known as G is preexistent to the ingestion of any chemicals, as you have put it. There is a situation in which the emotional body became convinced at a very tender age within incarnation that there were great dangers involved in feeling and experiencing deeply within incarnation. The role of the ingested substances then was not to initiate a wound within the psyche, as this instrument would call it, but rather to elucidate for the conscious mind the depth and extent of wounds already experienced but as yet unknown by the body.

The one known as G has mentioned that there is little remembrance of early childhood and this is indicative of the original difficulty which the ingestion of LSD simply brought to light. It is a case of awareness coming, light coming in, in a manner which was not regulated by the guidance of the self but rather by a substance which came in from without and created the capacity to experience truth, or light, of a certain intensity. That light was experienced and the intensity of it caused what could be described as an explosion or perhaps implosion within a system which created what the one known as B has described and the one known as G has also described as a hole within the self.

This is that which has needed to be healed gradually and it is perhaps at the limit of our ability to speak in this wise to say that, as the one known as G has said frequently, the current, supportive spiritual community is without any question the very best place in which to begin to tackle the healing of the self and the healing of the incarnation. The discomfort of this healing process is great. With any healing there comes the prickles of nerves becoming able to feel for the first time. That creates great pain and this has been experienced by the one known as G. However, the pain is a good pain in that it is giving notice to the one known as G that systems are coming alive again.

We find that there are, within this circle of seeking, entities who have had long practice in dealing with those prickles of awakening sensation. We speak especially of the one known as J. There is within this entity a great well of understanding of discomfort of a particular kind and therefore we find it helpful that the one known as G has arranged to work in harmony with the one known as J. Much of this particular entity's teach/learning capabilities dwells in silence, but simple observation and companionship with this entity shall be found to be extremely healing. We also find that the one known as B has an awareness of that particular kind of prison, although the relationship in this wise is more tangential or glancing. Indeed, each present within the community circle has gifts to give, yet it is these two entities, in this context, which have the greatest capacity to teach as a part of a teach/learning circle in which the one known as G has an equal ability to teach, so that there is a teach/learning circle that is genuinely taking place where relationships remain most mutually beneficial. This is also true of the one known as V, the one known as D, and the one known as C. Yet, at the same time, those three entities, for one reason or another, have less clarity in direct mentoring, shall we say, than the one known as B and the one known as J. Consequently, we would encourage observation of, and attentiveness to, these two individuals, not with an eye to absorbing their knowledge but with an eye to grasping the point of view which each has developed over a period of years of studying and learning.

When entities are in a state of nervousness or dread, they are hard-pressed; and you may watch both of those entities as they deal with that kind of catalyst to begin to see into the deep waters of patience, tolerance and grit, simple grit, upon which these entities call. But do not look at these entities in order to imitate but only in order to see another suffering soul which has found light, joy and peace, not as a steady state, perhaps, but often enough, and with impressive enough results, magically speaking. No one within your circle exists in a state of perfection. There is need in all entities still extant[88] upon your planet in incarnation for more learning, for more opportunities for service. Yet this does not mean that each imperfect entity does not have marvelous stories to share and wonderful insights

---

[88] Extant is defined as "Still in existence; not destroyed, lost or extinct."

that go beyond words. Listen not so much to the words of those for whom you have admiration, dear brother, but listen to their essence, to those honors and braveries and examples of courage and mettle that move beyond any particular circumstance and that speak to the nobility and the ideals within.

Your world of illusion is a world of action and in so many ways, your culture teaches you to appreciate jobs finished and advancements made. Yet within the process of spiritual evolution, there must be a realization that it is not in the doing but in the intending, not in the action but in the essence, that energy is transformed. It is in this wise that we would say that the light touch is ever and always important. The illusion, this instrument has often said, is cartoon-like and at times it needs to be seen as a cartoon with the only responsibility being that of supplying the correct caption for the happiest and most deeply felt laugh. See the laughability of the human condition. See the groping in the darkness that is designed into the illusion and know that it is only by a hint here and an inkling there that guidance most often chooses to share its information.

May we answer you further, my brother?

G: Treasures, Q'uo, you give me treasures. I am employing my discrimination and I disagree with nothing at all. You picked up on deeper layers to my previous question in your answer. I was going to ask you a question about referring me, if you couldn't answer, and you referred me to those that I live with and love.

In the interest of saving time and the instrument's energy I had a page written asking a question about a girl named T. I have it in my mind, I have it on paper, and B has read it so I hope that will suffice and I will just cut to the end of it and ask if there is anything that you can give, any clarity that you can offer, to my situation with her? Can you bring any light into these processes and offer me things to mull over so that I might come to a more balanced point of view about this deep and heartfelt love I feel for a girl who can't and/or won't reciprocate it as I feel and give it?

We are those of Q'uo, and are aware of your query, my brother. We may say little, but that which we may say we do say with a full and happy heart. There is no mistake in all that has occurred within the teach/learning relationship betwixt the one known as T and the one known as G. There is no lack of love or the ability to love. Indeed, the one known as T is fully and completely loving towards the one known as G. The one known as T, in her own processes, has encountered a stumbling block that this entity has encountered before within previous incarnations. This cannot be seen as that which is correct or incorrect about the one known as T. It is simply her incarnational lesson and her incarnation healing, which at this time she has chosen to ignore because of devotion to a higher ideal than the self.

The tangle for the one known as T, then, is within her own purview and not at all a reflection of anything which has to do with the one known as G. The love story, shall we say, of G and T, is a true one, regardless of the outcome upon the level of the physical illusion. The love has been healing, energizing and revivifying for both entities. Each has given all that each is able and that has not resulted in any expectation being met for either. Rather, each has felt disappointed and incomplete. Yet the energy exchange has been extremely beneficial and may well continue to be extremely beneficial if it is released into the creative Godhead principle. It is within Christ consciousness, as this instrument would say, or within the Godhead Itself, within the deepest aspects of your and the one known as T's experience, that this relationship has health, strength and meaning. It cannot be brought into the physical illusion in a way that is balanced for both entities and, consequently, it has been necessary to create space between the physical being or presence, of the one known as G and the one known as T.

There is no limit or end to love. And that has been felt purely and deeply. Allow that channel to be a source of living water, not because it is spoken, not because the other is present, but because the connection has been made. Love has been given and received and it has remained as pure as both know how to make it. Allow that gift to be what it is. There is no failure. There is no loss. There is only the expansion of two lives because of the love that each can feel in the other. Great gifts have been given and that which has not been given was not able to be given. This is perhaps all that we may say in this wise.

Is there a final query at this time, my brother?

G: You're good people, Q'uo. This is a spontaneous question. I don't know how to word it. I have this understanding that a single-pointed desire will accomplish the task which is desired by an entity, and in whatever time you could speak I am wondering if you could offer me anything about the desire that I try, and even more so lately, to instill into my day and the desire that I just try to hold on to moment after moment after moment, penetrating further into the mysteries that I don't understand about myself? If you could speak to the question of if that has anything to do with what you were talking about in the bulk portion of the reading where you cautioned against trying too hard or whether that is the "right" type of trying, that would be my final query. Thank you, Q'uo.

We are those of Q'uo and are aware of your query, my brother. Indeed, you have caught the drift of that line of thought that we were offering in the bulk of the first question in that it is vitally important to strive with all of one's heart, to as, the one known as Saint Paul said, "run the straight race," strive with one's very best at all times. The concept of excellence is a spiritual concept on a par with truth and beauty. Effort is a beautiful thing when it is given freely and with the utmost of one's ability to do something well. There is great value in that spiritually and we would never suggest in any way that you back off in this intensity. Indeed, we do not feel that you could, for it is your nature. On the other hand, balance in all things is a characteristic in general of health of the physical, health in a mental sense, and health in a spiritual sense more than anything else.

This instrument has often said, "Take it easy or you'll burn out." Now, there are two schools of thought on this and in truth we would, for the most part, agree with this instrument. Although there are nuances that this instrument has not yet grasped concerning real balance; the impulses to balance purity with laughter, and intensity with lightness, are good instincts. The choices are the same as, say, the choice of whether to live on the edge physically. If an entity wants to live hard and die young and burn the candle at both ends doing so, it is seen as a self-indulgent thing and if the entity does die because of taking risks, it is seen as a foolish incarnation brought to an end before its time because of poor judgment. On the other hand, when an entity moves into the spiritual realm and attempts to live hard and make great progress and burn the candle at both ends in the attempt to go further, know more, be more aware, the entity is inviting the same kind of early death in that the spiritual burnout, as this instrument would call it, is quick to appear when the entity has run through its own energy.

There is, shall we say, a tremendous amount of help available to the entity who releases its own effort after it has been made and rests in the fellowship of guidance, Godhead and the creation. The drive to intensity is in part based upon a perception that one is going it alone. Yet indeed there is never a solitude when it comes to spiritual evolution, for you dwell within a family of those seen and those unseen, in the inner planes and in those environments which were yours before coming to the planet you call Earth. We suggest that you lean into that peace that comes to one who has endeavored well. When the endeavor has been made, surround it with thankfulness and open that thankfulness to all of those, seen and unseen, especially those unseen who are part of the guidance system that is helping you with keels and rudders, that in truth you cannot know but that are there to help guide and point you in the right direction. Lean on that help, rest into that help, and when the aggravations and the irritations become great, allow yourself the escape, but at the same time, send a message to your family that help is needed. Do not attempt to go it alone. There is never a need to feel that one is alone. We are with you, the Creator is with you, many entities attracted to your hopes, your ideals, and your process are with you. The strength of that is palpable when called upon. And we encourage that source of comfort to be used when it is needed. We are all—incarnate, discarnate, inner planes, outer planes—one being. There is one love, one hope, one vision, one truth. It will never appear the same to two people, yet it is infinitely unitary.

We leave you in that unitary oneness, in the love and in the light of the one original Thought. Adonai. We are known to you as Q'uo. Adonai.

L/L Research

L/L Research is a subsidiary of Rock Creek Research & Development Laboratories, Inc.

P.O. Box 5195
Louisville, KY 40255-0195

www.llresearch.org

Rock Creek is a non-profit corporation dedicated to discovering and sharing information which may aid in the spiritual evolution of humankind.

ABOUT THE CONTENTS OF THIS TRANSCRIPT: This telepathic channeling has been taken from transcriptions of the weekly study and meditation meetings of the Rock Creek Research & Development Laboratories and L/L Research. It is offered in the hope that it may be useful to you. As the Confederation entities always make a point of saying, please use your discrimination and judgment in assessing this material. If something rings true to you, fine. If something does not resonate, please leave it behind, for neither we nor those of the Confederation would wish to be a stumbling block for any.

© 2009 L/L RESEARCH

Sunday Meditation
February 15, 2004

Group question: The question today has to do with changes of various kinds, whether it's changing a job or attitude or invoking a new presence of joy, peace and harmony. When we attempt these changes, when we make efforts in the third-density illusion to bring these changes about, we're wondering how we can know if we're being successful? Is there a predetermined path or way made for us already, or is this a choice we make from moment to moment totally of our own free will? How can we know if we're exactly on the beam or not?

(Carla channeling)

We are those of the principle known to you as Q'uo, and we greet you with full hearts and happy spirits in the love and in the light of the one infinite Creator, in Whose service we are. We thank you, each of you, for joining this circle of seeking today. It is our delight to be called to this group, and we would ask, as always, simply that you use your discrimination carefully in listening to our thoughts. For, as we share them, we need you to know that we are not authorities but fellow seekers and that we share opinions rather than proven fact. Please take those thoughts that you like from what we have to say, and leave the rest behind. That will enable us to speak without being concerned that we infringe upon your free will. It is well to guard carefully those portals wherein information is taken, for that which is believed is so. And when that which is believed is sufficiently different from that which is the more natural pattern of truth, the distortion can be difficult to comprehend and difficult to perceive and therefore difficult to extricate oneself from.

Indeed, this is a portion of that which you are asking this day, for you have asked about change and how to know when the appropriate change is manifesting; how to go about making sure that the changes are indeed appropriate in the pattern of your incarnation. This instrument was speaking with the one known as B concerning the piece of the Creator's creation which she calls "Avalon." The one known as B was saying that he had spoken with Avalon in that voice that has no words but expresses emotions and feelings, and he felt that the land itself had been somewhat abused in the past, misused and used too hard, so that the soil was depleted of those nutrients that it would wish to have in order to support life, and that it had been neglected and abandoned. Consequently, it was shy of humans and somewhat distrustful.

It had not occurred to this instrument that it was a two-way street, for, in this instrument's trusting and somewhat childlike way, she relates to all things and all qualities as though they were all very glad to see her, and the consequence that is indeed the reaction of the land called Avalon to the one known as Carla [is that] it is delighted to see this sprightly spirit and delighted to relate with her in any way she wishes. However, this instrument has not attempted to plant, nor has it asked of Avalon that which it wishes. And indeed this is something to think about when looking at a change that is large enough that it cannot entirely be imagined. When the question is asked, "What do you want?" or "What do I want?" the question throws the thinking mind back into the world of form and not into the world of substance. However, if the question is asked of the present moment, "What does it want?," "What does the life's situation at this moment want of me?" that is a blind and non-intellectual question, and consequently it has a big possibility of reaping a harvest of some sense. But that sense may well be a sense of substance rather than a sense of the form of the appropriate path to take. When the question is opened up so that it is clear that there is a relationship between the self and the creation, it enlists the cooperation of the creation which is, of course, an extension of the self, just as the self is an extension of the creation and just as both are holographic in nature, reflecting the Creator.

We have often said that all is one thing, and yet, when you relate to the outer world, that seemingly outer world of consensus reality, consciously including it in the decision-making process and asking it what it wishes, the question is made whole in a very special way. It is well to consult not only the inner self but that outer self that is the system of mirrors that reflects the Creator to you, that is, the outer creation, the Earth which you inhabit, the people which are your companions upon its surface. These energies and essences also have life, sentience and will. And, when cooperation is asked, it is immediately received. Then it is a question of continuing to listen, continuing to ask and continuing to have this living and protean dialogue that penetrates all forms and moves into the world of substance. The nature of coincidence or synchronicity or the unfolding of fate, if you will, is such that the more cooperation is asked and expected on a continuing basis, the more rich the sources of information will be that are eager to share information with you.

We have spoken many times about the fact that information can come through the natural world, and, indeed, it often does come through animals and elements that are in synch with the energy fields of your bodies, of your intentions, and of your hopes. So let us look at the area of intention and hope. There are two in this group, that is, three entities and two concerns, with an actual commitment of the self to a job or a new [business], and there are two other concerns within this group which have to do with attempting to create from nothing a network or cooperative or collaboration which is of a mixed nature, being partially spiritual and partially worldly. The process of visioning or envisioning is important.

From the business standpoint, of course, it is well known that one may go through a planning process in which the questions are asked of the self concerning what goals are intended, what resources come to the table to promote those goals, and so forth. It is perhaps less well understood that the same process must be followed with the environment about one and with the energies surrounding the present moment. The nexus of each present moment for each person is the self. This is why truth is so infinitely individual and personal. One is always coming from that place [where the environment is known to one] that has never been walked in before. The present moment finds each of you and each of us in a new world. It has taken aeons and densities and many, many incarnations and teachers and thoughts to bring each of us, each of you, to this precise tuning with which you greet this present moment. Consequently, your world is brand new, and nothing can be taken for granted. So it is well to look at this new world of the present moment with new eyes, innocent of supposition and without the blinders of cynicism and manic zeal, resting, relaxing and moving into the center of self.

Move with us, if you will, in the clockwise motion about the circle, feeling the energy of the group moving, growing and forming a temple of light about you. Now continue that exercise, but move only within the orbit of your being, and feel the part of the temple of the group that you are. Feel that smaller temple whose light moves into the group energy. Now, move deeper and deeper within that holy and sacred space within until you come to the very center of that being that you are and rest there. Stop, and sense into that quiet, living center of self which is your heart. Here is your place of rest, recuperation and healing. Here is your place to reach out your hand to the Creator and to feel Its hand in yours before the reaching has ever been done. This is the center of your connection to guidance, truth and stability. Were we never to speak with you another word, were there no perceived authority to offer wisdom, this center of self would be entirely sufficient to guide you, in terms of that which your desires for this incarnation were before you ever came into the experience of life with its hectic breath and its beating heart (and we may say, because of this instrument's allergies, its itching nose). Before all of the sensations of life, the center is the place of rest and the platform from which one may spring into action, spring into expanded being, spiral into those lessons to be learned and those services to be performed.

When one is able to come to the center of self and rest, then one is much more able to ask in that sacred space, "What lies before me? What is right action? What shall I see that will enable me to have more of the sense of who I am and why I am here?" When you open your eyes from this prayer, we would ask you to be open to guidance. Keep a paper and pencil handy, ready to jot down those things that come to you in this particular moment, after this particular time of centering and resting. When you get up from such a rest, keep the center open even as you become active again in the world of consensus reality. The creation is ready to expand into those areas which fascinate you, which draw you. It is sensitive to all kinds of energy, so, if there are conflicts within your desires, these will show up in the seeming cross-purposes and the [ambivalent] nature of the hints and the inklings that your guidance seems to be giving you. Consequently, there is contemplation involved in attempting to discern right action and right being, contemplation of what cross-purposes there may be.

If there is a dynamic where things seemingly are partially indicating one path and partially indicating another, sit and rest with that dynamic, letting the mind relax away from forms and looking at some of the underlying issues which might surround and inform this dynamic. Allow time for this procedure. Ask not simply on one day or on one occasion. Assume [not] that you have received the full wisdom that is available. There is a continual questing for those who wish to remain in the center of their beings, for you move on, the stream of time moves on, and the spiral of evolution moves on so that each day there is new information, there are new metamorphoses to be contemplating. And there are what this instrument has come to call distortion leavings to be released. Often that which muddies the picture for those questing for right action or right being is an over-affection for the pain, the pleasure, for the [shape] in general of the past, those things that have affected one in the past for weal or for woe.

It is just as important to release the self from past excellent experiences as it is to release the self from past misery and suffering. Does the good time in the past create or add into the reality of your present moment? If so, why? Does the pain and the sorrow that are remembered from past experiences affect, in a living and breathing way, the present moment for you? Ask yourself that. It is important to release that which has been harvested in terms of catalyst and experience. It is a natural thing to take in the food of catalyst and to digest it and work with it and get the good out of it. It is equally important to release the distortion leavings of these experiences from the system. Otherwise, they may well clog the system, making it impossible for your evolutionary energy body to absorb the nutrients of experience and be ready to take in more. If there is any lack of hunger for new things, it is entirely possible that it is because that which has been thoroughly and completely digested in one's life has not yet been eliminated from the system. When the value of the excellent times and the difficult times of one's past has been completely appreciated, it then becomes far easier to release these experiences.

Releasing negative experiences is especially important, in many cases, in terms of creating the possibility for fearlessness. When an entity has been bound into a contraction around any issue by fear, it becomes much more difficult to see clearly the colors and shapes of the issue and its resolution. This instrument recently experienced a visit to the Cathedral of Chartres in France, and she sat at the very center of a glyph which, in that enormous sacred space, takes up perhaps half a football field in its actual size.[89] It is a round maze, and its walking is considered a sacred practice. At the very center of that maze is a blinding point of light which this instrument was quick to feel. The achieving of that center is the achieving of the stable place of rest, the stable point of view from which [leverage] may be

---

[89] The Labyrinth of Chartres is built in stone into the floor of the nave. According to the site, www.beloit.edu/~arthist/historyofart/gothic/chartrescath.htm#artifact12, "The pilgrim could recreate a pilgrimage to a more distant land—like Jerusalem—by moving along the path while saying prayers. You'll notice that it is not a maze, but a single continuous path."

applied in any direction spiritually or metaphysically speaking. So much about knowing when one is on the right track, or on the beam, as the one known as V [has] said, is engaged in this pre-mental attitude, something that lives below the surface of thoughts and ideas. It is a matter of preparing the place upon which the sacred, heartfelt decisions will be made, moving into the sacredness of that, rounding oneself into that sacred place and letting in the light so that one is literally on the beam, that beam being the light that has been called from guidance, from what this instrument would call the Holy Spirit or from the higher self, as many have called it, from that place of inpouring light, [preparing] a place to stand, a place to rest when [the] calling for the light is extremely heartfelt.

In terms of knowing that you are on the beam, there is a talent in being able to look without looking, to know without knowing, and to walk between worlds. It is a lifting away from assumption, a lifting away from presupposition, and an opening into the possibilities that surround the moment. These possibilities are literally infinite. But which is that direction which calls? Which is that direction which wants you as much as you wish it? It is a matter of asking and asking again, centering and asking, centering and asking, until the life process contains the centering and the asking, the centering and the asking far beyond even a habit and more into a way of breathing life in and breathing life out. Ask … rest … ask … rest … as a way of being, so that you are asking yourself to open to the sense of rightness, the sense of resonance that you may get through your body and any of your senses, within your heart and various energy centers, in those signs and wonders which mean something subjectively to you personally. When the asking has become a part of the in breath and the resting has become a part of the out breath and the time between breaths, then you have entered a state of mind, a way of being, that has the best possibility of bringing to you a richer load or harvest of information concerning the issue about which you are asking. Sometimes it is a very subtle thing and occurs over a period of time, while in other cases there are sudden and sharp epiphanies in which whole systems of the future are seen for the first time in wonderful delineation.

It is never known ahead of time what pattern shall emerge from the chaos of asking without expectation. Yet, when it comes, there is that sense of a converging pattern that will let you know that the pieces, as the one known as S said, seem to be coming together. Chaos seems to be melting into a certain quantum, a certain situation that has, to say it one way, the blessing of guidance; to say it another way, the resonance of a good pattern that fits within those parameters of your incarnation which you set up before birth. It is not that there is a fate laid out for you. The possibilities are always infinite. It is that you have created for yourself what this instrument would loosely call a mission, a personal plan of service and learning. And, when that mission is being materially addressed, with whatever success, there is a sense of being in the right place that is unmistakable. Wait for that sense, and do not attempt to think it into place or feel it into place or in any way force the swirling mists to clear. If there is to be a misty and mysterious time, enjoy it as you would a great snow storm or a down-pouring and enriching summer rain. The vision goes away, but the heavens have opened to give life-giving moisture to the dry and thirsty soil.

Sometimes a great deal of the moisture of spiritual water must come and, for a time, blind the vision, and it is then that faith is a powerful support, that faith that all is well. It is not a faith that things will turn out appropriately, because things actually never turn out. You may have noticed this quality of life. Things spiral continuously, moving through many scenes and moods. Nothing ends or, to put it another way, everything ends, and the story moves on without missing a beat. There is no grand finale; there is no dénouement. There is simply the ongoing spiral of light and dark, laughter and tears, suffering and joy. Yet, beneath all of those experiences, surrounding all of that seemingly outward miasma of confusion, there remains always the place of center to which you may go. It is the closest thing to you. You may amputate arms and legs and not lose your center. You may glow incandescent as a candle without clothing, without occupation, with only the consciousness with which you came into the world of consensus reality, and you will have that center, that center that links you to all that is, to all that has been and all that will be. All you need is in that center. Perhaps that is the fundamental message we have to share this day. Rest and know all is love. All is one; all is love.

You are magical beings, my friends. You are not at risk, as it may seem that you are in terms of a physical life. You are citizens of eternity. You are in a very precious and hard-won place. You have cast aside all else, because you felt that this incarnation was important enough to invest your eternal self in, to go through a great deal of inconvenience and suffering just so that you might improve the balance of your own personality and serve in the consensus reality about you, to fulfill goals which you have set long ago, goals that have to do with being helpful. Rest in the knowledge that these things are in place and that there are many, many sources of information that are very dedicated to communicating with you and with the groups with which you associate.

Notice those groups about you. For this instrument, it has been a year or more of very obvious building up of the group, but, in all of the years of this instrument's life, there has been that same process going on, and, in each of those in this circle this day, this process has been taking place. Gradually the currents of self and other-self have circled and spiraled until each has met each, and each has been drawn into this group on this day. Each entity that you meet is a portion of a group, a soul group, as the one known as S has called it, or a group of those who have often incarnated together, to work together and to serve together. So, when you are touching entities, you are touching the groups with which they are involved, and you are binding yourself and others in streams of love and mutual hope and ideals. As you go about your daily life, and as you meet each entity, see the relationship in its deeper terms, and know that energies are involved that are far, far below the level of one's awareness. They may be sensed, and they may be followed, but they may usually not be understood. Follow those relationships, and consider the relationship and your part in it, in each case looking for the ways to support and encourage each other. There are higher selves involved in each of these groups as well and higher hopes that each of these groups may have in terms of the service of the members of that group to the planet and its people. Trust this network to be there, and expect to meet old friends as you move through the days ahead.

Above all, sharpen the energies with which you move through life by offering yourself the solace of meditation. Time in the silence cannot be overrated for returning one to that precious center, what the one known as G would call the "power of now."[90] Enlist the help of Gaia, as the one known as B calls the planet upon which you dwell. Walk within its precincts and allow the trees and the wind and the small animals to sooth you, to connect with you, and to bring you back to that precious center.

This instrument informs us that we need at this time to open the meeting to questions. Are there questions at this time beyond that which we have spoken?

G: Q'uo, I'm not sure of how exactly it is that the quarantine works around this planet, but, working within those principles, is it possible that an entity or a group of incarnate entities could request and create a physical meeting with beings of an extraterrestrial nature or higher density beings of a positive nature on this planet?

We are those of Q'uo, and are aware of your query, my brother. We do not choose to give this instrument any information upon this point for two reasons. Firstly, attempts of this nature create an energy that we do not consider particularly desirable. Secondly, the attempt to create such a meeting is much like sending out a "CQ" on a ham radio.[91] The entities who are monitoring these particular ham radio bands are, however, for the most part negative.

The infringement upon free will in giving further information is such that we find that we are not able to speak further. However we would say that the energies of the one known as B have already brought to you, the one known as G, experiences of meetings with entities that are not human and are certainly very positive, and we speak now of those entities on Avalon which this instrument has often called devas and which have a great deal of life and reality of their own. This kind of open questing is quite desirable, and we would recommend that, instead of attempting to meet an extraterrestrial, you simply attempt to meet the many, many entities around you with which you have not yet become acquainted.

May we answer you further, my brother?

---

[90] Eckhart Tolle, *The Power of Now*, Novato, CA, New World Library, [c1999]. This is a favorite inspirational book of G's.

[91] In ham radio, signaling the Morse code for the letters "CQ" is signaling a desire to speak with any other ham radio operator within range.

G: No, that was cool. I don't think I or anybody else has big plans to do so. I was just curious. Thank you, Q'uo.

We thank you, my brother. Is there a query at this time?

B: I have one that's not directly on this topic. I was wondering what the role of the social memory complex was in the development of consciousness?

We are aware of your query, my brother, but are having trouble with a response because of the fact that, as far as we are aware, consciousness is, and it is not in need of being, shall we say, developed.

B: Growth is perhaps a better term?

Would you rephrase the question, my brother?

B: I was examining the social memory complex, and, as we enter the seventh sub-density of the third density, Ra has said that we can actually form these structures, and I was wondering how that would interact with our conscious spiritual growth? I mean, why does the social memory dominate in the fourth density? What do we learn from this experience?

We are now far more aware of your query, my brother. The social memory complex is as if you had opened your arms and said, "Everybody in," as if you were the Creator and you had accepted everyone that was about you into your heaven. The energy of this formation enhances and intensifies the purity and the clarity of the individual's ability to open into unconditional love, or, in other words, to become a part of the social memory complex. So, as soon as a social memory complex begins to be formed, simply by leaning into the power of that group being or essence, you are allowing the self to become more and more attuned to that sublime or supernal nature of the self which truly feeds into the social memory complex.

You see, my brother, when experience is taken in at the level of consensus reality and conscious thought, much of the detail of the actual transactions taking place between entities is lost. The nuances are washed away by the grossness of words and actions, and the intentions, the energies that are being exchanged between two people, or a person and a place, or a person and a situation, are grossly oversimplified so that they can be consciously understood. Even in the most subtle and quick mind, there is that limit of rapidity of the accumulation of fact and the intuition, the ability for direct insight, is hampered. What the social memory complex does as entities move into it and begin to, shall we say, "get it" is to empower and enable the personal shell of personality to relax and lift away from specificity so that it may become less reactive and more stable. The personality shell of third density is unnecessary in fourth density, and the great gift of the seventh sub-octave of third density is that the social memory complex has enough energy now to be accessed by intention.

May we answer you further, my brother?

B: One quick point. Would the attempts to form a social memory complex here or, more specifically, at Avalon, be in any way disruptive to the non-human life that's there now, that which you referred to as devas and the plants and animals being of lower densities?

We are those of Q'uo, and are aware of your query, my brother. Indeed, were social memory being attempted, as if in a vacuum, as if only with people, certainly this would be perhaps less than optimal in terms of the energy of that portion of Gaia to which you refer, and this is why the instrument, in its talk with you at an earlier time, had the intuition that the land must be a portion of the questing for the social memory complex being formed upon its sacred ground. To form a social memory complex with the full cooperation of the earth that it contains is to make each place so included a sacred space. It most definitely would be appropriate to include the Earth itself as a part of the social memory complex, for the Earth is a very sentient and very conscious being.

May we answer you further, my brother?

B: So you would see no problem with second-density life being exposed to a fourth-density concept, thinking basically of the plants and things we would like to grow there. Now, my concern is this: a lot of times when higher concepts are introduced too early in a developmental stage, they might bias the development as I see here, when the Confederation introduced entities from other worlds to our planet. Do you understand what I'm trying to get at?

We are those of Q'uo, and are aware of your query, my brother. If it were forced upon this entity, Gaia, that such and such a group wished to do such and such a thing here and it was simply told to the land, then, yes, my brother, there would be the lack of respect. However, the second density and the first density, unlike the third density, dwell within the creation of the Father that the fourth density dwells within, so that in a way, moving into the social memory complex energy is returning to oneness with the creation of the Father. And indeed this works more synergistically than third density is able to with these nature spirits and with the planet itself.

May we answer you further, my brother?

B: That clarified it sufficiently, thank you.

We thank you, my brother. Is there a query at this time?

G: Q'uo, I usually wouldn't ask a question like this, but I'm just really curious. How did it come to be that the three of us, B, V and I, all had a dream about a volcano, and two of us had a dream about a Polynesian named Bob? Could you maybe speak to the symbolism and why it was that we had really similar dreams, please?

We are those of Q'uo, and are aware of your query, my brother, and, as you perhaps surmised, we leave this work to you.

Is there a final query at this time?

S: I have a question. We've noticed of late that the difficult times Carla calls psychic greeting, or what has been termed the dark brotherhood, have given very intensive interference to myself and those of my soul family group. I have asked the guidance source whom I call "The Seven Dwarves" about this. They were quite reluctant to give me any specific details. I recall that, similarly, I had asked you at one time, and you were also reluctant to give me specific information and just your opinion and your ideas. What is the meaning or spiritual reason behind that?

We are those of Q'uo, and are aware of your query, my brother. The nature of so-called psychic greeting or psychic attack or the influence of darkness is such that it seems to be coming in from without and seems to be a threat that is outer to one's own self. And yet the mechanism by which these greetings are attracted is the desire to stand in the light. The harder and more fervent the desire to be of the light and to serve at one's highest and best, the more sharply delineated are those portions of the shadow side of yourself that have not come into full harmony and acceptance within the self as loved, forgiven and redeemed. Only you as a self, falling in love with the self and going through a full circuit of forgiving, accepting, redeeming of self, can do the work that enables one not to have the chinks in the armor, as this instrument would say, of light. That armor of light shall always have chinks. It shall always, within third-density incarnation, be imperfect, because, were you able to be perfect, it would be time for you to move on, and you would simply not any longer be of third density. You would go through the experience of physical death so that your energy body, your soul, would be free to move into a more appropriate garment for continuing your experience.

Consequently, those who seek to stand the closest to the light are those who shall bring about the rightness or readiness for the experience of being tried, tested, greeted, attacked or overshadowed. These are all subjective terms which describe a situation where one feels invaded or intruded upon or encroached upon. What is encroaching upon the self in a metaphysical sense in psychic greeting is the shadow side of one's own self. So, when it is experienced from without, then it is well to take that mirror that is the dog barking at one, the wolf biting at one, and look to see within the self what portion of that shadow side, what vagrant part of the past, what relationship that has not been thought upon sufficiently, is truly causing the distortion within that has caused the wolf to bite just in such and such a way, so that responsibility is taken. And then, once responsibility is taken and it is seen that there is nothing to fear, for it is only the self, then it is helpful to be able to release the fear and the contraction around this [greeting], so that it no longer is a threat, it is simply that which is occurring. Then the work towards healing of the situation may be done without the additional stumbling block of fear blocking one's own path of forward progress.

May we answer you further, my brother?

S: It's an interesting thing for me to consider. I will have to think on it. Thank you very much.

We thank you, my brother. We find it is time to depart from this group, as this group's energy wanes somewhat, and it is well to leave this instrument while there is still plenty of energy to make a good farewell. And so we do offer you farewell, reminding you always that we are with you whenever you should mentally request it, to strengthen and support you, without words but with love and energy.

We leave you in the love and in the light of the one infinite Creator. We are those known to you as the principle of Q'uo. Adonai. Adonai. ✣

L/L Research

Sunday Meditation
March 7, 2004

Group question: The question today has to do with change, perhaps even change to the point of self-healing. We are wondering if Q'uo could talk to us about the decision-making process that goes into this type of change. Could you explore the concepts of honor and duty and how discovering what our honor and duty in a certain situation is might help us to make the choices that would lead to this change and perhaps healing ourselves, finding a direction to be of service to others?

(Carla channeling)

We are those of the principle known to you as Q'uo, and we greet you in the love and in the light of the one infinite Creator, in Whose service we come to you this day. We thank you so much for the privilege, the honor, and the duty of being called to this group this day. It is a blessing to us to be able to serve as we had hoped to and a call from your group is most welcome. We ask, as always, that each of you guard the portals of your discrimination very carefully, listening to the personal resonance that comes with your unique truth and not for any perceived outer authority. If you are able to guard those things that you keep of what we say and those things that you discard, then we will feel far more free to be able to share with you without infringing upon your free will.

The freedom of will has been a sticking point for many in the creation of a satisfying and rewarding spiritual practice. Free will can be a bewildering thing. The chore of determining what one truly wishes to do can be awe-inspiring and mind-boggling, for it is as though one were pulled in different directions by many different opinions and strains of thought in almost every situation. It is not too difficult to imagine the choices of many things: what to eat, what to wear, and so forth. However, there are levels of choice that affect more than just a moment or a day. It is as the choices become more ponderous and seem to carry more weight for the present and the future that the predicament of making what this instrument would call the "right" choice is more and more substantial a challenge.

The one known as B invoked the principle of the honor/duty that the ones of Ra had spoken of before with this group in saying that every honor is a duty and every duty an honor. It was the one known as B's thought that perhaps when one is attempting to make a truly correct choice for the self, however one wishes to define that word "correct," that perhaps one would do well to think of what one feels one's honor would require in a certain situation or what one's duty might require. It might also and equally be suggested to invoke the principle of unconditional love. Where is the love in a decision? It was the one known as T's hope that, in making the decision for his own right livelihood, he would be able to find that choice that most truly and deeply opened and revealed his heart, a deep and true center of self.

Certainly when one views the question that you asked and looks at the level of depth that is suggested when one is attempting to make decisions for the healing of one's self, any and all ways of looking at a situation, feeling into it, sensing the nuances of it, and so forth, are helpful. All resources are helpful when approaching a decision that has the capacity to affect one's path not just in this next day or next week, but in the rest of the incarnation to come.

We would perhaps start with that of which the one known as D was speaking, in terms of his own process, of his discovery that in the very pain of the dramatically and unconsciously lived life, where events seem to overtake one and toss one about with tremendous force and seeming carelessness, there is an aspect to this suffering that is attractive and that actually can begin to create the impression that it is this pain that is actually a sign of life and that, when the pain or the critical or difficult nature of the situation eases, the meaning of life has somehow been taken away from one and that, somehow, that meaning must be sought again, even though that meaning is a meaning that is felt in suffering and pain. This entity was discussing a way of looking at one's relationship with others that is called "co-dependant."

We would suggest that, if one may take a step back from a specific co-dependency or addiction that is specifically geared to one person, one may perhaps see that in each incarnational pattern there is that tendency to divide the self into the good self and the bad self, the light self and the dark self, the peaceful self and the disturbed self, and so forth, creating out of a universal and infinitely graded being with no seam or rip in the make-up of that being a being that has separations and isolations of parts of the self from other parts of the self, so that there seems to be more going on, shall we say, than in truth there really is. It is so endemic to your peoples that we would suggest that instead of the term "co-dependency" one may perhaps think more generally in terms of addictions. For the addiction to pain is no more of a puzzle than the addiction to any substance that one begins to see as not being helpful for the self. Why would entities with good sense and good balance choose to inculcate within the self a continuance of pain in order to feel more alive? It is simply because it it is the observed method upon your planet, in the culture in which you enjoy living, for entities to embrace those things which are destructive such as overwork, a dependence upon substances, and other imbalances, because they seem to be appropriate and even necessary for the functioning of the organism and the being, in the job, in the family, and in the environment. The habit of looking outward for meaning, of depending upon ideas, people or things for a feeling of rightness and a sense of meaning is that which has been accepted among your peoples as the appropriate way of behaving and thinking.

It is astounding to most entities who are living at this unconscious level to conceive that they may perhaps not be in a carefully engineered situation, in a certain, shall we say, "house," or environment of job and family and personal details for the reason that they may feel is so. They may not be in the job, for instance, because that is the correct job, they may be in that job because it seemed appropriate and it has seemed to be adequate to the life. The thought that one could simply walk out of this "house" of arrangements and relationships and "the way things are" would indeed seem not only astounding but somehow deeply wrong. Yet it is true that entities build their houses to include the pain that seems necessary in order for them to feel alive, normal and functioning.

So when one attempts to begin healing the self, it may perhaps be seen that a substantial amount of deconstruction becomes necessary. There is a stage that one goes through that is analogous to that which the one known as B, G, and D have been doing within the structure of the dwelling place in which this meeting is now taking place, the house that this instrument calls the Magic Kingdom. Indeed, it has been remarked often within the last few weeks, as disaster after disaster has been narrowly averted and repaired, that the angels that have stationed themselves as part of the loving system of guidance that surrounds this group have been working overtime! And each time that the one known as B has identified an electrical fault or found a gas leak or the one known as D has seen a fire start and put it out, that the house itself is expressing the desire to heal. The people within the house have banded together in an increasingly tight-knit group with the desire to create new life, new energy, a higher and a truer sense of self for each and for the group as a whole. And in this increasingly intense environment of idea, ideal and focus, the house itself is experiencing a deconstruction as old wires are pulled out and new wires must be put in, new wires that can hold more of a charge; that can sustain more of an effort. And indeed when one is attempting to heal, it is as though one were going back into the wiring of the self and needing to deconstruct some of that wiring, pulling out the inadequate wiring, checking the system for leaks, checking the system for truth, shall we say, checking the new "wire" that one is putting in to carry energy, to see if it indeed has more strength, if it indeed can carry more energy safely and at a stable manner and level.

One is doing the internal rewiring of various patterns of thinking, attempting to pull out of the self those tangles of old wiring that are no longer attached to anything that is helpful but that still may be carrying power, but oh so poorly and so inadequately. So this process must begin with a careful, conscious period of releasing that which is outmoded within one's thinking, within one's feelings, within one's being. And for each entity this will require different resources and different approaches, for no two people approach the mirror of the self in the same way. Each entity approaches the mirror and looks into the eyes of the self with a different bias. Each has a slightly different slant. Even each within oneself, from time to time, will be able to access different levels of self and be able to see into different levels of patterning and what the patterns of the past have to offer in terms of health, wellness and healing. Perhaps there are some old patterns that are extremely helpful. Not all things that are old are poor. Some of the oldest patterns within you may be some of your best work.

So it is not that one pulls everything out in order to toss it and to start over completely but rather that one looks into that mirror, into the eyes and not at the image; for one can get lost in mental images as well as one can in the image of the mirror. Your face does not tell the story of your soul, but the face of your personality also does not tell the story of your true essence, especially when one seeks to move into a better balance with the self, into a self-healing mode. One must not simply go with preconceived notions about the self. Rather, it is good to do that of which the one known as G has been speaking, the going on a quest for personal vision, a quest to see into that essence of self that is the gift which you have brought in the package that is your personality, your body, and what the ones known as B and V were calling your identity.

You have a location for your incarnation in space and time. The fact that in order to have a location you also have to buy into the illusion of life and death is simply a fact of the matter, a condition in which all incarnation is held. There is an illusion implicit in drawing breath and that illusion is that you are a location, an identity, a personality, a face. These concepts of self, in terms of your spiritual center, are and remain illusory right through the incarnation. Even in the midst of the illusion of incarnation you may know yourself as an illusory personality. Were this to be the beginning and end of the soul, there would be no point in working towards the evolution of that soul. However, you are, even within incarnation, a real essence, part of what this instrument calls the Godhead principle, part of the Creator. That you have a package makes you seem very singular and indeed you are unique; yet at the same time, you are a holograph of the Creator.

So in many ways the journey towards meaning is a journey down through layers of decreasing selfhood as more of the shell, the illusion, the body, the face, the personality, is seen for what it is and allowed to loosen its hold upon self-identity. What is your identity? Much of the decision-making process has to do with the stance from which you view the creation and that begins with your self-concept. If you conceive of yourself in thus and thus a way, then you begin to build that "house," that narrowness, that stricture that we were speaking of earlier. You begin to construct your location and seemingly to block yourself from making certain choices because they would not be appropriate to someone in this particular kind of house, this particular kind of personality.

Once you feel that you have gone through a time of coming to your own essence, once you feel that you have begun to be able to identify what it is to be you, that you that you will know as well ten thousand years from now in another incarnation as you do this day, then you can begin to ask the questions that the one known as B was asking, but only then. You cannot simply begin by saying, "This is who I am and therefore these are my duties and these are my responsibilities." First and foremost you must come into a relationship with yourself that is loving, unified and compassionate. In the words of this particular instrument, you must "redeem" yourself. For as long as you feel that there are parts of your personality that are the shadow side, that have not yet been claimed, they will continue to indicate their lack of being integrated by expressing themselves as negatives within your life experience and they will draw to you catalyst that is designed to uncover and delineate the particulars of these biases.

However, there does come a time when that first cluster of work is done and you sit, shall we say, in terms of the Native American way, on your blanket, in meditation, with the creation and the twelve directions spread out, the creation emanating from the center of the self and the wheel of unity spinning endlessly and fruitfully around that center in a way that feels powerful and full of life. In that centered position, then, you may ask yourself, truly, "Where is the love? Where is my heart? What are my duties? What do I wish to honor in my life?" And all of these questions are worth time and contemplation and a process of asking, and resting, and asking again. For such questions will remain with you as part of the spiral of learning and service that is the evolution of mind, body and spirit within incarnation.

How can you know that you are on the right track? We cannot give you a thumbnail rule for being in self-healing mode. We can speak of certain characteristics of being "on the beam." We've spoken often to this group about fear. When there is a feeling of attachment, urgency, desperation or necessity, these energies are suspect. It is to the peaceful, resting spirit that a balanced pattern is more likely to come and it is to the questing soul who rests with such a vision and allows it to mature that the inevitable difficulties of such a process will seem less demanding, less difficult. This instrument was speaking earlier of a level of peace that she has experienced recently and she was finding difficulty in describing it, yet it has to do with relaxing attachments to all outcomes in the growing understanding or grasp of the fact that there is no true attachment, there is no true necessity. What there is, is a spectrum of infinite possibility, which acts either without focus or with focus. Without focus, it is not as powerful in terms of interacting with other sources of energy. It moves and makes connections and will ally itself with like-minded energies. Yet it is to an entity who has done the work to have brought focus to that feeling of sitting in the center of the blanket with the energies of self very openly and tidily arranged about one like the pattern upon that blanket, that the connections will be stronger, the click of recognition between people will be more powerful, the ability to communicate ideas will be more pointed and more obvious. And when more than one entity in a group has begun to get that inner centering and that feeling of focus, the possibilities for deeper and deeper collaborations that are part of the hoped-for service and learning of the incarnational plan become more and more prominent and likely to prosper.

The one known as Dewey[92], in speaking of how his learning as a physicist affected his own thoughts about spiritual matters, chose to describe the way he saw the "new man" as an ethical biological unit. The "old man," he said, "was simply a biological unit." It worked from instinct, it made its choices, and it protected that which was its own and saw to the survival of itself and its family unit. However, when one moves into the new definition of self that is the conscious self, that self that is aware of itself as a soul, the word that is added is "ethical." An ethical biological unit is one who does look to the honors, to the duties, and to the love that is theirs to judge and deem appropriate and choose.

How true it is that one must, at some point, make a positive choice or the choice will simply make you and that choice may be a choice in which all of the old unconscious patternings of what the one known as Eckhart Tolle called the "pain body" may be thriving in glorious health. So it is well to take hold of the decision-making process, especially in such deep matters as right livelihood and self-healing, and to move through the most conscious effort possible of gazing within the self, moving the self to the best-judged center of self that can be found, and from that point, asking the self, "What do I love and where is the love pulling me? What do I honor and how can I [give] honor to those things that I do so honor? What are my just and fair responsibilities and how can I best fulfill those?"

This instrument has thought sometimes about the concept of responsibility, for she has seen many entities who are on spiritual quests who find themselves choosing to walk away from situations

---

[92] Referring to Dewey Larson, author of the Reciprocal Theory of physics that Don Elkins and the Ra group discussed in the Ra material.

without taking responsibility for them. Within her own life it has never seemed that this would be possible for her. Yet for many, the effort of becoming conscious is that effort which, in the terms of their own thinking at the time, cannot be made unless a clean and sharp break is made between the past and the present. And therefore, it cannot be said to be incorrect for such dramatic choices to be made. On the other hand, if there is sufficient time and space and patience for a slower and more careful process, it is very much a help to that process to move slowly, to move gently, and to ask the self frequently, "How does this feel? Do I feel centered? Do I feel open? Do I feel in any way hindered or bound by my belief system?"

Think of a root system that may be fouling a structure like a sidewalk or a pipe system. Some roots need to go deep, perhaps some pipes need to be moved. You must determine in the system of your own working spirit and its connections with the body, with the mind, and with the emotions, what is working and what is not working. "Where do I need to focus my redeeming love? Where do I need to embrace a part of myself of which I have been unconscious and which has been leading me around into dark places?" For indeed it is very true that the structures of suffering have to do with the thinking of the individual. It is not that you would not experience pain if you were completely without bias and exposed to fire. You would still burn. However, when the entity can see fire not as something from which to contract but as a brother or a sister, then certainly appropriate action may be taken to avoid immolation by such a force in one's life but at the same time there is nothing to fear, literally, no thing to fear, for you are an entity far beyond the limitations of these illusory husks, the personality, the body, the face, the package. Do not identify overly with the package but seek to begin to know what is inside and let that center of self begin to act as the gyroscope that is whirling inside in rhythm with the heart of the Creator so that, as the Creator seeks to know Itself, so do you seek to know yourself. And from that center all things have their right pattern.

May it be so for each of you in increasing levels of harmony and strength. For each is part of a beautiful dance, that dance of creation in which every flower and tree and bird and being has its part.

We would at this time open the meeting to further questions, if there be any at this time.

G: Q'uo, would you have any recommendations for concerning the preparation for my upcoming vision quest at Avalon and how I might best maximize the experience while there?

We are those of Q'uo, and are aware of your query, my brother. We would say to this instrument, trust the self and be unafraid to open the self to unfamiliar things. It is not an easy thing to move quickly from the surface of life to that level of consciousness where subconscious processes are available to the conscious mind. In something like a vision quest that you have spoken of, the basic effort is to open the doors of perception, as the one known as William James has said it, so that one has more information available. The concept of the quest has to do with the concept of the self as having many floors of being, shall we say, like a tall building that has quite a few different levels, not only above ground but also below the level that may be perceived as the ground floor. It is those deep, subterranean floors of self that one is attempting to access. Now, when one goes down the stairs into the basement, it is a very straight-forward thing. There is a certain angle to the steps and they are at a certain a distance from each other. It is a very regularized, geometric structure, the stair steps having so many degrees of declination, angles of turning, and so forth. It is not unlike that within the layers or floors of the self, below the level of the conscious mind. There is a very definite geometry and there is a way to move down into the deeper levels of the mind.

The one known as B was discussing one of these ways, the idea being to read in the mythology that affects one's blood ancestry. The thinking behind this is correct in that the body and its structure, down to the cell structure, is a gift from the ancestors of that body. Each cell in the body is instinct with the knowledge, the life, and the experience of all of those entities that have shared those cells, those inherited strands of what this instrument would call, DNA. So you are, as a body, as a being within incarnation, a part of the Earth from which these beings sprang, the mountains, the lakes, the air. And as one grows up within a certain environment, the geography, the topography of the land becomes written in the DNA and becomes part of you in a way that is magical, so that connecting with the Earth, connecting with the surroundings which are part of your heritage, places you in an optimal situation for stability in moving down into the roots of self. Certainly the roots of the body are not necessarily the roots of the mind or the spirit. But one is in the body and one needs the grounding of that body in order to fuel that quest for vision. Further, one has, in the stories told by the ancestors of your body, material that describes the geometry, shall we say, of a very deep level which this instrument would call the archetypal level, in that subconscious being which is a part of you. You are attempting to ask for vision from this larger part of self to which you do not have access in conscious, daily life. Consequently, the one known as B was suggesting that one steep oneself in the mythology and stories of one's ancestors. And certainly this is one way to approach such a quest.

There are other strengths into which one may lean in order to achieve this deep opening. Such alternatives include music, art and the creation itself. They include as well many other things and we do not feel we may be much more specific than this without infringing as you go about creating what needs to be for you a very self chosen, consciously chosen, experience. Within these parameters, may we answer you any further, my brother?

G: No, thank you very much, Q'uo.

We thank you, my brother.

G: I have one from the one known as J who asks, "How does one go about creating a ritual that allows you to effectively configure your mind for sacred workings and donning the magical personality?"

We are aware of your query, my brother, and we thank you for the question. It certainly is one with which the one known as J has been working for some time. We would say to the one known as J that the preceding discussion may help in somewhat delineating the field of action for becoming a conscious, magical being. The essence of seeing the self as magical and experiencing the self as magical is that great step of believing that the self is magical. If one moves from that assumption, then one must take responsibility for each thought. Not simply each action, but each thought. For the magical personality is often defined, at least by this instrument, as one who is able to effect changes in consciousness by thought alone. This again requires a time of deconstruction to loosen the bonds of shallow attachments and reconstruction in attaching to far more sturdy sources of power, or conduits for power.

We believe that this may be sufficient for now but we would be glad to revisit the question with the one known as J in the future.

Is there another query at this time?

G: A quick one, Q'uo. With enough work can an entity become a crystalline entity in one incarnation and is that goal worthy of pursuit?

We are those of Q'uo, and are aware of your query, my brother. Indeed, each of you is a crystal, it is a matter of mining for it, finding it, polishing it up, and allowing it to shine.

Is there another query at this time?

G: Q'uo, is this instrument hard-pressed to continue these channelings on her own?

We are those of Q'uo, and aware of your query, my brother. In gazing into this instrument's state of mind we find that she is as she has always been: one who sincerely wishes to serve. This instrument is convinced and has been convinced for a number of years that one of her right livelihoods or means of service is indeed this channeling of which you ask. It therefore is that which she does see the honor and the duty of doing. She does not find it at all burdensome. She does not find it, shall we say, fun; it is not something that draws her and consequently she must make a conscious effort to align herself with the gift which has been given her. There are times we find that she regrets the effort that it takes to move into this alignment and at the same time she would not forgo the honor even upon the point of death. Consequently, we would say no, this instrument does not find it difficult to serve. She would find it difficult not to serve.

May we answer you further, my brother?

G: Not on that line, thank you, Q'uo.

We thank you, my brother.

G: Sorry to hog it all but if nobody else is asking, I'll take it again. Q'uo I was just curious if for a wanderer to awaken to their status as being from elsewhere they need to be first of a 51% service-to-others vibratory nature before awakening to the truth of their identity?

We are aware of your query, my brother, and we do not find that to be necessary. Indeed, it is not necessarily at all linked that one be aware of polarity and that one be aware of not belonging to this planetary system. The two strains of learning are not necessarily connected.

May we answer you further, my brother?

G: I don't think I meant awareness of the workings of polarity but that they must be vibrating at 51% service to others. Must they be harvestable in order to awaken consciously to who they are?

We are those of Q'uo, and believe we are more aware of your query, my brother. Again, it is not necessary to have any awareness except the discomfort of being in a difficult place that does not feel right to be aware that one does not belong some place. The tendency is for those who wander to move into incarnation within third density with some of the overlays of the previous density which would suggest that many a wanderer has much information flowing through about service to others and so forth. And so there is a tendency for service-to-others entities to be those who are wanderers or shall we say it more properly, for those who are wanderers to be aware of desiring to be of service to others. Indeed, it is almost a part of desiring to be of service to others. Indeed, it is almost a part of the wanderer's syndrome, shall we say. However, there are many who awaken first to their discomfort and have not yet done that work of choosing a polarity.

May we answer you further, my brother?

G: No, thank you very much.

Is there a query from any in the group at this time?

G: So, for my vision quest, would you say that arming myself with a question, the question, my set of questions, would be sufficient? To go there with my questions for the Creator [and let the Creator do the answering]?

We are those of Q'uo, and are aware of your query, my brother. It is not for us to say what is sufficient. We believe that the thought of sufficiency is not helpful at this time. We would suggest that you allow yourself to be undefended, and unclothed with suppositions concerning what is enough and so forth. Beyond that, we find that we cannot speak.

Is there a final query at this time?

T: Q'uo, this is not a query. It's just an expression of thanks for your presence and help … in the last few weeks.

We are those of Q'uo, and aware of your most kind thoughts, my brother, and we thank you for them. We are indeed most pleased that we have been a resource for you at this time and we hope that we may continue so. Indeed, we hope that we may continue to serve each of you as a part of your system of guidance and strength. Please know that, whatever your self-doubt and whatever your process, we are there and so much is there for you. You are surrounded by a great web of love and we cannot tell you how strong and how bright that web is and how far it goes. Indeed, in the end all are connected to all.

We offer each of you blessings and love. We thank you with all of our hearts and we leave you in the love and in the light of the one infinite Creator. Adonai. Adonai. ♣

L/L Research is a subsidiary of Rock Creek Research & Development Laboratories, Inc.

P.O. Box 5195
Louisville, KY 40255-0195

L/L Research

www.llresearch.org

Rock Creek is a non-profit corporation dedicated to discovering and sharing information which may aid in the spiritual evolution of humankind.

ABOUT THE CONTENTS OF THIS TRANSCRIPT: This telepathic channeling has been taken from transcriptions of the weekly study and meditation meetings of the Rock Creek Research & Development Laboratories and L/L Research. It is offered in the hope that it may be useful to you. As the Confederation entities always make a point of saying, please use your discrimination and judgment in assessing this material. If something rings true to you, fine. If something does not resonate, please leave it behind, for neither we nor those of the Confederation would wish to be a stumbling block for any.

© 2009 L/L Research

Special Meditation
March 11, 2004

Question from C: Events seem to be preparing me for a new direction in my life and I would like Q'uo to speak to that direction as much as possible.

(Carla channeling)

We are thus known to you as the principle of the Q'uo, and we greet you in the love and light of the one infinite Creator, in Whose service we come to you this day. May we say, my brother, what a true privilege it is to be called to have a conversation with you concerning the question of what new directions to which you may be called. It is a question that is a joy to address, as it is open, straightforward and moving to the heart of things, releasing and embracing that which is, and that which is to be.

We would only ask one thing of you at this time and that would be that, as you listen to these humble words, you are able to release any thoughts of our being authorities over you in any way. We may have opinions and we are most happy to share all that we know and think. Yet is not knowledge and truth a very subjective thing, my brother? Consequently, though we aim to speak directly to your soul, at the same time we realize that some arrows will miss their mark. Therefore, please, as you listen, take care to discard these ideas which do not have resonance for you at this time. With that understood we shall feel free to express ourselves and not be concerned with infringing upon the freedom of your will and your process.

Within the question of new directions lies an assumption that that which is old may need to be discarded. For as the one known as C wrote in a letter to this instrument, it seems that there is a pattern of taking on new directions without appropriately evaluating that repositioning of oneself within the nexus of those activities that had at one time seemed like new directions and so had been followed with passion and joy. Yet in one life there is only so much energy and the wise entity looks not back but forward, for it is in the present and in that which the present seeds for the future of the self. Thus, the concern is justly brought to bear for the seeker of evolution for the self. Consequently, we would ask the one known as C what true evaluation can this entity give of his passion for each and every item that is upon the game board, shall we speak, as a piece that is moved and that takes up the time and the energy which the player of the game is willing to expend and has the time to expend? What is the harmony of that particular piece of the game of right livelihood? Or to move the field further, the game of right moving-hood, relative to the other pieces that are upon the board?

This instrument recently was encouraged to do this kind of evaluation of those things that were upon her mind and upon her heart and she found that they were, when gazed at steadily and with an analytical mind, quite prey to being sorted in one of several ways. In the end the criterion which this instrument chose was primarily that of passion. The question became one of those things for which she felt passion. How did she prioritize them in terms of their importance? It was this exercise that relieved this instrument of continuing feelings of being overwhelmed and swept by those things which she had on her agenda and we might fruitfully suggest that this tactic may be a preliminary to more deep and searching ways of evaluating the contents of a rich and fully lived life at this particular time. Some items, as noted by the one known as C, do need to fall off the back of the wagon but why and in what order? This sort of conscious, intellectually based analysis cannot go deep, cannot dive into the essence of the underlying questions that are presupposed in such a query. Yet it can, perhaps, in some helpful way, order and organize a picture of the situation within the mind so that there is a grasp of the whole that can be had at an intellectual level.

In moving deeper into the query of new directions and what we can say about them, you may perhaps have anticipated that we would be unable to be specific concerning new directions for it is not our work to do your work. Nor would we take that tremendous privilege and responsibility from you. There is an honor to being faced with this question in one's life and it presupposes a "life of significant soil" as the poet has said[93], that life that has dug into itself to produce things of value that are valued and have the history of being valued by others. Consequently, when one wishes to embrace new directions there are those deeper questions that are concerned in such a gaze. One wishes to gaze at the process of thinking which is the habitual nature of the one known as C, gazing at the self through time, looking at those patterns of thought that repeat themselves and beginning to sit with them and identify the themes of those thoughts. Many times there are patterns that have been used, and perhaps used fully, that, because of affection, are retained within the active mind and in some cases these need to be reevaluated in terms of the living and energetic center of the self which seems to be moving on and trying to move, shall we say, into new directions and in new ways of thinking and being.

You do not consider these things as quantities only. For each line of inquiry, each avenue of spending time fruitfully, is an entire world full of qualities and not simply a unit of fact. When things are valued they are far more than fact. When avenues of progress are valued they are far more than streets. There is an aura, a presence, a world that is implied with each turning and each new project. What roads are needed by the one known as C at this time for his learning and service? This is the proper question and we believe it is precisely that which you ask. But realize that you ask about a far more subtle and complex thing than simply that which can be said in a disposition that expresses quantity or essence.

We would move back to the word about which we had some discussion before and that word is "passion." It is always well to identify the center of one's passion and in order to do that it is often necessary to release all suppositions concerning the self and to begin from a place of simple inquiry into the self.

This past weekend this instrument was channeling for its group meditation at the regular Sunday afternoon time and a very similar question was asked of us by several within the group who were pondering new directions as well as the one known as C. And to them as well as to you we discuss the experience this instrument is having, of having the wiring within the house in which she lives redone because the previous wiring was not strong enough to carry enough power to do those things which this instrument wished to do within the house. When new directions are intended, quite often before they can be followed there must occur a period of deconstruction within the house of the personality, shall we say, or the ego, the aspects of self that are the shell of the self and that need sometimes gently to be evaluated and perhaps repositioned in a more helpful configuration for telling the truth about the

---

[93] T. S. Eliot, the ending of *Four Quartets; The Dry Salvages*:

> Here the impossible union
> Of spheres of existence is actual,
> Here the past and future
> Are conquered, and reconciled,
> Where action were otherwise movement
> Of that which is only moved
> And has in it no source of movement–
> Driven by demonic, chthonic
> Powers. And right action is freedom
> From past and future also.
> For most of us, this is the aim
> Never here to be realized;
> Who are only undefeated
> Because we have gone on trying;
> We, content to the last
> If our temporal reversion nourish
> (Not too far from the yew tree)
> The life of significant soil.

substance of being that dwells within the house of personality and name and identity. And so we would suggest to you that you take a gently ruminating and thoughtful look at the energy entity that is yourself, the nuclear level of personality, the level of the surface of the life experience. It is well to ask the self, "Who am I and what is it that feels the most deeply a part of myself? And what is it, on the other hand, that begins to feel like a part of a role which I am playing, a mask which I am wearing, a reputation which becomes, though true, most tiresome?" Often the expectations of others, as pleasing and flattering as they may be, are also those things which unconsciously limit the essential energies of the self from moving outside what this instrument would call the box of consensus reality and its conventions of thinking.

It is often helpful in searching for results not to forget the search for essence. Results are something that occur almost as an offshoot of that entity whose process is on the beam in terms of following the resonance of the needs of that essential being and energy that you are. Involved in the hoopla and the tap dancing of speech and expression and ratiocinations of all kinds, beneath the shell of words and the easy glibness of surface eloquence and meaning no matter how attractive, there lies a hungry and thirsty soul and spirit whose essence is aching to explore not further, but deeper, not more broadly, but in a more focused manner. And as the searchlight of one's everyday consciousness becomes charmed and intrigued into attaching itself to the focus of a deep inner search, that spotlight may sharpen and delineate much that upon the surface of things is impossible or certainly improbable to see.

In some cases it is a matter of almost seducing oneself away from the joys of thinking and into a position of utter surrender to that darkness that accepts the mystery of the self and the infinite possibilities of what that self may do if allowed to bloom as the Creator has prepared for you to bloom. Not that there is one destiny for you or one choice that is right. Quite the opposite. There is certainly one destiny in terms of a general incarnational design but it is rather that chances for that design to be fulfilled are bursting at every corner so that there is never an end to the possibility to, as this instrument would say from the old Shaker hymn, "come round right."[94]

There is more than one configuration that is appropriate at this time. However, one needs to be chosen and we encourage the one known as C to go deeply into that country that is unknown within himself. It can be done by something as simple as an exercise this instrument has done from time to time in just such a situation. The simple exercise is that of standing in front of the mirror and gazing, not at the self, but into the eyes or more particularly into the left eye, choosing one eye and gazing within it. This is a technique that aids in the focusing which moves the entity from [the attitude of] looking at an image or a form into the attitude of looking into an essence. For that which lies within the sparkle of the eye is the one infinite Creator, of which that sparkle is a little holographic unit.

We pause while this instrument awaits the removal of two feuding cats from the immediate vicinity of the instrument and the one known as V.

(Pause)

We are again with the instrument. Gazing into a mirror is gazing into the eyes of the Creator. Implicit in that flash of light that you are able to see into, in the eye in that mirror, is the gaze of The Lovers[95] which has been given flesh and is fascinated to find what it may find. This is your quest. To be and to learn and then, with the harvest that you have learned, to offer the gift of your observations to the one infinite Creator. For in learning about yourself you give the Creator the opportunity to learn about Itself in ever richer detail of understanding.

When you are in this state you have only to rest in the connection in order for that which is in your heart to be asked of that web of guidance that lies within that sparkle that you see in the mirror. It is a very physical way of identifying for you that consciousness that indwells you, dwells within your

---

[94] A Shaker song of the 18th century:

'Tis the gift to be simple, 'tis the gift to be free,
'Tis the gift to come down where we ought to be,
And when we find ourselves in the place just right,
Twill be in the valley of love and delight.
When true simplicity is gained
To bow and to bend we shan't be ashamed,
To turn, turn will be our delight
Till by turning, turning, we come round right.

[95] The nineteenth tarot image.

body, yet is closer to you than any cell in your body. For it is that essence that is you and out of it can be spun a thousand or a million bodies that may experience incarnation. That light in your eye, as you gaze into it, is all that there is. And so you have direct access to grasp that which is not able to be grasped by the intellect, that all is truly one and that all information that you need will come to you as you need it. Rest in that looking and in that receiving until you begin to get a sense of yourself as consciousness, not the [you of the] physical eye but the great, the universal eye that is a citizen of eternity and that has come to this particular place at this particular time hoping to do certain things.

It struck the one who is the instrument when she was reading the very helpful note which the one known as C had so kindly sent her, that in the query about the writing of songs the evaluation of that song writing took only one criterion and that was the possibility for popular success of the writing of these songs and these screen plays. Why, the one known as C wondered, would an urge to write these things be there if it were so inappropriate in terms of creating that green energy which the instrument calls money. And yet we would say to the one known as C, while it is the form of things that you wish to write songs or screen plays, what is the essence of that which you wish to communicate? Having achieved an age of seventy, it's a good time to move not into the mundane but into the metaphysical, not into the practical but into the philosophical, not into the outer world but into the essence of the inner world that contains the roots of consciousness. It cannot be said that there's any harm in outer achievement. Often such outer gifts to the world are most needed and most appreciated and most helpful in lightening the consciousness of the planet. Yet many times the essence of one's incarnational service to the planet, to its people, that for which one took breath in a very deep sense, has to do not with outer gifts but with inner gifts and their development. Many times in the attempts to be productive the self is not allowed fully to come into its bloom. That which blooms, that which is unseen, also lightens the planet.

And so we encourage the one known as C to open into a wider point of view so that there are more points to evaluate and a deeper puzzle to solve. We do not wish to solve this for you, my brother, but we do wish for you to see the justness of the question and the depth of its ramifications. We wish you great joy in moving into this time of choice with full awareness of your freedom to do that which truly creates for you the right environment in which to bloom.

May we answer any further queries at this time, my brother?

Questioner: Yes, can you tell me, if you can, when the human population of the earth will be reduced?

We are those of Q'uo, and are aware of your query, my brother. We may say, ironically enough, that the human population of this planet is already in the process of being reduced. For as those entities which are born come into incarnation, the structure of their cells are somewhat altered in such a way as to better enable them to enjoy fourth-density vibrations, which are becoming increasingly transparent to the third density of vibration upon your planet at this time.

We are not able to offer information concerning the possible sudden removal of entities from the planet which you know as Earth or Gaia. There are no more than possibilities or, as the one known as Ra called them, possibility/probability [vortices]. There is a wide range of possible futures for your peoples. May we say that much has changed simply because of the events since the turn of this last millennium in that while the outer situation has seemed to become darker and darker, the situation as regards the lightness of its peoples has improved in that the sheer darkness of the situation and the relative simplicity of identifying the darkness and the light have helped to quicken the pace of awakening those who were, shall we say, sitting on the fence, half asleep and half awake.

The sheer outrageousness of some of the patterns has been as the snooze alarm on the alarm clock saying, "Just wake up a minute and check out this one thing. Then you may go back to sleep." However, one snooze alarm after another has to bring one into a more wakeful state in which underlying patterns of planetary madness begin to become more obvious. Consequently, it is completely unknown to us at what rate entities will continue to awaken and at what rate the ensuing lightness of the planetary atmosphere will begin to cause what this instrument would call the "Hundredth Monkey Effect[96],"

---

[96] From *The Hundredth Monkey* by Ken Keyes Jr:

thereby causing rapid positive changes within planetary policies of all kinds. This could occur as well as those events which would set off rapid reductions in the population of humans upon the planet Earth.

May we answer you further upon this, my brother?

Questioner: Please tell me what you can about Western civilization and where it is heading.

We are those of Q'uo, and are aware of your query, my brother. We can say somewhat elliptically that your Western civilization has been heading nowhere for its entire sojourn upon your planet. Before your planet experienced its first orbit about this particular, shall we say, rut into which your third-density entities have fallen, the planet known to you as Mars had completed the pattern of choosing aggression over peace and territorial separation over unity as a society. And when those of what this instrument would call Babylon, Rome, the Holy Roman Empire, Germany, and finally, America, started and moved through the pattern of dominance and warfare and societal destruction, their orbits changed not, only the costumes worn by those who move through this particular pattern.

We are of the hope, as are many within your peoples, that at this particular time those within your societies, not only of America but of the entire globe, are able to move away from the old way of increasing polarity, war and destruction. It is not that this pattern is a complete disaster, for it has been most instructive in terms of the Creator discovering those things which do and which do not work to the betterment of the evolution of mind, body and spirit. It becomes obvious that there are aspects to the complete lack of guidance concerning polarity that encourage that which is known by this instrument as the dark side to have a seductive value that it would otherwise not have. Be that as it may, it has been so that your planet has included a nugatory[97], useless pattern so many times that its entire society has been quarantined and put to one side of, shall we say, the usual timeline. It is as if time itself had been suspended for these entities while they are moving through this pattern again and again. So it is a matter, more or less, of taking back the mind from those who would keep it distracted, polarized and asleep.

May we answer you further, my brother?

Questioner: You have been very enlightening and I thank you very much. Is there anything further that you would like to say to me?

We are those of Q'uo, and are aware of your query, my brother. We find we have only to say to you, "Be of good heart." There are many about you in the unseen world and some of those in the seen world who are angels and who wish only to help you. There are many ways of giving messages and leaving one's opinion to mix into the thinking process and those who are in that web of love about you are actively attempting to find ways to send a symbol, a hint, an inkling or even something very obvious to let you know that they are supporting, encouraging and attempting in all ways to help bring you into alignment with those things which are most deeply within your heart and within your incarnational plan. We would say to you, simply, "Take heart." Rest in quietness and confidence in that peace that the world knows not of. And from that consciousness know that all is well and all will be well. That which you need shall come to you and you shall, no matter what it looks like from the outside, be making those choices which help …"

(Tape ends.)

Although the exact number may vary, this Hundredth Monkey Phenomenon means that when only a limited number of individuals knows a "new way," it remains the conscious property of those individuals. However, when one more individual manifests this new awareness, the field is strengthened, a critical mass is reached, and the awareness becomes the conscious property of all. This new awareness is communicated mind to mind.

[97] nugatory: of little or no importance; trifling, or having no force; invalid.

L/L Research

L/L Research is a subsidiary of Rock Creek Research & Development Laboratories, Inc.

P.O. Box 5195
Louisville, KY 40255-0195

www.llresearch.org

Rock Creek is a non-profit corporation dedicated to discovering and sharing information which may aid in the spiritual evolution of humankind.

ABOUT THE CONTENTS OF THIS TRANSCRIPT: This telepathic channeling has been taken from transcriptions of the weekly study and meditation meetings of the Rock Creek Research & Development Laboratories and L/L Research. It is offered in the hope that it may be useful to you. As the Confederation entities always make a point of saying, please use your discrimination and judgment in assessing this material. If something rings true to you, fine. If something does not resonate, please leave it behind, for neither we nor those of the Confederation would wish to be a stumbling block for any.

© 2009 L/L Research

Sunday Meditation
March 21, 2004

Group question: Q'uo, today we've been discussing the interaction and relationship between the universe and the seeker. We would like you to discuss how it is that the universe answers the seeker's questions of identity, service and transformation and how it is that the seeker can best listen for, respond and know those answers that the universe offers. Additionally, what do these lessons teach of patience and how may we invoke and implement that quality in our lives?

(Carla channeling)

We are known to you as those of the principle of Q'uo and we greet you in the love and in the light of the one infinite Creator, in Whose service we come to you today. We thank each of you for taking the time and the energy to dedicate this working to the seeking of truth. It is a great privilege to enter meditation with you and to be a part of that still, small voice that speaks in the quiet of such times. We are most happy to speak with you this day concerning the nature of the relationship between the seeker and the creation, the questioner and the answerer, and thank you for that opportunity to speak. As always, we would ask that each of you govern those things which you would take in of what we would have to say with exquisite discrimination, for each of you has a very good power of discrimination and can feel the resonance of those thoughts that are helpful at a particular time. We would ask that, unless you feel that resonance, you allow the thoughts simply to pass by and be dropped without further thought. In this way we feel that we can share our hearts with you without being concerned that we will infringe upon your free will, for we truly do not wish to constitute a stumbling block for anyone.

Your query this day is one which drives to the heart of the nature of being. Perhaps it was not intended that this question probe so deeply, yet the question was that of the relationship betwixt the seeker and the system of information which constitutes the creative principle, the godhead principle, or the one infinite Creator. So we would first back up to gaze at that one infinite Creator, for that concept, in and of itself, is a key to that question that was asked. Each who is taking breath in and letting breath out within this circle of seeking and each who may read these words as a part of their life experience of a particular moment: at the moment you hear or read these words, each is a part of the one infinite Creator. The realest part of each spirit or soul in manifestation or third-density incarnation, alike and equally, is a part of the Godhead, a part that has never been separated from the Godhead, a spark that shall never know separation from the original Thought that created the "house" that you experience as the universe and all of the furnishings or dimensions or densities of it.

Becoming able to realize one's part in the creative principle is, within waking consciousness, virtually impossible, the limitations of body, flesh, and physical senses narrowing the doors of perception and, in many cases, closing them entirely. All of the massive indoctrination that you as very young entities within incarnation are carefully taken through by parents and teachers guarantee that if there are any who may come to awareness free of bias and full of the knowledge of the self as Creator, then that is a very tiny group. For the rest of those upon your sphere at this time, we believe it is safe to say that each has lost that direct sense of insight and union with the one infinite Creator. Yet there is a unity there. Perhaps each is not leaning into that unity, yet it subsists. It cannot be shed, it is not a skin that can be molted, and it is nothing that shall ever be renewed. The human experience, shall we say, the third-density incarnational experience, is all about death and renewal, endings and beginnings. Yet throughout the process of incarnational living, the most fundamental part of your essential being is not that which will change, grow or alter. Rather, it is that which is. How in the holy work that this instrument knows as the Bible did the Creator express itself? "I AM."

So part of each of you is an I AM. Can you feel the difference between "I" and "I AM"? Can you feel the shift from personhood to essence? It is an important shift of which to remain aware, not simply for the purpose of this discussion but in terms of the basic skills of living life awake and conscious of who you are and why you are here. What this instrument would say about the relationship between the I and the I AM is that she hopes, in each day, to allow the I that is I AM, to become her, so that the I of her is what she would call the Christ or Christ Consciousness or unconditional love. It is not a taking of the self, tossing the self away, and then replacing it with the Creator, the Christ, or the Christ principle. Rather, it is allowing oneself to remember that the I AM is the deepest essential self that is a true part of the whole being that is the one known as Carla.

Now, we feel that each within the circle has hopes along similar lines, that is, each has hopes of expanding personal consciousness into a truer, more whole and deeper consciousness; expressing a more essential and more vital self. If infinite consciousness is living your life, then there is no questioner and no answerer but rather a state of being which is unitary; in which there is no necessity for questioning, for waiting, for looking, for all is perfect. This is a valuable tool and resource. No matter what the circumstances, this level of consciousness is always a powerful resource in centering the self and allowing the self to lift away from peripheral details of a particular given situation that has the energy of a bubble of topical interest at the time. One cannot, for the most part, stay within unitary consciousness, within the I AM, a hundred percent of the time within consensus reality. Consensus reality was specifically designed to pull one away from calm, smugness and the acceptance of things as they are. Consensus reality is carefully designed to pull one's energies out of their comfort zone not once, but again, and again, in cycles, from birth until the death of the physical body. Consequently, we do not suggest that each attempt at all times to remain completely submerged in the I AM of Creatorship. Yet when there is that forest of confusion out of which one cannot find a way, when there seems to be a failure of the rational way of gazing at a situation, we encourage each to take a moment to rest the self from all of the labors of the mind and emotions, to sit or rest while walking, and simply allow that consciousness of I AM to permeate and take over the mind and the focus of the mind, for in that utter lack of personality or condition lies the deepest treasure of the incarnate spirit, the connection with all that there is.

Now let us move into gazing at a less unitary and more dualistic view of spiritual process, that view which posits that the seeker is the questioner and the universe, the creation, or guidance, is that which is responding the question. This is much closer to the level of consensus reality. This offers no challenge to the personality that is locked into the roles that he or she is playing and that have perhaps have been thrust upon him or her. Many times, the way the creation chooses to respond to the questions which seekers ask depends upon the most flimsy, fragile nuances in the way questions are put. Many times as this instrument has given personal channelings, private readings, for individuals she has asked for the entity asking the question to go back and study again the question that has been asked to be sure that it catches the absolute center of that concern with which the entity has come to request the reading. And this entity is correct to do so, for that which the universe naturally can flower into in response to a question is completely dependant upon the shape of the intent, the mood, the very tiniest wording of the question asked. And when that shape is heard by the creation it brings about an absolutely automatic, natural process of response. It is not a response that can be detailed in a linear fashion—first this happens, then that, and then the other—for it is a response upon as many levels of intent as the energy of the question discloses. What entity can truly know all of the levels at which he is asking a question? How can an entity truly penetrate so deeply into the unknown country of his own archetypical mind that he is even aware of the full nature of that which he seeks?

Earlier there was a discussion of a movie recently seen concerning the life of the one known as Jesus the Christ and in that movie the character of Pontius Pilate asks the question, "What is truth?" And this is basically what we are saying to you, "What is your question?" It is difficult to know the truth of a situation or a question. It is almost impossible to know what you are asking to the full limit of that question. Hidden within the folds of the silence between the words lie worlds of requested information that is pointed very precisely by the attitude, the hopes, and the feelings that go into that moment of asking.

So one thing that we would say about the relationship between questioner and response is that the questioner has the deepest of personal individual power and responsibility for the quest, the question, the intent of the question, and everything that surrounds the moment of coming to crux, coming to crisis, and accepting that there is a cusp which must be met. Then when that is realized, it is well to take that realization and employ that patience of which you asked first, in the forming of your question. How deeply can you probe into your secret heart? How carefully can you sense those feelings that perhaps have not seen the light of day? What work might there be for you to do in reaching out to those dark places within yourself where questions have not been fully asked because the essence beneath those questions has not yet been fully redeemed within the self, to the self? What powers of forgiveness can your heart bring to the process of coming into the present moment and releasing the past? How high can you hold up your hope, your intent, and your aim? And to what sharpness of focus can you bring that part of yourself that carries pride, so that you are able to give it as a gift, as you kneel in humility with empty hands at last before the truth itself.

Once the seeker has asked the question there is that time of release and then, skill and art lie in that which the one known as G referred to as the light touch. Once you have awakened the universe to your need, you may be sure that the universe will find many ways to communicate with you concerning your query. Again, because it is the universe of the Creator, rather than the universe of humankind, it is often that this information does not come in words at all, but rather in coincidences, signs, hints, chance thoughts heard in unusual circumstances, and many subjectively interesting occurrences such as the dreams of yourself and others about you, the chance comments of others about you upon topics that do not seem to have a relationship to your question but yet which angle in tangentially and have their own eerie but very true meaning in terms of your situation. Many are the times that we have discussed within this group all of the amazing ways in which the world of nature as well as the world of humankind finds ways to express its connectedness with you, its care for you, and its affiliation with you.

When there is a question which seems to be intensely important, it is especially difficult to retain a sense of proportion, a sense of peace, a sense of patience, shall we say. There is the feeling of a need for immediate change. And while we have complete sympathy for that wish to see results, at the same time we would encourage each to consider the possibility that the question that has been asked is expressing on many different levels, only one of which shows above the ground of the conscious mind, the limen or threshold of the waking consciousness. Most of the information that comes into the deeper self to inform and prepare that self for the changes in energy that are taking place come into the web of the self below the level of conscious awareness and only bubble up into conscious awareness in that very subtle way of yeast bubbling up into bread in order to make the situation rise, shall we say. One becomes aware that there is space where there had not been space, there is information, or an opinion, or a feeling where previously there had not been a feeling. Look for and lean into those perceptions that seem simply to be bubbling up from within because that is the end result of a fairly lengthy process of information-gathering by the self from the creation. It has bubbled in through notice of coincidences of conversations, the messengers of animals and flowers, the speaking of trees and the blowing of the wind. All of these things move into the web of self and touch various inner bodies of the energy-body system that is instinct within the outer physical shell that each of you enjoys.

It is a tremendous gift simply to have faith that this process is taking place. One may see that such a process shall, through the limitations of the physical body, take time. It takes time to wake and sleep and wake and sleep and wake again, allowing this process of recovery of information through dreams and through subtle processes that occur inwardly to have time to complete themselves. So it is not simply patience within a vacuum that we encourage you to adopt but rather patience that is a knowing patience, a patience that contains the awareness that things are occurring of which the conscious mind cannot know. The ability to take on faith that this [is the] way the spirit works within entities is a tremendous asset. Use it if you have it and attempt to cultivate it if you do not. How can you cultivate the faith in these subtle processes but by taking the leap of faith, taking the effort and the time to have patience with the process of seeking the answer to the question, and then evaluating, after the fact, what sources of information in fact came through to you and what kind of efficacy those processes have had in bringing into manifestation the blooming and development of that which was a budding situation of which there was great question as to the appropriate way of blooming or maturing.

When seeking the truth, there is much to be said for leaning into the interiority of the process. Much energy can be wasted in the reaching outward, for outer authority and outer knowledge. When there is a question of spiritual evolution involved it is seldom that the outer world will have a *prima facie*[98], direct way of speaking to the heart of the problem, the situation, or the question. The deeper the question, the less effective consulting outer authority shall be.

Yet there is a system of inner authority to which one may go in mind and in heart. And we would not limit this for entities by saying it is this or it is that. To many, a guidance system is a unitary or singular phenomenon. This instrument would call it the Holy Spirit. The one known as David would call it the Guidance System, and so forth. And yet we assure each that the guidance system of each of you is massive and tremendously complex, moving not simply into the inner planes of third density but into the family connections, shall we say, between those in soul groups and their connections in other densities and so forth, so that the guidance system that can be approached by the asking of a question amounts to the complete awareness of your own inner planes and [outer] densities as well as that center of guidance for each of you that is that self of sixth density that is looking back to self in third density and offering that harvest in awareness that it has within that particular illusion.

This massive family that backs up each of you may take some of your time to respond so that it manifests within your own awareness. And so we give to this instrument the image of that figure within the Bible of which the one known as Jesus spoke, of the one who goes into his room to pray in secret[99], to express suffering in secret, to offer in the utmost privacy of self, the heart of self, the suffering of self, and all of the self that can be brought to that room in the asking of what is the situation and what is the truth of the situation. Keeping it quiet, keeping it silent, keeping it completely inner is a very helpful technique for it allows a kind of intensity to build up within that tiny room of prayer. Perhaps each of you is familiar with the way that a materialization medium gathers ectoplasm within its closet so that it may manifest that which this entity would call a ghost or spirit in a séance. Just in such a way can you gather the energy of your prayer, keeping it within that tiny closet, within that point of union between you, the question, and the response system—that point that is the gateway to intelligent infinity—staying just there, just past the lions at the gate, just in the door, not anywhere nearer than moving into the interior, resting and allowing the process to move.

The one known as V was speaking the other day of the connectedness of all things, the labyrinth that turns out to be that which connects everything to everything. It is at that point, just within that tiny room of prayer, that that connection point is. So the more interior that you are able to make your seeking,

---

[98] *Prima facie* is defined as meaning "at first sight; before closer inspection."

[99] This reference is Matthew 6:18; "Whenever you fast, do not put on a gloomy face as the hypocrites do, for they neglect their appearance in order to be seen fasting by men. Truly I say to you, they have their reward in full. But you, when you fast, anoint your head, and wash your face so that you may not be seen fasting by men, but by your Father who is in secret; and your Father who sees in secret will repay you."

the more quiet, private and special, the more opportunity you will have to move into that deep rest that lifts you in a hammock just where you wish to be and allows you to rock, waiting in total comfort, resting in the cradle of the love of the infinite Creator. If you can do this for yourself, daily if possible, when working through a situation, you shall be touching into the most efficacious and helpful place within you for truly listening to that still, small voice of the one infinite Creator.

Each is aware of many techniques for determining the rightness of a particular fact or action. The use of the pendulum has been discussed often, the use of readings, whether they be tarot or astrology, and the use of psychic or spiritual counselors. All of these ways of getting more information are very helpful but you may see how diffused and outward they become and how quickly one loses that precious focus, that honed intent, and that quiet, listening ear. One may employ crystals, one may employ pyramids, one may employ such a large number of techniques for finding out more information concerning the outer details of a situation that we could not possibly mention them all. But each is aware of the size of the spiritual supermarket, about which this group has often joked and enjoyed conversation. There are many, many ways to know more about the energies around you. Yet, in terms of how the universe works, the best connection between questioner, question and guidance system is the gateway that lies within each of you.

At this time this instrument requests that we move on to ask if there are further questions that we may answer at this time. Is there a query that we may answer at this time?

B: I have one. When you were speaking initially, you spoke of a duality and you really only talked about one side. Would the other side be where the one infinite Creator becomes the seeker?

We are those of Q'uo. We are aware of your query, my brother. The duality of which we were speaking is that duality that is self perceived by the questioner, when the questioner sees itself as one dynamic of a duality and the answer as the other part of a duality. The unitary attitude, on the other hand, would see the questioner, the question, and the guidance as one system which is not at all separate from itself but which is a unit working to expand the self and, in that way, we would say that indeed when there is a unitary attitude the questioner is the Creator. This is correct, my brother.

Is there a further query?

G: Q'uo, I have one. Ra speaks about the will and says that it is paramount, it is not to be underestimated, and its use in faith can create change and can accelerate the path. Yet, I am feeling doubtful about the ritual that I want to undertake tonight, in which I would use the will to create a change or shift in consciousness. I know, reading through past transcripts, that this philosophical point between willing change [to occur] and waiting for change has been discussed much but I was wondering if you can speak more specifically to this particular situation?

We are those of Q'uo, my brother, and are aware of your query. The state of willing that which one feels is correct for the self is that state in which the entity is sure, in a way that this instrument would call "gnosis," of that which is intended. It is a matter of knowing one's own heart, knowing one's true feelings to the point where one is willing to stand upon the ground and say, "This is who I am. This is how I wish to express my will." In that way of offering the will, there is an inner knowing that lies behind that ability to cast off all fear and doubt and simply apply the will directly, straightforwardly, forthrightly, to the goal at hand. The purity with which one maintains honesty with the self is a great key to the achieving of this kind of gnosis or sure insight concerning the self.

When a situation is upcoming in which the will to serve is known by the person but not which situation needs to be served, [it] brings forth the second kind of use of will, which is to abnegate one's own will in favor of the will of the infinite Creator, the guidance system, and the basic incarnational plan that one has had in place for the entire incarnation and in which one does have faith. In this latter situation, it would be folly to force one outcome over another. In that case the will is involved simply in bringing the whole self to a point of surrender so that as the will of the Creator becomes obvious, it may be followed with a complete and full intensity of effort and focus.

May we answer you further my brother?

G: Yes. I think I was skillful enough to create the ritual so that I was not forcing one outcome or another or requesting any kind of specific unfolding of events but I did steer the will, especially at the end of it, to one of surrender to the Creator. So my question then is: if one feels that they are not fully, one hundred percent, in totality, surrendered to the Creator, can one then marshal what will that they are aware of within themselves to create a more full surrender to whatever outcome that the Creator will give, whatever catalyst that will come one's way, to bring the rest of that self lagging behind and up to that surrendered and accepted state to know the Creator's will?

We are those of Q'uo, and are aware of your query, my brother. Yes.

G: You're awesome. Thank you Q'uo.

We thank you, my brother. Is there a further query at this time?

B: Q'uo, you used the word, faith, on numerous occasions. Could you please define what you mean by faith?

We are those of Q'uo, and are aware of your query, my brother. We use the words that this instrument has in her vocabulary. Often there are intangible differences in the way we use that word which you may have noticed, my brother. Faith, in general, is intended to indicate surety. The way that this instrument sees faith is fairly acceptable to us. In her mind faith is connected with knowing that all is well. That is what this instrument tends to mean when she speaks of faith. It is not that she attaches any fact or dogmatic principle or tenet to the word, faith, but rather it is a noun expressing an attitude of inner surety of the reality of the perfection and the rightness of the pattern of creation in which she is involved and of which she is an active and creative part.

When we use that word we are attempting to express a sense of confidence that is not aggressive but rather rests in peace and confidence and sureness, so that the knowingness is not confrontive, argumentative or even filled with fact but is simply an attitude of mind which assumes and stands on the rightness and the goodness of creation, of each entity's place in it, and of the patterns of suffering and expression, and experience that seem to be moving about one at any particular time.

May we answer you further, my brother?

B: No, thank you, that was fine.

We thank you, my brother.

Is there a final query at this time?

T: Q'uo, I'm not sure how much you can say but are you able to comment at all upon the decisions that I've made in relation to employment and the idea that I'm now pursuing?

We are those of Q'uo, and the warmth of our affection for you makes this instrument smile, my brother. We are able to say that we feel that you do indeed stand on faith. We express our complete faith in you and in those decisions that you have made. And we are with you and with each as each moves into those areas which have been beyond the comfort zone and which now have the attraction of that which shall be and that which even now is growing into maturity within you.

May we answer you further, my brother?

T: No, no thank you, Q'uo. I just want to send my thanks and love to you and also to those of Hatonn.

We are those of Q'uo, and may we say, my brother, that your words are most welcome to those of Hatonn that are with us, as always, at this time.

We thank this group in our hearts for allowing us to be a part of your beautiful nature, your sweet meditation, and your community of seeking. It is such a privilege to us and such a blessing to be able to be of some small service within your patterns. We assure you that you are of tremendous service to us. And we thank you.

We leave each of you, as always, in the love and in the light of the one infinite Creator. Adonai. We are those known to you as the principle of Q'uo.

L/L Research

Sunday Meditation
April 4, 2004

Group question: The question today deals with change. We were talking around the circle about the different kinds of change that each of us is going through. It even seems that the Earth and the solar system and perhaps the galaxy are going through changes as well and it would seem to be the logical thing, considering all things are moving and growing. We are wondering if Q'uo could give us some information today on how we, in our own personal lives, can deal with change. It seems that whenever we want to change or when change faces us, that there is a practical side and an idealistic side to the change: things that we would like to do and things we feel like we have to do. Blending the two or balancing the two seems to be the real trick. So if Q'uo could talk to us some about how to look at the concept of change in both the practical and idealistic senses, we would appreciate that very much.

(Carla channeling)

We are those of the principle known to you as Q'uo, and we greet you in the love and in the light of the one infinite Creator, in Whose service we come to you this day. It is a great blessing to be among you, to experience your vibrations, and to share your meditation. We thank you for calling us to your circle this day to speak concerning the concept of change and we would ask one thing, as always, that will enable us to speak freely: we would ask each of you carefully to guard your own judgment and discrimination and to listen to those things that we say with a careful and jaundiced ear. Be cautious about absorbing new information. We are not authorities; we are those who seek, just as you are. We share our opinion and while you are welcome to it, we wish you to realize what we also realize that we are not without imperfections and it is possible for us to err. Consequently, guard those portals of your learning and accept only those things which resonate deeply within as being truths that are helpful for you at this time. Because truth is of the nature of a growing thing. It has a path of individual development and it is different for each individual. With that understood between us we feel that we can speak freely without infringing upon your free will and we appreciate that from each of you.

We gaze within this instrument's mind to find a starting point for that which we wish to say today and give her the image of the ivy that she was weeding from the planting of lilac trees that grows along the path of the side of this instrument's house. We see the thoughts that this instrument had while following the ivy around and around the lilac and gently disentangling it from the mass of other strands, or wires, of binding plant that spiral endlessly in the attempt to seek the sun and yet, in so doing, attempt to use all about it as a prop in order to have help in ascending to that source of light and food and warmth. Just in such innocent ways does each of you find comfort in the winding effect of some habits that have seemed at first to be helpful and then perhaps not so helpful and perhaps even narrowing or limiting in their effect upon you as a growing and changing person.

The change that is taking place is as a stream that has an energy of its own. Each nuance of attitude which you bring to the observation of and into relationship with this stream, affects the stream. When there is no resistance to that stream, which this instrument would loosely call "destiny," then it is as if that stream takes one quietly along with a minimum of distress or displacement because of the shift in the movement or flow of that river of destiny. It is as if quiet and self-confidence were the raft or the frail barque that keeps one high and dry in this river of destiny. Only those materials that build the canoe, quietness and confidence, are availing. In every other situation, one is either resisting the flow of destiny, which has little use since it moves directly against the process of change, or one may indeed embrace change with such a hectic ardor that the change cannot take place properly, or easily, shall we say, in the flow of things because the entity has taken up the oar, or the paddle, and begun furiously attempting to help the stream move forward. The first blocking energy is that energy of fear. The overeager energy is also, in a way, that of fear. The resting upon the pleasant seat in the canoe of quietness and confidence, then, is that path of least resistance which, in many cases, is the most difficult path to take. It is completely understandable that in many entity's minds, when one approaches a known process of change, one wishes first of all to create that process and move through it as quickly as possible.

So the first thing that we would suggest is to have a model within the mind of change as being affected very, very much by a process that is already flowing and that has flowed out of the wellspring of your past intentions and the focus you have attained in the past. For in the past you sow for the future and in the present you reap that which you have sown long ago. Allow this process to take place as it needs to in terms of the timing of things. Not in terms of how carefully you think about what is happening or how deeply you contemplate the nuances of the processes taking place. It is an excellent idea to ask the self daily, if it is on the mind daily, what one thinks, how one feels; to sense into the process that you are aware of, however imperfectly it is taking place, in order to keep the lines of communication within the self open. These lines of communication are most helpful and they are very sensitive to intention. Telling the self, asking the self, creating space within the self for learning more about such a process of change will yield results; whether they be from the portals of dream or waking vision or subjectively interesting coincidence.

Given that each day you are experiencing an increase in the transparency of the new energy to the energy of late third density, it is skillful, in working with the process of your accommodating and embracing change and of moving with the flow of your own destiny, to realize that you have increasing abilities to envision, to set intentions, to ask for help of far more subtle energies than were previously possible, and in many ways to link the deeper aspects of the self with the very considerable powers that are beginning to form up from fourth-density Gaia and from that fourth-density web of social memory that is nascent at this time and even now being experienced in brief flashes in groups such as this one. The subtlety of working with fourth-density energies while in a third-density body are not subtleties that will yield easily to the reasoning process of the logical mind. The third-density ability to generate thoughts that express in words, while a useful ability, is a third-density ability. And what you are attempting to do is make use of fourth-density-level information in approaching the process of change. This information does not come in processes that create words. There is a translation process that is necessary and entities such as this instrument have created ways to inform themselves of subconscious processes in a conscious manner which produces words. However, this a learned and not an automatic skill and, in general terms, the subconscious processes that feed into each of you are those processes that will not, at any time, approach the reasoning or logical mind.

Consequently, the challenge is how to take in fourth-density concepts when one has not yet become fully telepathic, shall we say, or sensitive to the voices in the trees and the wild animals and indeed in the elements, the "angry agate marble coffee table," and the sky. All things do have their voices and the one known as D is not altogether incorrect in assigning active personality to such things as the aforementioned table. The one known as D was unfortunate enough to come into contact in a painful manner with this particular table. Was the table therefore angry? Was the table therefore offering information? Or was the entire episode expressing that which was, shall we say, information which was most easily sent in that particular way in that particular moment.[100] All things that impend upon you can have a subjectively interesting meaning and can be looked at with profit for that which they bring, in terms of situations, emotions that have been brought up by such catalyst, and so forth.

The process of change is not simply a process of altering behavior or circumstance. Rather, it is a fairly complex series of small adjustments which allow an entity to balance with the flow of events and emotions. As the direction in which each is headed develops, the journey may bring sudden turns, sudden hills, "ups and downs," and surprises. The energy involved in finding grace and ease in attitude is that which helps to create an experience that is easy emotionally, physically, and so forth. The challenge again is in allowing without becoming passive. For it is not desired that an entity simply give oneself over to some blank Creatorship and say, "I have no more responsibility. It is all in the Creator's hands." There is wisdom in remaining personally interested and motivated towards discovering precisely what it is one desires. Serving the Creator and being a part of the spiritual principle does not mean denying the self but rather unveiling the self to the self and discovering the very heart of what you wish to do. And then, allowing the self to grow in awareness of the very best way to bring such a dream into manifestation. So we do not encourage you to abnegate any personal feelings in favor of the desire to serve the Creator. There is a co-creatorship that is important to the Creator as well as to you. It is important to the Creator that that which you desire is that for which you are aiming. Hone your desire once you find it. Until you are sure of it, pursue the knowledge of yourself. Pursue that question of the self as to what it truly does desire, what its motives truly are. Ask once but then ask a second time and a third time.

For the process of change is not that which occurs and then is over. It is that which will cycle through the experience until you are removed from this particular outer experience by the processes of death.

The body itself is irresistible in its relentless change. And as the one known as D has been discussing recently, the very system of planets and stars which are your physical home is in [the midst of] a relentless and inevitable series of changes.

The current atmosphere is one in which your best allies are your guidance system, your consciousness, and the world about you. The world about you, being first and second density, has never been separated from the love of the one Creator and it constitutes a powerful resource for those who are contemplating change. The guidance system that you experience has a great deal of information and many resources, many layers or levels of help that are available in various ways, in various times. As we have said before, we do not wish to pry too closely into that guidance system, which is a very individualized system. Yet it is there, whatever its characteristics are, whether it is, as this instrument would call it, a Holy Spirit or any other description, such as higher self, that you would wish to make as a characterization. This energy is a true part of who you are and it is never apart from you. So there is always information that is coming in that is fully intended to be helpful.

Consequently, those two allies are the most powerful. Your third ally is the consciousness that you carry. That consciousness is not your thoughts. Your thoughts are riding on that consciousness like whitecaps above the water. Your consciousness is that which lies beneath, around, permeating what you think of as your consciousness. It is your essence. It is that part of you that also has never been separated from the creative principle. Within it lies your sanctuary—that point of contact with the one infinite Creator, that tabernacle where you may go in at any time and find rest and comfort for your soul. This instrument likes to picture the one known as Jesus as having a huge hand and she climbs into that hand and falls asleep in that palm, resting in safety. In other times she imagines crawling into the lap of the Creator and being rocked like a little baby. And when she is feeling sore and weary she does go into her sanctuary. Each of you has that sanctuary within. Not because of what you think or because of how you feel. The water within you is deeper than any of those surface disturbances. You are also that deep water which is eternity and infinity. You are love. You are light. You are the one great original Thought, which is the Creator Itself. This asset is

---

[100] D was sitting down when he misjudged the distance and whacked his knee quite badly on the edge of our marble coffee table. At the time, we joked about the coffee table being angry. Perhaps it was not an entirely empty jest.

that which is so easily missed in the search for help without. And there is no entrance into this powerful ally except silence, time and asking. So we encourage those times of silence, and asking, and knowing that that which you are asking is being heard by the one infinite Creator Who is closer to you than your breath.

We would at this time ask if there are further queries about the opening question or whether we may answer another query at this time. We are those of Q'uo.

R: I don't have a question, Q'uo, but I do want to say that on the surface it seems good to be back in the group and hear your voice coming through the instrument, Carla. And I wanted to thank you for being with me during those two years in various places where I have been, being a quiet support, an inspiration.

We are those of Q'uo, and, my brother, may we say that it also has been inspirational for us for the one known as R has been a true knight who has polished his armor.

Is there another query at this time?

G: Q'uo, in the seeking of truth, could you comment on which of these two attitudes is more likely to be effective. A) The action of the seeker to seek after their own identity, that is, to commit themselves to the doing of the seeking of that identity, or B) To not necessarily search it out but to claim that knowing of identity—to affirm and state, "I know who I am." If you could respond to any of that I would be most appreciative.

We are those of Q'uo, my brother, and are aware of your query. The question of knowing is no light question and certainly there are as many answers to the question of right knowledge as there are philosophers. To state boldly that which you know is an excellent thing. To state boldly that of which you are not sure is premature. No one but the individual involved can know when unsureness and questing become absolute certainty within the self. One of the best ways to discover the degree of one's certainty is to ask the self if one would take a stance that might involve dying for taking that stance. If something is that which important enough to die for, this instrument has often said, then it is important enough to live for. This is one way of asking the self mentally how sure one is. Would one die for this principle? Would one die to be this entity?

May we answer you further, my brother?

G: No, excellent, thank you, Q'uo.

We are those of Q'uo, and we thank you, my brother. Is there another query at this time?

G: Q'uo, in your knowledge of all the many spiritual paths on this planet that all lead to one place, is there, in general, ever a point where a seeker needs to state what "price" they are willing to pay? Is there ever a price that needs to be decided upon before illumination or greater self-knowledge comes?

We are those of Q'uo, and are aware of your query, my brother. Indeed, if one gazes upon the archetypal images upon which the one known as G has been gazing recently[101], the material is rich in suggestion that the willingness to pay a price is a legitimate and even necessary part of an archetypal movement. This entity has recently seen that motion picture which is called Mel Gibson's *The Passion of the Christ*. And this entity indeed was asked what he would pay to express truth. This entity was not at first entirely settled in its mind that it was ready to pay that price. Yet it truly wished, as was expressed within the motion picture, to "make all things new." And that which made all things new, in this entity's way of thinking, was worth dying for. In this movement, this entity embraced that which eventually was indeed the physical death. Yet the story goes on to say that this price, having been paid, was redeemed and indeed was not price so much as gift; and the entity known as Jesus was not simply victim but also priest.

So, consequently the question, "What would you pay for this?" is that question which is as an archetypal key turner, that which changes energy, that which creates a bond between the self and the intention and indeed, in that way of thinking, and in those circumstances, it is indeed a legitimate and just query.

May we answer you further, my brother?

G: I'll have to look that over. Thank you, Q'uo.

We are those of Q'uo, and we thank you, my brother. Is there a final query at this time?

---

[101] G was preparing for a vision quest recently and reading mythological and philosophical material.

G: Q'uo, in the *Law of One* series they talked about the initiation that one goes through when one enters into the pyramid and Ra says, I believe, that it's in the Queen's Chamber that the "being must be centered upon the Creator," or there must be a commitment made to center the being upon the seeking of the Creator. While I don't expect direction from you, I believe that [the] seeking/centering [of which they speak] comes from within. Is that centering of the self upon the Creator the type of centering that is seen in saints—those people who spend every waking moment thinking about the Creator in adoration and reverence and worship, those who spend their time both in silence and conversing with the Creator in all ways inner and outer—is that something of what Ra meant by the centering of the being upon the seeking of the Creator?

We are those of Q'uo, and are aware of your query, my brother. Indeed, that would be one way of expressing such intention and devotion. The concept of devotion, we believe, is that with which you struggle at this time. There are as many ways to express devotion as there are ways of serving the Creator. For many, the ways of devotion are very ascetic and have almost no emotional aspects to them. For others, there is an almost hysterical amount of emotion within devotion. It depends upon the personality shell of each seeker in terms of what practice or daily rule of devotion, of keeping oneself fixed upon the Creator, will be most efficacious. For some, it as with this instrument, the daily reminders of morning and evening meditation and reading of spiritual material [are helpful]. For others, it is very much a twenty-four-hours-a-day, seven-days-a-week, experience of being lead from moment to moment, always within the feeling of being in direct contact with the one infinite Creator. There are many ways of expressing devotion. There are many levels and kinds of devotion and we encourage the one known as G to play with those feelings that he finds within the self, finding how his focus is honed and sharpened; finding how his particular emotional set is affected; finding how his particular "savage breast"[102] can be soothed—whether by music or by art, by beautiful words or by silence.

May we answer you further my brother?

G: No, thank you for being with us, Q'uo.

We are those of Q'uo, and we thank you, my brother, and thank each for the privilege of being able to share thoughts with you at this time. We would at this time leave each as we found you, in the love and in the light of the one infinite Creator. We are those known to you as the principle of Q'uo. Adonai, my friends. Adonai.

---

[102] William Congreve. 1670-1729. *The Mourning Bride.* Act i. Sc. 1. "Music hath charms to soothe the savage breast, to soften rocks, or bend a knotted oak."

L/L Research

L/L Research is a subsidiary of Rock Creek Research & Development Laboratories, Inc.

P.O. Box 5195
Louisville, KY 40255-0195

www.llresearch.org

Rock Creek is a non-profit corporation dedicated to discovering and sharing information which may aid in the spiritual evolution of humankind.

ABOUT THE CONTENTS OF THIS TRANSCRIPT: This telepathic channeling has been taken from transcriptions of the weekly study and meditation meetings of the Rock Creek Research & Development Laboratories and L/L Research. It is offered in the hope that it may be useful to you. As the Confederation entities always make a point of saying, please use your discrimination and judgment in assessing this material. If something rings true to you, fine. If something does not resonate, please leave it behind, for neither we nor those of the Confederation would wish to be a stumbling block for any.

© 2009 L/L Research

Sunday Meditation
April 18, 2004

Group question: Our question today has to do with the purpose of third density. As entities are graduated from the second density, where the way of being is the group mind, they come into third density with the opportunity of individuating, of developing an individualized consciousness that will be able to aid its own evolution by the choices that it makes, free will choices, and we would like Q'uo to give us information about how this individuation then will lead into another kind of group mind, a social memory complex, and maybe a little bit of information about how the group mind of second density differs from the social memory complex that we're moving towards as the result of the individual choices that we make in the third density. So could Q'uo give us a kind of overview of how this all works, of how the nature of the choice, the intention behind the choice, where does the metaphysical or magical personality come in here? We would appreciate anything you could tell us about how third density works.

(Carla channeling)

We are of those of the principle known to you as Q'uo and we greet you in the love and in the light of the one infinite Creator, in Whose service we come to you this day. We thank you for calling us to your group to talk about the function of the third-density experience and we are delighted to share our opinions upon this subject, with the request beforehand to each of you to guard your powers of discrimination well. We would ask that each of you be responsible for that which you take in and that which you leave behind. We cannot possibly hit the mark on all of our remarks. Some of them are bound to be useless to each of you. We ask you not to take them in without considering carefully whether they resonate in your own process and whether they feel like something that you might have forgotten but knew all along. If it feels like that, and resonates, then it is your truth for this particular point in your particular process. Otherwise, it perhaps bears no use whatsoever and would be best left behind. If you each will guard your free will and the processes by which you take in new concepts and make them your own, we will feel free to speak our mind. We thank each of you for allowing us this consideration.

Often the Confederation channels with which this group has long been associated have called third density the density of choice. It is a vivid, intense, rather brief period, in cosmic terms, during which an entity, as the question suggests, moves in consciousness from the consciousness of late second-density life-forms, such as your predecessor, the great ape, to the nascent life-form of an entity with a fourth-density body and fourth-density lessons to learn. In between that second-density experience of the animal kingdom and the vegetable and mineral worlds, and the experience of the density of love or understanding or compassion, lies the density of choice. That is the experience within which you are immersed at this time.

It is undoubtedly an experience that has not been tranquil, entirely, nor an experience in which the shape of the life [has] seemed at all times appropriate and desirable. It is an experience of artifice and illusion. One could almost call it a day at the carnival. And yet it is a carnival whose every ride has a carefully designed purpose and whose grounds are laid out in such a way as to provide an infinitely responsive feedback system to echo and intensify thoughts and desires that have more than a transitory value. It is an environment couched in forgetfulness. That is to say that a requirement for preparation to enter third density is the requirement to place in safe-keeping the detailed memory of that metaphysical or time/space world from which you came in order to enter incarnation in third density. Regardless of the density from which you came, whether it was from second density into third, or from a higher density, looping back into third density, for more work within that crucible, [the] preconditions of entering third density are alike. That direct knowledge, or as this instrument would say, *gnosis* of the Creator and of the self as an integral part of the Creator, must be placed aside and the veil of forgetting must drop, so that each entity that comes into third density comes into it blind and without the possibility of sight, in a very specific way; that being that, in terms of metaphysical as opposed to physical process, there is a carefully structured environment in which hints will constantly be given concerning the nature of that underlying ground of being which has been veiled over by the veil of forgetting, while keeping any sort of objective proof from muddying the waters of unknowing. There is a determined bias within the Creator, concerning this particular third density, towards keeping entities as much in the dark as possible concerning the way things really are underneath the appearance of things. It is a recipe that is designed to be confusing, frustrating, maddening and displacing.

It is felt, as the harvest of many experiences, that while more information and a more transparent third density is a more comfortable experience, in the end it is a more confusing, a less effective, and a less viable third-density experience in terms of serving as the ambiance within which seeking souls are able, consciously, to affect an acceleration of their learning and evolution. The third-density experience of this particular planet is extremely vivid. The consensus reality/illusion is extremely heavy and it is correspondingly difficult to penetrate. This means that there is great potential for experiencing intense emotions and desires. It is the production of these things: the feelings, the biases, the various elements of a person's make-up, that the environment of third density is designed to bring into greater and greater relief, so that each seeking entity has complete free will to look at the experience of living in any way that is chosen.

The Creator does not have to hope that something will occur because the experience of all previous creations has been that evolution is inevitable; change is inevitable. It may be change regressing towards the density left behind, [or] it may be change progressing towards the density ahead; but it is impossible for entities to remain completely stable. They must create novelty, they must move. That is the restless and insatiable nature of consciousness itself. It shall, by the machinations of endless free will, always have that curiosity about what else there may be to learn that pulls the entity onward, whether the entity is considered in terms of the microcosm or macrocosm. So each of you dwells now within a school that is carefully designed to give each entity its hard knocks on a regular basis. Not in order to indicate the cruelty or the judgment of the creative principle, but to create a schooling atmosphere in which entities are self-schooled by their own hand, by their own mind, by their own perceived problems and solutions.

Now let us look at this word "choice." What happens in terms of how third density functions as each entity comes to choices? This is a true key word for this density. Choice is at the center of learning here. For upon the choice of polarity rests the work of the next few millennia, the next few million years, shall we say, from your point of view. What is the nature of choice? From the second-density point of view, from the hive-mind, shall we say, choice has a certain cast in nature which may be understood best by seeing that species of animals and of plants have a common pool of being. The spirits that create growth and life using the elements of the Creator that have been provided, such as seeds and sunlight, are able to dip into this pool of type, or kind, and create specimens of that kind. These entities are created with a kind of consciousness that has a great deal of information in it, which is copied from the pool as a whole rather than being taken from any individual within the species. Consequently, it may be assumed, unless an animal, for instance, has had a great deal to do with humans who have altered the second-density programming for that animal, that an animal will act according to the actions of its species. While there are always rogues in any species that do not act according to the species, for the most part, one is dealing, in an animal of second density, with an entity that is making choices according to the choices programmed into its kind.

When an entity graduates from second density to third, it becomes an entity which has not been taken out of a pool of consciousness but rather must stand upon its own very shaky legs of individuality. It is still equipped with the second-density information but with the veil of forgetting over most of it. So in a way it has lost a great deal of valuable ground. Things that were obvious to second-density animals, because there was no conscious mentation in the genetic programming, become not at all obvious to an entity who is programmed heavily towards conscious and individualized thought. In other words, a third-density entity has complete freedom of will built into it.

Now when you gaze at an entity that has just entered third density, you are gazing at an entity who does not know what to do with free will. It does not know that it is free. It does not know that it was, at one time, pent in a cage of generic assumptions; and in fact, it may still be acting upon many of those assumptions, for they are part of the instinctual package that is dimly remembered if not clearly recalled. When such a third-density pioneer begins to make choices, they are likely to be made according to second-density programming. In other words a choice of action will generally be decided to protect the self and the tribe, or the family, and to secure for that family the resources necessary for its survival. While this is simple and even elementary programming, at the same time, the tentacles of the instinct for survival being so many and so far reaching, that simple programming may indeed control a large amount of the life decisions of an early third-density entity.

Slowly, usually, through a series of many incarnations, the third-density entity begins to develop a core sense of self that returns with a bit more strength from incarnation to incarnation so that there is not quite as much veil as there used to be and at some point, there is the experience of awakening. That awakening is an awakening to the possibilities that are, as this instrument would say according to the modern idiom, "outside the box." Now the box is simply the generic assumptions given in second density that have been accepted by the third-density entity. Society, as this instrument knows it and as each of you know it within your Western civilization, retains a great many of the characteristics of late second-density structure. The family structure, the way society is organized into extended family systems and into those who ally for survival, are structures which retain second-density characteristics.

However, as entities begin to awaken, they begin to see something very important for third-density work: that awakening begins when the realization occurs that the choice is not either/or. The choices are infinite. When the viewpoint begins to expand, when the mountain first disappears and then reappears, then that third-density soul begins to see that it is not a matter of becoming better at making choices, it is a matter of becoming more able to see the full range of choices. To see that it is not, for instance, a choice between belief in a creative principle and a belief in no creative principle. Rather the choice is an infinite range of possibilities concerning the godhead principle. There is the movement from a very firmly vectored angle of attack at things in making decisions to an increasingly loose, rounded and multi-directional way of looking at the present moment. It has often been noted in the conversations with this group that so many things are interconnected and that information is available virtually in everything that you lay your eyes on. The question then becomes, "What is that object, that word, that person, that catalyst actually attempting to tell you?" And as the third-density soul begins to grow in its maturity, it begins to realize the endless and infinite gradations of meaning that can be received when one peels away any present moment to see layer after layer after layer of insight, suggested, hinted at, sparkling on the wind, glistening in the trees—just waiting for the connection of heart and attention. The choice, then, is not simply a choice in a certain situation but, even more so, a choice of attitude, a choice of how to be, how to stand, how to express one's essence in the most full and honest way.

There is another key word that we would look at and that is "individuation." It was part of your query and it is a very tricky concept from a metaphysical point of view. Many times this instrument has tried to respond in letters to questions from people concerning whether it is service to self or service to others to take time for the self to learn, to study, and to begin to become familiar with the self deeply and to know the self in a non-transient manner. There is tremendous validity in this process of individuation, of researching and learning the self and indeed this process will go on as long as the individual retains flesh and blood around that particular personality shell. It is, then, a process that is never completed. It is not intended to be completed. Rather it is one of the ways of learning to serve and to grow within the third-density atmosphere. Until one has individuated, one cannot begin magical work, and yet one is never fully individuated. So, logically speaking, one could never begin magical work.

Yet there is, shall we say, a critical mass only that needs to be reached, and it is by no means a large percentage of the actual available will of an entity. It is a very powerful thing to become aware of one's own will and because of the use of it, even imperfectly and even incorrectly or without full knowledge, tremendous energies can be set in motion. So the magical process begins to take place as soon as an entity begins to ask of the Creator, or of perceived guidance directly, "Who am I? Why am I here and what would you have me do?" These kinds of queries are those that create a magical circumstance. Certainly it is well to be as mature as one may be before asking such questions and yet the glory of third density is that all are imperfect and yet all are asking those questions. These are the questions that drive third density.

Consequently, entities on the spiritual path are constantly asking for and getting much more information than they were prepared to deal with. Often they do not recognize that they are receiving that which they requested and feel that there is no sense to the experience. Yet, that, too, becomes perfectly acceptable, for no matter how the experiences that have been created by the questions are used, they in turn shall be that which will create the seeds that are sown for the next generation of learning. And those seeds will fall into good soil and have the possibility of growth, regardless of whether one road or another road is taken. Regardless of the choices made, the result will be a net gain in understanding. So it is in some ways a hard ambiance in which to learn and in other ways it is a very forgiving ambiance in that one cannot fail. One can become weary and rest, but one can always pick up the self when one feels again ready to enter the fray and again ask, and again receive the information, and again work with that information.

As the soul of third density begins to live consciously and make choices from a more aware standpoint as regards its own essence, the ability to do magical work increases and entities begin to have an inkling of what it is like to be a part of a living organism that has more than one center of consciousness. Many times this is first encountered in the small groups connected with family, that lucky family that happens to have a spiritual connection and experiences a common dedication to that which is beyond them. This occurs often in musical families, or in families of scholarship, or in healers such as medical doctors. These are the first nascent experiences of thinking as individuals and yet as one group, working as one, unified for a goal, whether it is to make music, to solve a complicated medical problem, or to resolve a fascinating scientific question. It is seldom, however, found that entities are able to enter into the unity of fourth density while within third-density bodies. And we note this present group, in attempting to create a fourth-density consciousness within its group, is indeed attempting that which is only marginally possible. Yet at the same time, the attempt not only creates a greatly advantageous learning situation for those attempting such a thing, it also creates, as the one known as V has suggested, that place where fourth-density qualities may dwell, survive and thrive. These kinds of desires to create heaven on Earth will hone and polish the honesty of each entity and will, if followed carefully, create a growing awareness of the fluidity and flexibility of truth.

The things that separate entities within third density are those things which are assumed. Some assumptions must be made in order to function. What assumptions entities have in common is very critical. The choices made by entities striving as this group is striving become more intense and more capable of making powerful changes in consciousness in the process of their being made because of the purity of the desire to stand in the light of love and be unified with the higher forces of love. This also creates an atmosphere in which experiences which are garnered from the ambience of such an atmosphere are very sharp and often painful.

It is, as this instrument would say, a very fast track, [one] that enables one to lift up and bring the self into an atmosphere of change and learning and energizing of that learning by conscious dedication. It is that which tests the mettle and the determination of the seeker. Any time an entity attempts to do what this instrument would call light work, to better the planet and its people, to serve as a beacon, and so forth, that choice brings into being a time of testing. And the more there is the desire to serve and to learn, the more the testing shall occur. It is a self-governing system that must operate as it does in order for free will to be preserved and in order for choices to be tested, refined and evolved. For a choice tends to move to another choice, to another choice, and so forth, so that it is a spiraling system that builds upon itself; each choice building upon itself or working to correct a previous choice made. Again, this is always at the discretion of the individual.

The late third-density entity then, the one who is ready for graduation, is an entity who knows itself well enough that it is ready to open itself completely to the offerings of all other entities with which it shall work. It has re-entered a group mind but it is not the same as any other of that group mind; rather, it is appreciated by the group for its flavors, no matter how harsh or pungent they may be. The group will use that uniqueness where it is needed according to the genius of that group. It is very difficult for a third-density entity even to believe in, much less experience, the power of the oversoul of a group and yet as soon as two entities make a true bond, there is a group soul. As soon as three entities are able to unify to a certain critical mass there is a group spirit, [just as there is one} to the L/L Research attendees that has grown over a period now of some 40 years and it is a very real source of guidance to those who call upon it. There are potential training wheels available for a nascent fourth-density type constructed at this time simply because this group has continued for a long period of time to attempt to unify itself, more and more, so that all within the group are attempting to serve together. There is a tremendous collaboration in service and in learning that comes into being as fourth-density ways are taken over from third density and at this time within your planet's experience, these possibilities for fourth-density structures and interactions become more and more viable as, as the one known as Bob Dylan said, "The times [they] are a changin'." The energy is changing, the vibration is changing, and fuller love is possible.

What choices shall you make? What polarity do you wish to study? This is the great choice and there is no issue too large or too small to contain grist for the mill and information that will be helpful in pursuing those choices.

This instrument informs us that we have talked as long as we should upon one subject and that it is time to open the meeting to further questions and so we would at this time do so and ask if there is a question at this time?

B: Q'uo, in a case where the messenger becomes more important than the message, what can the messenger do to correct the situation and bring the focus back to the message?

We are those of Q'uo, and we appreciate your query, my brother. It is a well-known phenomenon that often the face or the symbol of a very good thing may become mistaken for that quality and indeed there are times when the face must disappear. The technique of that disappearance is always at the choice of the entity who wishes to become less important. However the underlying difficulty is that difficulty of the easy versus the difficult, the obvious versus the subtle, the simplistic versus the real.

May we answer you further, my brother?

B: Are you aware of any specific techniques perhaps used by others in such a situation that could be helpful in understanding this?

We are those of Q'uo, and are aware of your query, my brother. We are aware of many techniques. However we find that this query runs very close to conscious work done by several of those present and therefore we run up against the bounds of free will. It is not acceptable to teach/learn for another.

May we answer you further my brother?

B: No, that's it, thank you.

Is there a further query at this time?

D: I had a question that I have wanted to ask for a long time. Are our prayers for blessings and guidance for the deceased a practice that is worthwhile?

We are those of Q'uo, and are aware of your query, my brother. Prayer of any kind is a very good idea in that it places one in the heart and places one in conversation with the godhead principle. Both of these are greatly desired orientations for spiritual seeking.

We would say perhaps the most skillful way to discuss blessings with the infinite Creator is to acknowledge them, for there are many blessings that abound even in the harshest circumstance. The attitude of thanksgiving and the claiming of great matters for which to be thankful are, as this instrument would say, a good idea. That attitude of affirming perfection as opposed to asking for blessings is the difference between knowing and being a needy child, asking for help. In one situation there is the claiming of the self as part of all that there is; in the other there is a separation between the asker and the one who has been asked. However, in general terms, any time that there is conversation with the Creator, it is a very positive and helpful resource upon which to draw.

May we answer you further my brother?

D: The general purpose of my question was more towards the deceased friends and loved ones. Does this apply in that area?

We are those of Q'uo, and this is correct, my brother. Is there a further query?

G: Q'uo, How does an entity in third density become qualified to serve as a higher agent, as a messenger of a message of service which is intended to be for your best and highest interest but which is given in what I would call a negative nature?

We are those of Q'uo, and are not grasping your query, my brother. Could you ask it in another way?

G: Reading your highest words I feel that opening the heart to another, accepting another unconditionally, and learning how to love is the crux of this density. I believe an entity may be mistaken to appoint themselves to a role in which they can administer a negative form of catalyst. So how does an entity, if an entity can indeed properly do this in a balanced manner, become so qualified? What in their being (experiential learning) makes this a balanced and loving service?

We are those of Q'uo, and are aware of your query, my brother. The ways of teachers and students do not run so much upon qualification as upon the movement of essence. Entities move into those roles for which they have a feeling. The question of qualification is not one which can apply for there is no system of qualification for spiritual work. It is truly a matter of each individual moving upon its own rhythms and upon its own track and attempting to serve as best as it may.

Consequently, all are teachers and all are students and all may indeed, in the process of expressing themselves, create negative catalyst for others, yet it is not upon the basis of qualification that such actions could be justified. Indeed, the concept of balance is perhaps helpful rather than the concept of justification.

May we answer you further, my brother?

G: Can an entity indeed act on your highest best, giving catalyst of a negative nature, and do that in a balanced manner?

We use the term of the one known as V and say, "Unknown, Captain." For indeed, you ask a question that we cannot answer. It moves us past the boundaries of free will and we apologize but can not go further than we have.

Is there another question, my brother?

G: Not on that particular topic. Thank you, Q'uo.

We thank you, my brother. Is there a final query at this time?

T: Q'uo, if you are able to answer without infringing upon my free will, are you able to offer any suggestions on how I may be able to better learn from the experiences of … times [when I needed] patience and tolerance?

We are those of Q'uo, and are aware of your query, my brother. The lessons of patience and tolerance are lessons that are slow, my brother. And therefore we encourage that feeling that you have for water to come forth for you, to picture within yourself the slow, slow movement of the breaking up of the ice of judgment and narrowness. Do not force the ice to melt, for it is spring, my brother, and the ice will melt. Rather, allow that process to take place even though it feels as if it were breaking you apart. For truly your nature must change from crystallized water to liquid water and from orthogonal angles to the spherical [drops] of the flowing water in which all things are able to rub along comfortably and make room for each other, whereas the crystallized nature of the ice is such that it must have a certain structure in order to exist in that form at all. You are experiencing, when you ask yourself to relax into non-judgment and patience, to move from that frozen condition to the liquid condition in which you do not have control such as you would feel that you had when you had that right-angled structure of the ice and its crystalline nature. It is not that you change from a crystalline nature. Water also is a crystal, yet it is able to radiate in a different way and is able to accept different structures in an enhanced way without disturbing its own nature.

May we answer you further, my brother?

T: No, thank you Q'uo, that's very helpful.

We thank you, my brother, and we thank each of those who has attended this group this day. We thank you for putting aside this time and for putting aside the daily grind and the concerns that have been on your hearts, simply to empty the self and to come into that place where questions are asked. It is hoped that resources have been added to your arsenal.

We leave each of you in the love and in the light of the one infinite Creator. We are known to you as those of Q'uo. Adonai. Adonai, my friends. ✤

L/L Research

L/L Research is a subsidiary of Rock Creek Research & Development Laboratories, Inc.

P.O. Box 5195
Louisville, KY 40255-0195

www.llresearch.org

Rock Creek is a non-profit corporation dedicated to discovering and sharing information which may aid in the spiritual evolution of humankind.

ABOUT THE CONTENTS OF THIS TRANSCRIPT: This telepathic channeling has been taken from transcriptions of the weekly study and meditation meetings of the Rock Creek Research & Development Laboratories and L/L Research. It is offered in the hope that it may be useful to you. As the Confederation entities always make a point of saying, please use your discrimination and judgment in assessing this material. If something rings true to you, fine. If something does not resonate, please leave it behind, for neither we nor those of the Confederation would wish to be a stumbling block for any.

© 2009 L/L RESEARCH

Sunday Meditation
May 2, 2004

Group question: The question today has to do with catalyst and determining what our catalyst is. We would like to have some information upon how we can determine what it is that is catalyst in our life and what we should be focusing on. The second part of the question has to do with the way catalyst can be processed: when it is successful, it seems as though the success comes from being able to look at the catalyst with a light touch; being able to look at it as catalyst and develop a certain sort of tolerance and patience with it as you work with it. And catalyst which has gone awry, as Ra said, tends to cause in us the feelings of frustration and anger and doubt and depression. So we would like for Q'uo to give us a bit of information about how to stay on the track where we develop the qualities of tolerance and patience and how to avoid the frustration and anger.

(Carla channeling)

We are those known to you as the principle of Q'uo, and we greet you in the love and in the light of the one infinite Creator, in Whose service we are. It is a great privilege and blessing to be called to your group this day and we thank you with all our hearts. To be able to be a part of your meditation and to share our thoughts with you is, to us, a powerful help, as it enables us to share our service as we hoped to do when we chose to undertake this time among your peoples. It has never been more pleasurable to undertake service to those of planet Earth than when we speak with this particular group and we thank you for maintaining the eagerness and the openness for truth that creates the vibration which calls us to you. As always, we would ask, in order to preserve free will, that each of you guard your own powers of discrimination carefully and use them well as you listen to those things which we would say to you this day. It is important to us that you realize that we are not authorities but rather your companions upon the way.

Your query this day is interesting to us and we thank you for asking us to speak upon the subject of catalyst. The message which we have to offer to those who would hear our voice remains very simple. There is a vibratory nature to creation. And the various fields of energy which comprise all of the complex parts of all of your bodies, be they physical or metaphysical, vibrate at a certain, shall we say, series of harmonics which, in total, add up to the complex of vibrations which is as an orchestra playing your song. We recognize each entity's melody fairly well. It is a signature like no other in its completeness. So each of you is a vibration that is at some harmonic, in general, with those about you, with the groups that comprise your planetary sphere and with the Creator and the creation as a whole. These vibrations are disturbed, or changed, by any number of stimuli, on any number of levels, speaking of the physical body, the mental, the emotional, the spiritual, and the inner bodies all together.

Catalyst, then, is a term to use to describe that which, while being unchanged, creates changes in this complex of energy fields and the vibrations thereof. Within a chemical experiment, there is a little arrow that is used to indicate that catalyst only goes one way. A chemical reaction does not go forwards and backwards, it only goes forwards, and so it is with the catalyst that you experience. One cannot look back. One cannot go back. One cannot possibly repeat one's experiences. One shall indeed meet each experience again, but it is a spiral of experience and catalyst, and experience and catalyst, and each time you meet the same type or class of catalyst you have a new opportunity to recognize the catalyst, to locate the trigger of the catalyst, to examine the equation of the catalyst: what is going into the chemical experiment, what's being "cooked," and what comes out at the other end. And you have the opportunity, if you choose to use the will and the discipline to take it, to alter by removing various, shall we say, chemicals of your emotions, your thoughts, and your triggers, thereby changing the equation and changing the result of this particular little experiment in the life of your self.

Now let us look at this model a bit more closely. We use the term, trigger, to describe the action of catalyst. A catalyst comes into the purview of the being. It does not come into the ambient environment of the entity on purpose. There is no innate consciousness to the way things occur from the level of their occurrence. There is a causative factor inherent in the carefully made agreements that were entered into before incarnation. Biases were set up in the very currents of destiny surrounding the particular nexus of energies that represents the opportunity for an incarnation. When the body and parents and so forth are chosen, this nexus becomes potentiated and that particular little destiny that is your pre-game game plan clicks into place and begins to unroll the scroll of space/time as you, as an entity, enter into a body, become embodied and enfleshed, take form by birth and begin to unravel the great tale that is the story of your life.

So one source of catalyst that is dependable and ongoing can loosely be called guidance or the higher self or destiny. For there has been implanted within your game plan, shall we say, repetitive cycles of the introduction of certain catalysts into the ambient environment so that you may work with certain balances and biases within one or more of your energy bodies. The inner work of an incarnation is primarily in those energy bodies in the inner planes, those bodies that are closer to the heart of why you are a being, or, shall we say, why the Creator finds it inevitable and useful to create beings such as yourselves. That is one source of catalyst and as you can identify those repetitive types of catalyst that point to incarnational level lessons, you as a seeker can begin to see into the game plan; to begin to think not like the victim of circumstance but the person who planned all this and finds that certain things have simply slipped her mind. If you can find this attitude in times of stress, that "you really have responsibility for this situation but, my goodness, you seemed to have forgotten just a bit of the pattern and now there is work to do," then you may do the work of identifying catalyst, locating the trigger, and, to the extent possible in situations, doing what you can to remove the trigger or to alter the circumstances. You have become far more a person of power than you were before.

Every time you are able to identify the catalyst and the trigger within you that caused an otherwise harmless detail to become powerful in your life, you have learned about yourself and have begun to take responsibility for learning in a conscious way what you would inevitably learn without consciousness, no matter what, by the sheer pressure of repetition. Each time you are able to get on board with the game plan beforehand, or during the catalyst's coming up, you become more able to retain your power. And eventually you become able to use that power wisely and with compassion. And this is particularly important regarding yourself. Although it is very helpful when you may achieve that same compassion for others, in the case of the identification and the working with catalyst, the primary player in the drama is the self and therefore the entity to be forgiven, accepted and loved unconditionally is the self.

We speak in terms of power here. Because when catalyst causes one to react, the catalyst, innocent though it may be, and unasking of power as it is, has the power. It is only as a person begins to be able to see into the process of these repetitive, cyclical testings, or introductions of catalyst into the environment, that one begins to be able to settle into a relationship with catalyst which sees catalyst, destiny and unexpected events in general, with an eagerness and a freshness of attitude that invites that which is to come and looks forward to the next lesson, the next test, the next introduction of discomfort into an otherwise serene atmosphere.

Within the confines of your illusion and the life which you experience consciously, awake and working with your day, there is a tremendous amount of power in becoming eager for that next piece of catalyst. When you at last find an appetite for change, for learning, for newness, then you are more able to invoke discipline when it would seem that difficult or unpleasant circumstances arise. Admittedly, as we gaze through this instrument's recent recollections we can see that it is not always an easy thing to create the environment for the self that is a safe environment for total honesty in looking at the catalyst of the self. It is often a lowering experience in terms of what this instrument would call, ego, to look into the mechanics or the psychology of the self, to see just how vulnerable the self is to catalyst which is at the level of the teenager or the child or even the toddler in some cases. And yet each entity retains all identities which have not proven themselves useless in terms of producing further learning.

So until you as an entity are through, completely through, with learning all of the lessons that are possible to learn within incarnation, you shall, according to the prerequisites of your own game plan, receive the spiraling, cycling opportunities to react to the catalyst. It shall come around again and again. This is not a ploy to drive the spiritual seeker crazy. It is a necessary way of checking the self to see where the self truly is, where the feet come down on the road in any given incarnational lesson. Thusly, catalyst may eventually, in a certain way, become that which enters the consciousness, proceeds through the consciousness and walks out the other side without causing any reaction. The entity is still aware of the catalyst and still aware of its trigger, which speaks but not loudly enough for the self to take seriously, for it has been worked so often and so well that there is no longer the potential for a reaction. Thusly and only in this way is catalyst at last neutralized. Until the energy in that catalyst's appearance is gone, there will be continuing work.

Thusly, we would suggest, whenever catalyst arises, that the most efficient attitude for the skillful worker in consciousness is to thank it, to open the self to it, to ask it to move through as quickly as possible, especially if it is difficult, but to put up no sort of resistance against it. The skillful seeker will sit with the catalyst while allowing it to move through the system and create the emotional changes and reactions that it will. The self can still be a witness to these reactions, these feelings, these worthy and needed expressions of the present moment. The purpose of working with catalyst is not to defeat the catalyst but to cooperate with the catalyst, to move into the catalyst, to move into that collection of energy, that node, that has been created by the catalyst and to see why the arrow is there, why the energy for reaction is there, what that energy is, where it comes from within the energy body in terms of the chakra involved, and so forth.

Then find that trigger, find that wounded part of the self that is not comfortable yet with the self and look at that trigger to see how deeply it goes into the self. And ask it once again—for those to whom we speak have in many cases identified several of the kinds of catalyst of which we speak—to enter into understanding it more and more, not to get rid of it but to learn from it. To absorb it. To be it. In the surrender to this node of concentrated energy, there is a magical component that increases as there is an increase in the confidence and faith within the seeker in the process that has been engaged by the activation of the catalyst. There is tremendous power in knowing why something is happening to one. Not in knowing what provoked a certain person to do something or what strange machinery created a coincidence that is complex and deep but rather knowing that one is in good hands, one is in the hands of guidance, and having faith in the process that will deliver one, at the end of that process, a greater gift to the Creator and a greater asset to the self because the balance of the energy body that has been worked on has improved, has come closer to that which was hoped before incarnation.

The question of how to recognize catalyst is almost that which we cannot answer for it seems too simple a thing to need a response and yet the query remains and so we would simply say that when one's tenor of thought or one's mood changes, the changes are either inconsequential, ephemeral and insubstantial, in which case there is no learning going on; or they are more substantial, consequential and meaningful, in which case there will be a plangent note to the moment of catalyst. There will be a sudden change in the vibration which you are putting out and giving to the world as your gift to it. In that change, the balance has shifted either more towards the vibration of the Creator or less towards the vibration of the Creator. When catalyst occurs, the result of which is that the entity is more in tune with the Creator, this normally is not seen as a situation which needs any concern for it is seen as a positive thing; it is enjoyable to feel bliss and joy and peace. When catalyst such as that occurs there is only rejoicing on the part of the seeker.

Yet, when there is catalyst that causes the exact opposite within the seeker, that causes a contraction in the self that pulls it away from a feeling of unity and oneness, then it is seen as a "bad thing." This attitude may always be examined. For locked within each seeker's deep mind is that collection of biases which, before incarnation, you genuinely and deeply intended to work with until you were more satisfied with the achieved balance.

Now, we speak repeatedly of balance and usually it is a balance that is between love and wisdom; between the green ray and the blue/indigo/violet trinity of rays. It is very attractive to many wanderers, especially in incarnation upon planet Earth, to stay within the upper triad of energies, using this system of seven chakras and an octave. It is similarly attractive to others who have come into incarnation from a point of different balance to lean into the green-ray open heart and to see everything in terms of keeping the heart open. Either focus, if taken to the extreme of not invoking the other, is unbalanced. So there are entities who are attempting to balance their energies more into the green ray, into an integration with green ray of their blue-ray strengths, and there are others who are doing precisely the opposite, attempting to soften their green ray with wisdom. Perhaps this may help in thinking about this very interesting subject. To become able to work with catalyst, be unafraid of catalyst, refrain from contracting when catalyst is felt, is a tremendous aid in becoming able to live consciously and she who lives consciously is she who is truly being that light that is upon the hill.

She who lives consciously is able to be more than one absorbed in a process and perhaps that is what we may say about the light touch. It is a very absorbing process to become aware of the self, to become at last one who is living consciously, magically, positively and constructively. This fascination, however, can blind one to the beauty, the wonder, the majesty of every moment that is lived, every heartbeat that is enjoyed, every tear and every laugh that is experienced. The gifts of life and thought are marvelous and the more that it can be seen that this catalyst and these sometimes dreary processes are taking place in the garden of Eden and in beauty indescribable, the more that this sojourn in the valley of the shadow of death, as this instrument would call life, becomes triumphant, funny, wonderful, delicious, a thing of real splendor. That is the potential of each breath. That is the shadow of what is possible when one becomes fully conscious and is able to express passion and excitement and equanimity and simply becomes able to enjoy the show. For upon a very substantial level, it is a show. It is a production. It is a performance.

There is an endless search within each for reality, the reality of the self, the reality of the life, that which is the ground of being. You shall never find it. You can only find images of it. You can, however, be the ground of being. You can be essence. You can be so much more than you can say! And in many ways the doing, the thinking, the working with catalyst and the whole process is aimed at delivering you at last to being.

The one known as G was talking with this instrument this morning concerning this instrument's bias against the use of feel-good music in church services. This instrument was saying that she appreciated the more complex sacred works which bring suffering and doubt and many complex and somewhat dark emotions into the singing of sacred thoughts so that the entire human experience is able to be brought into sacred space in such music, whereas in the so-called "praise music"[103] there is a seeming separation between the suffering person and the good feelings which are generated praising.

There are times, however, when praise music of whatever kind that lifts the spirits is very helpful. Perhaps for a certain entity it might be a country music song or a classical music piece or some other form of seeming distraction. Yet when chosen, such distractions are very helpful, whether they be good art, as this instrument—a born critic again—would call it, [or not]. That which lifts the spirit and changes the atmosphere is sometimes very helpful, as nonsensical and illogical as such things are. It is not

---

[103] Referring to a brand of contemporary Christian worship music that focuses not on the whole life and death of Jesus the Christ, but strictly upon his resurrection, his glory, and his awesomeness.

well to allow the self simply to rest in a state of panic or unhappiness or depression. There is a time for sitting with catalyst and when that time has come to an end—and for each entity the rhythms are different—there is the time of asking the self to rise up, give thanks, and move on into the rest of the day, into the rest of that which is available when one is not focused on a certain piece of catalyst. We encourage you not to allow yourselves to become so absorbed in the process of learning that you become unavailable to the present moment. This is a juggling act, in so many ways, as several within this group have said earlier this day. There is so much to think about and so much to do. As you juggle, you will drop balls, and as the one known as J says, when you drop the balls, that, too, is part of juggling. And the reaction to dropping them should not be that which is judgmental or harsh but simply to encourage the self to pick that dropped ball up with grace, style and humor.

Lastly, you questioned concerning how to avoid bitterness and how to encourage the self not to use catalyst awry. That is perhaps a topic we may save for another day in terms of really moving into it. But in general we may say that one is almost never able to see ahead of time that one is going to be bitter, defensive, angry and so forth. So one is not able to defend against such times. They simply come upon one and one finds oneself in the shadows and very unhappy for one reason or another and in one way or another, depending upon the personality shell. When you're in the soup there is no use objecting to yourself because you fell or because you're wet. Bitterness comes into the life because it is a way to keep the attention away from getting out of the soup. The energy of one who has run afoul of catalyst and is struggling can be focused in one of two ways. It can be focused in trying to stay afloat or it can be focused in trying to get out of the cup of soup. Climbing the slippery china walls of your cup is not easy and it requires far different skills than treading water.[104] However, those who tread water shall be doomed to repeat the exercise, never being allowed to drown and never, while treading water, able to garner the energy that is required for the tremendous effort needed to break the pattern and create a ladder of will and discipline that allows you to clamber over that china cup and get out of the soup. There is no question that it is easier to tread water, stay in the soup, and repine concerning the difficulty that one is in than it is to gather the energies and create, by will and faith alone, that ladder out of the situation and back to a sense of owning the self and not being a victim of circumstance. However, it is through such work that one is able to move through the refining fire, not burning to a cinder, but rather becoming more and more tempered …

(Side one of tape ends.)

(Carla channeling)

… more and more burnished, and more and more flexible.

We find that our time is up and it is time to open the meeting to [shorter additional] queries. Are there queries at this time?

J: On June 8 there's a Venus transit which lasts eight years, which will bring us right to the year 2012. I was wondering about your opinion. Is this an important event or is it just one of the many smaller events leading up to ascension? Is this event something that we should really look at to move us into a higher consciousness?

We are those of Q'uo, and we are aware of your query, my sister. We believe that information could be gleaned by those who have intuitive gifts and a wide and deep knowledge of astrology. There is always much to be learned from the movements of the stars and their influence upon the body of Earth itself and each of you as well. However, the chief excitement which remains upon our own minds is that great interest that we have in seeing the way entities are awakening and becoming more and more able to live consciously and radiate light. This is far more factored into the eventual outcome of your peoples and the, shall we say, end of the age than any cosmic influence. Much lies at this time in the hearts and the hands of entities upon planet Earth at this time.

May we answer you further, my sister?

J: No, thank you.

We thank you, my sister. Is there another query at this time?

G: Q'uo, I have a series of questions sent in from readers abroad but first, I know, knowing T1, that when he has a question he will hold his off and let

---

[104] Pardon the Q'uo for the mixed metaphor—soup, not water!

others ask their questions. I would like to ask if T1 has a question before I ask a series of questions.

T1: No, G, please go ahead.[105]

G: Okay. This question is from B. "In 1987 I lost my job, broke up my marriage, left my wife and children and lost my desire to live. I totally surrendered my life to the Source. It was my 'turning point.' And ever since I've been on my spiritual path, re-married and live happily. However, there is still some bitterness within my children and my ex-wife towards me, while sometimes I still feel guilty to have left them. I would appreciate it if Q'uo would throw some light on our relationship at soul level (karmic ties) and give us some guidance on how to heal the wounds."

We are those of Q'uo, and are aware of the query, my brother, and we thank you for vibrating that query for him. To the one known as B we would say that the true nature of the relationship betwixt you and your ex-spouse is oneness. The energies that you experience at this time may fruitfully be examined for just those things which we were speaking about earlier: the catalyst involved, the triggers involved, and the biases that are involved in the particular lesson that you and your ex-spouse share. Often this work cannot be done together with another in such a situation and so it is very helpful if the entity has the energy to step into the other-self's shoes to such an extent that the one known as B is able to see through the eyes of the ex-spouse, sitting there until there is as full an understanding on the conscious level of the dynamics involved in this particular node of catalyst as possible. The details of past lives and so forth are not those things with which we would prefer to deal as we would wish to limit comments to those that are helpful to all entities and at all times.

The spiritual principle involved here is the principle of responsibility for one's actions. When there is the full acceptance of the self, the full forgiveness of the self, and the full appreciation of the present moment, then such concerns as are expressed in the query become details which do not have the power to alter consciousness within the self. We encourage the reading of the channeling through this instrument that was given at the first part of this meditation.

---

[105] T calls from Australia to Kentucky each Sunday channeling, that he may be a part of the group. He joins us by speaker telephone.

Is there another query at this time, my brother?

G: This next one comes in from S. "I have only recently been exposed to the term 'Crystal Kids.' I would like to know as much information as possible on these children. Who are Crystal Kids? How are they different from the Indigo Kids and what can you tell us about their purpose on Earth? I thank you for the opportunity to ask this."

We are those of Q'uo, and are aware of your query, my sister. From our standpoint there is virtually no difference in those called Indigo Children and those called Crystal Kids. The designations indicate a double-activated third-density/fourth-density body, which makes such children, as they grow up, more able to access fourth-density reality. Since fourth density is here, since entities are living in a combined third-density/fourth-density atmosphere, there is an increasing ability for all people to work upon the, what this instrument would call, DNA; to work upon the self at the cellular level, lifting consciousness and asking it to take hold of the new reality that is interpenetrating third density.

These children are far more able to do this than those with only the yellow-ray body activated because their DNA is already altered to some extent. However, their purpose here is as pioneers. They come in, in terms of fourth density, within very basic and primitive conditions, and are giving their lives to help establish fourth density and to be bridges of light for those who would listen to that which they would have to say and to live in such a way as to follow such advice as they would give. To put it another way, they are here to radiate light and love, as are all entities. It is hoped by their higher selves that they will have more efficacy in doing so than those who have not the advantage of a double-activated body.

Is there another query at this time?

G: This is the last outside query. This one comes from T2. "Dr. Sun Yat-sen is the founding father of the Republic of China. This Republic is as short-lived as himself. However, he is respected by both Chinese and Taiwanese, both the Communist party and the Kuomin party. If it is possible, could Q'uo speak about Dr. Sun Yat-sen's life?"

We are those of Q'uo, and are aware of your query, my brother. This entity was one whose energy was that of the heart and yet whose abilities included communication. This entity was a brilliant blue-ray being who was able to inspire and to lead because his communication rested upon a compassionate and humane structure of character. This entity gave greatly of itself and was exemplary in its habits and inner disciplines, creating an incarnation of stature.

Is there another query at this time?

G: I have a personal one, Q'uo. In the last channeling you stated that, "Until one has individuated, one cannot begin magical work, and yet one is never fully individuated. So, logically speaking, one could never begin magical work. Yet there is, shall we say, a critical mass only that needs to be reached, and it is by no means a large percentage of the actual available will of an entity." Ra also spoke of a "set level of lack of distortion" required to tap intelligent energy through crystals, "or through any use." So the first part of my question is, are Q'uo and are Ra speaking of this same point? And the second part of the question is, can you describe more about this point and are there any tell-tale signs that will manifest in an entity when this point has been reached?

We are those of Q'uo, and are aware of your query, my brother. We cannot speak to the first part of your query in this setting, although, if you wish, we are able to address it at length at another time.

To respond to the second portion of your query: the tell-tale signs of magical working are sudden changes of a profound nature in circumstance which reflect a synchronicity that is obvious. Synchronicity is indeed a mark of one who has activated a certain magical-ness within its own nature.

May we answer you further, my brother?

G: Perhaps might that sudden change not only reflect through the outer physical in synchronicity but might that look or feel or give one the space, the freedom, to love that which was before was unlovable?

We are those of Q'uo, and are aware of your query, my brother. Such a circumstance might occur, my brother. May we answer you further?

G: No, thank you very much, Q'uo.

We thank you, my brother. Is there a final query at this time?

D: How may the distortions of pride and arrogance be recognized when you are the one experiencing them?

We are those of Q'uo, and are aware of your query, my brother. We smile because we are aware of this instrument's deep and intense involvement in this very query for the last little bit of her time. Because of this factor it is more difficult to answer your query, my brother. However, we may say that when the self, in its inner contemplations, begins to cast aspersions upon another, it is possible that pride and arrogance have been invoked and that there are more circumstances than one is aware of, which might change the attitude from that sourness to a more balanced and compassionate view. When that typical sourness which has that taste of judgment comes into the mouth, into the mind, then it may be that there are lessons in humility that could be easily taken up with advantage.

May we answer you further, my brother?

D: That's quite sufficient. Thank you.

We thank you, my brother, and we thank each of you. This group is such a blessing to us and it is such a pleasure to speak with you through this instrument. We thank you with all of our hearts and wish each of you to know that you are in our hearts. At any time that you wish to have our company during meditation, you have only to ask, for we are those who love each of you. Certainly the beauty of each of you is remarkable and we thank each of you for sharing the experience of this meeting with us.

We leave you in the love and in the light of the one infinite Creator. Adonai. We are those of Q'uo. ❧

L/L Research

L/L Research is a subsidiary of Rock Creek Research & Development Laboratories, Inc.

P.O. Box 5195
Louisville, KY 40255-0195

www.llresearch.org

Rock Creek is a non-profit corporation dedicated to discovering and sharing information which may aid in the spiritual evolution of humankind.

ABOUT THE CONTENTS OF THIS TRANSCRIPT: This telepathic channeling has been taken from transcriptions of the weekly study and meditation meetings of the Rock Creek Research & Development Laboratories and L/L Research. It is offered in the hope that it may be useful to you. As the Confederation entities always make a point of saying, please use your discrimination and judgment in assessing this material. If something rings true to you, fine. If something does not resonate, please leave it behind, for neither we nor those of the Confederation would wish to be a stumbling block for any.

© 2009 L/L Research

Sunday Meditation
May 16, 2004

Group question: Today, Q'uo, we have an interest in a couple of areas that might have a relationship. The first one we were talking about was the mirroring effect. In third density, since we have the veil of forgetting and aren't consciously aware of exactly what it is we're trying to do in our personal learning, each of us here is able to take advantage of the mirroring effect, where people reflect back to us that which we are attempting to learn. We're wondering if Q'uo could give us a bit more information about just how this works? Can we consciously affect the way we mirror to other people? Should we even try?

The other thing we were wondering about was, [in the discussion prior to this meditation,] there seemed to be a theme of new experiences, new jobs, new beginnings for everybody in our group today. We are wondering if there is any kind of connection between how we serve as mirrors in our general run of activities during the day and how we serve as mirrors when there is something new or changed, a different type of attitude or opportunity offered to us in our lives?

(Carla channeling)

We are those known to you as the principle of Q'uo and we greet you in the love and in the light of the one infinite Creator, in Whose service we are privileged to be. It is a distinct pleasure to share in your meditation and we bless each of you and thank you for inviting us to share our thoughts with you this day. As always, we would request that in order for free will to be observed, each of you guard the portals of your own belief system carefully, not taking those things that we have to say as truth but examining them for their resonance and their feeling of personal truth to you. Each entity has a personal truth, not so much a relative truth as an individual truth, a subjective truth. And words cannot begin to bridge the gap. Spiritual seeking takes place in the subjective realm and therefore it is not a matter of that which can be proven or disproven. And so the nature of truth itself becomes peculiarly key. Take care to guard those portals of your discrimination in order that those precepts that you do adopt are those which have had a long and careful review and a strong sense of remembering them as being true as opposed to learning them for the first time. We thank you for your attention to this detail which does give us a most satisfactory feeling of ethical probity.

You ask concerning mirrors and you ask concerning novelty. And indeed, on the surface, the two subjects would seem to have little in common and yet we find that they do intersect and we shall begin edging towards the first part of the intersection, the first subject, and that would be the subject of novelty. The question of newness would seem to be a patent one. When one asks what is new, one is fairly aware of the nature of novelty. However, there are different types of novelty. There is the expected novelty, such as the one known as T is experiencing, where the

347

activity is new and yet it is expected and prepared for aforetimes. The other type of novelty is that which takes one by surprise and indeed there are many surprises as the road of life twists and bends and the curves ahead cannot be seen.

The two have in common one characteristic and that is that in a novel situation, information is difficult to obtain relative to the speed of information retention when a situation is well known beforehand. We do not simply mean that it takes longer to obtain information because of the novelty of the details. Certainly, any time one were having to observe a new environment, there would be a longer adjustment time. However, added to this is the fact that when there is a novel environment, the eyes themselves, your physical eyes that behold a scene and transmit the information to the mind, are greatly handicapped because of the way the eyes work. When a view is completely new there is no pre-existing matrix of the view within the bio-computer of the entity's mind who is doing the looking. It is a relatively cumbersome thing to amass information about a new scene so that the brain can establish a kind of default setting for that scene and therefore when the eyes look upon the scene, far less data needs to be gathered before an entity is able to make sense of the scene itself.

This is the kind of handicap that one is encountering in a new situation. Consequently, the skill of an entity in a novel situation is that skill that slows the process of receiving information down, allowing for the self more time to orient the self to new places, new faces, new procedures, and new concepts. It is not the mark of a failing mind to take longer with everything that one does in any situation than usual. It is rather the inevitable mark of a mind having to amass many times the usual amount of data before a critical mass can be reached with which to address the next part of the process. What is to happen next is a question that cannot be answered quickly in a new situation. Oftentimes it may feel as though it were necessary to come to a conclusion about what one was seeing very quickly. In most cases, this is not so and we would encourage the slowing down of all those tempos that begin to feel as though they must speed up and hurry up. This is, in almost all situations, a false reading which has been the result of that spirit of eagerness to control a situation that is so much a part of the personality shell of most entities within third density. Many times there is more control in allowing the scene to build and continuing to amass information before making a decision, even though it may seem that one is somehow behindhand because of being less than rapid in the process of decision making.

Now we come to that point of intersection between the idea of novelty and the idea of mirrors. For, in the sense in which we would like to speak of mirrors, every situation has novel aspects. Every situation is one in which it is well to employ caution and find a sense of space and leisure in the process of looking, of looking into the mirror of a situation, [whether it be] another space, the challenge of a new job, or whatever one is looking at. It is always well to check the mirror again even if it is a mirror into which you have looked often and carefully.

The assumption that one has all aspects of the situation understood is wrong often enough that it is appropriate always to look again into that mirror which one is viewing with an eye to what one has missed, to what one has overlooked, to those things that have not been obvious but are part of the image at which one gazes. Allow yourself that moment of seeing a new world whenever you look into the images of life's mirror. For you gaze at reflections that have reflections that have reflections; and the echoing brilliance of meaning within these often convoluted expressions of image are most helpful in the process. And this is true in a fractal manner,[106] so that there is no end to the information that can be gleaned by an ever-closer inspection of thoughts, processes and images.

The mirroring aspect is worth looking at from the standpoint of mirrors themselves and the nature of entities as crystalline. Mirrors, being glass, are crystalline. The crystal is that which is transparent. The glass, the silicate, is that which is not able to be seen without a backing unless substances collect upon the surface of the glass and render it visible by its pattern of dirt. Without a smudge to identify a surface and without reflection to make it obvious that there is glass that can refract light, the glass itself is invisible and transparent and light simply moves through it. When a backing is put onto a plate of glass, it becomes a mirror.

---

[106] A fractal is any of various extremely irregular curves or shapes for which any suitably chosen part is similar in shape to a given larger or smaller part when magnified or reduced to the same size.

So to the question of whether there are different kinds of mirrors, the answer is yes. And the first way that we would note the difference between certain types of mirrors and others is that some mirrors have no backing. The ideal mirror, in fact, is a plate of glass that has lost its backing completely so that no matter what an entity gazing at the mirror of you looks at, all it sees is the sunlight shining through—the love and the light of the one infinite Creator that is able to pour right through that transparency of spirit and that openness of heart.

But there is another way in which mirrors differ, one from the other; for you are not simply a mirror with one face. The one known as G was, we believe, attempting to articulate a question concerning whether an entity always shows one mirror or whether an entity can affect the way his mirror images another self to itself. And we find that indeed an entity has a profound ability to affect what another entity will see when he looks into the mirror of you. Remember that all entities are one, so that what an entity is presenting or dwelling upon within the self has a strong effect upon how that entity is perceived. It is a complex formula involving an entity's assumptions about himself, which have been formed by gazing into the mirror of other selves. This creates a persona, the way that an entity thinks about himself and therefore puts himself forward.

If an entity does not do any disciplined work in consciousness, that mirror is as it is. And that which an entity will see gazing into your mirror is the reflective quality of glass sending light back; and that image will have been formed by the backing of all of the prejudices and biases within the personality shell of that entity that is the mirror. So if you are an unconsciously living entity, your mirror will be as it is and that which will be seen in it will tell a certain truth. That truth will be the simple summation of the moments of the self as it is, looking into the mirror of you as you are, with no possibility for anything but the inevitable result of those two energies.

When an entity begins to do conscious work in creating for itself a predisposition to a certain point of view, then the mirror of his self begins to refine what it shows. For the mirror of this particular type of crystal being that you are does not simply show a flat image, it also shows how that image feels. It shows how its essence wafts on the wind and what its odor is. It plays the melody that that particular nexus calls up. It is a full-service mirror in the way of expressing the nuances of attitude. And as you work on your attitude, you are creating an ever more articulate mirror which can show to an entity a more and more refined image. Perhaps each within this circle has met an entity whose love and light were such that in their presence you could see yourself in a different way. When you looked into that mirror, what you saw was a "you" that was only possible looking in that mirror. Was it an idealized portrait or image? No, it was a possible image of you aided by the positioning of an attitude with which that self was viewed. The more open you are able to lift the gates of the heart, the more compassion that you are able to let in when pride and arrogance are let out, the less the self chooses to partake of the judgment, the stronger will be the extra-dimensional aspects of mirroring that your mirror is capable of offering. Again, this is not something that can be consciously created at the time of the mirroring moment. Rather, it is that with which you come to the moment in all your own fresh novelty that defines what will occur when a mirroring moment happens.

There is a great deal that each entity may do to improve the mirroring quality of her nature and we recommend the work involved not only for its efficacy in creating a better mirror but also for the fascinating journey such disciplining of the personality constitutes. As always, it is helpful to use meditation or some form of sustained silence as part of any practice; but certainly, for doing work upon this mirroring ability—for employing, that is, the disciplines of the personality—daily silence to seat new thoughts and new learning is especially recommended.

At this time we would like to open the meeting to further questions. Are there further questions at this time?

G: Q'uo, twenty-three years ago, Ra confirmed Don's notion that we were soon approaching the end of third density when they said that in thirty years third density will be over and fourth will have begun. Now, apparently, the Confederation felt that it was within the limits of our free will that we could receive that approximate date at which the old would end and the new would begin. Knowing that, it can become problematic to those who sincerely believe that they are living in the "end times." It shouldn't, in my humble opinion, affect the seeker's inward journey. The disciplines of the personality must continue regardless of what is to come in the future. If anything, that date may only increase their desire to seek. But it becomes problematic to some, because it affects one's outward plans for the future, one's plans on the physical plane such as having kids and choosing a career. So, since the Confederation provided that little nugget of information, I was wondering if you might have any suggestions on how one could plan, how one could work around such a future occurrence?

We are those of Q'uo, and are aware of your query, my brother. The group known as Q'uo has limited abilities to examine the process of creating thoughts that were offered by those of Ra twenty-three years in your past. However, it is our feeling as well as of that of those within our principle known as the group of Ra that you are at this time indeed dwelling within fourth density. The intent of the original discussion, as the intent of this discussion, had nothing to do with creating a way to judge the making of plans within your physical universe. It was rather a discussion of a metaphysical process that is accompanying the physical process whereby the planet upon which you dwell chooses its needed, new magnetic alignment. That it is doing so in a far different manner than has been done in the past may perhaps be obvious to each of you. This moving of the magnetic north by very small increments over a period of time is the result of the attempt of many upon your planet to ease the passage or the birth of fourth density into reality. Its birth has gone relatively well considering the amount of chaotic or wasted energy amongst your peoples and the resulting metaphysical heat, shall we say, that has created so much discomfort among your peoples at this time. Naturally, the hope of the Confederation at this time is that this process may continue and that the Earth, as a planet, may reestablish a stable magnetic alignment without the necessity for planetary disaster. The possibility/probability vortex of this occurrence improves as more and more of your entities wake up and begin to polarize towards service to others, in response to the various wake-up calls, as the one known as J has termed them, that the various political injustices are occurring create.

We would suggest, insofar as our opinion would be useful, that entities do precisely what they feel to do in relation to their lives, assuming that all is well. If there is the kind of desire this group evinces towards making a more sustainable lifestyle in a more rural setting, that is certainly a sensible and logical plan when one suspects that there may be outages and lacks in the surrounding society. However, may we note that in no way is it possible for any group to plan for the future. This is true not only in a time of the birth of a new density and a new stellar cycle as well. This is true in every moment of every day of each incarnation. The processes of life and death are not in the hands of those whose breath touches the air of the planet but rather in the hands of the Creator of each spark of life. Resting in complete faith in the plan of the Creator, we would suggest, has the virtue of reflecting a high degree of ultimate truth.

May we answer you further, my brother?

G: No, that was great Q'uo, thank you.

We thank you, my brother, is there a further query?

G: Indeed. In the Ra series, Ra states that, "There are many Wanderers whom you may call adepts who do no conscious work in the present incarnation. It is a matter of attention. One may be a fine catcher of your game sphere, but if the eye is not turned as this sphere is tossed then perchance it will pass the entity by. If it turned its eyes upon the sphere, catching would be easy." Q'uo, my question is, what is the sphere that this analogy speaks of and where should the seeker be placing that attention?

We are those of Q'uo and are aware of your query, my brother. The query as to the definition of the game sphere is not a simple one for there is a continuing question in the minds of those who attempt to serve well as to whether the attention should be upon the outer detail or upon the inner reaction and response to that outer detail. It is a dance that is artful, to pick up all of the information that is being offered while at the same time being able to observe the self observing the outer information. For one is learning from how the self responds to the present moment as well as from the present moment. It is an exchange that can become quite convoluted and subtle.

The game sphere we suppose could best be described as the present moment itself. This pulls the mind's attention away from the self. The death of all new awareness is an over-absorption with the self. Getting into the moment is a matter of that balanced stance that looks inward and outward with an un-jaundiced and patient eye.

May we answer you further, my brother?

G: No, that was great, thank you.

We thank you, my brother. Is there another query at this time?

T: Do you have any suggestions to offer as I enter this period of intense study?

We are those of Q'uo, my brother, and are aware of your query. We encourage you to know that there is tremendous light in this process. We can see that the intensity of the learning process shall be that which could at times daunt [you] and perhaps [cause you to] feel as if there were a destabilizing influence in the concomitant additions of so many systems of thought and so many new and conflicting ways of looking at those qualities within illness which one wishes to heal. There is the possibility for the heart to become overly involved and there is the conflicting but also a very real possibility that one can shut away the heart in order to protect from the intensity of human knowledge being grasped. We recommend, therefore, the balancing, the allowing to come into balance, of often conflicting thoughts on any one particular item or process of study. Allowing the self to become too involved in the process is inviting a certain type of exhaustion which is not helpful in the learning process. Equally, allowing oneself to become cynical and dispassionate about that which is being learned is not skillful, especially in that the object of study is the human psyche, the human heart, the human soul. These are not those things about which one can be or ought to be dispassionate. So there is that balance that needs to be struck. Other than that piece of advice, my brother, we encourage you to enjoy and relish each moment of the blooming season that you embrace at this time. We are with you in your days and we will greatly enjoy the association with you and thank you for the continued invitation.

May we answer you further, my brother?

T: Thank you, Q'uo, that was very helpful. I do have one other question. I had a dream a few nights ago where I was reaching upwards and flying upwards until I eventually penetrated something like a threshold. And once through this I entered into another reality where I once again flew upwards to penetrate the next barrier and then continuing through that cycle. I wonder if you are able to comment at all upon that?

We are those of Q'uo, and are aware of your query, my brother. We find that we are not able to comment and merely encourage you to work with these materials as more information from other dreamscapes continues to filter in.

Is there another query at this time?

T: I understand and appreciate that. Thank you Q'uo, no more queries from me.

We thank you, my brother. Is there another query at this time?

G: As I understand what has occurred within the past 75,000 years there was a group of people known as the Elder Race who, through their own efforts, made the second cycle of harvest. And I was wondering if it was perhaps possible that those within this group or people work under a thinner veil than do the rest of the entities upon the planet because they were harvested and chose to stay?

We are those of Q'uo, and are aware of your query, my brother. Your supposition is not correct as the veil drops for all at the same rate and thickness. There are certainly strong personalities which find it more possible to see through parts of the veil. However, this is a characteristic not of the Elder Race or of any particular type of entrant to the human condition but is broad-based and throughout the gamut of those who take incarnation.

May we answer you further, my brother?

G: Not on that topic, thank you, Q'uo.

Is there a further query at this time?

G: There's one from T and he asks, "I wonder why God created mosquitoes. The Confederation has said that second-density beings are living in harmony with the original Thought. If that is the case, does the female mosquito represent a natural negative thought? Is there a divine purpose that mosquitoes must suck blood to survive?"

We are those of Q'uo, and are of your query, my brother. The poet known as Alfred wrote that nature is red in "tooth and claw"[107] and, indeed, the

---

[107] From Alfred Lord Tennyson's "In Memoriam":

Man, her last work, who seemed so fair,
Such splendid purpose in his eyes,
Who rolled the psalm to wintry skies,
Who built him fanes of fruitless prayer,

Who trusted God was Love indeed,
And love, Creation's final law,

patterns of life in the natural state are the patterns of eating and being eaten. The mosquito itself is prey for many creatures who would die were mosquitoes not available and mosquitoes would die if there were not prey for it to feed upon. So the shortest answer to your query is that the insect, the mosquito, is in its perfect place in a perfect creation, part of a food chain of eating and being eaten. Upon another level it is, however, true that mosquitoes, along with other small biting insects, are capable of being possessed by thought forms of a negative orientation and therefore it could be said that mosquitoes have the potential for acting as negatively-oriented harassers of targets chosen by entities using insect populations as henchman.

Is there a final query at this time?

G: Yes, Q'uo. In doing spiritual work one of the key aspects is trying to be as present as possible. And some days I'm really on the ball and I feel I'm living in the moment, as well as I can, and meditation goes hand in hand, each affecting the other. That kind of work feels like it takes energy. It really wears you down and burns you out. I would think that entering into the moment, connecting more into your true nature and the Creator, would be a rejuvenating activity. It would be one that refreshes and gives more energy and life. So, would Q'uo be able to tell me why it seems to be so wearying an activity?

We are those of Q'uo, and are aware of your query, my brother. We move into the discussion of novelty again when we address your query, my brother. For the effort taken to work with the self when the self has not yet accumulated a lot of experience in working with the self, is great. It is only as experience is gained through repetition of effort that it begins to feel less like work and more like resting comfortably in an easy chair and enjoying a particularly interesting ride. The factor which creates comfort is simply time. It is surprisingly difficult, from the standpoint of any entity within incarnation, to change that entity's biases one iota because of the almost unimaginable amount of repetition in a lifetime of creating the present system or structure of prejudices or biases. When one is attempting to address that structure, one has a large task ahead of one. One is basically changing the interior structure of the "house" in which one lives, taking out supporting walls and figuring out another way to support that weight in the house of the self. So allow that patience and that tolerance that one allows when one is working on constructing a remodeled and better house to live in.

May we answer you further, my brother?

G: No, excellent, Q'uo. And I'll say I'm going to miss you this summer.

J: Yeah, thank you, we'll see you in a couple months.

We are those of Q'uo, and we shall also miss our times of working with you within these walls. However, as each is able to call us to them for companionship and support, we expect to enjoy each of you during the time in which we are silent.

We leave each of you in the love and in the light of the one infinite Creator, thanking you for the joy of sharing this meditation and the privilege of sharing our thoughts. Take what you will and leave the rest and know always that we love you. Adonai. We are those of Q'uo. ❧

Though nature, red in tooth and claw,
With rapine, shrieked against his creed.

L/L Research

L/L Research is a subsidiary of Rock Creek Research & Development Laboratories, Inc.

P.O. Box 5195
Louisville, KY 40255-0195

www.llresearch.org

Rock Creek is a non-profit corporation dedicated to discovering and sharing information which may aid in the spiritual evolution of humankind.

ABOUT THE CONTENTS OF THIS TRANSCRIPT: This telepathic channeling has been taken from transcriptions of the weekly study and meditation meetings of the Rock Creek Research & Development Laboratories and L/L Research. It is offered in the hope that it may be useful to you. As the Confederation entities always make a point of saying, please use your discrimination and judgment in assessing this material. If something rings true to you, fine. If something does not resonate, please leave it behind, for neither we nor those of the Confederation would wish to be a stumbling block for any.

© 2009 L/L Research

Special Meditation
May 17, 2004

Question from D: There is a problem with my second chakra which is causing disruption in my job and in my communication and I would like to know how to work on it.

(Carla channeling)

We are those known to you as the principle of Q'uo, and we greet you in the love and in the light of the one infinite Creator, in Whose service we are and in Whose name we have been called to this group this day. We thank the one known as D and we thank each who sits within this circle this evening for the beauty of your nature and your meditation. It is a great privilege to be with this group and we would ask of you only that you guard well your powers of discrimination, allowing only those thoughts that we share with you that resonate to you to enter into your mind to be considered. If thoughts which we share with you do not seem to ring true to you then we would ask that you lay them aside, for we would not wish to constitute a stumbling block for any. If each will mind his powers of discrimination, than we will feel free to share our opinions without being concerned with infringing upon the free will of those within the circle.

The query from this entity is an interesting one in that the first portion of the query[108] is one, as this instrument has already said, to which we may not speak in any substantive form, for it does tread far too close to the line of free will in terms of affecting your actions in the future. Although it may, in the short run, be a great relief to have some seeming additional facts and figures to go on, to deal with the very difficult business situation that has arisen, yet at the same time, were we to interfere in this way, we would be crossing, shall we say, an invisible line drawn in the sand of eternity. And that line is that one does not share in the learning of another in such a way that the learning is lessoned in its intensity. Truly, for us to speak concerning the business concerns would be to step over that line and become as an Earth inhabitant and that we are not. We have the privilege only of sharing thoughts and are guests here, rather than inhabitants of your sphere. As guests, we must be very careful of our own polarity so that we can preserve our ability to be of service.

The second portion of the query, which the instrument vocalized to us, is that of which is far more within our ability to speak because it concerns the energy body, and while the query is concerning one particular entity, the one known as D, yet at the same time information concerning the energy vehicle and its intra-relationships amongst the chakras and so forth are pieces of information that may be useful resources for any which dwell within third density and are attempting to work with what sometimes feels like a run-away energy vehicle.

---

[108] D first asked a specific question about a business concern, and Carla told D, over the telephone, whereby he was attending his session, that the question would not be acceptable. D then asked the question which is above.

Now, let us step back just a step and gaze at some of the background of this query. We are assuming the various understandings connected with the Law of One; that is, that all things are one, that each entity has a full-spectrum of beingness—a 360-degree potentiated vehicle which contains the mind, body and the spirit portions. And in each of these portions there are connections within the inner bodies, or the chakra system of the inner planes bodies, that belong to the vehicle of each entity which dwells within third density. So when there is a query concerning that energy body, it is that portion of the body that dwells not in space/time, or in the physical world, but in time/space, or in the metaphysical world. And in the metaphysical world, the shape of reality is quite altered from the physical world. In the physical world, things are substantive and thoughts are dreams and visions and air, whereas in the metaphysical world, intentions, thoughts and focus are substantive and powerful things. The type of physical reality with which each is familiar in consensus reality is somewhat lacking in the metaphysical realm. And in the metaphysical realm, there is a potent bias which has grown up within the one known as D within the second chakra, indeed, in the first and second chakra and extending into the third chakra. However, the one known as D is correct in identifying the orange-ray or second chakra as that chakra which has born the brunt of over-activation and a concomitant level of confusion within the energy of that second chakra that is quite high.

Now let us gaze at this for a moment together. The red, orange and yellow chakras—the first, second and third chakras in this particular system of looking at the energy body—have basically to do with survival, with one's relationship with the self, and [with] one's relationship to groups. The pattern of this particular incarnation has been one which repeatedly brings up the incarnational question of self-worth. The entity has dealt with this internal sense of lacking worth throughout the incarnation repeatedly, in various shapes and forms, and has at times had better fortune in learning from the catalyst of low self-worth than others. Certainly, as the incarnation has continued to manifest, as experience has been gathered, there have been certain tendencies towards the hardening of that sense of a lack of self-worth, where there is the feeling of a need to purify, to prepare, to become more ready than one is for the highest and the best that lies within the immediate future of all entities. There is a feeling that one must reach, one must become more pure, more articulated in goodness. And this has, in some ways, been a very appropriate and useful attitude and process, resulting in the learning of much humility and an ever-increasing ability to, shall we say, stick with a desired result until an outcome has been reached.

However, when there is a tendency that has become energized through repetition throughout an incarnation towards a sense of real lack of being good enough, that very bias creates an over-activity within the chakra system wherein that confusion has begun to [become] solidified. That simple feeling that one is imperfect and humble is not, in and of itself, an incorrect thought in any way. It is an honest and accurate evaluation of the human condition. Yet at the same time, that human condition is precisely the condition that was greatly desired before incarnation and was greatly prized when the opportunity arose. Not only for the one known as D but for many of those within incarnation at this time, there was a real sense of achievement simply at having made "the team," shall we say, having been one of those who came to serve and who stayed true to that intention throughout the incarnation. This is that memory of mission, of which the one known as D may be pleased with himself and may assume that the time for being overly concerned with the worth of the self has passed for this particular incarnational experience. It is a desirable attitude to seek at this time within the life experience, to realize what the achievements of an incarnation already have become and to allow the self to come into an attitude which revolves around the question of finding balance rather than the question of how to achieve more purity or a higher way.

Now, were the one known as D young in years in terms of incarnational experience, this might not necessarily be so. However, there is a season for many things within incarnation and we would encourage the one known as D to consider the possibility that this is the time within incarnation when the work of learning the self has basically been done. The self is known and therefore the self may be set aside. There is nowhere to go. There is nothing to achieve. The achievement becomes coming into symmetry with the harmonics of the self so that the self is singing the truest, simplest and sweetest melody that lies within the heart. It is time within the incarnation of the one known as D to explore being, to accept the self as it is, and to begin to loosen those judgments that hold the one known as D to the confusion of lacking confidence in the goodness of the self. This is difficult to accept when there has been so much effort to improve the self and to come into a better harmony with the coming energies of fourth density.

However, we would ask the one known as D to consider that this is fourth density. There is no longer a struggle to come into a fourth-density environment because fourth density now interpenetrates third density and it is each entity's choice of which set of rules, shall we say, to play the game of living by. There is the third-density way in which, as the one known as D is fully aware, the rules of business are laid out, the rules of behavior are well laid out, and there is a very mechanical application of the self to the demands of the world. Within fourth density, gazing at the same world, the choices are seen to be the same, the options are the same, yet what changes is the point of view of the entity who witnesses these events coming into manifestation, and who has the power of choice as to what to do physically and what mentally to think concerning the worldly situation. This instrument would certainly lend her witness to the fact that thinking in fourth density while dealing with third density is a subtle and artful expression of awareness that calls forth much within a life experience, not only things of spirit but also things of the world.

We believe that this is the amount of information we wish to offer before we ask for a further query so we would ask the one known as D if there is a further query at this time.

D: Thank you. I have a map, as I understand, of the galaxy and I would like to find out if the map of the galaxy is actually of the Milky Way?

(Pause)

D: Hello?[109]

We are those of Q'uo, and are aware of your query, my brother, but are not able to deal with it for there is no spiritual portion that we may find upon which to comment. Therefore we find that we are not able to address this query and for that, my brother, we apologize.

Is there a further query at this time?

D: Yes, there is a further query. However, first I need to hang up and call on a different phone card. This phone card is running out. I will be calling you back in three minutes. Thank you.

(D returns.)

D: I would like to find out what is the correct angle of a pyramid that would be correct to be used relative to the condition that we are speaking of?

We are those of Q'uo, and we are aware of your query, my brother. What we are recommending for you at this time is a surrender and a release from the use of gadgets such as the pyramid. For the situation with your energy body is that it has stored a good deal of excess energy which it has no way to use. We would therefore recommend that rather than working further with pyramids to affect changes because of their shape, the most efficacious healing at this time would be that connection with the ocean and with water as a crystal, for there is a great deal of healing, within the salt water especially, where it is able to leach excess energy from a physical vehicle that has, not to put it too gently, been somewhat fried. The energies within portions of the energy body have actually—we try to give this instrument a vision of that which is arching and sparking over a gap but which is unable to disengage; and that need to disengage is that in which the water, especially the salt water, will aid. Indeed, any water is an excellent conductor of such energy and will gradually be able to improve the situation with regards to the health of the one known as D.

May we answer you further, my brother?

D: I would like to find out if I need to be in the water or if actually sleeping as close as I am to the water is sufficient?

We are those of Q'uo, and are aware of your query, my brother. The sleeping within sound of the water is excellent. However, we would recommend if at all possible that there be the immersion within the water, at least with a portion of the physical vehicle immersed in the water in order for the moving, cycling nature of the water to have its appropriate geometrical configuration.

May we answer you further, my brother?

---

[109] D attended this session by long-distance telephone.

D: I would like to know how many minutes is a minimum amount of time to actually have the correct effect in each particular usage.

We are those of Q'uo, and are aware of your query, my brother. In terms of the immersion within the waves, we would recommend a minimum of 20 to 25 minutes per day and if there is a desire to accelerate this process, it would be acceptable to have two 20 to 25-minute sessions within the swirling waters of the ocean in a diurnal period. As to the resting within sound of the ocean, this is acceptable at whatever length of time is the normal resting period.

May we answer further, my brother?

D: Yes, I would like to find out if my prior sleeping arrangement, the big long building that I'm actually speaking behind, is actually part of the problem?

We are those of Q'uo, and are aware of your query, my brother. We feel that there is a satisfactory resting place for the one known as D and that, in truth, any place which enjoyed the proximity to the ocean would be acceptable.

May we answer you further, my brother?

D: Yes, I would like the name of the individual I am speaking with.

We are those of Q'uo, my brother.

D: Say again.

We are those of the spelling "Q-u-o", Q'uo.

D: Thank you.

This entity is a principle and by that we mean are made up of three distinct social memory complexes: one from the level of love, one from the level of wisdom, and one from the level of unity. We who are speaking to you are those of Latwii, we are fifth-density entities. Our teacher is that entity known to this group as Ra and that entity is also a part of this principle. And the one known as Hatonn is most often with this group as well, not in order to express the self but in order to love and express that unconditional vibration that is so much needed within the Earth plane at this time. So we who speak to you are a principle that is made up of a range of entities, shall we say, a group of those who have learned and taught together for a very long time. Is this information satisfactory, my brother?

D: Yes, it's very insightful.

Is there a final query at this time?

D: My final inquiry is, I would like to have the oldest known name of Archangel Michael.

We are aware of your query, my brother. We are those of Q'uo, and find that our only relevant piece of information that may be of interest to you in this wise is that there are, in truth, only made-up or created names for all entities, so that when seeking the truth of an entity, it cannot be found at the level of the name. It cannot be found at the level of speaking and creating a shape and a timbre and a vibration. The actual name of the one known as Archangel Michael is an energy field of vibration that has its melody, that sings its characteristic song; and just in such a way is your nature that of a melody, an energy field, and a harmonic that is in exquisite and unending detail, so that it is a Word, it is a sub-logos, it is you. And that song is your name. We see that name when we greet you and when we call you by name, that is the name we use. That is actually why we always express it as the one "known as" D, the one "known as" the instrument, the one "known as" G, and the one "known as" J. The actuality is that each of those within the circle is a magical and brilliant crystal whose being is a name that shall be forever.

We give you this, my brother, because we are unable to discuss the question of the names of various entities. It is by far too confusing and meaningless at our level to deal with. We do not have great success in dealing with names.

We thank you, my brother, for this time together. It has been a great blessing to us. The time together has certainly been a pleasure and we hope that we have been able to share a few poor thoughts with you at this time. We are always with you and if you wish a deeper meditation or a deeper sleep, we ask for you to call upon us. We shall not speak with you. We simply shall be there, and it is as though there is a carrier wave that is helping you to meditate, helping you to sleep. That is what we are able to do and we are most happy to be with you. And we express love and blessing at this time.

We leave you in the love and in the light of the one infinite Creator. We are known to you as the principle of Q'uo. Adonai.

Special Meditation
August 4, 2004

Question from P: I would appreciate information regarding my experience on planet Earth. Can you confirm that I am a wanderer? Please talk with me about finding the right location, the right job, and the right service to fulfill my purpose of being.

(Carla channeling)

We are those known to you as the principle of Q'uo, and we greet you in the love and in the light of the one infinite Creator, in Whose service we come to you this day. We wish to thank the one known as P for calling us to this circle of seeking and, as well, to thank each of those who have joined this circle of seeking to support this entity and his spiritual evolution. It is our great privilege and blessing to be able to share our thoughts with you and, as always, we ask only that each realize fully that we are companions rather than authorities, not those to be obeyed or followed but those whose opinions have been considered helpful. And for that we thank you. In order for us to be able to share our opinions with you, however, we must know that your free will is not abridged in any way and that you are able to set aside any ideas that we may share with which you do not agree or resonate. As a general rule in this ever-shifting world of truths which have their proper location, personal truth is subjective and that which is someone's truth this day may not be someone's truth in the day to come. Consequently, truths and thoughts in general must be measured against that yardstick of your own powers of discrimination. Never simply assume that someone's opinion is good. Rather, ask yourself: does it resonate? Does it feel as if it were something that I already knew and had just been reminded of? If so, then it is time for that truth to be yours and you may claim it and use it and we hope you will find resources such as this today in that which we have to say. However, be proactive in setting aside anything that does not ring true. If you can do this we will be free to share our thoughts with you without being concerned for the issue of free will. For this care we do thank each of within the circle.

The one known as P has asked if he may have confirmation on his status as wanderer and we may say that this entity is indeed such. The energies and essences which are consonant with having entered into the incarnation from elsewhere have created their own challenges and catalysts within the life of the one known as P. Nevertheless, each aspect of this challenge and this catalyst has been chosen aforetimes in order to bring the self into an ever-improving ground which is that which not staples one into the environment but inserts one into a niche within that environment in such a way as to fit well, to ground one in a comfortable and ever more appropriate way. It is in this wise that we would confirm the feelings of the one known as P concerning his tendency to be one who develops an ever-stronger, shall we say, home within the particular geography within which he has found himself so that he may be ever more able to feel that safety which is connected with the concept of home in an emotional sense and also in a spiritual sense. The land and the energies of any area are quite individual and alive and the one known as P has been able to enter into the spirits of the land and the energies living upon that land wherever this entity has been. We would simply assure the one known as P that in any geographical location which resonates for this entity, the same enmeshing and familiarizing insertion into the niche within that particular geography will be forthcoming, as it is a gift connected with the challenge of being from elsewhere and has been brought into incarnation as a gift of personality where that ability to bond with the spirit of a location is given as an endowment of the personality shell.

This creates a situation in which an entity is free to choose the location of his dwelling without being overly concerned as to whether or not that particular location may hold power for the entity. We would only recommend against the insertion into a truly urbanized atmosphere as the efforts to insert oneself into the spirits of such a geographical location are greatly blunted by the density of those living entities present which inhabit that space without having any desire to so link with the spirits of that place. This, over time, causes the spirits of such a place as an urbanized dwelling to become insensitive and even resistant to the insertion into the true essences of that location, as these essences and entities have been ritually and habitually abused over long periods of your time. It is well, therefore, to focus upon dwelling in somewhat rural or completely rural locations where the land has been able to establish trust with the humans which dwell in that geographical location. Indeed, we believe that it is true that, for this entity as for many wanderers, the ability to insert the self into a place which has begun to awaken to the partnership possible between nature and humankind is the more desired location in order to be able to reap the harvest that has been sown by the unconditional love and the good work of those who went before.

To some extent, such a land as the Avalon Sacred Growth Center, which this instrument is so focused upon in her own path, has thusly been awakened, and that place which is in this instrument's mind is known Meher Baba's retreat also is of such a nature, in which much work has been done before this particular moment which has softened the level of distrust which land typically has of humankind at this stage in the development of third density and the human race upon this planet.

Your question also concerned right livelihood and, in truth, we have little to offer in this query except to reassure the one known as P that when an entity is serving the infinite Creator, in terms of his point of view, there is virtually no work that can be considered ill-chosen, even when an entity such as the one known as G, who is within this instrument's mind at this time, chooses to work in a situation in which he is, in the eyes of the world, a simple server of beverages and food. This entity, because of his attitude of service to others and his determination to make a difference with his open heart and his loving energy, has fulfilled the requirement of right livelihood, which is to serve the one infinite Creator with, as this instrument would say, singleness of heart. The purity of desire to serve is powerful in metaphysical terms and once this determination to serve the infinite Creator in all that is seen and in all that is sought and in all that is beheld is adopted, the service is established in a way that shall never be true within third density alone. For within third density, thoughts are not things. Thoughts remain in the mind and it is the doing of them that is therefore so impressive and so talked about within the consensus reality that this instrument and those within this circle enjoy. Nevertheless, what lies behind consensus reality is not a world of things. It is a world of thought. Thoughts are the objects of that realm which is entered in what those of Ra would call "time/space," or the metaphysical or inner realms of existence. Within those realms, we do not believe, my brother, that there is anything which you can do to earn money which would not be considered a right livelihood in terms of your intention to serve the one infinite Creator.

The establishment of that feeling of security is often the need which it is difficult to embrace in its totality. What is needed for the one known as P? What level of effort and labor does this entity need to put out in order to establish himself as one who is satisfied that he is taking care of tending to the self in a way which is honorable and appropriate? Certainly, we subscribe to the concept of each entity being sure that he or she is not a burden upon society at large if there is the possibility of doing work. It is rather that we wish to relax the entity's mind in terms of finding a specific right livelihood and rather redirect the thinking along the lines of where the joy of service seems to focus for this entity in terms of doing work for many. The gifts of this entity are numerous enough to make the choice between ways of making money a valid one. There are several options of how to fill the bank account and pay the bills. We encourage going within in this regard and asking with great sincerity to be given cues and clues and hints from spirit in whatever way would be most helpful so that the one known as P may enter into the question with more of his total or entire self.

The self is not simply the conscious mind, as the one known as P is well aware. It has also a subconscious mind that is shy of giving information in any conscious and rational manner. And yet, there is the world of synchronicity, coincidence and the half-hidden cues of street signs and birds' wings and the butterflies that move upon the wind and any other emblem of the Creator and Its ways that would be subjectively interesting and meaningful to the one known as P.

There is also the very valid avenue of dream work to pursue in entering into what the subconscious portions of the mind truly feel. It is very helpful in times of decision to pay special attention to these signals that are so rich in the environment about one sleeping and waking. Pay attention, watch and ask. Above all, remember to ask within the silence of a daily practice of such meditation or contemplation that seems appropriate to you as an entity. Ask, for the truth comes only when requested. Therefore, remember to ask and when the door is shut, remember to knock and when there is a need for help, remember to be a squeaky wheel and squeak.

Realize the incredible intimacy of your relationship with spirit. Realize that the Creator is closer to you than the voice of this instrument. Realize the power of your self. And take that power, take that magic, and use it well. Use it consciously, and lean into it always after asking, being sure to listen for the responses that silence gives. It may be that silence gives you nothing you can put your finger on, yet, coming out of such silence, coming out of such a time of asking, be aware that there will be communication but that you shall have to be attentive and follow it. Once followed, such communication opens like a flower and blooms and goes into other seeds of thought which, when followed, also bloom and flower. And, in the way of the repeating patterns of fractals, these odysseys of tracking information needed for spiritual growth will continue to develop as long as the attention continues to be put upon them. In truth, it is a never-ending seeking; it is a never-ending process. Learning does not stop because one query has been answered to the satisfaction of the seeker. For each answered question becomes the next generation's beginning to further inquiry, further challenges and further asking. You may expect and feel yourself a success to experience cyclical periods of unknowing and feeling that one is remiss and behind the power curve in knowledge of self. These seasons of unknowing are there in order that you may plant and fertilize and tend and weed and bring to bloom those precious energies that lie within you as seeds.

There was also the query as to the right companionship for this particular time within your life and, my brother, we may say to you on this point that it is correct that you are seeking proper companionship. However, the companion you seek is named P [himself] and he is hungering for your true dedication, commitment and love. This entity that is you is that first entity with whom you need to fall in love. For, indeed, it is true some entities must have that within their lives that is exciting and that nourishes in the companionship. However, my brother, there is a stumbling block when one begins to feel that without this companion one is less than one can be. This is in no case so. The value of an other-self who is loved and who is able to love you as you truly are is inestimable. And yet, until you, yourself, are able to be unconditional about your love of your self and able to embrace even the darkest shadow side of your personality, you shall not be able to nurture and cherish another soul. First you must learn to be your own best friend, your own lover, and, indeed, as this instrument has often said to many, to fall in love with yourself. This does not mean that you become blind to your warts and your immaturities; indeed, for this instrument, loving oneself is an ever-expanding adventure in learning more about those insecurities, those follies of self, those many, many warts and freckles, shall we say, of personality and point of view. How many, many ways there are to discover that one has been lazy in examining one's assumptions, that one has allowed many things that are not true about the self to become assumed as true.

But when one has fallen for the self in a big way, one is able to take those hits without being dismayed.

There is nothing disgraceful or discouraging about being imperfect and having work to do. Were you not imperfect you would not have been allowed into this environment called late third density on planet Earth. You had to earn your way here by having significant distortions which you wished to address within this incarnation for your own personal growth. Not simply are you here to help heal the Earth or to help bring light into a dark world which desperately needs it at this time. You are also here for personal balancing of energies and all that you can do is recommended by us to you in terms of, more and more, being able to move into your own self without that stumbling block of judgment. How many of those with whom you share third density at this time could say that they have become mature? How many entities could say with any accuracy that they have cleaned up their act and now, were they to stand before the great steps of light, they are absolutely positive that they would be in the first wave of ascension, as this instrument was aware that you spoke to the one known as V before this session?

We offer you a fairly accurate prospectus on that: the answer is none. There is no one within your Earthly sphere who is in any worldly sense worthy to move on. However, the challenge for one who wishes to evolve is not to be worthy but to be humble. It is not to become ransomed but to realize that one is hopelessly ignorant. It is not to succeed but to accept that the goal of becoming worthy is folly, vanity and as this instrument would say, "a striving after wind." She, like the teacher in Ecclesiastes, sees that all is vanity. All of the seeking for wisdom, all of the seeking to position oneself with right livelihood, with right geography, with right companionship, with right anything, is a seeking that is still engaged in justifying a structure which this instrument often calls the personality shell. We would not in any way scoff at the desire to do these things which is an endemic part of your culture. It is expected of entities that they will have a defensible reason for what they do, where they live, and with whom they associate. It is expected that one will have a rational path that one may trace with words in order to justify one's decisions. And yet we would say, my brother, to step back from the details of such consideration and, at least for a portion of time each day, allow yourself to rest in the entire system of self. Within that system, the whole, the integral self, emerges. The essence of self becomes that which is your true concern. You are here, to put it very shortly, to be here. It sounds redundant. However, the skill of being is almost atrophied within the human race. There's no cultural training; there is only cultural training in assuming masks, adopting roles, and fulfilling niches. You are far beyond that which can be confined into a niche or a persona or behind any mask. You are all that is. You are the Creator.

When one moves into incarnation, one is as a hologram. We move into this instrument's mind to capture part of a conversation this instrument had with the one known as V earlier this day, in which the one known as V was describing how even a tiny shard of the hologram, when lased or pierced by a laser in a coherent beam, allows one to see the entire pattern in three dimensions, of which that shard was originally a part. In just such a way are you a portion of the Creator that tells the truth about the Creator, even though you are a tiny sparkle, a tiny shard of that hologram. You have all within you which you seek. Therefore, in a very real sense, the seeking is a matter of moving into a position within the evolving self where you are able to listen to the drumbeats that come from the deep mind. You are able to listen to the helpers that cluster about one who is seeking consciously. You are able simply to be awake to the possibilities of an infinite universe. It impinges upon you, every moment, this infinity, this immensity of possibility, and yet it can also be dismissed if it is not seized and taken up and acknowledged and blessed. If thanks is not given for it and if it is not used, it will retreat and hide and in time, not even be available because of an atrophy of those points of entry within the self which have become clogged by ignorance, that is, by being ignored.

We would encourage the one known as P to lift up from considerations of the details of an incarnation, as important as those details are, for a time each day long enough to enter the silence as an infinitely aware, completely unhindered and unlimited citizen of eternity, resting in the essence of you, loving that, trusting that, knowing that it is part of what this instrument would call the true vine. This instrument's holy work, the Holy Bible, has a portion in several of the Gospels of the teacher known as Jesus the Christ, where this concept of the true vine is brought up by the teacher known as Jesus.[110] In this particular parable, the true vine is

---

[110] *Holy Bible*, John 15:1-12: "I am the true vine, and my Father is the vine-dresser. Every branch in Me that does not bear fruit,

seen as that which is of the kingdom of the Creator, and from this true vine grow true branches. Sometimes, grafted onto this true vine are other species that do not contain the virtue of the true vine. And for a time, these grafted branches may grow, yet they shall inevitably express themselves in such a way that the evolving seeker may come to the conclusion that indeed they are not part of the true vine of self and in that case the entity does not reject the self, the entity simply starts moving down the vine, past the graft. Where did it get grafted in? Where is the error in thinking? Move below that level of choice into the pre-choice self and the true vine is there in all of its vitality and health. It has not been compromised. It has not been ruined, and nothing has been lost. When time has passed and the questions have been asked and a sense of the self does come that says, "All right, here is where the graft lies and here is where I would like to make the cut to remove that false portion of self," then, strength will be given to the self to know just how to do the pruning, not the destruction or the rejection of self but the pruning of the undisciplined self so that the remaining self is true to the self. This is subtle work. This is work done over time and it cannot be done quickly or impulsively. Rather, let it be, as the Beatles wrote. Trust that things are moving as they should and that your job is not to be the director of the ship; rather, it is your job to learn the ship, to learn the ocean, and to penetrate, by instruments known only to you, your direction and your destiny enough that you may then cooperate with the time, the tide, the gifts of the particular barque upon which you have set sail.

You are a partner with many other unseen entities in this work of art that is your life. Take the time with it that you would take with any work of art. If you think of it as a poem, work endlessly to clean the language of your life. If you think of it as a complex image that you paint, take the time to place every stipple of light, every touch of the brush that shades and defines and reveals mystery so that your finished work shines with the deepest truth of you that an image can. And if you think of it as this instrument does, as a tapestry that she is weaving as she goes, not only with words but with the fragrance of her love and the touch of her heart and with all of those senses that each entity possesses that move far beyond the descriptions of words. She works to make a tapestry of real depth, truth and beauty. It is a challenge, for many truths are dark, many colors do not seem on the surface to be pretty or to be able to be wound into a tapestry in such a way as to make it better and yet, those are the challenges that make the finished tapestry interesting, and rich, and detailed, and textured. As you work with this concept of your life as a beautiful gift for the Creator, perhaps you shall begin to see what we mean by saying, work systemically, not always upon the details but at least a bit, daily, move into the truth of yourself as a whole being and see that the truth that lies there will endlessly deepen as you allow yourself to fall in love with yourself.

In general, the challenge of a wanderer who comes to this planet is duple. The first challenge is to engage the self with the environment in a way that honors that environment, that does not separate the self from the environment and that effects a positive connection between the self and the third-density milieu. This is the personal work that each entity has on his agenda when he arrives. It has to do with the balance of the vibrations between the fourth-density concepts of love and the fifth-density concepts of wisdom. Many sixth-density entities are here attempting, as is this instrument, to rebalance in favor of the true middle between wisdom and love. There is the personal judgment involved in this questing that there was room for improvement and each entity will have its own biases about the direction of such improvement. It is, however, not at all the majority of the reason for entering third-density incarnation.

He takes away; and every branch that bears fruit, He prunes it, that it may bear more fruit. You are already clean because of the Word [from the Greek, Logos, or unconditional love] which I have spoken to you. Abide in Me, and I in you. As the branch cannot bear fruit of itself, unless it abides in the vine, so neither can you, unless you abide in Me. I am the vine, you are the branches; he who abides in Me, and I in him, he bears much fruit; for apart from Me, you can do nothing. If anyone does not abide in Me, he is thrown away as a branch, and dries up; and they gather them, and cast them into the fire, and they are burned. If you abide in Me, and My word abides in you, ask whatever you wish and it shall be done for you. By this is My Father glorified, that you bear much fruit, and so prove to be My disciples. Just as the Father has loved Me, I have also loved you. Abide in My love. If you keep My commandments, you will abide in My love, just as I have kept My Father's commandments, and abide in His love. These things I have spoken to you, that My joy may be in you, and that your joy may be made full. This is My commandment, that you love one another, just as I have loved you."

The choice to do such is in no way shallow. It is a profoundly uncomfortable thing to enter third density from a higher density, especially upon your planet. There would be no reason to undergo such suffering and to put oneself into the maelstrom of such near insanity as this particular planet has entered into as a culture except to serve, and to serve in such a way that one person makes a difference. You are familiar with the concept of the Peace Corps where ordinary citizens go into a culture which seems to have needs which they can help satisfy. They have only themselves, their hearts, their willingness to serve and yet time and again if one interviews those who have been a part of such a program, they state that it has truly been a wonderful thing in that they really did feel that one person could make a difference and they saw that it was so. In this case, you came in as a member of a Peace Corps, a Peace, Love and Light Corps, shall we say, your aim being to make a difference even though you were only one being. You are already making a difference, as is everyone upon planet Earth. You are not part of an elite simply because you are a wanderer. All of those upon planet Earth at this time are harvestable. In terms of how they came into the incarnation, there are no hopeless souls here, all are able to make a difference, all have what it takes to love in a powerful and real way, to love beyond judgment, beyond limit, beyond holding back something for special people. Every entity here has the potential to make this difference.

The advantages of being a wanderer are that your memories of how things can be are much clearer, much closer to the surface and less veiled by the veil of forgetting than those who are native to the planet and are simply waking up for the first time. You have awakened once, you have done the work once, you are now in boot camp trying to get it back. "Where is that memory? What did I know before that I have lost?" These are the questions you are asking. But you do not have to reach for this knowledge. As with all wanderers, that knowledge is fairly close to the surface. You do remember better times; you do know how to love. It is just so dangerous in the way it feels to be so vulnerable and so open to criticism as to love without expectation of return in a world which is very cruel to those who love in such a way. Be prepared to feel the slings and arrows of those who would be cruel to idealists who refuse to become cynical. Be proud when you are reviled because you are an idealist, because you love when one could so easily judge, when one could so easily move into a separate and safe mental configuration where all is judgment and all is cynicism.

My brother, you are on trail, you are on task, more than you know. And yet you worry and you fret and this is understandable. We cannot wave a magic wand and cause you to stop doing so. We cannot wave a magic wand for this instrument and cause her to stop doing so. We can not do that for a single soul. You can probably not even do it for yourself, not all at once. But if you can repeat a few home truths when you are troubled, you may perhaps begin to change long-standing habits. If you can repeat, "All is well, all is well," when all is obviously not well, that will be a start. If you can ask yourself as those of Ra suggested, "Where is the love in this moment?" that is a start. These things are helpful, these short, pithy ways of nudging the mind into the act of remembrance of who you are and why you are here.

This instrument informs us that we have spent far too long on this question and we do apologize. However, it was a good question and we were enjoying ourselves.

We would at this time ask if there are follow-up questions which we may answer at this time. May we have the first one?

Questioner: Yes, Q'uo, you have already confirmed that P is a wanderer. Can you tell him from which density or which planetary system?

We are those of Q'uo, and are aware of your query, my brother, and we do not feel that this information would be at all helpful to you at this time. We believe that it is information that will come to you naturally and that, when it does come to you, it will be helpful at that time and not before. Trust the inner workings of synchronicity and coincidence [to bring you] gradually into more of a feeling of knowledge of where indeed you came from and what density that might be, if these things remain important to you in the future.

May we ask if there is another query at this time?

Questioner: Q'uo, P writes, "I have found myself to be lonely and seeking a true soul companion." You've somewhat addressed the subject of a companion. Can you speak more about his feeling of loneliness?

We are those of Q'uo, and we are aware of your query, my brother. Ah, my brother, to speak of loneliness, how we would wish to be able to express ourselves to the extent that you would know that we truly understand the agony of a wanderer who wanders in a strange land and who is often unable to speak words that resonate to those who would be able to hear that resonance and confirm the usefulness of such thoughts. How blessed it is when one simply feels understood and loved, encouraged and supported. It is part of the wanderer's suffering to feel isolated. And why should a wanderer not feel isolated? For he is the one known, as Heinlein phrased it, as "a stranger in a strange land." Of course you shall feel alienated by things that make no sense and that is all around you, my brother. We can only encourage you to move within and to begin to sense into the tremendous strength and power of the network of unseen entities that accompany you at all times. It is a crowded universe. No entity who is consciously attempting to stand close to the love and the light of the one infinite Creator shall ever be without a tremendous body of helpers. To this instrument, who is steeped in the Christian tradition, her mind goes to angels and archangels, seraphim and cherubim and all the hosts of heaven, and yet to one who is involved in other means of [religious] expression, it is just as valid to look at the animals who surround you, the elements of earth, air, wind and fire that surround you; to name those same energies and essences which this instrument would call angelic [thusly]. And, for those who worship the ancestors, for instance, in the process of acknowledging the enormous body of the roots of the physical being, the ancestors, the place from which one came and so forth, these essences and energies, in their own way, move into the same body of those who serve the Creator by serving those of the Godhead principle which are incarnate and sentient such as yourself, this instrument, or those within this circle and any living human being that is doing the work of third density.

Shall you ever be fully content within your isolation? This is unknown. This is more a question for the personality shell than for the essential being that you are. However, shall you be able to find joy and companionship within this incarnation? Yes, you must simply open to it. Work upon that love of self. Work upon truly being able to be in love with the self, to see the self in all of its flaws as a wonderful, brave and quirky oddity that is a treasure and that will always be the only one of its kind. See that as a wonderful thing and when you look up again you may see someone walking beside you that is also ready to embrace the self and in so doing, is ready to embrace a true companion of the soul.

May we ask if there is a further query at this time?

Questioner: Q'uo, is there anything else that you would like to communicate to P about himself?

My brother, we are satisfied that we have responded to those energies that are within you at this time. We welcome further queries but we would not volunteer information at this time. Is there a further query at this time?

Questioner: Q'uo, you've already answered the question that P had about whether he would be in the first wave of ascension, so then his final query is whether there is anything you would be able to share with him about his daughter or his relationship with her?

We are those of Q'uo, and, my brother, we would simply say that, as with virtually all children being born at this time upon your planet, your challenge is to respond to an entity which is half in third density and half in fourth density. This entity has a significantly different, shall we say, level of sophistication as a being. Therefore, it will have the typical difficulties of a new being who is dealing with beings which cannot possibly grasp the full brunt of what such an entity is going through. Know that often your best bet is to learn from her rather than assuming that you are an authority figure which will teach. Allow a teach/learning circle to develop where respect and honor is given by each, to each, and then simply be aware that, for all the sophistication inherent in a double-activated third-density/fourth-density being, entities who are young are unlearned, unskilled and untrained and that there are many, many simple ways in which you can encourage, support and help to offer discipline of mind to such an entity. Such an entity has a great need for discipline but it is a need for the discipline of the self, by the self. And in this teaching words are not helpful for the most part. Where you will be strong in helping this entity is in being yourself with honesty, integrity and depth. These things she will feel and respect.

Is there a final query at this time?

Questioner: Q'uo, I am not aware of another query by P at this time.

In that case, my brother, we now leave you in the love and in the light of the one infinite Creator, thanking you with all our hearts for this wonderful privilege of being able to share our thoughts with you. Your energy is a beautiful thing and we thank each within this circle for the beauty of their energies as well. It has been a delight to be with you and we leave you in the love and in the light of the one infinite Creator. We are those known to you as the principle of Q'uo. Adonai. Adonai. ✣

L/L Research

L/L Research is a subsidiary of Rock Creek Research & Development Laboratories, Inc.

P.O. Box 5195
Louisville, KY 40255-0195

www.llresearch.org

Rock Creek is a non-profit corporation dedicated to discovering and sharing information which may aid in the spiritual evolution of humankind.

ABOUT THE CONTENTS OF THIS TRANSCRIPT: This telepathic channeling has been taken from transcriptions of the weekly study and meditation meetings of the Rock Creek Research & Development Laboratories and L/L Research. It is offered in the hope that it may be useful to you. As the Confederation entities always make a point of saying, please use your discrimination and judgment in assessing this material. If something rings true to you, fine. If something does not resonate, please leave it behind, for neither we nor those of the Confederation would wish to be a stumbling block for any.

© 2009 L/L RESEARCH

SPECIAL MEDITATION
AUGUST 18, 2004

Question from T: I would like to receive information about the awakening and unfolding metamorphoses of self and its effects on myself and my family. How may one avoid trauma to one's family who may hold other views and to oneself as one tries to uphold the continuing duties and responsibilities of material life?

(Carla channeling)

We are those known to you as the principle of Q'uo, and we greet you in the love and in the light of the one infinite Creator, in Whose name we come to you this day and in Whose power and peace we serve. We thank the one known as T for calling us to this circle of seeking this day and we thank those who sit in this circle in his name and for his service.

It is a great privilege to speak with each of you and we would simply ask, as always, that you clear the way for us to feel completely free of any constraints concerned with the free will of any of you by guarding your own integrity and your powers of discrimination so that any thought which we offer that you take in be taken in quite consciously and with the knowledge that we are fallible beings such as yourselves, pilgrims along a very long path. We are perhaps a step or two ahead of you, but many steps away from becoming one once again with the infinite Creator. We all are part of that circle, that great Celtic knot[111] of evolution that begins and ends in the mystery and unity of the one infinite Creator.

This day there is a query concerning the shape of change in a person's life and how that shape can be experienced, not only be the self but by those about the self, with a minimum of difficulty and with an absence of trauma. My brother, were we the wisest of all advice givers, we would not have the solution to coming through transformation without suffering. And although we cannot say that any of your own processes properly can be considered to be the cause of trauma to others, we may also say that insofar as entities are unskilled at gazing in the mirrors which such change projects from your process into others, that too is a process that is likely not to be trouble-free or smooth. Certainly we can share some thoughts with you concerning how to visualize and work with these very laudable and appropriate desires to minimize the difficulty and trauma for the self and for other selves in the process of initiation. Yet at the same time, we wish to begin by stating firmly that we do not know a way for entities to move the way they think and their point of view from one system to another without creating considerable perceived chaos and pain. It is well to take this in and to realize the cost of transformation. It is always costly to attempt to stand closer to the

---
[111] A Celtic knot is a symmetrical pattern drawn without lifting pen from paper, so that although the pattern may be quite intricate, it is unitary.

light. It is always expensive to gain insight. It is always dislocating to widen one's point of view.

Now, with that said, let us turn to a more positive tack and sail our little boat of thought and words into the wind of change and see what we can find to suggest to you as you set your direction and work with the ocean upon which you now sail to bring you as handily as possible into the next port, and the next, and the next. Know always that you are in an archipelago[112] rather than a deep, uninhabited ocean when you are working with yourself and helping yourself cooperate with your destiny. You are not alone for long. There is always a place to stop and provender yourself, make sure of your direction and check your bearings, your equipment, and your own self for wellness and for trimness.

First, let us look at this little barque[113] that you sail at this time. Its sails have been the rising, the yearning of your own soul and heart for truth. Not for change in and of itself, but simply for a higher way, for a truer path. And when this kind of dedication of self is made, the door opens, the questions are asked, and the answers come pouring in. What is in your little boat? You have the sail of your desire and this is well set. What have you stashed in the hold for yourself? Have you kept for yourself a game or two, a chessboard, draughts[114], a deck of cards, something to pass the time, something to rest with, something light and meaningless? Have you packed some fun? Have you packed a box of taking things lightly? That would be good to pack away. If you have not done so, find yourself the pastimes that truly rest your mind and help your heart to stop racing, and keep them aboard. For there are times when only waiting will work and only unknowing will be the fruitful attitude. And in those times, it is well not to brood; it is well not to think too much; it is well to take things lightly and know that all is well and that there is time simply to have fun. If the fun is music, be sure and play it; if the fun is walking out of doors or working in the garden, be sure and pack that in, be sure and have that with you. This is a great tool to have when one is going through a process of intense change.

Have you packed sufficient inspiration for your journey? There are times when silence itself becomes too wearying and too intense. It is very helpful to have chosen a few written-down things that you may pick up and read, things that you may count on to give you food. In a metaphysical voyage, the food is ideas. Your food will be concepts that enable you to rest or to become restless but asking, and looking, and seeing a bit further.

Have you packed sufficient humility? There is a good deal of that needed on long voyages such as you have undertaken. In a way, the choice to seek is, in itself, prideful, or so it may seem from one point of view. It is a coming into oneself in such a bold and complete way that it startles and sometimes frightens the self or other selves who gaze upon such a one. And the thought is, perhaps, that such a bold move is not called for, is not necessary. It is impossible to explain to another self why must one set out upon metaphysical voyages. The self cannot even be explained to, if there are inner voices in the self that create resistance within the inner workings of the self. There may be a voice within the one known as T that is still saying, "You are not worthy of making such a bold and drastic change. You do not deserve to release the shoreline of previous ideas and to set forward in search of a new truth that is more all-encompassing, that seems to have more integrity." True humility, however, is that which allows all of the voices of oneself and of other selves to speak their piece to you without the need to defend. What is there to defend, after all? A sailor must set sail. Stays he upon land, he shall drown in the dry dirt. A sailor must take to the water, whatever the voyage, when it is called, when it is time. He simply has to set sail. That is the way with spiritual evolution for most people: when it comes, it is as the wake-up call and there is no going back to sleep. And so the sailor rigs out his boat, sets sail, and just hopes for the best. This is appropriate.

This is not a prideful act. The only prideful act connected with moving through transformation is the act of attempting to defend or justify to the self or to another self the reasons or the rightness of such a voyage. We do not say that there is no possibility of the one known as T choosing wrongly. We simply say that when there is the call for movement, there is no avoiding movement. It might be done awkwardly or smoothly; it might be done slowly or more quickly; it might be done with great joy or in great

---

[112] archipelago: "A sea, such as the Aegean, containing a large number of scattered islands."

[113] barque: "A small vessel that is propelled by oars or sails."

[114] draughts: "The game of checkers."

trepidation. But when the movement has come from the inside out, as the one known as T has expressed, then one is simply forced to sail, for better or for worse.

We ask the one known as T, therefore, to pack sufficient humility that he may rest from blame and rest from avenging those who would blame. It is perfectly understandable for inner voices and for outer voices to object to change. Change will always be uncomfortable. The status quo will always seem more comfortable, more sensible, more sane. It is to those who have been inspired in a certain way that the courage to enter into that zone of discomfort is given. Pack much of this humility, and along with it, my brother, pack much patience. Indeed, put a whole locker full of patience in. For your journey is not only a long journey, your journey is an everlasting journey, one that you have been on all the while and only at a certain point became aware of.

At the point at which you became aware, you also became able to affect the rate of change of your spiritual evolution. You became able to decide consciously to accelerate the pace of this change, to lean into the wind by asking, by seeking, by looking. Those things are as the powers that raise the winds in metaphysical waters: every focus of meditation, every focus of visualization, every focus of affirmation, and every moment of disciplining the personality, bring up the wind. And as you have set your sail by your desire, so the wind moves you in such and such a way. Consequently, check your desire, check the alignment of your sail, if you will, and see that it is working with the wind. When you get into port and have a moment, sit in silence and check, shall we say, in inner dry dock, the health of your vehicle. Are you creating wellness in your body? Are you creating enough rest for your emotional body? Are you creating enough lack of tension, enough balance between motion and stillness, seeking and resting, wisdom and love, attention paid to the self and attention paid to the milieu about one? This is what we would share with you upon working with yourself.

We come to a more difficult part of your question when we begin to look at the other selves about you. It is rare, indeed, on such a voyage, that one is able to take other selves with him. Most general is the case that you experience, where other selves that are dearly beloved to you and are part of your family are not able to take this voyage with you but must remain upon the shore which you have left. This simple separation of attitude and the direction of hopes for the future between mates and between family members has the strong and understandable tendency to create strife and discomfort on both the side of the self and the sides of other selves involved. Even if there are no hard feelings, the dislocation is felt and it must be dealt with by the other selves about you.

Certainly there are many things that you can do to lessen the apparent impact of your voyage. For your voyage is inner. It is not necessary for you to change your geographical location. It is not necessary for you to change the way that you earn money or the way that you participate in your community in order to sail far, far away in terms of the inner voyage of a self seeking the truth. However, as the voyage continues and as the sea miles pile up and the life experiences of these inner voyages begin to accumulate, there is an increasing distance in point of view from the old self. Those other selves who were fond of the old self and who miss the old self will begin missing that old self more and more.

It is rare to find mates, especially, but other selves in general, that are able to lift away from previously assumed knowledge of a person and replace that knowledge with the knowledge of the brand-new fledgling entity that is beginning to show himself. Certainly some are able to do it but for most—and for the one known as T—he will find that it is very difficult for those about him to embrace the changes that have already taken place and to embrace the continuing desire for further change. And so it is as though the other selves are acting as a drag upon the system, wanting always to regain what they consider to be lost ground, and being completely unable to do so because of the nature of metaphysical change. It is like a chemical reaction: it cannot reverse itself. Once started, it must play itself out. And, unfortunately for the peace of mind of those about the one known as T, this means that, insofar as this creates catalyst for those about the one known as T, they also will need to move through the processes of dealing with and finding ways to balance the perceived reality of these changes.

It is very helpful in such a case for the entity who is changing to refrain from attempting to explain or justify his journey, and indeed to refrain from speaking, unless asked, of the journey itself. It is very helpful to remember that beneath all of the chances and changes of living, the self is as a serene and unchanging stream, changing in surface ways, certainly, as things flow through, but unchanging in the sense of being a citizen of eternity with a certain vibratory nexus that is the pure essence of who you are. That vibration may change a very small bit because of hard work done throughout an incarnation, but you are truly an eternal being, and the magical energy of yourself is only partially brought into incarnation. It is connected through the silver cord into that well of self from which you came and in which you have tremendous power, wisdom and awareness. This is who you are, only seen through a cloud within incarnation. It is the quest of an entire incarnation simply to penetrate one's own personality shell so that one is able more and more to rest in the fuller expression of self that this instrument would call Christ consciousness. This is your essence. This is the kind of creature that you are. This is the facet of the Creator which you express.

What a blessing it is to be able to rest back in the essence of who you are. Rest in that essence as much as you can with your family. Stay at the soul level with them, relating to them as wonderful, unique sparks of the Creator, just as are you. So much is veiled, so much is unknown, and yet you can always love, you can always console, you can always lift up and support and encourage and offer hope. You can refuse to shut down, you can refuse to stop being vulnerable, you can refuse to close your heart against anyone or anything. You can endure whatever pain will help those about you as you listen to them express their difficulties and as you work endlessly and patiently, insofar as you can see a way to help them through what they are experiencing as they experience the catalyst of your change.

Be aware that what they say to you is a projection of what about themselves has the ability to confuse them. Each entity will react to what you are going through not in terms of you or anything to do with your journey but in terms of themselves and their own processes. Entities, for all that they think that they are working with other people, for the most part never get beyond their own heads. You will constantly be working to get outside of your own limitations into the broader vistas of a wider perspective. You cannot do this for others. What you can do with and for them is to be yourself, to stay as cheerful and positive as possible, to find patience where no patience seems to be and to find forgiveness for what seem to be unfair or unjust slings and arrows. This instrument has often said that it is a blessing when entities are unfair and unjust because it gives the self a perfect chance to work with that catalyst and to see that nothing needs to be taken personally and that all things are subject for prayer. When you can perceive no other way to serve your family, then remove yourself, sit in silence, and pray for their good, for their improvement of mind, for their healing of spirit, giving thanks, always, for every harsh word, every misunderstanding, every injustice, knowing that these are the things that refine one in the fire. These are the tempering agents that make one strong but flexible.

This instrument was talking to one of those within this circle earlier about the reason for continued tempering and continued testing in the fire. "Why," this instrument was asked, "would that be necessary on a continuing basis? What is the purpose for such a sharp edge when the desire is to love and to bring love to the planet?" And we say to this one, to this instrument and to the one known as T that the continued tempering is that which brings one into the present moment. It is not yesterday's tempering that will keep one flexible in the catalyst of the day. As each lesson is learned, a new vista opens and when the student is eager, those new vistas demand further tempering, further work, further catalyst, further opportunities for learning. Why is there no end to it? For the same reason that there is no end to spirit. When there is oneness, there is infinity. There are no markers, there are no stops, there are no categories, and that infinity becomes that great Celtic knot that moves from Creator to Creator with an octave of learning between.

It is a long, long road. It is a road that also is awash with joy and that is an experience that the one known as T has come into time and again, that sun-washed, light-filled experience of bliss and joy in the knowledge that one is in the right place, at the right time, and on the right journey. Bless and remember those times. That act of remembrance will be very helpful, and especially when one may be downhearted. Because one does see that one cannot make the proverbial omelet without breaking the eggs.

It is very helpful to remember that this experience is surrounded by supernal and infinite life. It is a blessed journey and even the pain of those about you is a blessing as you work in humility with the awareness of yourself as part of a pattern over which you have no control. Your only control is the choice to love and that choice of loving is endlessly subtle and always in the present moment.

At this time we would pause, for there are two questions this day. May we ask for the second question from T. We are those of Q'uo.

T: In this age of materialism, it seems our children often suffer greatly from a feeling of inadequacy and poor self-worth as they constantly compare themselves to the symbols of materialism. I would like to receive information on how parents of young children can best assist and guide the children in remembering and awakening to who they really are as they mature in this age of transition where materialism still has a strong influence.

We are those of Q'uo, and we are aware of your query, my brother. What a good query we find this! It is most appropriate to consider the raising of your young beings for, at this time, not only your being [and] those whom you have welcomed into your home and family, but also virtually all those coming into the world through incarnation's door as new to it are those who have, to some extent, opened their fourth-density bodies and so, are beings that are quite different than those who have come into incarnation with only the yellow-ray activated body[115]. When a person has a dual-activated body, certain things have changed for this entity. It may not be that these changes are consciously known by those who may be called Indigo Children, for a general term, but these changes are there. They include a thinner veiling, so that it is easier to remember preincarnative data, the ability to access psychic gifts largely because of the lighter veiling, the tendency to be impatient with third-density structures, especially those that seem to stand in their way, and some difficulty in cooperating with the strictures that make the least sense to them. Indeed, in some part, these have always been the characteristics of youth, but when there is a memory that is closer to the surface of a higher way and when the culture is mired in teachings that are directly counter to those sensings and half memories, it becomes fiendishly difficult for entities to make sense of their surroundings.

It may be considered unfortunate by the one known as T that such children do not come into incarnation equipped with what might be called maturity or common sense. Such children are children. They do not have an instinct for maturity. They do not have an instinct for right behavior. They are, as [are] all of the very young, self-involved, ever-questing, ever-impatient, and very inquisitive of knowledge, of ideas, of ways to be, of masks of all kinds. They are experimenters looking for ways to express that feel right to them. They are tremendously influenced by what is going on about them. And this is not simply the parents and the family but also contains the world of school and peers and the fads of a culture. If you add in the mass media and the tremendous amount of propaganda of mind-entraining material that exists within the programs and the commercials of television, the sum becomes a huge and unmanageable bundle of strictly third-density input for such children. There is nothing that the parents can do about this except keep them home, turn off the television set, and studiously home school. Some have put a great deal of time aside and actually done this. And yet those children will move out into the world of peers and fads and mass media because it is there in such abundant quantity. Consequently, we do not recommend such withdrawal from the society at large. We recommend, rather, some of that endless patience that you have taken with you on the journey. For you shall, as a parent, need to deal with situations one, by one, by one; and we are talking of hundreds and thousands and millions of situations in twenty years of raising a child. And in each of these situations, you will need to be creative and listen and find ways to offer positive suggestion and positive counsel when what you would really like to do is tear down structures that you feel are harmful for your children.

We recommend, most of all, that you yourself live in a way that you may endlessly explain and defend. This is painstaking work. If you would like them not to watch television, turn yours off, not once but as a habit. If you would like them to respect the rights of others, be sure that your converse and your

---

[115] The yellow-ray body is the physical body which we all have, and third density is the world of Earth life which we share. The fourth-density or green-ray body is that energy body which can work with fourth-density or higher vibrations. A dual-activated body is one in which both the third-density body and the fourth-density body are active.

comments constantly express the deepest love that you can find for every entity and every situation. Whatever it is that you are hoping for your children, rather than telling them, sit in counsel with yourself until you can find ways to live the life that you wish to embody for them. Be a living example to them, not by what you say, alone, but by how you are, by how you live your day. Do you, for instance, make a point of spending time with yourself and the Creator in silence, every day? If your children see you living a religiously or spiritually oriented life, they will know beyond a shadow of a doubt that that is of value to you and because you loom large in their small lives, that will have every reason to be considered as a value to them.

You may ask yourself, too, if you spend time with them where you do nothing but listen to them. If you can spend just a bit of time…

(Side one of tape ends.)

(Carla channeling)

…finding out what their process has been like this day, what their walk has led them to see and think about, what their dreams have told them, not with any view to commenting or improving upon their thoughts but simply to knowing them, they will feel worthy in a way that you cannot create by any other means. If you think that their small affairs are important, so will they know that they have a right to be and that what they do is worthwhile. These things cannot be taught. They have to be picked up from the attitude with which people hold them. As a parent you have tremendous ability to give them this kind of nourishment of self. As they talk themselves over with you, they begin to get their own bearings and the feeling that they have their own reality and their own process. As you give them credit for being people, even at a very young age, they are able to begin to grasp more of this double-activated nature. As you live a loving, radiant life, you are basically living in the fourth-density energy for which they so hunger since they are prepared to take it in and since your surface environment is so lacking in fuller light. See what you can do to be an unconscious but ever-present radiance in their life.

Again, it is nothing that you say that will mean as much in teaching children as how you are. How do you treat everything and everyone about you? How do you think of that world about you? In what way do you discuss the issues to which entities with double-activated bodies would be so sensitive? Damage to the environment, damage to other selves, lack of human rights, injustice and unfairness: these things will nag like thorns at a double-activated child. Do what you can to discover for yourself ways to talk about these shortcomings that can be perceived in outer society in such a way that hope is found and positive movement on a personal level is discussed. Never let children become cynical if you can possibly help it. And yet, at the same time, encourage good, straight, hard looks by these young children at what seem to you to be perhaps too adult areas or issues of consideration. For these children, things happen quickly. Ideas develop quickly, questions come up quickly. Expect this process to occur, when it does, with some speed and just see what you can do to maintain your own humor, patience and humility. You are not an authority figure to a double-activated entity, you are an advisor. You are, if you have been careful, considered to be a good one and you will be listened to, for there are deep threads of honor and respect that run through a double-activated child.

They can easily be distorted by disappointment and the typical disappointed, double-activated Indigo child can be a tough cookie. So we would just offer you the encouragement to stay within your own integrity, offer what encouragement that you can, and by all means do not assume that your child, being double-activated, has no need of guidance. Such children, like any children, do need persistent and firm limits. We simply say, make those limits loving, understandable, simple and then be willing to explain them, to stand by them, and to take insults and disagreement when it is inconvenient for other selves to observe those boundaries. Do not let that faze you, but keep the boundaries that you feel are important, not combatively but persistently, quietly and firmly.

Above all, find ways to express your own belief system in the tiny things of everyday. This way there is no preaching involved. There is no discussion of dogma or the lack of same, but only the expression in everyday life at the smallest level of thoughtfulness, desire to help the family system, and those other values that feed into a harmonious and loving family life. If you have not investigated fully the joys of doing laundry, scrubbing the toilet bowl, doing the dishes, or any of the other thousand and one things that a household takes to keep going, dig into it and investigate to the best of your ability all of the above and anything else that you can see that will help the family move more smoothly through the day. When entities are not afraid of cleaning a toilet with great love and great thoroughness and a delight in the result, then the entities around him can begin to see that all things are holy and that there is no unjust labor, or work to be scorned. In living a spiritually oriented life, this is a key concept and it cannot be gotten at with words. Those about you must see you participating in every way. This will enable them to find that same perspective within themselves gradually becoming more and more understandable.

Most of all, my brother, see to your own self. In the midst of all this concern for others, remember that you must tend to your own stability, wellness of mind, heart, body and soul, your own financial wellness, your own staying beforehand with the requirements of the world. What does it take to keep you grounded and balanced and ready for the new day? In most cases, there is that need for daily meditation, daily contemplation, a time that is sacred to oneself, a time spent in the temple of the inner heart, resting with the one infinite Creator. If you have to get up early, my brother, to do this, then set your alarm and give yourself a half hour to stare at a candle, to think over the day ahead, to make to-do lists, to do whatever it serves you to do to rise from your night ready for a new day, seeing into a new land filled with infinite possibility.

It has been a delight and a privilege to speak with you this day, my brother. And we thank those in the support group who have made this session of seeking possible. We are those of Q'uo, and we leave you in the love and in the light of the one infinite Creator. Adonai. Adonai. ✢

L/L Research

L/L Research is a subsidiary of Rock Creek Research & Development Laboratories, Inc.

P.O. Box 5195
Louisville, KY 40255-0195

www.llresearch.org

Rock Creek is a non-profit corporation dedicated to discovering and sharing information which may aid in the spiritual evolution of humankind.

ABOUT THE CONTENTS OF THIS TRANSCRIPT: This telepathic channeling has been taken from transcriptions of the weekly study and meditation meetings of the Rock Creek Research & Development Laboratories and L/L Research. It is offered in the hope that it may be useful to you. As the Confederation entities always make a point of saying, please use your discrimination and judgment in assessing this material. If something rings true to you, fine. If something does not resonate, please leave it behind, for neither we nor those of the Confederation would wish to be a stumbling block for any.

© 2009 L/L RESEARCH

Channeling Symposium, University of Louisville Belknap Campus
August 22, 2004

(Carla channeling)

We are those known to you as the principle of Q'uo, and we greet you in the love and in the light of the one infinite Creator, in Whose energy we come and in Whose service we are. It is our distinct privilege to be called to this circle of seeking and we thank each entity here for taking the time away from a very busy and tension-ridden life to stop a minute and just ask for the truth, for those things to come in that you hope will be resources and assets as you face the present moment. It is truly a present moment that is fascinating and challenging in many ways. And we are most glad to be here with you.

In order for us to be able to speak freely, we would add our voice to the one known as "Joy of Life"[116] and ask each to use your discrimination carefully. Do not assume that we or any other entity are authorities, for we are not. You are the authority over your own learning curve, over your own spiritual evolution. You have the right and the ownership of your truth. It is not like anyone else's truth and it is not the same truth for you from year to year and sometimes from moment to moment. Always listen with a new ear and see if you feel resonance with that which is being spoken. If so, take it in and work with it, make it your own. In the echoes of that resonance lie personal truth that is helpful for you now. If it does not resonate for you, drop it, leave it, walk away without a second thought. It is not your truth. It may be helpful to someone else but it didn't ring your bell, so let it be. This will enable us to speak freely without concern that we may be abridging your own free will for attempting to pretend that we can learn for you. We are only those who walk with you.

Before we take queries, we would simply suggest to each of you that you are the light of the world. There is illumination coming into this room from several sources and we would use some of these images to talk about how you are light. If you gaze behind this instrument, there is a decoration made of a tree into which there are pinned Christmas lights. It is a beautiful, aesthetically pleasing decoration. But more than that, it is a beautiful image of your planet and its people. Each of you is a radiant source of energy. When you are plugged in, how you shine! And you are connected one to the other, not visibly. Visibly, each entity is separate, each entity has limits, places where flesh and clothing meet the air, feet meet the ground. It is obvious that in the physical illusion each is separate. And yet you have, common to this incarnation, families, not nuclear or physical families alone, but spiritual families, larger groups of entities than you might suspect, who have chosen to come into incarnation to work in tandem with those whom they meet and with whom they seem to feel kinship and affinity and much more than that. With the

---

[116] Joy of Life is an inner-planes entity which had spoken through Sylvia Willett in a channeling offered by her prior to this channeling from Carla and those of Q'uo.

extended families of each of you, who in many cases share relatives, shall we say, on the unseen planes, you are connected in so many ways which you cannot see but can only feel. So know that, as you look into the eyes of those whom you have not yet touched into in terms of energy, with whom you have not exchanged energy, yet you do not look into the eyes of strangers. For beneath the surface of this seeming separateness of the physicality, you are strongly and powerfully connected by those families from which you came and to which you shall return.

You have come here to be a light, to lighten the planet known as Earth. Let us look at that Christmas lighting of the tree again, this image of all of you in incarnation being here and "holding the energy" or "holding the space."[117] Who are you linked into?

Look about you to the ceiling and you will see constellations of lighting that seem to come down from above. These might represent sources of integration. As the physical illusion becomes ever more complicated, reassurance and grounding, oddly enough, come from perceived sources of inspiration. One light may be a walk in the woods, another may be inspirational writings, and there are wonderful books offered in this very room that may be just what you might need at this time.[118] Touch the books, touch the materials, see if there is energy there for you and when you do perceive a source of energy, remember to use it. Open the book, take the walk, place yourself into engagement with the present moment. For you are a powerful and magical being. The light within you is that energy that is infinite. What are you plugged into? What infinite source are you plugged into?

And now look out the window and see the sunlight that pours a wasteful amount of energy infinitely into your plane, far more than any entities may use. The Creator is incredibly generous. There is no end to consciousness, there is no end to love, there is no end to that into which you are plugged. For you are as the vine branch; you are as the lamp that is lit. The vine branch moves down into the vine. The master known as Jesus said, "I am the true vine, and you are the branches."[119] And again, he said, "You are the light of the world,"[120] so do not hide your light under the bushel, do not tuck it away inside your house, inside your being, inside your practice, but allow that energy into which you are plugged in your inner heart to move ever [more] freely through the open heart and into the world around you.

All things are one and you are not only a personality shell, a being of a certain identified kind, living a certain kind of life. You are, as the one known as Father said, "a spark of the divine," a sparkle in the eye of the Creator. And you have come at no small inconvenience to yourself into what seems to be a fairly darkened atmosphere. Do not be fooled. Do not be dismayed. The "ascension" of which many have spoken is not coming. It is here. The energy of fourth density lives, as it can, in the corners, cracks and crevices of third-density Earth. It is an overpowering energy and it is moving far more energetically now than a year ago. Indeed, we may say that it is your choice as to which density in which you choose to live.

It is a delicate thing to change the point of view from third-density consensus reality to fourth-density perceived reality; to switch from living by fear into living by love; to move from a point of view in which one defends and guards into a point of view in which one sees oneself as a crystal being that is able to receive the love and the light of the one infinite Creator, bless it and allow it to go forth from the open heart without distortion. As you are able to express the unconditional love that fuels your light and that is the source of your light, you become the light of the world.

May I ask the one known as M at this time if there are queries for us?[121]

M: Yes, Q'uo, there are. "What is the next step for me to take, both personally and spiritually?"

We are those of Q'uo, and are aware of your query. The present moment is perfect. And yet it is as a seed that is in a process of growth. When one

---

[117] These are phrases channeled through Sylvia Willett in the previous segment of the symposium from her contact, "Father."

[118] All of the channelers had brought their materials for the audience to look over.

[119] *Holy Bible*, John 15: "I am the true vine, and my Father is the vine dresser. ... Abide in me, and I in you."

[120] *Holy Bible*, Matthew 5: "You are the light of the world. ... Let your light shine before men in such a way that they may see your good works, and glorify your Father who is in heaven."

[121] M was the moderator, and she had many question cards to read which the audience had filled out beforehand.

considers the next step, either personally or spiritually, the question becomes, "Where is the love in this moment?"

Your past has planted seeds in the work you have done, in the suffering you have undergone, the lessons you have learned. You have fertilized, watered and developed those seeds and they are what have bloomed into the present moment but they are not the end of the process—they are an exquisitely poignant picture that does not last except to give you wings to see your way to that next step. As you ask, "Where is the love?" you can begin to see into the relationships that you bring to this moment and the issues which you are pondering.

What help has been asked? If there is a request for service, that is always the next step. What are the energies surrounding this issue or this relationship? Where and how can the entity that you are and the gifts that you have be helpful? And do not forget yourself, for if you overwork yourself, if you exhaust your spiritual, your emotional, or your mental energies, not to mention your physical energies, how shall you serve at all?

So it is well to ask yourself, "What do I need to meet this moment?" It might be a very small thing that moves you from a feeling of being overworked, over-energized, exhausted, tense and even depressed, to good cheer and good energy. It might be a cup of tea. It might be anything that you sense into and realize, "You know, I've been thinking about everyone else but I really need to take a nap, take a bite, take a walk."

Focus, when looking at taking the next step, on how you are feeling, how your attitude is, and how you perceive this present moment. How do you see the system, as a whole, that is your energy field? Are you in health? You need to be in order to serve. If the answer to that is no, stop and ask for balance. If you are feeling bewildered, stop, sit in silence, and let the universe pour in. It might be the call of a bird; it might be spirits speaking directly to you in a voice you can hear. It might be anything in between. It might be a street sign that pops out at you in synchronicity with the thought that you were having. There are many, many ways that spirit connects with those who are listening, so listen, and listen to yourself, being sure, first, that the instrument is in good order, for you are instruments.

M: "What is my forward movement?"

We are those of Q'uo, and are aware of your query. The question of forwardness is interesting. A third-density consensus-reality way of thinking is always designed with an arrow: first this, then this, then this, a sequence in a straight line. However, spiritually speaking, there is a circle, or perhaps more rightly, a sphere, and all movement is forward. Think of yourself not as this lumbering great ape that is walking step, by step, by step. Think of the energy body that you are, for you have wings, and you fly. This energy body, or torus of energy, that is your basic metaphysical nature or body, can roll in any direction, and move from level to level, density to density, picking up the information and the resources that it needs. Certainly, most of this is not done consciously.

So a lot of moving forward is getting your preconceptions of what forward movement is out of the way and then opening to the resources about you: your dream work, your synchronicities, your reading, that which you pick up from conversations and from the silence when you tabernacle with the one infinite Creator and your guidance. It is so important to touch in frequently to your guidance and then listen. If you can, when you get an impression, take it seriously, write it down, go back and look at it and see if you have followed your own guidance yet. If not, hit it with ever more energy and enthusiasm, for you are connected, you do know in your inner heart where that next forward movement is. But you shall not know as fully unless you allow the roundness and the freedom of the being that you truly are as a citizen of eternity to come out.

M: "Will my financial situation resolve?"

We are those of Q'uo, and are aware of your query. The issue of supply is a ticklish one and certainly this instrument experiences many times of wondering precisely how the bills shall be paid, precisely how supply will manifest itself and yet, indeed it always has, for this instrument. It has sometimes been mighty close but somehow the wagon has continued to stay on the road in some way. And we would suggest that the visualizing of this state of perfection will encourage the richness of supply. We do not suggest a laundry list of needed things in your prayers to the Creator. When you think about the prayer that the master known as Jesus taught to his disciples, it only asked for today. Focus upon that which is needed this day and ask, without pride but also without shame, "May I have that which is needed in supply and in energy in all things this day, that I may serve?" Let that affirmation rest, knowing that, for this one day, you will be supplied with that which you truly need.

We apologize for not being more specific but we find that in order to keep the tuning of what this instrument would call the highest and best that she requested, we need to stay at the level of spiritual principles.

M: "Is this a special group? What can you tell us about what brought us together today?"

We are those of Q'uo, and are aware of your query. Indeed, we have spoken to some extent upon this subject and it is dear to our hearts. You are here this day because you are a family. You have not chosen each other in a conscious way. You do not have the entanglements with many of these here of family, previous friendships, and so forth. But there is a tabernacle in which all of you reside. It is that space or energy that is held together by those who seek the truth and who seek to serve at this time. You have come this day for reasons on the conscious level, but because of promptings also on the subconscious level. So we encourage you to see this event and this gathering as a family reunion of those who have not previously, perhaps, come into a gathering or re-uned. Yet you are all called by spirit to be witnesses to light and love. And each of you has worked and played and suffered and laughed and done the living that collects life experience. You have begun to gather about yourselves a kind of spiritual gravity, a weight, a density of being that holds the light. You see, when entities begin to wake up to their spiritual nature, they are perfectly capable of grasping the ideas because the ideas which concern spiritual evolution are fairly simple. It has often been called the universal wisdom, or the eternal wisdom. What we have to say, and indeed what each has to say this day has been said before and will be said again and yet, because of the nature of spirit, it must be said in the present moment as a spark that can ignite or as a germ that can infect.

Perhaps that is what we would say to you: each of you is a carrier of unconditional love. As one person becomes enlightened, awakened, and energized by the spirit, unconditional love pours through. Yet it cannot be held for long periods of time, at first. The tuning slips, the energy is exhausted, and rest must be taken. You are here to deepen your own spiritual density, to find those resources that work for you as you assume the discipline of your own personality and begin to learn how to persist in patience, in good humor, and in peace and compassion for yourself as a bozo and a mistake-maker of the first order. All of us, all of you, every iota of the creation of the Father, makes mistakes. If we did not have distortion, we would be resting in the allness of the creative principle. We would not be working our way back to the Source. You are between alpha and omega, and you are here to learn how to accelerate your pace of evolution. Each entity whom you meet this day is your teacher. Each eye that you look into is the eye of the Creator. You live in a hall of mirrors and these mirrors are wonderfully clear. Come, meet yourself here.

May we ask if there is another query at this time?

M: "Was Paladin a true energy encounter?"

We are those of Q'uo, and are aware of your query, my sister. Because of the degree of surety that you have at this time we would confirm that this is a helpful energy for you at this time.

We thank each of you and we leave each of you in the love and in the light of the one infinite Creator. We are known to you as those of Q'uo. Adonai, my friends. Adonai. ☙

L/L Research

L/L Research is a subsidiary of Rock Creek Research & Development Laboratories, Inc.

P.O. Box 5195
Louisville, KY 40255-0195

www.llresearch.org

Rock Creek is a non-profit corporation dedicated to discovering and sharing information which may aid in the spiritual evolution of humankind.

ABOUT THE CONTENTS OF THIS TRANSCRIPT: This telepathic channeling has been taken from transcriptions of the weekly study and meditation meetings of the Rock Creek Research & Development Laboratories and L/L Research. It is offered in the hope that it may be useful to you. As the Confederation entities always make a point of saying, please use your discrimination and judgment in assessing this material. If something rings true to you, fine. If something does not resonate, please leave it behind, for neither we nor those of the Confederation would wish to be a stumbling block for any.

© 2009 L/L Research

Special Meditation
August 30, 2004

Question from G: I would like to ask that you touch upon my desire and seeking to heal myself and my past, specifically delving into my search to discover the unknown traumatic learning and the primary cause of self-rejection developed within my formative years, the still-divided energies I feel within, and the hole I've described to you within my being, somewhere. Please feel free to leave these subjects and venture into any other topic you feel may be of benefit to me. I trust you. After which I'll have as many questions as you and the instrument have the time and energy for. Thank you.

(Carla channeling)

We are those of the principle known to you as Q'uo, and we greet you in the love and in the light of the one infinite Creator, in Whose service we come to you this day. It is our privilege to be called to your group and we thank you for the opportunity to share our thoughts on this search for self-healing that the one known as G is moving through at this time. As always, we would ask that each in this group exercise the utmost vigilance in using the discrimination of his own mind and heart, for those things which we offer are simply opinion rather than being authoritarian in nature and we need you to realize that our opinion is not necessarily the truth that is helpful for you at this time. If you find things that are helpful then by all means follow them and make them your own by working upon them and adding to them as new insights come to you. If they do not resonate to you with that familiar feel of an old friend newly remembered, then please let them drop away.

The beginning of an incarnation seems to be a simple thing and yet often it is somewhat more complicated than the simple beginning that it seems. Although many entities' processes of incarnation begin roughly at the time of the birth, for many, especially those who have a great deal of previous experience before this incarnation, the process of entering the body and starting the incarnation is begun somewhat prior to the actual birth of the fetus as it exits the womb of the mother. In the case of the one known as G, this was quite true. And, indeed, for each in this circle this was the case. A tremendous amount of awareness and even the basic personality shell was that which was given while the seeming fetus was yet in the womb. Indeed, by the time of the birth of the one known as G, much fairly complex work had been done and the beginning of the incarnation, therefore, was, shall we say, perhaps eight months or so prior to the birth of this entity into the world.

The bounds of free will do not permit us to discuss some of the complications that were occurring around the one known as G—and we mean that literally—during the pregnancy. Suffice it to say that there were disagreements and disharmonies betwixt the parents that alarmed and frightened the one known as G and convinced this entity that it would be better to turn partially away from full attention within the life experience in order to protect the tender sensibilities of this entity from the disharmonies that it was experiencing about it. It was not seen by this very young entity that this decision might become inconvenient at a later time. Nevertheless, the decision was made at a very deep level, prior to the actual birth of this entity, so that the one known as G came into incarnation with a substantive and very deep-set bias against paying full attention to that which was spoken by any entity about it that would have any possibility whatsoever of causing harm to this entity.

Because of the nature of the family system of the one known as G, this entity's decision to protect itself was only underlined and emphasized by the events of its early life. The climate of constant disagreement and disharmony continued and as the entity grew and became able to have friends and to begin moving through those cultural systems that you call school and education, more and more evidence seemed to point to the fact that disharmony was the standard operating environment that could be expected and, therefore, each time there came an opportunity to begin to second-guess that first basic decision to lift the attention away from any spoken word from any perceived authority figure, the decision was always made, once again, in favor of protecting the self and distancing the self from spoken communication.

The lifting away from dependence upon words had the positive aspect of creating, for this entity, an inner safe place. It had the apparently negative aspect of constituting a defect in the linkage between short term memory and long term memory so that there grew to be the impression within the one known as G of there being no memory of those things which had gone before. In fact, it is as though within the mind of the one known as G there are files that are locked away that have been designated as being, shall we say, contaminated or infected and therefore, that have been placed where they cannot be accessed. This has constituted in the adult life of the one known as G a real stumbling block. And when we gaze at those steps which can recover the so-called hole in the mind, or the gaps in the memory, we find that, in many ways, the effort needed to recover such locked-away memory might be considered excessive.

It is, however, more possible to look at working with changing the layers of decision-making, moving down through the tree of mind to reaccess that point before birth when the one known as G first made the decision to angle himself away from spoken communication. When one attempts to change a decision that one has made for one's own good, one must realize that one is asking of the self that it trust new information over old and trusted information. This is usually the most difficult part of altering a behavior and attitude of a point of view: that is, becoming able to trust the judgment of the self in its new configuration to the point where the self is able to gaze at the old configuration and the new configuration and have confidence that the new configuration will function properly. Therefore, we would suggest that the first step in clearing the old configuration is to move into a state of mind which is silent and to create, in that silence, shall we say, a workshop, a place within where this work can be held, gazed at, and considered.

For this instrument, such a workshop was her choice. She created her own workshop by moving into that silence of mind in which she contemplated her favorite places until she found her very favorite place and then, within her own mind, she constructed, detail by detail, the workshop she felt she needed to do work in consciousness. She provided for herself two rooms with a little bathroom off the side of the office. She offered to herself a room that was for records and for office work and for a comfortable chair that she could sit in and muse and prepare herself to do work in consciousness. And then, through a wide-open gateway, with no door but simply the arch of space that indicated that there were two rooms [she created] a working room where there were three seats and, in front of those three seats, a large screen. She created two doors in that second room through which the male and female aspects of her guidance might step. And when she invited those aspects in and they came in and were greeted, they took the three seats—one [aspect] on each side of her and her seat in the middle. When she was ready to do the work, she and her guidance, holding hands, would light the screen with their intention and when the screen lit, then the work could be visualized and done. This instrument created a color scheme, carpets, works of art, and everything that she could think of to make this space both sacred and beautiful. And it is a place to which she moves in consciousness each time that she tunes to work as she is working at this moment.

We give you this degree of detail not to indicate what the one known as G should design but to indicate that it is important in creating a place of working that it be created with great thought and attention to detail, so that the one known as G makes for himself a place that is truly his own, where he feels at home and safe, and where he feels safe in calling forth his guidance and his own power.

This instrument is glad to aid the one known as G in the creation of this sacred space but we do caution the one known as G that each detail of the work be his own and come from his heart and his soul and his mind.

When this workshop has been created, we would suggest that the one known as G move there in consciousness on a daily basis, if possible, while he is doing this work of attempting to recover the decision made before birth. We cannot say before incarnation, for this was an incarnative decision. But the fact that it was a decision made in the womb has serious consequences and creates, for the work at hand, a level of complexity that is not seen when the damage, shall we say, has been done to an entity's sense of self after birth.

It was also so, for the one known as Carla, that great alarm and dismay was felt before the incarnation properly began. In this instrument's case, the alarm was deep enough that it prolonged the pregnancy so that this instrument was born only after ten months in the womb. However, this instrument did not choose to create for herself that safe place that she would have had by deciding to reject some portion of the environment about her after birth. Rather, it created for her a deep sense of what this instrument would call resentment. It, therefore, can be seen that this instrument's personality shell is actually more warlike or warrior-like than the personality shell of the one known as G; it turned not towards flight but, in the end, towards fight, whereas the one known as G simply turned aside and slipped away from the danger it had perceived.

We would take time to note, to the one known as G, that there is no shame in perceiving as negative, or undesirable, that level of disharmony which makes words mean nothing. The ways of entities who use words to hurt are such that words lose their meaning. Words cannot be used logically or with common sense, for they are but markers or symbols for unspoken and perhaps unknown biases which drive the entity to use language in ways that are not consonant with logic. This is not an experience unique to his family system. It is relatively rampant within human society, in general, that words are used not to communicate but to control or to wound. Blessed indeed is the family system in which this is not true. The one known as G has now found his way into a spiritually-based family which holds the value of words used only for communication and not for control or for wounding. However, each of those in that family system makes frequent errors and has those moments when it does use words not purely to communicate but also to control, to persuade, or to wound. For the one known as G and for all of those within this family system, we could encourage careful thought when using words with the one known as G, realizing that this entity's wounds are of the nature of words being used as sticks and stones. If there is an energy there that can be perceived and that can be talked about, then we encourage, any time that such a slip from communication to persuasion to wounding is perceived, for there to be an honest and immediate effort to clean up communication and to reestablish communication as a clear and sweet channel of energy between two people.

That is the beautiful thing about communicating in clear blue ray, as this instrument would call it. When the heart is open and words are used well, each word carries that energy of the heart and can be perceived not as that which comes to wound but that which comes to aid. Gradually, through the time spent with this family system, the one known as G has found it more possible to listen to speech without becoming nervous or desiring to get away. And this is because that subconscious portion of the self recognizes the health and the attractiveness of these good words. It is an entirely new experience for this entity and is much appreciated on very deep levels. Yet still there is the backlog of two decades and more of difficulty and repetitive choices made to confirm the original choice that words are basically "bad" things. We overgeneralize here for the sake of the conversation.

We are giving this instrument the picture of the desert at night. It is dark. It is quiet. Indeed, it is silent. The stars stud the night sky as they do only in the desert when there are no cities about and no sources of artificial light and, indeed, no dwellings of any kind whatsoever. This is the environment of simplicity. This darkness, this quietness, may well be part of the place chosen for the workshop by the one known as G, for these are two outward markers of simplicity and the present blockages are a reaction against complexity. We move here in ways that this instrument does not understand and we ask her forgiveness for moving her beyond her comfort level but, in working with decisions made before birth, we are in a kind of shadow-land. Before birth, an entity is very close to the larger entity that it is before choosing a body and committing to the connection of the silver cord. Decisions made at this time are not irrevocable, for they did not come in as part of the personality shell. But they have that incredible strength of initial decisions that have never been circumvented or changed.

So, moving back into this space of darkness, it is perhaps not simply desert but more: the womb itself, that true darkness that has never seen any light. Realize that, to the one known as G, the womb itself was a dangerous place. There was no safety anywhere. The entity which carried the one known as G was angry and unhappy. This communicated itself, especially when this entity engaged in conversation with the one known as G's father. We do not suggest that either of these two parents were negative entities. Indeed, those who are parents to the one known as G are, as is he, beautiful, loving souls seeking to learn and to serve. However, they were chosen by the one known as G as part of a setup for an incarnational lesson that was designed to open the heart. And, indeed, this has, to some extent, misfired from the beginning because of this initial decision.

As the one known as G begins to engage in moving back into the layers of fear that prompted this early decision, we encourage a tremendous feeling of patience and compassion. Think of yourself as a doctor that has been called in to remove a splinter that has worked itself deep into the finger, or the toe, creating a tremendous amount of pain and an inability to use that particular appendage. Through time, that thorn has been unable to work itself out and it has festered in place. Indeed, it has encapsulated itself so that it is no longer able to be gotten at by a pair of pincers. It cannot be tweezed out.

Think of the work that you do in your workshop as a way of putting the appendage, the hand, or the foot, into the hot water of your silence, your darkness, your meditation and then think of asking for what would constitute a drawing solution such as the Epsom salts, for drawing out deep infection. What aspects of self would you call on to assist you in this work of healing? What aspects of your guidance would you call forth? If you were going to call forth a totem animal to give you courage to confront your deepest fears, what animal would you choose? Take the time to answer that question, to choose that totem animal and to make friends with it, so that you may ask it for help. What odor, what aroma, would you consider the best, the most inspirational for you to use in sweetening your mind and resting your heart as you do this work? Take the time to look at this question and choose an essential oil or incense that you may use when you do the work. Find as many ways as possible to set up for yourself a magical time, so that when you move into this workshop experience, you're using all of your senses and all of your help and all of the aspects of this personality shell that you bring to this work to bear on this question.

It may seem that you are dancing around this question by attending to so many details, but our feeling is that it is quite central that you create a place of safety in a new configuration of self that has as much attractiveness and soundness and substance, metaphysically speaking, as the safe place of the old configuration of thought has. For you cannot fool your subconscious self. It shall not heal itself because you ask it to, on a shallow basis. It takes time to convince that child self, that infant self, that it is safe to change from one closet to another. We say "closet" because we have used that metaphor before in discussing your particular difficulty. This instrument, just this morning, was editing the last special session which this group offered for the one known as G and in it we were using that term because it was a good thing at the time that it was chosen and it is only recently that it has become more and more of a prison than a closet, more of a limiting thing than a safe place.

So when that child self is offered a new safe place, because it is a safe place that is without those neat boundaries of the old safe place, the new safe place needs to be very detailed, very specific, very trustable. And this will take some serious repetition. This is not work done in a day or a week or even a month—it takes time to convince the self that one is serious when one is attempting to move at such a deep level within incarnation.

Outside of incarnation these alterations of thoughts are relatively simple because they are visible; the veil between conscious and subconscious does not hold. And work at very deep levels, even archetypical levels, can be done, certainly not quickly but consciously. Within incarnation, such attempts are not visible. One can work with that which shows above the level of consciousness but much of the real work is done under the threshold of consciousness and outside of the conscious awareness of the individual. Consequently, work that is done in these workshop meditations will be seated through sleep; and perhaps the one known as G will begin to have dream experiences that indicate that this material is being worked through.

It will be work that will be done completely on faith, for there will be no immediate result, and when results do begin to come into the conscious mind, it will be inkling by inkling and hint by hint rather than being a sudden and complete "aha!" experience. But we believe that the one known as G is on a good track. We agree with the one known as G that it would be helpful to move out of this closet, this previous safe place that has become such a limiting factor. For when this entity hears but does not hear, in each case, this is that same mechanism working perfectly to protect the one known as G from pain.

Think of what a daring thing it will be for the one known as G to ask to hear everything! After it asks this thing and has been given the boon of hearing all, it still shall be in a world in which many entities will speak words designed not to communicate but to persuade or to wound. That will not change. That basic truth of the environment of third density will remain as it is. Consequently, the challenge is to create, within the self, an intention that stands the test of time.

We offer to the one known as G our aid in being with him in his meditations and assure the one known as G that he has only to ask and we shall join him as that energy that deepens and stabilizes his level of meditation.

May we ask if there are other queries at this time?

G: Q'uo, I consider myself a very lucky person to be able to talk with a portion of the outer planes of the universe and to get some friendly advice. You stated in an earlier channeling that I had a considerable amount of spiritual energy available for my service, and that there was set up to be a near-complete natural reliance on accessing that. Can you comment at all about what this spiritual energy and how I may safely tap into it for its use?

We are those of Q'uo, and, my brother, that is the extent of that which we may say on that subject at this time. Is there a further query at this time?

G: That's cool. Yes, and I may get a similar response for this one too.

Sometimes I view my own particular path as possibly having some requirements, some voluntary limitations that I would do well to impose upon my actions for the sake of becoming what I think is the ultimate goal of where I view my seeking may lead me, and that's to become a purified channel for the Law of One. Can you tell me if any such requirements exist and possibly what they might be?

We are those of Q'uo, and are aware of your query, my brother. In general, the choice of paths to a goal is entirely up to the choice of the individual. For some, the choice of an abstemious lifestyle is as the outward marker for inward purity and, when that is sought, the practice of hewing to such ascetic disciplines is helpful. For others, such as this instrument, who have a naturally well-disciplined inner life, the opposite is true and this instrument works with itself to, shall we say, have fun and not to take the self so terribly seriously. What works for one person will not work for another. For one entity, monkhood, poverty, obedience, chastity, the classic giving up of the world, is tremendously comforting and healing and creates an inner space where the entity finally feels natural. For another entity, the world itself, with all of its excesses and imbalances, seems the Garden of Eden. We would simply ask that you stay in touch with your inner self to the point where you feel the rightness of choices such as abstemiousness or indulgence. Look for your own inner balance, not anyone else's, not any other system of thought's idea of what good behavior and spiritual environments are. But look within yourself and ask yourself and your guidance, "What do I need? What environment will serve me as I wish to serve the Creator?" Listen deeply and ask more than once and if you can, write down those impressions that you may get.

It is well to be in communication with yourself, to create a way for you to talk with yourself. This instrument, for instance, keeps a notebook and when she wishes to move a little more deeply into her guidance, she will actually sit down and write out a question and then simply ask for guidance. When that next thought comes into the mind, she begins to write it down as if it were not coming from her but through her and she has found this to be very helpful. We do not know what might work for the one known as G. It may be more helpful for this entity to work with the dreams and use that as the gateway to talking to the self about the self. Whatever mode of communication is chosen, we would suggest that it be pursued with perseverance, and as we said before, patience. These are long-term processes of the self, by the self. They do not have the shortcut of the authority of the teacher and this is that which could be seen as a time-consuming factor. And yet we say to the one known as G that no teacher from the outside can affect this particular difficulty. It will be the self working with the self that begins to balance this particular distortion that runs so deep.

May we answer you further, my brother?

G: Thank you, that's good advice. I understand what it means to discover for myself what is right or wrong. I have what may be an extension of that question. You may have an answer to this, you may not, but I would like to ask because I am not exactly sure myself. I am curious to know what effect these three substances have on me and my seeking: alcohol, cigarettes and refined sugar. Alcohol especially. I feel such a conflict, at times between filling in social needs and once-in-a-while occasion of drinking [alcohol] that goes along with that, and the seeming "harm" that sometimes it feels like it brings to my path.

We are those of Q'uo, and are aware of your query, my brother. We have discussed before that any substance that alters the mood can be seen as that which is a short-cut or a crutch. The cigarettes and the alcohol are both those types of things and that which you call refined sugar is, in a more subtle way, also that which alters the mood. However, we believe we would be moving beyond our proper limits in speaking further of such substances in this regard. They are not critical to the progress of this entity, one way or another. However, they have their impact, as does everything that affects the one known as G. We therefore leave it to the one known as G to assess the proper balance in the use of such substances. Does this entity feel that these substances are helpful? If so, what is the proper use, the appropriate balance, or the golden mean for the use of such substances?

Is there a final query at this time?

G: Yes. Last year I was a told by another local channel that, in my past somewhere, there was what this channel's source described as a cutting, decisive, split between my mother and I. I don't know how that operates or works or when it happened but the information seemed to resonate with me because, at some point in my life, I feel like there was a distance put between my mother and that I've never been able to breach. So many times when I am talking with her I can't help but feel an irritation and intolerance about who she is and I honestly have no clue where it's coming from. Why would I feel that way? Could you speak to this at all, Q'uo? And, thank you for your time spent with me today.

We are those of Q'uo, and are aware of your query, my brother. We see no harm in saying that this split was made with your mother as well as your father, but certainly more so with your mother, before birth and is part and parcel of this initial decision that you made to distance yourself from those whose nature was disharmonious. The weakness that was perceived by the infant, G, is no longer applicable to the one known as G at this time. However, as we said earlier, this early decision has never been rescinded and it shall be the work of some time for this entity to get to the depth of being at which this separation was chosen.

We thank the one known as G for his work, his love, and his calling upon us. It has been our distinct pleasure to be with each of you and to work with these questions. Our hearts go out to each of you and your poignant and never-ending efforts to be. There are many challenges to uncover being, many straws in the wind, many discouragements, and many trials. We commend each of you for your courage, your persistence, and your love. You are beautiful beings and we celebrate you. We hope we may help you to bloom. You are doing a beautiful job. We are with you.

We leave you in the love and in the light of the one infinite Creator. We are those known to you as the principle of Q'uo. Adonai. Adonai. ✣

L/L Research

L/L Research is a subsidiary of Rock Creek Research & Development Laboratories, Inc.

P.O. Box 5195
Louisville, KY 40255-0195

www.llresearch.org

Rock Creek is a non-profit corporation dedicated to discovering and sharing information which may aid in the spiritual evolution of humankind.

ABOUT THE CONTENTS OF THIS TRANSCRIPT: This telepathic channeling has been taken from transcriptions of the weekly study and meditation meetings of the Rock Creek Research & Development Laboratories and L/L Research. It is offered in the hope that it may be useful to you. As the Confederation entities always make a point of saying, please use your discrimination and judgment in assessing this material. If something rings true to you, fine. If something does not resonate, please leave it behind, for neither we nor those of the Confederation would wish to be a stumbling block for any.

© 2009 L/L Research

Sunday Meditation
September 5, 2004

Group question: We've talked a lot today about change: physical changes in our circumstances, moving to new residences, emotional changes, finding out a lot more about our deeper selves, spiritual changes, and learning to experience the world around us in new ways on new levels. We know that the Earth is going through a lot of change, also, and as beings on a path of service, we would like to know how best we can serve Earth as she's going through her change.

(Carla channeling)

We are those of the principle known to you as Q'uo, and we greet you in the love and in the light of the one infinite Creator, in Whose service we come to you this day. It is a great privilege to be called to your circle and we thank you so much for this privilege, and for the beauty of your souls as they sit in meditation. Truly you create a beautiful tabernacle made of your light, your seeking, and your hope for the truth. We are so happy to share our service with you, which is to share our thoughts. It is for this reason that we are in contact with instruments such as this one and we do hope to be able to offer opinions that may have some benefit in your own process. But in order for us to have the freedom to share these opinions we would ask that you carefully guard the gateway of your own perception and do not allow any of our thoughts to enter those gates. They need to pass the most careful discrimination of your own senses. Listen for resonance. When you feel that resonance in those thoughts that we share, then we welcome your working with those thoughts as may please you. Please, if there is no resonance there, if it has no feeling of being a personal memory that has somehow been reawakened, then please pass by those things that we say, for they are not yours and miss their mark and need to be left behind without a second thought. If you will all agree to do this mentally, then we will be free to speak with you without infringing upon your free will and your right to work as you need for your own acceleration of the process of spiritual evolution. For that is indeed what you are about this day.

Are you choosing to move a little bit faster along that infinite line that moves from the Creator to the Creator; from the Alpha of the beginning of this octave of creation to its end? All comes from that great potential that is the infinite Creator at rest. It all moves eventually back into the rest and the joy of ultimate unity. In between there are worlds and worlds to explore and the self is the Creator in all of those distorted ways of viewing the segmented or fractured creation. One falls through illusion, after illusion, after illusion to come to this precious moment, this illusion, this time together, this learning crux. As the one known as T. S. Eliot says, this "still point, where the dance is."[122]

---
[122] From Eliot's "Four Quartets":

Except for the point, the still point,
There would be no dance, and there is only the dance.

You ask this day concerning how each of you may be of service to the Earth as it moves through its own changes, its own transformation, its own new life. For indeed there is a birth occurring in the world, in the Earth, and in each soul that walks this Earth at this time. The very life that you live is a transformation. It is nothing more nor less than that, whether or not you choose to cooperate with this transformative process that shall occur, for it is the very warp and woof of the tapestry of your life. It is your reason for being here. You came to learn as well as to serve, or perhaps we should put it the other way around, you came to serve but also to learn. It is impossible to look at one without looking at the other. They are like the x-axis and the y-axis of the grid upon which your tapestry is sewn. Stitch by stitch, color by color, and texture by texture, this is your life and you do have the power to create that life.

This is at the heart of your question, for it is what the Earth itself is doing. It is creating new life. It is creating from its womb, from that womb of space and time and process, that inevitable transformation that comes when one cycle ends and another begins. This is an appropriate and a just process. It is going remarkably well considering the difficulties with which your planet has been dealing in terms of the harmony of its peoples and what that is doing to the harmony of this process of birthing through which your Earth is going. Quickly examine the conversation, as it went about your circle this day, [for] the kind of challenges and new events that are occurring in the lives of each within this circle. These are not simple changes, nor are they all on one level. There are multiple levels and great subtleties and complexities in each of these patterns, as you are exploring, as this instrument is very fond of asking, who you are and why you are here.

These two questions are questions that she has asked several people recently in working through mutually discussed issues and certainly it is a double question that she prays about in her own process each and every day, asking for focus, asking for the guidance of spirit on who she is and why she is here. For these things do not occur in a sequential process and then become finished. These are not questions you can finish answering within the confines of your present incarnation. The changes, the transformations, will continue. Certainly not relentlessly, moment by moment, but cyclically, so that there will be seasons of starting new seeds, seasons of fertilizing them and growing them, seasons of enjoying the abundance of full summer and watching the blooming and amazing growth and then seasons of reaping, harvesting and separating the wheat from the chaff. There are also those very difficult seasons of emotional, inner winter, when waiting and patience are the watchwords and where the pattern is not yet clear. And all these seasons are those that will occur not in any tidy order but certainly in cycles that vary depending upon how open each entity is to change and how skilled each entity is in discerning pattern from noise and organization from chaos.

Much of the seeming richness of detail in most change is not pattern but noise. It often does not add to the process to enumerate, detail by detail by detail, the outward appearance of a process of change through which one is moving. Often it is a more skillful approach to rest and sit with the apparent chaos of a new situation, not asking at all for order but being willing to sit in that winter's patience with that which has not yet manifested, with those patterns which have not yet come clear. There is no rush. There is no hurry. There is plenty of time, for change can happen in an instant, in a heartbeat, in a moment's time, but it is waiting for that moment that takes the skill and the patience. Those moments will burst upon you and realization will occur. Suddenly you will begin to see into the kingdom of the present moment in a way that you were not previously able to do. It cannot be coaxed forward. It cannot be produced on demand. It only comes when there is a surrender to that process, a surrender that says, "I don't care how long this process takes. In for a penny, in for a pound. I am here. I feel this is the right place for me to be and I am content to sit here with this for the rest of my life, if that is what it takes for this pattern to resolve." There is tremendous love and faith in that surrender and there is courage in the ability to persevere, in the waiting, in the asking, and in the knowing, by faith alone, that meanwhile, despite all apparent difficulties, all truly is well.

Your Earth, left to itself, would be fine. It would be going through this process with ease and rhythm. And indeed, the heart of the Earth is healthy and is attempting to do so, to follow its nature, to follow the signals of time and space and its own process. It is having difficulties because of generation upon generation and empire upon empire which holds the value of fear, possession, aggression, conquering and the willingness to pursue ends regardless of the means for the sake of result. These disharmonies have produced a tremendous burden among the peoples of the Earth who have experienced fear and anger and all of the harvest of a warlike and predatory culture.

From the beginnings of your recorded history, millennium upon millennium, your peoples have seemingly deepened their bias towards hasty and aggressive solutions to the differences of opinion betwixt those who were created as brothers and sisters of one flesh, one blood, one family. This has translated itself into the Earth itself as an increasing imbalance that generates a good deal of subterranean heat in the planet and creates an increasingly unbalanced energy situation which results in extreme violences of nature such as the hurricanes that you now are experiencing and the volcanoes which are erupting on your planet's surface at this time. As long as there is pain inflicted, [such as that inflicted] upon innocent school children, as has happened recently in your Chechnya, these energies will keep driving themselves deeper into the Earth and tending to constrict and make difficult the labor pains of Gaia, Mother Earth.

When groups such as nations and terrorists groups are in the news and washing through the media-driven culture of a great portion of the global surface, it may seem relatively improbable that individuals or small groups of people could make a difference in this picture. And yet we assure you that groups such as your own have long made a difference in this developing picture. It is not a new thing for groups to come together in order to generate unconditional love. The history of religions is rife with examples of groups who have been inspired so to get together and yet in many, many cases these groups have been co-opted by less than the highest and best interests of those groups of people. The energies of elitism and exclusion and divisions have crept into the unconditional love and compromised the light coming from these groups. Yet, somehow, in spite of all the resistance of an increasingly unloving surface culture, from the very heart and soul of each human there stems its divine nature.

The very nature of each of you is love. You are made of it. When there is a lack of that on the surface, you crave it, you hunger for it, you yearn for it and you know, somehow, that it is there. In the darkest prison, in the darkest night, in the deepest dark night of the soul, the spark of hope cannot be stamped out because your very heart is a lighthouse and it will relight if you allow it the slightest bit of silence, the tiniest room to be who it is. How much time have you spent today simply allowing yourself to be? Do you realize that this bare allowance of the self to be is that food which the mother of your flesh needs from you? It is being, it cannot help wearing its heart on its sleeve. That heart of nature has been abused but it beats strongly. And it must be itself. It has no choice. It exists without illusion and though it is deeply wounded and greatly and increasingly suspicious of that human energy which wishes to help; nevertheless, it cannot help reacting to, responding to, authentic being.

It sees you as you really are, not as a collection of bones and flesh and muscle and gristle; not as a collection of words and poses and attitudes, but as that texture and color and form, that sense in which you are a living flower or a work of art, an essence, an aroma in the nose of the Creator. You do not know how sweet you are, how beautifully your odor mingles with the truth of the odors of each other entity within this room to create a bouquet that we cannot describe in its beauty. Each of you shines like the gem that you are.

How can you know this when you are in the midst of the illusion in which you cannot see the gems of your soul or your heart but can only see the vainglory of flesh, the markers of eyes and nose and mouth and form. That which you see about you is, quite specifically, that which is the least real. That which you cannot grasp, cannot know, that which is lost in mystery, is the realest thing about you. What a backwards world it is for one who wishes to pin everything down! And yet your incarnation here is not about pinning things down. Your incarnation here is about learning to dance, learning to sing, learning to move in the rhythms that have no words but that move in harmony with every living thing in your world, starting with the air, the earth, the fire, and the water, moving through every created plant and animal, through yourselves and through those beings that exist without form that are those within the inner planes that are also part of the creation.

It is one great dance and one great song. You have heard of the music of the spheres. This is not a myth. This is the way things are in the world of what this instrument would call time/space, which coexists with and interpenetrates the consensus-reality illusion that you now enjoy. For each thing that you see, there are a million things that are interpenetrating that illusion that have more and more metaphysical substance. And you are not without the ability to begin to swim in and know these waters of spirit. You have within you great depths of ability to penetrate illusion and to begin to pick up the essence and the heart of the unseen mysteries that you seek. For you are an embodiment of these mysteries. You carry within you, as in a hologram, the one infinite Creator.

Certainly, that essence is well protected. There are gates through which one must pass in order to become more deeply and truly aware of the essence of self and of the increasing revelation of the Creator within. And there are lions that guard the gates to the temple that is your inner self. And occasionally you will be challenged. This is part of the process of transformation. It is a necessity for entities who are moving through transformation to have markers for these changes. And so when there is an initiation, so called, these initiations will have a certain form and symbols will come to you such as the hawks and the eagles of which you were speaking earlier. The symbols may be beast or bird or plant or words, street signs or chance-heard snatches of conversation that simply connect into your process synchronistically. It is impossible to know ahead of time what these markers of transformation will be. But when they come to you, note them and realize that you are on the right track. These processes are moving forward and no matter how dislocated you may feel in these movements that some times are swift, yet your feet are on the right track and you are moving well, and with honor and dignity.

When you come to those moments in which you are being yourself, those moments when you are tabernacling within your own sacred space, know that each moment you spend there is a direct and immediate help to the planet which is your mother in terms of your flesh and bone. The more that you can dwell in this awareness, the more your very being will be of service to Gaia. More than that, when you rise from your contemplation, meditation or whatever form of silence you have chosen as your own frame for being, we encourage you to lean into carrying that light with you as you go about the work of the day, whatever that may be.

This instrument was talking earlier about how she is able to feel Earth energy and has been aware of the Earth from her earliest memory. Becoming more and more aware of how Earth energy feels is a very helpful thing for the Earth as well as for you. That Earth energy is, mechanically speaking, that medium through which the love and the light of the one infinite Creator moves through the soles of your feet up into your body. It rushes up from the soles of the feet right into the red ray and directly from there, sequentially, through each chakra of the energy body. And when you are functioning well as an energy body, your chakras are balanced and opened. Full energy is moving through into the heart, and that heart is staying open no matter what hits it, so that the output, no matter how difficult your catalyst may be, is an output of love, joy and peace.

This is the energy that is coming into your physical vehicle and into your emotional and mental and spiritual vehicles as well. You can shape the way that you receive the catalyst that comes to you by how you choose to work with the energy body in responding to that catalyst. It is the most sensible and understandable thing in the world to react to incoming perceptions of anger and insult and difficulty by constricting and contracting the energy of the self in defensive and protective ways. Oftentimes, habits of defense and protection begin very early in one's incarnation as a response to the disharmonious experiences within the the birth family. That birth family may well have been chosen partially because of the disharmony within its system, for this sets up the arena for a lesson of incarnational level, whether it be patience, the learning to love without expectation of return, or any of the other incarnational lessons with which each of you may be working this time around, shall we say.

As habits begun early are repeated, the shell around them may harden so that it is seemingly at first very difficult to interrupt the habitual contraction around fear. There is no way to eliminate fear, for the incoming catalyst of any entity, no matter how well protected by wealth, circumstance or privilege, will contain those situations which produce fear. Fear is inevitable. The occasion for fear, shall we say, is inevitable. However, those who have spoken words of inspiration throughout the ages have shown over and over again that the reaction to conditions which would suggest fear need not be fearful. Such reactions can be loving under the most brutal circumstances, whether they be Holocaust, imprisonment, or any other oppressiveness or adversity. Prison cannot bind the free spirit. Prison is only a place. The spirit is a citizen of eternity and it can call from its larger self that knowledge of freedom and light and rightness that the world cannot know.

This willingness to explore the letting go of fear is a tremendous key in this process of transformation. What the Earth is going through is precisely what each of you is going through on a much smaller scale. For the Earth, a process taking approximately 76,000 of your years is coming to an end. The cosmic clock, shall we say, is striking the hour. And indeed a new hour has begun upon your planet at this time. It is having difficulty establishing itself. The labor is long and difficult. But it is going much better than expected because, at what this instrument would call the "grass roots" level, person by person, household by household, community by community, a choice is being made to embrace love and to practice a life that shines that love forth as best as those people, families and groups can muster the wisdom and the strength to allow.

Indeed, it is more a matter of allowing the self to cooperate with the energies about it than to frame this process as reaching for new things. The new things are here, the new things are a program all about you. It is a matter of allowing those new things to sift in through the cracks and crannies of the outer, still very strong, consensus reality of your old Earth, that which this instrument tends to call the "third-density Earth." The fourth-density Earth is at least as real, in the unseen or inner planes, as third density and it is getting stronger all the time. Entities have talked a good deal about the increasing movements, the literal movements of household and so forth, and it is understandable that every single thing in one's life would come up at this time to be questioned and perhaps to be changed. For it is, in microcosm, that which is occurring to the Earth.

And you are a part of that system, much more inextricably and organically than you realize. You are a crop that the Earth has produced, as much as the roses, the elms, the birds or the animals. Your process of spiritual evolution is a crop that you have at this time the chance to fertilize and encourage and, most of all, to allow. When you can open your heart and let go of the mental noise that is surrounding the details of your life, you are allowing the sunshine and the rain to come in and help your growth. When you can shut down, for a bit of time, the endless conversations that take place between the cast of thousands that live within that kingdom between your ears and just rest in the kingdom of the creation instead of that spiky, back-and-forth energy of what this instrument would call the monkey mind, there comes into being that wonderful kingdom that is the creation. And it is a land of harmony that is in infinite movement, swaying and dancing and singing its song. The more authentically you can sing your song, the more freely you can feel your energies dancing with the energies of all those about you and the Earth itself, the closer that you are to being that being that you came to be. You did not come here to find answers, you came here to participate in the dance, to be yourself, and as you dance and sing, to find ever more balanced ways to serve and to learn.

We thank you for asking this question and wish to say that our hearts are full of gratitude for the courage that you have as entities gazing upon a world that seemingly makes little sense at this time. Thank you for seeking ways to love and to serve the one infinite Creator, that wonderful entity which you call the Earth or Gaia, and each other as souls who have embarked together upon this journey around the sun in the spaceship of Earth, shall we say. It is well done of you to come to this moment and to ask for truth. Know that day by day, and realization by realization, you shall express more truth than you can ever know. For it shall come through you as light and beauty and love. Let those things roll through and bless them as they go, knowing that you shall make many mistakes but that you can never make a mistake if you are attempting to allow the love and the light of the one infinite Creator to flow through you unhindered by fear and blessed by your intention.

We are with you in attempting to share our love and our light and you give us great joy as we are able to offer our service to you, which is to share our very humble and imperfect thoughts. We would ask at this point if there are any queries that come out of this initial discussion or any queries at all. Is there a query at this time?

J: Hi, Q'uo. I know how we've talked about wants and desires as opposed to authentic need. I felt like I had all these wants and desires, and I got to experience that[123] and two weeks later I kind of feel empty. I guess I'd just like for you to speak about the difference. Is desire an empty hole that just can't be filled, compared to authentic need?

We are those of Q'uo, and are aware of your query, my sister. We say hello to you, the one known as J, for it is our great pleasure to touch into your energy.

The query that you ask is a subtle one and there is not a simple answer, for desire is not a fixed value. Desire is a custom-designed value. A desire can come from many different levels of being. There are natural desires that stem from the kind of physical vehicle which you now enjoy. The instincts of the physical body are perfectly natural and perfectly understandable. The desire for the life itself, the desire for survival, the desire for sexual expression: these things are at the very heart of the driving power of incarnation. Consequently it cannot be said in any way that those instinctual desires, including the sexual desires, are lesser than any other level of desire. And yet certainly the instinctual desires are not the ending of desire at all but the beginning, that which allows the light to proceed and sets the stage for much more subtle and complex forms of desire to arise. In a way, there is no moment without desire. It cannot be gotten rid of because the very physical vehicle that you enjoy has a constant desire to survive and every breath that you take is as the result of a desire for a continuation of that existence. Every pulse of the heart is an affirmative vote for [the] desire to live. It is impossible, in this body that you enjoy, that pulses and breathes and has many cycles of natural need, to avoid desire. The mind of your body, not even looking into that spiritual organ which is the consciousness, is in a constant state of desire. It is in a constant state of looking for the next thing and thinking about the last thing. It is in constant motion. The spiritual vehicle, as well, while not restless and desiring in that way, is resting in a steady heartbeat of creative and, what this instrument would call, godly, sacred desire to progress in its journey back towards its source and the ceasing of motion. You dwell in a sea which can be described as desire. It is the choice of what you desire and the level at which you desire that crafts the difference between empty and fulfilling, spiritually healthy, creative desire.

If one looks, for instance, at the tangle of discussion that you have shared with the one known as C concerning various aspects of this question, it can be seen that, in looking at freeing the red-ray energy and freeing that fundamental, healthy flow of the creative energy into the energy body, there is certainly a place for opening up those areas of that energy which were restricted by past abuse and difficulty with sexual expression. And yet, if it stops at the opening of that energy without moving into questions of where this opened energy might go, how it might be furthered, where it goes next in the energy body and how that works, then it shall be empty. For repetition of sheer red-ray desire and satisfaction of that desire are indeed an endless dropping of energy into a hole. Because that energy is a natural function and needs to be expressed again and again, it cannot be expressed once and then put to rest, although entities have found it helpful to do so under specialized conditions, where they were using the restraint from an open expression of sexuality as a marker for cleansing, purifying and enhancing the spiritual growth of the whole organism that is your mind, body and spirit.

When the energy stops at body work then the mind and the spirit have not yet been reckoned with. And the mind and the spirit also have great hopes and desires for being themselves. The more you work with moving through the chakra system, the more you see that this open red-ray energy moves into the opening of the orange-ray energy, which then moves into the opening of the yellow-ray energy, so that the energy moving up into the heart is whole and has not been hindered by fear at any of these three lower places. When energy is able to move up into the heart in full strength, then the whole world of higher chakra work begins to open up. It is very wise of the one known as J and the one known as T to investigate the opening up of red-ray sexuality, because it is the foundation for so much more sacred work. Yet the hunger remains for an expression that is sacred, an expression that has deeper meaning and higher purpose. There is that opening of the heart and that realization that each entity whom one meets is the Creator. There is then the opening of the heart to serving the Creator in each entity and most of all in one's mate, so that it comes full circle back to the sacredness of red ray, seen in the fullness

---

[123] J had attended a workshop whose purpose was to free the female orgasm.

of a system of living out that sacredness that is felt within the heart.

When desire has been disciplined and focused, it is the most powerful force in creation. It is that energy that moves the mountain. It is that energy that creates miracles, and it becomes more and more closely allied with those mysterious words of "faith" and "will." A great deal of time has been spent, in each of your incarnations, on trying to determine what it is that you seek, who it is that you are, what it is that you truly desire. These are wonderful energies; these are defining energies for you; these are key questions. And we greatly encourage this whole line of discussion and exploration.

May we answer you further, my sister?

J: Wow, that was amazing. Thank you, Q'uo. It's good to have you back.

My sister, it is good to have you back, also. Is there a further query at this time?

J: Not from me.

T1: I have a question, Q'uo. This is T. I think I might have got it, about some things you just said, and I guess, as far as the week that I had in California, where I was a little hung up is, they taught that not one person can sustain you sexually, therefore, monogamy was not of importance. And I have an issue with that, I don't know if that's right or wrong.

We are those of Q'uo, and are aware of your query, my sister. We shall attempt to answer, but this particular query lies very close to the surface of your own process and so there is a limit to that which we can say without breaking the trust that you give us not to infringe upon your own free will.

We give this instrument the image of a necklace of many jewels. Such is the experience of one who opens herself to many lovers. Each gem is lovely and beautiful of its own kind and the variety is dazzling and certainly most invigorating when one has been constricted by the moral fear and torpor of an unthinking, unquestioning and blind obedience to some moral code, these restraints and constraints that are placed from without have no value to the spiritual growth of an individual.

Consider, then, the beauty of a single, perfect stone that is hung upon a beautiful golden chain. It is not a blend of colors. It does not have that variety. It has been chosen because, out of all of the jewels that are possible to be had, this one gem has touched the heart, enlivened the soul, opened the heart to the possibilities of devotion, fidelity and the value of leaving behind the world of manyness and exploring the world of absolute value.

How dangerous it may seem to commit the self to one shining gem. It may indeed be a costly choice. It may well be that that one gem does not touch all of the possible ramifications of beauty that are possible to be recorded and appreciated by that incredibly sensitive instrument that is you as a person, as a mind/body/spirit complex, as the one known as Carla tends to call it. And yet, that choice opens the door to a higher way, a way which can be endlessly refined. It is difficult to be of service to a whole necklace full of entities, for each has its beauty, its flaws, its ways of relating, and its ways of resisting. Each is a conundrum, a mystery, with which one can only offer one's own conundrum, one's own mystery. Each, in that varied and beautiful necklace, could take up all of your attention and you would not be bored, nor would you stop learning. Yet, you have not the time to investigate deeply the many gems of this wonderful necklace. And so you look at the beautiful colors and you see the variety. And you enjoy this particular piece of jewelry that you have chosen as a way in which you honor and love the one infinite Creator. Yet there is a restlessness there, because there is not the ability to dive deep into the waters of another human soul. There is not the possibility of exploring how one may be devoted to the soul and the heart of another, not to the appearance, or the surface behavior. Those things will often challenge and puzzle any entity attempting to love. But they are those things that allow one to do deep work and to take the time to move more and more deeply into that house of mirrors that is the relationship between the self and the other self.

It is a question of moving horizontally and learning a little bit about a lot or moving vertically, going high, going deep, and learning in a different away about the self and about how to serve. Neither way is incorrect. Both ways are full of learning. It is a choice as to how you wish to express your own being and to direct your own considerable energies.

T1: Thank you.

Is there another query at this time?

T2: Q'uo, it's wonderful to hear your voice again. I'd just like to ask if there are any suggestions or advice that you can offer me in terms of how I can enhance my meditations, my connection and communication with my higher self, and improve inspiration in daily life?

We are those of Q'uo, and are aware of your query, my brother. Again, we do not wish to interfere with the learn/teaching process of the one known as T2 but we believe that we may suggest just one thing and that would be that, as the one known as T2 has such great sensitivity to sound and more specifically to the many sounds of water, that this entity find ways to link times of silence and the sensual experience of listening to water and experiencing water, whether that would be a walk along the water, a seat beside a splashing pond, or simply the soundtrack of the water that the one known as T2 might choose to use in times of silence. This particular element is very helpful to the one known as T2, as we are only confirming to one who has already created music in the key of water![124] Consequently, we simply encourage the one known as TM to continue in linking himself with that wonderful element and the naiads that dance about any expression of that magical substance which is water.

May we answer you further?

T2: No, thank you very much, Q'uo.

Oh, we thank you too, my brother. We are those of Q'uo, and would ask for a final query at this time if there is one.

T2: Since no one else has a question, is there any comment or information you might suggest for the one known as F?

We are those of Q'uo, and are aware of your query, my brother. And we find that there is little that we may say to the one known as F at this time except that all is well. It is sometimes, as this instrument was saying earlier in an email to a friend, seemingly silly to say that all is well, to say that it's okay, or it's all right. This, this instrument was saying, is what people say and yet, how intelligent is it to look at something that is causing difficulty and say, "It's okay." And we would say that patterns often do not look okay for periods of time and yet energies are in motion that shall become a good pattern, a helpful pattern, and a pattern in which the one known as F may thrive. And we simply would offer her this comfort if it will create within the one known as F any feeling of rest and peace.

We thank this instrument and this group for this opportunity and the beauty of these moments together. We leave each of you in the love and in the light of the one infinite Creator. We are known to you as the principle of Q'uo. Adonai. Adonai. ✻

---

[124] T2 recently produced a CD of original music entitled "Crystal Waters; Compositions Inspired by the Motion of Water."

Sunday Meditation
September 19, 2004

Group question: Today, Q'uo, our question has to do with how we might be able to determine, perhaps even define, our spiritual path through our daily round of activities. As we're immersed in all the things that we do during our regular days, it's so easy to get lost in the details and the ups and downs. Could you give us some little way or a shorthand way of reminding ourselves who we are and what we're doing, of how to find our way through the maze and to make a spiritual sense of it all?

(Carla channeling)

We are those of the principle known to you as Q'uo, and we greet you in the love and in the light of the one infinite Creator, in Whose service we come to you this day. It is a great privilege to be called to your circle of seeking and we thank each of you who has taken the time and the energy to seek the truth at this time. The beauty of your souls as you tabernacle together in silence and in unity of spirit is a beautiful, wonderful play of colors as your energies combine and swirl together to form a literal tabernacle of light. It is most inspiring to us. Your hearts and your souls express most beautifully the challenge of the tempering furnace and the extreme beauty of the subtle colors that are brought about by the interplay of tempering influences in that furnace of catalyst and experience.

You create a unique thing when you come together in groups such as this—a point of light that cannot be expressed in any physical sense, but which is an event and an occasion for rejoicing in the unseen planes, or as this instrument would call them, the inner planes. Such events as you as a group choosing to come together are as locations in time/space and beacons of light that strengthen the light of the whole of those unseen planes within your Earth energy. Thank you, for this expression of seeking and for the beauty of it. It inspires us greatly.

As always, we would ask each of you to listen carefully to those thoughts that we share, realizing that we make many mistakes. Please keep those thoughts that you find useful and discard the rest. This will enable us to share our thoughts freely without being concerned that you might see us as authority figures and try to follow thoughts that simply were not your own. If thoughts do not resonate to you then please leave them aside without a second thought. We thank you for this care.

You have asked this day concerning how to wend your path through the miasma of details and the seeming chaos of manyness that you are offered each day as you awaken and open your eyes to the kaleidoscope of events that will unfold. As you rise from the bed perhaps you cannot imagine what the day will bring. Certainly if you are thoroughly sure of what the day will bring you shall be surprised, for each day has its uniqueness and any hope of a perfectly conformable daily schedule is usually lost by midmorning. Much is occurring within your physical world and the ability of each entity to communicate with each other entity in a variety of ways and mediums creates a continuing atmosphere of surprise because, at any moment, entities might call or use the internet to write email or send paper mail so that you are constantly receiving a new voice or a new e-message or a new letter which changes the details of the day—adds to them and creates a new list of things to do and perhaps, a new way of prioritizing those things that you need to do. Seldom is it possible for any of those within this circle to arise, face the day, and go through the day with every aspect of the day being that which was expected and that which does not create any requirement for discipline or for the amalgamation of change.

Indeed, it has often been noted by many in this group and in your society in general that the rate of change seems to be accelerating and therefore time itself has the illusion of seeming to accelerate. There is a feeling of becoming swept up and carried away by the torrential waves of chaos and detail that wash over each of you. In this atmosphere, it is easy to lose one's balance and to surrender to a state of mind in which the requirement is simply to survive, to do the next thing on the list, and to make it to bed time without losing one's precarious and tenuous place in all of the bewildering array of detail.

Your request was to find ways to determine and define what the path was in the midst of all these details and there is, we would be quick to state, a path for each of you. Not a regimented, strait-and-narrow, straight-line path in which there are no deviations—this is not what we intend to suggest. But there is a path of … we are challenged, looking for a word within this instrument's vocabulary for what this path would be called. If we call it a path of rightness, that suggests that there is a wrong path. If we call it a path of resonance, that immediately places an entity upon very subjective ground. Let us work with this concept of a path. The one known as Lao-Tzu created a system of philosophy which is called *The Tao* or *The Way*, the word meaning, in general, the Path.

It might be posited by this general line of thinking that one's life itself is a path. And, inevitably, that path, that lifetime, that incarnation, wends its way up and down hills and around corners, many a time. There is no such thing as a broad, straight, easy incarnation. It is often hoped by entities in the midst of incarnation that their path might be straight and easy and clear, and yet, the essential requirement of an incarnation is mystery. Mystery was built into each entity's path by the entity himself along with that guidance which was consulted before the incarnation in drawing up the various aspects of the incarnation to come. Each of you carefully chose the relationships that would challenge and befuddle you in order to point up and bring forward incarnation lessons which you wished to tackle, not because you wished to defeat yourself or to confuse yourself, but because you wished to move the balance of your energies by decisions made within the incarnation.

Before the incarnation, you were able to have a good overview of the incarnation to come and of yourself as a soul entity. You looked at that entity that you are and you asked yourself, where you would like to go? What path that you would like to take from the beginning to the end of that very brief period of incarnation that you are looking at? Perhaps you felt that you had an overbalance of love and needed to learn wisdom; perhaps you felt that you had an overbalance of wisdom and needed to bring that balance between wisdom and love back more towards the true center in which love is informed by wisdom and wisdom is informed by love. We cannot define for you the basic direction of that path; each entity's path is unique. Each entity, however, has in common that it is seeking an improved, more balanced polarity as it approaches that great testing ground of graduation from third density to existence in fourth density. Each entity hopes that this incarnation will be the final incarnation within third density. Consequently, the concept of polarity is all-important in understanding how the mysteries of the path make themselves known to you.

In doing third-density work where you are attempting to improve your service-to-others polarity, you are always working against resistance. You are working against a potential difference. You are standing upon that which you envision as the desired ideal or the desired balance and you are pushing against the resistance to that change that is necessary in order to increase the polarity. Consequently, there must be the hidden corners, the blind defiles,[125] the ups and downs of a surprising and adventurous lifetime, in order for that deeper entity that you are to be constantly nudged towards

---

[125] A defile is a "narrow gorge or pass that restricts lateral movement, as of troops."

awakening to the deeper purposes, the deeper desires, that lie beneath the easy, soft and sweet of surface emotions. How easy it is, my friends, to move from the delight of a good conversation to the irritation of a bad conversation, and so forth. And how difficult it is sometimes to see through the surface details to the issues that are half-hidden and half-revealed by surface emotions, surface occasion, and surface reaction. Yet those surface expressions are as the foam upon the top of the waters. They have no substance. They have no longevity. They have no reality. Yet because they recur with such steady regularity over the course of the waves of the day, it is easy to become fixated upon watching them and surfing in them, to the exclusion of doing that work which deepens the requirements upon the self; which pulls the self into the more mysterious precincts of the deeper waters of the path.

So it is, indeed, a very good question that you ask in terms of how to find little ways to jog the memory, to create for the self a self-sustaining system of little alarm clocks that reawaken the memory of who you are and why you are here. This instrument was conversing with the one known as J the other day concerning football and in particular the comment of a football analyst that pressure is needed sometimes to change coal into the diamond that sparks the light.[126] The pressures of daily life are not random or unexpected. They are blessed and very much expected and anticipated, not by the conscious self but by the entity that you are beneath the conscious mind. For your consciousness is connected with all of eternity and is infinite, being part of the creative principle. As part of that creative principle, you have a far different schedule or calendar for your life than you as an egoic being with a personality shell might create from day to day. And these mysterious and winding ways of the spirit are very much planned upon and greeted with great thanksgiving and gratitude.

To move into that portion of the self where these things are true, then, is the challenge. And this instrument was saying to the one known as J that indeed it is interesting to reflect upon the difference between coal and the diamond in terms of emotions. For if the reaction of emotional nature to incoming catalyst is that of the coal, it will have generated heat; whereas if one's reaction to the incoming catalyst has the emotive qualities of the diamond, it will reflect and refract light. One quick way to determine where you are as a person with respect to the catalyst of the day, is to evaluate your emotional set. Has it generated heat or has it generated light? Have the emotions of the self been fiery and bright and sharp? Or has it been that emotional set which is as the diamond in taking the incoming catalyst and being with it in such a way that light is refracted through you from the catalyst to express light, color, beauty and those ineffable qualities that are part of a system of color and light. As the one known as T was saying earlier, the effort that this entity is making at this time is to decrease that heat and to increase the light that is produced in the soul's response to catalyst. When the self experiences heat, that in and of itself may be a good marker for activating that alarm clock that says, "There is work that I need to do on who I am and why I am here."

It is difficult sometimes, in the midst of a heated reaction, to corral the self. The reason for this is that much of the reaction to catalyst that is expressed by an entity is the result of habit. For instance, this entity has a habit of interpreting certain kinds of statements as a rejection of the self. This interpretation is biased in the extreme and has long been realized as such by this entity. Nevertheless, this entity often finds itself in the midst of a reaction to catalyst which can be seen in an instant evaluation as being that which has generated heat rather than light, that which is a colossal metaphysical mistake. And yet, because the habit began very long ago within this instrument's incarnation and because it has never completely been eradicated, it takes any opportunity in which it is given free rein, not simply to play for a moment but to play from beginning to end, as if it were a tape recording that, once started, must be played through. A good deal of retraining the self in the disciplining of the personality is in identifying and then going after those triggers to those old responses, those old tapes, that are so deeply buried within the upper reaches of the subconscious mind. A habit is a beautiful thing when it is working. A habit of diet and exercise have created continued health for many and certainly habits of healthful thinking are just as excellent. But when a habit has gotten out of control and is no longer useful, it can be a persistent and irritating difficulty which is constantly nudging that soul that

---

[126] Diamonds are the same element as coal, carbon. Great pressure upon coal, through time, creates the diamond.

you are off of its path and into the side road of useless, outdated, response.

How to counter these triggers is certainly a tremendous challenge. Mechanically speaking, there are ways to interrupt such tapes, shall we say, from rolling. Identifying the trigger is very helpful. And any work that can be done in honest communication with the self on identifying these triggers and the really deep nature of these triggers, will be a good resource for any. But more than that, when the trigger has been [pulled] and one has only identified that trigger after the fact, it is still possible, through the discipline of the personality, to halt long enough to say to the self, "I am being triggered," and to stop and celebrate the fact that you have realized this and are therefore taking the first step towards the actual eradication of this deeply buried trigger. It is helpful, then, if you take additional time to laugh at the self, to give the self a hug, and to ask the self, if it had the choice of any way of meeting this particular situation, what would be the highest and the best way? If there is time then for a little more thought and contemplation on seeing the best way, on envisioning the best way, and on, perhaps, moving forward in expressing this best way, then all of that is a great asset to your seeking. It has taken time to embed this habit. It will take much more time to bring it up, see it for what it is, and allow it to fall away. It must be pulled up into the light of day. It must be appreciated, and it must be loved and accepted as part of you before it can be released. So that which you can do when you find yourself expressing heat instead of light is, if you have the luxury of time, to take that time to interrupt that sequence and to redirect it.

Let us return to consideration of the path. The Path of Lao Tzu was ever undefined. Breathing in and out was the path. Listening and talking were the path. Doing and being were the path. All things were the path. Yet the fact that there is a path in this philosophy suggests that many things are not relevant to that path. And by various stories, the teacher known as Lao Tzu would attempt to describe the way that entities could find their way upon the path. We would suggest that it is impossible to be away from the path. It is possible, certainly, to stop by the side of the path and to amuse oneself without moving forward upon the path in meadows of side interest, places to rest, places to recreate and enjoy the self, places to sleep, and places to dream. It is good sometimes to stop in one of those places upon your path. It is not a path that one must embark upon a certain amount of time each day in order to be worthy. Indeed, in some ways, it can be conceived of as a path that does not have to be trod. It simply is, and you simply are. But the desire of anyone within a time-bound incarnation is to measure things by achievement and so, inevitably, that path is modeled as a path through space and time going somewhere. Try to remember that there are aspects of your path that never go anywhere, that you are always, if you choose to, able to operate from the very center of your being, having nowhere to go, no "what" to do, no "when" to do it, but simply being as you are, existing in essence and in truth. That is the heart of your path. Who you are is the essence of that path and what you are attempting to do as you wend your way through these mysterious turnings is not to do more but to do anything that you do with more truth.

Have you experienced entities that, when you met them, were within their integrity in a tremendously powerful way? Perhaps they did not even have to speak much for you to be able to feel the power of their being. That is the power that lies within each of you and the way to find that true nature of self is in the work that you do in determining and finding and defining what that path is through your crowded and busy days.

It helps, in a way that is difficult to define, for you to have some model within yourself for what that path that you are on is, and how it goes. This entity, for instance, being a mystical Christian, tends to model her rule of life and her path on the teachings of the one known as Jesus. And like all paths, and all models of paths, this model and this path has obvious flaws. The one known as Jesus walked the path of the martyr and while the path of the martyr is to be seen, in the case of the one known as Jesus, as an appropriate and a loving path, yet still it is not obvious, from the surface of the story of the one known as Jesus, that this entity was at all responsible or conservative in walking that path that eventually led towards a cross on a hilltop near Jerusalem. As this entity stretched its arms out upon that cross, it lost all ability to serve within this density. That is the difficulty of the bias of the path of a martyr. And so this entity must constantly ask itself where the appropriate balance is between service to others and martyrdom. Others following other paths must look at the biases that are connected with that model and that path and then ask the self what the issues are as one attempts to follow the way of a hero or an avatar.

The virtue of having a model or a hero for a path is simply that it is a shortcut, if you will, an icon on the desktop that you can click on in order to see deeper into the issues that you are facing. The cliché of modern day that this instrument would use, then, is "What would Jesus do?" Or as this instrument has altered it many a time, "What would Jesus be?" Asking the self what one's hero would do or how it would be is often very instructive to one's own private communication with the self. For one is working in deep waters and the light is dim. It is not easy to see one's way when one is attempting to sort signal from noise and truth from chaos. But we would suggest, if there is that feeling for a certain hero or avatar or icon of some kind, to use that, not blindly, but asking the self, "If I were thinking as this entity, how would I see my situation?" It helps to bring one up from the morass of confusion and give one a promontory upon which to stand, from which vantage point you may see the surrounding landscape of the moment that you are facing. If one does not have a hero, a master, an avatar, an icon, then one simply must move within the self and ask the guidance of the self, "What is the highest and best part of myself going to do in this situation?" And then await that wisdom in confidence and quietness.

It is very helpful when viewing this kind of deep and subtle work within the personality shell to avail oneself on a daily basis of silence. The uses of silence are many but the chief use is simple release. There is a silence in which there is no word. There is a deeper silence in which there is no sound and there is an even deeper silence in which there are no unspoken thoughts. Each of you has these levels of silence within. It is extremely helpful to the decompression of the stress of your daily life to release the self from words, from sounds, and from your own unspoken but certainly multitudinous thoughts. If you do not, they are as the taskmasters that have taken over your precious consciousness. Certainly they must have their reign. One must deal with words each day. One dwells within a welter of sound and, even as this instrument sits within this chair she is able to hear several different sounds that are expressive of the household working: the buzzing of the sound system, the buzzing of the air purifier, the computer system, and the refrigerator, and the sound that indicates that the fans and the heating elements of the house are working. Without this network of tiny sounds, the civilization factor would cease to exist and there would be no aids to comfort. The food would spoil, the house would become chilly or heated depending upon the weather, and so forth. So all of these subliminally heard tones are useful and helpful and certainly not of negative value. Yet, taken all together, they create a body tension that can not be ignored. It is a wonderful thing, my friends, to lift oneself away from civilization, from words, from sounds, and from your unspoken thoughts as well. If you are able to do this by gazing at a candle in meditation of the Eastern type, we encourage it. If your way is prayer and meditation in a more Christian sense, we encourage it. If your way is solitary walks in nature, we encourage them.

What we encourage is that you take the time for yourself, to give yourself the healing balm of silence. How blessed a thing that is. It is so alien to your culture that, in many cases, entities are left feeling very uncomfortable if there is true silence. And they will deliberately turn on the television, or the radio, or the sound system to banish that silence and to bring in the more desired energies of song or speech or drama. And in their place these are good things. But we do encourage the discipline that keeps the self away from distraction, even if it just be for five or ten minutes in a day. We would recommend, certainly, a period of fifteen minutes to a half an hour within each day. And if possible, we would recommend more than one of those places in the day in which spirit and that still, small voice of spirit might actually be able to bloom and to give unto your soul those silent words that are more precious than any sound or word could ever be.

This instrument informs us that we need at this time to open the meeting to other questions. We thank you for this wonderful question and the fun that we had in working on it and would ask at this time if there are any further queries?

S: *(Inaudible)* correct physical difficulties, could you elaborate or expound on the causes, perhaps the cures behind them?

We are those of Q'uo, and are aware of your query, my brother. The amount that we may say upon this subject, as you may understand, is quite limited for we do not wish to remove any learn/teaching opportunities for this entity. We may say that a goodly portion of this entity's experiences at this time have to do not with any particular present catalyst that is incoming but rather have to do with this entity's position within incarnation in that this entity has moved into the seventh decade of its incarnational age and is experiencing those systems within the body that are experiencing age and a less robust or youthful configuration and therefore are more open to damage.

The sources of stress within this instrument's incarnation, as the one known as N pointed out, have certainly been many and that stress is that which has been eagerly and thankfully embraced. This creates an atmosphere in which incoming catalyst has a depth and a sharpness which this instrument would call instant karma, and again this instrument has embraced the quickening and acceleration of these energies. To put it in short words, this instrument has agreed to play hardball and is therefore experiencing each and every part of the shadow side of its nature in ways that are much clearer than in some incarnational patterns. The challenge for this entity, as always, is that finding of the path that is in balance so that there is not an over-embracing of energies that would lead to martyrdom; nor is there an under-embracing of energies which would lead to slowing that acceleration of spiritual evolution that this instrument is most eager to accomplish.

The way towards healing is framed in thankfulness, gratitude and peace. And this is true not only of this instrument but is in general the attitude that most efficiently embraces and most skillfully makes use of the catalyst of the moment.

May we answer you further, my brother?

S: I think that's plenty for her to consider, thank you. Another question I had. If [the Q'uo] work with crystals, I gave one that I had to Carla to hold. I'm just curious if you can tune into its energy and tell me [what] its purpose is with Carla and with itself?

We are those of Q'uo, and aware of your query, my brother. As we do indeed tune into this entity we find that we are not able to work with this information without infringing upon the free will of those involved. May we answer you further, my brother?

S: Hmm, that's interesting then, surprising, but interesting. I have none at this time, thanks.

We thank you, my brother, and are most pleased to spend a brief moment of your physical space/time enjoying your presence. It is always a joy to greet you in person, my brother.

S: I'm curious, since the last time I was here, what do you see from your perspective, from your side, of how I've changed?

We are those of Q'uo, and are aware of your query, my brother. We find that the one known as S has somewhat matured in that there is a lessening of naiveté with no corresponding aggregation of cynicism. We find that, in greeting change, the maturing or evolving entity will accept becoming more complex whereas the entity that is attempting to avoid the maturation process will attempt to retain simplicity and in the resulting conflicts find itself becoming more and more bitter. It is that for which we would offer congratulations to the one known as S, that this entity has worked to deepen and to allow complexity within the self without the corresponding tendency towards bitterness.

May we answer you further, my brother?

S: No, I appreciate that thought and for what it's worth, for all that I've been and am becoming, I do want to express my love and gratitude because you are and have been a part of that and I just give you my love and appreciation.

We are those of Q'uo, and, my brother, we return your sentiments most heartily.

Is there a further query at this time?

S: Not from me.

R: I have a question, Q'uo, concerning a catalyst expressed in the physical body as a cancer. I remember reading some explanation of it in the *Law of One* book. I wanted to ask whether this cancer is in all cases the result of unprocessed catalyst and anger that expresses in the physical body as a growth of cells?

We are those of Q'uo, and are aware of your query, my brother. The query itself is difficult to get hold of because there are so many different kinds of anger. Some of them are obvious, some of them are very difficult to pin down and are almost a portion of the personality shell itself rather than being connected to certain situations or catalyst.

R: Can I refocus the query?

We are those of Q'uo, and would be delighted for you to do so, my brother.

R: Let's speak about an incarnation where an entity is offered catalyst of various kinds and finds an anger. I cannot describe the anger in more detail because it is a query that is partly hypothetical, but would it be correct to say that the cancer would be the result of unprocessed anger within that one's incarnation, discounting the effects of the previous one?

We are those of Q'uo, and are aware of your query, my brother. That query is easier to answer and we thank you for the change. That which you call disease, of which cancer is a kind, is literally uneasiness within the physical body. It is dis-ease. It is a moving away from the stasis of perfect balance in the body system. At heart, such disease is only partially physical. A large part of disease resides within the mind and the perceptions of that mind. When entities perceive disharmony in a way that is telling, it makes a mark upon the mind. That perception creates an actual change in each cell of the body. It creates an atmosphere in which any incoming agent of disease will be recognized more readily and grabbed onto by each cell of the body more readily. Conversely, when an entity begins to perceive that apparent disharmony has no reality and is therefore able to begin to change its perceptions, that lack of triggering of the perception of disharmony again communicates itself to every cell of the body and therefore when the agent of disease sends its signal to each cell the antennas of that cell do not reach out and grab the catalyst of disharmony because it perceives that there is no disharmony. Therefore, when one is working to lessen the impact of a perceived disease within the body, a part of the working has to do with changing the perceptions that gave rise to a feeling of disharmony.

May we answer you further, my brother?

R: With enough talent and focus each entity is able to find its disharmony within itself, then?

We are those of Q'uo. That is correct, my brother. In general, certainly it is a short discussion of a sometimes quite protracted process for each feeling entity.

May we answer you further, my brother?

R: In dealing with this catalyst, when one is able to bring love and acceptance to the process, is it part of the lessening of the over-activity of the antennas that you have mentioned?

We are those of Q'uo, and, this is correct, my brother. The perception is prior to physical reality and this may be seen, for instance, by the entity that is under hypnosis and is able to walk upon coals without having burned feet or to be stabbed by a needle without feeling pain or bleeding. The body is the creature of the mind.

May we answer you further, my brother?

R: No, Q'uo, that was good. I wanted to make it somewhat general rather than crossing over the threshold of personal data.

We are those of Q'uo, and applaud your discretion, my brother. It is very good to speak with you.

Is there a final query at this time?

R: Not a question but an invitation. Half seriously, if you would be interested to hang around and stay awhile and eat cookies afterwards, we would be delighted.

We are those of Q'uo, and, my brother, we must confess that we always stay for the tea and the cookies. Our hearts are full as we give our leave of you. It is such a blessing to be with you. We leave you in the love and in the light of the one infinite Creator. Adonai. ✤